The Game

The Association Game

A History of British Football

Matthew Taylor

PEARSON
Longman

Harlow, England • London • New York • Boston • San Francisco • Toronto
Sydney • Tokyo • Singapore • Hong Kong • Seoul • Taipei • New Delhi
Cape Town • Madrid • Mexico City • Amsterdam • Munich • Paris • Milan

PEARSON EDUCATION LIMITED

Edinburgh Gate
Harlow CM20 2JE
Tel: +44 (0)1279 623623
Fax: +44 (0)1279 431059
Website: www.pearsoned.co.uk

First published in Great Britain in 2008

© Pearson Education Limited 2008

The right of Matthew Taylor to be identified as author of this work has been asserted by him in accordance with the Copyright, Designs and Patents Act 1988.

ISBN: 978–0–582–50596–4

British Library Cataloguing-in-Publication Data
A catalogue record for this book is available from the British Library

Library of Congress Cataloging-in-Publication Data
A catalog record for this book is available from the Library of Congress

10 9 8 7 6 5 4 3 2 1
11 10 09 08 07

Typeset in 10pt Sabon by 3
Printed and bound in Malaysia (CTP - VVP)

The publisher's policy is to use paper manufactured from sustainable forests.

Contents

List of plates

Tables and figures

Acknowledgements

This book has benefited from the assistance of many colleagues and friends over a number of years. The initial proposal for the book was written while I was working at De Montfort University. Colleagues in the International Centre for Sports History and Culture and the history department were generous with ideas and advice and continued to be supportive after I had left to take up my present post. At Portsmouth, I have been lucky enough to work in a history team that takes research and scholarship seriously. Thanks go to former and present colleagues Dave Andress, Graham Attenborough, Brad Beaven, Sue Bruley, Rob James, Bob Kiehl, Ken Lunn, June Purvis, Gavin Schaffer, Heather Shore and James Thomas. Together with Barry Smart and Ben Oakley, I have run a cross-faculty unit at Portsmouth on 'Football and Society' since 2003. This has helped me to sharpen some of my ideas, particularly about the contemporary history of the game. Students on this and other units at Portsmouth have helped me to think through my ideas, providing a challenging and enjoyable environment in which to teach.

I owe a particular debt to Neil Carter, Fabio Chisari, Neal Garnham, Martin Johnes, Pierre Lanfranchi, Tony Mason, William Morgan, Dil Porter, Wray Vamplew and Jean Williams, who helped me out with sources and/or allowed me to consult work before publication. Pierre read drafts of some of the chapters and provided valuable advice. I would also like to thank the anonymous reviewers who offered useful suggestions for improving the original manuscript.

An interest in, and fascination with, football has been a common thread in many of my friendships over the years. I hope that my friends – from Lowestoft, York, Leicester and Portsmouth in particular – find something in this book that resonates with their understanding and experience of the game, although I suspect that many will think I've taken it far too seriously. Alex had the misfortune of experiencing her first World Cup with me at the same time as I was finishing the book. I am grateful to her for her patience and understanding of my temporary obsession with both. As always, my family has been a great support. My parents continue to show a genuine interest in my work and my brothers and their families have come to my aid on many occasions with free bed and board, and solutions to computer problems. This book could not have been completed without them.

Publisher's acknowledgements

The publishers are grateful to the following for permission to reproduce copyright material:

Plates 1, 2, 3, 4, 12, 13, 14, 15, 17, 18, 19, 20, 21, 22 and 23 courtesy of Popperfoto.com; plates 5, 6, 7, 8, 9, 10, 11 and 16 courtesy of the Hulton Archive/Getty.

In some instances we have been unable to trace the owners of copyright material, and we would appreciate any information that would enable us to do so.

Football, history and Britain

British football has a powerful sense of its own history. The culture of the game is replete with reminders of the past. We are constantly told of Britain's instrumental role in the development of what is now the 'world game': that it was the country that 'invented' football and then proceeded to bestow it upon the rest of the world. During major international championships, the English press focuses on the achievements of the 'boys of '66' and the 30 or 40 'years of hurt' since the last major triumph. The 'Wembley Wizards' of 1928 and 1967 hold a similar place in Scottish sporting folklore.[1] Football supporters are, in a sense, historians themselves; conveyors of particular forms of oral tradition and popular history. Even the most present-minded fans retain a keen awareness of the past, if only through the knowledge of the traditions, records and histories of their clubs and the competitions in which they play.

Football's late-twentieth-century rehabilitation, exemplified in its structural, economic and cultural overhaul, heightened this sense of history and popular nostalgia for the game's past.[2] Football became incorporated into a wider interest in public forms of history and what David Lowenthal termed the 'heritage crusade'.[3] Over recent years supporters have not only been able to read numerous official and unofficial histories of their club, they have also been able to visit museums dedicated to, and celebrating in, past glories, and sit in stands named after former players and directors. In an age of extensive refurbishment and relocation of stadiums, clubs have naturally been anxious to retain a link with the past, even if this is less a matter of preservation than reconstruction to suit the needs of the present. Such developments illustrate not only an awareness of the commercial value of the past but also 'a plea for history (or nostalgic versions of it) to remedy contemporary problems'.[4] Similarly, the new forms of football literature that emerged from the early 1990s were often obsessed with a perceived 'golden age' of football some 20 years earlier (or more specifically, during the childhood of the writer). Fanzines such as *When Saturday Comes* and books like Nick Hornby's best-selling *Fever Pitch* effectively mythologised the past, comparing it favourably with the degenerating 'modern' game.[5] A perfect example of such nostalgic evocations of football's past came when the legendary Stanley Matthews died in February 2000. Obituaries constructed Matthews as a committed and highly skilled artist and a modest gentleman who played fairly and with scrupulous honesty. As a symbol of 'the past', Matthews was then contrasted with the assumed inadequacies of the present. 'How different he was', wrote the *Daily Mail*, 'from the flamboyant, flashy, highly paid stars of today, with their Ferraris and celebrity wives'. For *The Sun*, he was 'a true hero, whose dedication and lifestyle shame the over-paid, over-rated players of today'.[6] For the British press, Matthews' death highlighted much about changes in football and society more broadly, reinforcing assumptions about the moral decay and decline of both.

Football and its histories

Academic historians of sport have been anxious to distance themselves from these more popular interpretations of the past and from notions of heritage and nostalgia. Eager to establish the credentials of their subject as a legitimate area for scholarly inquiry, they have focused on how sport fits into the broader social milieu and what it tells us about wider historical trends. Sport has been envisaged in this sense as a lens through which important aspects of social, cultural, economic and political life can be illuminated and set in sharper focus. In this manner, the historical study of sport in Britain has made considerable strides over the years. From the earliest forays of individual academics who in the 1960s and 1970s began to write journal articles and monographs, the history of sport has become established as a vibrant and productive subject for scholarly research. Taking their lead from more adventurous North American and Australian colleagues, British historians began to establish their own journals, associations and, latterly, research centres. Over time, the sub-discipline of 'sports history' has become recognised and the work of sports historians incorporated into the historical mainstream. It is hardly surprising that this research activity has been dominated by the study of football, by far the most prominent and popular sport in Britain today and, alongside perhaps cricket and horse racing, for much of the twentieth century.

For all this, there have been no more than a handful of academic histories of modern football in Britain or its constituent nations. The first to be written by a professional historian was James Walvin's *The People's Game*, published initially in 1975, and subsequently rewritten and republished in 1994.[7] This remains an important book, not least because it attempted to provide a serious social context to the sport, eschewing the popular 'scarf and rattle history' approach, and relating 'the game, in its many forms, to the society around it'.[8] Even in its revised form, however, *The People's Game* pays insufficient attention to the wealth of literature published since the 1970s and the corresponding debates that have raged among scholars of the game. Moreover, it is unfortunate that Walvin decided that in order to appeal to a general readership his book should be 'untrammeled by scholarship' and thus devoid of footnotes.[9] It was not until 1997 that another author attempted a complete history of the modern game spanning the nineteenth and twentieth centuries. Dave Russell's *Football and the English* was rather more successful in bridging the gap between the scholarly and lay audience.[10] It is an excellent study of the role of football in English social and cultural life, particularly alive to issues of local and regional identity and changing patterns of regional rivalry in a sport that also became seen to exemplify Englishness. Although Russell introduces it as a work of synthesis, *Football and the English* is much more than this. It is, in many respects, a landmark book, based on a considerable amount of new research and offering a number of original perspectives. Yet in other important areas, Russell's scope is relatively narrow. Its focus is on England and the professional game. As such, it rarely peers outward, to the rest of Britain, Europe or the wider world, or downward, to football at the amateur or grassroots level.

Studies of football over shorter periods of time, and in particular parts of Britain, have added detail and depth to our understanding of the game's development. Published in 1980, Tony Mason's *Association Football and English Society* remains the benchmark here.[11] Mason's close analysis of newspaper sources as well as private and public archives provided a model for future studies, as did his thematic treatment of clubs, players and supporters alongside consideration of the political and ideological ramifications of the game. Mason's influence can be traced in the structure and approach of a number of subsequent studies that deal with similar themes in different periods or places, notably Nicholas Fishwick's analysis of English football between 1910 and 1950, Martin Johnes's study of soccer in south Wales between 1900 and 1939 and Neal Garnham's history of Irish football up until the mid-1920s.[12] The origins of modern forms of football and the move toward professionalisation in the nineteenth century was considered first by the sociologist Eric Dunning in a series of articles, and later in collaboration with Kenneth Sheard in their 1979 book *Barbarians, Gentlemen and Players*. Stephen Tischler and Robert Lewis, meanwhile, developed our knowledge of the professionalisation and commercialisation of football from the 1870s.[13] More recently, the debate over the origins of football has been reignited by Adrian Harvey's work on popular football outside the public schools, while the more general studies of Wray Vamplew and Neil Tranter have helped set the pre-1914 game in its economic context.[14] The early periods may be the most comprehensively covered, but the studies of Fishwick and Johnes, Peter Beck's book on British and international football, my own work on professional football in England, and the attention given to these decades by Russell, has meant that the inter-war years are slowly catching up.[15]

The post-war years have been less well served. There is still no scholarly account of football in Britain post-1945, although an increasing number of journal articles and doctoral theses are being produced. A detailed study of the game's post-war boom and subsequent decline at professional and recreational level, assessing football's broader links with post-war patterns of austerity and affluence and perceptions of national and social decline, would certainly help to fill a major gap in the literature. It is perhaps not surprising that sociologists and social scientists have tended to provide the most insightful analyses of football's more recent history. Building on two provocative and influential essays by Ian Taylor and Chas Critcher, the sociological agenda has shifted from an initial focus on crowd disorder and hooliganism to assess broader aspects of football's cultural transformation in the 1980s and 1990s.[16] Anthony King's *The End of the Terraces* offers the most thorough account of these changes in England, while Richard Giulianotti's *Football: A Sociology of the Global Game* is more wide-ranging in its geographic sweep and thematic preoccupations.[17] Elsewhere, Alan Bairner, John Bale, H. F. Moorhouse, Alan Tomlinson, Stephen Wagg and John Williams, among others, have helped to establish the study of football as an important scholarly pursuit. What is more, although disciplinary barriers still undoubtedly exist, it is fair to say that the contemporary history of football has blossomed as a result of the input of perspectives from a range of disciplines, including economics, geography, anthropology, media studies and political science. To study the British game at the end of the twentieth century is to engage in an increasingly challenging and dynamic interdisciplinary debate.

As with the game itself, English perspectives have tended to dominate the historiography of British football. There have been quite valid criticisms that English writers erroneously equate 'Britain' and 'England' and draw British conclusions from English evidence. Yet whereas the earliest histories of football could be accused of extending a largely English narrative on to the whole of Britain, recent studies have been more sensitive to the crucial role of soccer in expressing feelings of national belonging and identity. Outside England, the interplay between nation and state has been a key theme in the emerging historiography of Welsh and Irish football, and in the work of Johnes and Garnham in particular.[18] But in neither case did the 'national' question overshadow attempts to address other crucial issues concerning patterns of participation, professionalisation and the civic and political importance of football, for example. The Scottish literature, by contrast, has tended to be more narrowly focused on a small number of established themes. Indeed, despite important studies of the 'Old Firm' rivalry, numerous detailed analyses of sectarianism in Scottish football and society, and an increasing interest in the relationship between soccer and Scottishness, there is still no academic history of the Scottish game in its totality.[19] It is not altogether clear why this should be the case. Scottish football has clearly not followed the same historical path as the English game and 'has meant different things' to Scots than to those in many other nations.[20] A book-length study of football in Scotland, charting either its entire history or a shorter period, would help to bring out more fully the assumed peculiarities in the Scottish game as well as revealing the extent to which aspects of the sport paralleled developments in the rest of the British Isles. At present, any historian of the British game unfortunately has to make do with a rather sketchy and skewed picture of football in Scotland.

Notwithstanding these imbalances and omissions, the literature on the history of British football is now vast. The main purpose of this book is to give the reader a firm grasp of the academic and popular writing on the subject. It aims to provide a synthesis of the existing literature and a guide to recent and current debates in the field. As such, it is not based primarily on original research, although details of my own work obviously feature throughout the text. Equally, it is important to state that the book is not intended as a narrative history of football. Readers seeking a straightforward linear account of the birth, rise and development of British football will have to look elsewhere. Indeed one of the basic points of the book is to show that in the study of football, as in all areas of history, contention, debate and controversy are rife. To put it simply, historians disagree. My aim is thus to weave together history and historiography: to describe, analyse and examine what happened, when and why, but also to draw attention at each stage to different interpretations, the strengths and weaknesses of these interpretations and the way in which the associated debates have affected our overall understanding of the topic. The intention is to try to incorporate a range of perspectives and highlight and examine alternative *histories* of football rather than attempt to arrive at a definitive *history*.

Football and its meanings

As the academic study of sport has matured, historians have begun to reassess how they conceive their subject and relate it to the wider social environment. The relationship between what people thought about a sport such as football and what they thought about other aspects of social, cultural and political life is inevitably hard to pin down. The appeal of the game for many who played, watched and read about it was precisely that it seemed to be an autonomous world without any obvious link to the arena of work or the realm of politics. It was a sanctuary to which they could escape from 'real life', at least for 90 minutes each week. Of course, as a product of the forces of modernisation and capitalist development, football could never be structurally separated in this way but this did not prevent some assuming that it might be. An alternative (and more convincing) approach has been to draw parallels and connections between football and society. It used to be common to think of sport as formed or shaped by powerful outside forces and developments, and valuable to historians primarily as a 'mirror' that reflected or, at most, a 'lens' that illuminated broader patterns of continuity and change. According to this view, the structures, relationships and values of a given society were simply imprinted upon football. It was thus 'determined' by society. Yet this approach has also been widely challenged.[21] Increasingly there has been an emphasis on the capacity of cultural forms such as football to bring about social and political change in their own right and some recognition that the relationship between the 'social and economic base' and the 'sporting superstructure' is circular and not unidirectional. As Russell argued: 'the football ground has been an important arena within which individuals can learn lessons about social and political roles and identities which are then carried "back" into other aspects of daily life'.[22]

In his *Sport, Leisure and Culture in Twentieth-Century Britain*, Jeffrey Hill has gone further by rejecting the marginal position often allocated to sport and instead emphasising its importance in determining how and what we think about the world. Sport and leisure, in Hill's view, should not be considered only in terms of the entertainment and pleasure they provide for people (important though this is) but also as 'cultural agencies with a power to work on their participants and consumers ideologically'. The texts and practices of sport are thus not ideologically empty but packed with meaning:

In their manifold activities are inscribed and structured habits of thought and behaviour which contribute to our ways of seeing ourselves and others, to a making sense of our social relationships, and to the piecing together of some notion of what we call 'society'.[23]

In his innovative application of the approaches of a range of political and cultural theorists, Hill has provided explicit theoretical support for an existing preoccupation among historians with what sport 'meant' to individuals and larger communities. But he is surely also right to note that in attempting to uncover the 'meaning' of sporting events and occasions, historians need to widen their methodological gaze and rethink what they are willing to accept as 'evidence'. Hill's own work on the FA Cup final as 'a "text" in which is inscribed a ceremonial expression of national identity', and in which the meanings of the songs and rituals of the occasion varied according to historical circumstance, provides a useful example of how the spectacle and symbolism of football might be investigated to good effect.[24]

Historians of football have been most comfortable in dealing with 'meaning' when articulating it via the notion of 'identity'. Understanding precisely what identity is, and how different identity categories are formed and interact with one another, can be complicated and problematic, but, as Simon Gunn has argued, identity remains a concept that historians 'can ill afford to do without'.[25] It seems a particularly appropriate concept in understanding a cultural activity such as football, where teams can easily be perceived as representatives of wider groups and communities and the key criteria of 'similarity' and 'difference' are given expression in the group solidarity of the crowd and the competition between opposing teams, supporters and, by extension, places. The public spectacle of football also appears to chime with the increasing emphasis on 'performance' in the construction of different types of social identity.[26] Scholars have focused mainly, though not exclusively, on five key identities in relation to football: class, gender, race, nationality and community. In line with prevailing historiographical trends, it was class that preoccupied the first historians of the game in the 1970s and 1980s. Much of the work of Walvin, Mason and Tischler, as well as the more general studies of John Hargreaves, Richard Holt and Stephen Jones, revolved around issues of sport, social relations and class identity.[27] In looking at the social diffusion of football in the nineteenth century, historians examined the contrasting ideas and meanings that different classes impressed upon the game. The issue of who really 'owned' the so-called 'people's game' as a commercial and cultural form has been at the heart of much of this discussion, equally essential to sociological assessment of the 1990s as historical debates concerning the 1890s. Notwithstanding its retreat in the mainstream of the discipline, concern with the role of social class has continued to be pervasive in the study of sport, even if here too it is no longer treated as the 'master' category it once was. The American scholar Steven Reiss's remark in 1994 that class was '*the* central issue in British sport historiography' is still largely true.[28] Identities of class remain key to the football historian's search for meaning.

Gender and race, by contrast, have not made anything like the mark on British sports history as on the historical mainstream.[29] The scholarship of soccer, like the game itself, has been dominated by white males, who have tended to deem the experiences of females and non-whites as marginal to the sport's overall impact and social meaning. Football's significance in forming and reinforcing masculine identity, and thus denying feminine input, has long been acknowledged but still requires more detailed exploration. Some of the most interesting recent work here has come from outside sports history. Holt's reference to 'the celebration of a distinctive brand of popular "masculinity"' through football, for example, has been touched upon in two studies of the inter-war period.[30] Adrian Bingham's study of gender and the national daily press has commented on the 'maleness of the sports pages' and the reference in football reports to notions of virility, masculinity, military heroism and national character. In most cases, 'women and "feminine" qualities were implicitly excluded'.[31] Pat Ayers, meanwhile, briefly touched on the importance of football in offering men in inter-war Liverpool 'a temporary escape from the responsibilities of daily life and an opportunity to reinforce the ties of male allegiance'. Watching and playing football was a form of male bonding which, when taken together with other leisure pursuits as well as drinking, gambling or socialising on street corners, helped 'to reinforce notions of a subliminal male self'.[32] As with gender, it is the sociological literature on football's recent history that has generally been best at addressing questions of race and ethnicity. There is some excellent work on sectarianism and ethnic identity in football in Scotland and Northern Ireland and an expanding literature on racism in British football since the 1970s. Phil Vasili has attempted to focus on these issues in earlier periods by tracing the history of black footballers, but much more work is needed to understand how the game's essential cultural 'whiteness' and institutional racism developed and operated over time.[33]

More developed is the literature on identities of place, particularly town or community identity and national identity, and the way in which these have meshed both with one another and with other forms of identity. In his *Town, City and Nation*, P. J. Waller used a footballing example to outline the meanings attached to place in the late nineteenth-century mind and the layers of consciousness and perception that could shift according to circumstance:

When citizens celebrated the relief of Mafeking they behaved as fellow nationals. When Manchester United Football Club played Manchester City the organizing principle changed. The association was no longer with Britons all, Lancastrians or Mancunians even, so much as with the closed world of the vendetta.[34]

Recent scholarship has demonstrated the multiplicity of identities – neighbourhood, locality, town, region and nation among others – exhibited through sport and the way in which particular forms of loyalty gave way to others as situation and context changed. In common with other social identities, those relating to place are no longer seen as fixed and definitive but increasingly envisaged as flexible if not fluid.[35] Neither is the notion of what constitutes 'community' in football as straightforward as might be assumed. In examining the creation by West Ham United of a special identity that emphasised the uniqueness and 'difference' of the club and the area in which it was located, Charles Korr nonetheless pointed out that the club always 'interacted with a variety of communities' and was 'a symbol of different things to different aspects of the population'.[36] Meanwhile, Gavin Mellor's work on the complex allegiances of football supporters in the post-war years, along with studies of those who 'follow' the game through newspapers, television, the Internet and other media, suggest that historians ought not to limit their understanding of football 'communities' to the immediate locale.[37] Similarly, while historians and sociologists have long been attuned to the importance of football as a focal point of national feeling and belonging, they are now examining in more detail how this relates to the pressures of both local and global identification. And, as we shall see below, the British anomaly of four nations representing a single state tells us a great deal about the history of football but equally as much about the complex character of national identity in Britain. It is for this reason that scholars of national identity place so much attention on this 'national' game.[38]

Football and its chronology

If notions of 'meaning' and 'identity' form a central thread in this book, so too does one of the historian's perennial concerns, continuity and change. Attempts to divide up, or periodise, football's past have tended to draw upon conventional historical markers, particularly the two world wars of the twentieth century. Many, though by no means all, historians have followed contemporaries in referring to pre-1914, inter-war and post-war soccer and organising their research projects and monographs accordingly. But the game has arguably provided its own crucial turning points – such as the legalisation of professionalism in 1885, the removal of the maximum wage law in 1961 and the Heysel Stadium disaster of 1985 – although it could be argued that these relate narrowly to the elite professional men's game in England. In his history of English football, Russell showed that there were a number of ways of conceptualising 'continuity' and 'change'. In one sense, he argued, the most significant changes in the structure, organisation and culture of football took place at the beginning and end of his period of study and, though hardly static and devoid of change, the intervening period between 1885 and 1961 was nonetheless 'marked by certain constant features'.[39] Giulianotti adopted a similar, if considerably more fluid, categorisation in his reference to the 'traditional', 'modern' and 'post-modern' stages of the game's development. His 'traditional' period, characterised by the emergence of common rules, their subsequent social and spatial diffusion and the formation of national associations, lasted until after the First World War. The 'modern' period – subdivided into shorter stages of 'early modernity', 'intermediate modernity' and 'late modernity' – spanned the middle of the twentieth century, from the 1920s to the late 1980s. The 'post-modern' epoch, meanwhile, was associated with the 'contemporary age' and linked to the apparent social, cultural and global transformation of football from the late 1980s.[40]

However, if we shift the focus of inquiry to wider perceptions of the game, and football's position in social and cultural life, the inter-war and post-1945 years emerge as dynamic eras in which the game became reha-bilitated via its association with notions of tolerance, decency, order and other positive expressions of national identity.[41] Football may still have been disliked by some socialists and religious leaders but, as Fishwick con-cluded, by the 1950s it was 'no longer out of favour with "public opinion" and seemed if anything to stand for much that was good in society'.[42] If we add to this the economic and financial development of football and the game's emergence as an important cultural phenomenon in parts of Scotland and Wales, the mid-twentieth century could easily be seen to rival earlier and later periods of 'change' as a defining era in the 'making' of British football.[43]

While recognising these chronological complexities, this book does not seek a radical departure in the periodisation of the history of football. It consists of six chapters that relate to fairly conventional, and broadly equal, units of time, divided either by the 'natural' boundaries of war or key markers in the game's history. Within this basic chronological struc-ture, a host of themes and issues are addressed, some weaving their way through each chapter, others recurring intermittently. Thus whereas dis-cussion of class and national identities, for instance, feature to some extent in each chapter, a theme such as crowd disorder and hooliganism is dealt with briefly in chapters 3 and 4, and in greater detail in chapter 5. Indeed although the chapters are meant to be read sequentially, sections such as those on 'Heroes and stars' (in Chapter 3) and 'The hooliganism debate' (in Chapter 5) are intended to act as short case studies: in-depth assessments of the literature that can easily be applied to earlier or later time periods. As such, the chronological boundaries of the chapters should be seen as relatively flexible and not as rigid barriers that enclose discussion and analysis.

Football and 'Britain'

Historians of sport are particularly sensitive to the distinction between the state of the United Kingdom and the separate nations of England, Scotland, Wales and Northern Ireland. Alexander Grant and Keith Stringer used sporting examples to outline the 'complexities and anom-alies' of this relationship in their collection of essays on British history, concluding that in sport 'the concept of the UK is a veritable enigma'.[44] The last two decades or so have witnessed an increasingly sophisticated approach to the study of the British Isles and a move away from the Anglocentric tendency to conflate 'English' and 'British' history towards what Keith Robbins has called the '"Britishing" of British history'.[45] This has involved an increasing recognition that if British history is to have any real meaning it should incorporate the different histories of England, Scotland, Ireland and Wales as well as their integration within a broader British perspective. For some historians this has meant taking an explicit 'four nations' approach that stresses the divisions between national and sub-national cultures; others have focused on the unifying perspective of Britishness and the blending of its constituent national cultures.[46]

At first glance, football appears more suited to a 'four nations' approach than one that uses Britain as a conceptual and organisational device. The existence of separate associations, competitions and representative teams in England, Scotland, Ireland and Wales by the 1890s, and the development of 'international' competition within Britain, meant that the game became a symbol of 'British' diversity rather than unity. However, certain aspects of football in Britain retained a crucial 'British' dimension that should not be overlooked. The migration of football talent from the poorer clubs in the peripheral nations to the English core, for example, meant that the experience of many players, and indeed supporters, was genuinely 'British'.[47] Likewise, the administration of the game and its rules took place in a wider British context that was to become important in determining relationships with football beyond British shores. Crucially, soccer was never sealed off and isolated in national cocoons: rather, a network of connections and influences bound the game in the four nations together. National and British football cultures thus coexisted, even if at times the latter seemed to disappear beneath the weight of the former.

The intention of this book is to examine football in Britain from both a 'British history' and a 'four nations' perspective, emphasising the cultural peculiarities and diversity of the sport's history in England, Scotland, Ireland and Wales while also tracing common developments and points of intersection between these 'national' footballing histories. This does not mean that each of the nations is given equal treatment in the text. For both practical and intellectual reasons, the game in England receives most attention, followed by Scotland, with Wales and (Northern) Ireland considered rather less frequently, although I have attempted where possible to make use of the more limited literature on these nations. Finally, we need to be clear about what we mean by 'British football'. Definitions of what constitutes 'Britain' are invariably slippery, with formal criteria rarely matching popular understandings. The 'Britain' dealt with in this book is the political state of the United Kingdom, consisting of Great Britain and

Ireland before 1922 and Great Britain and Northern Ireland after 1922. Soccer in the Irish Free State (later the Republic of Ireland) continued to be closely connected to the game in Britain, as we shall see, but the administrative split was sufficient to divide and isolate important aspects of the history of football in the south of Ireland from that in the north and the rest of Britain.

References

1 See Martin Polley, *Moving the Goalposts: A History of British Sport Since 1945* (London: Routledge, 1998), pp. 1–3; Stuart Cosgrove, *Hampden Babylon: Sex and Scandal in Scottish Football* (Edinburgh: Canongate, 2001 [1st edition, 1991]), p. 13; Bob Crampsey, *The Scottish Footballer* (Edinburgh: William Blackwood, 1978, pp. 58–9; John Rafferty, *One Hundred Years of Scottish Football* (London: Pan, 1973), pp. 58–64.

2 See Martin Johnes and Rhiannon Mason, 'Soccer, Public History and the National Football Museum', *Sport in History*, 23, 1 (Summer 2003), pp. 115–19; Dave Russell, '"We All Agree, Name the Stand after Shankly": Cultures of Commemoration in Late Twentieth-century English Football Culture', *Sport in History*, 26, 1 (April 2006), pp. 1–25; Matthew Taylor, 'Football, History and Memory: The Heroes of Manchester United', *Football Studies*, 3, 2 (2000), pp. 24, 36.

3 David Lowenthal, *The Heritage Crusade and the Spoils of History* (Cambridge: Cambridge University Press, 1998).

4 Dave Russell, 'Associating with Football: Social Identity in England, 1863–1998' in G. Armstrong and R. Giulianotti (eds), *Football Cultures and Identities* (Basingstoke: Macmillan, 1999), p. 22.

5 Nick Hornby, *Fever Pitch: A Fan's Life* (London: Victor Gollancz, 1992); Anthony King, *The End of the Terraces: The Transformation of English Football in the 1990s* (Leicester: Leicester University Press, 1998), pp. 180–3.

6 Cited in Garry Whannel, *Media Sport Stars: Masculinities and Moralities* (London: Routledge, 2002), pp. 103, 105.

7 James Walvin, *The People's Game: A Social History of British Football* (London: Allen Lane, 1975); *The People's Game: The History of Football Revisited* (Edinburgh: Mainstream, 1994).

8 Nicholas Fishwick, *English Football and Society, 1910–1950* (Manchester: Manchester University Press, 1989); Walvin, *People's Game* (1975), p. 7.

9 Walvin, *People's Game* (1994), p. 10.

10 Dave Russell, *Football and the English: A Social History of Association Football in England, 1863–1995* (Preston: Carnegie, 1997).

11 Tony Mason, *Association Football and English Society, 1863–1915* (Brighton: Harvester, 1980).

12 Fishwick, *English Football*; Martin Johnes, *Soccer and Society: South Wales, 1900–1939* (Cardiff: University of Wales Press, 2002); Neal Garnham, *Association Football and Society in Pre-Partition Ireland* (Belfast: Ulster Historical Foundation, 2004).

13 Eric Dunning, 'The Development of Modern Football' in E. Dunning (ed.), *The Sociology of Sport* (London; Frank Cass, 1971), pp. 133–51; Eric Dunning and Kenneth Sheard, *Barbarians, Gentlemen and Players: A Sociological Study of the Development of Rugby Football* (London: Routledge, 2005 [1st edition, 1979]); Stephen Tischler, *Footballers and Businessmen: The Origins of Professional Soccer in England* (New York: Holmes & Meier, 1981); Robert Lewis, 'The Development of Professional Football in Lancashire, 1870–1914', unpublished Ph.D. thesis, University of Lancaster, 1993.

14 Adrian Harvey, 'Football's Missing Link: The Real Story of the Evolution of Modern Football' in J. A. Mangan (ed.), *Sport in Europe: Politics, Class, Gender* (London: Frank Cass, 1999), pp. 92–116; *Football: The First Hundred Years* (London: Routledge, 2005); Wray Vamplew, *Pay Up and Play the Game: Professional Sport in Britain, 1875–1914* (Cambridge: Cambridge University Press, 1988); Neil Tranter, *Sport, Economy and Society in Britain, 1750–1914* (Cambridge: Cambridge University Press, 1998).

15 Fishwick, *English Football*; Johnes, *Soccer and Society*; Peter Beck, *Scoring for Britain: International Football and International Politics, 1900–1939* (London: Frank Cass, 1999); Matthew Taylor, *The Leaguers: The Making of Professional Football in England, 1900–1939* (Liverpool: Liverpool University Press, 2005); Russell, *Football and the English*, chapters 4 and 5.

16 Ian Taylor, '"Football Mad": A Speculative Sociology of Football Hooliganism' in Dunning (ed.), *Sociology of Sport*, pp. 352–77; Chas Critcher, 'Football Since the War' in J. Clarke, C. Critcher and R. Johnson (eds), *Working Class Culture: Studies in History and Theory* (London: Hutchinson, 1979), pp. 161–84.

17 King, *End of the Terraces*; Richard Giulianotti, *Football: A Sociology of the Global Game* (Cambridge: Polity, 1999).

18 Russell, *Football and the English*; Johnes, *Soccer and Society*, chapter 6; 'Eighty Minute Patriots?: National Identity and Sport in Modern Wales', *International Journal of the History of Sport*, 17, 4 (December 2000); Garnham, *Association Football*; 'Football and National Identity in Pre-Great

War Ireland', *Irish Economic and Social History*, 28 (2001), pp. 13–31. See also Mike Cronin, *Sport and Nationalism in Ireland: Gaelic Games, Soccer and Irish Identity Since 1884* (Dublin: Four Courts, 1999).

19 See, for example, Bill Murray, *The Old Firm: Sectarianism, Sport and Society in Scotland* (Edinburgh: John Donald, 2000 [1st edition, 1984]); G. P. T. Finn, 'Racism, Religion and Social Prejudice: Irish Catholic Clubs, Soccer and Scottish Society – 1 The Historical Roots of Prejudice', *International Journal of the History of Sport*, 8, 1 (May 1991); Joseph M. Bradley, *Ethnic and Religious Identity in Scotland: Politics, Culture and Football* (Aldershot: Avebury, 1995); 'Football in Scotland: A History of Political and Ethnic Identity', *International Journal of the History of Sport*, 12, 1 (April 1995), pp. 81–98; Graham Walker, 'Identity Questions in Contemporary Scotland: Faith, Football and Future Prospects', *Contemporary British History*, 15, 1 (Spring 2001), pp. 41–60; Grant Jarvie and Graham Walker (eds), *Scottish Sport in the Making of the Nation: Ninety-Minute Patriots?* (Leicester: Leicester University Press, 1994).

20 H. F. Moorhouse, 'On the Periphery: Scotland, Scottish Football and the New Europe' in J. Williams and S. Wagg (eds), *British Football and Social Change: Getting into Europe* (Leicester: Leicester University Press, 1991), p. 218.

21 See especially, Jeffrey Hill, 'British Sports History: A Post-Modern Future?', *Journal of Sport History*, 23, 1 (Spring 1996), pp. 1–19.

22 Russell, *Football and the English*, p. 237. See also Matthew Taylor, 'Football et culture politique en Grande-Bretagne' in Y. Gastaut and S. Mourlane (eds), *Le Football dans nos sociétés. Une culture populaire, 1914–1998* (Paris: Autrement, 2006), pp. 94–118; Johnes, *Soccer and Society*, p. 9.

23 Jeffrey Hill, *Sport, Leisure and Culture in Twentieth-Century Britain* (Basingstoke: Palgrave, 2002), p. 2.

24 See Jeffrey Hill, 'Cocks, Cats, Caps and Cups: A Semiotic Approach to Sport and National Identity', *Culture, Sport, Society*, 2, 2 (1999), pp. 1–21; quotation p. 16.

25 Simon Gunn, *History and Cultural Theory* (Harlow: Longman, 2006), p. 155.

26 Richard Jenkins, *Social Identity* (London: Routledge, 2004 [1st edition, 1996]), pp. 3–6; Peter Burke, *What is Cultural History?* (Cambridge: Polity, 2004), pp. 90–6. See also Christian Bromberger with Alain Hayot and Jan-Marc Mariottini, '"Allez l'O.M., Forza Juve": The Passion for Football in Marseille and Turin' in S. Redhead (ed.), *The Passion and the Fashion: Football Fandom in the New Europe* (Aldershot: Avebury, 1993), pp. 103–51.

27 Walvin, *People's Game*; Mason, *Association Football*; Tischler, *Footballers and Businessmen*; John Hargreaves, *Sport, Power and Culture: A Social and Historical Analysis of Popular Sports in Britain* (Cambridge: Polity, 1986); Richard Holt (ed.), *Sport and the Working Class in Modern Britain* (Manchester: Manchester University Press, 1990); *Sport and the British: A Modern History* (Oxford: Clarendon, 1989); Stephen Jones, *Sport, Politics and the Working Class: Organised Labour and Sport in Interwar Britain* (Manchester: Manchester University Press, 1988).

28 Steven Reiss, 'From Pitch to Putt: Sport and Class in Anglo-American Sport', *Journal of Sport History*, 21, 2 (Summer 1994), p. 138. See also Ross McKibbin, 'Class, Politics, Money: British Sport Since the First World War', *Twentieth Century British History*, 13, 2 (2002), pp. 191–200; John Lowerson, 'Opiate of the People and Stimulant for the Historian? – Some Issues in Sports History' in W. Lamont (ed.), *Historical Controversies and Historians* (London: UCL Press, 1998), p. 209.

29 See, for example, Hill, 'British Sports History', pp. 12–13; Richard Holt, 'Sport and History: The State of the Subject in Britain', *Twentieth Century British History*, 7, 2 (1996), pp. 284–5; Ben Carrington and Ian McDonald, 'Introduction: "Race", Sport and British Society' in B. Carrington and I. McDonald (eds), *'Race', Sport and British Society* (London: Routledge, 2001), pp. 1–26. For an Anglo-American perspective, see S. W. Pope, 'Decentring "Race" and (Re)presenting "Black" Performance in Sport History: Basketball and Jazz in American Culture, 1920–1950', p. 150 and Patricia Vertinsky, 'Time Gentlemen Please: The Space and Place of Gender in Sport History', p. 229, both in Murray G. Phillips (ed.), *Deconstructing Sport History: A Postmodern Analysis* (New York: SUNY Press, 2006).

30 Holt, *Sport and the British*, p. 366.

31 Adrian C. Bingham, 'Debating Gender: Approaches to Femininity and Masculinity in the Popular National Daily Press in Interwar Britain', unpublished D.Phil. thesis, University of Oxford, 2002, pp. 261, 258.

32 Pat Ayers, 'The Making of Men: Masculinities in Interwar Liverpool' in M. Walsh (ed.), *Working Out Gender: Perspectives from Labour History* (Aldershot: Ashgate, 1999), p. 75.

33 See references in note 19. Also John Sugden and Alan Bairner, *Sport, Sectarianism and Society in a Divided Ireland* (Leicester; Leicester University Press, 1993); Les Back, Tim Crabbe and John Solomos, *The Changing Face of Football: Racism, Identity and Multiculture in the English Game* (Oxford: Berg, 2001); Jon Garland and Michael Rowe, *Racism and Anti-Racism in Football* (Basingstoke: Palgrave, 2001); Phil Vasili, *Colouring Over the White Line: The History of Black Footballers in Britain* (Edinburgh: Mainstream, 2000).

34 P. J. Waller, *Town, City and Nation: England 1850–1914* (Oxford: Clarendon, 1983), p. 79.

35 See, for example, Dave Russell, 'Sport and Identity: The Case of Yorkshire County Cricket Club, 1890–1939', *Twentieth Century British History*, 7, 2 (1996), pp. 206–30; Jeff Hill and Jack Williams (eds), *Sport and Identity in the North of England* (Keele: Keele University Press, 1996); Matthew Taylor, 'Building a National League?: The Football League and the North of England, 1888–1939', *International Journal of Regional and Local Studies*, 1, 1 (2005), pp. 11–27; Johnes, *Soccer and Society*.

36 Charles P. Korr, 'A Different Kind of Success: West Ham United and the Creation of Tradition and Community' in Holt (ed.), *Sport and the Working Class*, p. 142.

37 Gavin Mellor, 'Football and its Supporters in the North West of England, 1945–1985', unpublished Ph.D. thesis, University of Central Lancashire, 2003; Garry Crawford, *Consuming Sport: Fans, Sport and Culture* (London: Routledge, 2004). See also Adam Brown, Tim Crabbe, Gavin Mellor, Tony Blackshaw and Chris Stone, *Football and Its Communities: Final Report* (Manchester: Football Foundation and Manchester Metropolitan University, 2006).

38 See, for example, Richard Weight, *Patriots: National Identity in Britain, 1940–2000* (London: Pan Macmillan, 2003); Paul Ward, *Britishness Since 1870* (London: Routledge, 2004).

39 Russell, *Football and the English*, p. 235.

40 Giulianotti, *Football*, pp. xiii–xiv, 166–9.

41 Russell, *Football and the English*, p. 238; Jeffrey Richards, 'Football and the Crisis of British Identity' in S. Caunce, E. Mazierska, S. Sydney-Smith and J. Walton (eds), *Relocating Britishness* (Manchester: Manchester University Press, 2004), p. 97.

42 Fishwick, *English Football*, p. 146.

43 See Stephen G. Jones, 'The Economic Aspects of Association Football in England, 1918–39', *British Journal of Sports History*, 1, 3 (December 1984), pp. 286–99; Taylor, *The Leaguers*, pp. 246–47.

44 Alexander Grant and Keith Stringer, 'Introduction: The Enigma of British History' in A. Grant and K. Stringer (eds), *Uniting the Kingdom?: The Making of British History* (London: Routledge, 1995), p. 3.

45 Keith Robbins, 'British History and the Generation of Change' in H. Brocklehurst and R. Phillips (eds), *History, Nationhood and the Question of Britain* (Basingstoke: Palgrave, 2004), p. 3.

46 See J. G. A Pocock, 'The Limits and Divisions of British History: In Search of

the Unknown Subject', *American Historical Review*, 87 (1982); Raphael
Samuel, 'British Dimensions: "Four Nations History" ', *History Workshop
Journal*, 40 (Autumn 1995); Hugh Kearney, *The British Isles: A History of
Four Nations* (Cambridge: Cambridge University Press, 1989); Norman
Davies, *The Isles* (Basingstoke: Permac, 1999); Linda Colley, *Britons:
Forging the Nation, 1707–1837* (London: Pimlico, 2003 [1st edition, 1992]);
Keith Robbins, *Nineteenth-Century Britain: Integration and Diversity*
(Oxford: Clarendon, 1988).

47 Robbins, *Nineteenth-Century Britain*, p. 166; Pierre Lanfranchi and
Matthew Taylor, *Moving With the Ball: The Migration of Professional
Footballers* (Oxford: Berg, 2001), pp. 38–45.

CHAPTER 1

Early years, *c.* 1863–85

When did football in Britain begin? The initial response to such a fundamental question is that it depends what we mean by the term 'football'. Historians make a mistake if they identify 'football' only with the association variant of the game. In spite of common usage, 'football' has become a generic term for a whole range of ball games, including rugby football, American football, Australian football and Gaelic football, as well as association football. The term dates back at least to 1314 and referred to the many pre-modern forms of ball game that were common throughout Britain and continental Europe and which were the antecedents of the nineteenth-century codes. Some of these early games involved mainly kicking, but pre-modern or folk football was never exclusively non-handling. One writer has speculated that the name may have derived from the ball itself rather than the nature of the game and that it might have referred to a game played on foot rather than on horseback.[1]

Many histories of association football thus begin by looking at medieval or early modern versions of the football game. Percy Young's 1968 history included chapters on tribal origins, the Middle Ages, the Renaissance and the Georgians and only reached the foundation of the Football Association (FA) on page 132. James Walvin's *The People's Game* starts with references to the twelfth and thirteenth centuries before examining the emergence of football-like games from the fourteenth century. Even the work of Tony Mason and Dave Russell, which focuses strictly on association football, gives some space to its folk roots.[2] This chapter takes a similar view. Any account of the modern association game needs to pay some attention to the question of its origins, a subject which has provoked a number of theses, articles and books in recent years and remains one of the most intense debates in the historiography of the game.

The 'origins' debate: the public schools and popular football

Determining a precise moment of origin for a sport such as football is a tricky, some would say futile, endeavour. Few sports were 'born' or 'invented' at a specific historical moment that can be clearly identified and accepted by all. They are less often the result of individual inspiration and invention than the culmination of various local initiatives, modifications and compromises. The contexts in which sports originate are thus crucial. As Martin Polley has noted, the origin of any sport 'needs to be linked to local and regional issues, and to the power relations of the individual game's promoters, rather than any moment of invention'.[3] In the case of association football, the foundation of the FA in 1863 serves as a convenient starting point but it is debatable whether it should be regarded as *the* date when a new game was created.[4] It was undoubtedly a key moment in the early history of football but some historians now identify different times and places as also (and often equally) significant. Football, as we shall see, had a prolonged, messy and complicated birth.

Orthodox interpretations

Traditional histories of football have been fairly clear about its basic origins and chronological development in Britain. An orthodox viewpoint has emerged which holds that the modern game as we know it is the product of the rationalisation and civilisation of a traditional folk activity in the nation's elite public schools and universities. The codified game that emerged then gained ground among working-class players and spectators and in time was transformed into a genuinely popular recreational activity. In the course of no more than a generation, it developed from an activity of a privileged elite into what Walvin could call 'the people's game'.[5]

One of the most influential versions of this orthodox approach comes from the work of the sociologist Eric Dunning. In an early essay, Dunning identified four stages in the development of modern football. During the first stage, broadly from the fourteenth to the nineteenth centuries, football existed as 'a relatively simple, wild and unruly folk game', which varied considerably from place to place according to local traditions and customs. The second stage, from 1750 to 1840, involved the adoption and adaptation by the public schools of the folk game, while during the third stage, between about 1840 and 1860, the game was organised in a more formal manner, particularly through the creation of the first written rules. Between approximately 1850 and 1890, the final stage, public school forms of football were popularised beyond the school gates, and associations were established at local and national levels to organise and regulate the sport. It was during this period that the game also developed a mass support of paying spectators, which in turn allowed clubs to fund the engagement of professional players.[6]

Central to this basic thesis is what Dunning has called the 'cultural marginalization' of the traditional folk game. Attempts to suppress football dated back to at least 1314 but it was not until the late eighteenth century that it fell foul of the twin 'state formation' and 'civilizing' processes. The introduction of new methods of policing meant more effective control over these unruly and violent games, which in any case were increasingly coming to be regarded, alongside other traditional pastimes and sports, as abhorrent and lacking in respectability. A further factor militating against the survival of folk football was the removal of aristocratic patronage. Challenged by the increasing influence and status of the urban bourgeoisie, it is argued that the landed aristocracy and gentry drew back from this cultural association with the working classes and withdrew the support upon which traditional sports, football included, had been based.[7]

Such an interpretation found considerable support in the work of the first historians of leisure and sport, who argued that the impact of industrialisation led to the decline and effective disappearance by the Victorian era of traditional working-class sport. According to this view, rapid economic and urban change devastated existing sporting cultures, limiting the opportunities and the inclination of working people to participate in sport. The first crucial element in this was the decline of time and space in which to play. While the growth of factories and the industrialisation of agriculture brought with them increased and more regular working hours, the move from a predominantly rural to an urban society had a profound effect on established recreational practices, particularly if seen alongside the widespread enclosure of the common land which had been such an important location for folk games. We can add to this the influence of Evangelical and Methodist thought, which tended to regard games of this type as fundamentally immoral, thwarting the spiritual development of those who participated and so impeding the creation of a civilised society. Such attitudes, for Mason, were the 'final nail in the coffin of rough football'.[8]

Anthony Delves's study of the suppression of street football in Derby provides a useful example of how these various factors combined in practice. A customary contest ostensibly between the two parishes of All Saints and St Peter's, Shrove Tuesday football in Derby had evolved by the early nineteenth century into 'a popular festival, an English *mardi gras*'. Involving hundreds of people and beginning with the throwing in of the ball in the marketplace, the game was typical of contemporary forms of football in its absence of spatial and temporal limits and, most significantly, the prominence of violent and criminal behaviour. Opposition to its continuance gained momentum from the 1830s, engineered by a coalition of local industrialists, tradesmen, shopkeepers and artisans. In their eyes the game not only seriously disrupted the local economy, forcing as it did the suspension of work for two days and the closure of shops and businesses, but it also encouraged drinking, public disorder and other forms of behaviour considered to be 'socially and morally corrosive'. By the 1840s, the hostility of teetotallers, Evangelicals and sections of the local bourgeoisie was reinforced by the new political gloss which could be placed on such activities. What may have previously been regarded as a relatively harmless popular festival, increasingly came to be seen by the authorities as a form of riot or collective violence in the context of rising trade unionism and Chartist demonstrations. With the death of the game's most influential supporter, the local industrialist Joseph Strutt, the opponents went on the offensive, persuading the Mayor in 1845 to declare it illegal. Despite some working-class resistance over the following decade, leading to riots and the calling in of troops, Derby street football had indeed been marginalised, even if, as Delves notes, it was far from extinguished entirely.[9]

With the evident decline of traditional forms of football, the narrative normally turns to the role of the elite public schools in reinventing the game. One account from 1906 suggested that 'football, in its modern form, is entirely the product ... of the various public school games', particularly those of Eton, Harrow, Westminster and Charterhouse.[10] Rough forms of football, similar to those existing throughout Britain, had long been played in many public schools. But they differed in a number of respects, the most significant of which was their connection to methods of pupil control, and in particular the prefect-fagging system. Football became one way in which senior boys exerted control over their younger counterparts. 'Fags' were forced to play and reduced to keeping goal or even used as a means of demarcating the goalposts or the boundary of the pitch. With the reform of the public schools during the 1830s and 1840s, organised games such as football came to assume a number of additional functions. First, it had the practical benefit of keeping boys occupied and out of mischief when not under the direct control of the masters. If boys were sent to bed tired, it was thought, the chances of them indulging in rowdy behaviour, or the twin 'evils' of masturbation and homosexuality, would be minimised. What is more, football became bound up in an influential cult of athleticism which, allied to the ideas of muscular Christianity and manliness, dominated the thinking of Victorian public school educators. Participating in football was thought to encourage a range of manly characteristics and qualities: from co-operation, teamwork and leadership to pluck, courage and self-restraint.[11] In T. C. Worsley's well-chosen phrase, organised games in the Victorian public school became 'the wheel around which the moral values turned'.[12]

New types of football began to develop in this context. These differed from earlier forms in a number of fundamental ways: first, they were based on written rules rather than oral ones; second, both the duration of matches and the size and shape of the playing area were subject to strict limitations; third, the number of players was reduced and the size of competing teams equalised; and finally the levels of physical violence permissible in the games were restricted. Of these, the writing down of the rules was to be most crucial of all, not just because it provided the masters with an indirect authority that they had not had when the senior boys controlled the game but also as it determined the form modern football would take. Historians have determined that Rugby was the first school to commit its version of football to writing, although they differ as to whether this occurred in 1845 or 1846.[13] The second, Eton, was an older and more prestigious institution, located next to Windsor and able to boast of a royal foundation. Its rules, produced in 1847, were different from Rugby's in three important respects. First, it allowed for a goal to be achieved when the ball was kicked between two goal sticks 'provided it is not over the level of the top of them' rather than above H-shaped posts. Second, it outlawed a practice known as 'sneaking' (Eton's version of 'offside'). Third, hands could only be used to stop the ball; carrying or running with the ball was strictly prohibited. Dunning has suggested that Eton's insistence on a kicking game antithetical to the Rugby handling game is explained by status competition between the two: 'by developing a form of football which was equally distinctive but in key respects diametrically opposite to the game at Rugby, the Etonians were deliberately attempting to put the "upstart" Rugbeians in their place and to "see off" this challenge to Eton's status as *the* leading public school *in all respects*.' While we should not conclude from this that rugby and soccer were thus established in their modern forms by the late 1840s, these rules might realistically be seen as embryonic versions. Dunning, for one, regards the Eton Field Game as 'probably the earliest prototype of soccer'.[14]

Historians often draw a straight line from these evolving public school games of the 1840s and 1850s to the creation of the Football Association in 1863, with Oxford and Cambridge Universities (the latter especially) providing the necessary institutional link. As in the public schools, sport emerged in these decades as a central feature of university life, with ball games like football gaining increasing acceptance from the 1850s. If undergraduates brought up on the peculiar footballing traditions of their former schools wished to play together, it was clear that common rules had to be developed. We know that this occurred at Cambridge between 1838 and 1842, in 1846, 1848, 1856, and again in 1863. The final of these, produced by a committee of undergraduates from Eton, Harrow, Rugby, Marlborough, Shrewsbury and Westminster, formed the basis of the discussions undertaken by the embryonic Football Association during the same year.[15] In other cases, the link between public school football and the FA came with the creation of 'old boys' teams. Charles Alcock and his brother John helped to found the Forest Football Club at the end of 1859, the year after Charles left Harrow. Based at Snaresbrook in Essex, the early members were all Old Harrovians who competed mainly against other teams of former public schoolboys based around London. The Alcock brothers represented Forest at the first meetings of the governing body and Charles was to become the FA's first secretary. The significance of metropolitan organisations such as Forest (reformed as Wanderers – the first FA Cup winners – in 1864) in the development of association football has been highlighted in the work of early historians of the game, one of whom was Charles Alcock himself. In 1890, he claimed that Forest had been 'the progenitor of all the now numerous clubs playing football of any kind throughout the kingdom'.[16]

Revisionist interpretations

In recent years, this orthodox account of the origins of the modern game has come under some scrutiny. Building on the findings of economic historians, there has been good reason to challenge the idea that 'traditional' forms of football disappeared in the manner previously assumed. Few now regard Britain's industrial growth from the late eighteenth century as revolutionary, preferring to portray it as a relatively slow, uneven and incomplete process. Certainly by the mid-nineteenth century only a small proportion of workers were engaged in the type of factory or other industrial enterprise in which hours were substantially increased and recreation thus became impossible. Neil Tranter has suggested that the limited nature of industrial and technological change for most meant that existing patterns of recreation remained largely intact. This was as true of places such as rural Oxfordshire as it was of Lancashire, where factory production and urbanisation was most pronounced: in both cases, those sports associated with local festivals and holidays survived well into the nineteenth century. In industrial Scotland, Tranter presents sport as 'more not less common in the 1830s/1840s than in the 1790s' and provides the example of a football match played in 1835 between the Blairdrummond estates and the Deanston cotton mills as evidence that even factory workers had the time to engage in customary sporting activities. Wray Vamplew has similarly highlighted the resilience of traditional sports, noting that 'despite a long period of attrition, many ... were still being played in the 1820s'.[17]

Adrian Harvey has undertaken a more thorough revisionism in his meticulous study of sporting culture before 1850.[18] Rather than stressing the continuation of traditional sporting practices, he concentrates on the development of a highly sophisticated sporting culture between the late 1790s and the middle of the nineteenth century that laid the basis for the supposed 'sporting revolution' of the 1850s onwards. This culture was characterised, Harvey argues, by commercial imperatives including large fee-paying crowds and professional players and by the creation of a 'modern' weekly schedule of events that owed little to the traditional recreational calendar based on annual holidays and festivals. Equally significant was the promotional role of the sporting press and the fact that many of these sports were governed by strict rules, supervised by referees and officials and characterised by an emphasis on 'scientific' techniques and skilful play. Moreover, although social segregation was the norm, all classes of British society participated as promoters, players and spectators. Thus, in contrast with those historians who regard early Victorian Britain as a recreational vacuum, Harvey's view is that 'the bulk of the ingredients required for the emergence of the nationally organized sporting culture that appeared in the 1880s was present' by 1850.[19] It was only after 1850 that this culture began to fragment, with the advocates of amateur sport distancing themselves from the commercial element and briefly interrupting the growth of a commercial sporting culture that was gradually to reassert itself from the 1870s onwards.

While this account has gone some way towards revising the accepted chronology of nineteenth-century sport, it has little to say specifically about football. Along with John Goulstone, however, Harvey has remedied this in a series of articles and a book that attack the orthodox interpretation at its empirical core. In essence, they challenge the centrality attached to the public schools in the codification and subsequent diffusion of association football. Underpinning their accounts are an emphasis on the existence during the middle decades of the nineteenth century of forms of popular football every bit as sophisticated, rational and influential as the games played in the public schools and universities. As such they question the tendency of historians to report football's progress purely 'within the limited context [of] establishment institutions' and ignore its evident flourishing beyond their walls.[20]

Some historians had long suspected a degree of continuity between traditional and modern forms of football. Even with limited concrete evidence, Hugh Cunningham felt it likely that older games continued to be played by working people between 1840 and 1860. 'Seeing things through public school spectacles', he has argued, 'ignores the continuous history of football as a popular sport'. We know, after all, that the most famous of the festive football occasions, such as the Derby Shrove Tuesday match, were subject to prohibition, but how can we be sure that football in its more casual and less visible guise simply disappeared? Richard Holt has gently suggested that scholars may have

taken on board too eagerly the heroic accounts of the public school men, who founded the Football Association in 1863, and assumed in consequence that traditional football was suppressed lock, stock and barrel during the first half of the nineteenth century to be re-invented and re-popularized in the second.[21]

The studies of Goulstone and Harvey provide some substance to this speculation. On the basis of a close reading of the weekly newspaper *Bell's Life in London*, both identify the existence of numerous football teams engaged in matches with varying regularity, often for stake money, throughout Britain. According to Harvey's data, eight such organisations emerged in the 1830s, 45 in the 1840s and a further 15 in the 1850s. A fair proportion of these were associated with educational institutions and pubs, while others derived from existing clubs and societies, occupational groups, the military and rural parishes. Significantly, many of these predated the formal organisation of public school football and, with one or two exceptions, there is little obvious evidence of public school influence in their rules or personnel.[22]

The football these teams played, according to the revised account, was also highly organised, bound by agreed (and often written) rules and no less civilised than its public school counterpart. Surrey Football Club, for example, was founded in 1849 as an adjunct to the county cricket club. At the club's first meeting, the chairman William Denison issued a set of six rules, which included the outlawing of 'wilful kicking', the capping of sides at 22 men each and arrangements for starting the game and deter- mining the winner (defined as 'that side which shall first kick the ball over the "goal rope" of their opponents'). The inspiration for this game was not, according to Denison, the football played at nearby Charterhouse and Westminster schools but that arranged by a Gymnastic Society, whose last match had taken place on Kennington Common 60 years earlier. Elsewhere, laws of the game which dealt with issues such as the size of pitch, dimensions of the goals, the use of substitutes and so on, were often agreed prior to the match, documented and signed by representatives of both sides, along with the stake that invariably accompanied any such game. One example taken from *Bell's Life in London* during 1852 recorded that

A meeting was held at the Clock public house, Bickenhill, Warwickshire, on the 15th instant, to draw up articles and decide upon the day and place for the match at football, between six gentlemen of the above parish and six gentlemen of Hampton, when it was decided to come off at Hampden at Arden, on the 2d of Nov., for a bottle of wine and dinner each. The length between the goals to be ten score yards, width of goals ten feet, height six feet, and to be the best of three goals.[23]

Most of these games were characterised by other features conventionally associated with public school innovation. Referees or umpires were common. At a match between the Bodyguards and Fearnoughts at Rochdale in 1842, there was one umpire for each team, while in 1846 a game at Ashton-under-Lyne made use of officials unrelated to either team. Although the size of teams varied considerably, the principle that they should be equal in number was well established. Most of the matches recorded in the period 1835 to 1859 by Harvey ranged from 6 to 20-a-side. Goulstone's meticulous research reveals that 11-a-side matches were being played by teams from Leicestershire, Berkshire, Northamptonshire and Hampshire during the same period, but 10 and 12-a-side competition seems to have been equally common. There is also evidence that many of these popular forms of football eschewed violence in favour of skill and scientific play. One Scottish commentator described a local game in which 'hacking and collaring' were unknown as 'less hazardous than shinty'.[24]

Another facet of the revisionist case concerns the role of Sheffield during this crucial formative period, a role which, it is argued, existing accounts have ignored, marginalised or else misunderstood. For Harvey, in particular, the development of an organised football culture in Sheffield from the 1850s, complete with a hegemonic club, significant popular support and a widely accepted code regulating games throughout the area, represents a powerful challenge to the public schools' claim to be the parent of modern football. If most histories recognise Sheffield Football Club (FC) as one of the first genuinely modern organisations, a great deal of confusion surrounds its origins and subsequent influence. The club seems to have emerged around 1855 when a number of players from the cricket club based at Bramall Lane decided to take up football. A separate club was probably founded in 1857, and according to Percy Young a code of rules was issued later the same year, although Harvey has found a slightly different set of regulations dated 1858. Greater disagreement exists over the provenance of these rules. Young and subsequent historians have regarded them as deriving from the public schools, either via the players themselves or through masters at the Sheffield Collegiate School where a number of the original members had been educated. The adoption from the Eton game of the 'rouge', a 4-yard area either side of the goal providing an additional means of scoring, offers further evidence of this. Harvey, however, has disputed that Sheffield FC was primarily a Collegiate old boys' club and claims that the first rules were 'principally of local origin'. Years later one of its founders, Major Nathaniel Creswick, revealed that the club had indeed contacted leading public schools for copies of their laws but rejected them as unintelligible. The absence of an offside rule, common in all public school forms of football, and the inclusion of a law penalising illegal play with a free kick, unknown in any, has further convinced Harvey of the popular derivation of the prototype Sheffield rules.[25]

What cannot be doubted is the impact the club and its rules had on the popularity of football in the Sheffield region. The main rivals of Sheffield were Hallam FC, formed between 1857 and 1860. One match between the teams in 1861 attracted a crowd of 600 spectators; a second the following year witnessed an exchange of blows between Major Creswick and a Hallam player called Waterfall, which was only stopped by the intervention of 'senior spectators' and the decision to reprimand Waterfall by putting him in goal. Although initially secondary to athletics as the winter sport, interest in football grew and by 1862 the region could boast 15 clubs. None of these matched Sheffield FC in either seniority or the social position of their membership and thus the club managed to retain its leadership amongst this embryonic association. This applied to its code, known as 'The Sheffield Rules', which, when updated and printed once again in 1862, was soon adopted as a standard code for all clubs in the area. Although the club was unable to standardise the length of matches, which ranged from one to three hours, or the number of players, with 14-a-side games more common than the favoured 11-a-side, Harvey has seen in Sheffield the development of a rationalised and uniform football culture which surpassed anything happening elsewhere, including within the public schools or the metropolitan old boys' teams.[26]

Soccer, rugby and 1863

In fact it was this absence of an agreed code that prompted the series of meetings leading to the creation of the Football Association in 1863. At the time, most teams in London played according to their own distinct rules. In order to compete on a wider basis, teams thus had either to agree on rules before playing or, as often happened, play both codes over one or two matches, switching rules, in the former case, halfway through. On 26 October 1863 a meeting took place at Freeman's Tavern in Lincoln Inn's Field involving captains and representatives of a number of London suburban clubs. The aim was to decide on a shared set of rules that would allow matches to take place without the problems that existed at the time. The clubs represented at the meeting were Barnes, Blackheath, Perceval House (Blackheath), Kensington School, the War Office, Crystal Palace, Blackheath Proprietary School, The Crusaders, Forest, Surbiton and No Names of Kilburn; Charterhouse School, meanwhile, sent a representative to observe proceedings but did not join. Ebenezer Morley of Barnes proposed the formation of an association, and this was carried by 11 votes to one. The FA was born, with Morley becoming its first honorary secretary and Arthur Pember of No Names its first president.[27]

However, the game discussed in meetings over the next month or so was not association football as it came to be recognised. Recent research suggests that Walvin was mistaken in his observation that, with the exception of Blackheath, 'all the clubs were committed to the dribbling game'.[28] The inclusion in the first rules, drawn up on 24 November, of elements of what later became rugby, especially the practices of 'hacking' (kicking the shins) and 'carrying', suggests that many of those attendant envisaged the creation of a composite game: most of the 14 rules were based on an amalgamation of those played by a variety of schools, universities and clubs. It was only when the Cambridge Rules, which outlawed running with the ball and hacking, were debated that the schism amongst the representatives was revealed. Seen by some as the essence of football's masculine toughness, hacking in particular was criticised by others as an uncivilised habit.[29] Following a series of stormy meetings, those in favour of the dribbling code were eventually victorious, although this may have been helped by the fact that a number of pro-handling delegates were absent at important stages in the deliberations.[30] The first set of rules was enshrined at a meeting on 8 December. Blackheath, the most vociferous supporters of hacking, immediately left the FA and became instrumental in the creation of the Rugby Football Union in 1871.

Despite some attempts to downplay its significance, the foundation of the FA in 1863 remains a major landmark in the development of the game. The claim that it amounted to the invention of association football, however, is open to debate. For Dunning and his colleagues, the incipient bifurcation of football into the separate games of soccer and rugby had occurred some time earlier, with the establishment of the rival Eton and Rugby codes in the 1840s; the 1863 disputes between dribbling and handling advocates merely formalised it.[31] In a powerful critique of this view, however, Tony Collins has suggested that it rests on limited factual evidence and that, in fact, the Rugby and Eton forms of football were less distinct from one another, and from other emerging codes, than Dunning et al. acknowledge. By taking the modern games of soccer and rugby as their starting point, Collins argues, Dunning et al. adopt a teleological perspective that leads them 'to emphasize the differences and downplay the similarities' between these early codes of football.[32] By contrast, there is, as we shall see, considerable evidence to suggest that these games continued to exist for a number of years either in an amalgamated form or alongside one another as alternative codes which 'football' teams played as and when they saw fit. Indeed Collins is probably correct to suggest that it was not until the 1870s, when the popularity of football spread throughout society and cup competitions were introduced, that divisions widened and the split between the association and rugby codes became definitive.[33]

To recognise the significance of 1863 does not mean that we should ignore the football cultures flourishing outside the capital and the public schools. It now appears that, at the very least, sophisticated and organised forms of popular football pre-dated the creation of the FA and were arguably equally as influential. Aspects of the revisionist case are certainly overstated. Previous historians have not marginalised Sheffield football nearly as much as Harvey suggests and neither is 'the established view' on the relationship between pre-modern and modern forms of football as monolithic and simplistic as he would have us believe. Nevertheless, this work has been crucial in contributing to a more complete understanding of the 'mixture of influences' that helped to create the association game and the recognition that football should no longer be regarded as having been made solely in the environment of the leading public schools and universities.[34] It would indeed be wise to take heed of the words of Holt, who has argued for football to be seen as an innovation based on popular traditions, or as 'a form of cultural continuity', rather than the invention of a privileged social group.[35] Despite the appeal of foundation myths and heroic law-makers, the creation of football in its modern guise was a more collaborative and complicated affair than we used to think.

Codes, clubs and the diffusion of football

The early impact of the FA on the growth and diffusion of association football was modest. 1863 may indeed be regarded as something of a false start in the game's development. Most authors, after all, have very little to say about the 1860s, a decade in which the game remained largely confined geographically to the home counties, Sheffield and one or two other pockets of England and Scotland. There is precious little evidence that the FA did much to spread or popularise its new code. The number of teams reported to be active in London increased from 31 in 1864 to 79 by 1867, but no more than a handful of these joined the FA or adopted its rules. This posed such a problem for the No Names club that it complained in 1866 of only being able to play two other teams – Barnes and Crystal Palace – under common FA rules. The public schools were no more impressed. Most were hostile to the association and its code and it was not until 1868 that the first major school sides – Charterhouse and Westminster – joined. In the provinces, Sheffield FC and its variant of football remained more influential than the FA. When the Sheffield Football Association was formed in 1867, it had more affiliated clubs and players than the FA itself. The club had already arranged matches with teams from Leeds, Lincoln, Nottingham and Manchester, usually based on using each club's code for alternate fixtures, and initiated a similar meeting against a London FA team in 1866. This too was based not on the FA code but on a composite set of rules: London won by the non-soccer-like score of two goals and four touchdowns to nil. By 1867 the FA's membership had slipped to ten teams – nine from London and Sheffield FC (which remained nonetheless attached to its own rules) – and Morley as chairman even suggested that, having achieved its aim of creating a code to govern football, the association should disband.[36]

That it did not was, according to Harvey at least, due to the influence of the Sheffield club, which was instrumental in the adoption of a series of measures designed to broaden the game's appeal. Central amongst these was the modification of its code to exclude touchdowns (or rouges) and the use of the hand to knock the ball on, both similar to aspects of the rugby game. Alongside a campaign to advertise the game by organising exhibition matches and sending its rules to club secretaries across the country, this had the immediate effect of pushing the FA's membership up to 30 by early 1868. But expansion remained slow. According to one interpretation of the data in Charles Alcock's *Football Annual* of 1873, only 122 clubs in Britain played a form of association football, making it less popular than rugby, which could claim 130. What is more, of these 122 no more than 74 played according to the FA code; the remainder either used local variations of the association game or, in the case of 36 English provincial sides and one from Scotland, adopted the Sheffield rules. Indeed the Sheffield association did not take up the FA code until April 1877.[37]

Charting and explaining the pattern of football's diffusion in these early years has proved to be a complex matter. The differential growth of the rugby and soccer codes appeared no more logical to contemporaries. A *Times* article from 1880 remarked that

the distribution of the game is sporadic and curious. The seed of the one or the other game has, for no visible reason, settled in some districts and been wholly driven out in others. In Nottingham and Sheffield the Rugby game is regarded with contempt but nothing else is played around most of the large towns in Yorkshire, while the same game again, is largely dominant in Lancashire. In Berkshire and Buckinghamshire there is a cup for Association clubs, while next to nothing is heard of the Rugby game.[38]

The theories offered by academics to explain the dissemination of sport are rarely satisfactory enough to account for such peculiar patterns. The geographer John Bale, for instance, has speculated that football's diffusion combined spatial and hierarchical factors: that is, the game spread outwards from neighbouring areas and downwards, from larger and more industrialised urban cities to smaller settlements.[39] In the north-east of England, there is supporting evidence for the former explanation but not for the latter. The first clubs were indeed established in the regional centres of Newcastle and Middlesbrough but beyond this it was often small towns such as Barnard Castle and Corbridge, or villages like Bishop Middleham and Haughton-le-Skerne, which followed, long before the bigger towns of Gateshead, Stockton and Darlington. The process of spatial diffusion can be seen in the Teeside case, where the formation of Middlesbrough FC in 1876 was followed two years later by the creation of three more clubs in the city (Lambton, St John's and Middlesbrough Pupil Teachers), before spreading outside Middlesbrough to neighbouring Linthorpe in 1879, North Ormesby in 1880 and Port Clarence in 1881. In Lancashire, similarly, diffusion to nearby places was more evident than dispersal down the urban hierarchy. The game began in the village of Turton, where a club was formed in 1871, and quickly spread to the nearby cotton towns of Darwen, Blackburn and Bolton. Along with three other small local centres, these towns provided all of the 28 founding clubs of the Lancashire FA in 1878. But the spread of soccer had its limits: in other parts of the county, rugby had got there first. In the Preston-Burnley-Colne area, for instance, it took the adoption of the association code by the village side of Padiham in 1879 to encourage a rapid and widespread switch to the FA rules. Among those who embraced soccer at this time was Preston North End, a club set to become the inaugural winner of the Football League ten years later.[40]

Distance from the place of innovation, or the game's 'culture hearth', thus appears a more convincing explanation for geographical diffusion than community size. Yet it fails to explain the late adoption of soccer in the West Riding of Yorkshire, located relatively close to the association heartlands of central and east Lancashire and South Yorkshire. Here another explanation has been advanced: the importance of cultural boundaries. Soccer's popularity in the Sheffield area did gradually extend northwards, with clubs established in Barnsley, Doncaster and Penistone from the early 1880s, but could barely penetrate the rugby culture of the textile towns further north. It may well be that the cultural boundaries that separated the two areas, in elements ranging from political traditions to popular music, can help us to understand the contrasting preference for rugby in the west and soccer in the south. As Dave Russell has noted, although only 20 miles apart, Huddersfield and Sheffield were located in separate cultural spheres. Equally, the Pennines could have acted as a barrier that 'placed the two sides into separate formations' and thus halted the association game's spread eastwards from Lancashire.[41] Similar cultural boundaries may explain the initial dichotomy between a soccer-playing north Wales, which maintained close economic, social and cultural links with Shropshire and north-west England, and a rugby-playing south. Indeed it was the influence of individuals from, or schooled in, England, as much as from the north of the country, which accounted for the earliest development of the association code in the south.[42]

Other explanations for the spread of soccer in the 1870s and 1880s have revolved around what Tranter called the 'social diffusionist' model.[43] In its crudest form, this involved the sons of the local elite returning home from school with a ball, or old boys from the public and grammar schools or universities wishing to continue to play in adulthood, and so forming a team. In time, the game then percolated down the social structure to the working class. This certainly did happen in some cases. Turton FC was co-founded by James Kay, the Harrow-educated son of a local landowner, whereas at Darwen it was the three sons of local millowner Nathaniel Walsh who formed a football club after they had played with workers during their holidays away from Harrow. Further down the social scale, John Lewis (later to become the most famous referee of the pre-war era) and Arthur Constantine, fresh from the local grammar school, were responsible for the foundation of Blackburn Rovers in 1874. Chester City and Leicester Fosse were similar products of the organising zeal and sporting enthusiasm of grammar school old boys.[44]

More often, however, the social diffusion of football seems to have occurred less directly. As Walvin noted, 'those who wished to encourage sporting activity among working people ... needed a point of entry to a social world which was often distant and generally alien'.[45] A range of social groups and institutions, the most prominent of which were connected to education, religion and the workplace, provided this point of entry. School teachers were to the forefront in establishing clubs in many areas. Here the process of geographical and social diffusion went hand in hand. The increase in the numbers of teacher training colleges undoubtedly had an enormous effect, yet to be fully explored by scholars, on the increasing popularity of the game. New teachers willing to establish football amongst their pupils were often equally eager to play the game themselves. Such was the case in Sunderland in 1879 where James Allan, a Scot, was instrumental in organising the Sunderland and District club which later became Sunderland FC. During the same year William Harrison, an elementary teacher originally from Liverpool, helped found the Redcar club, while a number of pupil teachers were heavily involved in the creation of Middlesbrough's earliest clubs and, after graduating, in popularising the game in the Durham area.[46]

The role of churches, chapels and other religious bodies in the foundation of football teams has long been known. Some of England's most famous clubs, such as Aston Villa, Birmingham City, Bolton Wanderers, Everton and Fulham, were established during the 1870s or early 1880s as church or Sunday School teams. Church-based teams were regular competitors in the nascent football cultures of Blackburn, Nottingham and Sheffield from the mid-1870s. D. D. Molyneux's research on Birmingham shows that of the clubs active in the 1876–7, 1879–80 and 1883–4 seasons, just under 24 per cent were connected to religious organisations. In 1885 in Liverpool, where football arrived relatively late, 25 of the city's 112 clubs were church-related. No doubt many of the clergy who became active here were inspired by a philosophy of 'muscular Christianity' and convinced of the moral value of sport. Some, like the vicar who became the first captain of the Durham village club Tow Law in 1881, were active players themselves, having learnt the game at school or university.[47]

Religious connections were particularly important in the formation of the earliest Scottish clubs. Scotland's senior club was Queen's Park, established in Glasgow in 1867 by members of the Young Men's Christian Association (YMCA). Its dominance over the early years of the game north of the border was immense. With few serious rivals, the club managed to avoid conceding a goal in its first five years of existence, and during the 1881–2 season its three teams remained unbeaten. Like Queen's Park, many of these clubs seem to have sprung from similar origins as their English counterparts. For instance, Moffatt FC was established in 1879 by the Rev. W. H. Churchill, a muscular Christian of some note who had captained the Cambridge University soccer eleven. He believed that the game helped to instil discipline and self-control in those who played and so, on returning to England, donated a cup to be competed for by local clubs with the gate receipts distributed to local charities.[48] However, the history of sectarianism in Scottish society places a rather different gloss on the religious roots of its clubs. Hibernian was formed in 1875 at St Patrick's Church, Edinburgh, among representatives of the Catholic equivalent of the YMCA, the Catholic Young Men's Society (CYMS). One historian has claimed that the chaplain Canon Edward Hannon 'had it written into the constitution of the club that its players must be practising Catholics', making Hibernian Scotland's first all-Catholic club, although others have rejected the notion that it was ever sectarian.[49] Similar debate exists over the creation of Rangers. Formed in 1873 ostensibly by a group of young men from Glasgow, Bill Murray has argued that 'there was nothing religious in the origins of Rangers, they were Protestant only in the sense that the vast majority of clubs in Scotland at that time were made up of Protestants'. Yet G.P.T. Finn has situated Rangers within a tradition of religious and politically affiliated clubs, such as the 3rd Edinburgh Rifle Volunteers, Larkhall Royal Albert and Clydebank. These clubs, Finn argues, had developed anti-Catholic and unionist tendencies that pre-dated the foundation of Irish–Scots clubs like Hibernian and Celtic.[50]

The workplace was also a common site for the formation of clubs. Students of the game are well aware of the origins of Arsenal and West Ham United at the Woolwich Arsenal and Thames Ironworks respectively, although both were founded beyond this period (in 1886 and 1895). While less numerous than church-based organisations, Molyneux still located 25 works teams competing in Birmingham football during 1871, 1875 and 1880. Tony Mason found a similar number playing in Sheffield in selected years between 1873 and 1885. The most prominent of these was the team of file steel and cutlery firm Lockwood Brothers, founded as early as 1870. By 1882 the club had 140 members and seems to have benefited from the support of George Francis Lockwood, grandson of the founder, who is reported to have played football at the Sheffield Collegiate School. In many cases, the precise nature of the link between firm and club is far from clear. We know little about the extent to which companies lent financial support or were closely involved in the decision making of 'their' clubs, although no doubt in certain cases the relationship was merely symbolic. Even companies that seem to have lent more than a name, such as the Birmingham brewers Mitchells (Mitchell St Georges) and the Midland Railway Company (Derby Midland), were only prepared to support sporting enterprise so long as the team was successful and the finances manageable.[51]

This often tenuous connection between clubs and the institutions from which they supposedly sprang represents a serious flaw in the downwards 'social diffusionist' model. As a number of historians have pointed out, new clubs were more often the product of the independent initiative of those who wanted to play than the work of rational recreationists.[52] The church or workplace provided the organisational locus for the formation of clubs but most of the impetus and organisation seems to have come from the membership or employees themselves. Thus Aston Villa may have 'originated ... from members of the Villa Cross Wesleyan Chapel', in Walvin's words, but the chapel seems to have played no part whatso-ever in the club's subsequent development. Certainly it was of less significance than a local butcher who provided the club with a playing field and a local publican who offered changing facilities. In response to Young's vision of the curate or vicar setting out to 'claim souls with a Bible in one hand and a football in the other', Peter Bailey has pointed out that the sporting churchman remained a rarity in Victorian Britain.[53] Even in the case of Scottish clubs where the religious connection appears much stronger, it tended to be the members who took the lead: Hibernian, we should remember, was founded by the players not by the chaplain. What is more, there is considerable evidence to suggest that many religious bodies and employers were keener to restrict rather than encourage involvement in sport and that where clubs did exist, membership was often restricted to regular churchgoers in the first case and 'reputable' employees in the second. Nor should we assume that the majority of foot-ball-playing public school and university graduates were anxious to teach the game to their social inferiors or that in William Baker's words, 'fired with the ideals of "muscular Christianity" [they] zealously introduced rugby and soccer to the masses outside the pale of southern refinement'.[54]

All this suggests that we need to be more sophisticated in our under-standing of the spread of football, recognising the likelihood that its expansion was driven by a combination of popular and elite initiative. The proliferation of teams focused not on institutions but on the suburb, neighbourhood or even the street, supports the suggestion that much of the momentum for diffusion came not from above but from below. In Birmingham, Liverpool and Sheffield, teams with street or place names were considerably more numerous than workplace or church clubs. Tranter's study of teams founded in Stirling between 1876 and 1895 revealed that 37 of the total of 68 were named after a part of the town, with at least five of these – Baker Street Rangers, Cowane Street Thistle, George Street, Shore Road Thistle and Wallace Street Thistle – centred on the street.[55] Although we should be wary of drawing firm conclusions simply on the basis of team names, there is enough evidence to suggest that the growth of association football throughout the country was the product not of simply copying or emulating upper and middle-class play but also of a genuine and largely autonomous popular enthusiasm for the game. Perhaps a passion for and understanding of the game among working people did not have to be learnt? Bearing in mind the emphasis we have already given to the continuity of popular forms of football into the mid-century, it may well be that Holt was accurate in his speculation that the game's rapid expansion from the mid-1870s onwards can be explained by the existence of a latent popular 'football' culture pre-dating the codification of the association game.[56]

More research is needed before we can be confident of grasping the intricacies of football's geographical and social diffusion over this period. What should be clear, however, is that simple monocausal explanations will no longer suffice. This is evident if we briefly look at the way in which soccer was established in Ireland. Conventional histories offer two main, though not necessarily incompatible, explanations.[57] The first prioritises the role of students who had experienced the English public school system, particularly those who came back to study at Trinity College in Dublin. John Sugden and Alan Bairner have suggested that 'Irish pupils at these schools brought this ... form of football [the kicking game] back to Ireland, either during their vacations or on completion of their studies'.[58] Yet, as in the English case, it remains unclear exactly how such elite sporting activity filtered down the social scale and spread across the country, particularly given the relatively fractured nature of Irish society and its geographical diversity. The second explanation provides Irish soccer with a precise place and date of birth. On 24 October 1878, the Scottish teams Caledonians and Queen's Park played an exhibition match at the Ulster Cricket Club in Belfast. The game had been arranged by J. A. McAlery, a clothes shop manager, who had apparently watched soccer on his honeymoon in Scotland. The following year McAlery helped to found Ireland's first association club, Cliftonville FC, and in November 1880 along with two other Belfast clubs, Avoniel and Knock, formed the Irish Football Association (IFA) to organise and promote the game.[59]

The game was late to arrive in Ireland and spread rather slowly, hampered somewhat by the popularity of not just one but two rival codes: rugby and Gaelic football (formally codified in 1885). Nonetheless we can detect even in the embryonic growth of Irish soccer the type of complex and often contradictory patterns that we have identified elsewhere in Britain. In Belfast, the centre of the early game, the role of Scottish migrants was crucial. The Avoniel team was said to be formed by Scotsmen building a new distillery of that name, while Queen's Island, the Irish Cup winners of 1882, was made up of Scottish employees in the city shipyard. The connection even extended to the adoption by the IFA of 'the Scotch Rule book' at one of its earliest meetings. Here the cultural and socio-economic connections and the relatively short distance between the west of Scotland and the north of Ireland may also have been significant. In Dublin, however, it was the public schoolboy and university student who played the key role, giving the game a more elite image than in Belfast. Elsewhere, military teams were often vital in early competition, even if this generated as much opposition to the game as it offered encouragement. Regional and social variations were thus marked in Irish soccer's early years. As Neal Garnham has observed, 'the means by which Association football was … disseminated across Ireland were many and varied'.[60]

Associations, cups and players

This is little doubt that from the mid-1870s football's popularity in Britain grew rapidly.[61] There are a number of ways of charting this rise. One is to look at the creation of national and local associations. The Scottish Football Association (SFA) was established in 1873, ten years after the English body, with the Football Association of Wales (FAW) created in 1876 and, as we have seen, the IFA following in 1880. On a regional level, there was an eight-year delay between the formation of the Sheffield FA in 1867 and the Birmingham FA in 1875, but thereafter associations were set up in quick succession. In the north and midlands of England, associations were established in Staffordshire in 1877, Cheshire and Lancashire in 1878, Durham and Northumberland in 1879, Cleveland and Lincolnshire in 1881, Liverpool, Shropshire, Northamptonshire, Nottinghamshire, Walsall and Scarborough and the East Riding in 1882 and Derbyshire in 1883. In the south, Surrey (1877), Berkshire and Buckinghamshire (1878), Norfolk (1881), London and Sussex (1882), Essex, Kent and Middlesex (1883), Cambridgeshire, South Hampshire and Dorset (1884) and Somerset and Suffolk (1885) all had their own football associations by the end of this period.[62] A second method is to judge participation rates by counting club and player numbers. Such evidence is notoriously patchy and difficult to interpret but we can certainly use it as a guide. The Lancashire FA's original 28 clubs in 1878 had increased to 62 by 1882 and 114 by 1886 while the Birmingham FA grew from 17 clubs in 1877 to 50 by 1880 and 63 by 1884–5. The smaller Northumberland and Durham association, meanwhile, leapt from a base of just three members in 1879 to 25 by the 1880–1 season. By 1879, there were 40 clubs and 5,000 players affiliated to the Sheffield FA, while its Nottinghamshire counterpart could claim to represent 36 clubs and 1,630 players six years later. The Stirlingshire FA, meanwhile, was founded with seven senior clubs in 1882, a number that had risen to 19, accounting for 1,200 players, by the end of 1884. In

PLATE 1 *Charles W. Alcock, Secretary of the Football Association from 1870 until 1895 (© Popperfoto.com).*

central Scotland more generally, Tranter has documented 66 football clubs in existence between 1871 and 1880. Over the course of the following decade, this figure increased over sevenfold, to 506.[63] Such surviving data, concerned as it is mainly with affiliated and registered clubs, cannot begin to account for the considerable number of teams and individuals who, as we shall see in the next chapter, played on a less permanent, less organised, even ad hoc basis.

Crucial to the growth and survival of clubs and associations was the development of cup competitions. The establishment of the FA Challenge Cup in 1871–2 has not surprisingly been regarded as pivotal here. The idea for a knock-out competition is normally supposed to have been taken by Alcock from his experience of the 'Cock House' competitions at Harrow. While there is no reason to doubt this explanation, it is important once again to acknowledge the additional influence that Sheffield football is likely to have had upon this innovation. A cup competition, apparently based on a knock-out system, had been launched by the music-hall proprietor Thomas Youdon as early as 1867 (to become the Cromwell Cup a year later). It would be surprising if Alcock, who had played against representatives of the Sheffield association and knew of the cup, did not derive some inspiration from its apparent success.[64] What is more, we should not overemphasise the initial impact of the FA Cup in broadening interest in the game. The inaugural competition attracted just 15 clubs. Most of these were formed around the teams of London-based public school old boys and only two, Donington Grammar School from Lincolnshire and Scotland's representative Queen's Park, were drawn from beyond the home counties. Alcock's own club, Wanderers, beat Royal Engineers 1–0 in the first final at the Oval in London. That these two clubs, along with Old Etonians and Oxford University, contested every one of the first seven finals, is surely evidence of elite domination over this particular competition rather than over the game as a whole. After all, even by 1876 the FA Cup attracted no more than 37 entrants, only four of which (the Druids from Ruabon in north Wales, Sheffield FC, Shropshire Wanderers and Queen's Park) were non-metropolitan. This contrasted rather poorly with the 40 clubs competing in the first round of the inaugural Lancashire Cup just four years later and with the Cromwell Cup, which could draw participants from well beyond Sheffield, including the Redcar and Middlesbrough clubs who first entered in 1879. It took some ten years for the FA Cup to evolve into a competition of genuinely national scope. Darwen was defeated in the 1881 semi-final by the eventual winners Old Carthusians, and the following year Blackburn Rovers became the first provincial side to make the final, losing 1–0 to Old Etonians. The 1883–4 competition, eventually won by Blackburn Rovers, saw 101 clubs entered, the vast majority of which were now situated in the north and midlands of England.[65]

Cups normally followed closely behind the creation of associations. In the Scottish case, they emerged simultaneously: the eight clubs that formed the national body in 1873 had met ostensibly to sponsor a cup competition. The Welsh Cup arrived in 1877–8, a year after the formation of the national association. In common with the earliest administrators and international teams, the cup was dominated by representatives from the north of the Principality. Wrexham won the first competition and of the 19 entrants only Swansea was drawn from the south, and it was primarily a rugby club that had apparently not realised that the tournament was to be based on association rules.[66] The rapid spread of regional associations brought with it a proliferation of cup competitions, which stood alongside more minor cups and other charity cup events on club fixture lists. Mike Huggins and Dave Russell have both regarded cups as a major fillip to the game by generating the necessary interest and excitement to sustain soccer as the main football code in the north-east and Lancashire respectively. Not only did the knock-out element of cup competition create greater enthusiasm than an ordinary 'friendly' match (and offer better gambling prospects) but it could also become closely associated with local and civic pride. When Redcar defeated Middlesbrough in 1880, a local newspaper commented on the 'astonishment and blank dismay of [Redcar's] defeated opponents, who until this day had held premier position among the association clubs for miles around'. Neither should we assume that this competitive spirit was entirely northern. By 1883, challenge cups on the FA model had also been established in Essex, London, Norfolk, Surrey and Sussex.[67]

It is difficult to be precise about the social background of the earliest football players. Not surprisingly, we know most about the ex-public school men who became the game's first administrators and historians; men such as Alcock of course but also the Old Etonian and Trinity graduate (later Lord and Baron) Arthur Kinnaird and N. L. 'Pa' Jackson, founder of the staunchly amateur Corinthians club in 1882. The elite status of some of the most prominent of the first association clubs is beyond dispute. From its beginnings, Queen's Park established an image as a club of social and sporting prestige. As the club's historian has argued, it tended to include its fair share of professionals – lawyers, doctors and teachers, as well as students, accountants and commercial travellers. Yet there were also some skilled workers, such as the right-winger and Scottish international James Weir, who was a carpenter.[68] Mason and Harvey have examined the occupations of members of Sheffield FC and both found them to be predominantly middle class. Manufacturers, solicitors, surgeons and brewers headed the 1858 and 1859 membership lists. Among the new members enrolling in 1870 were two gentlemen, two bankers, a coal company secretary and a timber merchant. The *Sheffield Daily Telegraph* described the club in 1867 as 'almost exclusively of the middle class', while it could apparently count on the support of 'most of the leading men in the neighbourhood'. Few clubs, outside London at least, were as socially selective as this but many were clearly middle class in complexion.[69] One reporter thought most of the players on the Tyne and Tees before 1886 'were of a certain class', namely professional men: bank clerks, clergymen, lawyers and teachers. There were indeed 21 teachers, nine vicars or curates and four doctors among the 39 captains and vice-captains of the teams identified by Huggins in the north-east between 1876 and 1883. Martin Johnes and Ian Garland's analysis of early Welsh soccer sides revealed a similar middle-class core but a significant working-class element as well. The Welsh Cup winning Oswestry team of 1884, for example, included a farmer's son, a blacksmith and a tannery worker alongside a schoolmaster, shopkeeper and future accountant. Some early football teams were thus clearly composed of a mixture of classes and occupational groups.[70]

It is telling that, although there may well have been many genuinely proletarian clubs – those that were, in Mason's words, 'working class in origin and run by working men for working men' – historians have found few examples. The most familiar is the Elswick Leather Works from Newcastle, described in 1881 by its secretary as 'a working men's club' with almost 90 members. Another possible candidate, the New Marske club in North Yorkshire, which maintained close links with the miners' institute, nonetheless included three farmers' sons and a grocer in its sides between 1881 and 1883 and had, like many clubs in the north-east, been founded by a group of pupil teachers. Even the celebrated Lancastrian sides, which began to make progress to the latter stages of the FA Cup in the late 1870s, are more accurately described as working-class *teams* rather than working-class clubs. The Darwen first eleven, which reached the quarter-finals in 1879 and the semi-finals in 1881, for example, may have been composed of workers in the local textile industry but the committee contained a sizeable middle-class element.[71]

It is in this respect that the 1883 FA Cup final is often presented as such a major watershed in the history of the game.[72] It pitted the Old Etonians, captained by Kinnaird and holders of the trophy, against Blackburn Olympic, a team which, in the phrase of one historian, supposedly 'came south with factory muck still on their brows'. The Etonians had been up against another Blackburn side, Rovers, in the previous year's final, but had triumphed 1–0. The scoreline was 2–1 in 1883 but on this occasion it was the northerners who won. Following the reaction of the contemporary press, historians have played with the contrasts of style, etiquette and class raised by the match. If Olympic's semi-final against the Old Carthusians had been dubbed by *Athletic News* a contest between 'patricians and plebeians', the final was all the more so. The *Blackburn Times* saw in the result

the meeting and vanquishing, in a most severe trial of athletic skill, of a Club composed of sons of some of the families of the upper class in the Kingdom . . . as the Old Etonian Club is, by a Provincial Club composed entirely, we believe, of Lancashire Lads of the manual working-class, sons of small tradesmen, artizans, and operatives.

The same newspaper had already outlined the precise occupations of the Olympic team: there were three weavers, two iron foundry workers, a loomer, a gilder, a master plumber, a clerk, a licensed victualler and a dental assistant. Yet the significance of the result was not that it symbolised the end of public school domination and the rise of the working-class game, a trend which was already firmly established, especially in the provinces. More important was its suggestion of a new, professional approach to the game. Sydney Yates, a local iron founder, and Councillor Boothman, had both contributed £100 to help the team prepare for the final. Under player-manager Jack Hunter, Olympic had engaged in three weeks of special training at Blackpool, Bournemouth and Richmond to improve their fitness and work on their tactical play. This was serious business and the *Eton College Chronicle* thought it unsporting but not altogether unsurprising, given the patronage of local employers, the passion of Olympic's supporters and their overwhelming will to win. Such sentiments were to be echoed and rejoined continually during the first half of the 1880s.[73]

Spectators, money and professionalisation

The introduction of professionalism in football is often presented as if it were an inevitable result of the game's increasing popularity. Popular enthusiasm, we are told, begat large crowds which lead to increased gate money income and ultimately to the need to reimburse, secure and even reward the best players. Yet recent research has shown the 'drift to professional football' to be less straightforward than this.[74] As the economic historian Wray Vamplew has shown, the enclosing of grounds, charging of entrance money and building of stadiums were not the inevitable outcome of impersonal structural forces. They resulted from the decisions of individual sports entrepreneurs responding to the economic stimuli which underpinned the growth of late nineteenth-century commercialised leisure.[75] And it was far from certain that prospective consumers would choose football over other recreational attractions in the numbers they did. Neither, as students of British sporting history are well aware, was there anything inevitable about the decision to legalise the practice of paying players, as the FA did in 1885. The debate between advocates of strict amateurism and open professionalism in the rugby fraternity a decade later was similarly polarised but ended rather differently, with a split into two separate bodies and, ultimately, games. Why was this avoided in football? Any adequate answer to this question needs to pay due attention both to the broader social and political environment of late Victorian Britain and the particular beliefs and actions of those who ran the clubs and governed the sport.

The watching, no less than the playing, of football on a mass scale was dependent upon changes in the time and money available to working people. Any attempt to identify general trends here is problematic, given the economic fluctuations over the period and the varieties of working experience in different industries and parts of the country. Yet what we can say is that, starting with the Ten Hours Act of 1847, a combination of government legislation and trade union agitation had led to a shortening of the working week in the more unionised industries by the 1870s. For sport to flourish, however, what was more important than reductions in the hours worked was when this time off was allocated in the course of the working week. In this respect, the granting of the Saturday half-holiday in most skilled trades was crucial. Saturday afternoons represented, in the absence of the adequate technology to provide flood-lighting for night games and a widespread opposition to Sunday sport, the only available time slot in which regular sporting events could be fitted. This needs to be seen alongside the general increase in the spending power of the working class, which, as with working hours, was subject to numerous regional, occupational and temporal variations. A very basic estimate suggests that real wages rose by about 60 per cent between 1870 and the 1890s, but this figure cannot begin to take account of fluctuations in the trade cycle and the periodic unemployment, lay-offs and short-term working which inevitably affected the actual money taken home. Economic historians have identified the major beneficiaries of increased prosperity and accompanying welfare schemes as textile and engineering workers and those employed in the shipbuilding, transport and mining industries. Such evidence may explain the centrality of the industrial heartland of Lancashire to the growth of the game and help us to understand the relatively late take-up of cities like Liverpool, with a large casual, non-unionised workforce, and parts of the north-east, where the Saturday half-day was only introduced from the mid-1880s.[76]

Historians have been slow to examine why workers with increased money and leisure time opted to watch football matches. Many of the explanations are necessarily speculative. We certainly need to know much more about the relationship between playing and spectating in this period.[77] Of course, the distinction between the two was largely a product of the codification of the modern game. Stephen Tischler has made the basic but fundamental point that with a reduced number of participants per side, and the limitation and demarcation of the playing area, 'participation' for most people was necessarily downgraded from playing to supporting. Lack of space in which to play was another consideration. Studies of late nineteenth-century Birmingham and Liverpool have emphasised the increasing provision of playing fields and of parks and open spaces where games could be played, but the expansion of facilities was not as rapid as some would have liked. The Open Space Movement complained of 'the chronic shortage of playing room in the towns', and the lack of playground space for children and youths in various parts of the country led to numerous instances of football being forced on to the streets, with the resulting social nuisance it caused. Such obstacles to play may indeed have 'inadvertently fostered the tendency to watch football', as Tischler believed.[78] Yet we should not assume that, especially at this early stage in the game's development, playing and watching were mutually exclusive. Most spectators had probably played the game at some stage and indeed many would surely have regarded it as a chance to learn new techniques and skills and to improve old ones. Even for those who did not play, however, the aesthetic appeal of the game was still significant. One newspaper report from 1882 was impressed by the popular

eagerness of witnessing play of the highest order and excellence. As the players themselves became educated in the intricacies of passing, dodging, and combination ... so do the thousands, who weekly cull enjoyment from witnessing a good game, become more and more appreciative of good play.[79]

Expertise in the stands developed alongside expertise on the field. Such expertise was no doubt acquired easily due to the relative simplicity of soccer. The 14 basic rules codified by the FA in 1863 compared with some 59 laws that accompanied the institutionalisation of rugby in 1871.[80]

Whatever the particular appeal of football (and it is likely to have varied from person to person), there is no doubt that there were large numbers of people willing to attend matches, and to pay to do so. The idea of gate-money sport was already well-established in cricket and athletics and was emerging in horse racing, where Sandown Park was opened in 1875 as the first enclosed course with spectators charged for entry. Although it is difficult to be precise about dates, we can be sure that by the early 1870s many clubs had fenced off the field or pitch on which they played, and created gates at which spectators paid to enter. At Aston Villa's Perry Barr ground a hedge originally encircled the field. Yet with increased crowds, and gaps in the hedge allowing a free view to potential paying customers, it was cut down in 1878 and replaced by boardings.[81]

The information we have on spectator numbers from this period is invariably based on newspaper estimates, making them notoriously unreliable. Yet bearing this in mind, we can still identify the general trend for the size of crowds to rise substantially from the mid to late-1870s, especially at the high-profile national and local cup-ties and special representative and exhibition matches. Gates of over 3,000 were extremely rare even in the early years of the FA and Scottish Cup. The very first English final tie at the Oval in 1872 drew only 2,000 and the inaugural Scotland–England international at Glasgow in the same year attracted no more than 4,000 spectators, many of whom were reported (with some surprise) to be 'ladies'. By the early 1880s, however, crowds of over 10,000 were not unknown. The largest attendances were to be found in Scotland and the north of England. The *Pall Mall Gazette*'s 'northern horde of uncouth garbe and strange oaths' which accompanied Blackburn Rovers' visit to the Oval for the 1882 Cup final helped to swell the metropolitan crowd to 6,000, but this could not match the 8,000 who attended Preston North End's Deepdale ground for its Lancashire Cup second-round clash with Great Lever in 1883 or the 20,000 reported to have purchased tickets for a match between Darwen and Blackburn Rovers in March 1882. At Aston Villa, Blackburn Rovers and Preston North End, crowds ranged from 4,000 to 6,000 in the early to mid-1880s and exceeded 15,000 on specific occasions at Bolton, Nottingham and Derby during 1884 and early 1885.[82]

The sheer scale of such crowds impressed observers. A reporter at a representative match between Birmingham and Scotland in March 1882 believed that the

enormous crowd was an imposing sight; they were closely packed all round the enclosure, the grandstands were full to repletion, and vehicles of all descriptions lined the track which circles the meadow. A small regiment of venturesome youths had perched themselves upon two sheds ... and all the persuasive eloquence of several policemen, and even stronger argument in the shape of a hose, failed to induce them to descend from their position ... The trees, and even the shrubs, too, were taken advantage of by hundreds of juveniles, perched in mid-air like so many crows overlooking a field.

Many others detected in such developments a threat to the game as it had, or ought to have been, organised. One London journalist regarded big gates as 'the curse of the game'; a Birmingham commentator saw in such contests a fundamental challenge to the character of sport, which should be conducted 'for the honour of victory alone without any ulterior thought as to how much the "gate" is worth'. What is more, as Tischler has outlined, the corollary of this emergent brand of gate-money football was the need to secure the best players possible. The football entrepreneur could not assume that his customer would continue to contribute to the gate if the team lost and/or the quality of play was poor. Local journalists recognised the discretionary and fickle nature of such support. 'The public', according to *The Athlete*, 'are bound to flock where they can see the best play.' A poor start to the 1884–5 season led *Athletic News* to advise the Blackburn Rovers committee that if the team were not strengthened they would 'not only lose a lot of engagements, but they will find a considerable falling off of gate receipts'. In such circumstances, the engagement of quality players was essential to ensure both sporting success and financial security.[83] 'Where you get big gates', Gibson and Pickford later commented, 'you must almost of necessity get professionalism.' The debate over professionalism emerged in this context.[84]

James Catton, sports journalist and one of the first historians of football, tells us that the original professionals in Britain were the Scottish pair of Peter Andrews and James Lang, who joined the Sheffield club Heeley around 1876.[85] Yet professionalism on a significant scale was centred on Lancashire; more precisely according to Robert Lewis, in the Bolton-Blackburn-Darwen triangle of cotton towns. Certainly we know that in 1878 Turton FC handed the £3 the club won for finishing second in a challenge cup tournament to one Fergie Suter, a Scotsman who claimed to have moved to the area as a stonemason but turned to football after finding that the local stone caused his hands and arms to swell. The following spring, Darwen FC played a benefit match 'for two Scotch gentlemen', the aforementioned Suter and Jimmy Love, who had apparently represented the club over the past season. At around the same time, a Darwen newspaper suggested Hugh McIntyre, a former captain of Glasgow Rangers who had played for Blackburn Rovers in a recent game, was engaged by that club as a professional. By the 1880s, certainly, such insinuations were commonplace.[86] 'Professionalism' at this time, as Dave Russell has observed, was not only about being paid to play. Rather, it was a catch-all phrase that embraced a range of supposed abuses of the rules and the spirit of the game.[87] The *Midland Athlete* captured this eloquently when it remarked in 1881 that although it knew of no obvious instances of direct money payment *we do know of cases where men have received more than legitimate expenses to play for a club. But though men are not often paid in cash they are in other ways; it is no uncommon thing for influential members of a club to obtain situations for good players as an inducement for them to play with certain clubs. Then it is not improbable that club funds may or have been used to find a small business for popular players who pose as 'mine host' before their admiring clubmates ... Men who can afford to give up business for football, who can travel here, there and everywhere at all times and seasons, men who receive payment for playing in certain matches, men who make a profit out of the game they play, are professionals.*[88]

Lewis has identified three practices that were indicative of the presence of professionalism in Lancashire: the 'importation' of players; the use of 'guest' players borrowed from other clubs; and the inducement or 'poaching' of players from rival clubs. The first of these was undoubtedly the most serious issue for contemporary observers, regarded as it was by many as a precursor of professionalism outright. As the examples cited above suggest, most of the 'imports' were Scottish nationals, widely regarded at the time as the most highly skilled 'professors' of the game. Bolton Wanderers certainly had six Scots on its books in 1882, one reporter joking that the team should in future sport kilts and be known as the 'Caledonians'. In May of that year the Lancashire FA had attempted to ban imports altogether, but after opposition from member clubs settled on a two-year residential qualification for players born outside the county who wished to appear in cup ties. Nevertheless, *Football Field* could list at least 55 Scottish players turning out for 11 Lancashire clubs in December 1884, 11 of whom were with Preston North End, 9 at Burnley and 7 at Halliwell (near Bolton). In keeping with the *Midland Athlete*'s implication, some seem to have been offered convenient employment positions. Burnley's former Vale of Leven man Dan Friel was landlord of the Footballers' Arms in Burnley and James McKernan worked at the Britannia Inn, the then headquarters of Bolton Wanderers. Great Lever, meanwhile, had the ex-Kilmarnock player Johnnie Goodall working at the club's meeting place – the Robin Hood Inn. Tot Rostron, another probable professional, though not an import, kept the bowling green at the same establishment. Accusations of professionalism were not confined to the north-west. In 1883 Nottingham Forest found an inventive way of publicising its suspicions that three of Sheffield Wednesday's team in a recent cup tie had not been bona fide players by mounting placards on the

Sheffield streets and offering a £20 reward for information. The Sheffield association required any player accused of professionalism to provide proof that he had not exceeded payment beyond travelling and hotel expenses. Along with the Lancashire body, it also attempted to prevent 'guesting' by ensuring that players could only represent one club in cup competitions over the course of a season. In 1884 the Scottish FA threatened players receiving remuneration 'beyond their reasonable and legitimate expenses' with a two-year ban.[89]

That so-called 'veiled' professionals certainly existed was revealed in November 1883 when the FA banned a player for receiving a financial sum to join Accrington and expelled the club from the national association. Over the course of 1884 and 1885 the debate became increasingly intense and threatened a split in the administration of the English game. The crucial development came in January 1884 when the amateur London club Upton Park protested to the governing body that their fourth-round FA Cup opponents Preston North End had included professionals in its line-up. Rather than deny the claim as many had before, the Preston secretary and local mill manager Major William Sudell admitted paying his players but denied that this practice was either wrong or unusual. Preston was banned from the competition, followed soon after by Burnley and Great Lever. Over a year of investigations, meetings, proposals and counter-proposals were not able to resolve the issue. Indeed an attempt to prohibit non-Englishmen from representing English teams in the FA Cup prompted a threatened formation of a separatist British National Association by some 40 northern clubs in the autumn of 1884. Finally, the pressure for change proved too great and in July 1885 the FA legalised professionalism. Yet the regulations placed stringent controls on the new professional player: appearances in cup games were dependent on birth or residential qualifications (two years living within 6 miles of the club headquarters); swapping clubs mid season was prohibited without express permission; and involvement in club or association committees was outlawed.[90]

It has been tempting to view the struggle over professionalism as fundamentally polarised along the lines of class and geography. For Tischler, certainly, opposition to professionalism was driven above all by class prejudice: the term 'professional came to be accepted as a euphemism for "working class"'. The oft-quoted remark of the Birmingham association's W. H. Jope that 'it was degrading for respectable men to play with professionals' lends support to such a view but his was an extreme voice amongst a range of gentlemen amateur opinion in the FA and the press.

Charles Alcock, for one, thought that most amateurs had no problem playing alongside professionals and rejected that the latter were 'the utter outcasts some people represent them to be'. Indeed, throughout the debate there was a clear split within the public school-dominated FA hierarchy over how to deal with the professional threat. Lewis categorised this as a division between 'liberals' and 'conservatives'; for Mason, it was really about tactical differences over whether to fight or contain the 'monster' of professionalism.[91]

Similarly, the issue can hardly be reduced to simple north–south or Lancashire–London rivalries. The language of regional identity and anti-metropolitanism was certainly to the fore in the pages of the Lancashire press. One newspaper had no doubt about what was at stake: 'Is the Lancashire Association going to stand quietly by while Lancashire clubs are interfered with – many think unlawfully – by a caucus of South Country footballers?' Another felt that the whole crisis was the creation of 'a few mashers who wish to have the English cup back in London'.[92] At an FA meeting in early 1885 the rift was symbolised by the decision of the northern delegates to sit to the right of the president and the southern representatives to the left. Yet, just as in the case of class, there were complications to this neat dichotomy. We know that some London representatives voted for professionalism and that one or two Lancashire clubs – particularly Blackburn Rovers and Darwen – stood apart from the movement for legalisation. What is more, some of Lancashire's staunchest opponents came not from the capital but from the provinces, particularly Birmingham, Sheffield and Scotland, where rumours of veiled professionalism were rife. We certainly need more detailed information on who voted for what at the key FA meetings, and a greater understanding of the local debates over professionalism in these other crucial regions. As was to continue to be the case, the amateur–professional issue in soccer was infused with aspects of class and regional identity and antagonism, but not in any reductionist, straightforward way.[93]

How can we explain the FA's decision to control and contain rather than fight professionalism, as the amateur rugby authorities chose to do in the 1890s? Dunning and Sheard have posited two possibilities. The first, that the more elevated social and educational background of football's leaders – drawn from the upper classes and the very best public schools such as Eton and Harrow – made them more socially assured and thus willing to embrace the professional element than was the case with the Rugby Football Union, remains short on evidence and inconclusive. Their second explanation, though equally speculative, has more to commend itself to the historian. They point to the relatively quiescent and harmonious social, political and industrial relations of the early to mid-1880s in comparison with a less stable environment by the 1890s brought on by the impact of 'new unionism', increasing industrial militancy and the growing influence of socialist and independent labour politics.[94] Another leading historian of rugby has made a similar observation. Britain in the mid-1890s was, according to Collins, 'a very different society from that which it had been in 1886', one in which 'industrial conflict and class antagonism were to the fore', the old certainties 'disappearing and the fear of the mob was rising'.[95] In such circumstances, conceding to the predominantly working-class, professional element of the sport may have taken on a much different resonance.

Another explanation is that football's administrators already had a model provided by another major sport in which professionalism had been accepted but controlled: cricket. County committees and the MCC (Marylebone Cricket Club), as the game's governing body, managed the behaviour, working conditions and earnings of the cricket professionals extremely tightly. Amateurism and social exclusivity were retained. The idea that football's administrators may have been influenced by this state of affairs is not entirely fanciful. A number, particularly Alcock who was secretary of Surrey CCC, were more than familiar with the way in which cricket governed its professionals. Moreover, some writers have commented on the similarities between the FA's first professional rules and county cricket's existing birth and residential qualifications.[96] A decade later, by contrast, it was the experience of soccer's professionalisation that influenced the thinking of rugby's opinion formers and decision makers. Views were split on whether professionalism had ruined or improved the association game but there were certainly those who felt it proved that open professionalism marginalised the amateur and destroyed the finances of clubs.[97] The next chapter looks at how these debates were played out within soccer circles, examining the game's fortunes in the professional era.

References

1 Eric Dunning, *Sport Matters: Sociological Studies of Sport, Violence and Civilization* (London: Routledge, 1999), p. 88. The term 'soccer', often dismissed erroneously as an 'Americanisation', was actually a nineteenth-century derivation of '*association* football'. It will be used interchangeably with 'football' in this book.

2 Percy Young, *A History of British Football* (London: Arrow, 1973 [1st edition, 1968]); James Walvin, *The People's Game: The History of Football Revisited* (Edinburgh: Mainstream, 1994); Tony Mason, *Association Football and English Society, 1863–1915* (Brighton: Harvester, 1980); Dave Russell, *Football and the English: A Social History of Association Football in England, 1863–1995* (Preston: Carnegie, 1997).

3 Martin Polley, 'History and Sport' in B. Houlihan (ed.), *Sport and Society: A Student Introduction* (London: Sage, 2003), p. 59.

4 Two recent popular histories take 1863 as the unequivocal beginning of modern football: Philip Gibbons, *Association Football in Victorian England: A History of the Game from 1863–1900* (Leicestershire: Upfront, 2002); John Blythe Smart, *The Wow Factor: A Concise History of Early Soccer and the Men Who Made It* (Hailsham: Blythe Smart, 2003).

5 Walvin, *People's Game*.

6 Eric Dunning, 'The Development of Modern Football' in E. Dunning (ed.), *The Sociology of Sport* (London: Frank Cass, 1971), pp. 133–4. For an updated version, see Eric Dunning and Kenneth Sheard, *Barbarians, Gentlemen and Players: A Sociological Study of the Development of Rugby Football* (London: Routledge, 2005 [1st edition, 1979]), pp. 2–3.

7 Dunning, *Sport Matters*, pp. 90–1; Dunning and Sheard, *Barbarians, Gentlemen and Players*, pp. 36–8; Eric Dunning and Graham Curry, 'Public Schools, Status Rivalry and the Development of Football' in E. Dunning, D. Malcolm and I. Waddington (eds), *Sport Histories: Figurational Studies of the Development of Modern Sports* (London: Routledge, 2004), pp. 38–9.

8 R. W. Malcolmson, *Popular Recreations in English Society, 1700–1850* (Cambridge: Cambridge University Press, 1973), pp. 89–117; James Walvin, *Leisure and Society, 1830–1915* (Harlow: Longman, 1978), pp. 3–11; Neil Tranter, *Sport, Economy and Society in Britain, 1750–1914* (Cambridge: Cambridge University Press, 1998), pp. 3–12; Mason, *Association Football*, p. 10.

9 Anthony Delves, 'Popular Recreation and Social Conflict in Derby, 1800–1850' in E. Yeo and S. Yeo (eds), *Popular Culture and Class Conflict, 1590–1914* (Brighton: Harvester, 1981), pp. 89–127.

10 J. E. Vincent, 'The Antiquities of Football' in C. Leatherdale (ed.), *The Book of Football* (Westcliff-on-Sea: Desert Island, 1997 [1st edition, 1906]), p. 5.

11 Dunning and Sheard, *Barbarians, Gentlemen and Players*, pp. 45–51; Dunning and Curry, 'Public Schools', pp. 41–2; Dunning, *Sport Matters*, p. 92; J. A. Mangan, *Athleticism in the Victorian and Edwardian Public School* (London: Frank Cass, 2002 [1st edition, 1981]); Richard Holt, *Sport and the British: A Modern History* (Oxford: Clarendon, 1989), pp. 89–97.

12 Quoted in Mangan, *Athleticism*, p. 9.

13 Dunning and Curry, 'Public Schools', p. 42; Young, *History of British Football*, p. 99; Dunning and Sheard, *Barbarians, Gentlemen and Players*, p. 79.

14 Dunning, *Sport Matters*, pp. 94–6; Dunning and Curry, 'Public Schools', pp. 44–6; Dunning and Sheard, *Barbarians, Gentlemen and Players*, pp. 85–8; The quotations are from Dunning, *Sport Matters*, p. 96.

15 Graham Curry, 'The Trinity Connection: An Analysis of the Role of Members of Cambridge University in the Development of Football in the Mid-Nineteenth Century', *The Sports Historian*, 22, 2 (November 2002), pp. 46–74; Graham Curry, Eric Dunning and Kenneth Sheard, 'Sociological Versus Empiricist History: Some Comments on Tony Collins's "History, Theory and the 'Civilizing Process'" ', *Sport in History*, 26, 1 (April 2006), pp. 118–20; Timothy J. L. Chandler, 'The Structuring of Manliness and the Development of Rugby Football at the Public Schools and Oxbridge, 1830–1880' in J. Nauright and T. J. L. Chandler (eds), *Making Men: Rugby and Masculine Identity* (London: Frank Cass, 1996), pp. 20–1; Dunning and Curry, 'Public Schools', pp. 48–9; Dunning and Sheard, *Barbarians, Gentlemen and Players*, pp. 89–91.

16 Young, *History of British Football*, pp. 127–8; Dunning and Sheard, *Barbarians, Gentlemen and Players*, pp. 91–3; Alcock quoted in Keith Booth, *The Father of Modern Sport: The Life and Times of Charles W. Alcock* (Manchester: Parrs Wood, 2002), p. 44.

17 Tranter, *Sport, Economy and Society*, p. 8; Wray Vamplew, 'Sport and Industrialization: An Economic Interpretation of the Changes in Popular Sport in Nineteenth-Century England' in J. A. Mangan (ed.), *Pleasure, Profit and Proselytism: British Culture and Sport at Home and Abroad, 1700–1914* (London: Frank Cass, 1988), p. 10.

18 Adrian Harvey, *The Beginnings of a Commercial Sporting Culture in Britain, 1793–1850* (Aldershot: Ashgate, 2004).

19 Harvey, *Beginnings*, p. 5.

20 See, in particular, John Goulstone, 'The Working Class Origins of Modern Football', *International Journal of the History of Sport*, 17, 1

(March 2000), pp. 135–43 and *Football's Secret History* (Upminster: 3–2 Books, 2001); Adrian Harvey, 'Football's Missing Link: The Real Story of the Evolution of Modern Football' in J. A. Mangan (ed.), *Sport in Europe: Politics, Class, Gender* (London: Frank Cass, 1999), pp. 92–116; '"An Epoch in the Annals of National Sport": Football in Sheffield and the Creation of Modern Soccer and Rugby', *International Journal of the History of Sport*, 18, 4 (December 2001), pp. 53–87; *Football: The First Hundred Years* (London: Routledge, 2005). The quotation is from Goulstone, *Football's Secret History*, p. 5.

21 Hugh Cunningham, *Leisure in the Industrial Revolution*, (London: Croom Helm, 1980), p. 127; Richard Holt, 'Football and the Urban Way of Life in Nineteenth-Century Britain', in Mangan (ed.), *Pleasure, Profit and Proselytism*, p. 70. On the continuation of folk football, see Douglas Reid, 'Folk Football, the Aristocracy and Cultural Change: A Critique of Dunning and Sheard', *International Journal of the History of Sport*, 5, 2 (1988), pp. 224–38; Neal Garnham, 'Patronage, Politics and the Modernization of Leisure in Northern England: The Case of Alnwick's Shrove Tuesday Football Match' *English Historical Review*, 117, 474 (2002) pp. 1228–46.

22 Harvey, 'Football's Missing Link', pp. 97–9. See also Harvey, *Football*, pp. 55–75.

23 Goulstone, 'Working-Class Origins', p. 141.

24 Harvey, 'Football's Missing Link', pp. 103, 107; Goulstone, *Football's Secret History*, pp. 29–33.

25 Harvey, 'An Epoch in the Annals', pp. 59–61 and *Football*, pp. 92–100; Percy M. Young, *Football in Sheffield* (London: Sportsmans Book Club, 1964), pp. 17–18; *History of British Football*, pp. 115–18. The quotation is from Harvey, *Football*, p. 97. For the debate over Harvey's interpretation of the role of Sheffield in the early history of football, see Eric Dunning, 'Something of a Curate's Egg', *International Journal of the History of Sport*, 18, 4 (December 2001), pp. 88–94; Adrian Harvey, 'The Curate's Egg Put Back Together: Comments on Eric Dunning's Response to "An Epoch in the Annals of National Sport"', pp. 192–9 and Eric Dunning and Graham Curry, 'The Curate's Egg Scrambled Again: Comments on "The Curate's Egg Put Back Together"!', pp. 200–4, both in *International Journal of the History of Sport*, 19, 4 (December 2002); Adrian Harvey, 'Curate's Egg Pursued by Red Herrings: A Reply to Eric Dunning and Graham Curry', *International Journal of the History of Sport*, 21, 1 (January 2004), pp. 127–31.

26 Young, *History of British Football*, pp. 117–18; Harvey, *Football*, pp. 103–20; 'An Epoch in the Annals'.

27 On the early meetings of the FA, see Geoffrey Green, *The History of the Football Association* (London: Naldrett, 1953), pp. 19–33; Harvey, *Football*, pp. 134–49; Young, *History of British Football*, pp. 132–8; Dunning and Sheard, *Barbarians, Gentlemen and Players*, pp. 93–6.

28 Walvin, *People's Game*, p. 43.

29 See Dunning and Curry, 'Public Schools', pp. 49–50; Chandler, 'Structuring of Manliness', pp. 21–4; Russell, *Football and the English*, pp. 9–10.

30 Harvey has argued that at the fifth meeting of the FA, on 1 December 1863, Morley and Pember 'staged what was effectively a coup against the existing consensus regarding the rules' by pushing through changes which outlawed hacking and carrying the ball. Harvey, *Football*, p. 144.

31 Dunning and Sheard, *Barbarians, Gentlemen and Players*, p. 87; Dunning and Curry, 'Public Schools', p. 47.

32 Tony Collins, 'History, Theory and the "Civilizing Process"', *Sport in History*, 25, 2 (August 2005), p. 296. For a reply, see Curry, Dunning and Sheard, 'Sociological Versus Empiricist History', pp. 110–23.

33 Collins, 'History, Theory', pp. 295–6.

34 Harvey, *Football*, pp. 54–6, 232.

35 Holt, 'Football and the Urban Way of Life', p. 70.

36 Harvey, 'An Epoch in the Annals', pp. 70–4; Graham Williams, *The Code War: English Football Under the Historical Spotlight* (Harefield: Yore, 1994), p. 28; Young, *History of British Football*, p. 147; Tony Collins, *Rugby's Great Split: Class, Culture and the Origins of Rugby League Football* (London: Frank Cass, 1998), p. 12. See also Harvey, *Football*, pp. 120–5, 159–66.

37 Quoted in Harvey, 'An Epoch in the Annals', pp. 75–6. Harvey provides slightly different figures in *Football*, pp. 185–9, and suggests that the number of clubs playing the association and rugby codes were similar between 1868–73. Dunning and Sheard's interpretation of the 1873 data is based on English clubs alone. They calculate 132 rugby-playing clubs, 91 association clubs (of which 22 played according to Sheffield rules) and 7 playing both rugby and association or another variant. But they argue that the larger number of adult association players listed (6,076 compared to rugby's 3,702) suggests that 'soccer was increasing more in popularity as an adult game'. Dunning and Sheard, *Barbarians, Gentlemen and Players*, pp. 108–9.

38 Cited in David Russell, '"Sporadic and Curious": The Emergence of Rugby and Soccer Zones in Yorkshire and Lancashire, *c*.1860–1914',

International Journal of the History of Sport, 5, 2 (September 1988), p. 192.

39 John Bale, *Sport and Place: A Geography of Sport in England, Scotland and Wales* (London: C. Hurst, 1982), p. 23.

40 Mike Huggins, 'The Spread of Association Football in North-East England, 1876–90: The Pattern of Diffusion', *International Journal of the History of Sport*, 6, 3 (December 1989), p. 302; Russell, 'Sporadic and Curious', pp. 186–9; Collins, *Rugby's Great Split*, p. 38.

41 Tranter, *Sport, Economy and Society*, p. 30; Russell, 'Sporadic and Curious', p. 196.

42 Martin Johnes, *A History of Sport in Wales* (Cardiff: University of Wales Press, 2005), pp. 17–21, 34; Martin Johnes and Ian Garland, '"The New Craze": Football and Society in North-East Wales, *c.*1870–90', *Welsh History Review*, 22, 2 (December 2004), pp. 278–304.

43 Tranter, *Sport, Economy and Society*, p. 26.

44 Mason, *Association Football*, p. 24; Walvin, *People's Game*, p. 61.

45 Walvin, *People's Game*, p. 59.

46 Peter Bilsborough, 'The Development of Sport in Glasgow, 1850–1914', unpublished M.Litt. thesis, University of Stirling, 1983, pp. 101–2; Huggins, 'Spread of Association Football', pp. 305–6.

47 Mason, *Association Football*, p. 25; P. J. Waller, *Town, City and Nation: England, 1850–1914* (Oxford: Clarendon, 1983), p. 103; D. D. Molyneux, 'The Development of Physical Recreation in the Birmingham District from 1871 to 1892', Unpublished MA thesis, University of Birmingham, 1957, pp. 39–40; Huggins, 'Spread of Association Football', p. 306. See also Johnes and Garland, 'New Craze', pp. 289–90.

48 Young, *History of British Football*, p. 149; R. M. Connell, 'The Association Game in Scotland' in Leatherdale (ed.), *Book of Football*, p. 46; G. P. T. Finn, 'Racism, Religion and Social Prejudice: Irish Catholic Clubs, Soccer and Scottish Society – 1 The Historical Roots of Prejudice', *International Journal of the History of Sport*, 8, 1 (May 1991), pp. 81–2.

49 Bill Murray, *The Old Firm: Sectarianism, Sport and Society in Scotland* (Edinburgh: John Donald, 2000 [1st edition 1984]), p. 12.

50 Bill Murray, *The Old Firm in the New Age* (Edinburgh: Mainstream, 1998), p. 34; Finn, 'Racism, Religion and Social Prejudice', p. 82. Also see Richard Giulianotti and Michael Gerrard, 'Cruel Britannia?: Glasgow Rangers, Scotland and "Hot" Football Rivalries', in G. Armstrong and

R. Giulianotti (eds), *Fear and Loathing in World Football* (Oxford: Berg, 2001), pp. 23–42.

51 Mason, *Association Football*, pp. 28–9.

52 See Peter Bailey, *Leisure and Class in Victorian England: Rational Recreation and the Contest for Control, 1830–1885* (London: Methuen, 1987 [1st edition, 1978]), p. 147; Cunningham, *Leisure*, p. 128; Russell, *Football and the English*, p. 16; Tranter, *Sport, Economy and Society*, pp. 28–9.

53 Walvin, *People's Game*, p. 59; Young, *History of British Football*, p. 161; Bailey, *Leisure and Class*, pp. 145–6.

54 William J. Baker, 'The Making of a Working-Class Football Culture in Victorian England', *Journal of Social History*, 13 (Winter 1979), p. 243.

55 Holt, *Sport and the British*, pp. 150–1; Tranter cited in Holt, 'Football and the Urban Way of Life', p. 25.

56 Holt, 'Football and the Urban Way of Life', p. 72; Johnes and Garland, 'New Craze', p. 289; Collins, *Rugby's Great Split*, p. 4.

57 For an assessment of these, see Mike Cronin, *Sport and Nationalism in Ireland: Gaelic Games, Soccer and Irish Identity since 1884* (Dublin: Four Courts, 1999), pp. 118–21.

58 John Sugden and Alan Bairner, *Sport, Sectarianism and Society in a Divided Ireland* (Leicester: Leicester University Press, 1993), p. 71.

59 Neal Garnham, 'The Origins and Development of Irish Football', in N. Garnham (ed.), *The Origins and Development of Football in Ireland* (Belfast: Ulster Historical Foundation, 1999), pp. 7–8; Malcolm Brodie, *100 Years of Irish Football* (Belfast: Blackstaff, 1980), pp. 1–2.

60 Neal Garnham, *Association Football and Society in Pre-Partition Ireland* (Belfast: Ulster Historical Foundation, 2004) pp. 4–32; quotation p. 15.

61 Although this is not to deny that rugby grew faster, and was the dominant code, in parts of Britain. In the north of England, according to Collins, rugby 'towered over soccer' as a popular sport for most of the 1870s and the early 1880s. Collins, *Rugby's Great Split*, pp. 37–9.

62 The dates of the foundation of local and regional football associations vary from source to source. This may be explained by a time lag in their actual formation and their subsequent affiliation to the FA. These dates are taken from Tranter, *Sport, Economy and Society*, pp. 24–5.

63 Mason, *Association Football*, p. 31; Harvey, *Football*, pp. 208–10; Neil Tranter, 'The Chronology of Organized Sport in Nineteenth-century Scotland: A Regional Study, 1 – Patterns', *International Journal of the History of Sport*, 7, 2 (September 1990), pp. 198, 189.

64 Harvey, 'An Epoch in the Annals', p. 62; Booth, *Father of Modern Sport*, pp. 109–11; Harvey, *Football*, pp. 124, 171–2, 271.

65 Williams, *Code War*, p. 62; C. E. Sutcliffe and F. Hargreaves, *History of the Lancashire Football Association, 1878–1928* (Harefield: Yore, 1992 [1st edition, 1928]), pp. 50–1; Tony Mason, 'Football, Sport of the North?', in J. Hill and J. Williams (eds), *Sport and Identity in the North of England* (Keele: Keele University Press, 1996), p. 44; Johnes and Garland, 'New Craze', p. 282.

66 Bob Crampsey, *The First 100 Years: The Scottish Football League* (Glasgow: Scottish Football League, 1990), p. 3; Johnes and Garland, 'New Craze', pp. 284–5; Johnes, *History of Sport in Wales*, p. 34; John Harris, 'The Early History and Development of Association Football in Breconshire', in C. Harte (ed.), *One Day in Leicester* (Association of Sport Historians, 1996), p. 41.

67 Cited in Huggins, 'Spread of Association Football', p. 307; Russell, 'Sporadic and Curious', pp. 194–5; Williams, *Code War*, p. 86. See also Harvey, *Football*, p. 209; Collins, *Rugby's Great Split*, p. 38.

68 Bob Crampsey, *The Scottish Footballer* (Edinburgh: William Blackwood, 1978), pp. 13, 16; Archie Hunter, *Triumphs of the Football Field* (Smethwick: Sports Projects, 1997 [reprinted from *Birmingham Weekly Mercury*, 1890]), p. 25.

69 Cited in Mason, *Association Football*, pp. 22–3; Harvey, *Football*, pp. 100–1.

70 Huggins, 'Spread of Association Football', pp. 305–6; Johnes and Garland, 'New Craze', pp. 287–9

71 Mason, *Association Football*, pp. 32–3; Huggins, 'Spread of Association Football', p. 307.

72 See, for example, H. E. Meller, *Leisure and the Changing City, 1870–1914* (London: Routledge & Kegan Paul, 1976), p. 234; Waller, *Town, City and Nation*, p. 103; Eric Hobsbawm, 'Mass-Producing Traditions: Europe, 1870–1914' in E. Hobsbawm and T. Ranger (eds), *The Invention of Tradition* (Cambridge; Cambridge University Press, 1983), p. 289.

73 Mason, *Association Football*, pp. 33, 54 (note 52); Christopher Andrew, '1883 Cup Final: "Patricians" v "Plebeians"', *History Today* (May 1983), pp. 21–4.

74 Walvin, *People's Game*, pp. 81, 82.

75 Wray Vamplew, *Pay Up and Play the Game: Professional Sport in Britain, 1875–1914* (Cambridge: Cambridge University Press, 1988), p. 54.

76 Vamplew, *Pay Up*, pp. 53–4; John Hutchinson, *The Football Industry* (Edinburgh: Richard Drew, 1982), pp. 13–15; Russell, *Football and the English*, pp. 13–14; Donald M. MacRaild and David E. Martin, *Labour in British Society* (London: Macmillan, 2000), pp. 45–7; John Benson, *The Working Class in Britain, 1850–1939* (London: Longman, 1989), pp. 40–4.

77 See Hobsbawm, 'Mass-Producing Traditions', pp. 289–90.

78 Stephen Tischler, *Footballers and Businessmen: The Origins of Professional Soccer in England* (New York: Holmes & Meier, 1981), p. 38; Vamplew, *Pay Up*, p. 52; Bailey, *Leisure and Class*, p. 146.

79 Cited in Tischler, *Footballers and Businessmen*, p. 38.

80 Patrick Murphy, John Williams and Eric Dunning, *Football on Trial: Spectator Violence and Development in the Football World* (London: Routledge, 1990), p. 3.

81 Vamplew, *Pay Up*, pp. 56–8; Neil Carter, *The Football Manager: A History* (London: Routledge, 2006), p. 15.

82 Young, *History of British Football*, pp. 156–7; Williams, *Code War*, pp. 78–9, 82; Tischler, *Footballers and Businessmen*, pp. 31, 46.

83 All cited in Tischler, *Footballers and Businessmen*, pp. 41–2.

84 Alfred Gibson and William Pickford, *Association Football and the Men Who Made It*, Vol. 2 (London: Caxton, 1906), p. 160.

85 'Tityrus', *The Rise of the Leaguers, 1863–1897* (London: Sporting Chronicle, 1897), pp. 105–6. For a detailed analysis of Lang and emergent professionalism, see Graham Curry, 'Playing for Money: James J. Lang and Emergent Soccer Professionalism in Sheffield', *Soccer and Society*, 5, 3 (Autumn 2004), pp. 336–55.

86 Robert W. Lewis, 'The Genesis of Professional Football: Bolton-Blackburn-Darwen, the Centre of Innovation, 1878–85', *International Journal of the History of Sport*, 14, 1 (April 1997), pp. 21–54; Mason, *Association Football*, p. 69.

87 Russell, *Football and the English*, p. 23.

88 *Midland Athlete*, 12 October, 29 December 1881, cited in Mason, *Association Football*, p. 70.

89 Lewis, 'Genesis of Professional Football', pp. 32–7, 54 (Appendix F); Tischler, *Footballers and Businessmen*, p. 46; Mason, *Association Football*, pp. 71–2; Vamplew, *Pay Up*, p. 193.

90 See Mason, *Association Football*, pp. 72–81; Tischler, *Footballers and Businessmen*, pp. 51–8; Harvey, *Football*, pp. 216–17; Matthew Taylor, 'Little Englanders: Tradition, Identity and Professional Football in

Lancashire, 1880–1930' in S. Gehrmann (ed.), *Football and Regional Identity in Europe* (Münster: Lit Verlag, 1997), pp. 36–40.

91 Tischler, *Footballers and Businessmen*, p. 43; Williams, *Code War*, pp. 91–2; Lewis, 'Genesis of Professional Football', p. 25; Mason, *Association Football*, p. 75.

92 Lewis, 'Genesis of Professional Football', p. 38; Bailey, *Leisure and Class*, p. 150.

93 R. W. Lewis, 'The Development of Professional Football in Lancashire, 1870–1914', unpublished Ph.D. thesis, University of Lancaster, 1993, p. 56; Mason, 'Football, sport of the North?'; Dave Russell, *Looking North: Northern England and the National Imagination* (Manchester: Manchester University Press, 2004), pp. 251–2.

94 Dunning and Sheard, *Barbarians, Gentlemen and Players*, pp. 155–70.

95 Collins, *Rugby's Great Split*, p. 112.

96 Mason, *Association Football*, p. 70; Williams, *Code War*, p. 93; Booth, *Father of Modern Sport*, p. 190.

97 Collins, *Rugby's Great Split*, pp. 134–6; Harvey, *Football*, pp. 226–7.

CHAPTER 2

The making of British football, 1885–1914

Association football may have come a long way in the years from its initial codification to the acceptance of profession-alism but this was nothing compared with the developments of the three decades preceding the First World War. Some historians have regarded this as the period in which the game was 'made' in its modern form. Such a phrase is inevitably imprecise but at the very least it refers to expansion in terms of numbers playing, watching and writing about the game, the emergence of new commercial and financial dimensions, and the geographical growth of clubs and competitions. And all these forms of football, from the playground match to the professional cup final, were arranged according to a uniform set of rules. At a qualitative level, football's 'making' is normally taken to mean an increasing centrality in the lifestyle and culture of some, if not all, social classes. Dave Russell has categorised football's transformation thus: 'In 1875, it was still largely a game for a leisured elite; by 1914, it lay at the heart of much English male culture'.[1] Such a view has much to recommend it and indeed few historians would deny that by the outbreak of the First World War association football had acquired much of the shape and the meaning that was to define its role in the course of the twentieth century. Yet there is a danger of adopting a Whiggish view of history here; of identifying broad patterns of growth and progress while paying little attention to regional variations and uneven development. This is compounded by the tendency to focus on England (even particular areas such as the north and the midlands) and the professional game to the neglect of what was happening in other parts of the British Isles and at the recreational and amateur level.

This chapter will critically assess the social significance of football over the period and its relationship to notions of class, community and nation. In so doing, it will engage with a number of questions that have preoccupied scholars of the game. What were the motives of those who invested time and money in clubs as shareholders, directors, and of course, supporters? What sort of men became professional footballers and how were they treated? To what extent did football reflect or contribute to senses of class or community consciousness? How did Britain's social, economic and political elite perceive the game and how significant was it in the construction of community and national identities? At the heart of these questions is the issue of the 'ownership' of football. In what senses can the sport be said to have 'belonged' to a particular social or national grouping? Was it a working-class game or a people's game? To what extent had it become a national game or even *the* national game?

Professional football

Writing in 1899, the amateur international G. O. Smith measured the benefits brought to association football by the introduction of professionalism. In spite of its harmful effects on the game and the manner in which it was played, Smith could accept that professionalism had

made it possible for thousands to enjoy a game which would otherwise have been altogether out of their reach. To many, thus, it has given not only a means of livelihood, but also the opportunity, in all probability, of gratifying a long-cherished desire. To countless people besides it has given the chance of watching games, and has aroused in them a love of sport which otherwise had never been brought to the surface. The keen and friendly rivalry between town and town, the desire to play your hardest for your side, the subservience of self to the common good – all these good emotions have been made possible for men who, without the introduction of professionalism, might have had small chance of experiencing them.[2]

Yet it would be wrong to assume that professionalism immediately changed the face of British football and swept away the amateur game. For one thing, as with the introduction of football in the first place, professionalism was an innovation that took time to spread. Unsurprisingly, Lancashire clubs were among the first to register paid players. By October 1887 at least 47 clubs in the county were engaging some 424 professionals; these figures had risen to 61 clubs and 570 professionals by

September 1888. From Lancashire as the 'centre of innovation', Robert Lewis has argued, professional football then spread outwards, 'only reaching rural, outlying districts much later'. The first clubs outside the county to adopt professionalism were those geographically close by and related both to Lancashire and to one another through an existing network of competition: Stoke and Burslem Port Vale in the Potteries; West Bromwich Albion, Aston Villa and Small Heath Alliance in the Black Country and Birmingham; and across to Derby County and Notts County in the east midlands. Early professionalism, as John Bale has noted, was a phenomenon 'confined to the north-west and the midlands'.[3]

What Bale has termed 'regional peculiarities of culture and values' were undoubtedly important in explaining the timing of the arrival of professionalism in various parts of Britain. In many cases, professionalism was checked by the strength of the amateur ethos among football's early participants and administrators. The Sheffield FA, for example, remained steadfastly amateur until 1887 when plans for a new professional club prompted The Wednesday to turn professional and resign from the local body. Similarly, the London FA's unyielding opposition to professionalism hampered clubs in the English capital. Arsenal's decision to adopt professionalism in 1891 – the first London club to do so – 'brought down the vials of wraths of the London FA on the heads of the Arsenal executive', leading to the club's expulsion from the London body and its cup competitions. In addition, many of its southern rivals cancelled fixtures with the club in protest. Millwall Athletic followed soon after, but these metropolitan professionals were very much in the minority. Bale has consequently identified a ten-year time lag in the adoption of professionalism in London, with the majority of clubs remaining amateur until at least 1900.[4] In Scotland, initial resistance at the associational level served to delay the official recognition of payment for play rather than prevent its actual practice. Archie Hunter, one of Aston Villa's leading players during the 1880s, revealed in 1890 that 'professional footballists are plentiful enough in Scotland and it is not much of a secret. Most people know what is going on'. Investigations the same year uncovered over 200 cases of irregular payments to players, although in a strange twist of logic the Scottish FA was still able to proclaim that 'professionalism does not exist in Scotland'.[5] It was, however, finally sanctioned in 1893, with 560 professionals instantly registered to some 50 Scottish clubs. By the 1895–6 season, this had increased to 936 professionals attached to 89 clubs. Progress in Ireland was much slower, despite the official legalisation of professionalism by the national association in 1894. As in parts of southern England, a number of regional bodies, such as Londonderry's North West FA, refused to sanction professionalism in the competitions they controlled until the 1900s. Even official professionalism failed to catch on immediately in the way it had in Lancashire and Scotland, possibly because players preferred unofficial forms of payment and a system where they were not compelled to attach themselves contractually to a particular club. This might explain why the Irish FA had only registered 16 professionals by the first week of its first 'open' season. Similar resistance to the professional game was evident in south Wales, where the local association outlawed player payment until 1900, even though its own chairman admitted that veiled professionalism was 'not only rife but rampant'.[6]

Other reasons have been proffered for professional soccer's relatively late appearance in one of England's major industrial regions, the West Riding of Yorkshire. Here the game was faced with the success of rugby (more particularly, after 1895, the Northern Union or rugby league), which by the 1890s had already entrenched itself as the region's favoured brand of football. Yet, according to Russell, the nationalising tendencies of the sporting and general press combined with the increasing role of soccer as the chosen team game at many schools to loosen the grip of the rugby code and encourage the development of professional soccer clubs. A. J. Arnold, meanwhile, has emphasised the commercial imperatives that encouraged the foundation of new soccer clubs and convinced a number of professional club directorates to switch to the supposedly more lucrative association game. The establishment of Bradford City (formerly the rugby side Manningham) in 1903 and Leeds City (previously Holbeck) in 1905 encouraged a delayed diffusion of the professional game to neighbouring Huddersfield and Halifax in the late 1900s. Although it could not displace rugby, within a decade professional soccer had established a foothold in a region from which it had been conspicuously absent.[7]

More than any other factor, early professional football benefited from the establishment of league competition. Without doubt, the two developments were closely linked. The Football League, Britain's first and most significant competition of its kind, was created essentially to solve the administrative and financial difficulties that had arisen in the wake of professionalism. The most important of these was the fact that clubs lacked a reliable and permanent fixture list. Those now facing large wage bills in addition to other expenses could no longer depend on a haphazard schedule of local cup games in which opponents might be too weak to attract a crowd, or 'friendly' matches where visiting teams could arrive

PLATE 2 *Blackburn Rovers, the 1886 English FA Cup winners. Rovers beat West Bromich Albion 2–1 in the replayed final at Derby's Racecourse Ground (© Popperfoto.com).*

with less than a full side, if they showed up at all. In a situation where 'fixtures were kept and cancelled in a capricious way', some degree of order was needed. It arrived in March 1888 when William McGregor, an exiled Scot and director of Aston Villa, circulated a letter suggesting that 'ten or twelve of the most prominent clubs in England combine to arrange home and away fixtures each season'. The idea was not entirely new. A similar system already existed in US baseball but McGregor himself claimed that cricket's County Championship had provided the main inspiration. Whatever the case, it was an idea that appealed to a number of leading clubs in professionalism's heartland of the north and the midlands. Of the 12 chosen to begin the first season, six were drawn from Lancashire (Accrington, Bolton Wanderers, Blackburn Rovers, Burnley, Everton and Preston North End), three from Staffordshire (Stoke, West Bromwich Albion and Wolverhampton Wanderers) and one each from Warwickshire (Aston Villa), Nottinghamshire (Notts County) and Derbyshire (Derby County). It seems likely that playing ability was less significant in the final choice than good facilities, location and the potential to draw large crowds. After all, only three of the founder members – Aston Villa, Blackburn Rovers and West Bromwich Albion – had won the FA Cup before 1888 and a number of those left out were considered to have better claims for inclusion than some of those chosen. Two of these – Halliwell and Nottingham Forest – were nearly admitted at the last minute but lost out to close neighbours. The former suffered from competition with Bolton Wanderers, whose ground was closer to the town centre; Notts County was apparently preferred because its Trent Bridge ground had a better tram service than Forest's Lenton headquarters.[8]

Despite initial press scepticism, the Football League proved an immediate financial success. One commentator remarked after the inaugural season that 'inclusion in the League means an almost safe exchequer for the season for a club ... and a very great addition in interest in its matches'. Such was the case for Wolverhampton Wanderers, where gate receipts of £821 in its last non-League season had leapt to £3,356 by 1893–4. As the leading sports journalist James Catton noted, the establishment of the League 'galvanised the dry bones of club football into life and endowed the game'. Imitators soon followed. In 1889 the Football Alliance, the Lancashire League, the Midland Counties League, the Northern Football League and the North Eastern Football League were all established, although the latter lasted just a season. Three years later the most prestigious of these, the Football Alliance, was elected en bloc to form the basis of a new Football League Second Division. Expansion continued apace over the course of the Football League's first decade, with membership increasing threefold to 36 clubs (divided equally into two divisions) by 1898. Geographically, however, its membership was regional rather than national. With the exception of Arsenal and Luton Town from the south and Sunderland, Newcastle United and Middlesbrough in the north-east, by the turn of the century the Football League consisted of clubs drawn mainly from its original areas. Of the 32 member clubs in the 1899–1900 season, 16 were from the midlands and 9 came from Lancashire. As such, Bale has observed that its coverage at this time 'had scarcely spread beyond a triangular belt between the Mersey and the Humber'.[9]

Alongside professionalism, the formation of leagues faced considerable resistance in the south of England. As the first attempt in 1890 to create a league under the auspices of the London FA shows, league football in the south, though closely associated with professionalism, was not inextricable from it. Indeed of the nine clubs to form the Southern League's First Division in its inaugural season in 1894–5, four were amateur. Yet as was the case with all Britain's major leagues, it soon became a vehicle for the rise of the professional game. According to the Southern League's first historian, its *raison d'être* was the problem faced by Millwall Athletic in securing competitive fixtures due to a boycott by Football League clubs. Without the attraction of visitors from the north and the midlands, professional clubs in London and the south were faced with depleted fixture lists and, potentially at least, financial ruin. The Southern League's rivalry with its northern counterpart was evident straight away, on the pitch as well as in the transfer market. Southampton and Tottenham Hotspur were particularly successful in the FA Cup, the former reaching one semi-final and two finals between 1898 and 1902, the latter actually defeating Sheffield United of the Football League to win the 1901 competition. However, such equality between the two bodies was shortlived. By 1907 one observer from the south could comment that the Southern League 'has seen its best days' and that its football was 'ping-pong' compared to that practised in the Football League. During the 1900s a number of Southern League members (Bristol City in 1901, Clapton Orient in 1905, Fulham in 1907 and Tottenham Hotspur in 1908) were poached by the senior league. The Southern League's junior status was underscored by the fact that 18 of its clubs were so anxious to join the Football League in 1909 that they considered being appended en bloc as a new Third Division.[10]

Yet despite the mutual antagonism, by 1914 the Football League and the Southern League had established a virtual monopoly over elite professional football in England and Wales. From 1893 until 1914 the two leagues provided the last eight clubs in the FA Cup each season and by the turn of the century its players took all but a few of the positions in England international line-ups. Numerically, the Football League had expanded to 40 clubs in two equally sized divisions, while the Southern body had grown from 16 clubs to 36 in just two decades. Both had also spread significantly beyond their original geographical constituencies. The Football League now embraced five clubs from London and Bristol City in the south-west along with four from the West Riding textile district. More dramatically, the Southern League had grown out from its base in London, the Home Counties, Wiltshire and the Hampshire coast to include representatives from as far afield as Norwich, Plymouth, Northampton, Coventry, Stoke and, most important of all, south Wales. Shorn of its best metropolitan clubs, the league identified south Wales as an area of potential growth in the professional game, and proceeded to court existing clubs and encourage the formation of new ones. Aberdare,

Merthyr Town and Ton Pentre were the first to be admitted in 1909 and by the 1913–14 season there were 14 sides from south Wales competing in the Southern League. Neither competition was national in scope but, taken together, by the First World War the Football and Southern Leagues covered most of the major towns, cities and regions. The creation of a unified English and Welsh league competition had to wait until the 1920s.[11]

In Scotland, the creation of a 'national' league preceded the legalisation of professionalism. The success of the Football League had been closely watched north of the border, as had its tendency to employ many of the best Scottish players as professionals. More specifically, the fact that in 1889 Celtic and Queen's Park, two of the leading sides of the day, had been drawn together in the first round of the Scottish Cup, prompted calls for a more reliable programme of matches to place clubs on a sounder financial footing. Critics of the scheme, such as Queen's Park who snubbed invitations to join, saw it as a covert attempt to wrest administrative control from the Scottish FA and introduce professionalism. With fewer clubs to choose from and a less overtly commercial purpose than in England, the nine founder members were picked as much on the basis of past reputation as on crowd support and financial potential. Vale of Leven, for example, had won the Scottish Cup three times in succession during the 1870s. Renton were also former cup winners and had famously proclaimed themselves 'Champions of the World' after defeating the English Cup winners West Bromwich Albion in 1888. But with little more than village populations, these clubs struggled to survive, especially following the legalisation of professionalism. By the turn of the century, founders Cambuslang, Cowlairs, Renton and Vale of Leven had all dropped out of the Scottish League. Vale of Leven returned to the Second Division in 1905 but performances were undistinguished and in 1926 the club slipped quietly out of top-level football. The turnover of members was indeed to be a feature of the first 25 years of the Scottish League: ten clubs, including such long-forgotten names as Ayr Parkhouse, Dundee Wanderers, Linthouse, Northern and Thistle, were voted out of the league before the First World War. The Scottish League's nine founder members were, like much of the population, concentrated in a central belt between the Forth and Clyde rivers. Only slowly did it expand eastwards and northwards, taking in representatives from Fife, Dundee and Aberdeen as the league expanded gradually in size to 22 clubs in 1901 and 32 by 1912. A Second Division had been established in the 1893–4 season but it remained more independent and free to manage its own affairs than

its English equivalent. An effect of this was that promotion was by election rather than automatic merit, meaning that both Hibernian and
Kilmarnock had to win the title in consecutive seasons during the 1890s
before they were deemed worthy of joining the highest group.[12]

The role of the league system in boosting football's popularity has been
rather underplayed by historians. There has been a tendency to associate
it entirely with the elite professional game from which it sprang, but its
impact was undoubtedly much wider. By 1900 Britain was 'criss-crossed
by a network of leagues professional, semi-professional and amateur, providing the competitive structure that proved such a vital dynamic to the
game's expansion'.[13] The league principle of an ordered calendar of
matches arranged across the season complemented the sudden-death
appeal of cup competition. Where the cup rewarded the successful one-off
performance, the league repaid consistency over the season. Above all,
leagues provided a competitive structure absent in the friendly encounters
that had previously filled the gaps in club fixture lists between the all-
important cup ties.

The football 'business'

Supporters and critics of professional football alike agreed that it was a
commercial enterprise. Some saw it as business, pure and simple. Even
McGregor, the 'father' of the Football League, acknowledged in 1906 that
the game had become 'a big business'. 'The turnover of some of our clubs',
he remarked, 'is considerably larger than the turnover of many an
important trading concern.'[14] The issue for historians of football has been
to determine to what extent these clubs operated like conventional businesses. Stephen Tischler has argued that football represented 'a
microcosm of the larger business environment' and that it 'dealt in sports
in much the way other enterprises traded in houses, food and pencils'.[15] A
more influential interpretation has come from those historians who
emphasise the 'peculiar economics' of football. Prominent among these
has been Wray Vamplew, who concluded that professional clubs tended
to be what economists call utility maximisers rather than profit maximisers; more interested, in other words, in sporting progress than
financial gain.[16]

Originally clubs were voluntary organisations run by a committee
elected from the broader membership. The extra costs associated with
gate-money and professionalism, however, led most of the leading outfits
to reorganise themselves as limited liability companies, with shareholders

and a board of directors. This was done, as Richard Holt has noted, not to 'speculate in the entertainment business' but legally to secure the cost of existing expenses, buying a ground or improving facilities.[17] In any case, it has been argued, the financial returns to be made from football were slight. In England, the FA prevented the payment of directors and restricted dividends to shareholders to 5 per cent (7.5 per cent after 1918). *Athletic News* noted that during the 1908–9 season only six of the 63 top clubs paid the maximum dividend to shareholders. It went on to reflect that the majority of those who invested in football considered 'financial obligations as of secondary importance to the sport they get ... No one who is out for a business return would look at football shares'.[18] No such restrictions were placed on Scottish clubs but, even so, few shareholders received direct returns. Only Celtic and Rangers, whose 'Old Firm' label derived from their joint commercial might, paid dividends on anything like a regular basis. In its first year as a company (1897–8), Celtic paid 20 per cent, followed by 10 per cent for the next seven years, while in 1913 each senior director received £50. Yet even these relatively modest payments were exceptional. In his survey of financial statements, Vamplew found only two other Scottish clubs who paid dividends between the 1906–7 and 1913–14 seasons and neither of these did so more than twice.[19]

If historians concur over the limited direct financial returns that could be made by football investors, less agreement exists over the indirect benefits. Tischler has stressed the benefit in the form of contracts and extra sales to be made by directors involved in the building, catering or sports outfitting trades. Certainly a high proportion of brewers and builders bought shares and became directors of clubs throughout Britain, but it is by no means clear that they did so for pecuniary advantage. The most obvious profiteer of this type was Harry Mears, who set up the Chelsea club at the Stamford Bridge ground he owned but ensured that the rent was high and that it was his own Chelsea FC Catering Company that provided for the large crowds which the club attracted. Shareholders could also benefit. The architect of Rangers' Ibrox stadium, Archibald Leitch, was also a shareholder, as were the Penman brothers at Celtic, for whom they were conveniently the playing kit suppliers. Likewise, it may not be a coincidence that among the shareholders of the Belfast club Glentoran, which by the mid-1900s had one of Ireland's premier cycle tracks encircling the pitch, were a number of individuals involved in the cycle trade.[20] Yet on the evidence we have it is unlikely that very many businessmen became shareholders or directors primarily for financial reasons. Only a handful of clubs specifically prohibited contracting with directors but many more doubtless regarded it as 'morally unacceptable'. The Football League president certainly felt that such instances were rare: 'here and there you will find a man who is a director for the money he indirectly makes out of it; but that cannot always be avoided'.[21]

Profits could be made, of course, but not by every club and certainly not in every season. At the elite end of the spectrum, Everton recorded a surplus in each year bar one between 1891 and 1914. Chelsea did likewise between 1908 and 1915, achieving a record profit for any league club of £22,826 during the first year of this run. A sample of 14 First Division clubs in 1904–5 revealed losses for five and modest returns for the rest; a similar sample of 19 clubs from 1913–14 showed that most were making a small profit of between £1,000 and £5,000. The highest return in the latter sample came from Burnley, whose £12,883 was largely a result of its victorious FA Cup run.[22] These figures were easily eclipsed by Scotland's 'Old Firm': by 1907, Celtic was able to yield £18,884 with rivals Rangers returning £14,076 the next year. Yet many more clubs at a lower level faced a continual struggle to make ends meet. West Bromwich Albion was one such case, requiring fund-raising and public appeals to stem the continual financial difficulties it suffered for much of the period. Reading, of the Southern League, similarly spent its first two decades as a professional club in an alternating state of financial deficit and full-blown crisis. It was nearly wound up in 1900 and its loss of some £300 in 1906 was not untypical. Some organisations fared much worse. Of the 47 professional clubs whose shareholdings were analysed by Tony Mason, 17 had gone bust by 1914. *The Times* remarked in September 1910 that 'more [Football] League teams are in pecuniary difficulties than has been the case before, and the syndicates are beginning to see that football is not really a money-making business'.[23] On the whole, most historians would agree with Neil Tranter that, except at the highest level, 'debt was the norm and survival usually precarious'.[24]

Any profits that were made were invariably ploughed back into the club, normally to strengthen the playing squad or improve the ground. It is worth noting that as many as 58 leading professional clubs in England and 19 in Scotland moved to new grounds between 1889 and 1910. Such evidence, when placed alongside the lack of price competition, the commitment to friendly or minor cup fixtures which made little money and the reluctance to utilise grounds for non-footballing activities, has led to Vamplew's thesis that utility took precedence over profit making in British football. English clubs, according to Vamplew, were generally more obvious profit maximisers and indeed there were some isolated examples of patent profit orientation, such as Small Heath's decision in 1892 to forgo home advantage in its FA Cup tie with Sheffield Wednesday for a sum of £200 and Arsenal's 1913 move from Woolwich to the highly populated Highbury area of north London.[25] But the notion of football as a business of a rather unusual type remains persuasive. Certainly, when we compare it with other sectors of the emerging leisure industry, such as the music hall, professional football emerges as considerably less thoroughly commercialised and freer from the control of profit-seeking capitalists.[26]

Another important strand in the debate over the nature of the professional football 'business' involves the position of the players themselves. Most historians have chosen to categorise footballers as industrial workers whose relations with their employers were in most respects not unlike those in the factory or on the shop floor. What made them unique, however, was the existence of a series of measures designed to curtail their economic freedom. The most important of these were the retain-and-transfer system, which effectively prevented a player from choosing his own employer, and the maximum wage (applicable only in England and Wales from the early 1900s), which denied him the opportunity of selling his labour to the highest bidder. The former regulation, in particular, first developed in English football during the early 1890s, left the player at the mercy of his employer. If it wished to 'retain' him, he had little choice but to accept; if placed on the transfer list, he could be left for months without wages until a rival club was willing to pay the designated fee. Once registered for a club, one commentator noted, the player is then 'tied up, "cribbed, cabined and confined" ' and forced 'to obey club orders and do what he is told'.[27] In 1912 Syd Owen, secretary of the recently established Association Football Players' and Trainers' Union (AFPTU), remarked in a similar vein that 'the professional player is the slave of the club and they can do practically anything they want with him'.[28]

Football's early industrial relations system has not endeared itself any more to scholars. It has been described variously as 'quasi-feudal' and 'draconian', with the players regarded as 'servants', 'wage slaves' and 'bonded men'.[29] Without doubt, the power in the professional game resided with the clubs, in tandem with the leagues, which acted effectively as employers' associations. Discipline and control, both on and off the field, could be harsh. Players were expected to follow the orders of the board, sometimes delegated to the trainer or captain. Failure to do so could mean a warning at best, a fine, suspension or dismissal at worst. We know that at the Edinburgh club Hearts 'any player misbehaving or who refused to obey orders' was reported immediately to the club chairman. In 1913 George Travers was suspended by Barnsley *sine die* for 'absence from training and using insulting language to the directors' and never played for the club again. An equally serious fate befell Aston Villa's Christopher Buckley, who was fined £24 and suspended for two seasons by a Football League Commission as a result of a dispute with a director over bonus payments. In such cases, players had no right to legal representation and no recourse to legal action without the express permission of the respective national association. Away from the pitch, many clubs instigated rules that forbade players visiting pubs or racecourses, determined where they could live and circumscribed their leisure time through curfews and the organisation of club-run social events. Some were not averse to employing private detectives to check on the behaviour of players away from the clubhouse. At Celtic, the board issued employees with details of training regulations and dietary advice and warned them that 'the player who cannot conduct himself on and off the park has no peg for his suit at Celtic Park'.[30]

Discussions of how to categorise such managerial behaviour have generally settled on the notion of paternalism. One historian has talked of 'a strange kind of paternalism in which players were treated rather like some Victorian middle-class wives; stifling their independence perhaps but cushioning them from some of the natural contingencies of life which most working people could rarely face with equanimity'.[31] There were indeed many cases of clubs treating their employees well. Some clubs kept more than an eye on the personal finances of their 'boys': Sheffield United paid off the debts of one of its players while the West Ham United board held in fund the wages of any player with a drinking problem. Most made financial and medical arrangements to look after injured or sick players. Increasingly injuries were treated in-house but in serious cases players were sent to local hospitals or those specialising in sports injuries, such as the renowned Matlock House in Manchester, which was run by a Manchester City director. The Sheffield clubs were generous enough to send injured players to the seaside to recuperate. Towards the end of the period, however, the preference of individual clubs for informal welfare arrangements were giving way to a more formalised and centralised system. The inclusion in 1906 of professional footballers within the provisions of the Workmen's Compensation Act was crucial in this, leading for instance to the formation a year later of the Football Mutual Insurance Federation (FMIF) by representatives of Football League, Southern

League and Scottish League clubs. Henceforth welfare provision tended to be subject more to central control and left less to the discretionary power of club committees. In this area, as in the organisation of the labour market, payment scales for players and even disciplinary rules, the paternalism of the club was increasingly supplemented by the bureaucratic control of leagues and national associations.[32]

Any restrictions faced by professional players were, according to some, more than compensated for by high levels of pay. Generalisations here are best avoided, but we do have enough information to indicate basic trends and comparisons. In England the maximum wage rule, introduced for the beginning of the 1901–2 season, had a major impact on the earnings of players. Unrestricted by such limits, the Liverpool players who won the 1900–1 Football League title were receiving up to £10 a week, although for most players in the same division a wage of between £3 and £4 a week was more common during the late 1890s. With wages capped at £4 per week, a number of the leading players received a drop in basic wages, although benefit payments, bonuses and, for the very best, international match fees, could boost earnings substantially. Others were no doubt paid extra in breach of the regulations. The Welsh international winger Billy Meredith, for one, was on £6 per week (£2 above the maximum) with Manchester City between 1902 and 1906. But at the very least we know that in 1910 573 of an estimated 6,800 professional footballers in England were in receipt of the £4 maximum. Although there was no maximum wage in Scotland, earnings were generally no higher than those in England. Even at the top clubs, such as Celtic, Rangers and Hearts, £4 was the average weekly wage, although the latter's international Bobby Walker received a guaranteed £6. Irish clubs could hardly compete with such sums. In 1906 the Distillery goalkeeper Donald Sloan was offered £3 per week throughout the year to keep him from moving to England and some Linfield players were receiving £4 by 1914, but elsewhere wages rarely rose above £2 a week. Throughout Britain, it must be said, earnings at the bottom of the hierarchy were so low that football could only ever be a part-time profession used to supplement more regular employment. Yet as contemporaries recognised, such rewards, real and potential, placed many footballers in a better financial position than even the most skilled workers and, still taking into account the lack of job security and the limited length of a playing career, provided most with 'a fairly comfortable lifestyle'.[33] 'Professional footballers', wrote the former England international William Bassett, 'are a handsomely remunerated set of men, and call for the commiseration of no one.'[34]

Amateur football

The label of 'amateur football' covers a wide variety of the soccer taking place in Britain at this time, from the unorganised and impromptu street or park game to schoolboy football, and from the normally localised game often described as junior football to the virulently anti-professional version advocated by the Amateur Football Association (AFA). In some respects, the only thing these varieties of football had in common was that they were *not* professional, although even here the dividing line was often blurred, with some clubs and players moving between the professional and amateur ranks or, in Alan Metcalfe's words, straddling 'the thin line between amateurism and professionalism'.[35] What is not in doubt, however, is that football below the elite professional level constituted an important part of the game's development in this period. Playing football was, as Martin Johnes has noted, 'the leading physical pastime of a con-siderable proportion of the male population', without which 'the thousands who flocked to see the professionals would never have emerged in the numbers they did'. As such, non-professional football represented 'the backbone' of the game as a whole.[36]

The recreational game

It is impossible to know exactly how many people played football in Britain over this period. Even the governing bodies of the sport could only provide a general estimation. The English FA claimed a few years before the First World War to administer over 12,000 clubs and between 300,000 and 500,000 players. On the face of it, this might seem an impressive figure, but becomes less so if we consider that in 1911 the country's male population aged between 15 and 39 amounted to some 7¼ million. According to these statistics, therefore, only one in 14 Englishmen at most played football. Participation in Scotland appears to have been higher. According to Neil Tranter, one in four Scottish males aged 14–29 were attached to a football club by the 1880s. His study of the Stirling district indicates the particularly rapid institutionalisation of junior and juvenile soccer. While in 1885 there was one club for every 850 males aged 15–44 and every 530 aged 15–29, by 1900 the figures were 250 and 160 respect-ively; this, it is noted, despite the reduction of the number of senior and professional teams affiliated to the local association.[37]

Perhaps not surprisingly, recreational football in northern England seems to have had its highest concentration in areas that could boast

Football League clubs, suggesting 'a connection between a high level of interest in professional football and a desire to play recreational sport'. Jack Williams has thus found more soccer clubs in Bolton, Burnley and Sunderland than in St Helens and Wigan.[38] Yet in the rugby-dominated Yorkshire textile district at least, growth at the junior and schoolboy level was as impressive as in many soccer districts and, as we have seen, stimulated the move to professional football, not vice-versa. By the early twentieth century, the West Yorkshire FA controlled over nine junior leagues spread throughout the district, and in 1906 the *Brighouse Echo* noted that 'there are now in this locality more football clubs that play under association rules than under the rugby code'.[39] What is more, local working patterns always affected levels of participation. In the iron and steel industry of the north-east, the establishment of the Saturday half-day came relatively late, towards the end of the 1880s, but seems to have stimulated the local football scene. Robert Poole has identified a 'fresh wave' of club formation in Bolton with the establishment in 1890 of a Wednesday half-holiday for shops. This allowed the creation of a Bolton and District Amateur League and, in 1900, a Bolton Wednesday League, which included as members Bolton Co-op, Bolton Pawn-Brokers' Assistants and Bolton Post Office Recreation Club.[40]

The lack of precision in the available figures points to a key characteristic of much of the amateur football at the time: its transient and non-official nature. Evidence from a number of localities has revealed how significant this 'hidden' form of football was. In the East Northumberland coalfields, unaffiliated and non-league teams outnumbered the organised and semi-permanent ones. Many were put together for specific occasions, such as the region's annual flower shows or community and charity events. Were it not for Metcalfe's meticulous research, we might not have been aware of teams such as Shankhouse Rising Blacks and Dinnington War Cry or the Levisons Pilgrims and Spion Kop Jumpers, which were formed in 1913 by workers at New Delaval for a benefit match in aid of two workmates. The development of permanent league and cup competitions during the 1890s provided some degree of stability, but most football continued to be played outside this institutionalised framework. Indeed only 15 of the 408 clubs from the coalfields who entered the Northumberland FA Cup between 1890 and 1913 survived for ten or more consecutive seasons. Mike Huggins has shown that few junior clubs in the north-east of England joined county associations or entered major cups and leagues. The situation was similar in central Scotland, where clubs were formed, disbanded and often reformed 'with the regularity of a yo-yo'. The Doune Vale of Teith FC, for example, had been established in 1878 but was dissolved in 1886 and then re-emerged again in 1890, 1894 and 1898. The Irish Football Association (IFA), meanwhile, exercised jurisdiction over 37 clubs in 1887, 101 in 1895 and 420 by 1910, but there were many more which were not affiliated. Only 18 of the 51 junior clubs thought to be active in Ulster in 1891 were actually members of the IFA. Jack Williams has suggested that, in the north of England at least, 'unaffiliated' football was not particularly widespread by the early twentieth century and certainly there does seem to have been a general move towards joining local associations by 1914. Affiliation, however, was no guarantee of stability.[41]

The primary reason for the precarious existence of so many amateur football clubs was financial. Subscriptions from players and fund-raising might have been adequate for survival for a short time but any club with ambitions of long-term viability required some form of patronage from local institutions, wealthy individuals or fee-paying supporters. The workplace and the church or chapel remained common sponsors, accounting respectively for 27.5 and 23.8 per cent of the clubs active in Teeside during the 1888–9 season. Nicholas Fishwick has stated that by 1910 religious institutions were 'the single most important patrons of junior football', an argument supported by the research of Williams on northern England, though less so by Johnes's work on south Wales.[42] The level of patronage varied but almost certainly included the provision of basic equipment (shirts and balls) and some form of financial support or perhaps a playing field. At Ashington FC, colliery officials and town councillors stepped in to stave off financial collapse in 1895. As a result of such community support, financial as well as symbolic, the club managed to increase crowds and gate receipts, built a new ground and by 1914 had been elected to the professional North Eastern League. Most junior clubs at lower levels tried to survive without such assistance. This proved impossible for New Star Delaval, which in 1913 resigned from the Ashington and District League citing a financial deficit. The costs for the rent of a field and changing rooms, referees' pay and ball repairs were hardly great by many clubs' standards, but were considerably more than the income raised from gate receipts, a lottery and the players' own pockets.[43]

The problems of finding a place to play remained one of the most significant obstacles to the growth of recreational football and the stability of amateur clubs throughout the twentieth century. For the ambitious club wishing to climb the local and regional league system, an enclosed ground was essential because without it gate-money could not be charged. The survival of smaller clubs likewise often depended on sympathetic local landowners being prepared to rent ground at a reasonable rate. In large industrial cities the main problem was one that had existed throughout the nineteenth century: the paucity of open space for recreational purposes. In Birmingham, at least, there was a marked improvement over the period, from 10 open spaces covering 222 acres in 1886 to 63 spaces and 1,298 acres by 1913. A London Playing Fields Association was established in 1891 to help 'the clerks, working men and boys' of the capital gain access to more pitches in parks and public spaces. Similar bodies had been set up in Birmingham and Manchester by 1907. By 1914 the Manchester body administered some 100 cricket and football pitches, which with the 30 pitches provided free of charge in the city's major parks and the 260 grounds controlled by the Manchester and Salford Parks Committees, represented a considerable resource that few other cities could match. Claims of the inadequacy of the existing provision led the Dublin authorities to lay out some 29 soccer pitches (compared, incidentally, with only two for Gaelic football) with dressing-room facilities at Phoenix Park in the north of the city. But even then the quality and location of the pitches could make things difficult. The following observation from 1904 was doubtless a fairly typical experience: 'The boys get off work at irregular times from varying distances and it is good luck if both teams have assembled by 3.30 to commence in winter a half hour's game in semi-darkness on a dismal swamp miscalled a football pitch'.[44]

The schoolboy game

Underpinning the popularity of both professional and amateur football was the schoolboy game. One historian has posited the adoption of football in British state schools as 'perhaps *the* most important factor in guaranteeing the future of football as a mass game' and 'a determining factor in making football the national game'.[45] The 1870 Education Act had provided for the creation of local school boards throughout England and Wales to organise elementary education for children of the working classes. No provision, however, had been made for the playing of organised games as a part of the curriculum. Physical education instead took the form of drill, often of a military nature, which was valued mainly for the discipline it was supposed to instil in the children. Only gradually did the Board of Education come to recognise that team games could offer, in the words of its own 1898 Report, a 'simple, ready, and pleasant means of physical education'. In 1900 games, supervised appropriately by members of staff, were finally advocated as an alternative to Swedish drill or physical exercises, although it was not until 1906 that cricket, hockey and football were introduced and promoted as a formal part of the school curriculum, which could be practised in school hours. Much of this change in official attitude was due to the role of individuals such as Robert Morant, the Permanent Secretary of the Board of Education and a former Winchester pupil, who advocated the educational value of team games and the role of athleticism in encouraging discipline and fair play.[46]

Notwithstanding its belated acceptance by educational authorities, football was far from absent in elementary schools before the twentieth century. Rather, it had relied on the role of enthusiastic teachers convinced of the moral and physical benefits of games, as well as students willing to dedicate their own time to play. Many of these teachers were the product of the rise in teacher training colleges and, as mentioned in the previous chapter, were closely involved in the creation of adult clubs as well as in the institutionalisation of the schoolboy game. Two such products of St Peter's College in Birmingham during the 1870s were C. S. Johnstone and J. Adams. Johnstone was a player, committeeman and director of Aston Villa, while Adams was a referee and treasurer of the Brimingham FA in 1883. Both took up headmaster's posts at Birmingham schools. George Sharples, a native of Bolton and an alumni of St John's Teacher Training College in Battersea, secured headships at schools in Bolton, Huddersfield and Manchester, as well as captaining Bolton Wanderers in 1882 and becoming a Football League referee. He promoted football everywhere he went, suggesting in 1898 that the growth of the schoolboy game 'has done more for the real well-being of the boys of this country than all the drill and calisthenics exercises yet introduced'. A recent study has discussed the influence of two pioneers of schools football in London, W. J. Wilson of Oldridge Road Board School in Balham and J. G. Timms of Rosendale Road Board School in Lambeth. Both were active in the development of games playing at their own schools and in the growth of inter-school competition. Wilson, for example, founded the South London Schools' Football Association (the first schools body in Britain) in 1885 and the London Schools' Football Association in 1892, and used the official journal of the National Union of Teachers to promote both organisations. The log book of the Rosendale Road School, meanwhile, reveals the prominence of games in general, and football in particular, in the daily lives of the pupils. One entry from September 1906 noted that Mr Bartlett, an assistant master, took the boys 'in an excellent match of football with properly laid out ground poles, flags etc. and with sides and captains of each team appointed'. The pupils apparently returned 'looking bright and fresh and having thoroughly entered into the games'.[47]

We can only speculate about what most pupils thought of the introduction of school football. James Walvin has suggested that 'football proved to be the attraction which drew many boys to school and to school activities'.[48] This was no doubt true for some but many others probably regarded sport in general as no more than a welcome break from academic lessons, while others would have positively detested it. One former elementary school pupil from Bristol later recalled that

I was proud of the school, I used to play football for the school. On Friday afternoons we would 'ave school assembly and whoever was picked for the team, their name was called out and you had to march to the front. The teacher would give you out your 'shirties' as we used to call them. No football knickers or nothing like that, an' we had no football boots. We used to play in our ordinary shoes ... We'd play in the park ... The teachers would arrange the teams. We 'ad a captain of the team an' positions. We had out own colours, green shirt, 'St Silas for honour, for loyalty, for courage, for courtesy. Play up, play fair, play the game.' When I left school they had one of the finest teams in England.

Stephen Humphries has interpreted such comments as evidence of both 'the internalization of the public-school ethos by a working-class boy' and a type of subjugation to hierarchical control through the 'corporate and competitive spirit' of school football. Yet it could also be read as evidence of the considerable commitment and enthusiasm displayed by young males towards a game which, we must remember, was mostly played outside school time.[49]

Although Mason has highlighted the breakthrough work of the Birmingham School Board in financing the establishment of school teams in the area during the early 1880s and a cup for elementary schools in 1885, London seems to have been the epicentre of the emerging schoolboy game. Under the influence of headteachers like Wilson and Timms, inter-district competition was promoted through the inauguration of the Corinthian Shield in 1893 and the Dewar Cup, started in 1898, which was contested by individual school teams throughout the capital. Sheffield could also claim to have been a forerunner, with the creation in 1890 of the Clegg Shield for local schools. Schools associations were subsequently formed rapidly in most of Britain's major cities and football centres over the course of the 1890s. The Manchester, Salford and District Elementary Schools Football Association, created in 1890, was said to have been modelled specifically on the London and Sheffield bodies. Inter-regional contests soon followed, the first pitting the boys of Leeds against those of South London. These often took place at major grounds and drew crowds comparable with the professional game. Ten thousand spectators, for example, came to Hampden Park in 1905 to watch Glasgow schoolboys beat London 4–2. It took until 1904 for an English Schools Football Association (ESFA) to be formed, with 21 towns and districts affiliated, increasing to 41 within two years.[50] The Welsh Schools Football Association (WSFA) emerged in 1912 and within a year could count 45 schools as members. The relationship of schools football with the professional game remained tenuous at this stage. An early historian of schools football stated that its aim was 'to provide the youthful Britons with a healthy exercise in the open air' rather than to 'manufacture' professionals. Grounds were offered for matches and cups donated for local competition but it is not clear how far professional organisations were successful in tapping this reservoir of young talent. Colm Kerrigan's research on London certainly suggests that progress was slow. George Hilsdon was the first prominent London schoolboy to graduate into the professional and international arena with Chelsea and England from 1906, while only Millwall Athletic and West Ham United regularly recruited from the successful schoolboy teams in the capital.[51]

Amateurs and professionals

The kinds of football thus far discussed were essentially non-professional rather than amateur in any strict, ideological sense. However, for an important group of individuals and clubs based mainly around the English Home Counties, amateur football existed not as a resource for the professional arm of the sport but as an antithesis to it. It was considered, in many ways, to be a different game entirely. The roots of this opposition can be traced back to the decision of the FA and its sister British associations to 'manage' professionalism. This proved unsatisfactory for men like the FA president Major Francis Marindin, an Old Etonian, and five southern-based vice-presidents, who resigned from the governing body in 1890 when the residential qualifications on professionals were loosened. The rapid growth of what amateur critics regarded as 'business football', and its alleged embrace by the leaders of the FA, prompted calls for separate professional and amateur sections within the governing body. Others advocated full-scale amateur secession. An FA Amateur Cup was established in 1893 but soon came to be dominated by proletarian teams from the north-east such as Bishop Auckland, Stockton, Middlesbrough and West Hartlepool.

The pride of the gentlemen amateur game was the Corinthian FC, founded in 1882 by N. L. Jackson as a kind of amateur 'superclub' which brought the best ex-public school and university players, including the England centre-forward G. O. Smith and the well-known cricketer and athlete C. B. Fry, together in regular competition.[52] Significantly, the Corinthians chose not to enter cup competitions, opting instead for schedules of friendly matches against professional and amateur sides at home and abroad. It was probably one of the best teams in the country during the last decade of the nineteenth century, providing the entire England eleven for matches against Wales in 1894 and 1895 and even managing to beat the English FA Cup holders Bury 10–3 in 1904. In its opposition to the penalty kick, introduced in 1891, the Corinthians and other amateur

PLATE 3 *Portrait of G. O. Smith, circa 1905, centre-forward for Oxford University, Old Carthusians, Corinthians and England (© Popperfoto.com)*

clubs demonstrated how uncomfortably their brand of amateurism sat with the changing priorities of the governing bodies. The very idea of penalising a team for a deliberate foul was anathema to the notion of gentlemanly sporting behaviour and the Corinthians, for one, are said to have actively resisted the new law by deliberately shooting wide if awarded a penalty kick and withdrawing the goalkeeper if one was conceded. The dissatisfaction of old boys' teams with the existing competitions led to the creation of the exclusive Arthur Dunn Cup in 1902, which may have allowed those involved to play according to more conducive codes of behaviour but, in Derek Birley's words, 'did nothing for the strength of amateur soccer generally'.[53]

The simmering resentment felt by the 'pure' amateurs towards the FA finally boiled over in 1905. It sprang from the refusal of the Middlesex and Surrey associations to comply with an FA resolution requiring all county FAs to absorb professional clubs located within its jurisdiction. In 1906 an Amateur Football Defence Federation was formed by a collection of the recalcitrant clubs from Surrey, Middlesex and other parts of London which, having been expelled by the governing body, was reformed as the Amateur Football Association (AFA) in the summer of 1907. The new body gained some influential support, in the form of the Rugby Football Union and the Hockey Association and southern-based periodicals such as *Truth*, *Amateur Sport Illustrated* and *Amateur Football*, the latter effectively becoming an AFA mouthpiece. *The Times* also apparently welcomed its foundation. By October 1909 the secretary of the Hockey Association claimed that the AFA had 900 affiliated clubs, including the Corinthians, Oxford and Cambridge Universities and all the principal 'old boy' and public school teams, with a total player membership of 80,000. *C. B. Fry's Magazine* suggested a much more realistic figure of 500 clubs and 20,000 players. The vast majority of amateur sides, however, remained with the FA and the AFA failed to make much impact at all beyond its southern base, with its northernmost club by 1913 based in Nottinghamshire. Critics of the AFA were found throughout the amateur football world. Captain W. S. Masterman, a former captain of Tunbridge Wells FC, itself an affiliate of the rebel body, wrote in 1911 that 'No one takes The AFA seriously', noting that the 'purest' amateur association of all, the Army FA, had stayed loyal to the parent body.[54] Alongside low membership, the AFA suffered through its inability to wrest control of international selection at the 1908 and 1912 Olympics from the FA and by 1914 was forced to return to the FA as an affiliated body.

As John Lowerson has shown, this was less a conflict between amateurism and professionalism than 'an intra-middle-class debate' between different groups of amateurs. One supporter of the breakaway reasoned that the quarrel was not with the professional player, whom the amateur admired, but with 'the professionals' myopic administrators'. *Amateur Sports Illustrated* even accused the old Etonian and FA president Lord Kinnaird of betraying his class.[55] Other authors have seen the whole episode in a much broader social and political context. For Russell, the AFA's stout defence of amateurism represented 'a rebellion of the old order' which, as in politics, had seen their power and influence wittled away by the emergence of new reforming forces. The rise of the Labour Party and new Liberalism, it is speculatively suggested, posed the same fundamental challenge to the social and political role of this 'old order' as the threat of business football and managed professionalism did within the game. Walvin has likewise seen the move towards exclusive amateur cups and associations as emblematic of wider social developments and class relations in Edwardian Britain: 'Unable to exert their traditional control within a changing world, the . . . gentlemen players withdrew into a contracting world of their own – or quit football entirely'.[56] We should remember of course that the Corinthians and the AFA were hardly typical of amateur football at the time. It may be that historians have paid rather too much attention to what was in fact a relatively small, regional clique of extremist amateurs. In most cases, amateurism and professionalism co-existed, sometimes awkwardly but often easily, on the field and in the committee room.

The game of football

Academic writing on sport is sometimes assailed for neglecting what actually happens on the field of play. Fishwick, in response, has asserted that 'social historians ought not to feel obliged to describe matches which they never saw or to engage in second-hand discussions of tactics and the like'. Yet the critics surely have a point. There is a danger of spending so much time on contextual developments that we forget the important changes in the actual game that was played, watched and organised. Trying to decipher what 'football meant and why it mattered' surely requires an examination of the nature of the play located at the centre of most people's lived experience of the sport.[57] Indeed there is a strong case for treating the game of football itself as a 'text' upon which particular cultural and sporting values were inscribed. Styles of play, certainly, are rarely considered to be ideologically neutral, while the codes and rules of sport have also been described as a type of 'landscape' through which culture and meaning is often expressed.[58] Some of these ideas remain rather speculative at present, but they do point to the fact that we should take the game itself seriously. This section will focus on related developments in the rules of the game, the organisation of teams and the styles of play adopted in British football before 1914, and the various ways in which these have been interpreted.

In his chapter on 'The Game' in *Association Football and English Society*, Mason described the spectacle which the imaginary spectator at the 1872 English FA Cup final would have been likely to witness. Mason's intention was doubtless to provide a 'representative' snapshot of the game of football at the time, but there is a limit to how typical this example was, even in England. As we noted in Chapter 1, a fair proportion (over a third according to one estimate) of matches in Britain where the FA's jurisdiction had not yet reached were still played according to particular local codes. In Sheffield, for instance, an equivalent spectator in 1872 would have seen a goal with a bar pitched 9 feet above the ground (rather than a tape 8 feet above) and witnessed players of the opposite side to the one who kicked it into touch throwing the ball back into play (rather than the first to reach the ball). The Scottish FA, similarly, developed its own variations to the FA code over the course of the 1870s. Particular disagreement arose over conflicting definitions of the offside rule as well as the English body's adoption of a new throw-in law in 1877, which now required a one-handed throw in any direction rather than at right-angles to the touchline. These may have only been minor differences to the same basic game but it is important to recognise that it was not until 1882 that a uniform set of rules was guaranteed and a forum for their revision established, through the creation of an International Board incorporating representatives of all the UK associations (and representatives of the world-governing body FIFA – Fédération Internationale de Football Association – from 1913).[59]

The International Board faced its busiest time of all in these early decades. Most of the changes were the simple rationalisation of what remained a relatively simple game to play and understand. The basic dimensions of the pitch (with maximum and minimum length and breadth for both regular and international matches) were not officially laid down until 1897. There was now less latitude in the size of pitches, and a reduction in the maximum length from 200 to 130 yards meant that many were considerably shorter than had previously been the case. Flags at each corner, possibly supplemented by others along the sideline, initially indicated the basic layout of the pitch. It was not until 1883 that lines were placed at the border of the pitch, with the first internal markings indicating a centre line and 12-yard lines and 6-yard semicircles from either goal arriving in 1892. In 1902 the interior markings assumed a more recognisable form to twenty-first century eyes, with the introduction of a rectangular penalty area (to replace the 12-yard line), a six-yard box (instead of the semicircles) and a penalty spot. Most of these changes resulted from the increasing instances of infringements of the laws of the game and foul play. Free kicks were rare in the 1870s but increased as the International Board undertook a specific policy of rule revision from the late 1880s. By 1901 the penalty kick (effectively a direct free kick with all players bar the goalkeeper 6 yards behind the ball) could be awarded for seven offences: intentional tripping, pushing, kicking, charging from behind, holding, jumping at an opponent and handling. Between 1889 and 1891 the referee, initially a peripheral figure whose job was to adjudicate from the side of the pitch in the event of disagreement between the two officials in either half, was given the power to police the game from within the playing area. He assumed the right to award free kicks and send players off for foul play, with the umpires becoming linesmen whose role was reduced to indicating when a player was caught offside or the ball crossed the touchline.[60]

Complementary to this rationalisation of the laws of football was the move from a dribbling game based on individual prowess to a passing game underpinned by an emphasis on teamwork, or what contemporaries referred to as 'combination'. Geoffrey Green provided a succinct description of the former approach:

The good dribbler retained the ball as long as possible, especially if he combined speed with control. Long runs were the thing of the day. There was, however, a system of 'backing up', that of a player who followed up the dribbler, ready to receive the ball if it came to him, or to hustle and ward off any interference by the opposing forwards or back.[61]

Such was the primacy of the dribbler that when in the course of the 1877 England–Scotland fixture W. Mosforth complained to his colleague the Hon. Alfred Lyttleton that his dribbling was excessive and he was not passing to teammates in space, Lyttleton is said to have replied that 'I am playing purely for my own pleasure, Sir!' Attacking here was the principal concern and so most teams in the 1870s consisted of seven or perhaps six forwards with the remainder of the outfield team operating as half-backs and backs. A number of sources have been claimed for the introduction of the passing game. FA secretary Charles Alcock emphasised the role of teams from Scotland and the north of England. He highlighted three particular progenitors: the Sheffield team of the late 1860s; the Queen's Park and Vale of Leven clubs of the 1870s, who developed a short passing game; and the Blackburn Olympic side of the early 1880s, with its 'alternation of long passing and vigorous rushes'. An alternative view, advocated among others by a later FA secretary Frederick Wall and Sheffield's W. E. Clegg, has it that the London amateurs Royal Engineers 'were the first football team to introduce the "combination" style of play'. Walvin's suggestion that the crucial period of transformation was between 1874 and 1876 rules out the influence of Blackburn Olympic, although it is doubtful whether he is right that by the latter date 'the passing game had replaced the dribbling game' altogether. Certainly the 2–3–5 formation most connected with combination play, with a third centre half-back withdrawn from the forward line to act as a link between attack and defence, was not firmly established in England and Scotland until the mid to late 1880s.[62]

Combination, as against individualism, may indeed have become the norm by the early 1880s but there was more than one way of combining. It is telling that the epithet 'scientific' was used to describe the play of many of the nascent professional sides of the late Victorian and Edwardian period. To be 'scientific' was not only to take seriously the business of developing and practising skills and techniques but also to employ effective manoeuvres, ploys and tactics to achieve victory. In the first decades of professionalism, scientific football was associated above all with the Scottish short passing game, considered by many to be the best means of combating the prescriptive offside law. It was adopted by some of the best English professional sides, such as Preston North End in the late 1880s, Aston Villa during the 1890s and Newcastle United in the early 1900s. Yet there were alternative models for success. The so-called 'kick and rush' style, related first of all with West Bromwich Albion in the 1890s, was not, its advocates opined, a return to the unsophisticated 'rushing' of previous decades. Rather, it was the methodical employment of a system of long crossfield passing – 'from the inside-left to the outside-right, and from the inside-right to the outside-left' – designed to confuse defenders, outflank defences and force mistakes. Aston Villa had apparently used the system to good effect in their FA Cup final victory against Newcastle in 1905. Such systems of play were not mutually exclusive: many teams seem to have adopted a combination of tactical approaches. As the former England international William Bassett wrote in 1906:

the one-style team is not the successful one. The team which is successful today is the one which manifests most resource. Certain methods only suit certain conditions, and if forwards cannot adapt themselves to all conditions they are not likely to be permanently successful.[63]

Whether the clampdown on fouls and the introduction of a more 'scientific' approach led to the reduction of the physical side of the game is open to debate. G. O. Smith certainly felt that players in the late 1890s were overprotected from rough but fair charging and looked back longingly to the days when 'it used to be a matter of skill to avoid heavy charges, and of excitement to be on the lookout for them; one had to be constantly on the alert so as not to be bowled over and damaged'.[64] The shoulder charge had not been outlawed but its practice was curtailed: by 1905 the charge was permissible providing it was not 'violent or dangerous' or came from behind. Goalkeepers received little special treatment in this respect, although from 1893 they could only be charged when in contact with the ball or obstructing an opponent. Above all, the central role of the tackle as a means of winning possession of the ball ensured that British football in this period remained a highly tough, physical game.[65]

How can we interpret these developments in the aesthetic dimension of football? One approach is simply to regard football play as developing in an autonomous world generating 'its own panoply of actions, styles and productive creativity'.[66] Any variations in the way the game was played would thus be the result of straightforward technical decisions designed to achieve sporting success. Yet many writers have seen in the playing styles of football teams a reflection or reproduction of broader social and cultural values. For the French anthropologist Christian Bromberger, the football team 'is perceived, through its playing style, as a symbol of a specific mode of collective existence'. On a similar note, Richard Giulianotti has proposed that because 'body culture and social environment are closely related', considerable emphasis ought to be placed on the meanings which can be derived from playing styles.[67] At present, such analyses of late nineteenth and early twentieth-century British football are no more than tentative. Percy Young has seen the dribbling method as 'a derivant from the "leadership" philosophy' of the public schools at which it was cultivated; another author has, somewhat misguidedly, seen in dribbling the values of individualism and risk associated with the entrepreneur.[68] For Walvin, meanwhile, the introduction of 'combination' had a clear ideological resonance amongst the working class:

teamwork, with its strict allocation of positions and division of labour among the players, suited the style, attitudes and practices of working-class life. Working men were accustomed to a crude division of labour, to fulfil specific roles and functions; they were not expected to take upon themselves the individualistic responsibilities of their social superiors. The game which working men proceeded to colonize fitted this order of social relations; by the late 1870s the game had begun to reflect the qualities of their experience.[69]

We could add that the more 'scientific' approach to football combined an attention to skill and a dedication to hard, physical work which might well have appealed to the higher echelons of the manual working class throughout the country. Yet provocative though they may be, it is not clear how seriously we can take such speculative interpretations. What we can say is that in such contexts winning overrode any stylistic consider-ations. In the final analysis passing probably replaced dribbling not for aesthetic reasons but due to the simple fact that it worked.

Football, class and community

It has become almost a cliché to refer to association football as 'the people's game'. Walvin of course used the phrase as the title of his history of British football, but it has rarely been seriously questioned or subjected to sustained criticism.[70] The notion of 'the people' is an ambiguous and contested one in British social history. Patrick Joyce is one who has advo-cated its adoption as a more inclusive and universalising alternative to the category of class.[71] Yet in both general and academic usage the notion of 'the people' often overlaps with that of 'the working class'. There is an implication in the way in which it is used in the context of football, by Walvin and others, that 'the people' in this sense refers not to the popu-lace as a whole but a certain section of it – the ordinary folk, the lower ranks, the workers. It is telling, however, that both Walvin and Mason, who tend to favour the descriptive notions of 'the workers' or 'working people', generally avoid the language and concept of class. Few would claim that association football pre-1914 was a game exclusively of the working class, however this was defined. If it can be regarded as a people's game at all, the consensus is that it would be in the nature of its support and consumption rather than in the way it was organised and controlled.[72]

Football and class

Football was certainly a people's game in the sense that the majority of those who played and watched were working class. On the evidence we have, it appears that the first generation of professional footballers in Britain came originally from what might be called the skilled working class. Most of the imported Scots and Welshmen who moved to Lancashire clubs in the 1880s were skilled artisans rather than labourers. Mason's analysis of 67 players attached to elite English professional clubs between 1884 and 1900 shows a proliferation of skilled manual workers such as bricklayers, plumbers, slaters and upholsterers, although there was also a fair sprinkling of white-collar workers, professionals and the self-employed.[73] Similarly, as we can see from Table 2.1, almost half of the 123 players listed in H. R. Brown's *Football Who's Who* in 1907–8, and *Athletic News* articles over the next few years, were broadly drawn from skilled work; the 14 coal miners (fitting easily into neither a skilled nor unskilled category) suggesting the emergence of what was to become an important source for professional footballers over the course of the century. Irish footballers were considerably more likely to have been unskilled workers or labourers than their English counterparts, a disparity possibly accounted for by the limited rewards available relative to other skilled occupations and the low status of the job. We have less detailed evidence on Scottish players but it has been argued that they 'almost always came from industrial backgrounds'.[74]

Our knowledge of the composition of football crowds is even more sketchy but the overwhelming impression once again is that the bulk of those who regularly attended were working class 'in origin, occupation and life style'. Despite their limitations, press reports and commentaries are the most important source we have in this respect. At an 1886 match between

TABLE 2.1 *Occupational backgrounds of professional footballers in England and Ireland, c. 1900–10*

Occupational category	England, 1907–10		Ireland, c.1900	
Skilled	53	43.1%	21	38.2%
Labourers/unskilled	14	11.4%	20	36.4%
Artisans			7	12.7%
White collar			7	12.7%
Unclassified	12	9.7%		
Others	44	35.8%		

Source: Tony Mason, *Association Football and English Society, 1863–1915* (Brighton: Harvester, 1980) p. 93 (Table 4.2); Neal Garnham, *Association Football and Society in Pre-Partition Ireland* (Belfast: Ulster Historical Foundation, 2004), p. 96 (Table 3.3).

West Bromwich and Aston Villa, the crowd was depicted as that 'vast concourse of the British Artisan Class'; at Sunderland in 1890 'the horny-handed in the shipyards' were thought to be the most numerous supporters; and at the 1893 Sheffield 'derby' 'the working element was undoubtedly in the ascendent'. When Belfast newspapers described the city's football crowds as 'the great unwashed' this was partly social prejudice but confirmed more balanced observations concerning the working-class nature of spectatorship. Elements of the middle class and well-to-do did go to football, especially for special occasions such as Cup finals and international fixtures, but they were often physically segregated in the stand, representing 'a bourgeois island in a sea of working-class faces'.[75] It has been calculated that in the Stirling region at least, fewer than 5 per cent of football supporters at this time were middle-class males. What concrete data we do have on the social and occupational make-up of the crowd in this period comes from Scotland and Ireland. First, the police and newspapers recorded details of the casualties of the Ibrox disaster of 1902, when part of the terracing collapsed at the Scotland–England international, with 26 killed and over 500 injured. Of the 249 victims whose occupations were noted, 166 have been classified as skilled workers as against 59 unskilled and 30 in white-collar, middle-class or other employment. If we add photographic evidence to this, what seems to emerge is a picture of football crowds as dominated by the skilled and 'respectable' sectors of the working class, whose stable and relatively well-paid jobs would have enabled them to purchase the regular 6d match tickets on a habitual basis.[76]

A slight corrective to this view is provided by Neil Tranter's examination of the riot that took place at Greenock Morton's Cappielow ground in 1899. A subsequent report estimated that the 1,200 Port Glasgow fans in the 6,000 strong crowd were made up of 'the roughest class of shipyard workers, labourers and persons of that stamp' and that 37 per cent of the rioters arrested were unskilled workers. In a similar vein, Neal Garnham has shown that 32 per cent of those injured following a disturbance at the Belfast Celtic–Linfield fixture in 1912 were from the labouring and unskilled category. Although these latter examples were in various ways untypical, it should warn us not to underplay the attendance of what have been called the 'rougher' sections of the working class.[77]

If players and spectators were by and large working class, the same cannot be said of administrators, directors and shareholders. By the beginning of the twentieth century the English FA was less the preserve of a southern public-school elite than it had been in the 1870s. In 1903 its decision-making forum, the FA Council, included more schoolmasters, accountants and clerks than lords and gentlemen. The Football League's Management Committee consisted of a range of manufacturers and small businessmen but was dominated by a core of journalists, solicitors and other professionals. Suffice it to say that no working men were to be found represented in either body.[78] Mason, Tischler and Vamplew have highlighted the prevalence of proprietors and employers on English club boards, representing between 47.8 to 53.8 per cent of all directors according to their different calculations. The highest estimate identified only 11.8 per cent coming from the ranks of manual workers, although working-class representation was considerably higher in Scotland, at 28.8 per cent in 1914. Similarly, the financial control of professional clubs, through ownership of shares, lay firmly with the middle class. Manual workers accounted for 36.8 per cent of the shareholders and only 17.8 per cent of the shares at English clubs; the comparative Scottish figures were 47.2 and 24.0 per cent. The size of this 'sprinkling of working class shareholders' impressed and rather surprised Mason but recent research on clubs in Newcastle, Sunderland and Middlesbrough suggests that calculations based on occupation alone may in fact have inflated the working-class presence. In any case, such small shareholdings could hardly be equated with any degree of influence or control in the way a club was run, especially if, as was the case of most workers, no more than a couple of shares were purchased. As has often been pointed out, shareholding in this instance was little more than an extension of being a fan.[79]

Looking beyond the averages, we can detect isolated examples where working-class shareholders were in the majority, as at Darwen, Dartford and Woolwich Arsenal. The latter's self-image as 'a working-class club' was reflected in its shareholding and even the constituency of its board of directors, which initially included six engineers. Financial problems, however, forced Arsenal to go the way of so many other clubs by seeking the assistance of local patrons from the business community and the professions. By the beginning of the twentieth century, the familiar social division of roles in British professional football had been resolutely adopted, with the bourgeoisie located in the boardroom and stands and the proletariat manning the terraces and the dressing room.[80]

A working-class game?

There has been a tendency when faced with such evidence of the lack of working-class authority and autonomy in the organisation of 'their' game to resort to a rather crude model of social control. Tischler, for one, has argued that scholars ought to reconsider the assumption that football was a workingman's game 'in anything other than a superficial sense'. Rather, in its professional guise at least, it operated as an instrument of bourgeois control, acting as 'a safety valve through which pressure generated by industrial capitalism could pass safely, without endangering the basic relationships of society'. Contemporaries occasionally articulated the view that football could be used to keep workers out of trouble but rarely saw it as a means of staving off revolution. One reporter referred to the importance of match attendance as an 'innocent recreation for a couple of hours a week for men who might otherwise be in worse places'.[81] The Conservative politician F. E. Smith (later Lord Birkenhead) mused over the issue in 1911:

What would the devotees of athletics do if their present amusements were abolished? The policeman, the police magistrate, the social worker, the minister of religion, the public schoolmaster and the University don would each ... contemplate such a prospect with dismay ... The poorer classes have not got the tastes which superior people or a Royal Commission would choose for them and were cricket and football abolished, it would bring upon the masses nothing but misery, depression, sloth, indiscipline and disorder.[82]

As Holt and Mason point out, however, the airing of such sentiments is not the same as showing that football actually operated as an 'opiate'. It was quite possible to be both a football supporter and a socialist and there is little evidence that watching the game made people docile and politically inert. Indeed as Gareth Stedman Jones has pointed out, it was Glasgow, the very place where football arguably received the greatest popular support before 1914, which also witnessed the most significant industrial unrest and militancy before and during the First World War.[83]

An alternative view is to see football as a people's game in the sense that it bore the stamp of working-class ideals and characteristics. Soccer appears in this account as a cultural experience that the people 'made' themselves rather than one which was imposed upon them. John Hargreaves, for instance, has argued that although working people achieved little genuine control, they invested games like football 'with their own character and transformed them in some ways into a means of expression of values opposed to the bourgeois athleticist tradition'. Stephen Jones felt that the labouring classes were able to take from sport 'those elements, rituals and values which fitted into their own culture'. Walvin hinted at the same basic point in his reference to the successful working-class 'colonisation' of the association game.[84] The partisanship of spectators and the emphasis on winning were just two aspects of this fledgling popular football culture, which were widely commented upon, and more often than not denigrated, in contemporary 'gentlemen's magazines'. 'There is no sportsmanship in a football crowd', wrote one observer in 1913:

Partisanship has dulled its idea of sport and warped its moral sense. It cannot enjoy a game that has been won by the visiting team. A referee is good or bad (with adjectives), according to the manner in which his decisions affect the home side.

Another noted that 'doubtful tactics by the home team are applauded to the echo, while the same actions by the opponents are met with hooting and groans'. Discussing what he called 'The New Football Mania' in 1892, Charles Edwardes highlighted the shouts, abuse and 'encouragement' directed by spectators at the players: '"Down him!" "Sit on his chest!" "Knock their ribs in!" are invitations often addressed to them, and in no playful mode be it understood'.[85]

The football terrace also seems to have been the site for the development of particular ways and styles of supporting. Much of the game's visceral attraction – the colour, noise and excitement – was the creation of its working-class patrons. We cannot be sure when club colours, rosettes and scarves were first worn or when rattles and mascots initially became a part of the match day experience but they seem to have been prominent enough in pre-1914 written and visual sources. Supporters often 'borrowed' songs and catchphrases from the music hall, some over time becoming associated with particular teams. The drinking song, the 'Rowdy Dowdy Boys', for example, was taken up by followers of Sheffield United, and Southampton fans had apparently by 1902 developed what one reporter called their 'distinctive Yi! Yi! Yi! chant'. We also know from contemporary accounts that drinking and gambling were part and parcel of supporting culture at this time, although we can only speculate whether this had yet formed part of a broader weekend cultural routine (involving, perhaps, the public house, the bookmaker's shop, the sporting newspaper and the music hall as well as the match itself) for any more than the most affluent workers.[86]

Russell has seen in this the rejection of football as a middle-class 'school of moral instruction' and its transformation into a form of 'popular theatre'.[87] Others might extend the discussion further, perceiving football in this sense as one element of Eric Hobsbawm's traditional and standardised working-class culture, which cohered in the latter decades of the nineteenth century and persisted almost unchanged until the 1950s. Alongside the pub, the music hall, fish and chip shops, the 'palais-de-danse', betting, the seaside holiday and so on, watching and playing football was, it is argued, an important part of what set the working class apart from the rest of society. Although not obviously 'radical' or 'political' in itself, it provided workers with yet another example of the wider sense of difference between 'us' and 'them' which permeated their lives.[88] As such, it might be regarded as an important site of class expression, even class-consciousness. Historians have wrestled with these ideas for decades. Critical analyses from a range of topic areas have stressed the considerable fractures and divisions in this supposedly homogeneous working-class culture. Andrew Davies is just one who has highlighted the diversity of popular cultural experiences on the ground, and the fact that commercialised forms of leisure such as football were heavily structured by gender, ethnicity and poverty.[89] More sympathetic to Hobsbawm's thesis, Neville Kirk has restated the mutuality and collectivism in workers' lives and criticised Davies and others for isolating culture and leisure from broader patterns of social change and nationalising tendencies.[90]

Football and place

A fruitful way of engaging with these debates is to look at the role played by the game at the town or community level. The notion of civic culture has been a major preoccupation of social and urban historians. Often associated with the construction of public buildings such as town halls, museums, libraries and concert halls, civic culture was also important in the creation and projection of identities of place. Through the built structures of civic culture, elite groups were able to demonstrate their power and status over the working class and simultaneously define their image of the town or city. But through civic culture, elites could also signal their achievement to rival elites in surrounding towns and beyond. In this way, it was crucial to notions of place identity, place promotion and what has been termed civic boosterism. At the popular level, there is no doubt that sport generally, and football specifically, played a leading role in providing a sense of place and belonging in the urban environment as well as constructing and promoting broader town and city identities.[91]

The classic statement of the significance of football in the creation of urban, civic and community identities comes from Holt. He has suggested that the game provided supporters with 'a reassuring feeling of being part of something even if the crowd itself were for the great part strangers to one another'. It generated a 'sense of urban community' through which supporters achieved a form of 'symbolic citizenship'.[92] Williams has helped to flesh out these ideas in his study of sport and town identity. Focusing mainly on Lancashire and the north of England, he has outlined football's ability to reflect and articulate, perhaps even help to define, civic identity and encourage both pride in one's place of residence and a wider sense of social harmony. This was best displayed of course when teams were successful, and especially when victory was achieved on a national stage. Hence an estimated crowd of 30–40,000 packed the centre of Blackburn to welcome home the Rovers players in 1890 following their 6–1 FA Cup final defeat of Sheffield Wednesday. By this time celebrations of this kind had become an established and ritualised practice.[93] Such loyalties demonstrated through football were easier to assert in small towns with a single professional club than in large cities with many. In Glasgow, Edinburgh, Belfast, Manchester, Liverpool, Sheffield, Nottingham, Bristol and elsewhere, there is at least the possibility that professional football actually worked to divide rather than unite communities. Yet even here, Holt has argued that 'derby' matches between city rivals 'strengthened rather than weakened civic pride'. Thus the 'Old Firm' match is seen here as a spectacle that Glaswegians celebrated as being something particular and unique to the city. Similarly, while there was a fervent division of loyalties in Liverpool between the blues and the reds, this may have ultimately contributed to create an even stronger pride in the city, as evidenced by the triumphant reaction of the local press in 1906 when Liverpool won the First Division and Everton the FA Cup.[94]

Studies of individual towns and cities have deepened our understanding of the relationship between football and urban culture. An analysis of male working-class leisure in Coventry by Brad Beaven has focused on the role played by the local football club in providing a sense of attachment to the city. In Coventry, a city dealing with high levels of immigration, football conveyed 'a popular form of citizenship which constructed assumptions about the ... city's achievements' and simultaneously 'developed ideas about the "otherness" of those from outside the town'.[95] Originally based around the Singer's bicycle works, Coventry City (as the club was renamed in 1898) soon became sufficiently popular and successful to represent the city in district and then national competition. Civic approval was achieved when a number of city councillors took control of the club in 1905, starting a process that formally connected 'local patriotism, good citizenship and support for the city's football team'. Indeed supporting Coventry

City, Beaven concludes, did more to foster civic pride and city loyalty than numerous municipal schemes of social citizenship were able to achieve.[96] Andy Croll's study of the town of Merthyr in south Wales, meanwhile, links football more explicitly with notions of public space. Followers of the local football club were not confined to the ground alone: they increasingly began to appropriate the streets of the town. Whether on the way to the match, or 'greeting' visiting teams as they arrived at the railway station, Merthyr Town supporters in their red and green colours became a new visible (and audible) presence in the streets and public spaces of the town in the first decade of the twentieth century. These increasing demands upon urban space were paralleled by the discursive space the game began to take up in the local newspapers. Coverage increased as the game became more popular but, significantly, also because football increasingly came to be viewed by editors as an element in the construction of a united civic identity. In these different ways, Croll argues, football began to occupy an enhanced position in local urban culture that was readily utilised by projectors of 'civic Merthyr'.[97]

Yet the question remains whether this identification of football with place was in fact compatible with working-class solidarity. As Joanna Bourke notes, many historians have seen a clear correlation between community consciousness and class consciousness. Williams, for one, concludes that 'town identities based on sport were a form of solidarity among working men'. Robbie Gray argued that in Victorian Edinburgh the rise of football 'made for a more homogeneous urban working-class culture'.[98] Metcalfe, meanwhile, has shown the complex way in which community pride and class identity complemented one another among the miners of East Northumberland. At the recreational and junior level, interest in football was based on intense rivalries between clubs representing the different mining villages. Yet these divisions were set aside when senior clubs such as Ashington and Blyth Spartans represented the area in the Northern Alliance and the North-Eastern League, when the East Northumberland Schoolboys competed in the English Schools Shield and when miners travelled to St James's Park to support Newcastle United. But class was not an irrelevance here. Underpinning these multiple affiliations was a feeling among the miners that football 'belonged to them'. 'It was', for Metcalfe, 'the first game that was solidly rooted in the working class: it was their own game, not one visibly associated with the "superior" classes like rugby and cricket.'[99] Such arguments are difficult to refute. They lend concrete support to the notion of the centrality of football as a unifying force within working-class cultural life.[100]

Divisions: gender, religion and ethnicity

However, we should be wary of painting too idealised a picture of the game as an expression of worker solidarity. The broader criticisms of this supposed 'traditional' working-class culture remain pertinent here. In particular, football was often divided on the basis of gender and religion. The values associated with football were indisputably male and masculine. In Jeff Hill's words, 'few other pastimes ... served more to generate a feeling of male sociability and exclusiveness than football, whether in its participant or spectating forms'. The terrace and the changing room have been regarded in this way not just as an important site for the construction of male identity but 'a locale into which men could escape from domestic and family obligation'.[101] One analysis has suggested that involvement in the football company through shareholding, dominated as it was by married men, provided similar masculine camaraderie and a refuge from home life.[102] All this is not to say that football was exclusively male. There are plentiful examples that women did watch and indeed play football. In Scotland, they were admitted free of charge up until 1918 and often gained half-price entry elsewhere. Two thousand women attended a Preston match in 1885, and at Leicester in 1899, 'the fair sex' were reportedly observed 'in every part of the ground'. Mason and Taylor have argued that female attendance fell as the overall size of crowds increased and that, in any case, the practical and financial constraints on the 'leisure' opportunities of working-class women militated against regular attendance.[103] Touring teams, such as the 'British Ladies' organised by Lady Florence Dixie and the 'Original Lady Footballers' under Mrs Graham, were playing mainly charity matches across England and Scotland from the 1890s. Yet almost universally they were treated with disdain by both the media and the game's governing bodies, the English and Scottish FAs actually advising its members not to partake in such events in 1902. There is thus a good case for perceiving football at this time as a gendered activity, with female involvement even at the margins threatening the game's essential cultural and masculine values.[104]

In parts of Scotland and Ireland, football's main cleavage was based on religious and ethnic affiliations. The sectarian rivalry between Glasgow's premier clubs, Celtic and Rangers, provides the best and most obvious example here. Early writers traced the beginning of the trouble between the two groups of supporters to the arrival of the Belfast-based Harland and Wolff shipbuilders, and its immigrant and largely Protestant workforce, on the Clyde in 1912. Yet as Bill Murray has shown, the religious and ethnic characteristics of both clubs were long established before this time: Celtic originating and drawing its support from the Catholic Irish community and Rangers associated with Protestant Scotland and the anti-Catholicism of the Orange Order. The 'Old Firm' reflected, and in time reinforced, the divisions and polarities of Glasgow and Scottish society more generally. By the beginning of the twentieth century, the two clubs had become 'standard bearers for their respective societies'. This sectarianism was reproduced in a milder form in Edinburgh's Hearts–Hibs rivalry and that between Dundee FC and Dundee Hibs (later United).[105] It acquired a harder political edge in Belfast, where the rivalries between the Protestant-allied Linfield and Glentoran and the Catholic Belfast Celtic were caught up, particularly from 1912 onwards, in the politics of Irish Home Rule. In September 1912 a league match between Belfast Celtic and Linfield was abandoned at half-time when fighting between rival supporters led to over 50 casualties, some with gunshot wounds. Contemporary reports revealed that the disturbance was infused with a particular politico-sectarian character, involving the chanting of political slogans and the unfurling by the respective parties of nationalist and unionist banners. Most thought that it had little to do with football. In essence, it was a clash 'between two groups of young men of differing religious and political views, but with a possible common sporting interest'. This was a particularly violent incident but its sectarian dimension was not exceptional in British football at the time. The aforementioned Cappielow Riot has largely been explained as 'a clash between two different cultures': the Irish, Catholic, working-class Port Glasgow population and the Scottish, Protestant, more 'respectable' people of Greenock. Similarly, violent clashes at 'Old Firm' matches were commonplace from the mid-1890s, even if the most notorious of all, the Hampden Riot of 1909 (described by H. F. Moorhouse as 'one of the most spectacular instances of violence around a British football match') stemmed more from collective frustration at the failure to play extra time.[106]

In many ways, Belfast and Glasgow were untypical. British football was hardly riven by ethnic and sectarian divisions but, even where it was, it could still be an important element of working-class culture. A multitude of loyalties – overlapping and cross-cutting – were expressed through the game. Football could feed on or be built around a whole range of affiliations and identities, based on gender, religion and locality as well as class and, as we shall see below, nationality. Likewise, it could unite and divide. By 1914 football was indeed a working-class game played and watched predominantly in working-class communities. But it is difficult to argue that it was working class in a more political or ideological sense. It was, as Mason put it so well, 'one of those things which working men did', articulating a consciousness of class but possibly not class consciousness.[107] If it was 'the people's game', we must accept this as a relatively narrow and exclusive definition of 'the people', which had little place for women and many men, and could divide and subdivide along regional, communal and ethnic lines. Association football had become an important cultural activity in Britain by the First World War but it was still a minority interest, attracting perhaps no more than 5 per cent of the entire population on a regular basis as players or spectators.[108] Its meanings, of course, spread much wider than this.

Football and nation

Football was a British game but there was no British cup, no British league and (with the exception of the early Olympic tournaments) no British team. By the 1890s the game in the British Isles had been established on a national basis, with Scottish, Irish and Welsh associations and competitions modelled on the English examples. The first Scotland–England match took place at the West of Scotland Cricket Ground in Glasgow in 1872 and thereafter became an annual encounter. Wales played Scotland for the first time in 1876 and England in 1879. Ireland first competed against England and Wales in 1882 and Scotland in 1884. In a territory incorporating a single nation-state but four separate nations, this particular game had gone along the latter route. Yet it had not been inevitable that this would happen. Neither the Football Association nor the Football League assumed the epithet 'English' nor regarded themselves as restricted to English clubs. Indeed the FA Cup was from its beginnings open to Scottish, Irish and Welsh competitors. Queen's Park affiliated to the FA and, as we have seen, played in the first 1872 competition, but could not afford to travel down to London to play Wanderers for a replay of their semi-final tie and had to withdraw. Linfield became the first Irish side to reach the first round proper of the competition after defeating Nottingham Forest in Belfast in 1888, but had to concede its place as there were insufficient funds to finance the designated trip to Kent.[109] Early on, the main obstacles in the way of a genuinely 'British' competition were thus financial and logistical rather than emotional.

Yet nationalist sentiments were never far below the surface. Historians of Scottish nationalism have highlighted the importance of one particular incident that took place on 30 October 1886 at Hampden Park in

Glasgow. During the match, a third-round FA Cup tie between Queen's Park and Preston North End, the visitors' exiled Scot Jimmy Ross fouled the home team's centre-forward, after which the crowd invaded the pitch and Ross had to be protected as he left the ground. Already aggravated by the acceptance of professionalism south of the border, the Scottish FA subsequently banned its clubs from affiliating to other national associations and, as such, prohibited them from entering the FA Cup. According to Christopher Harvie, this decision amounted to 'a declaration of independence'. The die had been cast. Football, Harvie argues, was henceforth to be run along national rather than British lines and to become a fertile source of Scottish working-class nationalism.[110]

The idea that sport and nationalism are closely linked and that sport can be a key force in defining and sustaining national identity is a potent one. Yet the issue is complicated and eludes easy generalisation. Mike Cronin has discussed the numerous and diverse ways in which nationalism connects with sport: 'it can be representative of many different themes, groups and ideas, and ... formed and shaped by a multitude of forces'. Eric Hobsbawm got to the heart of the matter when he suggested that 'the imagined community of millions seems more real as a team of eleven named people'.[111] A football team could have added meaning for those 'submerged nations' that had no unifying ethnicity or language and were governed from afar. As Johnes notes, for those located in Britain's Celtic fringes, eleven men in national colours offers 'one of the few pieces of tangible evidence that their nation exists'.[112] Football, however, was not suddenly shorn of its British dimension with the creation of national governing bodies, leagues and representative teams. Any sense of Scottishness, Irishness, Welshness or even Englishness which might have been articulated through football was restrained and held in balance by a broader British context. Central to this was the British International Championship, better known as the home internationals, which began in the 1883–4 season. Along with the Inter-League fixtures, the home internationals ensured that competition between the British nations became an essential element of the annual football calendar, simultaneously promoting the distinctive identity of the rival nations and their unity within a British whole. The constant flow of playing talent, generally but not exclusively from the peripheral nations to the English centre, was another constant reminder that soccer could not be contained within national borders. Thus national identities in the British game were far from straightforward. Michael Lynch's assessment of the Scottish case summarises this ambivalence. By 1914 football was 'Scottish but, in a sense,

PLATE 4 *Hampden Park, 1910. Spectators queue to see the Scotland–England international. Scotland won 2–0 (© Popperfoto.com).*

British too – for it was both a "national game" and the British national game ... it was an emblem of the condition of a nation living within a larger nation-state'.[113]

It was probably more popular in Scotland than anywhere else in Britain. In the Celtic–Rangers and Scotland–England matches, Glasgow could claim some of the most passionate and most of the highest crowds in the country each season. At Celtic Park in 1912, 74,000 were present and 65,000 packed Ibrox a year later. Twenty thousand attended the first Hampden Park international between Scotland and England in 1878 but by 1906 the figure had reached a massive 100,000 and in 1912 a record 127,000 attended. Yet football's relationship to Scottish identity can hardly be explained quantitatively. One commentator from 1906 remarked that 'the enthusiasm of the Scot for the Association game is without parallel in any race for any particular sport or pastime'.[114] Hyperbolic though they may have been, such views were commonplace among reporters, observers and players north of the border. As Alan Bairner has commented, 'the game's importance to the nation's psyche far exceeds normal relationships between sport and national identity'.[115] This alleged passion for football was often compared favourably with that of the English. Aston Villa's Archie Hunter considered the matter at some length in 1890:

all Scotchmen are athletes. They develop plenty of muscle and they seem to get strength and stability from their mode of living and very often from their occupations also. Then they have a genuine love of the sport – a deep love for it which lasts a long time, not a passing fancy. They are different to many Englishmen in this way, who like cricket for a few seasons and then football for a few seasons and then something else for a few seasons. Scotchmen grow up playing football and they stick to it all their lives. They prefer it to all outdoor sports. In some towns you may see all the boys playing football, although they have no shoes to their feet. I think the national character has something to do with their success. They are steady and persevering, and they always play to win. My experience of English players lends me to think that they can't be depended upon to do their best after a certain time. They will play excellently one season, or two, or three; but sooner or later their enthusiasm dies off and they get lazy, or want to change.[116]

This may help explain the success of Scotland against the 'auld enemy' in this period: they won 17 and drew 12 of the 42 matches with England between 1872 and 1914. The game was unquestionably the most important of the season in Scotland, though less so in England, where attendances were always much lower. Its obsessive appeal to the Scots, Holt has argued, sprang from three main sources: the history of conflict between the nations; the chance to defeat a more powerful and politically and economically dominant neighbour; and the need to escape the disunity of domestic club football, exemplified by the 'Old Firm' games. Yet to beat England was also a periodic reaffirmation of what the Scottish liked to think of as their primacy over the game. It may have been part of a shared British culture but for the Scots it was 'emotionally *their* property'.[117]

The Welsh and Irish relationship with football was rather more ambiguous. In neither case could soccer claim to be the national game in quite the way it could in Scotland. Rugby assumed that mantle in Wales, buttressed by a famous victory over the touring New Zealand 'All Blacks' in 1905 and confirmed by consistent success in competition with its British neighbours. The national soccer team, by contrast, was uncompetitive in playing terms and unrepresentative of the country as a whole. It only won the home international championship once, in 1907, and failed to beat England at all between 1883 and 1914. Moreover, most of the players picked were born and employed in north Wales, or else, like the famous winger Billy Meredith, were north Walians with English clubs. Small wonder, then, that a south Wales newspaper could bemoan the failure to produce 'an eleven from regular players in the principality to uphold the honour of the country'. What is more, although there was a Welsh Cup and, from 1912, a Welsh League, the leading clubs played in English competitions and judged their success in an English rather than a Welsh context. Kenneth Morgan is thus surely right that it was rugby, and not football, that provided the Welsh with their main 'popular source of national sporting esteem' pre-1914.[118]

In Ireland, the existence of the Gaelic Athletic Association (GAA), with its explicit political nationalism and its ban on what were regarded as 'foreign' sports, served to marginalise soccer in certain respects as a unionist and a British, which in this context meant a 'foreign', game. The fact that the Irish FA and most of the leading clubs were based in Belfast, rather than the capital Dublin, also marked it out, in Cronin's words, as 'identifiable with a specific sector of Irish society'.[119] As with Wales, the poor performances of the Irish side did not help to engender national pride and identity. The first international fixture in 1882 was a 13–0 defeat against England in Belfast and it was not until 1887 that the Irish won their first match, 4–1 against Wales. Triumphs over Scotland and England had to wait until 1903 and 1913 respectively, although Ireland did manage to tie the 1902–3 championship with both of the senior nations.[120] Garnham has provided a particularly nuanced account of how Irish identity in all its complexity related to soccer. He shows how the rejection of soccer by some nationalists was linked to broader questions of morality, race and masculinity *as well as* the explicit criticism of it as a foreign game linked administratively to the 'imperial centre'. It was never likely to become a nationalist symbol for a united Ireland, but as the game spread among both Catholics and Protestants and across the social spectrum, it came to develop (in the north of Ireland at least) a significant appeal for nationalists and unionists alike. For the former, administrative parity and the occasional victory over the English, as in 1913 and 1914, was taken as evidence of the equality of Ireland and England, while the latter could be satisfied by the success of Irish players abroad and the British context of competition. Soccer was a case, Garnham argues, where 'rival nationalisms could coalesce in their support for a single sporting code'.[121]

In England, football was emerging as an important vehicle for expressing an attachment to community, town and even region but rarely to the nation. In stark contrast to Scotland, football, at least until the inter-war years, 'carried a limited burden in relation to the reinforcement and construction of national identity'. English representative sides were reasonably well supported and journalists, players and supporters did seem to care if the team won or lost but rarely with the same loyalty and passion as they treated club encounters. It has been suggested that English football was often too wrapped up in parochial and regional rivalries 'to give itself whole-heartedly to the national cause'.[122] It hardly helped that the national team rarely played and that, when it did, it was usually against the same opponents in the annual home internationals. The first full international against non-British opposition was not until 1908 (a 6–1 away victory in Austria), although there were numerous amateur internationals during the 1900s. The English press took some pride in victories against its neighbours, but such matches were hardly likely to mean the same as they did for the Scottish, Irish or Welsh or ignite a dormant English nationalism. What is more, it is evident that the emerging 'Englishness' rediscovered by writers and poets from the late nineteenth century hardly chimed with the character of football. This was an Englishness that celebrated the rural, the ancient and, above all, the countryside of the south of England. Football's connections with the urban and industrial, the north and midlands and the working-class city 'had no place in the image of Englishness that was created'.[123] It was cricket, rather than football, that fitted this variant of English identity. In England at least, football had yet to become *the* national game.

References

1 Dave Russell, *Football and the English: A Social History of Association Football in England, 1863–1995* (Preston: Carnegie, 1997), p. 30.

2 G. O. Smith, 'Origin and Benefits of the League and the Effects of Professionalism on the Game', in Montague Shearman (ed.), *Football* (London: Badminton Library Series, 1899), p. 173.

3 Robert W. Lewis, 'The Genesis of Professional Football: Bolton-Blackburn-Darwen, the Centre of Innovation, 1878–85', *International Journal of the History of Sport*, 14, 1 (April 1997), pp. 41, 50–1 (Tables 1 and 2); 'The Development of Professional Football in Lancashire, 1870–1914', unpublished Ph.D. thesis, University of Lancaster, 1993, chapters 2, 3 and conclusion; Graham Williams, *The Code War: English Football Under the Historical Spotlight* (Harefield: Yore, 1994), p. 94; John Bale, 'Geographical Diffusion and the Adoption of Professionalism in Football in

England and Wales', *Geography*, 63 (1978), pp. 191–2; *Sport and Place: A Geography of Sport in England, Scotland and Wales* (London: C. Hurst, 1982), p. 25.

4 Bale, *Sport and Place*, p. 25; Williams, *Code War*, p. 94; A. E. Kennedy, 'The History of Woolwich Arsenal' in C. Leatherdale (ed.), *The Book of Football* (Westcliff-on-Sea: Desert Island, 1997 [1st edition, 1906]), p. 17.

5 Archie Hunter, *Triumphs of the Football Field* (Smethwick: Sports Projects, 1997 [first published in *Birmingham Weekly Mercury*, 1890]), p. 22; Wray Vamplew, *Pay Up and Play the Game: Professional Sport in Britain, 1875–1914* (Cambridge; Cambridge University Press, 1988), p. 194.

6 Neal Garnham, 'Professionals and Professionalism in Pre-Great War Irish Soccer', *Journal of Sport History*, 29, 1 (Spring 2002), pp. 81–2; *Association Football and Society in Pre-Partition Ireland* (Belfast: Ulster Historical Foundation, 2004), pp. 72–4; Brian Lile and David Farmer, 'The Early Development of Association Football in South Wales, 1890–1906', *Transactions of the Honourable Society of Cymmrodorion* (1984), p. 206.

7 David Russell, '"Sporadic and Curious": The Emergence of Rugby and Soccer Zones in Yorkshire and Lancashire, *c*. 1860–1914', *International Journal of the History of Sport*, 5, 2 (September 1988), pp. 196–201; A. J. Arnold, 'The Belated Entry of Professional Soccer into the West Riding Textile District of Northern England: Commercial Imperatives and Problems', *International Journal of the History of Sport*, 6, 3 (December 1989), pp. 319–34.

8 Matthew Taylor, *The Leaguers: The Making of Professional Football in England, 1900–39* (Liverpool: Liverpool University Press, 2005), pp. 3–5; Simon Inglis, *League Football and the Men Who Made It: The Official Centenary History of the Football League, 1888–1988* (London: Collins Willow, 1988), pp. 6–10; Adrian Harvey, *Football: The First Hundred Years* (London: Routledge, 2005), p. 220.

9 Taylor, *The Leaguers*, pp. 5–12; Brian Hunt, *Northern Goalfields Revisited: The Millennium History of the Northern Football League, 1889–2000* (Northern Football League, 2000), p. 2; Russell, *Football and the English*, p. 34; John Coyle, 'English Sports Leagues, Franchising and the Management of Expansion: The Football League and the Northern Union up to 1923', unpublished MA dissertation, De Montfort University, 1997, chapter 2; Bale, *Sport and Place*, p. 28.

10 Alfred Davis, 'The Southern League: Its Rise and Progress' in Leatherdale (ed.), *Book of Football*, pp. 284–6; Paul Harrison, *Southern League Football: The First Fifty Years* (Gravesend: P. Harrison, 1989), pp. 5–20; *Football Chat*, 22 January 1907; Taylor, *The Leaguers*, pp. 12–14.

11 Harrison, *Southern League Football*, pp. 20–4; Martin Johnes, *Soccer and*

Society: South Wales, 1900–1939 (Cardiff: University of Wales Press, 2002), pp. 36–40.

12 Bob Crampsey, *The First 100 Years: The Scottish Football League* (Glasgow: Scottish Football League, 1990); R. M. Connell, 'The Scottish Football League and its History' in Leatherdale (ed.), *Book of Football*, pp. 266–9; John Rafferty, *One Hundred Years of Scottish Football* (London: Pan, 1973), pp. 27–8.

13 Russell, *Football and the English*, p. 34.

14 William McGregor, 'The £ s. d. of Football' in Leatherdale (ed.), *Book of Football*, p. 60.

15 Stephen Tischler, *Footballers and Businessmen: The Origins of Professional Soccer in England* (New York: Holmes & Meier, 1981), pp. 86, 69.

16 Vamplew, *Pay Up*, chapter 8.

17 Richard Holt, *Sport and the British: A Modern History* (Oxford: Clarendon, 1989), p. 282.

18 Cited in Tony Mason, *Association Football and English Society, 1863–1915* (Brighton: Harvester, 1980), p. 48.

19 Bill Murray, *The Old Firm: Sectarianism, Sport and Society in Scotland* (Edinburgh: John Donald, 2000 [1st edition, 1984]), p. 25 (n. 53); Vamplew, *Pay Up*, p. 86.

20 Tischler, *Footballers and Businessmen*, 76–8; Mason, *Association Football*, 45–6; Neil Tranter, *Sport, Economy and Society, 1750–1914* (Cambridge: Cambridge University Press, 1998), p. 72; Garnham, *Association Football*, p. 55.

21 Holt, *Sport and the British*, p. 283; McGregor, '£ s. d. of Football', p. 60.

22 Mason, *Association Football*, p. 46–7; McGregor, '£ s. d. of Football', p. 61; Tischler, *Footballers and Businessmen*, p. 84 (Table 5).

23 Murray, *Old Firm*, p. 22; Stephen Yeo, *Religion and Voluntary Organisations in Crisis* (London: Croom Helm, 1976), pp. 195–6; Mason, *Association Football*, p. 38, 78 (n. 55); *The Times* cited in Arnold, 'Belated Entry', p. 331.

24 Tranter, *Sport, Economy and Society*, p. 74.

25 Simon Inglis, *The Football Grounds of Britain* (London: Collins Willow, 1993 [1st edition, 1983]), p. 10; Wray Vamplew, 'The Economics of a Sports Industry: Scottish Gate-Money Football, 1890–1914', *Economic History Review*, 35 (1982), p. 566; William McGregor, 'Birmingham (late Small Heath) Football Club' in Leatherdale (ed.), *Book of Football*, p. 120; Vamplew, *Pay Up*, pp. 85–6.

26 Andrew Crowhurst, 'The "Portly Grabbers of 75 per cent": Capital Investment in the British Entertainment Industry, 1885–1914', *Leisure Studies*, 20 (2001), pp. 107–23.

27 Charles Korr, 'West Ham United Football Club and the Beginnings of Professional Football in East London, 1895–1914', *Journal of Contemporary History*, 13 (1978), pp. 229–30; Taylor, *The Leaguers*, pp. 98–101; Tischler, *Footballers and Businessmen*, p. 89; Alfred Gibson and William Pickford, *Association Football and the Men Who Made It*, Vol 2, (London: Caxton, 1906), p. 200.

28 Geoffrey Green, *The History of the Football Association* (London: Naldrett, 1953), p. 419.

29 John Hargreaves, *Sport, Power and Culture: A Social and Historical Analysis of Popular Sports in Britain* (Cambridge: Polity, 1986), p. 69; Jeffrey Hill, *Sport, Leisure and Culture in Twentieth-Century Britain* (Basingstoke: Palgrave, 2002), p. 28; Mason, *Association Football*, p. 77; Vamplew, *Pay Up*, pp. 254–6.

30 Vamplew, *Pay Up*, p. 240; Matthew Taylor, 'Labour Relations and Managerial Control in English Professional Football, 1890–1939', *Sport History Review*, 31, 2 (November 2000), pp. 86–90; Crampsey, *First 100 Years*, p. 25.

31 Mason, *Association Football*, pp. 106–7.

32 Korr, 'West Ham United', pp. 229–30; Taylor, *The Leaguers*, pp. 129–30, 147–8.

33 Wray Vamplew, 'Playing for Pay: The Earnings of Professional Sportsmen in England, 1870–1914' in R. Cashman and M. McKernan, *Sport: Money, Morality and the Media* (Brisbane: New South Wales University Press, 1981), pp. 118–24; Matthew Taylor, 'Beyond the Maximum Wage: The Earnings of Football Professionals in England, 1900–1939', *Soccer and Society*, 2, 3 (Autumn 2001), pp. 102–3, 110–11; Bob Crampsey, *The Scottish Footballer* (Edinburgh: William Blackwood, 1978), p. 26; Vamplew, *Pay Up*, 224; Garnham, 'Professionals and Professionalism', p. 83; P. J. Waller, *Town, City and Nation: England, 1850–1914* (Oxford: Clarendon, 1983), p. 104.

34 William Bassett, 'Big Transfers and the Transfer System' in Leatherdale (ed.) *Book of Football*, p. 160.

35 Alan Metcalfe, 'Football in the Mining Communities of East Northumberland, 1882–1914', *International Journal of the History of Sport*, 5, 3 (December 1988), p. 277.

36 Johnes, *Soccer and Society*, p. 81; Nicholas Fishwick, *English Football and Society, 1910–1950* (Manchester: Manchester University Press, 1989), p. 1.

37 Green, *History of the Football Association*, pp. 251, 261; Vamplew, *Pay Up*, p. 52; W. Hamish Fraser, 'Developments in Leisure' in W. Hamish Fraser and R. J. Morris (eds), *People and Society in Scotland*, Vol. 2: *1830–1914* (Edinburgh: John Donald, 1990), p. 253; Neil Tranter, 'The Chronology of Organized Sport in Nineteenth-Century Scotland: A Regional Study, I – Patterns', *International Journal of the History of Sport*, 7, 2 (September 1990), pp. 194, 198.

38 Jack Williams, 'Churches, Sport and Identities in the North, 1900–1939', in J. Hill and J. Williams (eds), *Sport and Identity in the North of England* (Keele: Keele University Press, 1996), p. 119, 115 (Table 1).

39 Russell, 'Sporadic and Curious', p. 197.

40 Mike Huggins, 'The Spread of Association Football in North-East England, 1876–90: The Pattern of Diffusion', *International Journal of the History of Sport*, 6, 3 (December 1989), pp. 304–5; Robert Poole, *Popular Leisure and the Music Hall in Nineteenth-Century Bolton* (University of Lancaster: Centre for North-West Regional Studies, Occasional Paper No. 12, 1982), p. 36.

41 Metcalfe, 'Football in the Mining Communities', pp. 270–1, 274; Huggins, 'Spread of Association Football', p. 311; Tranter, 'Chronology of Organized Sport', p. 200; Garnham, *Association Football*, pp. 43–4; Williams, 'Churches, Sport and Identities', p. 120.

42 Fishwick, *English Football*, p. 12; Williams, 'Churches, Sport and Identities'; Johnes, *Soccer and Society*, p. 102. H. E. Meller's fixture list from Bristol in 1901 shows old boys' teams, firms' teams, church, chapel and YMCA sides and trade union teams alongside those representing districts of the city. H.E. Meller, *Leisure and the Changing City, 1870–1914* (London: Routledge & Kegan Paul, 1976), pp. 232–3. Recent research by Roger Munting, however, suggests that the role of companies in providing sporting opportunities for their employees before 1914 has been underestimated and that football (and other sports) played a key part in the early development of welfare capitalism. See Roger Munting, 'The Games Ethic and Industrial Capitalism before 1914: The Provision of Company Sports', *Sport in History*, 23, 1 (Summer 2003), pp. 45–63.

43 Metcalfe, 'Football in the Mining Communities', pp. 277–8, 275.

44 Mason, *Association Football*, pp. 87–8; Garnham, *Association Football*, p. 12. See also Meller, *Leisure and the Changing City*, p. 233.

45 Walvin, *People's Game*, p. 62.

46 J. A. Mangan and Colm Hickey, 'English Elementary Education Revisited and Revised: Drill and Athleticism in Tandem' in J. A. Mangan (ed.), *Sport in Europe: Politics, Class, Gender* (London: Frank Cass, 1999), pp. 63–9;

Mason, *Association Football*, pp. 85–6; Colm Kerrigan, '"Thoroughly Good Football": Teachers and the Origins of Elementary School Football', *History of Education*, 29, 1 (2000), pp. 523, 533.

47 Mason, *Association Football*, p. 84; Mangan and Hickey, 'English Elementary Education', pp. 87–8, 75–9. On the development of schools football in London, see Kerrigan, 'Thoroughly Good Football', pp. 525–32.

48 Walvin, *People's Game*, p. 62.

49 Stephen Humphries, *Hooligans or Rebels?: An Oral History of Working-Class Childhood and Youth, 1889–1939* (Oxford: Basil Blackwell, 1981), p. 42; Mangan and Hickey, 'English Elementary Education', p. 83.

50 Mason, *Association Game*, pp. 84–5; H. J. W. Offord, 'Schoolboy Football' in Leatherdale (ed.), *Book of Football*, pp. 151–2; Kerrigan, 'Thoroughly Good Football', pp. 530–3; Colm Kerrigan, *A History of the English Schools' Football Association, 1904–2004* (Trowbridge: English Schools' Football Association, 2004), pp. 10–14, 16–21.

51 Johnes, *Soccer and Society*, pp. 86–7; Offord, 'Schoolboy Football', p. 152; Colm Kerrigan, 'London Schoolboys and Professional Football', *International Journal of the History of Sport*, 11, 2 (August 1994), pp. 287–97.

52 See Edward Grayson, *Corinthians and Cricketers* (London: Sportsmans Book Club, 1957), pp. 26–9, 132–4, 137–40.

53 Derek Birley, *Land of Sport and Glory: Sport and British Society, 1887–1910* (Manchester: Manchester University Press, 1995), pp. 36, 238; Mason, *Association Football*, p. 216; Grayson, *Corinthians*, pp. 100–1.

54 Green, *History of the Football Association*, pp. 203–28; John Lowerson, *Sport and the English Middle Classes, 1870–1914* (Manchester: Manchester University Press, 1993), pp. 185–6.

55 Lowerson, *Sport and the English Middle Classes*, pp. 181, 186; Birley, *Land of Sport and Glory*, p. 239.

56 Russell, *Football and the English*, p. 41; Walvin, *People's Game*, pp. 91–2.

57 Fishwick, *English Football*, pp. xi–xii.

58 Tony Collins, 'The End of the "Creeping Barrage": The Introduction of Rugby League's Limited Tackle Rule', paper presented to the British Society of Sports History Annual Conference, University of Southampton, April 2003.

59 Mason, *Association Football*, p. 207; Green, *History of the Football Association*, pp. 94, 74–8; Adrian Harvey, '"An Epoch in the Annals of National Sport": Football in Sheffield and the Creation of Modern Soccer

and Rugby', *International Journal of the History of Sport*, 18, 4 (December 2001), pp. 70–2.

60   Green, *History of the Football Association*, pp. 558–65, 577–83; Tony Mason, 'Football' in T. Mason (ed.), *Sport in Britain: A Social History* (Cambridge: Cambridge University Press, 1989), pp. 154–5.

61   Green, *History of the Football Association*, p. 58.

62   Mason, *Association Football*, p. 213; Russell, *Football and the English*, pp. 20–1; Young, *History of British Football*, pp. 160–1; Walvin, *People's Game*, p. 76; Green, *History of the Football Association*, p. 60.

63   Tony Mason, 'Kick and Rush or Revolt into Style?: Football Playing Among the English Professionals from Great Power to Image of Decline', paper presented to the Jeu et société conference, INSEP Paris, May 1998: published in France as 'Grandeur et déclin du Kick and Rush Anglais ou la revolt d'un style' in H. Hélal and P. Mignon (eds), *Football: Jeu et société* (Paris: INSEP, 1999), pp. 47–64; W. I. Bassett, 'The Making of a Player: Part 1 – The Forward Game' in Leatherdale (ed.), *Book of Football*, p. 20.

64   Smith, 'Origin and Benefits of the League', p. 177.

65   Green, *History of the Football Association*, pp. 582, 580.

66   Richard Giulianotti, *Football: A Sociology of the Global Game* (Cambridge: Polity, 1999), p. 128.

67   Christian Bromberger with Alain Hayot and Jean-Marc Mariottini, '"Allez l'O.M., Forza Juve": The Passion for Football in Marseille and Turin', in S. Redhead, *The Passion and the Fashion: Football Fandom in the New Europe* (Aldershot: Avebury, 1993), p. 119; Giulianotti, *Football*, pp. 128–9.

68   Young, *History of British Football*, p. 159; Giulianotti, *Football*, p. 129.

69   Walvin, *People's Game*, p. 77.

70   Walvin, *People's Game*. Some critics have suggested that the title ought to have included a question mark. For example, Tony Mason, 'Football and the Historians', *International Journal of the History of Sport*, 5, (1988), p. 138 and 'Sport and Recreation' in P. Johnson (ed.), *Twentieth-Century Britain: Economic, Social and Cultural Change* (London: Longman, 1994), pp. 122–3.

71   Patrick Joyce, *Visions of the People: Industrial England and the Question of Class, 1848–1914* (Cambridge: Cambridge University Press, 1991).

72   See, for example, Tony Mason, 'Football and the Workers in England, 1880–1914' in Cashman and McKernan (eds), *Sport*, pp. 248–71; Dave Russell, 'Associating with Football: Social Identity in England, 1863–1998'

in G. Armstrong and R. Giulianotti (eds), *Football Cultures and Identities* (Basingstoke: Macmillan, 1999), p. 16.

73 Lewis, 'Genesis of Professional Football', pp. 33–4; Mason, *Association Football*, pp. 90–1.

74 Garnham, *Association Football*, pp. 95–7; Crampsey, *Scottish Footballer*, p. 25.

75 Mason, *Association Football*, pp. 153, 154–6; Garnham, *Association Football*, pp. 110–11.

76 Neil Tranter, 'The Cappielow Riot and the Composition and Behaviour of Soccer Crowds in Late Victorian Scotland', *International Journal of the History of Sport*, 12, 3 (December 1995), p. 127; John Hutchinson, 'Some Aspects of Football Crowds before 1914', Paper presented to the Society for the Study of Labour History, University of Sussex, 1975.

77 Tranter, 'The Cappielow Riot', pp. 127–8; Garnham, *Association Football*, pp. 114–16.

78 Green, *History of the Football Association*, pp. 194–5; Inglis, *League Football*, passim; Taylor, *The Leaguers*, pp. 52–62.

79 Vamplew, *Pay Up*, pp. 155–70; Mason, *Association Football*, pp. 37–43; Tischler, *Footballers and Businessmen*, pp. 72–6; Pamela Dixon, Neal Garnham and Andrew Jackson, 'Shareholders and Shareholding: The Case of the Football Company in Late Victorian England', *Business History*, 46, 4 (October 2004), pp. 503–24; Neal Garnham and Andrew Jackson, 'Who Invested in Victorian Football Clubs?: The Case of Newcastle-upon-Tyne', *Soccer and Society*, 4, 1 (Spring 2003), pp. 57–70.

80 Mason, *Association Football*, pp. 34–5, 37–9.

81 Tischler, *Footballers and Businessmen*, pp. 137, 136, 134. On social control, see F. M. L. Thompson, 'Social Control in Victorian Britain', *Economic History Review*, 34 (1981), pp. 189–208; Waller, *Town, City and Nation*, p. 103; Roy Hay, 'Soccer and Social Control in Scotland, 1873–1978', in Cashman and McKernan (eds), *Sport*, pp. 223–47.

82 Mason, 'Sport and Recreation', p. 123.

83 Holt, *Sport and the British*, p. 364; Mason, 'Sport and Recreation', p. 123; Eric Hobsbawm, 'Mass-Producing Traditions: Europe, 1870–1914' in E. Hobsbawm and T. Ranger, *The Invention of Tradition* (Cambridge: Cambridge University Press, 1983), p. 290; Gareth Stedman Jones, *Languages of Class: Studies of English Working-Class History, 1832–1982* (Cambridge: Cambridge University Press, 1983), p. 87.

84 Hargreaves, *Sport, Power and Culture*, p. 67; Stephen Jones, *Sport, Politics and the Working Class: Organised Labour and Sport in Interwar Britain*

(Manchester: Manchester University Press, 1988), p. 25; Walvin, *People's Game*, p. 77. See also Christopher J. Nottingham, 'More Important Than Life or Death: Football, the British Working Class and the Social Order' in L. H. van Voss and F. van Holthoon (eds), *Working Class and Popular Culture* (Amsterdam: Stichting Beheer IISG, 1988), pp. 150–1.

85 Robert W. Lewis, '"Touched Pitch and Been Shockingly Defiled": Football, Class, Social Darwinism and Decadence in England, 1880–1914' in Mangan (ed.), *Sport in Europe*, pp. 117–43; quotation p. 135; Mason, *Association Football*, p. 231; Charles Edwardes, 'The New Football Mania', *Nineteenth Century* (1892), reprinted in Ian Hamilton (ed.), *The Faber Book of Soccer* (London: Faber & Faber, 1992), pp. 6–11. See also Johnes and Garland, 'New Craze', pp. 295–6.

86 Russell, *Football and the English*, pp. 18–19.

87 Russell, *Football and the English*, p. 71.

88 Eric Hobsbawm, *Worlds of Labour: Further Studies in the History of Labour* (London: Weidenfeld & Nicolson, 1984), chapters 10 and 11. For the alternative notion that popular leisure provided a 'culture of consolation' that engendered conservatism rather than radicalism within the working class, see Gareth Stedman Jones, 'Working-Class Culture and Working-Class Politics in London, 1870–1900', *Journal of Social History*, 7 (1975), reprinted in his *Languages of Class*, pp. 179–238.

89 Andrew Davies, *Leisure, Gender and Poverty: Working Class Culture in Salford and Manchester, 1900–1939* (Buckingham: Open University Press, 1992); Andrew Davies and Steven Fielding (eds), *Workers' Worlds: Cultures and Communities in Manchester and Salford, 1880–1939* (Manchester: Manchester University Press, 1992). See also Steven Fielding, *Class and Ethnicity: Irish Catholics in England, 1880–1939* (Buckingham: Open University Press, 1993); T. Griffiths, *The Lancashire Working Classes, c.1880–1930* (Oxford: Clarendon, 2001).

90 Neville Kirk, '"Traditional" Working-Class Culture and "the Rise of Labour": Some Preliminary Questions and Observations', *Social History*, 16, 2 (May 1991), pp. 203–16; *Change, Continuity and Class: Labour in British Society, 1850–1920* (Manchester: Manchester University Press, 1998), chapter 9. See also Mike Savage and Andrew Miles, *The Remaking of the British Working Class, 1840–1940* (London: Routledge, 1994)

91 Jon Stobart, 'Building an Urban Identity: Cultural Space and Civic Boosterism in a "New" Industrial Town. Burslem, 1761–1911', *Social History*, 29, 4 (November 2004), pp. 485–98; Kate Hill, '"Thoroughly Imbued with the Spirit of Ancient Greece": Symbolism and Space in Victorian Civic Culture' in A. Kidd and D. Nicholls (eds), *Gender, Civic Culture and Consumerism: Middle Class Identity in Britain, 1800–1940*

(Manchester: Manchester University Press, 1999), pp. 99–111; Andy Croll, *Civilizing the Urban: Popular Culture and Public Space in Merthyr, c. 1870–1914* (Cardiff: University of Wales Press, 2000); Helen Meller, *European Cities 1890s–1930s: History, Culture and the Built Environment* (Chichester: John Wiley, 2001).

92 Holt, *Sport and the British*, p. 172.

93 Jack Williams, '"One Could Literally Have Walked on the Heads of the People Congregated There": Sport, the Town and Identity', in K. Laybourn (eds), *Social Conditions, Status and Community, 1860–c.1920* (Stroud: Sutton, 1997), pp. 123–38.

94 Russell, *Football and the English*, pp. 66–7; Richard Holt, 'Football and the Urban Way of Life in Nineteenth-Century Britain', in J. A. Mangan (ed.), *Pleasure, Profit and Proselytism: British Culture and Sport at Home and Abroad, 1700–1914* (London: Frank Cass, 1988), p. 80.

95 Brad Beaven, *Leisure, Citizenship and Working-Class Men in Britain, 1850–1945* (Manchester: Manchester University Press, 2005), p. 79.

96 Beaven, *Leisure*, pp. 72–80; quotation p. 77.

97 Croll, *Civilizing the Urban*, pp. 136–75.

98 Joanna Bourke, *Working-Class Cultures in Britain, 1890–1960: Gender, Class and Ethnicity* (London: Routledge, 1994), pp. 138–9; Williams, 'Sport, the Town and Identity', p. 129; Robert Gray, *The Labour Aristocracy in Victorian Edinburgh* (Oxford: Clarendon, 1976), p. 117.

99 Metcalfe, 'Football in the Mining Communities', pp. 285–7, 290.

100 Ross McKibbin, *Classes and Cultures: England, 1918–1951* (Oxford: Oxford University Press, 1998), p. 340.

101 Jeff Hill, 'Rite of Spring: Cup Finals and Community in the North of England' in Hill and Williams (eds), *Sport and Identity*, p. 107; Russell, *Football and the English*, p. 64.

102 Dixon, Garnham and Jackson, 'Shareholders and Shareholding', p. 520.

103 Crampsey, *Scottish Footballer*, p. 19; Mason, *Association Football*, pp. 152–3; Rogan Taylor, *Football and Its Fans: Supporters and their Relations with the Game, 1885–1985* (Leicester: Leicester University Press, 1992), p. 7.

104 Jessica Macbeth, 'The Development of Women's Football in Scotland', *The Sports Historian*, 22, 2 (November 2002), pp. 151–2; Jean Williams, *A Game for Rough Girls?: A History of Women's Football in Britain* (London: Routledge, 2003), pp. 26–7.

105 Murray, *Old Firm*, pp. 46–69; W. W. Knox, *Industrial Nation: Work,*

Culture and Society in Scotland, 1800–Present (Edinburgh: Edinburgh University Press, 1999), p. 141.

106   Garnham, *Association Football*, pp. 125–7; John Sugden and Alan Bairner, *Sport, Sectarianism and Society in a Divided Ireland* (Leicester: Leicester University Press, 1993), pp. 81–2; Tranter, 'Cappielow Riot', p. 133; Murray, *Old Firm*, pp. 138–9; H. F. Moorhouse, 'Football Hooliganism: Old Bottle, New Whines?', *Sociological Review*, 39 (1991).

107   Mason, *Association Football*, p. 222; Russell, *Football and the English*, p. 72.

108   Hugh Cunningham, 'Leisure' in J. Benson (ed.), *Working Class in England, 1875–1914* (London: Croom Helm, 1984), p. 143; Hay, 'Soccer and Social Control', p. 233.

109   Keith Robbins, *Nineteenth-Century Britain: Integration and Diversity* (Oxford: Clarendon, 1988), pp. 162–8; Young, *History of British Football*, p. 155; Garnham, *Association Football*, p. 32.

110   Christopher Harvie, *Scotland and Nationalism: Scottish Society and Politics, 1707–1994* (London: Routledge, 1994 [1st edition, 1977]), p. 19. See also Grant Jarvie and Irene Reid, 'Sport, Nationalism and Culture in Scotland', *The Sports Historian*, 19, 1 (May 1999), pp. 97–124.

111   Cronin, *Sport and Nationalism*, p. 56; Eric Hobsbawm, *Nations and Nationalism Since 1870: Programme, Myth, Reality* (Cambridge: Cambridge University Press, 1990), p. 143.

112   H. F. Moorhouse, 'Scotland, Football and Identities: The National Team and Club Sides', in S. Gehrmann (ed.), *Football and Regional Identity in Europe* (Münster: Lit Verlag, 1997), p. 181; Martin Johnes, 'Eighty Minute Patriots?: National Identity and Sport in Modern Wales', *International Journal of the History of Sport*, 17, 4 (December 2000), p. 93.

113   Michael Lynch, *Scotland: A New History* (London: Pimlico, 1992), pp. 360–1.

114   Fraser, 'Developments in Leisure', p. 255; Vamplew, *Pay Up*, pp. 64, 324 (n. 61); P. Bilsborough, 'The Development of Sport in Glasgow, 1850–1914', unpublished M.Litt. thesis, University of Stirling, 1983, p. 230 (Table 7.3); R. M. Connell, 'The Association Game in Scotland' in Leatherdale (ed.), *Book of Football*, p. 45.

115   Alan Bairner, 'Football' in G. Jarvie and J. Burnett (eds), *Sport, Scotland and the Scots* (East Linton: Tuckwell, 2000), p. 88.

116   Hunter, *Triumphs of the Football Field*, pp. 22–3.

117   Holt, *Sport and the British*, pp. 256–8.

118   Johnes, *Soccer and Society*, pp. 184–7; *A History of Sport in Wales*

(Cardiff: University of Wales Press, 2005), pp. 34–5; Kenneth O. Morgan, *Rebirth of a Nation: Wales 1880–1980* (Oxford: Clarendon, 1980), p. 133.

119 Cronin, *Sport and Nationalism*, p. 121.

120 Garnham, *Association Football*, pp. 32–8.

121 Neal Garnham, 'Football and National Identity in Pre-Great War Ireland', *Irish Economic and Social History*, 28 (2001), pp. 13–31; quotation p. 31.

122 Russell, 'Associating with Football', p. 21; Holt, *Sport and the British*, p. 273.

123 Peter Beck, *Scoring for Britain: International Football and International Politics, 1900–1939* (London: Frank Cass, 1999), pp. 52–5; Dave Russell, *Looking North: Northern England and the National Imagination* (Manchester: Manchester University Press, 2004), pp. 7–8, 267; 'Associating with Football', p. 21; Peter Beck, 'Leisure and Sport in Britain, 1900–1939' in C. Wrigley (ed.), *A Companion to Early Twentieth-Century Britain* (London: Blackwell, 2003), pp. 462–3; Krishan Kumar, *The Making of English Identity* (Cambridge: Cambridge University Press, 2003), pp. 209–12; quotation p. 211.

CHAPTER 3

Football between the wars, 1914–39

Until the late 1980s, historians of sport in general, and football in particular, had tended to overlook the inter-war years. Much of the initial work had focused on the origins and embryonic growth of sport in the Victorian and Edwardian period – the 'making' of games in their recognisably 'modern' forms – and seemed to find a natural ending with the outbreak of war. Underlying this has been an assumption, particularly in football, of continuity between the pre- and post-1914 periods. The way in which the game was played, watched, understood and identified with seemed to be much the same in 1935 as it had been in 1905. Yet the work of Nicholas Fishwick, Stephen Jones and Dave Russell has emphasised the changes that took place in the game and its social role, changes which in Russell's opinion 'almost seem to lead into a new era'.[1] Martin Johnes's study of south Wales, meanwhile, provides an important reminder of the uneven development of football. Here, as in many parts of Britain outside what Fishwick loosely refers to as the 'traditional areas', it was not before but *after* 1914 that football matured into a game with a genuinely mass following and popular profile.[2]

The socio-economic and political context is of course crucial in all this. The British economy underwent considerable fluctuations, from a short post-war boom to a severe slump between 1920 and 1922. Thereafter the 1920s witnessed a mild recovery which ended with the worldwide depression from 1929, reaching its British nadir in 1932, before a revival from the mid-1930s. The resultant unemployment and social distress, which still dominate the collective memory of the period, was also structured according to region, industrial sector and occupation. While the staple industries of coal, shipbuilding, iron and steel and textiles, located mainly in Scotland, Wales, Lancashire and the north-east of England, suffered contraction, there was a growth in the newer motor manufacturing, electrical engineering and chemical industries based around the midlands and the south. If Britain between the wars was thus a complicated, diverse and heterogeneous nation, this was reflected in its football. As in the previous chapter, we need to set aside simplistic notions of 'progress' or 'development' and recognise the contrasts, contradictions and irregularities that patterned the game at all levels.

We return here to a number of themes introduced in the previous chapters but also explore some new ones. Consideration is given first of all to the position of the game during the First World War before we examine the advance of football at the grassroots, amateur and professional levels, its relationship with various parts of the media and with the emerging international game. A number of key issues are considered in the course of the discussion. Should we regard elite players as budding media heroes or as soccer slaves? Were those who visited matches and read about the game consumers, supporters or hooligans? What was the British attitude to international football and what role did international competition play in the construction and expression of national and British identities? Running throughout the chapter is an insistence on the diversity of experience, which should guard against assuming that the period was marked by an irresistible popularity and boom in the game.

The First World War

Rather than a parenthesis in the history of football, the First World War actually had fundamental repercussions for public, especially middle-class and elite, perceptions of the sport. Indeed football's so-called 'crisis season' of 1914–15 was arguably one of its most damaging. With little guidance from the government, the controlling bodies of British sport were left to decide how to react to the outbreak of war and were judged by public and press accordingly. The different paths taken by the amateur and professional arms of sport were dictated to a considerable degree by contrasting responsibilities. All expected a short war. The hockey, golf, rugby union and lawn tennis associations stopped their competitions immediately and dedicated their resources and manpower to the war effort. By contrast, sports like football, horse racing, rugby league and cricket employed professional staff and were run along business lines and as such had little choice but to carry on until the war ended.[3] The decision to continue playing may have received the support of the War Office but was attacked as unpatriotic and counterproductive to the war effort by influential sections of the press. As the voice of the political and cultural establishment, *The Times* led the assault. In its letter pages of 7 November 1914, the historian and former Oxford rower A. F. Pollard wrote that

there is no excuse for diverting from the front thousands of athletes in order to feast the eyes of crowds of inactive spectators, who are either unfit to fight or unfit to be fought for ... Every club that employs a professional football player is bribing a needed recruit to refrain from enlistment, and every spectator who pays his gate money is contributing so much towards a German victory.

The recruitment record of football was compared unfavourably with that of cricket, rugby union and rowing, despite attempts to encourage enlistment by having public figures address match-day crowds. Incensed by such criticism, football's defenders launched a vigorous counter-attack. The Manchester-based *Athletic News* proclaimed the criticism as 'nothing less than an attempt by the classes to stop the recreation on one day a week of the masses'. The FA claimed in November 1914 to have contributed some 100,000 recruits, including 2,000 professionals, to the forces, a higher figure than any other sport. A Footballers' Battalion was formed in December at a meeting attended by 4–5,000 but by March the colonel in charge claimed that, in what amounted to a 'public scandal', just 122 of 1,800 professionals had come forward. Ian Nannestad has gone so far as to see the Battalion as 'little more than a publicity exercise' designed to appease public sentiment and provide propaganda for the War Office.[4]

Some accounts have downplayed the broader impact of this anti-football agitation. Colin Veitch saw it largely as the attack of a 'vocal minority' of amateurs on the professional and working-class ethos of sport, while Derek Birley explained it as 'pre-war snobbery decked in patriotic uniform'. Others have detected limited hostility to football beyond the pages of patriotic sections of the press. Nevertheless, the anti-football campaign clearly had some effect. Not all newspapers and politicians were critical of the game, especially outside London, but Birley is probably right in his view that the football authorities were 'losing the argument hands down'.[5] The Scottish FA certainly thought so. In its opinion there was 'a large body of public opinion against the continuance of the game' and this criticism 'was not confined to the non-football public'. It agitated determinedly within official football circles for the suspension of cup competitions and international fixtures, fearing that 'any contrary decision will imprint a stigma upon the greatest of all sports from which it may never recover'.[6] Yet its English counterpart, in particular, remained convinced until late in the season that by providing a full programme of organised sport it was ensuring normality, soothing disquiet, facilitating enlistment and thus helping rather than hindering the war effort. Against accusations of simple money-making, the Football League likewise answered that its games were 'of national service in counteracting any tendency to panic and monomania'.[7] As Fishwick points out, it took the more practical considerations of falling attendances and meagre gate receipts to convince them otherwise. The FA estimated that by November 1914 average attendances in England had halved. War work and declining incomes also led to declining gates among Belfast clubs. To cut costs, players' wages were reduced by between 15 and 5 per cent in England and 25 per cent in Ireland, with a maximum wage set for the first time in Scotland. But to no avail. In the end, the decision to suspend the regular football schedule from the beginning of the 1915–16 season rested on economic reasoning rather than patriotic pressure.[8]

Top-level football survived the war by modifying its rules and truncating its competitions. In England there was to be no League championship, no FA Cup and no international fixtures, and trophies and medals were not awarded. Neither was the payment of players allowed, although football employees were free to guest for other clubs 'as a matter of convenience of work and residence'.[9] For the 1915–16 season 30 Football League clubs competed in regional competitions based around northern and midland sections, while the leading metropolitan clubs joined together to form the London Combination. Newcastle United, Middlesbrough and Sunderland, relatively isolated in the north-east and with a majority of players engaged in war work, chose not to compete, as did clubs like Aston Villa, West Bromwich Albion and Blackburn Rovers, which considered the organisation of competitive football both financially impractical and immoral. Nevertheless, these skeletal competitions continued throughout the war, partly as a result of the imposition of income-sharing arrangements whereby the richer and better-supported clubs helped out the weak. Less successful was the regional league set up in south Wales and south-west England, which faced poor attendances and travel restrictions and folded within a season.[10]

The Scottish League, meanwhile, abandoned its second division, but the top division continued to function throughout the war years. Sacrifices, however, had to be made. Wages were reduced in 1915 to £1 per week, and in 1917 Aberdeen, Dundee and Raith Rovers (from Kirkcaldy) were persuaded to retire so as to reduce travel expenses for the majority of clubs based in the central belt between Glasgow and Edinburgh. The Irish Cup continued but the senior clubs adopted a regional league structure based around a Belfast and District Football League and a Leinster Football League, which absorbed the two Dublin-based Irish League sides Bohemians and Shelbourne. This north–south split was to have profound consequences in the immediate post-war years. By 1915, the basic partition that was to define Irish football for the rest of the century had been effected.[11]

Russell is right to conclude that football ultimately survived its wartime test but this is not to say it was left unscathed. First, a large number of public schools and grammar schools adopted rugby union in preference to soccer during and after the war. This 1920s 'rush to rugby' seems to have been a positive response to rugby's patriotic war record and its overt association with militarism as much as a rejection of soccer as unpatriotic. One headmaster praised rugby as 'unequalled by any other game as a school of true manhood and leadership' and bemoaned the fact 'that there should still be some great schools that follow the less inspiring and less severe discipline of Association'.[12] Second, the professional game suffered a series of scandals which provided valuable ammunition for those middle-class critics who regarded it as essentially corrupt and guided by money. The most significant of these arose from the Good Friday match between Manchester United and Liverpool in 1915, which finished 2–0 to United but was later revealed as 'a complete fraud'. It turned out that four Liverpool players, three from United and one from Chester, had arranged a substantial bet on a 2–0 outcome and did everything in their power to ensure that result: this included kicking the ball into the stands, deliberately missing a penalty and chastising one player not in on the plan who had tried to score a late goal. All those involved were suspended *sine die* from football. Leeds City, meanwhile, became the first club to be expelled from the Football League in 1919 after it came to light that the club had paid its players throughout the war in contravention of the FA ban. The rather harsh treatment of the club by the game's authorities, exacerbated by the refusal of Leeds directors to hand over key documents to the investigating commission, has been explained by A. J. Arnold as an attempt to rehabilitate football's public profile. It was, in his view, a 'dramatic gesture by men who knew they had badly misjudged the political symbolism of professional soccer in the early years of the Great War'.[13]

If the image of football was tarnished to some extent on the home front, its reputation was, by contrast, consolidated and bolstered in the services. J. G. Fuller's research has demonstrated the crucial role of football and other sports in providing recreation and entertainment for, and upholding the morale of, the British forces behind the front lines. Such was its popularity in the working-class communities from which the majority of troops in the regular and civilian army came that football naturally accompanied the forces 'to every fighting front'. Matches were initially informal and spontaneous and were often greeted with disapproval by senior commanders such as Douglas Haig, who bemoaned the tendency of men to 'run around and play football' when they ought to have been resting.[14] Yet both Fuller and James Roberts have shown how as the war progressed officers came to accept and, in time, encourage the organisation of football for both participants and spectators. Matches became increasingly competitive and drew significant crowds: attendances of 1,500–2,500 were not uncommon by 1917 for games between battalion representative sides, while 3,000 watched the first final of the inter-divisional Fanshawe Cup in 1916. Such activity undoubtedly built to some extent upon an established system and culture of regimental army football. Yet Roberts is right to distinguish the proletarian values and motives enshrined in wartime football from the largely amateur and public school values prevalent in pre-war army sport. Along with other working-class pastimes such as concert parties and fairs, playing and watching football was thus important in the wartime 'proletarianisation' of military culture. In helping to relieve boredom, providing a sense of cultural normality and escape from the horrors of the front line and reinforcing the necessary *esprit de corps* and group loyalty among new recruits, it also played a key role in sustaining the morale of British troops.[15]

Football at the grassroots

Street, park and schoolboy football

For most forms of recreational football, the inter-war years as a whole were a period of growth. Its simplest form was the informal, sometimes impromptu and always unaffiliated street or park game. Various types of evidence – from oral testimony and players' autobiographies to police records – point to the ubiquity of children and even adults playing in the street. Often this led to conflict with the authorities, ranging from a ticking off from the bobby on the beat to convictions and fines imposed by the local magistrate. In 1922, 216 of the 447 under-16-year-olds charged by the Cardiff Police were arrested for football playing. Such arrests were not confined to boys: 238 Cardiff men were similarly charged in 1934, while two girls were among the seven youngsters summoned for playing street football in Highgate in 1922.[16] The street football match, with makeshift equipment and hastily arranged sides, has become the stuff of legend, representing a type of stereotypical shorthand for 'traditional' ways of playing. The Labour MP George Thomas's recollection of childhood games in the Rhondda valley – 'coats down on the ground in the street to mark out goal posts with one boy on the lookout for Bobby Jones [the policeman]' – is fairly typical, as is the future England international Raich Carter's description of rudimentary streets games in 1920s Sunderland 'where the lamp-posts served according to season as wickets or goalposts, and the ball was often homemade with rags and newspapers'. Some young men played football informally almost every day: in such cases, the streets of working-class towns doubled up as 'impromptu football pitches'.[17]

Yet Ross McKibbin is probably correct to surmise that street football in this period gradually gave way to matches on waste ground or public parks. In Bristol, gangs of youths walked or travelled by tram to play games in nearby parks. According to oral interviews conducted by Andrew Davies, games on scraps of waste ground between pub teams were common in Salford between the wars. There may have been no referee, no proper pitch and no playing kit, but with bets waged on the outcome and spectators shouting on the teams, these were nonetheless serious contests for those involved, capable of arousing 'passions as strong as any professional encounter'.[18] Such informal varieties of football possibly complemented the more formalised schoolboy and junior games more than has been recognised. Players and indeed spectators did not have to step from one to the other: if they had the time and perhaps the money they could enjoy both. The fact that many of these street and park games took place on a Sunday, when all organised competition was normally prohibited, suggests that different levels and experiences of the game could co-exist for the ardent footballer.

Notwithstanding the move to rugby in many public schools, the rise of organised school and youth soccer between the wars was significant. By 1928 the English Schools Football Association (ESFA) incorporated 6,000 schools in England and Wales, a figure that had increased by 1939 to 7,000 schools and an estimated one million schoolboy players. In 1930–1, 310 schools football associations were attached to the ESFA. A Lancashire county body was established in 1920, consisting of 50 affiliated associations and over 1,000 schools. Some 160 school teams in Sheffield were competing for the district cup during the 1930s. Despite stiff competition from rugby at secondary school level, around 300 schools in 27 affiliated leagues were active in Wales during the early 1920s. School football developed its own hierarchical structure with representative and international matches mirroring the elite professional game. Stimulated by local patriotism, large crowds continued to be common, especially in the latter stages of national competitions. Fifteen thousand spectators watched the Brighton boys play North Staffordshire for the English schools shield at the Goldstone Ground in 1928, while 20,000 packed the Vetch Field in Swansea to witness the local side triumph in the 1939 final. Some supporters actually preferred the spectacle of the schoolboy game because, unlike its professional version, the players were 'truly representative, born and bred in the county they represent'. The ESFA tried to keep its distance from adult football, particularly the professional game, but senior clubs were coming to recognise the value in scouting at youth level. County, divisional and national schools sides provided particularly rich pickings: 11 of those who appeared in the England–Wales schoolboy match in April

PLATE 5 *A West Ham schoolboy heading the ball during a 1936 match against Romford Boys in the Corinthian Shield competition (© Hulton Archive/Getty).*

1927 went on to play for Football League clubs and seven to represent their respective nation. In 1939 the ESFA complained to the FA of the nuisance caused by scouts from professional and minor football and it was agreed that while in formal education a boy's first loyalty was to play for his school.[19]

Despite such progress, the provision of school football remained patchy and largely dependent upon adequate facilities and the enthusiasm of individual teachers. The Sheffield Physical Training Department was successful in increasing the acreage of school playing fields in the city from 95 in 1928 to 256 (equivalent to 130 football pitches) by 1938, but overwhelmingly poverty, kit shortages and travelling problems meant that still only a third of Sheffield schoolchildren played team sport on a weekly basis. Pay cuts in 1931 apparently curbed the willingness of Oxford teachers to organise sport outside school hours. Girls aside, the most significant gap in provision was for boys between the ages of 14 and 18. Young talent was being lost, it was felt, in that important period between leaving school and entering adult football. In his dual role as a schoolteacher and a director of Swindon Town, A. E. Bullock supported the creation of a local youth competition in 1933: 'At present boys between the ages of 14 and 16 were running wild, and by the time they got back into football they had lost a lot of promise, and consequently none of them were worthy to play for the Town'.[20] Organisations such as the Boy Scouts, Church Lads' and Boys' Brigades or youth clubs often stepped in where school sport ended, intent on providing recreation for moral and behavioural as well as physical purposes. The English FA attempted to coordinate these activities on a national level in 1927 with the creation of its Minor Football Committee, but most of the initiative was left to county associations, which generally lacked the resources to expand the youth game. As a result, youth football seems to have stagnated, if not declined, during the 1930s, especially in the more depressed counties and districts.[21]

Money, time and space: recreational football

Any general statement about the rising popularity of recreational and junior football between the wars needs to be hedged around with explanations and exceptions. Bald figures tell us very little. Frederick Wall, for instance, estimated that 750,000 amateurs played football every Saturday in England in 1937 but Fishwick has suggested that only about 350,000–500,000 actually took to the field on a regular basis. Similarly, the comparison between 12,000 clubs in 1910 and 35,000 in 1937 hides a number of important variations across time and space. Johnes has identified a 'spiralling growth in localized teams' in south Wales and the secretary of the Welsh FA was able to claim in 1933 that 'there is scarcely a town, hamlet or village in Wales that is without a soccer team'. There were substantial increases in the number of clubs affiliated to county associations in the so-called 'non-traditional areas', such as Oxfordshire and Wiltshire, where football's pre-1914 growth had been limited. Yet expansion is less easy to identify in football's heartlands. The Lancashire FA controlled 50 leagues in the 1914-15 season, a figure that had risen to 74 leagues and over 2,000 clubs by 1921-2 but had barely changed by 1927-8.[22] Table 3.1 shows that in at least eight localities in the north of England there was no pattern of continuous growth in recreational football. In five cases, the number of football teams reached its peak in 1922 and in all but two localities there were fewer teams playing in 1939 than in 1914. On the basis of this evidence, it would appear that recreational football was actually in decline in Barnsley, Bolton, Burnley, Oldham and Sunderland over the course of the inter-war period.

These complicated patterns of football activity can be partly explained by changing economic circumstances. Unemployment was a mixed blessing for the recreational footballer, bringing more spare time but little money to spend on non-enforced leisure activities. It certainly does not seem to have led inevitably to falling numbers of clubs and players. In seven of the eight localities in Table 3.1 there were more clubs in 1930 when unemployment was high than in 1939 when it was much lower. In Sheffield, club formation seems to have been inversely related to the state of local trade and industry. The County FA recorded a 1920s peak of 748 affiliated clubs during the 1926 coal strike, a rise explained by the 'abnormal conditions prevailing during the season, many clubs being tem-

TABLE 3.1 *Football teams in selected localities, 1914-39*

Locality	1914	1922	1930	1939
Barnsley	75	143	99	69
Bolton	136	255	192	127
Burnley	133	136	73	51
Halifax	78	30	42	54
Oldham	57	199	78	35
St Helens	50	88	95	80
Sunderland	226	307	189	142
Wigan	41	55	72	54

Source: Adapted from Jack Williams, 'Churches, Sport and Identities in the North, 1900-1939' in J. Hill and J. Williams (eds), *Sport and Identity in the North of England* (Keele: Keele University Press, 1996), pp. 115, 123-4 (Tables 1 and 2).

porarily formed in the mining areas'. Numbers rose during the worst depression years of the early 1930s, reaching a peak of 874 in 1933–4, but fell the following season due partly to 'improvements in trade' and failed to increase much in the relative prosperity of the late 1930s.[23] On the other hand, sustained economic hardship naturally hit some junior clubs hard. A local south Wales newspaper thought it a 'miracle' that those clubs below the top division of the Newport and District League did not fold during the slump of 1922, and in 1928–9 a quarter were unable to finish the season as a result of financial difficulties. Here high levels of unemployment and the migration of men away from the region to find work hampered rather than stimulated recreational football, to the extent that the number of leagues attached to the South Wales association dropped from 21 in 1926 to 12 in 1938. Rising unemployment similarly led to the closure of a number of the Great Western Railway works leagues in Swindon between 1929 and 1931.[24]

Alongside the impact of unemployment, limited access to playing space continued to obstruct the growth of grassroots football. In line with his general thesis of the increased state role in the provision of leisure, Jones has argued that municipal facilities expanded, in the larger cities at least. In Liverpool, the corporation provided 154 football plots in 1921 and 172 by 1930, while the London County Council recorded 420 football pitches in its various parks.[25] Yet elsewhere the playing field shortage was identified as one of the main problems facing local and national authorities in England. Improvements in local economies leading to an increase in house building was a major issue here. One explanation for the decline of clubs in Sheffield during the mid to late 1930s was that 'a large number of grounds have been taken for building and have not been replaced'. House building, it was pointed out in 1939, had also led to the disappearance of 130 football pitches in six West Riding towns and the hiving off of parts of Hackney Marshes in London. Space was at a premium too in the valleys of south Wales, particularly as the mining companies took over flat land previously set aside for sport to use as coal tips. Such developments only exacerbated the existing deficiency of resources in many areas. There were only 6 pitches to share between 30 clubs in Barry in 1923, 11 pitches between 34 teams in Swindon in 1935 and 12 between 120 in the Rhondda in 1936. In Ashton-under-Lyne, a Lancashire textile town with a population of over 60,000, there were no municipal football pitches at all until the 1930s and no more than eight or nine by the end of the decade.[26]

Neither were the facilities provided always adequate. One Wiltshire club's pitch was described as 'Quagmire Park'. Another in south Wales was 'solid in some places and a quagmire in others', and in Cardiff teams were turning out on a pitch which was 'little more than a thin layer of earth over concrete'. It was not uncommon to find other surfaces covered with refuse and glass, while goal nets and changing facilities were often the exception rather than the rule. Despite such conditions, local authorities were reluctant to spend ratepayers' money on public playing fields even when they recognised the benefits in terms of health and social order. A national solution was attempted with the creation in 1925 of the National Playing Fields Association (NPFA). Yet its aim, to increase playing field space through its own funding (backed by the Carnegie Trust) and the promotion of local initiatives, met with only limited success. It led to some improvements in playing field provision, in the Cardiff and Oxford districts for example, but elsewhere the NPFA's work was often hindered by a lack of local financial backing and the apathy of the local authorities. In Ashton, for instance, both the Richmond Street and the King George V playing fields were left unfinished at the end of the 1930s, despite a £4,000 loan from the Ministry of Health and £3,500 in grants from the NPFA and other bodies.[27]

With limited municipal provision, many clubs depended, as they had before 1914, on the patronage of social institutions. Much of this institutional support remained based on the patterns established in the late nineteenth and early twentieth centuries. Yet there were some important changes. A number of local studies have outlined the growth of works football. This has been partly explained by the increasing prominence of industrial welfare schemes, especially in the larger firms that could afford to sustain extensive recreational facilities.[28] The Sheffield Works' Sports Association, founded to shape the behaviour of young workers in the First World War, claimed a membership of 80 companies and 86 teams by 1936. Workshop leagues and tournaments were organised in the 1920s by cotton employers in Blackburn, Bolton and Stockport, while the National Council for the Pottery Industry similarly developed inter-factory competitions for its employees. Company teams were also common in south Wales, although here the trend was away from separate workers' leagues and towards integration in local competition: works teams accounted for just under 14 per cent of those in the Cardiff and District League in 1924–5 but a little over a quarter ten years later.[29] Colliery companies invested indirectly in recreation through semi-autonomous welfare schemes and funds, run jointly by employers and mining unions. In some areas, such as Durham and Yorkshire, this led to substantial sums allocated to the provision of sports clubs and facilities. The welfare club of the

Ashington Coal Company could thus boast 27 football teams in 1924. In the main, employers used such clubs as a means of promoting company loyalty and discipline and thus improving economic efficiency. But success on the football field could also be an important source of publicity for the firm. This was taken to its extreme in Newport and Oxford, where the teams of the confectioners Lovell's and the motor manufacturers Morris outgrew their recreational basis and briefly came to rival the senior city clubs. In the latter case, there were complaints in the local press that this drive for success had led to the marginalisation of football for the ordinary worker.[30]

A number of historians have linked the rise of work-based football to the decline of the church or chapel team. Williams, for instance, observed a correlation in some, but by no means all, of the northern localities he studied (Table 3.2). The chairman of the Bolton Sunday Schools Social League was one who believed that some players were leaving for the better facilities available in the works' welfare leagues. Such problems forced the Merthyr Sunday School League to merge in 1923 with the local welfare league and led to the replacement of the Swindon Sunday School League in 1932 by a secular competition. The general decline in organised religion over the period was undoubtedly a factor here. The insistence of many clubs and leagues that players should be regular church attenders may have convinced some to move on, as it did in the case of the Sheffield Churches League, but it would be a mistake to dismiss the continued significance of religious-based football throughout Britain. Table 3.2 shows that despite a relative decline, the church continued to be an important patron of junior football at the end of the 1930s.[31] The religious link was probably most evident in Scotland, particularly Glasgow, where Boys' Brigade teams and competitions were well established and by the 1950s allegedly involved 200 teams in 'the largest football league in the world'. Certainly, the young George Raynor's decision to join the local Elsecar Bible Class because it boasted one of the best teams in Barnsley was hardly uncommon and illustrated that in many areas churches and chapels of all denominations represented the best opportunity to play organised football.[32]

If we look beyond the workplace and the church, we find that the patrons of grassroots football were many and varied. Stephen Jones has outlined the role of the Communist-inspired British Workers' Sports Foundation (BWSF) and the National Workers' Sports Association (NWSA), allied to the Labour Party and the Trade Unions Congress (TUC), as important providers of recreational sport. The BWSF estab-

TABLE 3.2 *Church-based and works football teams in selected localities, 1914–39*

Locality	1914		1922		1930		1939	
	Church	Work	Church	Work	Church	Work	Church	Work
Barnsley	28	5	69	8	21	9	1	28
Bolton	75	4	167	13	92	32	63	34
Burnley	28	4	69	5	41	10	23	16
Halifax	39	9	3	2	16	7	20	13
Oldham	37	5	115	10	48	3	22	3
St Helens	30	4	55	3	51	8	24	19
Sunderland	40	10	72	37	60	62	24	53
Wigan	27	4	37	0	59	3	33	1

Source: Adapted from Williams, 'Churches, Sport and Identities', pp. 115, 123–4 (Tables 1 and 2).

lished workers' leagues in London, Derby, south Wales and Glasgow (and played a key role in the successful campaign for Sunday football on London County Council pitches in the 1930s) while the NWSA had its own labour leagues and a national cup competition, but in most areas this activity was marginal and rarely challenged the existing institutions of recreational football. Elsewhere there were clubs, leagues and cup competitions organised around licensed victuallers, working men's clubs and institutes, co-operative societies and so on. Football at this level was, in Johnes's words, 'rooted in, and a reflection of, the complex social networks of male urban life'. For all the evidence of patronage 'from above', the most important networks were probably friendship and neighbourhood ones. Whether named after a street or district, or a pub, church or political institution, the majority of clubs were the work of small enthusiastic groups of friends and acquaintances. Some lasted for many years and built up their own reputation and tradition in local football, but others were what Fishwick calls 'mayfly' teams, lasting a season or two and disappearing as finances became stretched or key individuals moved on (geographically or socially).[33]

Semi-professional and amateur football

Beyond the level of local town and district leagues, football was much more than mere recreation. The highest amateur leagues and cups in England and Wales, and the semi-professional junior tournaments in Scotland, vied with the lower echelons of the professional game for spectators, players and newspaper coverage. By the 1922–3 season there were a number of major county and regional junior leagues north of the border and 412 entries to the national Junior Cup, won that season by Musselburgh Bruntonians in front of a 20,000 crowd at Heart of

Midlothian's Tynecastle ground. As in the senior game, clubs from Glasgow were the most successful on the field, winning 13 of the 22 Scottish Junior Cups between 1918 and 1939. Such was the competitive nature of junior football that the best leagues and clubs acted as the main source of playing talent for Scottish League clubs. Few turned professional without graduating through the ranks of junior football. Schoolboy friends in the Lanarkshire mining village of Bellshill, Hughie Gallacher and Alex James turned out respectively for Bellshill Athletic and the Glasgow junior outfit Ashfield in their late teens and early twenties before being scouted by senior clubs Airdrieonians and Raith Rovers. Ashfield, in fact, acted as the nursery for a stream of future professionals and Scottish internationals during the 1920s and 1930s, including George Brown of Rangers, Alex Massie of Hearts and Aston Villa and Jackie Milne of Arsenal and Middlesbrough.[34]

Yet the relationship between the elite and the grassroots was far from harmonious. The frequency with which junior players were 'snatched' by senior clubs, English as well as Scottish, and the related issue of compensation, initiated a major dispute and a split in the junior game between 1925 and 1931. Complaining of little protection from either the Scottish FA or the Junior FA, over 60 clubs from Glasgow and the west of Scotland left the parent bodies, forming a new Intermediate Association and creating their own league and cup competitions. Most of these 'rebels' had suffered a continual loss of players to the senior ranks. A Shieldmuir Celtic official claimed that 11 players had left the club for senior contracts between 1923 and 1925, with just £50 received as compensation. Plymouth Argyle paid the club the meagre sum of £5 for Frank Sloan, one of the best junior footballers of his day, but Bradford, Clyde and Dundee among others neither approached Shieldmuir nor offered compensation. A resolution to the conflict came in 1931 with a standardisation of aspects of the junior–senior relationship such as registration forms, procedures for approaching players and compensatory fees.[35]

The higher echelons of English amateur football were dominated by the clubs of the south-east and the north-east. Dulwich Hamlet and Bishop Auckland carried away four Amateur Cups each between 1920 and 1939 while Leyton appeared in five finals over the same period. The Northern League was particularly strong, providing nine Amateur Cup finalists between the wars, including both clubs in the 1922 and 1939 finals. Some of its members had been among the first of Britain's football tourists at the beginning of the century and continued to play continental opposition on a regular basis. Crook Town, for example, toured Spain in

1921, playing no less than four matches against FC Barcelona at the latter's Campo de la Calle de la Industria stadium, while Stockton made regular Easter visits to the continent.[36] Yet as in Scotland relations with the national governing body were often strained. The main cause of disagreement was over the interpretation of amateurism, an issue which, as we shall see later in the chapter, also led to the British split with FIFA (the world governing body). A major dispute erupted in 1927 when an anonymous letter was sent to the Durham FA accusing Crook Town of flouting the rules concerning legitimate expenses to amateur players. The club was suspended, but it responded by alleging that a further 20 north-eastern clubs had also made illegal payments to its players. An FA investigation in 1928 led to the suspension of an unprecedented 341 players and numerous club officials. Bishop Auckland and Ferryhill each had 46 players suspended and declared 'professional', while Cockfield, Stanley United and Willington similarly lost 37, 29 and 16 players respectively. Even Football League clubs such as Durham City, Hartlepools United, Darlington and South Shields were affected. The local reaction was indignant. The *Northern Echo* felt that it would lead to the extinction of amateur football in the area and mean that many players would never kick a ball in competitive football again. The widespread practice of paying a flat rate fee in expenses, commonly known as tea money, could hardly be seen as a form of 'shamateurism': 'If tea money means professional football then ... there is not a single amateur team in the County of Durham' wrote one commentator. The Cockfield captain R. W. Harrison outlined the social discrimination embedded in the FA's definition of amateurism:

The amateur who sports plus-fours and knows the best people, travels in comfort, lunches before the match, dines after it and stays at the best hotel keeps his status. The stocky built, bow-legged Durham pit lad goes without lunch, crowds into a United bus, receives five shillings for tea, contents himself with a pie or a snack in a side-street and consequently is a professional.

William McKeag, vice-chairman of Durham City, objected to the FA's autocratic governing of the game, likening them to 'a group of psuedo Mussolinis'. Eventually the FA lifted most of the suspensions, but the whole incident had revealed the regional and class-based tensions that still existed over the issue of amateurism.[37]

Women and football

One of the most significant developments in this period was the rise of the women's game. Most historians have understood its take-off as a response to the particular opportunities provided by women's wartime work. In the absence of the organised male game, women's football could be more easily accepted as a means of boosting patriotism and morale, entertaining the workers and, most importantly of all, raising money for charity. Most of the teams were tied to industrial firms, particularly munitions work, such as the famous Dick, Kerr Ladies of Preston, Ley's Ladies of Nottingham and Bennett's of London. Huddersfield Atalanta, however, was made up of secretaries and teachers, while a number of Lyon's café teams emerged in London. Rather than fading away, the women's game increased in popularity after the war, experiencing a boom in participation and spectatorship. Matches moved out of factory yards and farmers' fields and on to the grounds of professional men's clubs. It received a further boost in parts of Lancashire, Durham and Northumberland during the coal lock-out of the summer of 1921, when

PLATE 6 *Members of the Lyon's football team outside the clubhouse, 1921 (© Hulton Archive/Getty).*

women's matches played a vital role in raising money for strike funds. By the end of 1921 there were an estimated 150 teams in England, 25 of which met in December to form the shortlived English Ladies Football Association. Teams had also been formed in Cardiff, Llanelly, Merthyr, Newport and Swansea and in Cowdenbeath, Edinburgh, Glasgow and Renfrew. A match between the ladies' clubs of Aberdeen and Belfast during Christmas 1920 was just one of a series of 'international' fixtures.[38]

Yet, it is the Dick, Kerr team that dominates historical accounts of the boom period.[39] John Williams and Jackie Woodhouse have argued that by early 1920 it had effectively become the unofficial English women's team, defeating a Scottish representative side over two matches by an aggregate score of 22–0. The team played some 30 matches that year, including four against a French representative side in front of a total of 61,000 spectators, with a reciprocal visit to France in October. The following year it attracted over 70,000 spectators to its five-match Scottish tour and drew crowds of 18,000 and 25,000 respectively to fixtures at Cardiff and Swansea. The acknowledged high point, however, was the 1920 Boxing Day charity match at Goodison Park against St Helen's, which attracted 53,000 (with many thousands more locked out) paying over £3,000 in gate receipts. David Williamson thought that by the beginning of 1921 Britain was 'gripped by ladies' football fever' and that every week in almost every part of the country 'there was a ladies' match being played somewhere'.[40]

Yet opposition towards the women's game was never far from the surface. Players and clubs often faced a level of contempt from the press and the public that reflected deep-rooted prejudices concerning gender roles and appropriate female behaviour. That which under abnormal wartime conditions could be easily rationalised as a novel spectacle or a harmless form of fun took on a rather different complexion in the postwar return to normality. A Welsh woman thought that there were 'plenty of pastimes for girls without indulging in such masculine games as football and I don't think any really nice girls would play it'. One spectator wrote in disgust to the *Western Morning News* in 1921: 'It was the most ludicrous exhibition of the noble sport I have ever witnessed'.[41] The English FA was equally critical. In December 1921 it prohibited the grounds of its affiliated clubs being used for women's games on the basis that 'the game of football is quite unsuitable for females and ought not to be encouraged'. Jean Williams has argued that the ban was 'a rather clumsy attempt . . . to reinforce the masculine image of football'.[42] Indeed it is unlikely that many of the FA's administrators were comfortable with sanctioning female involvement in what they regarded fundamentally as a man's game. But there were other considerations. The pretext for the decision had been the insinuation that the money raised at women's fixtures was being used for non-charitable purposes; it was even suggested that some players were being paid. More significantly, at a time when many amateur and professional male clubs were suffering a slump in attendances, the women's game was beginning to be perceived by some as a serious distraction, possibly even a rival, although Alethea Melling's view that the ban was an attempt to 'subjugate a sport that was strongly competing with male football in terms of skill, crowds and gate receipts' is surely overstated.[43]

While the FA's ban undoubtedly had a profound effect on women's football, it did not lead to its disappearance. The practical difficulties of finding places to play, together with the perceived removal of legitimacy that had come from association with the male game, reduced women's football in many cases to a rather irregular, ad hoc occurrence. Melling has suggested that it effectively became a 'subculture'. Established teams such as Bolton Ladies, Manchester Ladies and Liverpool Ladies disbanded and the game appears at first glance to have gone into a sharp decline. Yet Dick, Kerr Ladies continued to play regularly and even undertook a successful US tour in 1922 where they competed against men's teams. Joan Whalley was one player who turned out for the team throughout the inter-war years. Together with the striker Lily Parr and six teammates, she supported herself as a nurse at Whittingham Hospital during the period. Elsewhere, Williams has talked about the 'embryonic national community' of women's football and the success of clubs such as Bridgett's United, later Stoke Ladies, in initially ignoring the FA ban.[44] Teams had to make use of rugby stadiums, local recreation grounds and any other public space they could find in order to continue. Many failed to do so, but women's football certainly survived on a modest scale away from the official gaze. Indeed recent research on Wales and Scotland has hinted that during the 1930s, at least, it was less sporadic than we might assume. The Welsh FA actually relaxed its ban periodically to allow charity matches, while international fixtures pitting England and Great Britain teams against France were staged in Pontypool (in 1935) and Pontypridd (in 1937). Edinburgh Ladies played home and away games against Dick, Kerr Ladies to determine the 'Champions of the World' in 1937 and 1938. This was clearly more than a one-off for an Edinburgh side that claimed to have played 20 times during the year of the first meeting. Lovell's of

Newport similarly organised a permanent team for its young female workers, while a number of Norwich shoe factories maintained ladies' football teams into the early 1930s and played occasional 'friendly' matches.[45]

Melling and Russell have suggested that even after the ban the notion of women's participation was beginning to impress itself upon the broader culture of the game through adventure stories such as *Bess of Blacktown*, *Ray of the Rovers* and *Meg Foster Footballer*. What is interesting about such stories is that rather than conforming to existing patriarchal structures, they subtly challenged them, transforming 'the working class heroine figure, cultivated as part of the war effort, into a symbol of feminist consciousness'.[46] More research is needed before we can determine whether such examples represent the tip of a much bigger subcultural iceberg, but they do suggest that we need to reconsider the view that in the prevailing economic, cultural and ideological climate of the late 1920s and 1930s 'there was no room for women's football'.[47]

Spectators and supporters

The academic discussion about football supporters in the first few decades of the twentieth century has revolved around three interrelated issues: the composition of the crowd; the nature of its support; and its behaviour. As regards the first of these, Fishwick's categorisation of football spectators as 'working class men of working age' implies a degree of continuity with earlier periods. The conclusions drawn by historians from the impressionistic evidence contained in match reports and newspaper commentaries certainly support the idea that the professional match was the domain of 'decent workaday folk'.[48] Crowd scenes often showed spectators wearing the peaked flat caps which, according to Eric Hobsbawm, had become 'the virtual uniform of the British worker at leisure'. Popular sections of grounds in south Wales were likewise dominated by a 'sea of cloth caps'. The majority of these supporters (up to an estimated 90 per cent at some clubs) were coal miners, the primary skilled workers of the region. What is less clear is how far football's core constituency of skilled workers broadened out between the wars to embrace 'all sections of working men more or less in proportion', as Mason has speculated.[49] A number of historians have outlined the limitations on regular working-class attendance, particularly in areas of poverty and high unemployment. The increase in minimum entrance charges in the Football League – from 6d. to 9d. in 1917 and then 1s. after the First World War – seems to have been beyond the means of even some skilled workers. One of Andrew Davies' intervie-wees recalled that his father, a former amateur footballer, 'never went to City, or Manchester [United]. Quite honestly I don't think a lot of people could afford it, even in those days it was a shilling, or one and six to get in.' The situation was worse for those living on the outskirts of the city, who faced additional transport costs.[50]

While workers certainly dominated the popular sections of most grounds, football also had its supporters among the more affluent. Journalists often highlighted the heterogeneity of football crowds and compared the character and behaviour of the 'popular side' with that of the 'wealthier element'. The quickest of glances at relative income and living standards tells us that only a minority could afford to purchase higher-priced stand and season tickets. It is doubtful, for instance, whether the budgets of many local railway workers extended to the 10s. 6d. a young Evelyn Waugh had paid for a seat at a Swindon cup-tie in 1920, although there is evidence that the less wealthy were prepared to pay more for the big one-off match. The existence of a sizeable section of affluent middle-class support is also hinted at by the increasing reports of motor traffic around grounds on match days from the 1920s and the con-struction of car parks, such as that at Preston's Deepdale ground, to accommodate motoring patrons. Another factor was the development of supporters' clubs. Such bodies were invariably organised by sections of the respectable lower-middle and middle class and many were drawn from similar social backgrounds as club directors. Wrexham's supporters' club was founded in 1926 by a former town clerk and alderman, while the first officers of the National Federation of Supporters' Clubs (NFSC) included the Lord Mayor of Brighton, a Justice of the Peace from Northampton and a councillor from Bournemouth.[51]

All this evidence points towards a significant – albeit minority – bour-geois presence at football matches between the wars. Few clubs could claim to attract the fashionable middle-class clientele associated with Arsenal between the wars, but a number of important studies have pointed to the broadening of the crowd's social composition to embrace sections of the 'respectable' middle class. Eric Dunning and his colleagues have found hints in the regional press that Leicester City was increas-ingly recruiting its audience 'not just from the working class, but from higher up the social scale' and that in Birmingham the 'hat and collar' crowd was replacing the 'old cap-filling, collar-lacking "gate"'.[52] In fact, the accumulation of such evidence has led Russell to posit that the inter-war years (and more particularly the 1930s) may have been an important moment in what he calls the long-term 'embourgeoisification' of football.[53]

Some agreement exists over the extent of female spectatorship during the 1920s and 1930s. Dunning *et al.* have pointed to 'a body of evidence' that women attended matches in greater numbers over the period, while Williams and Woodhouse refer to the partial 'feminisation' of the inter-war football crowd.[54] The female spectator was certainly an increasing feature of press reports. One provincial newspaper remarked at the 'number of women who had accompanied their sweethearts and husbands' to the 1927 FA Cup final and a London publication confirmed that 'The girls have come to town!' Females were estimated to have made up 50 per cent of the Bolton and Portsmouth supporters who travelled to Wembley two years later, while at the 1935 final 'there seemed as many women as men.' In 1936 the Leicester press termed Brentford 'the ladies team' on account of the number of female fans who travelled to the east midlands to watch a cup-tie.[55] The *South Wales Echo* noted a rise of female support during the early 1920s and in 1938 the Cardiff City match programme could refer to the ladies 'who attend in great numbers'. It could be argued of course that such instances attracted press attention precisely because they were unusual. There was certainly a touch of the novelty in references to the 75-year-old Cardiff fan who attended all home games and to 70-year-old Mrs Catterall, who brought along a canary and cage adorned in club colours to Blackburn Rovers' 1928 Cup final appearance. Some female spectators claimed to attend so that they could spend more time with partners, but this does not mean that they were any less committed or knowledgeable than their male counterparts. Two female 'shilling supporters' responded to suggestions in a Sheffield paper that they refrain from discussing 'men's affairs' like football by stating that 'women will never cease to "butt into men's affairs" so long as they interest them'.[56] Fragmentary evidence can also be drawn from crowd photographs, such as those of the popular side at Swindon Town which show eight females out of a total 55 spectators in 1927 and 11 out of 50 in 1938. Significantly, some of these were gathered in female groups rather than attending as part of a male–female couple. The problems inherent in extrapolating general trends from such fragments may explain Russell's circumspection about the claim of increased female attendance. Certainly the presence of women on the terraces alongside men hardly amounts to the 'feminisation' of the crowd. Yet despite Fishwick's suggestion that female spectators were regarded as 'alien, unnatural Amazons', there are sufficient signs that women were becoming recognised as an accepted and an acceptable feature of football spectatorship at many grounds.[57]

What was it like to visit a football match between the wars? Much of the appeal undoubtedly came from the excitement of the game and the accompanying colour and noise. Some saw it as a form of escapism from the monotony and drudgery of everyday life. As one Sheffield newspaper observed in 1928: 'People dress themselves up in strange garb, carry painted umbrellas, blow bugles, swing rattles and handbells, and perform in a manner they would not think of doing at any other time'.[58] Some important matches, particularly local 'derbies', bore all the hallmarks of traditional communal events and have been likened to local festivals or carnivals. Trips to away matches, which increased over this period, provided one of the best opportunities to dress up and display one's allegiance. Arsenal's contingent of travelling support in the 1930s included Jimmy Clayton and Les Jessop, both of whom dressed in red and white suits, the former carrying a white duck to all matches. Huddersfield Town fans travelling down to Wembley in 1928 covered not just the train carriages but also the engine and the guard's van with balloons and slogans in support of the team. Some 2,500 Bradford City supporters visiting Burnley in 1921 were arranged in train compartments belonging to groupings calling themselves 'The Swankers', 'The Toffs' and 'Jock's Pals'. Yet there was no direct equivalent in England to the brake clubs, a long-established and important facet of Scottish fan culture. Dating from the 1890s, brake clubs were forerunners of the supporters' clubs of the twentieth century. They took their name from the festooned horse-drawn 'brakes' which transported spectators to matches, and which invariably carried banners identifying the particular brake club and celebrating one of the club's leading players. By the inter-war years they had become motorised, and in Glasgow at least, as we shall see, were closely associated with instances of disturbance and violence.[59]

Bill Murray has suggested that pre-Second World War crowds may well have been as noisy, if not as colourful, as they are today. The extroverts and 'characters' aside, photographs show relatively few spectators departing from plain dress and hardly any wearing the colours of their team. On visual evidence alone, there was little that differentiated supporters of opposing teams. A notable exception to this was the 'Old Firm' encounter. Descriptions of Celtic–Rangers games from the start of the twentieth century highlighted the spectacle of the occasion. The journalist 'Gulliver' found himself in the Rangers end at a New Year's Day match in the 1930s: 'Blue was the predominant colour, and innumerable blue handkerchiefs were in evidence, and soon began to wave defiance at the other end of the field, where green handkerchiefs were soon answering'. Alongside the wearing of colours and the waving of banners and flags, singing and chanting were common features of 'Old Firm' games. Press accounts drew attention to the significance of the rival 'choirs', although as often in criticism as in celebration. One Catholic newspaper, for example, urged Celtic supporters to 'cut out singing at matches [and the] chanting of childish ditties ... It merely gives an excuse for the enemy to reply with their ribald doggerel and insulting challenges'. The television commentator Kenneth Wolstenholme recalled his astonishment when attending the final of the Empire Exhibition Cup between Celtic and Everton in 1938. It was his 'first taste of the Scottish fervour ... especially the brand turned on by the Celtic fans. They waved their banners, they waved their flags, and they sang their revolutionary songs and their special war-cry of "The Dear Little Shamrock" '.[60]

Barracking was a common characteristic of inter-war crowds, although in England and Wales there was little of the continual mass-chanting of later years. Nonetheless, the considerable noise generated by large football crowds belied the assumption of some critics that spectatorship was a passive activity. Sheffield Wednesday's Billy Walker was one who acknowledged the inspiration derived by him and his teammates when the 'Hillsborough Roar' reached its crescendo. The most celebrated and noisy 'crowd' of all was probably that which packed Glasgow's Hampden Park, especially for the biannual Scotland–England fixture. Tommy Lawton was awed by his first experience of the 'Hampden Roar': 'I thought to myself, what a noise ... that is when I *could* think. The noise echoes and eddies round this giant bowl, and smashes into your eardrums.' Stanley Matthews attributed England's 3–1 reverse at Hampden in 1937 to the noise and enthusiasm of the home crowd, which seemed to be 'transfused into the veins of the Scottish players'. According to Matthews, those 'who have never heard the "Roar" cannot appreciate the effect it has on a player. It shook me and my colleagues in the England team'.[61]

For all the attractions of watching football, we should avoid idealising the experience. As Johnes has pointed out, spectating could also be frustrating, uncomfortable and even dangerous. The popular areas of many grounds offered a poor view of the action and little or no protection from the elements. Spectators stood on raised banks of earth, often built upon refuse, clay, rubble or dust, which quickly turned into mud in wet weather. Many of these popular banks were gradually levelled out and then tiered into a terrace, but concrete terracing was rare before the 1940s. The experience was hardly improved by the general lack of adequate toilet facilities and the consequent use made by some male fans of rolled-up newspapers. Large crowds may have improved the atmosphere and spectacle of a game but they could also adversely affect the overall view and comfort of those standing to watch. Any sight of play was unlikely for the smaller spectator, such as the writer to a Welsh newspaper who, being only 5 foot 2 inches, had been limited to 'the view of hats and heads' at a recent match. Significantly, however, what alarmed the writer much more had been the crush caused by too many spectators packed tightly into the ground. Neither Swansea's Vetch Field nor Cardiff City's Ninian Park could easily accommodate the club's largest crowds and even Arsenal's redeveloped Highbury stadium was considered 'not big enough to be comfortable on big match days' during the late 1930s. Crushing increased when spectators grouped together at the best vantage points or surged forward in response to a goal or near-miss. At times, serious injury was only prevented by an overflow of spectators from the terrace to the edge of the pitch.[62]

Such instances were common throughout the inter-war years. The most notorious example came at the first Wembley FA Cup final of 1923 when at least 126,047, and possibly as many as 250,000 according to some estimates, were in attendance. There were no deaths but an estimated 1,000 spectators were injured, with some witnesses suggesting that greater casualties were prevented only by the absence of barriers and the good behaviour of the crowd. Yet concerns over ground safety usually fell on deaf ears. Despite an inquiry into the Wembley debacle, the football authorities opposed the imposition of safety regulations or the licensing of grounds by outside agencies, preferring to leave the matter to the clubs themselves. Unlike in the music hall and theatre, the safety of football crowds was not deemed worthy of governmental regulation and the game thus continued to deal with the problems of poor facilities and over-crowding through a rather haphazard and unsatisfactory form of self-regulation.[63]

That people were prepared to pay to watch football in spite of conditions that would be tolerated (according to one newspaper) 'in no other department of the entertainment world' has been explained by the peculiar nature of the game's audience.[64] Many regarded themselves, and were seen by others, as 'supporters' of particular clubs rather than spectators in a general sense. This distinction was of some significance: 'supporters' were loyal and committed enthusiasts rather than casual consumers of a product. Supporting a football club was often described in terms of the 'passion' and 'devotion' it generated. It arguably involved a degree of emotional investment absent in other forms of entertainment. Supporters were attached to, and indeed part of, the unfolding drama (of both the 90-minute game and the nine-month season) in a way that cinema audiences, for example, could not possibly be. As Arthur Hopcraft memorably suggested, football was in this sense more than merely a 'game' or a form of 'entertainment': it engaged the personality and became a source of meaning and identity in people's lives.[65] The most celebrated depiction of what football 'meant' to those who attended between the wars comes from J. B. Priestley's 1929 novel *The Good Companions*. It is worth quoting here at length:

For a shilling the Bruddersford United AFC offered you Conflict and Art; it turned you into a critic, happy in your judgment of the fine points, ready in a second to estimate the worth of a well-judged pass, a run down the touch-line, a lightning shot, a clearance kick by the back or goalkeeper; it turned you into a partisan, holding your breath when the ball came sailing into your own goalmouth, ecstatic when your forwards raced towards the opposite goal, elated, downcast, bitter, triumphant by turns at the fortunes of your side, watching a ball shape Iliads and Odysseys for you ...

And what is more, it turned you into a member of a new community, all brothers together for an hour and a half, for not only had you escaped from the clanking machinery of this lesser life, from work, wages, rent, dole, sick pay, insurance-cards, nagging wives, ailing children, bad bosses, idle workmen, but you had escaped with most of your mates and neighbours, with half the town, and there you were, cheering together, thumping one another on the shoulders, swapping judgments like lords of the earth, having pushed your way through a turnstile into another and altogether more splendid kind of life, hurtling with Conflict and yet passionate and beautiful in its Art.

Moreover, it offered you more than a shilling's worth of material for talk during the rest of the week. A man who had missed the last home match of 't'United' had to enter social life on tiptoe in Bruddersford.[66]

Priestley's description may be fictional but it should not be regarded as having less historical value for that, even if we accept it primarily as a 'discursive device': an 'idealised' portrayal of the football crowd used by the author to represent the authentic values of northern working-class and, by extension, English life. What it brings out most vividly is the central position football occupied in the lives of those who watched. In this sense, they were certainly not like other leisure consumers. Football supporters, it is often emphasised, were hardly likely to take their shillings elsewhere if the product on offer proved unsatisfactory. As Richard Holt has suggested, in this important cultural sense supporters were as much 'members' as 'customers' of football clubs.[67]

There were of course many levels of this kind of club 'membership'. It is perhaps no surprise that writers have focused their attention on the most loyal or core groups of supporters: those that attended every week, possibly including reserve games, and extended their involvement by buying shares in the club or regularly discussing its fortunes in the letter pages of the local press. For such men and women, supporting 'their' club provided an important sense of collective identity, which could merge with and act alongside other significant social, geographical and ideological identities. Johnes has gone further by highlighting the deep attachment such supporters developed towards the ground itself, even the particular area of the ground where they stood each week and the people they stood with. Such evidence suggests that a fan's sense of place could be extremely strong and bears out John Bale's observation that supporters have often exhibited a similar bond with 'their' stadium as with their home.[68]

But not all supporters were as faithful and loyal as this. For the less committed, bad weather, transport difficulties and the poor recent form of the team could all act as a disincentive to attend. The notion of the 'calculating' or 'fickle' supporter was commonplace to club and league officials and sports journalists. Attendances tended to follow a familiar seasonal pattern. Crowds were invariably largest at the beginning of each season and declined as the weather got worse and initial expectations were dashed. Cup ties, local derbies and holiday fixtures often led to a resurgence of support while crowds normally increased for those clubs involved in relegation and promotion battles during the final few weeks of the season, but overall the high gates of late summer and early autumn were rarely matched after Christmas. When combined with serious economic problems, poor weather and poor results could have a catastrophic effect on attendances. Thus Preston North End's normal home gate of 10,000 fell to just 3,000 when Bury visited on a particularly cold and windy day in February 1932. When Nelson and Wigan Borough both left the Football League in 1931, the poor crowds brought on by weak performances and unemployment had cast doubts on the strength of local support for the clubs. Rochdale, meanwhile, managed to maintain reasonable gates over the course of the 1931–2 season despite finding itself in considerable debt, conceding 135 goals in 40 matches and plummeting to the bottom of the Third Division North. Patterns of support could thus be extremely complex and uneven, with an increased sense of loyalty and commitment re-emerging amongst some supporters precisely when a club was struggling most.[69]

Followers and hooligans

There has been a tendency in the existing literature to associate football support entirely with spectatorship. This might seem an obvious approach to take, especially for the historian of the pre-television age, but it fails to take account of the various ways in which contemporaries identified with and followed the game. Watching an event live is only one of a number of levels at which people 'witness' or 'consume' sport. One recent study focused on US sport, for instance, differentiated between those 'sport *spectators*' who actually witness events as they happen, and those 'sport *fans*' who might simply 'be interested in and follow a sport, team, and/or athlete'. Within the former category, the study also distinguished the 'direct sport consumer' who attends an event in person, from the 'indirect sport consumer' who engages with sport through some form of media, mainly radio or television.[70] Such classifications can be easily applied to British soccer in this period. Certainly, in the 1920s and 1930s people 'followed' football in a variety of ways that did not involve passing through turnstiles. One of the most obvious of these was reading about the game in the press. A host of writers have outlined the symbiotic relationship that developed from the last quarter of the nineteenth century between sport and the press. Tony Mason has suggested that 'modern sport and the modern press grew up together' and his work and that of others has given us a clear understanding of the close relationship forged between what we might call the football world and a myriad of local, national and specialist sporting newspapers. The press provided a crucial source of free publicity for the game through the straightforward task of covering matches and publishing scores and was also central to the early organis-ation and management of the sport. The growth of the popular press between the wars, and the role of sporting coverage in subsequent circu-lation battles, further increased the significance of this relationship. By 1940 national dailies such as the *Express*, *Herald*, *Mirror* and *Mail* could each boast circulations of between 1.45 and 2.6 million, while both the Sunday papers *News of the World* and the *People* reached well over 3 million. In each case, the space devoted to football increased as circulation grew, reaching about 10 per cent of the overall coverage in the two popular Sunday titles by the end of the 1930s.[71]

We will never know exactly how many people read the football pages but such evidence lends much support to Fishwick's argument that the press was key in the 'transformation of football into a national game of importance to more people of different classes'.[72] Press coverage could work both as a supplement to, and in lieu of, an individual's actual attendance at matches. For those who did not watch their team on a regular basis, newspapers offered relatively quick and detailed access to the progress of a favourite team and the fluctuating narrative of a league championship. Football specials, established in most towns and cities during the 1890s and 1900s and flourishing by the 1920s, provided instant news of local and national competition to readers on Saturday evenings. By the mid-1920s the *Football Pink* in Swindon was publishing same-day reports, along with the results, of every Football League match. The *Sheffield Telegraph* revealed in 1925 how a telephone, a special messenger and a shorthand typist made it possible for a journalist at the other end of the country to have a 1,500-word match report in print within an hour of the final whistle. The nature of football 'news' was virtually transformed in the 1930s by the pioneering style of the *People*, and its preference for transfer gossip and exclusives and sensational stories involving money, corruption and violence. For most readers this new style of reporting complemented the more traditional patterns of the build-up to fixtures through the week and then reflection upon results and performances on Sundays and Mondays. To borrow the categories outlined by David Rowe in his study of contemporary sports journalism, 'soft news' and 'reflexive analysis' – a form of writing that challenged and criticised rather than eulogised sport – emerged alongside the established 'hard news' agenda of football reporting.[73]

Few scholars would thus deny that newspapers were crucial agents in the increasing popularity of the game. Yet there is more to this relationship than is normally recognised. What happened on a football pitch could of course never be transparently 'viewed' by readers through a newspaper report. Rather, the game was presented to its followers in a 'mediated' form: they 'saw' football via the language of the journalist and the visual images of the illustrator, photographer or editor. What newspapers offered were subjective and powerful 'representations' of football, which, as Jeffrey Hill has convincingly argued, were central in helping to shape and construct what people thought and understood about the game.

We might take this a step further. In his study of American football and the popular press in the late nineteenth and early twentieth centuries, Michael Oriard has argued that the game 'was created as a popular spectacle by the daily newspaper' and that most Americans' primary experience of their version of football was through reading about it in newspapers.[74] One could, tentatively, make a similar claim about British soccer. Certainly, it is likely that more people read about football than watched it and we can probably safely assume that a fair percentage of these followed the game *primarily* through the pages of the press, even as aggregate live attendances increased in the first half of the twentieth century. Further research is certainly needed before we can make any confident assertions about the nature of press representations of football and the way in which readers reacted to them. At the very least, however, we need to acknowledge the significance of those who, while perhaps not regarded as 'supporters' by contemporaries, can nonetheless be termed 'followers' of football by virtue of their engagement with the game through different strands of the media.

Also of importance in this respect were those who followed the game by watching newsreels or listening to radio broadcasts. Although less obviously cinematic than other sports such as boxing and horse racing, the first films of football matches were made in the late 1890s and the FA Cup final was regularly filmed from 1899. During the 1920s and 1930s major sporting events became an important element of the newsreel footage that helped to fill cinema programmes. Football historians have rather downplayed the significance of newsreels, observing that their brief, incomplete and retrospective nature 'left them as no substitute for going to a … ground'. Yet the point is surely rather that newsreels offered a further means by which the game could reach mass audiences, many of whom may never have been inclined to visit a match themselves. Indeed, given the relatively poor quality of photo-journalism at the time, newsreel and film offered the best opportunity for many to actually 'see' football, both as a sport and as a popular spectacle.[75]

Radio's relationship with the game was rather different. Not only was its introduction in 1922 a challenge to the existing dissemination of sports news by the print media but also the subsequent development of running commentaries posed a potential threat to live attendances. The BBC's first live outside broadcast of a professional match was Arsenal's home fixture with Sheffield United in January 1927, with the FA Cup final between Cardiff City and Arsenal following a few months later. There was no denying the enormous impact radio broadcasting had both on the public awareness of, and interest in, football. Initially confined mainly to the middle class, wireless licences rose from two million in 1927 to 9 million by 1939, representing 71 per cent of all UK households. According to one account, the weekly round-up of football results had already reached the status of a 'national institution' by the Second World War. The BBC argued that eye-witness accounts and running commentaries served to popularise the game, bringing the immediate thrill of a match to new social groups, as well as those who by virtue of age or disability were unable to watch at first-hand. Its director of Outside Broadcasting claimed in 1931 to have 'indisputable evidence of a growing interest in Association Football directly due to broadcast running commentaries'. We certainly know that it appealed to a broad spectrum of listeners, including some unlikely 'followers' such as the novelist and feminist Winifred Holtby: 'I know that if ever I want a really exciting sport, I have to wait to put my feet on the footstool, push the six cats out of the armchair, and listen for that astonishing crescendo which rises and breaks about the great shout, "Goal" '.[76]

PLATE 7 *A BBC camera filming the 1938 England–Scotland international at Wembley (© Hulton Archive/Getty).*

By contrast, the main concern of the football authorities was that radio reduced attendances by turning existing spectators into passive 'armchair supporters'. The Football League, in particular, maintained a consistent resistance to live broadcasting, arguing not only that it threatened the financial future of its poorer lower division members but also that it altered the fundamental nature of football support. For Charles Sutcliffe, vice-president of the League, radio was transforming soccer 'into a parlour game' and challenging the commitment of the dedicated spectator: 'When the weather is cold and the elements unkind, a man must be an enthusiast to turn up at a match, but it really needs no enthusiasm to sit at ease with slippers on, peacefully smoking and listening in.' Arguments of this kind led the League to ban the broadcasting of all its matches in 1931, a decision which remained in force for all UK listeners for the rest of the decade. The Scottish League took an even firmer line, rejecting requests to cover all representative and domestic fixtures and prohibiting the BBC from contacting its clubs directly.[77] The FA Cup final at Wembley was the one match exempted from the general ban on running commentaries, mainly due to the FA's recognition that its showpiece had become an event of national (in England and Wales at least) significance alongside the Grand National, the Derby, the Boat Race, Wimbledon and Cricket Tests. All contributed to form the basis of a British national sporting culture which was to a considerable extent *created* by the BBC. By the late 1930s, the FA had also sanctioned the broadcast of the second-half of certain international fixtures and cup-ties, as well as highlights of amateur games and the previously private FA Cup draws. Whether the relatively rapid growth of football broadcasting in the 1930s can be said to have changed the nature of football fandom, as Richard Haynes has argued, is open to debate. Like the press, radio was instrumental in opening up the football experience behind the turnstiles to a larger and more diverse audience. It reached a large number of people: some 50 per cent of all listeners according to a 1939 BBC survey. Yet we know little at present of the precise relationship between those who watched and listened to the game and, as such, Haynes's contention that radio successfully 'brought a football community together, stitching together the public and the private spheres' is rather premature.[78]

The press and the radio were closely connected to the other major medium through which public interest in football was developed and sustained between the wars: the pools. People had always wagered money on football matches but the sheer scale of the pools brought the practice into the mainstream. It developed in the early 1920s as a form of fixed-odds

coupon betting through which companies could evade the 1920 prohibition on ready-money betting by receiving stake money in arrears.
Well-marketed and appealing to a wide range of existing and new punters,
the pools expanded quickly into a vast industry and a national obsession.
Although technically a 'commercial spin-off' or 'economic by-product' of
football, it rapidly overshadowed the game itself as both an industry and
a leisure pursuit. The annual national turnover of its companies, led by the
Liverpool-based Littlewoods and Vernons, grew from approximately £10
million in 1934 to £40 million by 1938. The £30 million yearly turnover
identified by *The Economist* in 1936 represented 20 times the annual
income of the entire 88-club membership of the Football League.[79]

The number of 'poolites' was equally impressive. One estimate was
that between 5 and 7 million filled in a coupon every week by the mid-
1930s. By the end of the decade 10 million were listed as clients of the
various firms, and possibly one in three of the entire population returned
a coupon at one time or another. 'Doing the pools' was as common a
habit as smoking in some communities, and those that did not partake
were deemed 'outsiders' or 'bad sports'. It is accepted that many more
people were involved in the football pools than in watching matches.
While 20,000 coupons were distributed every week in Swindon in 1937,
only 9,000 saw Swindon Town play every fortnight; in Sheffield, the
figures were 100,000 coupons, with the United and Wednesday attracting
a much smaller 20,000. Nationally, Walvin has estimated that 16.5 as
many people were gambling on football during the mid-1930s as were
watching it. It also seems to have been spread more widely across the
social spectrum than actual match attendance, with greater numbers of
both poor and rich punters, as well as considerable female participation.
In spite of the opposition of powerful sections of the football and religious
establishment, the pools were central in reinforcing football's status as the
people's game. The association of pools betting with immorality may have
tarnished football's image for some, but ultimately the weekly flutter did
more to help than to hinder the popularity of the sport. As Walvin has
succinctly stated, it 'widened even further the national interest in the game
and gave many millions of people, who would otherwise not have taken
an interest in it, a personal, albeit distant, commitment to the weekly
progress of matches'.[80]

Above all else, it is the issue of hooliganism that has dominated academic discussion of spectator activity. The work of Dunning and the
Leicester sociologists is the obvious starting point here. The basic argument, outlined in their major work *The Roots of Football Hooliganism*,

has been termed by others the 'continuity thesis': disorder and violence, they argue, have always taken place at football matches and as such 'modern' manifestations from the 1960s should be understood as rooted in (though certainly not identical to) practices established during the late nineteenth century.[81] Drawing on a combination of press reports and official documents, they argue that crowd misconduct and disorder, though hardly the norm, were frequent occurrences in British soccer before the First World War. Our concern in this chapter, of course, is the inter-war period. Here Dunning *et al.* suggest that the behaviour of crowds, in England at least, generally improved and that serious incidents of disorder were less prevalent than before. Taken on face value, the figures unearthed from FA records and *Leicester Mercury* match reports suggest an increase in spectator misconduct and disorderliness (see Tables 3.3 and 3.4). Yet Dunning *et al.* show that other factors need to be considered – namely the overall increase in the game's national popularity (with more matches played and increasing spectator numbers) and the seriousness of the alleged instances of 'hooliganism'. On the latter point, the decline in the ratio of ground closures and the increasing reference to relatively minor indiscretions such as 'barracking' and 'unsporting' conduct in the Leicester data are all suggestive of an overall improvement in crowd behaviour. Dunning *et al.* explain this in a number of ways. First, they point to the changing composition of the crowd, which they argue (as outlined earlier) included more members of the middle and even

TABLE 3.3 *Incidents of spectator misconduct and disorderliness at Football League matches recorded by the FA, 1895–1915 and 1921–39*

Period	No. of seasons	No. of incidents		Totals
		Closures	Warnings	
1895–1915	18.5	8	17	25
1921–39	18.0	8	64	72

Source: Eric Dunning, Patrick Murphy and John Williams, *The Roots of Football Hooliganism: An Historical and Sociological Study* (London: Routledge & Kegan Paul, 1988), p. 95 (Table 5.1).

TABLE 3.4 *Incidents of spectator misconduct and disorderliness reported in the Leicester (Daily) Mercury, 1894–1914 and 1921–39*

Period	Filbert Street	Elsewhere in Leicestershire	Elsewhere in England
1894–1914	20	39	84
1921–39	43*	22	35

*Includes two incidents that occurred in connection with travel to and from away matches.
Source: Dunning, Murphy and Williams, *Roots of Football Hooliganism*

upper class and a greater proportion of females. Second, they focus on broader societal changes, placing particular emphasis on what they see as the increasing 'incorporation' of the working class. Improvements in living standards and the softening of industrial relations combined with the move towards a more consumerist, home-centred and educated mass culture to create the beginnings of a genuinely integrated and affluent society. Absorbing the values of the dominant upper and middle classes, working-class people thus came to behave, and were portrayed as behaving, in an increasingly 'respectable' and less unruly manner, both inside and outside the football ground.[82]

This notion of the orderly and peaceful inter-war crowd has been a popular one. Although more impressed by the fundamental differences between crowds of the past and the present, the studies of Fishwick, Holt and McKibbin all endorse this idea of relative quiescence. Their explanations prioritise the role of older supporters as a mediating influence, the absence of gangs of disaffected youths congregated at a particular end of the ground and the rarity of 'away' support. Indeed, despite what the Leicester researchers called the 'subterranean existence' of crowd disorder, the impression that comes from the reading of both contemporary sources and scholarly accounts is of the overwhelming restraint and discipline of the English football spectator.[83] The contribution of the events surrounding the 1923 FA Cup final to the construction of this image can hardly be underestimated. Notwithstanding the serious danger to life resulting from the massive overcrowding blamed on organisational ineptitude and the presence of so many gatecrashers, the events of the day quickly came to be covered with a more positive gloss. In particular, the two most significant 'myths' of Wembley 1923 – that the arrival of the King calmed the crowd and that the single policeman on his white horse was able to clear the pitch – were rapidly etched into the popular memory of the game. People soon recalled it as 'The White Horse Cup Final', with an accepted narrative that 'the king and a horse had saved the day'. What is more, as Hill has noted in his perceptive study, initial reports of disorder, injury and the 'threat of the crowd' were soon 'transformed into a reassuring image of the virtues of the nation'. The conduct of the Wembley crowd seemed to embody the way in which the English saw themselves as a people: 'self-disciplined, peaceable [and] essentially cooperative'.[84]

By contrast, Scottish football was more susceptible to disorderly and violent behaviour. As Murray has shown, a particular brand of hooligan activity was endemic in the sectarian rivalry between Celtic and Rangers

supporters from at least the turn of the century. This increased between
the wars and became particularly associated with the growing prominence
of the brake clubs and the so-called 'razor gangs' of the period. One report
of an incident from 1922 involving a returning Rangers brake suggests a
level of violence far beyond anything that existed south of the border: the
occupants were said to be carrying iron bars, swords and bayonets along
with the usual stones and bottles. Likewise, the operation of street gangs
such as the Protestant 'Bridgeton Billy Boys' on the fringes of the game
had no contemporary equivalent in England. Originating in 1924, the
gang apparently numbered some 800 and was represented for some years
at Orange Walks as well as Rangers matches. They were notorious, in
Murray's words, for 'picking fights before, during or after the exploits of
their sporting heroes'. One of the worst incidents of the period involved a
confrontation between Morton and Celtic fans at Greenock in April 1922.
In need of a single point to take the championship, visiting supporters
arrived in brakes, blowing bugles and sporting colours but also waving
Sinn Fein flags. They were met by Morton supporters from the Protestant
areas of Port Glasgow 'armed with bags of rivets and other missiles'.
Fighting apparently broke out during the first half, and at the half-time
interval the west terracing 'expolded into violence', with hundreds of spectators from both sides spilling on to the pitch. The game resumed with
Celtic gaining the necessary draw, but fighting continued outside the
ground, on the approach to the station and on some of the special trains
back to Glasgow.[85] While it would be misleading to downplay the peculiar sectarian dimension of such confrontations, Dunning *et al.* have
nonetheless located them in the context of the recurrent patterns of masculinity, group loyalty and heavy drinking which were to become such a
feature of hooliganism in the twentieth century. In their view, the greater
incidence of football-related violence north of the border was less notable
than its high degree of organisation and premeditation, making it closer
in many respects to its English variant of the 1960s and 1970s than the
1920s and 1930s.[86]

Recent local studies have added a great deal to our understanding of
crowd disorder, generally downplaying the seriousness of early manifestations of hooliganism and challenging the 'continuity thesis' of the
Leicester researchers.[87] Johnes's work on south Wales, for example, has
emphasised the importance of situating the misbehaviour of football spectators within the social and cultural values of the day. Broadly in line with
the chronology suggested by Dunning *et al.*, he argues that disorder was
highest in the early 1920s at a time when industrial unrest and inter-class

tension was at its height, but declined from the mid-1920s as order returned to the pits and streets of the region and remained a rarity for the rest of the period. Incidents actually involving violence, moreover, were much less frequent than the routine barracking of players and referees, which in itself tended to be exaggerated by the moralistic administrators of the game and the press. Such behaviour is best understood, for Johnes, in the context of the working lives and social norms of the crowd. The skilled workers, mostly miners, who populated the 'bob banks' at Ninian Park and the Vetch Field thus felt entitled to criticise the performance of home players in the same way as they would be chastised when standards slipped in their own jobs, using the same colourful language of the work-place. In a similar way, verbal or even physical retaliation to a perceived wrong (be it a refereeing decision or a bad tackle) was considered legiti-mate in soccer as it was on the picket-line or the public house. It did not take place very often but when it did, football-related violence exhibited many of the characteristics of the violent behaviour that was part of everyday life in the south Wales coalfield (and many other parts of Britain). Overall, Johnes contends that crowd disorder was not a particu-larly serious problem in south Wales before 1939. It was 'simply an extension of the general rowdiness elsewhere in society and never on the scale of the disorder in contemporary industrial disputes or indeed modern soccer violence'.[88] Here, as in other parts of Britain, the police and political authorities barely considered it worthy of their attention. Even in Glasgow, exuberance was normally restrained, and violence in and around football grounds was extremely rare. Hooliganism, in short, was marginal to most people's experiences of and concerns about inter-war British football. To pay it too much attention is to distort the historical record.

Heroes and stars

Richard Holt and J. A. Mangan have argued that 'a sport without a hero is like Hamlet without the Prince'. Football may be a team game but out-standing individual performance has always been celebrated by the sporting public and the media. Yet sports historians were until recently relatively uninterested in the actual exploits of individuals, preferring to concentrate on the 'social, cultural and political *context* of performance rather than the performers themselves'.[89] Over the last decade or so, however, a more self-confident approach to the subject has meshed with a number of historiographical trends and led to the emergence of the football hero or star as a legitimate subject of analysis. The relationship between biography, life-history and mainstream academic history has been a vibrant area of scholarly debate pertinent to the study of sport.[90] Although few British sports historians have attempted book-length biographies, the inclusion of over 80 nineteenth and twentieth-century footballers (rugby and association) in the *Oxford Dictionary of National Biography* shows the increasing significance attached to the life stories of individual players. Another important influence has, perhaps ironically, been the move towards 'a people's history' and the impact of 'history from below'. Sports heroes, in the writing that has emerged, are not viewed in the same way as the 'great men', politicians and military leaders of the more conventional political history but rather as 'ordinary people' who, in Mason's words, happened to be able to 'do one thing supremely well'.[91] As such it is what these people stood for in the eyes of those who watched or read about them that has been seen as important. Post-modern approaches to history have also been influential. While few have adopted the methodologies of the most extreme post-modern historians, Hill in particular has urged historians to treat sporting heroes as 'texts' that have no fixed meanings but can be interpreted and reinterpreted by readers who bring particular chronological and spatial influences to bear on the text. In this sense the way in which heroes were represented in the press, biographies and other media, and the precise language used, are seen as fundamental in understanding what they actually 'meant' to the public.[92]

When applied to sporting activity, 'hero' can be a problematic and slippery term. The classical Greek heroes were legendary individuals – born to greatness and favoured by the gods – who undertook tasks of awesome significance. Such ancient heroes were, according to one writer, 'distinguished for exceptional courage, fortitude, enterprise, superior qualities or deeds'.[93] Twentieth-century heroes, sporting or otherwise, could hardly match such criteria, but the idea of the 'hero' was still prevalent. The meaning of the term has been subject to change across time and between cultures: in Holt's words, sporting heroes 'are both universal and particular. They resemble each other and differ from each other'.[94] Steven Reiss has noted that heroes in American sport were not only expected to display outstanding performance over a long period but also to have moral and social responsibilities and act as role models. The achievements of figures like baseball's Babe Ruth and football's Red Grange simultaneously demonstrated the continuing merit of traditional American ideals such as individualism, hard work and self-reliance and the significance of newer modern traits like co-operation and teamwork.[95] In

Europe, grit and determination and style in performance were all prerequisites but fairness and decency (in sport and life) were also highly prized in a way that was less obvious of many of their US counterparts. Other writers have emphasised the role of failure and destruction in the making of sporting heroism. For Pierre Lanfranchi, tragedy is 'one of the requirements to transform a champion into a hero' and death the ultimate heroic sacrifice. The anthropologist Eduardo Archetti concurs, identifying the Argentinian footballer Diego Maradona's construction as 'a tragic hero' during the collapse of his personal life and playing career as fundamental to his overall status as a mythical heroic figure to many Argentinians and some Italians.[96]

Sports heroes have generally been regarded as symbolic of wider values and identities. As H. F. Moorhouse has argued, they are 'not just superior athletes but emblematic figures' who could represent and communicate ideas about class and masculinity, region or nation. Holt suggests that their lives 'are woven into stories we tell ourselves about ourselves'.[97] It was the cricketer rather than the footballer that became exemplar of the British (or more accurately the English) heroic ideal. Cricket had a genuinely national, cross-class appeal which soccer had yet to attain and its leading players such as Jack Hobbs and Len Hutton came to be identified with the modesty, respectability and basic decency so closely associated with the greatest Victorian explorers and soldiers.[98] The earliest football heroes, by contrast, were more proletarian and parochial. Chas Critcher has referred to the professional as 'traditionally a kind of working-class folk hero', and Mason's study of the Edwardian players Stephen Bloomer and Harold Fleming has revealed their significance as essentially local heroes. Although both competed internationally for England, they were regarded above all as local lads, known affectionately as 'our Stephen' and 'our Harold', who succeeded in giving their respective provincial towns (Derby and Swindon) a national prominence by virtue of their footballing skills. The qualities they displayed – loyalty, reliability and 'steadiness' – were not dissimilar to those of the cricketing idol, yet had a different resonance in the context of football's more localised working-class support.[99] Goal-scorers like Bloomer and Fleming, and skilful ball artists such as Alex James or the young Stanley Matthews, were perhaps the archetypal terrace idols, but heroes needed to be neither spectacular nor particularly entertaining, as Holt's analysis of northern footballers like the former blacksmith Frank Barson indicates. A central defender for Barnsley, Aston Villa and Manchester United over nearly 20 years, Barson suffered numerous injuries and had one of the worst disciplinary records ever, even ending his career by being sent off in his own benefit match. Fred Keenor, a strong, hard and courageous centre-half with Cardiff City and Wales, may have been in a similar mould but was arguably a more complex kind of hero. As team captain, he personified the success of Cardiff's 1927 FA Cup victory, in his robust and tireless play epitomised the struggles of life in south Wales during the years of depression and on leaving the club was to remain 'a symbol of past glories'. Like many others who were remembered as heroes of club and community, Keenor was less important for what he was and what he did than for what he represented.[100]

In Scotland, a local or club hero could more easily become a national idol. Playing for Scotland mattered more to the Scots than playing for England did to the English. Alan Morton, for instance, came to be regarded as '*the* Rangers star of the inter-war years'. In his skilful style of play, he arguably stood outside the Rangers tradition for power and strength, but his middle-class background, teetotalism and immaculate appearance – he always wore a bowler hat and suit – fitted the club's reputation for discipline and respectability. But Morton's popularity in Scotland was enhanced most through his performances against England, and reinforced by the fact that he was a 'home' player rather than an 'Anglo' earning his living south of the border. Consequently, he was 'revered as much as a Scottish wizard as a Rangers immortal' whereas players such as Alex James and Hughie Gallacher, who often had their 'Scottishness' called into question by the press and the public, came to be identified more with their English employers than with Scotland.[101] Gallacher's life reveals another dimension that seems particularly pronounced in the construction of Scottish heroes: tragedy. With a fiery temper and a disdain for authority to match his bravery and skill, Gallacher has been presented as 'the epitome of the great Scottish footballer'. Yet his story was marked by personal and professional scandal, fuelled by a drink problem and ultimately the taking of his own life. His headless body was found on a Gateshead railway line in 1957 amidst allegations that he had maltreated his son. John Thomson, the 'Prince of Goalkeepers', was a tragic hero of a very different kind. The young Celtic player died as the result of a collision with the Rangers forward Sam English during an 'Old Firm' match in September 1931 and was quickly elevated to iconic status. Over the years he has been remembered through anniversaries and memorials and honoured in the songs of the Parkhead crowd. However, Thomson was also rather more than a club hero. Moorhouse has suggested that his tragic death became significant not just for Celtic followers but for the 'Old Firm' collectively, feeding the tradition that their encounter was indeed something special: 'the greatest club game in the world'.[102]

If inter-war footballers are frequently understood as 'heroes', they are less often defined as 'stars'. One problem is that scholars can be inconsistent in their use of the terms. Some adopt 'hero' and 'star' as neutral descriptors that can be used interchangeably; for others there is a linear relationship between the two, with the working-class hero transforming under the increasing gaze of the media into a genuine classless star. Richard Giulianotti, for example, framed part of his discussion of football players in terms of the move '*from* heroes to stars'. Less explicitly, in his typology of the post-Second World War footballer, Critcher has positioned the traditional 'hero' as the forerunner of the 'star' and 'superstar' of the 1960s and beyond. Recent research has challenged this assumption that the rise of the soccer star was a post-war phenomenon. Moorhouse has argued that many of the characteristics of the so-called 'superstars' of the 1960s – widespread fame, problems on and off the field and personal dislocation from the traditional working-class milieu from which they came – were actually nothing particularly new but rather a feature of the lives of many earlier 'stars'.[103] Joyce Woolridge has taken the argument a step further in a paper focusing on English footballers. Drawing on methodologies developed in film studies, she argues for a more sophisticated understanding of the nature of football stardom and a new chronology of its development. According to this view, the earliest footballers were performers or entertainers as well as workers, who, like film actors, achieved star status not only by virtue of their intrinsic talent but also through the public recognition of their image. Audiences thus came to 'know' the footballer as much via the subsidiary circulation of his image, through newspaper reports, magazine articles and other football ephemera such as cigarette cards and player photographs, as by his weekly performance on the pitch. Furthermore, Woolridge argues that a prominent group of football stars emerged from the Edwardian era onwards and rejects McKibbin's view that there were 'only a handful of players who were national figures' by the Second World War.[104]

Although admittedly highly speculative, there is a lot for historians to heed in Woolridge's analysis. Her emphasis on a more precise definition of 'stars' (as 'those players who were known in special ways, locally, regionally and sometimes nationally, to followers of football'), and the way in which the star was distinguished culturally as well as economically from the ordinary player, are both important.[105] What is more, the widespread dissemination of players' names and images via the medium of cigarette cards, newspaper popularity polls, music-hall posters and so on, provides convincing evidence of the existence of nationally recognised football stars before 1914. The Welsh winger Billy Meredith certainly falls into this category. His biographer John Harding has described him as 'a star during a period when publicity was rudimentary' and 'a national celebrity'. Joining Manchester City as a professional in 1894, he played for the best part of the next 30 years, appearing 50 times for Wales and in two FA Cup finals, finally bowing out in a 1924 semi-final at the age of almost 50. Yet Meredith was known as much for his image as for his achievements. With his bandy legs and trademark toothpick in the mouth while playing, he was a favourite subject for cartoonists. He was also a friend of music-hall stars such as George Robey, Fred Karno and Harry Wheldon, contributed regularly to newspaper columns, endorsed a range of sporting and non-sporting brands and even starred in a feature film, *The Ball of Fortune*, during retirement in 1926. In contradistinction to Mason, Woolridge also argues that the other great Edwardian footballer, Stephen Bloomer, was as much a national star as a local hero. Known as 'Paleface' on account of his ghost-like complexion, Bloomer may not have looked like the modern star but he was certainly well known. He scored an extraordinary 23 times for England in 28 matches between 1895 and 1907, exploiting his fame by appearing in advertisements for the tonic Phosferine and a range of football products. Woolridge also claims that Bloomer was a 'showman', leaping in the air and turning cartwheels after scoring as a young striker, and kicking the ball into the air to mark his entrance to the pitch later in his career. His biographer has called him 'football's first superstar', although Woolridge restricts this label to a later period when players received national recognition beyond the football world.[106]

Surprisingly, Woolridge has relatively little to say about the inter-war soccer star. She accepts that players such as Everton's high-scoring 'Dixie' Dean, Arsenal's Cliff Bastin and Tommy Lawton, Dean's replacement at Goodison Park, were all recognisable to a national audience due to the circulation of their images in newspapers and through endorsing a range of commercial products. The increasing coverage directed to the game in various forms of the inter-war print and broadcast media is crucial here. Radio not only promoted the game itself but also helped to construct a new raft of football personalities, the most notable of whom was not in fact a player but the commentator and then Arsenal manager George Allison. Cartoons and caricatures of players became ever more popular during the period and were essential in defining and disseminating the 'image' of the star footballer: according to Fishwick, 'Alex James's baggy trousers were as important in making his name in the 1930s as Billy Meredith's toothpick had been before 1920'.[107] Yet what was perhaps most striking about the inter-war period was the increasing attention given by the local and national press to 'human interest' stories about players. The inclusion of an article in the *Lancashire Daily Post* in 1937 on the wives of Cup-finalists Preston North End exemplified, for Russell, the growing focus of the northern press on the domestic lives of footballers. On a national level, *Topical Times* had long included articles on the non-work aspects of players' lives. Alongside features on 'Best Dressed Footballers' and 'Players and their Families', its series on the 'Private Lives' and 'Human Side' of players during the 1930s revealed something of the character, beliefs and interests of its subjects outside the game. According to Woolridge's own criteria, the 'consumption of the football star through knowledge of his personal life is a key element in establishing the existence of a more developed and wider stardom'. This desire to 'know' something about stars beyond what they did as performers may well have begun to transform the best-known footballers into genuine personalities and certainly suggests that the football 'star' was a more widespread phenomenon of the inter-war years, and especially the 1930s, than we used to think.[108]

British and international football

Recent research has shown the relationship between British football and the emerging game beyond its shores as more complex than was previously recognised. Popular accounts tend to regard Britain as the originator and pioneer: the nation that gave the game of football to the world. Walvin's claim that soccer was Britain's 'most durable export' and that the game followed the British flag around the globe has become a familiar one. In an important article, Mason argued that in the international diffusion of football

the feet of the English [sic.] were everywhere, playing the game in schools, playing it among themselves in the adult world outside ... and playing it in factories and railway yards. British soldiers carried footballs in their knapsacks and British sailors tucked them in their kitbags. British teams and British coaches were in demand all over Europe and beyond.[109]

The basic elements of this argument are undisputed. Significantly, the spread of the game followed the routes of trade rather than those of

Empire. As Bill Murray has observed, it was those countries with close commercial, educational and cultural links with Britain that adopted football first: Switzerland, Belgium and Denmark in Europe (with the Netherlands, Scandinavia, Germany and France close on their heels) and Argentina and Uruguay in South America. The process of dissemination seems to have followed a similar pattern in each case. First, expatriate Britons, particularly bankers, entrepreneurs, engineers, managers and technicians as well as teachers and students, began to play matches against one another. In time, members of the local aristocracy or traditional elites were drawn in, initially simply to make up the numbers or provide opposition for the British-dominated teams. Finally, these new indigenous groups assumed control of the game and the influence of the British declined. In this orthodox account, football emerges as a gift that the British generously bestowed on their less developed trading partners. On an individual level, British citizens were undoubtedly central in the foundation and initial development of football throughout the world. The names of Britons are to the forefront in national and club histories throughout Europe and South America. In Russia, it was the Lancastrian brothers Clement and Harry Charnock who in 1887 established a football team among workers at a textile factory in Orekhovo-Zuevo near Moscow. Alexander Watson Hutton, a teacher from Scotland, was involved in the introduction of school soccer and the development of Argentina's earliest organised competitions, becoming the first president of the Argentine Association Football League (later to become the Argentine Football Association) in 1893. The accepted founding father of Brazilian football was Charles Miller, who had been born in São Paulo but had an English father and played for Hampshire and the Corinthians while studying in England. Elsewhere, men such as the professor William Leslie Poole in Montevideo, the doctor James Spensley in Genoa and the student Tom Griffith in Zurich are all credited as local 'founders' of the association game.[110]

However, the impact of the British in the spread of world football was not necessarily so straightforward. Where older studies emphasise the direct role of the British, more recent interpretations have highlighted the broader appeal of football as an embodiment of British values and culture. In a series of articles, Lanfranchi has examined the complex processes through which the game was exported to a range of European regions and countries. He argues that Britons on the spot were in fact less important than those members of the continental elite who associated all things English (football included) with innovation and modernity. For these groups, playing football embodied a cosmopolitan and modern way of life to be contrasted with the traditional conventions of the nationalistic gymnastic organisations. Joining a football club was part of a broader mood of anglophilia among the continental bourgeoisie which also included wearing English clothes, giving English first names to their sons and adopting terms such as 'gentleman' and 'fair play'. The very first teams to be formed in Bologna, Bari, Naples, Milan, Lyons and Irun in Spain took on English names – such as 'Sporting Club', 'Black Star', 'Football Club' and 'Racing Club' – but significantly had no other connections with Britain. Likewise, the English-sounding Grasshoppers of Zurich, Young Boys of Bern and Be Quick of Groningen actually included few British players. For Lanfranchi, the most striking characteristic of these early European clubs was not their 'Britishness' but their cosmopolitanism. To take just one example, FC Barcelona was founded in 1899 by the Swiss accountant Hans Gamper and included in its first team players originating from Switzerland, Austria and Germany as well as Britain. Club founders such as Gamper were highly mobile, educated young men who exemplified 'the integration of a modern, urban and transnational society' rather than any particular form of British influence.[111] The case of Vittorio Pozzo, manager of Italy during their World Cup victories in the 1930s and a leading figure in the early development of European soccer, is revealing in this respect. Walvin has suggested that Pozzo developed a passion for football during his time studying English in Manchester and Bradford, yet, as Lanfranchi points out, he had learned about and played the game earlier than this, during his years at technical college in the Swiss town of Winterthur.[112]

That football was not transferred from Britain in any direct or straightforward manner is supported by the fact that a very different social constituency was drawn to the game abroad. Studies of football in the importing countries of Europe and South America show it as a largely middle-class and elite game well into the twentieth century, in contrast to its predominantly working-class character in Britain. As Christiane Eisenberg has noted, this was partly because industrialisation outside Britain was less advanced but also due to the limited contact between social classes (on and off the sports field) in countries like Germany and Russia and the marginal appeal of soccer elsewhere among workers who remained loyal to gymnastic clubs or indigenous sports. For this and other reasons, we need to adopt a broader perspective of the British influence on the beginnings of world football. To argue, as Walvin did, that the spread of football was the result of 'the missionary zeal of travelling Britons' is to oversimplify the complicated processes of dissemination, adaptation and modification that occurred on the ground in each of the importing countries.[113]

After the initial period of international diffusion in the late nineteenth and early twentieth centuries, Britain's relationship with the burgeoning game overseas cooled. Most writers have stressed the isolation and introversion of British football in this period. Alan Tomlinson put it thus: 'As the game took a grip on the world ... Britain stayed at home'. Walvin, meanwhile, dubbed the years 1915 to 1939 as the era of 'the insular game'.[114] British isolationism was manifest in the early history of the world governing body FIFA (Fédération Internationale de Football Association). Established in 1904 by representatives of seven European nations, FIFA was without British involvement for its first two years. Yet sensing that the new international body would be a permanent one, the British football associations finally joined in 1906, even proceeding to have their own man, D. B. Woolfall, elected as president. The British withdrew from FIFA in 1920 over the issue of how to treat the defeated wartime nations but rejoined in 1924, only to leave again in 1928 when disagreement surfaced over conflicting definitions of amateurism and the vexed issue of 'broken time' payments. The hauteur of the UK associations was illustrated in their letter of resignation, which rather patronisingly noted that as most of the FIFA's member associations were of recent formation, they 'cannot have the knowledge which only experience can bring'. A similar attitude was displayed in the British stance towards the World Cup: they rejected invitations to the first tournament in Uruguay in 1930, the second in Italy in 1934 and the third in France in 1938. Charles Sutcliffe, a leading figure in the Football League, dismissed the 1934 competition as 'a joke' and suggested that the British home internationals amounted to 'a far better World Championship than the one to be staged in Rome'. Matches against 'foreign' sides were consequently accorded a low priority. England was the most willing to face foreign competition but Scotland waited until 1929 for its first match against non-British opposition and Wales did not play abroad until 1933.[115]

Peter Beck has argued that this strain of isolationism – 'based on a strong concept of Britishness, a belief in the fundamental superiority of British football, and the primacy of the domestic leagues programmes' – dominated the thinking of the football authorities in this period.[116] However, we should not overlook the less formal connections that many British clubs, coaches and players established and retained with the developing game abroad. Above all, it was the twin impact of touring teams and migrant coaches that consolidated the British influence. The first regular football tourists were amateur sides from the south of England, such as Middlesex Wanderers and the famous Corinthians. The latter team of mostly public school students and teachers was rare in having the necessary time and money to venture beyond Europe, making their first overseas trip to South Africa in 1897 and returning in 1903 and 1907. They also visited Canada and the USA and Brazil several times before and after the First World War. Wherever they went, the Corinthians attracted considerable local interest and large crowds. They donated cups for local amateur clubs after visiting Hungary and Sweden and even passed on their name to a now famous team in São Paulo.[117] Professional clubs soon followed their amateur counterparts abroad. In his book *Soccer Revolution*, Willy Meisl recorded the pre-1914 visits of British clubs to his native Vienna: Southampton came in 1900, followed by Rangers and Celtic in 1904, Everton and Tottenham in 1905, Manchester United in 1908, Sunderland in 1909, Barnsley in 1910 and Blackburn Rovers, Oldham Athletic and Celtic again in 1911. Southampton, Everton and Tottenham likewise toured South America, as did Nottingham Forest, Swindon Town and Exeter City. Overseas tours increased in frequency and ranged in destination between the wars: North America joined South America and Europe as a common destination for representative and club sides. In 1938 alone, the FA sanctioned 197 Easter holiday matches between English and continental clubs and 20 close season tours. In some cases, long-standing cross-Channel relationships could be forged, as when Arsenal began its annual Armistice Day fixture against Racing Club de Paris, which was to last until the 1960s. Yet although clubs and associations still claimed to be promoting the game and building friendships when travelling abroad, the profit motive seems to have become decisive. Even the 'missionary' tours to the British dominions (Australia, Canada, New Zealand and South Africa) were becoming as much about covering expenses as about popularising the game.[118]

The expatriate British coach was arguably even more influential. According to Mason, Britons 'were to be found everywhere, from Spain to Hungary, to Italy and Uruguay'. Lanfranchi has seen them as 'representative of the wider pattern by which British technical and practical knowledge was exported by her engineers all over the globe'.[119] Jimmy Hogan was perhaps the best known to contemporaries. He retired from Bolton Wanderers as a player in 1911 and moved to Holland as coach of the national side, before going on to train national and club sides in Austria, Hungary, Germany, France and Switzerland throughout the inter-war period. He coached the Austrian side that finished runners-up at the 1936 Berlin Olympics and was involved with Hugo Meisl in the success of the Austrian 'Wonderteam' of the 1930s. A former Blackburn Rovers and Arsenal player, William Garbutt was equally influential as an itinerant coach. He joined Genoa in 1912, going on to coach Naples, Roma, Milan and Bilbao over a 36-year career. Although barely remembered in England, his legacy in Italy is as the first genuine football manager and a key figure in the rise of the professional game. According to one account, Garbutt 'brought the heritage of English football to Italy'. Similar observations could be made about the Scots John Madden, who managed Slavia Prague between 1905 and 1938, and John Hurley, who as coach of Penarol for over 50 years became a leading figure in the development of Uruguayan football.[120]

The 1920s and 1930s witnessed a boom in the export of British coaches as well as players, boosted by the general progress of football abroad and, more particularly, the creation of professional leagues in the USA and France. As many as 108 Scottish, Irish and English players were engaged by clubs in the American Soccer League in 1926–7, while some 43 British players and several British coaches lined up for the first French league season in 1932. Though relatively unknown in Britain, former professionals such as G. S. Kimpton, Ted Magner and Curtis Booth went on to acquire prestigious jobs with club and national sides in France, Belgium, Holland and Turkey. For all this, we should once again be careful of overestimating the role of the British. By the inter-war years, Britons were certainly not the only peripatetic footballers. Austrians, Czechs and Hungarians quickly nudged out the British as the dominant national groups in French football over the course of the 1930s. By 1933, Garbutt was the sole British representative alongside 45 Hungarian coaches in Italian football, while there were only two Britons among 500 coaches in Germany. Most contemporaries recognised that Central Europe had replaced Britain as the main reservoir of coaching talent throughout the continent by the Second World War.[121]

A further area of interest for historians has been the role of the British government in the emerging footballing relations between Britain and other countries. It used to be thought that sport in Britain was relatively free from mainstream politics and state intervention. At a time when it was thoroughly politicised in Nazi Germany, Fascist Italy and the Soviet Union, sport was still portrayed as a predominantly autonomous activity in Britain, subject to the control of voluntary and private sporting bodies and free of the input of politicians and civil servants. In this view, the infamous Nazi salute given by the England team before their victory over Germany in Berlin in May 1938 (under the advice of the British ambassador Nevile Henderson) has been regarded as 'an exception', a rare example of the Foreign Office using football as a diplomatic tool.[122] Studies by Stephen Jones, Martin Polley and Peter Beck offer a rather different picture. Jones has argued that the British government 'used football as an integral part of overseas cultural propaganda, seeking to portray Britain as a nation of justice and fair play and to support diplomatic objectives'.[123] A more recent study by Beck has outlined in painstaking detail the increasing intervention by the Foreign Office in the fixtures of the British, especially the English, national teams between the wars. As inter-war governments began to recognise that football could be used to support British interests and project a favourable image of the nation abroad, so they made attempts behind the scenes to influence the organisation of England fixtures by the FA, especially high-profile matches such as those with Germany in 1935 and 1938 and Italy in 1934. The Foreign Office claimed in 1938 that it had tried 'to discourage the staging of football matches with foreigners and that on more than one occasion we have drawn attention to the embarrassing situation created as the result of the visits abroad of poor teams'. Yet despite an increasing recognition in Whitehall that 'international football was too important to be left entirely to sporting bodies', there was a limit to the extent to which the state was able or willing to direct the actions of administrators and the performances of players. Beck has termed this approach 'an interventionist interpretation of non-intervention'.[124] In truth, it was only certain nationalistic sections of the press and some government officials who seriously regarded footballers in this period as ambassadors of the nation. Ultimately for a large part of the media, and most fans and players, overseas football was of little real interest and was only ever regarded as a temporary distraction from the more important concerns of domestic competition.[125]

The tendency to equate 'international' football with the annual championship between the representatives of England, Scotland, Ireland and Wales rather than matches against 'continental' or 'foreign' opponents continued to be a feature of the inter-war period. In Scotland particularly, the annual fixture with England grew in this period into a major popular cultural event. The success of the Scots – winning 12 of the 20 encounters between the wars – has led Christopher Harvie to refer to the years 1920–39 as the 'golden age' of Scottish football.[126] But the match was always about more than winning and it acquired a greater symbolic resonance in the context of two developments: the increasing flight of Scottish players to English clubs and the biannual trip to Wembley Stadium. We have seen in earlier chapters that the movement of Scots south of the border had always been a feature of British football but its significance grew between the wars, to a point where some 362 were employed in the four divisions of the English Football League in 1929. As Moorhouse points out, this has always provoked complex and contradictory reactions in Scotland: 'A fatalistic sense of loss mingles with the pride that the English simply cannot get by without taking Scottish talent'. National sentiment and recruitment problems led to the fielding of 'all-tartan teams' (Scots employed by Scottish clubs) against England in 1925, 1931 and 1932, but the greatest Scottish success of the period came in 1928 when a team consisting mainly of Anglo-Scots defeated the 'auld enemy' 5–1 at Wembley, the new home of English football. By the early 1930s, the trip to Wembley had already established itself as a sporting tradition and a ritualistic expression of national feeling. By 1936 some 30,000 Scots were travelling south for the fixture, many resplendent in tam o' shanters and scarves, decked in thistles and some carrying rattles, accordions and tin frying pans to make their presence felt outside and inside the stadium. There was little crowd trouble at these games, but Moorhouse notes that the war-like metaphors employed by Scottish newspapers and in the banners and chants of the fans revealed it as 'much more than "a day out"'. Scottish resentment of its richer and more powerful footballing neighbour was channelled into the biannual raid on London and the sporting 'battle' with England that was its centrepiece.[127]

The progress of Welsh football was the result of the success of club sides more than the national team. Cardiff City became the first Welsh club to enter the English Football League in 1920 and was joined a year later by Swansea Town, Newport County, Aberdare Athletic, Merthyr Town and Wrexham. That the best professional clubs in the principality were anxious to test themselves in English company, and willing to treat the Welsh leagues and cups as nothing more than reserve competitions, was revealing of the inequitable economic and political relationship between the two countries. Yet it also shows that Welsh and British identities could easily coexist in Welsh football. The success of Cardiff in the 1920s offers an excellent example of this. The club narrowly missed out on the Football League championship in 1924 but reached the FA Cup final a year later and in 1927 became the first and only non-English side to win the trophy. That match, against Arsenal, had been presented as a battle between Wales and England. The 40,000 or so fans who descended on London (from all parts of Wales) wore leeks, carried Welsh flags and sang 'Land of my fathers'. The press in both countries portrayed this as a metaphorical Welsh invasion to take away the English cup. Cardiff won the game 1–0 with a team consisting of only three Welshmen alongside four Irishmen, three Scots and an Englishman, but the victory was still perceived by press and supporters alike as a national achievement. Yet while celebrating Welshness, such events also emphasised a broader sense of British unity. The FA Cup final at Wembley was an English event but also part of a wider British popular culture. In this case, as elsewhere in Welsh football, 'a pride in Wales sat comfortably alongside a sense of Britishness'.[128]

The performance of Wales in the home international championship was much better than it had been before 1914. Despite the perennial problem of obtaining the release of players with English clubs, Wales took the trophy home in 1920, 1924, 1928, 1933, 1934 and 1937, shared it in 1939, and defeated the English Goliath on no less than eight occasions between the wars. Yet neither the size of crowds nor the enthusiasm of press and supporters matched the club game. A crowd of just 8,000 watched the home side defeat England at Swansea in 1925, while the Cardiff press claimed that the fate of their club in the First Division was more important to the national cause than a Welsh victory that day. Attendances improved along with performances from the mid-1930s, but Johnes has claimed that with so many players based in England any victory was tinged with an element of sadness. International football had not yet reached the same level of national significance ascribed to rugby union and no triumph by the national side could match the 'unrestrained national celebration' associated with Cardiff's 1927 success.[129]

Perhaps the most noteworthy issue within British football in this period involved the position of the Irish game in the wake of political partition in 1922. During the previous year the Leinster FA had seceded from the Irish Football Association (IFA) in the north to form the Football Association of Ireland (FAI). A separate League of Ireland consisting of Dublin clubs was also established, leaving the Irish League an entirely northern preserve. Football in Ireland was thus effectively separated between the six counties of Ulster in the north and the 26 counties of the new Irish Free State in the south. Most writers have regarded this division as a straightforward consequence of the wider political partition. Thus the Irish historian Dermot Keogh argued that the game became 'a victim of political tensions' while for Mike Cronin 'Ireland's politics ... divided soccer along the lines of partition'.[130] Neal Garnham has recently articulated an alternative view. Like most writers, he places considerable emphasis on the Belfast–Dublin tensions of the early 1920s, particularly the IFA's controversial decision that Dublin side Shelbourne should return to Belfast for its 1921 Irish Cup semi-final replay, but suggests that these merely built upon a history of mutual distrust and a long-standing power struggle between the two centres. Rather than initiating the football split, Garnham concludes that the political situation 'provided a window of opportunity through which the various proponents of the game could leap'. Indeed even after 1921 it was far from inevitable that the Irish game would develop along separate paths. Most sports in Ireland either retained an all-Ireland structure (Gaelic games and rugby) or actually unified for the first time during the political pressures of the period (athletics and cricket), while in soccer two years of negotiations between the IFA and FAI 'came within a hair's breath' of reunifying the game.[131] In 1923, however, the division hardened when the renamed Football Association of the Irish Free State (FAIFS) was admitted into membership of FIFA and formally recognised as the authority of the game within its borders. It may have been accepted by the world governing body but it is significant that the FAIFS remained excluded from the British football fraternity throughout the inter-war years. In spite of political partition, the IFA continued to regard itself, and to be recognised by its sister associations, as the 'national association' of Ireland and its representative on the rule-making International Board and in the home international championship. The team we now call Northern Ireland played internationally as 'Ireland' and selected its players from the whole of Ireland, including those born in the Irish Free State. As far as the British football authorities were concerned, there was only one Ireland.[132]

References

1 Nicholas Fishwick, *English Football and Society, 1910–1950* (Manchester: Manchester University Press, 1989); Stephen Jones, *Sport, Politics and the Working Class: Organised Labour and Sport in Interwar Britain* (Manchester: Manchester University Press, 1988); Dave Russell, *Football and the English: A Social History of Association Football in England, 1863–1995* (Preston: Carnegie, 1997), chapters 4 and 5.

2 Martin Johnes, *Soccer and Society: South Wales, 1900–1939* (Cardiff: University of Wales Press, 2002); Fishwick, *English Football*, p. 1.

3 Derek Birley, *Playing the Game: Sport and British Society, 1910–45*

(Manchester: Manchester University Press, 1995), pp. 56–76; Matthew Taylor, 'Leisure and Entertainment' in J. Bourne, P. Liddle and I. Whitehead (eds), *The Great World War, 1914–45*, Vol. 2: *The People's Experience* (London: HarperCollins, 2001), pp. 378–94.

4 Tony Mason, *Association Football and English Society, 1863–1915* (Brighton: Harvester, 1980), pp. 251–5; Colin Veitch, '"Play Up! Play Up! And Win the War!": Football, the Nation and the First World War, 1914–15', *Journal of Contemporary History*, 20, 3 (July 1985), pp. 363–78; John M. Osborne, '"To Keep the Life of the Nation on the Old Lines": *The Athletic News* and the First World War', *Journal of Sport History*, 14, 2 (Summer 1987), pp. 143–4; Simon Inglis, *League Football and the Men Who Made It: The Official History of the Football League, 1888–1988* (London: Collins Willow, 1988), p. 96; Ian Nannestad, '"The Charge at Football is Good, That With the Bayonet Finer": The Formation of the Footballers' Battalion, 1914', *Soccer History*, 1 (Spring 2002), pp. 3–6.

5 Veitch, 'Play Up', pp. 370, 375; Birley, *Playing the Game*, pp. 72–3; Fishwick, *English Football*, pp. 144–5; Johnes, *Soccer and Society*, p. 52.

6 Football Association Minute Books 1914–15, Scottish Football Association, The War and Football: Delegates' Report, 14 December 1914.

7 A. J. Arnold, '"Not Playing the Game"?: Leeds City in the Great War', *International Journal of the History of Sport*, 7 (May 1990), p. 112.

8 Fishwick, *English Football*, p. 145; Mason, *Association Football*, 253; Neal Garnham, *Association Football and Society in Pre-Partition Ireland* (Belfast: Irish Historical Foundation, 2004), p. 169; Bob Crampsey, *The First 100 Years: The Scottish Football League* (Glasgow: Scottish Football League, 1990), p. 58.

9 *Athletic News*, 26 July 1915.

10 Inglis, *League Football*, pp. 97–100; Matthew Taylor, *The Leaguers: The Making of Professional Football in England, 1900–1939* (Liverpool: Liverpool University Press, 2005), pp. 70–1; Johnes, *Soccer and Society*, p. 53.

11 Crampsey, *First 100 Years*, pp. 57–70; Garnham, *Association Football*, p. 168.

12 Russell, *Football and the English*, 75; Mason, *Association Football*, p. 242; Tony Collins, 'English Rugby Union and the First World War', *The Historical Journal*, 45, 4 (2002), pp. 815–16.

13 Simon Inglis, *Soccer in the Dock* (London: Willow, 1985); Arnold, 'Not Playing the Game', p. 117.

14 J. G. Fuller, *Troop Morale and Popular Culture in the British and*

Dominion Armies 1914–1918 (Oxford: Clarendon, 1991), pp. 85–94; quotations pp. 85, 87.

15 Fuller, *Troop Morale*, pp. 88–94, 175; James Roberts, '"The Best Football Team, The Best Platoon": The Role of Football in the Proletarianization of the British Expeditionary Force, 1914–1918', *Sport in History*, 26, 1 (April 2006), pp. 26–46; J. D. Campbell, '"Training for Sport is Training for War": Sport and the Transformation of the British Army, 1860–1914', *International Journal of the History of Sport*, 17, 4 (December 2000), pp. 21–58.

16 Johnes, *Soccer and Society*, pp. 82–3; Tony Mason, 'Football' in T. Mason (ed.), *Sport in Britain: A Social History* (Cambridge: Cambridge University Press, 1989), pp. 150, 182 (n. 6).

17 Johnes, *Soccer and Society*, p. 82; Raich Carter, *Footballer's Progress* (London: Sporting Handbooks, 1950), 19; Brad Beaven, *Leisure, Citizenship and Working-Class Men in Britain* (Manchester: Manchester University Press, 2005), p. 107.

18 Ross McKibbin, *Classes and Cultures: England 1918–1950* (Oxford: Oxford University Press, 1998), 340; Stephen Humphries, *Hooligans or Rebels?: An Oral History of Working-Class Childhood and Youth, 1889–1939* (Oxford: Basil Blackwell, 1981), p. 204; Andrew Davies, 'Leisure in the "Classic Slum", 1900–1939' in A. Davies and S. Fielding (eds), *Workers' Worlds: Cultures and Communities in Manchester and Salford, 1880–1939* (Manchester: Manchester University Press), 1992), p. 126. See also Stephen G. Jones, *Workers at Play: A Social and Economic History of Leisure, 1918–1939* (London: Routledge & Kegan Paul, 1986), pp. 75–80.

19 Fishwick, *English Football*, p. 6; Geoffrey Green, *The History of the Football Association* (London: Naldrett, 1953), pp. 440, 443; Colm Kerrigan, *A History of the English Schools' Football Association, 1904–2004* (Trowbridge: English Schools' Football Association, 2004), p. 50; C. E. Sutcliffe and F. Hargreaves, *History of the Lancashire Football Association, 1878–1928* (Harefield: Yore, 1992 [1st edition, 1928]), p. 228; Alec E. Whitcher, *The Voice of Soccer* (Brighton: Southern Publishing, 1946), pp. 110–11; Johnes, *Soccer and Society*, p. 88; Carter, *Footballer's Progress*, p. 22. The quotation is from Whitcher, *Voice of Soccer*, p. 110.

20 Fishwick, *English Football*, pp. 4–7.

21 Green, *History of the Football Association*, pp. 432–5.

22 Fishwick, *English Football*, pp. 1–2; Johnes, *Soccer and Society*, p. 90; Sutcliffe and Hargreaves, *Lancashire Football Association*, pp. 22, 25, 127–8.

23 Fishwick, *English Football*, p. 15; Jack Williams, 'Churches, Sport and Identities in the North, 1900–1939' in J. Hill and J. Williams (eds), *Sport and Identity in the North of England* (Keele: Keele University Press, 1996), pp. 122–3.

24 Johnes, *Soccer and Society*, p. 108; Fishwick, *English Football*, p. 14.

25 Jones, *Workers at Play*, pp. 94–5 (Table 4.2). He has offered an equally optimistic overview of provision in Manchester, where the city parks alone could boast 201 football and hockey pitches to accommodate 400 or so teams. See Stephen Jones, 'Working-Class Sport in Manchester Between the Wars' in R. Holt (ed.), *Sport and the Working Class in Modern Britain* (Manchester: Manchester University Press, 1990), pp. 75, 78.

26 Fishwick, *English Football*, pp. 7–11; Williams, 'Church, Sport and Identities', p. 123; Jones, *Workers at Play*, p. 97; Johnes, *Soccer and Society*, p. 100; David Bowker, 'Parks and Baths: Sport, Recreation and Municipal Government in Ashton-under-Lyme Between the Wars' in Holt (ed.), *Sport and the Working Class*, p. 91.

27 Fishwick, *English Football*, pp. 8–10; Johnes, *Soccer and Society*, pp. 100–1; Bowker, 'Parks and Baths', p. 92.

28 See Roger Munting, 'The Games Ethic and Industrial Capitalism before 1914: The Provision of Company Sports', *Sport in History*, 23, 1 (Summer 2003), pp. 58, 62; Simon Phillips, '"Fellowship in Recreation, Fellowship in Ideals": Sport, Leisure and Culture at Boots Pure Drug Company, Nottingham *c.* 1883–1945', *Midland History*, 29 (2004), pp. 107–23.

29 McKibbin, *Classes and Cultures*, p. 341; Stephen Jones, 'Cotton Employers and Industrial Welfare Between the Wars' in J. A. Jowitt and A. J. McIvor, *Employers and Labour in the English Textile Industries, 1850–1939* (London: Routledge, 1988), p. 71; Mason, 'Football', p. 149; Johnes, *Soccer and Society*, pp. 91 (Table 3.2).

30 Williams, 'Churches, Sport and Identities', p. 124; Mason, 'Football', p. 149; Johnes, *Soccer and Society*, pp. 103–4; Fishwick, *English Football*, pp. 12–14.

31 Williams, 'Churches, Sport and Identities', p. 124; Johnes, *Soccer and Society*, p. 103; Fishwick, *English Football*, p. 12

32 Peter Bilsborough, 'The Development of Sport in Glasgow, 1850–1914', unpublished M.Litt. thesis, University of Stirling, 1983, pp. 144–8; Chris Harvie, 'Sport and the Scottish State' in G. Jarvie and G. Walker (eds), *Scottish Sport in the Making of the Nation: Ninety-Minute Patriots?* (Leicester: Leicester University Press, 1994), p. 53; George Raynor, *Football Ambassador at Large* (London: Soccer Book Club, 1960), p. 9.

33 Stephen Jones, *Sport, Politics and the Working Class: Organised Labour*

and Sport in Interwar Britain (Manchester: Manchester University Press, 1988), pp. 93, 108, 150–4; *Daily Worker*, 2, 16 October 1934; Williams, 'Church, Sport and Identities', pp. 120–1; Jones, 'Working-Class Sport in Manchester', p. 76; Johnes, *Soccer and Society*, pp. 90–2, 106–7; Fishwick, *English Football*, p. 16.

34 David McGlone and Bill McLure, *The Juniors – 100 Years: A Centenary History of Scottish Junior Football* (Edinburgh: Mainstream, 1987); John Harding, *Alex James: Life of a Football Legend* (London: Robson, 1988), pp. 15–27.

35 McGlone and McLure, *The Juniors*, pp. 125–33.

36 Green, *History of the Football Association*, pp. 453–4; Brian Hunt, *Northern Goalfields Revisited: The Millennium History of the Northern Football League, 1889–2000* (Northern Football League, 2000), pp. 108, 172.

37 Mason, 'Football', p. 148; Mike Amos, 'Storms in a Tea Cup' in Hunt, *Northern Goalfields*, pp. 484–90.

38 John Williams and Jackie Woodhouse, 'Can Play, Will Play?: Women and Football in Britain', in J. Williams and S. Wagg, *British Football and Social Change: Getting into Europe* (Leicester: Leicester University Press, 1991), pp. 90–1; Jean Williams, *A Game for Rough Girls?: A History of Women's Football in Britain* (London: Routledge, 2003), pp. 31–3; Alethea Melling, '"Plucky Lasses", "Pea Soup" and Politics: The Role of Ladies' Football during the 1921 Miners' Lock-Out in Wigan and Leigh', *International Journal of the History of Sport*, 16, 1 (March 1999), pp. 38–64; Tony Mason, 'Rise and Strange Decline of Women's Football', unpublished paper, n.d.; David Williamson, *Belles of the Ball* (Devon: R & D Associates, 1991), p. 83; Johnes, *Soccer and Society*, p. 109; Jessica Macbeth, 'The Development of Women's Football in Scotland', *The Sports Historian*, 22, 2 (November 2002), p. 153.

39 See Gail J. Newsham, *In a League of Their Own!: The Dick, Kerr Ladies Football Team* (London: Scarlet, 1997 [1st edition, 1994]), chapters 1–5.

40 Williams and Woodhouse, 'Can Play, Will Play', p. 91; Macbeth, 'Women's Football in Scotland', p. 154; Johnes, *Soccer and Society*, p. 110; Alethea Melling, 'Cultural Differentiation, Shared Aspiration: The Entente Cordiale of International Ladies' Football, 1920–45' in J. A. Mangan, *Sport in Europe: Politics, Class, Gender* (London: Frank Cass, 1999), pp. 27–53; Williamson, *Belles of the Ball*, p. 15.

41 Johnes, *Soccer and Society*, p. 110.

42 Newsham, *League of Their Own*, p. 49; Williams, *Game for Rough Girls*, p. 34.

43 Williams and Woodhouse, 'Can Play, Will Play', p. 92; Alethea Melling, '"Ray of the Rovers": The Working-Class Heroine in Popular Football Fiction, 1915–25', *International Journal of the History of Sport*, 15, 1 (April 1998), p. 98. See also Newsham, *League of Their Own*, p. 51.

44 Melling, 'Cultural Differentiation', p. 44; Newsham, *League of Their Own*, pp. 55–69; Williams, *Game for Rough Girls*, pp. 31, 46–7.

45 Williams, *Game for Rough Girls*, p. 36; Johnes, *Soccer and Society*, p. 111; Macbeth, 'Women's Football in Scotland', p. 157; Munting, 'Games Ethic', p. 61.

46 Russell, *Football and the English*, pp. 96–7; Melling, 'Ray of the Rovers', p. 119.

47 Gertrud Pfister, Kari Fasting, Sheila Scraton and Benilde Vzquez, 'Women and Football – A Contradiction?: The Beginnings of Women's Football in Four European Countries' in Mangan (ed.), *Sport in Europe*, p. 22.

48 Fishwick, *English Football*, pp. 56, 58.

49 Eric Hobsbawm, *Worlds of Labour: Further Studies in the History of Labour* (London: Weidenfeld & Nicolson, 1984), p. 186 and 'Mass-Producing Traditions: Europe, 1870–1914', in E. Hobsbawm and T. Ranger, *The Invention of Tradition* (Cambridge: Cambridge University Press, 1983), p. 287; Johnes, *Soccer and Society*, p. 115; Mason, *Association Football*, p. 157.

50 Russell, *Football and the English*, p. 98; Davies, 'Leisure in the "Classic Slum"', p. 111.

51 Johnes, *Soccer and Society*, pp. 119–20; Fishwick, *English Football*, p. 56; Dave Russell, 'Football and Society in the North-West, 1919–1939', *North West Labour History*, 24 (1999/2000), p. 11; Rogan Taylor, *Football and its Fans: Supporters and their Relations with the Game* (Leicester: Leicester University Press, 1992), pp. 38, 44–5.

52 Tom Watt, *The End: 80 Years of Life on the Terraces* (Edinburgh: Mainstream, 1993), p. 44; Eric Dunning, Patrick Murphy and John Williams, *The Roots of Football Hooliganism: An Historical and Sociological Study* (London: Routledge & Kegan Paul, 1988), pp. 118–19.

53 Russell, 'Football and Society', p. 11.

54 Patrick Murphy, John Williams and Eric Dunning, *Football on Trial: Spectator Violence and Development in the Football World* (London: Routledge, 1990), p. 78; Williams and Woodhouse, 'Can Play, Will Play?', p. 95.

55 Dunning, Murphy and Williams, *Roots of Football Hooliganism*,

pp. 100–1; Claire Langhamer, *Women's Leisure in England, 1920–60* (Manchester: Manchester University Press, 2000), p. 83.

56 Johnes, *Soccer and Society*, p. 117–19; Russell, *Football and the English*, p. 99; Fishwick, *English Football*, p. 58.

57 Fishwick, *English Football*, p. 58; Russell, *Football and the English*, p. 99.

58 Fishwick, *English Football*, p. 59

59 Watt, *The End*, p. 55; Russell, *Football and the English*, p. 99–100; Bill Murray, *The Old Firm: Sectarianism, Sport and Society in Scotland* (Edinburgh: John Donald, 2000 [1st edition, 1984]), p. 18.

60 Murray, *Old Firm*, pp. 144–6; Kenneth Wolstenholme, *Sports Special* (London: Sportsmans Book Club, 1958), p. 82.

61 Fishwick, *English Football*, p. 60; Tommy Lawton, *Football is my Business* (London: Sporting Handbooks, 1946), pp. 74–5; Stanley Matthews, *Feet First Again* (London: Nicholas Kaye, 1952), p. 29.

62 Johnes, *Soccer and Society*, pp. 120–3; Simon Inglis, *The Football Grounds of Britain* (London: Collins Willow, 1993 [1st edition, 1983]), pp. 18–19; Watt, *The End*, pp. 33, 52.

63 Martin Johnes, '"Heads in the Sand": Football, Politics and Crowd Disasters in Twentieth-Century Britain', pp. 12–13 and Jeffrey Hill, '"The Day was an Ugly One": Wembley, 28th April 1923', pp. 28–44, both in P. Darby, M. Johnes and G. Mellor (eds), *Soccer and Disasters: International Perspectives* (London: Routledge, 2005); Callum G. Brown, 'Sport and the Scottish Office in the Twentieth Century' in Mangan (ed.), *Sport in Europe*, pp. 173–4.

64 Quoted in Watt, *The End*, p. 52.

65 Arthur Hopcraft, *The Football Man: People and Passions in Soccer* (London: Simon & Schuster, 1988 [1st edition, 1968]), p. 9.

66 J. B. Priestley, *The Good Companions* (London: Heinemann, 1976 [1st edition, 1929]), pp. 13–14.

67 Russell, *Football and the English*, p. 122; Richard Holt, *Sport and the British: A Modern History* (Oxford: Clarendon, 1989), p. 165.

68 Johnes, *Soccer and Society*, pp. 126–7; John Bale, 'Playing at Home: British Football and a Sense of Place', in Williams and Wagg, *British Football and Social Change*, pp. 130–44.

69 Russell, 'Football and Society', pp. 6–8; Holt, *Sport and the British*, p. 172; Fishwick, *English Football*, pp. 52–3.

70 Daniel L. Wann, Merrill J. Melnick, Gordon W. Russell and Dale G. Pease,

Sport Fans: The Psychology and Social Impact of Spectators (London: Routledge, 2001), pp. 2–3.

71 Tony Mason, 'All the Winners and the Half Times . . .', *The Sports Historian*, 13 (May 1993), pp. 3–13; *Association Football*, pp. 187–95; Holt, *Sport and the British*, pp. 306–11; Russell, *Football and the English*, pp. 103–4; Fishwick, *English Football*, pp. 100–1.

72 Fishwick, *English Football*, p. 94.

73 Mason, 'All the Winners', pp. 6–7; Fishwick, *English Football*, pp. 96–7, 101–4; Johnes, *Soccer and Society*, pp. 11–13; David Rowe, 'Modes of Sports Writing', in P. Dahlgren and C. Sparks (eds), *Journalism and Popular Culture* (London: Sage, 1992), pp. 96–112; *Sport, Culture and the Media: The Unruly Trinity* (Maidenhead: Open University Press, 1999), pp. 106–14.

74 Jeffrey Hill, *Sport, Leisure and Culture in Twentieth-Century Britain* (Basingstoke: Palgrave, 2002), chapter 3 and 'Anecdotal Evidence: Sport, the Newspaper Press and History' in Murray G. Phillips (eds), *Deconstructing Sport History: A Postmodern Analysis* (New York: SUNY Press, 2006), pp. 117–29; Michael Oriard, *Reading Football: How the Popular Press Created an American Spectacle* (Chapel Hill: University of North Carolina Press, 1993), pp. xviii–xxiii. See also Johnes, *Soccer and Society*, p. 10.

75 Luke McKernan, 'Sport and the First Films', in C. Williams (ed.), *Cinema: The Beginnings and the Future* (London: University of Westminster Press, 1996), pp. 113–15; Fishwick, *English Football*, pp. 110–11. On early football on film and the relationship between football and the world of feature film and the music hall, see respectively Vanessa Toulmin, '"Vivid and Realistic": Edwardian Sport in Film', *Sport in History*, 26, 1 (April 2006), pp. 124–49; Andrew Horrall, *Popular Culture in London, c.1890–1918: The Transformation of Entertainment* (Manchester: Manchester University Press, 2001), chapter 11.

76 Russell, *Football and the English*, pp. 106–7; Holt, *Sport and the British*, p. 311–14; Fishwick, *English Football*, pp. 107–10; Stephen Wagg, *The Football World: A Contemporary Social History* (Brighton: Harvester, 1984), pp. 41–2; Richard Haynes, '"There's Many a Slip 'Twixt the Eye and the Lip": An Exploratory History of Football Broadcasts and Running Commentaries on BBC Radio, 1927–1939', *International Review for the Sociology of Sport*, 34, 2 (1999), p. 144.

77 Fishwick, *English Football*, pp. 108–9; Matthew Taylor, *The Leaguers: The Making of Professional Football in England, 1900–1939* (Liverpool: Liverpool University Press, 2005), p. 269; Crampsey, *First 100 Years*, pp. 87–8.

78 Haynes, 'There's Many a Slip', pp. 147, 152; Holt, *Sport and the British*,
    p. 312.

79 Mark Clapson, *A Bit of a Flutter: Popular Gambling and English Society,
    c.1823–1961* (Manchester: Manchester University Press, 1992), chapter 7;
    Walvin, *People's Game*, pp. 125–8; Russell, *Football and the English*,
    p. 105; Stephen Jones, 'The Economic Aspects of Association Football in
    England, 1918–1939', *British Journal of Sports History*, 1, 3 (December
    1984), p. 295; *The Economist*, 29 February 1936, 17 April 1937. See also
    Graham Sharpe, *Gambling on Goals: A Century of Football Betting*
    (Edinburgh: Mainstream, 1997).

80 Walvin, *People's Game*, p. 127; McKibbin, *Classes and Cultures*, p. 374;
    Clapson, *Bit of a Flutter*, pp. 174, 176–7; Fishwick, *English Football*,
    pp. 122–3.

81 Dunning, Murphy and Williams, *Roots of Football Hooliganism*. For
    discussions of the Leicester work see Richard Giulianotti, 'Social Identity
    and Public Order: Political and Academic Discourses on Football Violence',
    in R. Giulianotti, N. Bonney and M. Hepworth, *Football, Violence and
    Social Identity* (London: Routledge, 1994), pp. 10–36 and in the same
    volume, Eric Dunning, 'The Social Roots of Football Hooliganism: A Reply
    to the Critics of the "Leicester School" ', pp. 128–57; Richard Giulianotti,
    Football: A Sociology of the Global Game (Cambridge: Polity, 1999),
    pp. 44–7.

82 Dunning, Murphy and Williams, *Roots of Football Hooliganism*, chapters
    5 and 6; Murphy, Williams and Dunning, *Football on Trial*, pp. 74–7.

83 Fishwick, *English Football*, pp. 62–5; Holt, *Sport and the British*,
    pp. 331–6; McKibbin, *Classes and Cultures*, p. 343; Dunning, Murphy and
    Williams, *Roots of Football Hooliganism*, p. 131. See also Jeffrey Richards,
    'Football and the Crisis of British Identity' in S. Caunce, E. Mazierska,
    S. Sydney-Smith and J. Walton (eds), *Relocating Britishness* (Manchester:
    Manchester University Press, 2004), p. 97.

84 Russell, *Football and the English*, p. 121; Hill, 'Wembley', pp. 35, 36.

85 Murray, *Old Firm*, pp. 119–20, 139–44

86 Dunning, Murphy and Williams, *Roots of Football Hooliganism*,
    pp. 113–17.

87 See R. W. Lewis, 'Football Hooliganism in England before 1914: A
    Critique of the Dunning Thesis', *International Journal of the History of
    Sport*, 13, 3 (1996), pp. 310–19; Martin Johnes, 'Hooligans and
    Barrackers: Crowd Disorder and Soccer in South Wales, c.1906–36', *Soccer
    and Society*, 1, 2 (Summer 2000), pp. 19–35.

88 Johnes, 'Hooligans and Barrackers', p. 31.

89 Richard Holt and J. A. Mangan, 'Prologue: Heroes of a European Past', in R. Holt, J. A. Mangan and P. Lanfranchi (eds), *European Heroes: Myth, Identity, Sport* (London: Frank Cass, 1996), p. 5.

90 See John Bale, Mette K. Christiansen and Gertrud Pfister (eds), *Writing Lives in Sport: Biographies, Life-Histories and Methods* (Langelandsgade: Aarhus University Press, 2004).

91 Tony Mason, '"Our Stephen and Our Harold": Edwardian Footballers as Local Heroes', in Holt, Mangan and Lanfranchi (eds), *European Heroes*, p. 71.

92 Jeff Hill, 'Reading the Stars: Towards a Post-Modernist Approach to Sports History', *The Sports Historian*, 14 (May 1994), pp. 45–55; 'British Sports History: A Post-Modern Future?', *Journal of Sport History*, 23, 1 (Spring 1996), pp. 1–19; '"Brylcreem Boy": Inter-Textual Signification in the Life of Denis Compton' in Bale, Christiansen and Pfister (eds), *Writing Lives*, pp. 171–8.

93 Leah R. Vande Berg, 'The Sports Hero Meets Mediated Celebrityhood', in L. A. Wenner (ed.), *MediaSport* (London: Routledge, 1998), p. 134.

94 Richard Holt, 'Champions, Heroes and Celebrities: Sporting Greatness and the British Public', in *The Book of British Sporting Heroes* (London: National Portrait Gallery, 1998), p. 12.

95 Steven Reiss, *Sport in Industrial America, 1850–1920* (Wheeling, Illinois: Harlan Davidson, 1995), p. 10.

96 Holt and Mangan, 'Prologue', p. 6; Pierre Lanfranchi, 'Unaccomplished Heroes: Three Sporting Biographies between Algeria and France', unpublished paper, n.d.; Eduardo P. Archetti, 'The Spectacle of a Heroic Life: The Case of Diego Maradona', in D. L. Andrews and S. J. Jackson (eds), *Sports Stars: The Cultural Politics of Sporting Celebrity* (London: Routledge, 2001), pp. 151–63.

97 H. F. Moorhouse, 'Shooting Stars: Footballers and Working-Class Culture in Twentieth-Century Scotland', in Holt (ed.), *Sport and the Working Class*, p. 180; Holt, 'Champions, Heroes and Celebrities', p. 12.

98 Richard Holt, 'Cricket and Englishness: The Batsman as Hero', in Holt, Mangan and Lanfranchi (eds), *European Heroes*, pp. 48–70; 'The Batsman as Gentleman: Inter-War Cricket and the English Hero', in G. Cubitt and A. Warren (eds), *Heroic Reputations and Exemplary Lives* (Manchester: Manchester University Press, 2000), pp. 225–40.

99 Chas Critcher, 'Football Since the War', in J. Clarke, C. Critcher and R. Johnson (eds), *Working-Class Culture: Studies in History and Theory* (London: Hutchinson, 1979), p. 163; Mason, 'Our Stephen and Our Harold'.

100 Richard Holt, 'Heroes of the North: Sport and the Shaping of Regional Identity', in Hill and Williams (eds), *Sport and Identity*, pp. 150–7; Fishwick, *English Football*, p. 84; Percy Young, *A History of British Football* (London: Arrow, 1973 [1st edition, 1968]), pp. 235–6; Martin Johnes, 'Fred Keenor: A Welsh Soccer Hero', *The Sports Historian*, 18, 1 (1998), pp. 105–19. On the different types of 'terrace hero', see Graham Kelly, *Terrace Heroes: The Life and Times of the 1930s Professional Footballer* (London: Routledge, 2005), pp. 1–5. Holt's notion of the particular traits of 'northern' heroes is challenged in Nicholas A. Phelps, 'The Southern Football Hero and the Shaping of Local and Regional Identity in the South of England', *Soccer and Society*, 2, 3 (Autumn 2001), pp. 44–57.

101 Moorhouse, 'Shooting Stars', pp. 189, 185–6; Bob Crampsey, *The Scottish Footballer* (Edinburgh: William Blackwood, 1978), p. 11.

102 Moorhouse, 'Shooting Stars', pp. 192–3, 188; Alan Bairner, 'Football', in G. Jarvie and J. Burnett (eds), *Sport, Scotland and the Scots* (East Linton: Tuckwell, 2000), p. 98.

103 Giulianotti, *Football*, pp. 116–21; Critcher, 'Football since the War', pp. 164–5; Moorhouse, 'Shooting Stars', pp. 181, 191.

104 Joyce Woolridge, 'Mapping the Stars: Stardom in English Professional Football, 1890–1946', *Soccer and Society*, 3, 2 (Summer 2002), pp. 51–69; McKibbin, *Classes and Cultures*, p. 344. For views similar to those of McKibbin, see Holt, *Sport and the British*, p. 324; Hobsbawm, 'Mass-Producing Traditions', p. 289.

105 Woolridge, 'Mapping the Stars', pp. 53.

106 Woolridge, 'Mapping the Stars', pp. 56–61; John Harding, 'Billy Meredith', in P. Stead and H. Richards (eds), *For Club and Country: Welsh Football Greats* (Cardiff: University of Wales Press, 2000), p. 16; John Harding, *Football Wizard: The Story of Billy Meredith* (Derby: Breedon, 1985); Peter Seddon, *Steve Bloomer: The Story of Football's First Superstar* (Derby: Breedon, 1999).

107 Woolridge, 'Mapping the Stars', p. 61; Kelly, *Terrace Heroes*, pp. 43–50, 153; Fishwick, *English Football*, p. 106.

108 Russell, *Football and the English*, pp. 104–5; Matthew Taylor, 'Work and Play: The Professional Footballer in England, *c*.1900–1950', *The Sports Historian*, 22, 1 (May 2002), pp. 30–1; Woolridge, 'Mapping the Stars', pp. 52–3.

109 Walvin, *People's Game*, chapter 5; Willy Meisl, *Soccer Revolution* (London: Panther Edition, 1957 [1st edition, 1955]), chapter 5; Tony Mason, 'Some Englishmen and Scotsmen Abroad: The Spread of World Football', in A. Tomlinson and G. Whannel (eds), *Off the Ball: The Football World Cup* (London: Pluto, 1986), pp. 67–82.

110 Bill Murray, *The World's Game: A History of Soccer* (Urbana: University of Illinois Press, 1998), pp. 22–35; Christiane Eisenberg, 'From England to the World: The Spread of Modern Football, 1863–2000', *Moving Bodies*, 1, 1 (2003), pp. 12–13; Walvin, *People's Game*, pp. 97–109; Tony Mason, *Passion of the People?: Football in South America* (London: Verso, 1995), chapter 1. On the British influence on Russian and Brazilian football respectively, see Peter A. Frykholm, 'Soccer and Social Identity in Pre-Revolutionary Moscow', *Journal of Sport History*, 24, 2 (Summer 1997), pp. 143–54; Aidan Hamilton, *An Entirely Different Game: The British Influence on Brazilian Football* (Edinburgh: Mainstream, 1998).

111 Pierre Lanfranchi, 'Exporting Football: Notes on the Development of Football in Europe', in R. Giulianotti and J. Williams (eds), *Game Without Frontiers: Football, Identity and Modernity* (Aldershot: Arena, 1994), pp. 23–45; Pierre Lanfranchi, with Stephen Wagg, 'Cathedrals in Concrete: Football in Southern European Society', in S. Wagg (ed.), *Giving the Game Away: Football, Politics and Culture on Five Continents* (Leicester: Leicester University Press, 1995), pp. 125–6; Pierre Lanfranchi and Matthew Taylor, *Moving With the Ball: The Migration of Professional Footballers* (Oxford: Berg, 2001), p. 20.

112 Walvin, *People's Game*, p. 99; Lanfranchi, 'Exporting Football', p. 28.

113 Lanfranchi, 'Exporting Football'; Eisenberg, 'From England to the World', p. 13; Walvin, *People's Game*, p. 97.

114 Alan Tomlinson, 'Going Global: The FIFA Story', in Tomlinson and Whannel (eds), *Off the Ball*, p. 84; Walvin, *People's Game*, chapter 6.

115 Tomlinson, 'Going Global', pp. 85–93; Mason, 'Football', pp. 176–7; Taylor, *The Leaguers*, pp. 217–18; Peter Beck, *Scoring for Britain: International Football and International Politics, 1900–1939* (London: Frank Cass, 1999), pp. 28–33.

116 Beck, *Scoring for Britain*, p. 102.

117 Mason, 'Some Englishmen and Scotsmen Abroad', pp. 72–3; Walvin, *People's Game*, pp. 109–10.

118 Meisl, *Soccer Revolution*, pp. 54–5; Mason, *Passion of the People?*, pp. 15–26; S. F. Rous, 'Football as an International Sport', *The Listener*, 4 May 1938; Lanfranchi and Taylor, *Moving With the Ball*, pp. 46–7; Beck, *Scoring for Britain*, p. 107.

119 Mason, 'Some Englishmen and Scotsmen Abroad', p. 74; Pierre Lanfranchi, '"Mister" Garbutt: The First European Manager', *The Sports Historian*, 22, 1 (May 2002), p. 45.

120 Lanfranchi, 'Mister Garbutt', pp. 44–59; quotation p. 56; Walvin, *People's Game*, pp. 110–11.

121 Lanfranchi and Taylor, *Moving With the Ball*, pp. 148 (Table 5.1), 54; Lanfranchi, 'Mister Garbutt', p. 45; W. Capel-Kirby and Frederick W. Carter, *The Mighty Kick: Romance, History and Humour of Football* (London: Jarrolds, 1933), p. 140.

122 See John Hargreaves, 'The State and Sport: Programmed and Non-Programmed Intervention in Britain', in L. Allison (ed.), *The Politics of Sport* (Manchester: Manchester University Press, 1986), p. 248.

123 Martin Polley, 'The Foreign Office and International Sport, 1918–1948', unpublished Ph.D. thesis, St David's University College, University of Wales, 1991; Stephen G. Jones, 'State Intervention in Sport and Leisure in Britain between the Wars', *Journal of Contemporary History*, 22 (1987), p. 170; *Workers at Play*, pp. 183–8; p. 183. See also Richard Holt, 'The Foreign Office and the Football Association: British Sport and Appeasement, 1935–1938' in P. Arnaud and J. Riordan (eds), *Sport and International Politics: The Impact of Fascism and Communism on Sport* (London: E & FN Spon, 1998), pp. 51–66.

124 Beck, *Scoring for Britain*, p. 279; Mason, 'Football', p. 177.

125 Taylor, *The Leaguers*, p. 225.

126 Christopher Harvie, *No Gods and Precious Few Heroes: Twentieth-Century Scotland* (Edinburgh: Edinburgh University Press, 2000 [1st edition, 1981]), p. 120.

127 H. F. Moorhouse, 'Scotland against England: Football and Popular Culture', *International Journal of the History of Sport*, 4, 2 (September 1987), pp. 189–202; Crampsey, *Scottish Footballer*, p. 32; H. F. Moorhouse, 'Blue Bonnets over the Border: Scotland and the Migration of Footballers', in J. Bale and J. Maguire (eds), *The Global Sports Arena: Athletic Talent Migration in an Interdependent World* (London: Frank Cass, 1994), p. 93.

128 Johnes, *Soccer and Society*, pp. 173–7, 195, 201; *A History of Sport in Wales* (Cardiff: University of Wales Press, 2005), pp. 49–51.

129 Johnes, *Soccer and Society*, pp. 184–93; quotation p. 191; *Sport in Wales*, p. 61.

130 Dermot Keogh, *Twentieth-Century Ireland: Nation and State* (Dublin: Gill & Macmillan, 1994), p. 35; Mike Cronin, *Sport and Nationalism in Ireland: Gaelic Games, Soccer and Irish Identity since 1884* (Dublin: Four Courts, 1999), p. 121.

131 Garnham, *Association Football*, pp. 177–95, 196; 'The Origins and Development of Irish Football' in N. Garnham (ed.), *The Origins and Development of Football in Ireland* (Belfast: Ulster Historical Foundation, 1999), p. 28

132 H. F. Moorhouse, 'One State, Several Countries: Soccer and Identities in the "United" Kingdom', European University Institute Colloquium Papers, 1989, pp. 4–5; Beck, *Scoring for Britain*, p. 102; Garnham, *Association Football*, pp. 181–2; Cronin, *Sport and Nationalism*, pp. 122–3; Pierre Lanfranchi, Christiane Eisenberg, Tony Mason and Alfred Wahl, *100 Years of Football: The FIFA Centennial Book* (London: Weidenfeld & Nicolson, 2004), p. 274.

CHAPTER 4

The golden age of British football? 1939–61

The 1940s and 1950s hold a special place in the popular memory of British football. Although similar in many respects to the pre-war years, the game seemed to enjoy a higher public profile, and certainly a greater popularity, than had previously been the case. Conventional wisdom has it that the crowds flocked to watch players earning little more than an average skilled worker performing for teams to whom they were loyal and for communities of which they felt a part. Given the fact that there are increasingly fewer people alive in the twenty-first century who witnessed the game before the Second World War, it is the clubs and players of this period that are generally taken to represent football's 'past'. The post-war years are often celebrated as much for what they did not represent as for what they did. In popular memory, this was the age before the creation of the superstar footballer and the all-powerful 'superclub', before the intrusion of television, before the emergence of hooliganism and before the rampant commercialisation that turned a 'sport' into a 'business'. These were the 'good old days' of British football, after which money and violence arrived to tarnish the game.[1]

Yet as with all alleged 'golden ages', the mythology is more potent than the reality. Rather than being seen as the final throw, perhaps even the highpoint, of the 'traditional' game before the emergence of 'modern' soccer from the 1960s, the period actually witnessed an intricate mixture of continuity and change. The best accounts treat this era as one of transition between the old and the new. Dave Russell's study of English football outlines the game's continuities through the war years and the

1940s and then focuses on the 1950s as the decade when 'a set of crucial changes were set in train which were to usher in the "modern" game in the 1960s'. Concentrating mainly on domestic football, he charts developments in coaching, shifts in patterns of support, increased media scrutiny and the changing attitude towards the treatment of players which resulted in the abolition of the maximum wage in 1961.[2] With more of an eye on the place of British football on the international stage, Percy Young and James Walvin have identified specific turning points in the history of the game. For Young, it was 25 November 1953 when the England national team suffered its first ever home defeat by a continental side, losing 6–3 to Hungary at Wembley Stadium. Walvin highlighted another famous date – 6 February 1958, the night of the Munich air crash – which represented, in his words, 'a defining moment in the story of English football'. In this view, the significance of the event went much deeper than its immediate tragic effect on the Manchester United and England teams of the day. When set alongside the recent impact of European club competition and British involvement in the World Cup, Walvin argues that 1958 marks 'a clear break with the past'. Followers of the game

had become aware as never before of a wider footballing world. They learned from visiting teams and televised football that it was a world game and that some of the greatest teams and finest players plied their trade far beyond English shores.

Indeed the presence of all four UK sides at the 1958 World Cup in Sweden could be read as a belated acceptance of the international game and the end of Britain's era of insularity.[3]

This chapter will critically assess both the popular view of 1939–61 as a golden age and the academic view of it as a transitional period. The earlier sections consider the role of football in war and reconstruction and the subsequent post-war spectator boom which was so crucial in helping to mark out this period as a golden age. The core of the chapter focuses on three interconnected issues central to the so-called transition from the traditional to the modern: relations with European and world football; the role of managers, coaching and the game itself; and the position of players and their fight (in England and Wales) to end the maximum wage. The chapter ends with a discussion of the place of football in the national life of Britain viewed through the lens of the media and its portrayal of the famous English Cup final of 1953.

War and reconstruction

John Walton has written that histories of leisure towns treat wars 'as anomalous interludes breaking up a smooth narrative flow, which can then be resumed when normality returns'. A similar point could be made about studies of sport. Yet as Walton points out, and as we saw of the 1914–18 conflict, it would be a mistake to bracket such periods off as if they were unconnected with what preceded and followed.[4] Indeed the vast literature on war and social change demands that scholars of sport look closely not just at how games survived or 'made do' but also the ways in which the abnormal conditions of wartime fed into post-war developments. Richard Holt and Tony Mason's book on sport since 1945 and Norman Baker's study of sport during and after the Second World War have been important in this respect by linking wartime and post-war developments through an analysis of the process of reconstruction.[5] This section follows a similar route by discussing the practical difficulties involved in, and moral questions raised by, the continuation of football, as well as considering the impact of wartime planning for peace in the immediate post-war years.

Much has been made of the contrasting fortunes of football during the two world wars. That most surveys depict 1939–45 as a 'good' war for sport as a whole in a way that 1914–18 had not been is partly explained by contrasting circumstances.[6] While the First World War had been focused on the trenches of the Western Front, the second conflict involved the entire military and civilian population experiencing war at first hand. State intervention was always likely to be more pronounced in this context of 'total war', but it was the risk of air attack that guaranteed government control over the organisation of sport. The fear of mass gatherings led the Home Office to ban all football at the outbreak of hostilities on 3 September 1939, but within a week grounds in low-risk areas were allowed to reopen. On 21 September a revised programme of football was sanctioned, with tight restrictions placed on attendances. Crowds were limited to 8,000 for most clubs in evacuation areas, or 15,000 for those with large stadiums, and all matches were subject to authorisation by the local police. In addition, the requisitioning of grounds, the scarcity of equipment as well as blackout and transport restrictions had an immediate effect on the nature of sporting activity. In his acclaimed survey of the people's war, Angus Calder thought that 'no national institution of comparable importance had been so badly hit by the outbreak of war' as sport. John Ross Schleppi likewise found little evidence of planning between the state and the football authorities, concluding that most decisions concerning the nature of the wartime game 'were made in reaction to government edicts'.[7] Indeed as the war progressed, government policy became the crucial factor in determining restrictions on sport. Regulations were tightened and eased in line with the changing fortunes of war but if we contrast football with other forms of public entertainment such as the cinema and radio which acted as useful sources of propaganda, it was nonetheless left relatively untouched and free to run its own affairs.

As in the First World War, football continued in a modified form, involving a mixture of home internationals, representative fixtures, interservice games and a limited league and cup programme. A series of regional groupings was created in England and Wales, which included all but six of the Football League's 88 member clubs, while special wartime cup competitions were established. The decision in 1942 to divide clubs into simple north–south sections was less well received, especially by those from the capital, who broke away to form their own London War League. In Scotland, teams divided into regional east and west sections for the 1939–40 season before reorganising as separate Southern and North-Eastern Leagues outside the auspices of the Scottish Football League. A number of Scottish clubs closed down for the duration of the war, and two, the Stirling club King's Park and the Edinburgh outfit St Bernard, disbanded for good.[8] Despite the fact that organised football continued to be played throughout the conflict, it was affected by wartime conditions in a number of ways. Even if the immediate threat of air attack failed to materialise, disruption was common in areas where air raids were frequent. The Home Office initially ordered that play should stop every time an alert was sounded, a situation that caused delays and even led to the abandonment of some matches. At the height of the Battle of Britain, one match at Stamford Bridge apparently took three hours to complete; Joe Mercer, one of the players, related that the sirens were heard so often that 'we were in and out, in and out'. In May 1940 at least 60,000 ticket holders stayed away from an international fixture at Hampden Park, Glasgow, amidst widespread rumours and German radio propoganda forecasting a Luftwaffe raid on the ground in the second half. For all this, the adoption of the 'spotter' system at most grounds, which gave warning of imminent danger, and the reduction of daylight bombing after 1942 led to a significant increase in attendances and a safer atmosphere at most matches.[9]

Travel restrictions were less easy to solve. Rail services were limited and could be withdrawn from time to time. Professional teams could only travel by road within a 50-mile radius, with amateur teams restricted to 25 miles. The transport authorities were loath to treat football teams with any favour. The Ministry of War Transport informed the Football League in December 1941 that the game ultimately had 'to bow to more essential considerations' and asked the League 'to consider the effect on public opinion in the USA, where petrol had been rationed so that it could be sent to England, if it were known that the petrol was being used to convey football teams'. Celtic, meanwhile, had its official permit for a bus to transport its players withdrawn in November 1942. Under such circumstances, players were known to arrive at matches by any means necessary, some finding lifts on milk lorries, fire engines and even in aeroplanes.[10]

The outbreak of war undoubtedly had a major effect on the lives of professional footballers. The future looked bleak and uncertain for many. Peter Doherty, an inside-forward with Manchester City, later recalled:

the cleavage was a harsh one; contracts were automatically torn up, and for those players who had families to support and no savings to fall back on, the immediate prospect was grave. It was a grim lesson for professionals ... Without a scrap of consideration or sentiment, our means of livelihood were simply jettisoned, and we were left to find fresh ones as best we could.[11]

When regular football resumed, the rewards for players were limited. They received no more than 30s. per match in England (£2 in Scotland), in contrast with the pre-war limit of £8. The Players' Union reported that 'many players could not get a game nor find employment' and that some 'had no income whatsoever'.[12] Few players had other skills to fall back on. Only one of Heart of Midlothian's eight internationals, for example, had an occupation other than football. It would be wrong, however, to suggest that all footballers suffered to the same extent. Some of the leading players became Physical Training Instructors (PTIs) in the Army or the RAF. By March 1940 the FA could report that 154 footballers had been accepted as PTIs in the services. Matt Busby, a 32-year old Scottish international when the war began, was one of the first batch to undergo training at Aldershot. When the Allies invaded Italy in 1944, Busby was made officer-in-charge of the British Army team sent to entertain the troops in battle areas. He was responsible for the training, tactics and selection of the team and also for the general discipline of the footballer-soldiers under his command. This proved to be invaluable experience for Busby's subsequent position as manager of Manchester United, which he began a month after demobilisation in October 1945. Joining the forces did not prevent suggestions that footballers (and sportsmen more generally) were having it easy. The playing of football was rarely considered to be unpatriotic in the way it had been in 1914–18, but it remained a sensitive issue. Even in the course of defending football's contribution to the war effort, the editor of the West Bromwich Albion programme could comment that 'some famous footballers who had joined the army seem to be doing more football than military service'.[13] Willie Watson, a member of Busby's Army team in Italy, remembered being derided by shouts of 'Come on the D-Day Dodgers' during one match, and Tom Finney also admitted that during his time with the Royal Armoured Corps in Egypt and the Middle East he 'often wondered if it was right that I should go on playing while others were fighting'.[14]

Some writers have assumed rather too readily that there was little debate over whether to continue playing and watching football during the Second World War. Walvin, for example, maintained there had been 'a sea-change' in opinion since the previous war about the vital role of football (and sport generally) in sustaining morale, while Russell detected no significant wartime criticism of a game whose status had risen in the eyes of the ruling classes. Another account suggested that in contrast with its earlier marginalisation, soccer was actually encouraged by the government during the second war as 'at once a signal of normality and a practical resource in the war effort'.[15] For others, the issue is less clear-cut. In his doctoral thesis on the wartime game, Schleppi concludes that the British government, dominated by a form of 'war puritanism', initially had little interest in the role of football. Only as the conflict progressed, he argues, did it come to acknowledge the game's cultural importance and morale-boosting qualities.[16] In analysing what he calls the wartime debate over the 'appropriateness' of sporting activity, meanwhile, Baker has shown that there was considerable political opposition to the continuation of spectator sport. Criticism of sport peaked during the war's low points, such as in February 1942 when a press campaign to strengthen restrictions on sport coincided with a parliamentary debate on the subject. Sir Stafford Cripps, Lord President and Leader of the House of Commons, made the case for the opponents when he argued that sports such as dog racing and boxing 'are completely out of accord with the true spirit of determination of the people'. As such, they should 'no longer be allowed to offend the solid and serious intention of the country to achieve victory'. Undoubtedly, football was regarded more kindly even by the likes of Cripps and, as a national sport, it benefited more than most from the position of tolerance that came to characterise government policy towards civilian sport.[17]

The link between football and morale was a common feature of the statements of the governing bodies and the work of research organisations such as Mass-Observation. One of the latter's most quoted reports from 1940 maintained that

Sports like football have an absolute major effect on the morale of the people, and one Saturday afternoon of League matches could probably do more to affect people's spirits than the recent £50,000 Government poster campaign urging cheerfulness.[18]

Yet it is worth noting that histories of civilian morale have almost nothing to say about football. Robert Mackay's recent study is particularly down-beat about football's role in the maintenance of morale. Like Baker, Mackay argues that within governmental circles there was 'ambivalence about the place of sport in war' and that many continued to think that sport wasted vital resources and acted as an unnecessary and frivolous distraction from the war effort. What is more, rather than lauding the game's ability to struggle on and contribute to a feeling of normality, he points out the impoverished state of football for both spectators and players. For Mackay, the ramshackle state of wartime sport did little to lift the spirits of the British people: on the contrary, it was 'just one more way in which the war threatened to wear down the Dunkirk spirit and nibble away at civilian morale'.[19] Such interpretations serve as a useful corrective to those that view the game uncontroversially as part of the orthodox consensus whereby the nation was united by its fortitude, adaptability and resolve. Much of what we know about the game during this time can be explained by the football authorities' success in managing its wartime image and publicising its war record. It is only in this context that the FA chairman Lord Athlone could claim that soccer 'acted as a strong link in combining the forces which brought victory'.[20] Yet on balance football's contribution to the war was rather small. Attendances increased as the war progressed but were still nowhere near the numbers who listened to the radio or visited the cinema. Nor was the game co-opted into formal government attempts to 'ease the strain' of war as other types of entertainment were. Guest players, regional leagues and represen-tative matches were tolerated as temporary features but wartime soccer lacked the essential competitiveness that came from local partisanship within a national context and the league system of promotion and relega-tion. Thomas Taw has thus described it as 'ersatz – acceptable, but not authentic'. Football continued and more than survived but it can hardly be said to have flourished.[21]

Football was the first British sport to consider seriously how it might be organised and played when peace returned. Post-war planning was one of the key topics of debate in sport as it was in so many areas of social and political life, and football's Beveridge was the FA secretary Stanley Rous. On speaking terms with influential figures in the government and beyond, Rous had been involved before the war in cross-sport bodies such as the National Playing Fields Association and the Central Council for Recreative Physical Training, and assumed chairmanship of the Civil Defence Sports Committee during the conflict. The war represented for him an opportunity to secure the position of the game in British society through a series of constructive reforms. In May 1943 he presented a memorandum on 'Post-War Development' through the War Emergency Committee for consideration by the FA Council. Covering topics ranging from players, facilities and coaching to relations with international bodies, the pools and the press, the memorandum has been described by Baker as a 'cautious, conservative document, reflecting a powerful Corinthian influence'. Certainly, its two most radical proposals – the use of pools money to improve the game at grassroots level and the incorporation of a Sunday football association within the FA – were rejected out of hand, and the 1943–4 annual report concluded that there should be no 'revolutionary changes' or 'unnecessary innovations' to the way in which the game was played and administered.[22]

Yet, as Holt and Mason point out, a number of elements of the 1943 reconstruction plan were in fact taken up in the immediate post-war years. In coaching, Walter Winterbottom became the first FA director of coaching and England team manager in 1946, and at the same time the *Bulletin* was established to publicise the role of coaching and the work of the FA. The Moscow Dynamo tour of 1945 and the readmission of the UK associations to FIFA in 1946 reflected Rous's stated commitment to the internationalisation of the British game. The Football League established its own Post-War Planning Committee in 1943, but those progressive ideas which were floated – such as a British league, a League Cup and the transfer of its headquarters from Preston to London – came to nothing at the 1945 AGM. In what Simon Inglis described as 'its greatest error of the early post-war period', the League also snubbed the pools companies' offer to pay £100,000 per year for the use of its match fixtures. The English League was happy enough with the status quo to revert to its 1939 structure and fixture list for the resumption of normal competition in 1946, but its Scottish counterpart contemplated a new elite super league before deciding on A and B divisions that took account of wartime commitment as well as pre-war playing records. The Scottish Southern League's cup competition was one wartime innovation that was successfully carried over to peacetime.[23]

Planning for reconstruction was one thing, but change has also been identified with the general social upheaval of war. Following the work of Arthur Marwick, a host of scholars have looked at the effect of war in breaking down barriers of class, gender, race and so on. As far as football was concerned, long-term changes of any significance are not easy to uncover. The playing of women's football was limited during the Second World War and any hints of a post-war revival were quashed when the FA reaffirmed its 1921 ban in December 1946. According to Sue Lopez, only 17 women's teams were still in operation by the following year. Football remained, in Baker's words, 'entrenched at the core of concepts of masculinity'.[24] The influx of refugees and military personnel as a result of war and its aftermath certainly impacted upon both amateur and professional soccer, although there is no indication that it led to changed attitudes to race and nationality. Phil Vasili has shown that non-white players were rare and subject to various forms of discrimination, but nevertheless, as in industry, football's post-war labour force was more open to foreigners than it had been. The most famous foreign player of the post-war period was the German goalkeeper Bert Trautmann. A captured paratrooper, Trautmann spent the last year of the conflict in a prisoner-of-war camp in Lancashire, played for St Helens Town after his release and was then signed up by Manchester City in 1949 as replacement for the England international Frank Swift. Polish Army exiles Alfie Lesz and Feliks Starocsik and internationals such as Switzerland's Willi Steffan and Iceland's Albert Gudmundsson were others who played for some time in top-level Scottish and English football after the war, but the British leagues continued to be more parochial than cosmopolitan in personnel and outlook.[25]

Some historians have suggested that the war had a democratising effect on the social relations of the game. Russell, for instance, has hinted at the development of a less deferential relationship between directors and the new breed of former players who became managers. This may have been due, in part at least, to 'the more egalitarian social and political climate of the war and the immediate post-war years'.[26] According to another article, the line between players and spectators became more blurred than ever as the former took up ordinary wartime posts and the latter were occasionally called on to make up numbers. Under such circumstances, the connection between the football hero and the normal citizen may have reached its peak. For players too, the war arguably offered a chance for the novice to compete alongside the established star and international. Leading figures of the post-war game, such as Billy Wright, Nat Lofthouse, Stan Mortensen and Henry Cockburn, certainly credited wartime football with speeding up their development. Indeed, although clubs generally disliked it, the guest player system 'probably had an equalising effect on the professional hierarchy within football'.[27] In complete contrast, Joyce Woolridge has contended that one of the main outcomes of wartime football was 'a demonstrable widening of the gap in status between the ordinary player and the star professional'.[28] In this view, constantly changing team-sheets, the prevalence of star 'guests' and the increasing prominence of representative and international fixtures combined to create a new elite group of soccer superstars which went on to dominate the post-war era. There was even some intimation from contemporaries that the game itself acquired a new spirit of co-operation – 'a kind of footballing citizenship' – reflecting the unity of wartime Britain. Some have claimed that it was from the camaraderie of war that the convention of shaking hands after the game began.[29] But for all this we should be wary of overstating the effect of wartime experience on British football. Most of what is outlined above is awash with speculation but short on real evidence. Not everything returned to the way it had been before the war, but Baker is probably right to argue that 'on balance, continuity prevailed over change' in the immediate years after 1945.[30] Any wholesale transformation of the British game would have to wait.

Football's boom and beyond

In many respects, the game's post-war history has been defined by the sharp increase in attendances that occurred during the late 1940s. The three seasons following the end of hostilities witnessed a massive rise in crowds in the Football League, from an annual aggregate total of 27 million in the last pre-war season to 35.6 million in 1946–7, and then a jump to the historic peak of 41.2 million during 1948–9. Newcastle United topped the attendance tables in these seasons, with an average crowd of 56,283 watching the side gain promotion from the Second Division in 1947–8 and as many as 30,000 turning up for some reserve team matches. But large gates were not confined to the most successful clubs. Hull City attracted average crowds of over 36,700 in the Third Division North, and Notts County pulled in more than 30,000 in the Third Division South during 1948–9. In total 23 English and Welsh clubs recorded their highest average attendances of all-time between the 1947–8 and 1948–9 seasons. Scottish attendances were equally impressive. Such was the appeal of the game that Celtic and Third Lanark could attract a crowd of 87,000 to Hampden Park for the minor Glasgow Cup final in 1948, while Queen's Park was able to draw 28,000 for a lowly B Division match with Kilmarnock. The first half of the 1950s was particularly successful, with 12 clubs (including B Division Arbroath and Stenhousemuir alongside Aberdeen, Dundee and Hibernian) achieving record crowds in this period. The attendance boom extended to amateur and junior football. The Amateur Cup final attracted crowds almost twice the pre-1939 record in the immediate post-war years, leading the FA to switch the final in 1949 to Wembley. Bromley and Romford attracted 95,000 on that occasion, while 100,000 attended the 1951 final between Bishop Auckland and Pegasus, including some 15,000 who travelled the long distance south from County Durham. Based close to a number of professional and amateur rivals in east London, Leytonstone still managed to attract 5,000 regularly during the late 1940s, while a 1951 report claimed that, without a professional club close by, nearly a fifth of the

PLATE 8 *Football spectators watching Colchester United play Norwich City at Colchester, 1950 (© Hulton Archive/Getty).*

population of High Wycombe (approximately 7,000 people) attended amateur football matches on a Saturday afternoon. Crowds for the Scottish Junior Cup final similarly soared with the game moving permanently to Hampden Park. Nearly 69,000 watched the 1949 finale, while a record 77,650 witnessed Petershill's defeat of Irvine Meadow two years later.[31]

The game itself has featured but little in attempts to explain this attendance boom. Few have claimed that crowds flocked through the turnstiles because the quality of play had dramatically improved or because matches were any more entertaining. Rather, most have agreed with Walvin that the rise in gates was 'part of a much broader outburst of pleasure-seeking'.[32] In the unusual conditions of late 1940s Britain – with minimal unemployment but continued rationing – people had money to spend but little to spend it on. An economic study summed up the accepted view:

Demobilisation and the relaxation of restrictions after the Second World War released a widespread and unprecedented pent-up demand for recreation and entertainment, which manifested itself not only in booming football attendances, but also in record-breaking cinema audience figures and packed beaches at British seaside resorts during the summers.[33]

In some areas, such as the north-east of England, football's rising popularity undoubtedly stood out even in the context of this general boom in leisure. Here, high employment in the region's heavy industries coincided with football's cheap admission rates and the absence of counter-attractions to create extraordinary popular interest in the game. For Neil Wigglesworth, it was the role of football as 'a manifestation of social solidarity' that explains its post-war fortunes. Attendances rose in line with the Attlee government's espousal of working-class communal values, and declined as greater prosperity served to fracture social and cultural loyalties.[34]

The decline from this highpoint was slow at first and uneven between clubs and across divisions but it was to be sustained. Eight million spectators were lost to Football League matches in the seasons between 1948–9 and 1956–7 and, following a mild recovery, a further sharp decline of nearly 4 million (representing a massive 12 per cent drop in crowd size) took place during the 1960–1 season. The fall was faster among clubs in the lower divisions: the Second Division share of aggregate attendances dropped from 30.5 per cent in 1947–8 to 24.5 per cent in 1960–1 at the same time as the First Division share rose from 41.5 per cent to 45.3. Equivalent data on the Scottish League is difficult to come by but the pattern of decline seems to have been similar, with the smaller clubs shedding supporters at a faster rate than their larger rivals. A 33.5 per cent drop in senior Scottish attendances was recorded between 1948–9 and 1965–6. There were of course numerous exceptions to this general downward trend, such as when Everton recorded its highest average attendance during the championship-winning 1962–3 season or when Manchester United and Leeds United did likewise in 1967–8 and 1970–1 respectively. Large crowds were certainly not consigned to history after the mid-1950s, particularly for cup-ties and internationals, but such consistent levels of support throughout the top British leagues were never to be approached again.[35]

In the search for football's 'missing millions', as with the post-war boom, most writers have looked beyond the game itself and emphasised the effect of broader socio-economic change. The emergence of a society of relative affluence in place of the poverty of the 1930s and the austerity of the 1940s paved the way for profound changes in the way in which people spent their leisure time. The new affluent worker was fundamentally individualistic and consumerist, increasingly opting for the domestic space of home and family in preference to the public world of the pub and the football terrace. The growth of home ownership and the building of new public housing based on suburban estates encouraged this retreat into privacy. J. H. Goldthorpe and his colleagues noted that the most popular activities among workers in the new estates of Luton in the early 1960s were gardening, doing 'odd jobs' and watching television. The TV, along with the car, was one of the most important symbols of this new affluent society. Both mushroomed in popularity over this period: from 2.3 million private vehicles in 1950, there were 5.6 million by 1960, while ownership of television sets, negligible in 1950, had reached three-quarters of all British households by 1961. Both also offered a potentially more satisfying and relaxing way of spending a Saturday afternoon than standing on an often wet and crowded football terrace.[36] 'Quite apart from the direct competition', observed one regional newspaper in 1961, 'people conditioned to comfortable cars and fireside entertainment are going to be an increasingly tough proposition for soccer and its spartan conditions to retain and recapture.' Rather more speculative is Walvin's suggestion that 'changes in female demands and expectations' had something to do with the declining numbers.[37] It may well be that in the post-war world many men were less free and indeed less willing to spend their precious spare time away from family and spouse, indulging in male-dominated pursuits like watching football. Yet, as Russell has pointed out, it is doubtful whether this necessarily represented progress for women so much as 'the transfer of male energies from a public to a private sphere' and the substitution of 'deeds with tenon saw, hi-fi and wall-papering brush' for 'tales of dipping volleys and chipped free kicks'. More convincing is Russell's suggestion that alongside those increasingly affluent supporters who were financially able to choose alternative forms of entertainment were poorer fans who may well have been priced out of the game, as minimum admission charges rose from 1s. 3d. in 1946 to 1s. 9d. in 1952 and then 2s. 6d. by 1960.[38]

Few authors have had much to say on the subject of post-war football crowds. Fishwick's study of the English game extends to 1950 but makes no distinction between the pre- and post-war crowd, while both Russell and Walvin are more concerned with the number of spectators than with their social composition and behaviour.[39] What has been written has tended to be impressionistic and based on ahistorical assumptions and received wisdom rather than empirical research. An exception to this is Gavin Mellor's recent work on the north-west of England. Drawing on local newspapers, photographic testimony and interviews with spectators of the time, he argues that crowds in the immediate post-war era were less socially homogenous than had been thought. In common with the most recent studies of the inter-war period, which we looked at in the last chapter, Mellor identifies a sprinkling of middle-class, 'affluent' or 'professional' people among the predominantly working-class supporters. Manchester United's Old Trafford ground, for instance, was apparently 'a place to be seen' for members of the local industrial and commercial classes, while newspaper reports showed increasing numbers of supporters travelling to both home and away matches by car, at a time when car ownership was largely restricted to sections of the middle class. Another significant discovery of Mellor's research is that many football spectators during this era were drawn from beyond the immediate locale of the club. Burnley was thus able to draw regular support from other towns in east and north Lancashire and even areas of West Yorkshire, while Everton apparently attracted travelling fans from Blackburn and even Dublin for its home matches during the 1950s. The directors of Preston North End, meanwhile, seem to have had a long-standing policy of trying to garner support from Lancaster, Morecambe, Kendal, Barrow and other cities and towns in the north of the county.[40]

This phenomenon of 'out of town' support needs to be considered alongside another tendency identified by Mellor: that of regional support,

PLATE 9 *Manchester United supporters, published in* Picture Post, *1948 (© Hulton Archive/Getty).*

whereby some spectators watched more than one club on a regular basis and felt a general attachment to football in Lancashire or the north-west rather than loyalty to a particular club. One interviewee had season tickets at both Bolton and Stockport and visited a range of other Lancashire clubs when their home matches did not clash. This may be an extreme case, but there are other examples of Preston fans travelling to Blackburn or Blackpool on days when North End were playing away or of supporters in Manchester visiting Maine Road and Old Trafford on alternate Saturdays.[41] Fans could thus enjoy a sense of attachment or belonging 'to a regional or ... countywide "family" of clubs'.[42] Neither was this a north-western peculiarity, as Peter Hutchins's doctoral work on football in the north-east of England shows. The 'floating fan' who supported the game rather than just one club was a recognised feature of the sport in this region from at least the 1930s and seems to have remained so until the 1960s. 'Floating fans' were especially common, it is claimed, in the Durham and Northumberland pit villages, where miners chose between Newcastle and Sunderland on the basis of current position and form.[43]

In stressing the social diversity of football crowds in at least one part of Britain during the 1940s and 1950s, Mellor's work complements studies of earlier periods. A bourgeois presence at grounds was sustained in this era: as he admits, 'some middle-class people attended some football matches some of the time', although not necessarily in great numbers or in larger percentages than before the war. It is Mellor's focus on geographical diversity, however, that raises the most stimulating questions. The suggestion that some clubs could boast a significant regional catchment area for spectators during the 1940s and 1950s casts some doubt on the theory that so-called regional or national 'super-clubs' only began to arrive towards the end of this period with improvements in public and private transport, the construction of a more reliable road network and other changes in demography and personal mobility. In drawing attention to multi-club and regional affiliation, Mellor also suggests that academics should rethink the assumptions they make about patterns of football support and the link between clubs and town or civic identities.[44] Although the majority of spectators may well have been loyal throughout their lives to a single club in the town in which they lived, we should not assume that they all were or dismiss the experiences of those who were not. As in earlier periods, football supporters in the 1940s and 1950s were not a homogenous mass but a complex and varied group about which academics still have much to understand.

The behaviour of post-war soccer crowds was also more variable than popular wisdom would have us believe. According to Geoffrey Gorer, writing in 1955, the English football crowd was 'as orderly as church meetings'.[45] In England, the years 1946–60 have been perceived as 'the halcyon days of the "sporting" ... crowd' and incidents of crowd trouble were certainly low. The FA recorded just 195 cases of disorderly spectator behaviour (an average of 13 each season) in this period. Eric Dunning and his colleagues have detected a mounting moral panic about spectator misconduct towards the end of the 1950s, articulated by sections of the media in the context of a broader concern with the behaviour of working-class youths. Sensationalist reports of fans wrecking trains and committing other acts of vandalism were increasingly common, but such disorder was still regarded by the authorities as a relatively minor problem.[46] Trouble among Northern Irish and Scottish crowds was more pronounced, marked as it often was by a sharp sectarian edge. In the former case, the rivalry between the two leading clubs – Belfast Celtic and Linfield – was so intense that matches 'always held the potential for serious spectator violence'.[47] Tensions reached a head at an infamous fixture at Windsor

Park in 1948. The game ended in a 1–1 draw, but the most significant event occurred when Linfield's Bob Bryson had his ankle broken accidentally in a clash with Celtic's Jimmy Jones. As the Celtic players tried to leave the pitch after the final whistle, they were set upon by Linfield fans: the main target was Jones, who had his leg broken and was left unconscious. To avoid any repeat of such an extreme incident, the directors of Belfast Celtic took the unprecedented step of withdrawing from the Irish League. They were never to return.[48]

In Scotland, concern over the behaviour and safety of crowds rose during the 1940s and 1950s and was almost invariably centred on the clashes of the 'Old Firm'. After a particularly disorderly New Year's Day encounter in 1952, at which bottles were thrown from the Celtic end and fans encircled the pitch, the Glasgow magistrates launched an inquiry into the 'Old Firm' disturbances. The subsequent recommendations to the Scottish FA and Scottish League included the prohibition of the traditional New Year's Day fixture, limitations on crowd numbers and the banning of flags 'which might incite feeling among the spectators'. Most of these ideas were rejected, although there was a shortlived and controversial ban on Celtic flying the Irish tricolour at Parkhead. Other suggested solutions included the playing of matches behind closed doors, the clubs swapping their strips and the closure of grounds, with the latter considered impractical in view of the importance of the 'Old Firm' to the overall financial well-being of the Scottish senior game. Celtic supporters were particular subjects of criticism. A Scottish Home and Health Department memorandum from 1953 noted that rowdyism was likely 'on any ground on which the Celtic Football Club is playing', and in the aftermath of one 1961 fixture with Dundee, in which some 50 fans were allegedly slashed by bottles and one later died, a Scottish MP even called for the dissolution of the Parkhead club.[49]

Assessments of football's rise and fall in this period have tended to focus exclusively on the professional level with no more than an occasional glance at the recreational game. When compared with both earlier and later periods, we know very little about the scale and make-up of grassroots soccer during the mid twentieth-century. Indeed we still await a comprehensive study of the game in any part of the British Isles in the post-war period, which would allow a more thorough understanding of developments and trends over a reasonable timescale. Most studies assume that levels of participation increased in the immediate post-war years, but the evidence to support this view is not altogether convincing. The figure of 31,219 affiliated clubs (excluding the services, university and public school teams but including over 8,000 other school teams) recorded by the FA in November 1949, though described as 'amazing' by one historian, actually indicates a drop of a few thousand from William Pickford's 1937 estimate.[50] Not surprisingly, the established associations of Birmingham (1,669 clubs), Lancashire (1,140), West Riding (913) and Sheffield and Hallamshire (897) in the north and midlands were among the best represented but, with nearly 2,000 clubs, London was the largest association and those in the south-east were probably the fastest growing. Considerable growth was evident in areas such as schoolboy and youth football. Membership of the ESFA had risen to over 8,000 by 1949 and youth football between the ages of 16 and 18 was strengthened by the creation of a plethora of new competitions – a County Youth Championship, International Youth tournaments and a youth equivalent of the Home International Championships – and the extension of coaching schemes to schools and youth clubs through the services of (by 1953) over 200 visiting professional coaches. Another flourishing facet of British football, in both qualitative and quantitative terms, was the university game. This benefited from the surge of mature students who were able to renew their undergraduate education after the war and the increasing prominence, at Oxford and Cambridge especially, of ex-grammar school soccer players. Such was the strength of varsity football that Pegasus, the joint Oxford and Cambridge University team founded in 1948, could win the FA Amateur Cup in 1951 and 1953 and be rated by *The Times* football correspondent Geoffrey Green as one of the most influential teams of the 1950s.[51]

According to both the Central Council of Physical Recreation (CCPR) in England and Wales and the Scottish Council for Physical Recreation (SCPR), participation in sport rose over the 1950s and early 1960s as live attendance declined. Yet in football at least there remained some significant barriers to participation. At one level, amateur competitions continued to be closely guarded against the supposedly corrupting influence of the so-called 'shamateur'. Dilwyn Porter has shown that the FA remained vigilant in the post-war years over the amateur–professional distinction, by controlling the role of ex-professionals in amateur soccer and attempting to eradicate 'gifts' to players and other forms of 'boot money' payment. Players who had competed at professional or semi-professional level could find themselves suspended from amateur competition, as could the clubs employing them. A system existed whereby professionals could be reinstated as amateurs through application to the governing body, but even these 'permit' players were outlawed by some of the best amateur competitions, such as the Isthmian, Athenian, Spartan and Corinthian Leagues. Despite the best efforts of the game's authorities, 'shamateurism' could not be expunged and towards the end of the period some leading figures even began to advocate a move away from the rigid application of regulations relating to amateurism. As early as 1949 the editor of *Amateur Sport* had expressed some sympathy for 'the talented amateur footballer of modest means who has no wish to become a professional, who enjoys the game, but is not averse to a little pocket money', while a minority voice on the 1960 Wolfenden Committee Report into *Sport and the Community* advocated the abolition of 'the formal distinction between amateur and professional'.[52]

At the recreational level, the prohibition of Sunday football was probably the most significant obstacle to regular participation. From 1910 the rules of the English FA had explicitly denied recognition of any player or club involved in Sunday competition. Even though unaffiliated games were organised in some parts of the country during the 1920s and 1930s, notably on council pitches in London, the governing body stood firm in declaring itself 'unable officially to recognise Sunday football'. Regulations were relaxed during the Second World War to allow servicemen and those working throughout the rest of the week to play on Sundays, and when hostilities ended the FA Council briefly toyed with the idea of removing the ban on a permanent basis. At a 1946 conference of county FA officials, advocates of a change of rule contended that playing field shortages and the increase of shift work 'was compelling clubs to play on Sundays or not at all'. A continuation of the ban, they argued, would not only force large numbers of recreational players (as many as 50 per cent according to one estimate) into unaffiliated football but also tarnish the game's image and challenge the FA's control over the grassroots. The moral opposition to Sunday football rested on its alleged connections with public houses and the payment of players and, above all, the fear that football would be endorsing the unpopular notion of the continental Sunday. After some debate, the ban was reaffirmed in 1948, with 200 registered players being disciplined for participating in outlawed Sunday leagues the following year.[53] Despite the claim of one county association that there was 'no demand' for Sunday football, an estimated 2,547 clubs were playing in 73 Sunday leagues throughout Britain by the end of the 1940s and its popularity continued to rise during the 1950s. A National Sunday Football Association was established, representing, according to its advocates, some half a million young players rather than those who simply 'play for pints'. The journalists Archie Ledbrooke and

Edgar Turner suggested that failure to recognise the Sunday game could threaten the FA's national authority, and indeed a further attempt to assume control over the Sunday leagues was made during the late 1950s but proved unsuccessful amidst accusations from the governing body that the leagues were badly organised, poorly refereed and marred by bad language and violent behaviour.[54]

Britain, Europe and the world

If British football embraced the world game in the post-war decades, it did so only hesitantly and with a continuing assumption of its administrative and sporting superiority. The decision of the four UK associations to return to FIFA in 1946 was the most salient of a series of developments aimed to extend contacts with overseas football and encourage an international perspective on the British game. The increased number of international matches during wartime, often involving service teams, and the collaboration with government departments and international organisations had convinced Rous and other football legislators of the opportunities for international development in the post-war world. Aware of Britain's declining political power and imperial interests, it has been argued that Rous 'saw in football a chance to retain some influence over world culture'.[55] British clubs, coaches and referees were dispatched abroad to help reconstruct and promote the game. The FA sent 15 coaches to Norway and Sweden in 1946, including the former Rotherham and Bury outside-right George Raynor, who went on to guide the Swedish national side to victory at the 1948 London Olympics and third and second place respectively at the World Cups of 1950 and 1958. By December 1947 there were at least 34 British coaches employed by clubs and associations in Europe and beyond, with the national teams of the Netherlands, Portugal, Costa Rica, Trinidad and Egypt all managed by Britons. International contacts were cemented by events such as the 1951 Festival of Britain, during which club sides hosted exhibition matches with 'sister' clubs from abroad, and a special 'International Day' pitted the home nations against a range of continental opponents. Rous later claimed that the Festival matches enhanced the 'fund of goodwill for British soccer throughout Europe, and indeed ... the world'.[56] The decision of the British associations to compete for the World Cup from the 1950s and Arthur Drewry's assumption of the FIFA presidency in 1956 doubtless also helped to boost the international profile of the British game.

The tension between British football's emerging international focus and its traditional self-obsession and introversion had been manifest when Moscow Dynamo toured Britain in 1945. Suspected by some of being a national team in disguise, the Soviet side defeated Cardiff City (10–1) and Arsenal (4–3) and drew with Chelsea and Rangers before crowds ranging from 45,000 to 90,000. Despite their success, assessments of the ability of the 'mysterious' visitors varied. The *Sunday Chronicle* marvelled at the combination, teamwork and attacking flair of the tourists, rating them as better than the Austrian 'Wonderteam' of the 1930s. Stanley Matthews, who played as a guest in the Arsenal team, reckoned Dynamo to be 'the finest team to have visited this island'. Chelsea's Tommy Lawton considered them one of the quickest teams he had ever played against, praising their speed of thought and accurate passing and commenting on the effectiveness of their 'concertina' tactics, whereby the team as a whole contracted into defence and expanded rapidly into attacking positions when required. But they were let down by poor shooting, and under different circumstances and with more players available Lawton believed the

PLATE 10 *The Moscow Dynamo team walking onto the pitch at Stamford Bridge with bouquets of flowers to present to the Chelsea team before their match in 1945 (© Hulton Archive/Getty).*

British would have put up a better show. Dynamo, he concluded, were 'a very good football team ... but not a super-side'.[57] The press likewise tended to downplay the achievements of the Soviet side, comparing their style and talent to British sides of earlier periods. According to the *Daily Herald*, the best pre-1939 teams would have 'comfortably' beaten Dynamo: they were talented but 'not a world-shaking perfect football machine'.[58]

The tour has also been remembered for its off-the-field events. Initial reactions to the visitors (both official and popular) were positive, stressing the importance of extending British contacts with its wartime ally. Most sections of the press were impressed at first, not least because the tourists made good print. Observers stressed the novel features of their approach to the game, such as the long pre-match warm-up, use of substitutes and presentations of bouquets of flowers to opponents before the game. Even their appearance – in 'Baltic Blue' strip with a large 'D' emblazoned on the left breast and long baggy shorts – was interpreted as 'exotic'. But disputes over tour arrangements, refereeing decisions and unsporting play served to taint the initial feeling of goodwill on both sides. The 14 stipulations laid down by the delegation before a ball was kicked – including the presence of a Russian referee for one match, a 50 per cent share of gate receipts and the decision to eat all meals at the Russian Embassy – had raised some eyebrows amongst the British and disagreements continued over a range of issues, including Arsenal's selection of a number of guest players (including Matthews and his Blackpool teammate Stan Mortensen) and Dynamo's 'accidental' fielding of a twelfth player on more than one occasion. In an article on 'The Sporting Spirit', the novelist George Orwell wrote that sport, as exemplified by the Dynamo tour, 'is an unfailing cause of ill-will, and that if such visits as this had any effect at all on Anglo-Soviet relations, it could only be to make them slightly worse than before'. Basing his view on what he had been told about the Arsenal and Rangers encounters, Orwell probably overplayed the political ill-effects of the tour but it certainly soured relations at some levels and, in the short term at least, discouraged further Anglo-Soviet sporting contacts. 'Neither the government nor the FA', in Peter Beck's view, 'felt inclined to repeat the experience of the Dynamo tour in a hurry'. Proposals for a return visit in 1946 were scuppered and it was not until 1954 that Arsenal became the first British club to play in the Soviet Union.[59]

Getting into Europe

Contrary to one recent account, the 1950s were not marked by British hostility to the international game.[60] The situation was more complicated than this. As had been the case in the 1920s and 1930s, club sides took the lead in sustaining contacts on the continent. The appetite for football against foreign opposition, whetted by the Moscow Dynamo tour, was satisfied by a series of mid-week evening friendlies arranged to take advantage of the FA's withdrawal of its ban on floodlighting in 1950 and often given additional publicity through being televised by the BBC. In London alone, Arsenal took on Hapoel Tel Aviv in September 1951, Tottenham Hotspur invited Racing Club de Paris to White Hart Lane in September 1953 and Chelsea and West Ham played host to Vörös Lobogo ('Red Banner' in English) of Hungary and Milan respectively in December 1954. But it was Wolverhampton Wanderers, one of the most successful Football League sides of the 1950s, which became recognised as the British pioneer of European competition. Victories over Moscow Spartak, Moscow Dynamo and Honved of Hungary under floodlights and in front of television cameras at Molineux were widely interpreted at home as evidence of the continued superiority of the British game. The Honved match of December 1954 was especially important as the visitors included six players who had helped the Hungarian national team defeat England 6–3 at Wembley just over a year earlier (see below). In broadcasting the match, the BBC 'had positioned its audience as witnesses to the salubrious event, the health of the nation riding on the back of a single club's fortunes'.[61] On a muddy pitch in front of 55,000 spectators, the English champions Wolves came from 2–0 down at half-time to win 3–2 and were duly proclaimed by the English press as unofficial champions of Europe, if not the world. 'English soccer', according to the *Daily Express*, 'the genuine, original, unbeatable article, is still the best of its kind in the world.'[62] It was barely mentioned that the bulk of the Honved side had played an international against Scotland a week earlier or that the supposedly 'invincible' Hungarians had lost by the same 3–2 scoreline to Partizan Belgrade, placed seventh at the time in the Yugoslav league, just two weeks before that. The Austrian journalist Willy Meisl thought it inconceivable that his English counterparts could make such a claim 'on the strength of *one* victory ... won on home ground under most pronounced "home" conditions without even waiting for the result of the return away game'.[63]

Writing in the French sports paper *L'Equipe*, Gabriel Hanot, another influential journalist, agreed. He cast doubt on the English assumption of superiority and advocated the creation of a European Championship to test the comparative strength of the continent's best club sides. Support for Hanot's idea grew and soon received the authorisation of FIFA and the newly established European governing body, UEFA (Union of European Football Associations). The idea was not exactly new, drawing inspiration from competitions such as the Mitropa Cup, contested by central European teams since 1927, and a Latin Cup for the top French, Italian, Spanish and Portuguese clubs, which had begun in 1949. Together with Jean-Bernard Lévy, the president of Racing Club de Paris, Hanot had advocated the creation of a knock-out competition for European clubs during the 1930s and even then recognised that the biggest obstacle would be to persuade the inward-looking English clubs to take part.[64] The clubs, however, were less of a problem than the leagues. As prospective champions, Chelsea were invited to take part but withdrew after pressure from the Football League Management Committee, who regarded European football as 'something of a joke and, at best, a nine days' wonder'. The League thought that the proposed cup would disrupt its already packed fixture schedule but also saw in it a more fundamental threat to its own competition, fearing the creation of a European-leaning elite within its own ranks.[65] There was no such objection from north of the border, and so Hibernian joined 15 clubs from 15 different national leagues to compete in the first European Champion Clubs' Cup, popularly known as the European Cup, during the 1955–6 season.

British soccer's decision makers remained divided in their attitude to Europe. The following season, Manchester United, supported by the FA, resisted continued League opposition by becoming the first English club to compete in the European Cup. But the League blocked a move by Aston Villa to participate in a tournament for national cup winners (three years before the creation of the European Cup-Winners' Cup) and prevented Manchester United taking an invited place because of the Munich air crash alongside champions Wolves in the 1958–9 European Cup. The FA was far more positive. Indeed it was Rous who, with colleagues from Italy and Switzerland, drew up the rules for the Inter-Cities' Fairs Cup, a competition originally designed for teams representing cities that had staged industrial trade fairs. The first competition began in June 1955 but was not completed until May 1958, when a London eleven consisting of players from five metropolitan clubs, including Chelsea's Jimmy Greaves and Fulham's Johnny Haynes, were defeated over two legs by a Barcelona representative side. For League secretary Alan Hardaker, the Fairs Cup was 'a ponderous, rather messy competition' and in its early years it certainly had limited appeal beyond the cities involved.[66] Yet such was the allure of European football that over 45,000 turned up to Stamford Bridge to watch the London–Barcelona tie and 40,500 saw Birmingham City host Barcelona in the first leg of the competition's second final in March 1960. In Glasgow, 80,000 watched Rangers play Fiorentina in the first leg of the final of the new Cup Winners' Cup the following May. The attraction of European competition, and the possible financial reward, was quickly becoming apparent to British clubs. By the 1960–1 season, Britain (Northern Ireland included) could boast seven representatives in various European competitions.

Two clubs in particular – Manchester United and Real Madrid – were instrumental in impressing the European game into the consciousness of the British football follower. United may not have won the European Cup in this period – their campaigns in 1956–7 and 1957–8 both finishing at the semi-final stage – but their exploits certainly helped to transform a competition initially regarded as a distraction and a gimmick into 'an essential part of the British season'. To the appeal of fixtures that pitted the local and familiar against the foreign and exotic was added the lure of real competition against opponents of the highest quality. The former United player and writer Eamon Dunphy has described the sense of occasion and glamour associated with the ties against Athletic Bilbao and Real Madrid during the first campaign: an adventure which, in his words, 'transformed English football forever'.[67] Another crucial component of this transformation ironically came out of the tragedy of 6 February 1958, when eight of the Manchester United team were killed on a Munich runway returning from a European Cup tie in Belgrade. The historian Richard Weight has recently suggested that the tragedy contributed to an anti-European mood in British sport, leading some to debate the benefits of future involvement in such competitions. Yet despite its undeniable impact on the club itself and the British game more generally, there is little evidence of a retreat from Europe in the aftermath of Munich. More convincing is the view that it contributed to a growing recognition of the centrality of European competition to British clubs, players and supporters. After 1958, European football was increasingly seen as an end in itself, bound to domestic league and cup competition through widespread acceptance of the principle of entry into Europe on merit rather than invitation or reputation. In a relatively short time Europe become, in Walvin's words, 'the prime ambition of Britain's leading clubs'.[68]

Real Madrid exemplified the appeal of European football during the 1950s and early 1960s. With a team drawn from across Europe and South America – including the Argentinian Alfredo De Stefano, French winger

Raymond Kopa and the Hungarian star Ferenc Puskas – Real were phe-
nomenally successful, winning the European Cup for the first five years of
its existence. The way in which they looked and played was a revelation
to British eyes. Dressed in an all-white kit 'that looked custom-made and
streamlined' and wearing boots reminiscent of 'highly-polished light-
weight leather carpet slippers', Real simply overwhelmed their opponents
with football that 'seemed to have come from another world'.[69] The highpoint of their achievement was the stunning 7–3 victory over an
impressive Eintract Frankfurt side in the 1960 European Cup final at
Glasgow's Hampden Park. The German side had defeated Scottish champions Rangers 12–4 over two legs in the semi-final but were swept aside
before a crowd of 135,000 and a television audience of millions in Britain
and beyond. To this day, it remains one of the most famous football
matches ever played on British shores. It certainly helped to consolidate
the 'legend' of Real Madrid in Britain. Such was the influence of the
Spanish club in the early 1960s that new Leeds United manager Don Revie
was inspired to adopt their all-white kit, and a *Real Madrid Book of
Football* could be marketed for 'all British fans who have watched them
at Molineux, Old Trafford or on Television'.[70]

National teams and World Cups

The European exploits of clubs may have been important but the true
standing of the British game was increasingly being measured by the
success of national teams. Holt and Mason have argued that in the
decade after the Second World War the fortunes of the England team
were regarded with a degree of detachment. The team was supported
but never with the same passion as club sides. Thus the reaction to
failure at the 1950 World Cup in Brazil was 'surprisingly measured' and
'strangely muted'.[71] Bob Ferrier claimed that the team's shock 1–0
defeat by 500–1 outsiders the USA, as well as the 1–0 reverse against
Spain, had 'mortified if not humiliated the national consciousness in a
way that was quite new', but there is in fact little evidence that it provoked such emotions in the English press or among the public. The
media showed limited interest in the tournament: there was no BBC
radio commentary or television broadcasts and some newspapers, such
as *The Times*, did not even send a correspondent. If the Scottish
national team was already regarded as a focus for national sentiment,
this related to its encounters with England more than its contacts with
other international teams. Indeed the Scottish FA showed its ambiva-

PLATE 11 *George Young and Billy Wright, Britain's most capped players at the time, lead their teams onto Wembley in 1957 (© Hulton Archive/Getty).*

lence to international competition by refusing to send a team to Brazil in 1950 because it had only finished runner-up to England in the home international championship.[72]

English football's self-confidence took its greatest blow, possibly of all time, with the famous 6–3 home defeat by Hungary in November 1953. In purely sporting terms, the outcome could have been predicted. Despite some impressive results, including a 4–0 victory over Italy in Turin in 1948, England had lost to a number of continental opponents on its travels and struggled against others at home. The Republic of Ireland became the first non-British national side to win on English soil in 1949 and home defeats against Yugoslavia, Austria, France and a Rest of the World eleven were narrowly avoided in the early 1950s. The latter of these, in October 1953, became a portent for the Hungary game the following month. Critics regarded it as 'a moral defeat for England' with the English players 'chasing shadows as the continentals flashed the ball from man to man'.[73] With an unbeaten record stretching nearly four years, and as Olympic champions, the Hungarian 'Golden Team' was recognised as one of the world's best. Why, then, did the result seem so unexpected? Some have pointed to the role of the English press, which managed to convince its readers (the players included) that England would have little trouble winning the match. Willy Meisl described this as the 'igno-arrogance' of the English, who for decades had 'ignored the glaring facts of European and international football'. Jeffrey Hill has shown how the dominant newspaper theme of 'mastery' allowed previous failures to be dismissed as 'adventitious occurrences' and the 'myth' of English footballing superiority to be maintained.[74] With defeat at Wembley, and an arguably more humiliating 7–1 loss in Budapest the following May, however, the deficiencies of the English game had been cruelly exposed. Geoffrey Green of *The Times* proclaimed that England was 'no longer a major world power in the game'. Arthur Hopcraft was equally succinct: 'We could not play football better than any other country, after all. Far from knowing all there was to know about the game we found that we had been left years behind by it.'[75]

The impact of 1953 can hardly be underestimated. It led to decades of soul-searching by those who coached, played and wrote about the game in England. Stephen Wagg has called it 'the symbolic moment when it became clear that English football would have to "go back to school" and learn to play in the modern, scientific way'. The most damning critique of all came from the pen of Meisl. In his book *Soccer Revolution*, first published in 1955, Meisl traced the decline of English football back to changes in the offside law introduced in 1925 and the subsequent introduction of a negative 'safety first' attitude. He argued that English players had become devoted to a rigid system with an emphasis on stopping opponents rather than creating attacking opportunities and had thus lost the very qualities of clever positioning, precision passing and team combination which were displayed so impressively by the new Hungarian 'masters'.[76] Although undoubtedly a team of excellent players – especially the inside-forwards Puskas and Sandor Kocsis and the deep-lying centre-forward Nandor Hidegkuti – it was the overall approach of the Hungarians that impressed many commentators. Bernard Joy, the former Arsenal and England amateur and *Evening Standard* football correspondent, pointed to the successful combination of tactical awareness, fitness and mastery of the ball, but also argued that Hungary brought a 'new conception of the game', whereby the football interests of the country were devoted entirely to the cause of the national team. Some of these observations were certainly taken on board. An under-23 side was established to aid the process of team-building at international level and, after defeat by Uruguay in the quarter-finals of the 1954 World Cup in Switzerland, plans were made to give Walter Winterbottom more time to prepare his squad for international fixtures. Possibly as a result of these developments, the England team went 16 matches undefeated between November 1955 and November 1957, with a new generation of players including the likes of Ron Clayton, Johnny Haynes and Manchester United's teenage star Duncan Edwards.[77]

Yet the reaction to the Hungarian defeat was about more than preparation and tactics. Looked at from a broader perspective, 1953 can be seen as a decisive moment in the relationship between football and English national identity. At a time when Britain was retreating from its empire and losing its political influence on the world stage, the England football team increasingly came to be regarded as an embodiment of the nation itself. As *The Times* observed in early 1955: 'The ordinary man finds the form of our professional footballers a more convenient indication of the state of the nation than all the economist's soundings'.[78] Holt and Mason have suggested that in the wake of the combined shock of defeat by Hungary and the Suez crisis of 1956, there was a change in the way in which the England team was perceived by public and popular press alike. Matches against foreign opposition were taken more seriously and 'winning became more important'.[79] For Weight, the significance of 1953 was greater still, helping 'to alter the trajectory of Britishness'. Not only, in his view, was it a catalyst for consolidating soccer's supremacy over cricket as the national game of the English populace, but it also led to football replacing institutions such as the monarchy, church and parliament as '*the* focal point of English national identity'. Logically, according to Weight's argument, football's new patriotic dimension in England also had an effect on Anglo-Scottish relations, converting the game 'from a shared leisure pursuit to the crucible of national tensions within the Union'. Weight's narrative does simplify matters by telescoping a number of complicated developments occurring over decades into a single event, but the fundamental point - that the Hungary defeat was instrumental in linking the fortunes of the England team to those of the English nation – is not really in doubt.[80]

The Scottish national team also suffered a number of defeats against foreign opposition in the early 1950s but *its* 'Hungary' was to come during its first World Cup appearance in 1954. A 1–0 defeat by Austria, followed by a 7–0 thrashing at the hands of Uruguay, left the Scots humiliated and regarded, according to one account, as 'the laughing-stock of the world'. For journalist John Rafferty, Scotland's participation was a 'shambles': 'an embarrassing affair, reluctantly conceived and ill-managed'. The BBC commentator Kenneth Wolstenholme felt that the Scottish preparations for the tournament gave the impression 'that they really didn't want anything to do with this nonsense'.[81] There is certainly little indication that the Scottish FA took it seriously. It not only allowed Rangers to take its best players on a tour of the USA while the competition was in progress but also made do with a squad of only 13 (including just one goalkeeper) rather than the 22 permitted under FIFA rules. The squad also apparently travelled without training gear and thus many players trained in their club jerseys. Moreover, internal disputes within the party led to the resignation of manager Andy Beattie on the eve of the Uruguay fiasco. Dismissed along with Korea and Turkey as one of the competition's minnows, Scotland found its football reputation shattered by the humiliation of 1954.[82]

It is possible to read the 1958 World Cup in Sweden as heralding the deferred arrival of British football on to the international stage. For the first (and only) time, all four nations qualified. With an inexperienced squad depleted by the loss of several key Manchester United players

PLATE 12 *The Wales team before a World Cup qualifying game against Israel at Ninian Park, Cardiff, in February 1958. Wales won the match and qualified for the World Cup finals that summer in Sweden (© Popperfoto.com).*

months earlier at Munich, England failed to progress beyond the group phase, but its performances have been described as creditable under the circumstances and deserving of sympathy. Scotland also went out in the first round, but Northern Ireland and Wales were more successful, proceeding to the quarter-final stage after play-offs. Hampered by injuries and poor travel arrangements, the Irish team was well beaten (4–0) by France while, without its best player John Charles, Wales went down 1–0 to champions elect Brazil, courtesy of a goal by a 17-year old Pele. But these were major achievements nonetheless. Jimmy McIlroy, one of Northern Ireland's stars, thought the competition had transformed his nation from 'soccer nonentities' into a 'world soccer power' and that 'those three weeks in Scandinavia did more for Irish football than all the seventy-odd years that had gone before'. For the Welsh, the tournament remains the highpoint of its soccer history.[83]

More generally, however, the 1958 World Cup only served to underline the comparative weakness of British football. Television once again played a crucial role here. The establishment of 'Eurovision' in 1954 by the continent's leading national broadcasters allowed viewers to watch the world's best sides and players in Switzerland and Sweden rather than second-hand via press reports and radio commentary. As well as broadening the horizons of British fans, television also alerted them to the vast gap in quality between the home nations and the best international sides such as Uruguay, Germany, Brazil and France. It is instructive that the most strident criticism of England's performances in 1958 came from television reporters, who, for instance, considered England lucky to get away with a goalless draw in the opening match against Brazil when the press had considered it a magnificent performance.[84] A couple of years after the finals, George Raynor, coach of the runners-up, wrote a penetrating attack on the 'failure' of the British sides in 1958. He admonished the associations for sloppy preparation and poor team selection but pointed to more fundamental difficulties relating to perceptions of the world game. Despite the lessons of the early and mid-1950s, the British still underestimated the rest of the world and refused to take international football sufficiently seriously. Club football still mattered more. In terms of both ability and attitude, Raynor suggested, the British teams were 'not yet equipped to win world competitions'.[85]

Managers, coaching and the game

The age of the manager

The changing role of the football manager offers a particularly revealing insight into what has been termed the modernisation of the British game in the post-war years. While his position was established before the First World War, and consolidated in the 1920s and 1930s, the manager only emerged as an autonomous and central figure in the world of professional football during this period. Aided by the move towards technocracy and the spread of coaching, Stephen Wagg has argued that control and responsibility for team affairs, previously the preserve of the directors at most clubs, increasingly shifted to the manager. It was now the manager who bought the players, selected the team, communicated with supporters and the media and was ultimately held responsible for the results. But the rise of the manager was gradual and uneven. Neil Carter has recently suggested that, despite discernable changes, football management in the post-war years was 'slow to modernise', retaining many of the character-istics of its Victorian inheritance. Football managers, in his view, shared the tradition of practical experience characteristic of British industrial managers more generally. They acquired expertise by learning on the job rather than through qualifications or formal training. Carter also stresses that, despite closer relationships between 'the boss' and 'the lads', an authoritarian style of man-management based on nineteenth-century notions of control and obedience continued to dominate the industrial relations of British football.[86]

Without doubt, the most important individual in the history of foot-ball management was Herbert Chapman. Not only was he extremely successful – achieving three consecutive championships with Huddersfield Town in the 1920s and laying the foundations for a similar feat at Arsenal before his death in January 1934 – he was also instrumental in defining the boundaries of the position as we understand it today. Secretary-man-agers had existed since the late nineteenth century and some of these, such as Tom Watson of Sunderland and Liverpool, played an active role in the recruitment, selection and training of players but continued to operate under the authority of the board of directors. Chapman ultimately changed all this. For some he was a 'football revolutionary', providing new tactical perspectives on the playing side but also advocating a range of innovations in the structure, administration and public relations of the sport. One of the earliest assessments of his career was subtitled 'A Study in the Origins of Modern Soccer' and claimed him to be 'the first, and perhaps the greatest, of the modern-style football managers'.[87] According to Carter, Chapman effectively modernised the manager's role and became the prototype for its future. Others have highlighted the role of another inter-war manager, Major Frank Buckley of Wolverhampton Wanderers, who shared Chapman's autonomy over team matters, his concern for the discipline and welfare of his players and his eye for publicity. In Scotland, Bill Struth of Rangers achieved a similar autonomy over team affairs, ruling through fear and force of personality, aided by a carefully chosen hierarchy of senior players and a substantial shareholding in the company. Yet all writers tend to agree that, in Russell's words, these developments 'represented the beginning of a trend rather than a full-blown change' and that the process of 'Chapmanisation' was resisted at most British clubs between the wars. Thus during the 1930s the manager's powers at Newport County were limited to 'recommending' the players for selection, while the Sheffield Wednesday directors did no more than 'consider' the opinion of manager Billy Walker on team matters. The Everton team was under the organisational and tactical control of its leading director William Cuff before 1939, while West Bromwich Albion did not appoint a manager in name until 1948 and Aston Villa until 1958. Most clubs may have employed a manager under one guise or another by the Second World War, but few enjoyed the range of powers allowed to men like Chapman, Buckley or Struth.[88]

Percy Young dubbed the inter-war years 'the age of the manager' but it is an epithet arguably more applicable to the post-war decades.[89] Alongside their increasing employment at all professional clubs, the turnover of managers grew considerably, a consequence of the tendency of the media, supporters and, most importantly, directors to identify them with the fortunes (good and bad) of the team. The vast majority of these new appointees were former professional players, with no management training or expertise save for the fact that they themselves had played the game. Ex-internationals were particularly popular with club directorates

on the principle that either a good player would be able to pass on his talents to other players, or that he would provide inspiration, or, more pragmatically, that the presence of a big name in the manager's chair would put a few thousand on the gate.[90]

The FA tried to establish formal training courses for managers from the late 1950s. It was supported in its endeavours by managers such as Wolves' Stan Cullis, who bemoaned the fact that 'former players become managers almost overnight' and advocated the study by prospective

PLATE 13 *Stan Cullis, manager of Wolverhampton Wanderers, pictured in 1955 in the dressing room at Molineux talking tactics with (l–r) Billy Wright, Ray Swinburne, Ron Flowers and Jimmy Mullen (© Popperfoto.com).*

recruits of 'tactics, business administration, laws and regulations of the Football Association and Football League [and] the art of handling men'. There was also probably an eye on developments on the continent, where most clubs and national sides only employed qualified coaches, and in Italy particularly, where the first courses and diplomas for football management had been introduced in the late 1940s.[91] Yet for all this, the response within the game was lukewarm and so what might have developed into a system of professional qualifications and a formal appointments procedure for football was ultimately rejected in favour of the existing ad hoc arrangements which left directors free to appoint as manager whomever they wanted.[92]

Many football managers adopted personas and techniques reminiscent of the armed forces. The 'sergeant-major' style of management prevalent in the inter-war years remained a popular approach for a generation who had either served during the Second World War, often as physical training instructors, or experienced national service afterwards.[93] The most successful managers of the period – such as Cullis at Wolves and, to a lesser extent, Matt Busby at Manchester United – were authoritarians with charismatic personalities who believed that discipline lay at the heart of managing groups of young working-class men. In certain respects Cullis, for instance, adopted a similar approach to Buckley, his mentor and predecessor at Wolves. He was a 'hard man' who was unquestionably disliked by some of his charges: one former player, Dennis Wilshaw, believed that the team spirit 'stemmed from the fact that we hated his guts'. His demands on players could lead to mistreatment, such as when he ordered Ted Farmer to play on after an injury which left him urinating blood, telling the club doctor: 'Wait till it comes through his backside before you take him off'.[94] Yet many post-war managers differed from their inter-war counterparts in that they combined an authoritarian hand with a personal touch, perhaps reflecting the less deferential nature of British society after 1945. Cullis, who was in his early thirties when he took the manager's seat at Wolves in 1948, was in daily contact with his players, training with them and encouraging them to voice their opinions during weekly team talks. England international Ron Flowers thought that, despite the rigid discipline, there was 'a warm heart' at Molineux (the Wolves home ground) and that the welfare of the players was the manager's main concern. Jimmy McIlroy described Harry Potts, his manager at Burnley, as 'one of the boys': 'Off the field, we are not subjected to petty restrictions ... He trusts us'. Elsewhere, managers such as Bill Nicholson at Tottenham Hotspur and Bedford Jezzard at Fulham were on first-name terms with their players.[95]

Post-war managers tended to present themselves less as distant autocrats and more as caring father figures. Matt Busby's reign at Manchester United provides the perfect example. He was often described as a 'patriarch'; in Arthur Hopcraft's portrait, he was the 'stern, devoted grandfather, making all the big decisions, ordering and disciplining in some huge, unpredictably gifted household'. Busby endeavoured to minimise the gulf between management and players and adopt a more humane approach to the role, such as that which he had experienced as a player under George Kay at Liverpool. Like Cullis, he was thus a regular presence on the training ground; indeed he is often regarded as the very first 'tracksuit' manager.[96] He attended reserve team matches and showed a genuine interest in the fortunes of the young footballers under his control. One author has written of the 'omniscient presence' of Busby and argued that his 'paternal solicitude' was crucial in forming a bond with the playing staff. He also involved himself closely in their personal lives, dealing with any domestic problems and identifying vices that could potentially affect the performance of his players. This concern with the welfare of players was bound up in the rhetoric of the 'family'. Eamon Dunphy has succinctly summed up this aspect of the Busby management philosophy: 'The club was a family, *his* family, there would be no secrets, no gaps in communication, no misunderstandings. His office door was always open ... not just for football problems, for anything, however personal and seemingly remote from the game.' As a young player, Bobby Charlton was particularly impressed by Busby's ability to recall the Christian names of everyone at the club and by the family spirit 'created and nurtured by the boss'. Yet Busby was also ruthless in excluding those who did not fit into his family. Thus the talented but independently minded Johnny Morris was transfer-listed in 1949 after a training ground argument, while two years later Charlie Mitten was excluded from Old Trafford and transferred to Fulham, despite asking Busby for a pardon for breaking his contract and moving to the outlawed Colombian league.[97]

Carter has described the move towards managerial autonomy in British football as a complex and 'almost imperceptible process' dependent upon the management culture of individual clubs and the influence of powerful personalities. In 1961 an FA Technical Committee defined a manager's responsibilities to include the signing of players approved by the board, the organisation of the scouting system and players' salaries, the planning of tactics and coaching and the overall control of all staff. In practice, however, these were still often checked by directorial interference. On his return to English football in the mid-1950s with Coventry City, George Raynor found his directors meddling in the payment of players' benefits, transfer decisions and even half-time team talks. When a general manager was appointed, thus reducing his role to that of team manager, Raynor resigned, complaining of the interference and impatience of the board. The right to intervene was explicitly written into Raich Carter's 1955 contract with Leeds United, by making him 'subject to any orders given to him by the Board of Directors'. At lowly Darlington, a Third Division North and Fourth Division club during the 1950s, the records of board meetings show that team selection and transfer decisions were never fully relinquished, even when contracts were signed that ensured managers full control.[98] This is not to deny that the old role of the manager as 'front man and office boy' was becoming increasingly difficult to justify by the 1950s and early 1960s. Wagg has convincingly argued that the establishment of managers as 'arbiters of team affairs *in fact*, not just in theory' was aided by the changing attitudes of the media and club directors. First, the manager rather than the club was increasingly pivotal to any newspaper story: managers bought players, devised tactical schemes and thus won or lost matches. Teams were equated with their manager: Manchester United became 'Matt Busby United' and then 'The Busby Babes'; West Ham United under Ron Greenwood were known as 'Greenwood Men'. Men like Busby and Cullis, and later Bill Nicholson at Tottenham Hotspur, were portrayed as 'Great Team Makers' in the same tradition as Chapman. Football managers, in short, were more famous than they had ever been. Second, as crowds declined, wage demands increased and competition for players intensified, directors increasingly looked to a single expert who could take on the burden of expectation and be held individually responsible for a club's fortunes. All this served to transform the manager from a marginal to a central figure in British football culture and encouraged the idea, if not always reflecting the reality, that 'the managerial hand alone guided team performance'.[99]

Attitudes to coaching

The emergence of the modern manager was closely connected to the development of coaching and what Wagg called the 'coming of technocracy'. By this, he was referring to the creation of a body of accumulated technical knowledge related to the tactical and preparatory side of the game and the accompanying formation of a network of football 'specialists' or 'experts'.[100] The FA, under its first coaching guru Walter Winterbottom, was at the heart of these changes. It had run coaching courses directed mainly at tuition for schoolboys from the mid-1930s, but extended these after 1945 to include more professional players and managers. Qualifications were established through a system of preliminary and full certificates and badges. Official publications such as the FA Bulletin and the FA Book for Boys, and instructional films on football skills and techniques, worked alongside these schemes, helping the English governing body to establish a coterie of experienced coaches and to 'spread the coaching gospel' more broadly. This was an important aspect of the FA's work – accounting for £10,000 of its annual budget from the late 1940s – and part of its mission under Rous 'to meet contemporary challenges and slough off at least some of its conservative traditions'. Under Winterbottom, coaching also became central to the preparation of the England team. According to Bob Ferrier, the pre-match training sessions were well received by even the senior players:

Lawton, Carter, Swift, Matthews, Scott, all fell to with a will and enjoyed the new approach and the fun and games of preparation ... The fact that such men, established stars of the highest class, could relish these practices was highly encouraging.

Coaching at this level, Ferrier revealed, was about blending the skills of the players rather than teaching them to tackle, dribble and shoot. The coach (Winterbottom in this case) thus acted as 'the third party' whose role it was 'to build a high co-ordination factor in the team by directing practice and preparation'.[101]

Resistance to the idea of coaching was certainly a feature of both the pre- and post-war periods but its significance has probably been over-stated. Many players objected to coaching quite simply because to accept it would imply that football talent might be based on something other than the innate skill of the individual. This was a view that assumed that great players were born or self-made not taught: it owed much to that strand of working-class anti-intellectualism which had little time for 'book learners, chalkers on blackboards and purveyors of purely theoretical knowledge'. Because the anti-coaching lobby within the game had support in the popular press, its claims may have been magnified. We know that some of those players portrayed by Ferrier as advocates of the new approach were actually among its harshest critics. Tommy Lawton and Raich Carter were less convinced than most by Winterbottom's first England team meetings.[102] Stanley Matthews, meanwhile, included a chapter in his 1952 autobiography railing against the 'modern craze' of coaching. The players of his generation had done without tuition but instead relied on natural ability and hard practice: 'A lad who is a born footballer will succeed, but I defy any coach to make a really good player out of a youngster who hasn't got what it takes'. Other leading players made similar public statements. Wilf Mannion thought coaches entirely unnecessary for professional players: 'No one coached Raich Carter. No one coached Stanley Matthews. If a lad can't play at eighteen or twenty, he'll never play.' Tom Finney was one of many who believed that players could be over-coached and that rigid and regimented instruction did more harm than good. 'It is a fact', Finney argued in 1960, 'that British football produced more great players in the days when coaching on a national scale was almost non-existent than it does today.'[103]

Yet for all this ideological opposition, there is evidence that the intro-duction of coaching actually received as much support as criticism. Even in the early days of the FA's scheme, advocates were to be found at numerous professional clubs: Sheffield United and Oldham Athletic were impressed enough to send their entire training staffs to the summer schools at the Carnegie Physical Training College in Leeds during the late 1930s. By 1947, 300 were graduating annually with full coaching badges, many of them senior professional players who then returned to their clubs and put the new methods learnt into practice.[104] Despite the opinions outlined above, Wagg has shown that the majority of England players under Winterbottom were similarly receptive to these ideas. Nat Lofthouse, Billy Wright, Frank Swift, Johnny Haynes, George Hardwick and Bobby Robson all spoke of their enthusiasm for Winterbottom's methods and coaching in general. Bill Nicholson and Joe Mercer, meanwhile, were two who soon acquired FA badges, the latter after having previously doubted the benefit of any preparation other than match play experience itself. The Rangers and Scotland captain George Young thought that the success of the FA's work meant that 'coaching is no longer looked upon with a certain amount of suspicion by a large section of the soccer community' in England and advocated the creation of an equivalent structure north of the border.[105] Such was the impact of these new approaches on players that they often took a central role in developing styles and systems of play. At West Ham United, the brand of 'entertaining football' associated with the club from the mid-1950s was a product of the discussions of the professionals themselves, led by Malcolm Allison, whose 'classroom' was the local Cassatarri café close to the Upton Park ground. The 'West Ham Academy', as it was to be called, with the 'passive encouragement' of manager Ted Fenton, not only determined how the team was to play but also became the breeding ground for a number of influential coaches and managers of the future, including Allison himself, Frank O'Farrell, John Bond and Dave Sexton.[106]

Tactics and playing styles

We can see that much of the division over coaching arose because the term was flexible enough to encompass a range of meanings. For those who saw it primarily as the teaching of skills, the idea of coaching in terms of tactical preparation for matches was less problematic. Indeed few now objected to the notion that teams should have a basic plan of how to play before they set foot on the field. Conventional wisdom has it that English football at least, if not the British game more generally, was characterised by a fundamental uniformity of tactics and styles before the 1960s. The introduction of the so-called 'stopper' or 'third back' as a new defensive centre-half effectively revolutionised the way the game was played in Britain. Most closely associated with Arsenal under Chapman, the innovation arose to combat the increased goal-scoring opportunities resulting from the 1925 change in the offside law and led to the widespread adoption of a new WM formation, incorporating three backs, two half-backs, two withdrawn inside-forwards and a three-man attacking line. The Arsenal system was widely imitated, with most British teams moving over to some version of the 'third back game' by the 1930s, but often suffered due to its replication by less talented players and a tendency to neglect the crucial linking role of the deep-lying forwards.[107] What resulted, according to critics like Meisl, was a game 'built mainly on destructive, defensive, spoiling tactics, in short, on negative football'. Others bemoaned the predominance of a crude and dreary 'kick-and-rush' game based on the speed and strength of forwards and the long punting of defenders. By the 1950s this had become recognised by some as a quintessential English style of football. Chas Critcher, for one, has argued that the approach pioneered by Chapman remained the unchallenged tactical orthodoxy for almost four decades.[108]

Other accounts have dismissed the 'kick-and-rush' label as simplistic, stressing the proliferation of different playing styles in the post-war years. In contrast to the stereotypical view of English football as 'all neanderthal vigour, high tempo, and the big boot', intelligent interplay and short passing were hardly uncommon. Under Cliff Britton, Burnley adopted the so-called 'clockwork method', which involved positioning the whole team behind the ball when on the defensive and then, when possession was regained, moving up the field by the means of short passes (in a 'tick-tock fashion') from player to player. Arguably more attractive and certainly more effective was the 'push-and-run' style developed at Tottenham Hotspur by Arthur Rowe, which brought the club consecutive Second and First Division championships in 1949–50 and 1950–1. Based on first-time passing over short distances and constant movement off the ball, 'push-and-run' was likened to continental football generally, and the style of the 1945 Moscow Dynamo team specifically. Practice and tactical preparation were fundamental to the club's success. Rowe's philosophy was exemplified in a number of key slogans – such as 'Move the ball, move yourself' and 'Make it simple, make it quick' – and relied on the linking together of all 11 players as a team unit when defending and attacking. West Bromwich Albion, whose combination of Rowe's short-passing game with the occasional 40-yard ball nearly brought the League and Cup double in the 1953–4 season, showed how 'push-and-run' could be modified to suit the particular talents of the available players. Hibernian won the Scottish League in 1950–1 and 1951–2 with an approach not dissimilar from Tottenham's: Bernard Joy described it as the traditional Scottish style of accurate distribution along the ground and clever wing-play merged with 'sharp inter-passing and inter-changing on the Continental pattern'. At Manchester City, the overseas influence was more direct, with Don Revie employed in the role of retreating centre-forward popularised a few years earlier by Hidegkuti for Hungary.[109] Some thought this tactical diversity damaging to the British game. Ledbrooke and Turner complained that 'in this country, we have too many styles' and suggested that as national coach Winterbottom should be empowered, like his continental counterparts, to dictate patterns of play from the national eleven to schoolboy football.[110]

Even Wolves, the archetypal 1950s 'kick-and-rush' side, adopted a more technical and tactically sophisticated approach to the game than is often supposed. The long-ball game favoured by Cullis was much more than a 'traditional' English style of play: it was in fact a highly scientific approach based on the detailed analysis of match performance and the most efficient use of the available resources. Aided by the statistical data of soccer's first performance analyst, Wing-Commander Charles Reep, Cullis developed a tactical system based on harrying and pressing the opposition and sending the ball as quickly as possible into the opponents' penalty area. This was to be done ideally in less than three passes, invariably via a long ball out of defence for fast wingers to run on to. Cullis himself accepted that this could be called 'scientific kick-and-rush football' based on the crucial principle that the team 'went for goal in a direct, incisive fashion which contained scarcely any frills'.[111] Wolves did employ a number of talented ball players and, in wingers Johnny Hancocks and Jimmy Mullen, had two of the most accurate passers of the long ball in the game. But their talent was harnessed to the team effort. Indeed Cullis was even prepared gently to chide individualists such as the great Stanley Matthews:

If a young Matthews came to Molineux tomorrow, I would endeavour to use his tremendous skill to a greater effect than perhaps it has been used in the past. With his speed, superlative ball-control, ability to slip easily past a defender and accurate shot, Matthews should surely have scored many more goals than he has done.

Whatever critics thought of the Wolves tactics, they were certainly effective. The club was First Division champions three times during the 1950s and scored over one hundred league goals each season from 1957–8 to 1960–1. Nor was Wolves alone in making intelligent use of the long ball. Newcastle United adopted this method to exploit the pace of centre-forward Jackie Milburn, while Johnny Haynes became 'the master of the long distance pass' for Fulham and England, regularly splitting opposing defences by releasing wingers or centre-forwards with accurate passes of some 50 yards. This way of playing was technical, scientific and certainly much more than simple 'kick-and-rush'. It reflected a progressive way of thinking about the game which formed a fundamental part of the modernisation of British football. For Cullis, as for Rowe and other new thinkers, winning had to be managed and planned. Few clubs adopted the rigid models of play feared by critics of coaching, but by the early 1960s fewer still risked facing opponents without adequate preparation and some form of tactical plan.[112]

Players and the end of football slavery?
Work and play

Evidence of modernisation is less easy to find in the employment conditions and social status of the players themselves. In many respects, their experience of work and their associated lifestyle and occupational culture had not altered significantly since the 1920s. The basic job was much the same as it had always been. Players trained intensely over three to four weeks in pre-season and then settled into a weekly schedule which varied from club to club but normally involved some combination of running, physical exercises and ball work over four or five days every week. The length and intensity of the season, particularly in England, led to a traditional emphasis on maintaining fitness and stamina at the exclusion of ball practice. Accounts of training sessions from the pre-1939 period indicate the predominance of sprinting, running, walking, skipping and some work with weights alongside less frequent bouts of ball work. Dave Willis, a trainer at Raith Rovers, Nottingham Forest and Derby County between the wars, articulated the seemingly bizarre but commonly held view that players who practised too much with the ball during the week got bored of the sight of it and were consequently less eager to get hold of it come Saturday. We know from contemporary accounts that many players regarded training as monotonous and lacking in imagination. Particular antipathy was reserved for the practice of lapping the perimeter of the field in order to harden the muscles and improve general stamina and fitness. Some clubs required players to circle the pitch as often as 50 or 60 times a day.[113]

Training regimes at many clubs did change after 1945, with a new breed of young trainers, coaches and managers, some with overseas experience, ushering in a range of methods designed to improve the fitness and maintain the interest of their players. Hull City's player-manager Raich Carter, for example, had little time for lapping, consigning it to the Thursday schedule alongside dribbling, sprinting and body exercises. For him, ball practice was 'the correct way to do training' as it was 'ideal for keeping players interested in their work'. At Doncaster Rovers, Peter Doherty combined established routines with team games such as basketball, volleyball and football tennis, while another young player-manager, Ronnie Rooke, introduced competitive ball races at Crystal Palace and replaced lapping with 10-mile hikes on a variety of routes.[114] Stan Cullis claimed that training at most clubs during the 1950s and early 1960s was 'far removed from the old days when three or four laps and half a dozen sprints each morning and a bit of kicking comprised the programme'. At Wolves, training was organised 'scientifically' into six categories relating to factors such as speed, stamina, agility and utilisation of ground coverage. The normal weekly schedule consisted of:

Monday: Light ball-work for 100 minutes in the morning.
Tuesday: A three-mile run, sprinting, hurdling and agility training for 100 minutes in the morning. Weight-training and ball-work for a similar spell in the afternoon.
Wednesday: A morning practice match or training in football boots for two hours in the morning.
Thursday: Sprinting and running, ball-work in the morning. Positional and individual coaching in the afternoon.
Friday: Sprinting, exercises and light ball-work for an hour.[115]

One writer has described this emphasis on physical endurance, power and dexterity as 'ahead of its time'. Certainly most training was nowhere near as intense, as Danny Blanchflower found during his time at Barnsley, where he was prevented by the trainer from doing extra ball practice in the afternoons on the grounds that other players might then want to join him.[116]

The increasing pace of the game led to greater demands on the bodies of footballers. Even over the course of the 1930s, the secretary of the Players' Union could comment on the increasing 'craze for speed' in the professional game, which led to more and more knocks and serious injuries and threw scores of footballers 'on the scrap heap'. The fear of injury had always been paramount in the minds of players, who faced the potential loss both of their source of income and their health. Most clubs employed doctors, masseurs and later, physiotherapists, to treat injured players as well as paying the costs for surgery and recuperation. Under the Workmen's Compensation Act of 1906, injured players were entitled to continued income and medical expenses and, when forced to retire, received a lump-sum payment as compensation. A joint FA–Union accident insurance scheme funded out of television money was established in 1956 which, when set alongside the Provident Fund founded in 1949, offered a degree of financial protection for injured players or those forced to quit the game prematurely.[117] For all this, the increasing demand for results meant that the physical well-being of players was not always the foremost consideration of employers. In the masculine environment of the dressing-room, players were expected to endure 'hard knocks', and suffer pain and discomfort without complaint. A number of autobiographies have revealed the poor medical treatment metered out to employees. Charlie Williams remembered being strapped up and told to walk to and from training, rather than being put in plaster, when he ripped his tendons playing for Doncaster Rovers in the 1950s. At Portsmouth, Derek Dougan trained and played with an undetected broken ankle for ten weeks, while Ted Farmer recalls a number of incidents as a young player at Wolves during the early 1960s when he was stitched up, injected with cortisone and sent out to play regardless of his symptoms and pain. The last straw came when Farmer's own doctor discovered that he had suffered a broken fibula in a match five weeks earlier. The club had detected a more minor injury, accused him of hypochondria and forced him to resume playing despite continual pain. Three years and a series of poorly diagnosed injuries later, Farmer was forced to retire at the age of 25.[118]

Theorists writing from a Marxist perspective have seen in all this evidence of the control and exploitation of footballers' bodies. According to this view, players are transformed into alienated 'workers' in the capitalist enterprise of the professional football industry. As the source of their labour power, their bodies are subjected to close supervision and discipline, monitored, tuned and programmed by managers, trainers and physiotherapists. Gerhard Vinnai has written of footballers as 'machines' who are trained and regulated to fit with the overarching tactical system of the team. The rhetoric of the game emphasises the technical and the mechanical: players with high levels of stamina are described as having a 'good engine' while others, conversely, have 'nothing left in the tank'. Even the acquisition of ball skills and technique act to constrain the individual freedom of the footballer and prevent him from controlling his own body movements. For Vinnai, the professional is thus no more than a part of the rationalised machinery of the football production line. Moreover, football in this context has been perceived as a form of work rather than play. For writers such as Bruno Rigauer and Jean-Marie Brohm, the patterns and structures of sporting competition fundamentally replicate those of work. According to the latter, sport 'removes all bodily freedom, all creative spontaneity, every aesthetic dimension and every playful impulse'. Writing in the early 1970s, Vinnai likewise considered the term 'play' inappropriate in the context of professional sport: 'The element of play, which could still find a place in the early days of football, has increasingly disappeared'.[119]

In reality, however, the relationship between notions of 'work' and 'play' in football was much more ambiguous than Vinnai and others assume. Most observers have recognised the peculiar nature of the footballer's occupation: as employees whose job it was to try to win for their team but who were nonetheless described as 'players' engaged in a 'game'. In 1934 a high court case reversed the existing legal definition of professional footballers as 'workmen' employed 'by way of manual labour'. The presiding judge, Justice Roach, found that footballers 'are engaged not in work but in play. They are playing for reward and payment . . . but they are still playing a game'. Many professionals were likewise able to look on football as both a sport at which they 'played' and a job at which they 'worked'. Dick Walker, whose career lasted from 1934 until 1953, told Charles Korr that 'he enjoyed playing for West Ham and getting paid for it'. Yet, Korr noted, 'at no time did he ever regard what he was doing as amusement or a game. He was on the pitch to perform attractively *and* to do a job'.[120] Although footballers were undeniably workers in some respects, there is little evidence that they became alienated from their productive labour in a Marxist sense. In spite of tactical and disciplinary constraints, they enjoyed relative freedom over the way they played and prepared for matches. The leading post-war players were described as 'entertainers' or 'artists' with exceptional talent rather than as labourers performing routine tasks. Even when the language of work was employed, emphasis was placed on the commitment to football as a trade, a craft or a vocation as well as the 'hard graft' associated with manual work. Stanley Matthews, for example, has been portrayed as a professional 'dedicated to fitness and training' with 'the qualities of an artisan who kept his tools in order'. Training well, watching one's weight and keeping oneself physically fit were important elements of the job but also a source of professional pride. These were characteristics of the craftsman or skilled worker who controlled his labour and applied his skill. In such circumstances, it seems more appropriate to speak of bodily expression through football than bodily subjugation.[121]

Fighting for freedom

As far as conditions of employment were concerned, control lay firmly in the hands of the employers. Labouring under maximum wage restrictions and the retain-and-transfer system, post-war footballers in England continued to be considered by many as 'slaves' of management. The better players had always expressed dissatisfaction with these conditions, if only through their union, but unrest grew in the context of general wage rises in industry and the widespread belief that they should be treated and rewarded in the same manner as other entertainers. Newspaper articles and autobiographies decried the unfairness of the existing system. Advocating the concept of 'star pay for star play', Tom Finney accused the game's leaders of 'violating every basic principle of economics with their archaic maximum wage restriction':

Imagine Mr Rex Harrison appearing in My Fair Lady at the Theatre Royal Drury Lane, for £20-a-week ... (winter only, of course!) Ridiculous? Yet Stanley Matthews, in his own field, is as great a star as Rex Harrison. He should be paid accordingly.[122]

Len Shackleton referred in his controversial autobiography to the player's contract as 'an evil document' that led 'unrest and dissatisfaction to spread through soccer, season after season'. Adopting a more restrained tone, Charlton's veteran goalkeeper Sam Bartram nonetheless believed that 'a footballer should have the normal right of every working man to give notice and change his job'.[123] Although free from a maximum wage, Scottish footballers faced the same contractual restrictions as in England and had less opportunity to move to a club outside the major league if in dispute with their employers. Other grievances set out by the Scottish Players' Union in 1951 included the poor share of transfer fees received and the taxing of benefit payments.[124]

Pressure from the unions and outside bodies led to increases in the maximum wage in England after 1945. The National Arbitration Tribunal raised the maximum to £12 a week during the playing season and £10 in the summer break, with a minimum introduced for the first time of between £3 and £7 depending on the player's age. By 1958, the maximum had reached £20 and £17 in the close season, but there were considerable differentials between divisions and clubs and even within teams. Cullis claimed that the members of his 1958–9 championship squad at Wolves were on £1,600 a year, made up of a basic wage, win bonuses, talent money and benefit payments. With the addition of international match fees, Wolves and England captain Billy Wright was estimated to have made as much as £2,100 that season. For the same season, Political and Economic Planning calculated average annual earnings at £1,150 for First Division regulars but only £875 in the Fourth Division. The Football League noted at the beginning of the 1950s that 25 per cent of its players were in receipt of the maximum wage, but the figure was much lower outside the first team and the top division. Only one player at Bradford City, in the Third Division North, was paid the £12 maximum in 1949–50; five years later there were only four on over £12 (the maximum now at £15) while eight of the squad were on a miserly sum of £5 per week or less.[125] The leading Scottish clubs established individual payment ceilings, with £16 a week and a £2 win bonus the limit at Rangers during the mid-1950s. George Young considered that he had earned 'far more than I ever could have done had I joined an English club', while professionals in the top division, on between £10 and £14 per week during the early 1950s, were certainly better off than most of those who watched. Yet the income gap between professional footballers and industrial workers was undoubtedly narrowing: a comparative pay rate of £8 and £4 respectively in 1939 had become £20 and £15 by 1960. Whereas his earning capacity rendered the footballer 'a privileged member of the community' before the Second World War, by the 1950s there was a perception that his standard of living and 'standing in the community' were under threat. Even Arsenal manager Tom Whittaker advocated higher wages for players who 'although living in nice houses in good-class districts, find it hard to keep up appearances, especially during the summer period when there is a substantial drop in their earnings'.[126]

Resentment at wage levels was stoked up by the perception that large attendances, together with the twin boosts of the abolition of the Entertainment Tax and the introduction of pools money in 1957, meant that clubs were in a buoyant financial state. Yet it would be wide of the mark to think that footballers were on the verge of rebellion during the 1950s. Russell has argued that most made what they could from the game 'with varying degrees of acceptance and contentment'.[127] John Harding has similarly noted that even the most disgruntled players tried to circumvent or escape their restrictions rather than confront the system head-on. Thus Wilf Mannion's five-month long one-man strike during 1949, precipitated by his employer Middlesbrough's refusal to allow him to move to the club of his choice, was an exceptional occurrence. The England international's attempt to secure his own financial future and at the same time to show up the absurdities of the transfer system generated considerable press support, but ultimately faltered as Middlesbrough placed a prohibitive £25,000 fee on his head and held firm in its decision not to let him go.[128]

Others opted to move abroad, with or without the consent of their clubs. When seven British professionals, including the Stoke City and England centre-half Neil Franklin, broke their contracts at home and accepted offers in the summer of 1950 to join clubs in the outlawed Colombian soccer league, the fear of a mass exodus of likewise dissatisfied players appeared very real. Franklin claimed to have been paid a £1,500 signing-on fee and £150 a month plus bonuses, while another of the exiles, Manchester United's Charlie Mitten, on an annual salary of £5,000 plus a £25 win bonus, was said to be making more in one season than in his previous decade and a half as a professional. Failing to adapt to a different climate, culture and attitude to the game, most of the Colombian rebels returned home quickly, but the emigration of players did not end. Suspended as a result of the controversial claims of illegal payments included in his autobiography, Welsh centre-forward Trevor Ford moved to Holland with PSV Eindhoven, but Italy proved the most popular destination. Only a handful of lesser-known Britons had played in Italy when Eddie Firmani joined Sampdoria from Charlton Athletic in 1955. Two years later he was joined by the Welsh international John Charles, whose success at Juventus, winning three championships in his first four seasons, encouraged the transfer of other top names, such as Jimmy Greaves and Denis Law, at the beginning of the 1960s. Italian football undoubtedly promised a better income and lifestyle than in Britain. Charles was provided with a Fiat car, a rent-free family apartment and a Mediterranean villa alongside other gifts. His basic wage of £18 may have been £2 less than that at Leeds, but on top of that he received bonuses of £15 for home and £25 for away wins, and up to £500 for special matches, as well as £10,000 of his £65,000 transfer fee. Charles played down the financial gap between the two leagues in his first autobiography but noted that the wage limit offered little incentive to improve and that there was consequently 'precious little future in being a professional footballer in Britain'.[129]

The main vehicle for the articulation of the players' grievances was its union. Established in England in 1907 (a Scottish counterpart followed in

1913), the Association Football Players' Union had instigated an initial wave of militancy, leading to the threat of a nationwide strike in 1909 and a failed attempt to challenge the legality of the transfer system in 1912. Thereafter it eschewed confrontation with the football authorities, largely restricting its activities to membership drives and compensation claims on behalf of members. The short time span and uncertainties of a career in sport had always worked to limit the likelihood of collective action. According to one historian, the Players' Union resembled 'a Red Cross rather than a Red Army' before 1950, while Holt and Mason have portrayed it as 'more of a gadfly on the flank of the Football League than a guided missile'.[130] It became more militant after 1945 but faced tactical and leadership problems. Under its radical chairman Jimmy Guthrie, a cup winner with Portsmouth in 1939, the union increased its public profile, gained the support of politicians such as the Labour MP J. P. W. Mallalieu and courted key sections of the popular press. Yet its lack of experience at the negotiating table and limited gains in collective bargaining with the FA and the Football League necessitated a new approach. In 1957 Guthrie was replaced by Jimmy Hill, an articulate, grammar-school educated Fulham player with a background in business and connections in the media, advertising and public relations industries. Whether or not Hill was 'marginal to football culture', as one writer suggests, there is no doubting his role in uniting the players behind the union and communicating its case to an increasingly sympathetic and receptive public.[131] From the late 1950s, a concerted effort was made to secure the 'two freedoms' of payment and movement. By the middle of 1960 the players were officially in dispute with their employers, and, after a series of failed negotiations overseen by the Ministry of Labour, a strike notice was issued for January 1961. This forced the Football League to concede on a number of issues, culminating in an agreement finally to remove the maximum wage.

Explanations of the players' achievement in 1961 have focused on the union's ability to win influential backing and publicity. Much has rightly been made of the 1957 decision to drop its 'union' title in favour of the more respectable sounding Professional Footballers' Association (PFA) and under Hill it continued to display a sound grasp of public relations. Within the game, the support of the star players alongside the PFA's rank-and-file was imperative, with the respected Stanley Matthews' decision to back strike action most important of all. Television provided the forum for well-known players, such as Tommy Docherty, Phil Woosnam and Don Howe, to put the PFA case, while Hill made regular media

appearances, even discussing the issue on BBC's flagship sports programme *Grandstand* with presenter David Coleman. Support for the
PFA's case also came from the TUC, which called for members to boycott
matches involving blackleg labour if a strike took place.[132] On the other
side of the political spectrum, the Conservative MP Philip Goodhart made
an impassioned parliamentary speech in support of the players; Wagg has
argued that, in the context of increasing working-class affluence and
embourgeoisement, the Conservative government actually 'had more to
gain in prestige from a PFA victory'. The League's Alan Hardaker claimed
in his autobiography that the players' victory was primarily the result of
its superior public relations, 'which clouded opinion in the House of
Commons as well as on the terraces'.[133] Yet the PFA's official historian
has dismissed Hardaker's view that the players 'won' because of
favourable media coverage and instead suggests that it was the strength of
the argument itself that swayed opinion: 'common sense could no longer
accept conditions of employment rooted in the attitudes of nineteenth-
century mill-owners'. Russell has likewise concluded that it was the 'broad
public support' for the players' arguments that eventually forced the football authorities to abolish the wage limit.[134]

A rather different perspective emerges if we consider the events from
the employers' side rather than that of the players. Simon Inglis has
argued that the lack of agreement between the clubs and their failure to
relinquish authority to the League Management Committee were crucial
in the final outcome. In a similar vein, Hill himself thought that the main
responsibility for the dispute lay with 'the unwieldy machinery of the
Football League'. The unwillingness of clubs seriously to consider a
negotiated settlement, whether involving an increased and graduated
maximum or a phasing out of the wage limit over a number of years,
combined with the intransigence of some to push the PFA towards a
more radical solution. In Inglis's view, 'the clubs almost goaded the
players into fighting to the death'.[135] Hardaker similarly bemoaned the
lack of solidarity and long-term planning amongst the employers, suggesting that the historic decision to remove the maximum wage occurred
in a 'period of duress and muddled thinking'. Indeed there is some evidence that Hardaker's own preference for a higher maximum with
unlimited incentives and bonuses may well have been accepted by the
PFA early on in the dispute and that it was the League's obstinate refusal
to consider any change on the principles of the transfer system and the
maximum wage that radicalised the players to the point of strike
action.[136]

While one freedom had been achieved in 1961, the other was some way off. Not for the first time, however, the retain-and-transfer system was facing imminent challenge in the law courts. As noted above, a 1912 case involving a former Aston Villa player, Charles Kingaby, had been won by the employers, leaving the system intact and the union on the verge of bankruptcy. Yet by the 1950s informed opinion had it that a legal challenge that focused on the system itself rather than the motives of the club (as had been the case in 1912) would probably succeed. A number of opportunities presented themselves; legal action was considered by the respective unions in the cases of Allan Brown and George Aitken of East Fife, who wished to transfer to English clubs, and Newcastle's Frank Brennan and Aldershot's Ralph Banks, both of whom had refused terms but were nonetheless retained by their employers and prevented from moving to their club of choice. When the chance finally arose it involved one of the Football League's most talented players, George Eastham, a centre-forward with Newcastle United. In many respects the situation was a familiar one. Eastham wanted a move to London but the directors refused and placed him on the club's retained list. Determined to leave Newcastle but unable to play for anyone else, Eastham left the game entirely and for five months worked as a salesman in London. Although Newcastle eventually freed him to join Arsenal in November 1960, he pursued the case and, with PFA assistance, issued a writ against his former employers on the grounds of restraint of trade. Presided over by Justice Wilberforce, the Eastham case finally reached the High Court in the summer of 1963. While convinced of the principles underlying the transfer system, Wilberforce found it 'an unjustifiable restraint of trade' when combined with the retention system. The rules were not technically deemed illegal but rather *ultra vires*, that is, beyond the legal power of the employers. Retain and transfer was condemned as 'an employer's system set up in an industry where the employers have established a monolithic front and where it is clear for the purposes of negotiation the employers are more strongly organized than the employees'.[137] In the wake of these conclusions, the system as it had existed for some 70 years could no longer continue: Eastham himself thought that its ramifications would 'change the face of football for all time'.[138]

Yet the view of the Eastham case as a pivotal moment in the game's history, representing the end of football slavery, has come under considerable scrutiny. Some have pointed to the ambiguities and limitations of the ruling. Nobody has gone so far as Hardaker in seeing Wilberforce's judgment as a complete validation of the transfer system, but most have

observed that it was far from a complete condemnation. As a result, the
football authorities felt justified in modifying the system rather than abol-
ishing it, leaving the professional some way short of freedom of contract.
A new system of option contracts was introduced in 1964, allowing clubs
to renew a player's contract as long as it was for the same period and on
equivalent terms as those previously offered. Free transfers were to be
granted by clubs not wishing to take up its option and players in the
process of being transferred were to continue to receive their contracted
terms. A new Independent Tribunal was established, consisting of representatives of the leagues and unions under the authority of an independent
chairman, to adjudicate on any contractual or transfer disputes that might
arise. This all undoubtedly improved the players' lot, but did it amount to
a revolution in their position? Harding thought not, preferring to see the
Eastham case as 'a significant victory in a very long war', with genuine
freedom of contract having to wait until the late 1970s. Steve Redhead has
put the case even more powerfully. He has argued against seeing the successes of the early 1960s as indicative of a new phase in the history of the
game, symbolised by the death of 'football feudalism' and 'the forward
march of sporting labour'. These were, the argument runs, 'symbolic
breakthroughs rather than fundamental changes in the legal and social
status of professional footballers'. Players continued to be bought and
sold by clubs and were still subject to a range of restrictions that would
hardly have been accepted anywhere outside the football world.[139] For all
its merits, however, this argument should not be taken too far. Most
writers continue to recognise the changes of 1961 and 1963 as important
turning points in the development of the game. They certainly heralded a
transformation in soccer's industrial relations, with the football employee
on a more equal footing with his employer than ever before. For Steve
Greenfield and Guy Osborn, the abolition of the maximum wage and the
Eastham case allowed players to 'partially release the strict grip that the
clubs had previously exerted'.[140] The shackles of football slavery were significantly loosened but the chains had not been broken.

Football, nation and modernity: the 1953 Cup final

One match that was particularly emblematic of the supposed 'golden age'
of British football was the English FA Cup final of 1953. That it has featured so prominently in popular histories of the game is at least partly
explained by the excitement and drama of what happened on the pitch. It

PLATE 14 *Stanley Matthews carried by teammates Jackie Mudie and Stan Mortensen, having collected his winners' medal at the 1953 FA Cup final (© Popperfoto.com).*

was certainly one of the most incredible recoveries by one team in a Wembley final. Bolton Wanderers led 3–1 with just 20 minutes remaining but, with the assistance of their renowned winger Stanley Matthews and a Stan Mortensen hat-trick, Blackpool came back to win 4–3 in the dying seconds. Yet the game alone is hardly sufficient to explain its impact and meaning for contemporaries and historians or why it seems to have held the interest and engaged the emotions of so many inside and outside the stadium.

More significant were the various historical contexts in which the match was set. First, it was the first Cup final that managed to attract a substantial television audience. Disputes between the football authorities and the BBC had led to the showing of only the second half of the 1951 final and none of the 1952 final, but an audience of 10 million watched in 1953 – most in a communal setting with family and friends and many on televisions purchased specifically to watch the coronation of Elizabeth II the same year. Many have seen this as a turning point in the relationship between television, football and the nation. What was already a popular national sporting occasion was thus transformed by television into 'a genuinely shared event' witnessed by millions.[141] Second, the match saw one of England's most celebrated footballers, Stanley Matthews, obtain the Cup Winner's medal that had eluded him in a long and distinguished career. Such was Matthews' popularity and standing within the football world and beyond that the game was framed by the media at the time, and has subsequently been remembered, as 'the Matthews Final'.[142] Third, the match became closely associated with a series of political and sporting celebrations that took place during the same year, principally the coronation but also the British-led conquest of Mount Everest and the English cricket team's regaining of the Ashes. The much-publicised attendance at the final of the Queen and the Duke of Edinburgh provided the match with a particular symbolic significance, binding it in the public mind to the monarchy and the coronation. As Martin Johnes and Gavin Mellor have pointed out, it was the combination of these various contexts, and the manner in which they were reported and narrated in the press, that ensured the game's 'historic' status and dimension.[143]

Much has been made of the link between the 1953 Cup final and ideas of national and social unity. Dave Russell has argued for the match to be seen not only as a key event in sporting history but a defining moment in the history of the English nation, reflecting the unity and consensus of its people and thus elevating the status of football higher than ever in the public mind. For Richard Holt and Tony Mason, this was the point at which football was able to finally shed its working-class skin and be embraced 'as the equal of cricket as a part of English national culture'. The cricket writer Neville Cardus certainly thought that the drama of the 1953 final might have helped football to replace cricket as the 'game of the people', while others have seen it as a crucial moment in making soccer seem more respectable and palatable to middle-class taste.[144] It was important that the Cup final was already established as an 'icon of nationality'. The royal connection had begun in 1914, when George V attended the final at Crystal Palace and, although the link was relatively restrained, this, together with its permanent relocation to the Empire stadium at Wembley (in 1923) and the communal singing of the Victorian hymn 'Abide With Me' (from 1927), clearly helped to define the Cup final as a national event. FA secretary Frederick Wall could describe it as a 'national football festival' in the 1930s and by 1953 it was widely recognised as a national institution, providing the opportunity 'for the people to celebrate their sport and way of life in the capital city and in front of the monarch'.

Underpinning this was a contemporary sense of social unity and harmony derived at least partly from the supposed collective experiences of the Second World War and the political consensus of the post-war years. These strands were woven into the media narratives that saw the 1953 match as an opportunity for 'national rejoicing' and the coming together of a nation at play.[145]

Away from the pages of the national press, other narratives were offered. Research on the north of England has shown the importance of the Cup final from its beginnings in reinforcing ideas of civic unity and identity. Particularly significant in this respect were the stories and myths developed by the local press around the 'invasion' of the capital by travelling northern fans and the celebratory homecoming of winning (and losing) teams. Such discourses were present in 1953, with the Blackpool and Bolton press both presenting the Cup final as a shared civic occasion and an opportunity to raise the profiles of each town, as well as a vehicle for asserting a combined Lancashire identity. Moreover, they complemented rather than clashed with the feelings of national solidarity mentioned above. In this as in earlier, and later, Cup finals, 'local and national converged naturally'.[146] Yet while it embraced notions of Britishness as well as Englishness, there is little evidence that the final had the same symbolic resonance outside England. The Scottish, at least, had their own Cup final to concern themselves with: Rangers drew 1–1 with Aberdeen at Hampden Park but won the subsequent replay 1–0. The sense of nationhood evoked by 1953 seems to have been a largely English one.

Johnes and Mellor have argued that the match 'symbolised the dominant political and social currents of 1953 Britain', particularly the post-war celebration of both tradition and modernity.[147] The connection with royalty and the coronation, for example, blended a respect for the past and the traditions associated with the monarchy with a recently acquired popular enthusiasm, personified by the young Queen and encapsulated in the notion of 'a new Elizabethan age in which . . . Britain would still retain a glorious place in the world'.[148] This sense of optimism and hope for the future was reflected in the technological progress that allowed television to bring the coronation and the Cup final into the homes of millions. Yet in other important respects, such as the adulation bestowed upon Matthews, the Cup final reflected a longing for the past. Matthews had begun his career in the early 1930s and was 37 years old at the time of the final. More importantly, he was an exemplar of the type of ordinary, honest and decent English football hero mentioned in

Chapter 3. In his serious attitude to work and deference to authority he was also representative of a certain strand of working-class respectability. He was symbolic of the mores of a previous age and the importance of valuing tradition even at a time of modernisation and change. The Cup final of 1953 thus captured the popular mood of post-war Britain perfectly, reflecting a pride in past achievements and optimism in the future.[149] But six months later, as we have seen, the England team was soundly beaten by Hungary at the same venue, and within a few years the country had suffered the political shock of the Suez crisis. Confidence in British traditions and capabilities, in football and beyond, was never to be as high again.

References

1 On the notion of the 'golden age', 'golden years' or 'good old days' of football, see Lincoln Allison, *Condition of England: Essays and Impressions* (London: Junction, 1981), p. 125; John Williams, 'Having an Away Day: English Football Spectators and the Hooligan Debate' in J. Williams and S. Wagg, *British Football and Social Change: Getting into Europe* (Leicester: Leicester University Press, 1991), pp. 163–5; John Williams, 'The Changing Face of Football: A Case for National Regulation?', pp. 94–7 and Kevin Jaquiss, 'Football, Fans and Fat Cats: Whose Football Club is it Anyway?', p. 113, both in S. Hamil, J. Michie, C. Oughton and S. Warby (eds), *Football in the Digital Age: Whose Game is it Anyway?* (Edinburgh: Mainstream, 2000); N. A. Phelps, 'Professional Football and Local Identity in the "Golden Age": Portsmouth in the Mid-Twentieth Century', *Urban History*, 32, 3 (2005), pp. 459–80. John Tennant, *Football: The Golden Age* (London: Cassell, 2001) extends the 'golden age' from 1900 to 1985.

2 Dave Russell, *Football and the English: A Social History of Association Football in England, 1863–1995* (Preston: Carnegie, 1997), chapter 6.

3 Percy Young, *A History of British Football* (London: Arrow Edition, 1973 [1st edition, 1968]), p. 263; James Walvin, *The Only Game: Football in Our Times* (Harlow: Longman, 2001), pp. 125–6.

4 John K. Walton, 'Leisure Towns in Wartime: The Impact of the First World War in Blackpool and San Sebastián', *Journal of Contemporary History*, 31, 4 (1996), pp. 603–4.

5 Richard Holt and Tony Mason, *Sport in Britain, 1945–2000* (London: Blackwell, 2000), chapter 2; Norman Baker, 'A More Even Playing Field?: Sport During and After the War', in N. Hayes and J. Hill (eds), *'Millions*

Like Us'?: British Culture in the Second World War (Liverpool: Liverpool University Press, 1999), pp. 125–55.

6 See Matthew Taylor, 'Leisure and Entertainment', in J. Bourne, P. Liddle and I. Whitehead (eds), *The Great World War, 1914–45*: Vol. 2: *The People's Experience* (London: Harper Collins, 2001), pp. 378–94; Derek Birley, *Playing the Game: Sport and British Society, 1910–45* (Manchester: Manchester University Press, 1995), pp. 317–33.

7 Angus Calder, *The People's War: Britain 1939–45* (London: Jonathan Cape, 1969), p. 374; John Ross Schleppi, 'A History of Professional Association Football in England during the Second World War', unpublished Ph.D. thesis, Ohio State University, 1972, Vol. 2, p. 439.

8 Simon Inglis, *League Football and the Men Who Made It* (London: Collins Willow, 1988), pp. 165–70; Bob Crampsey, *The First 100 Years: The Scottish Football League* (Glasgow: Scottish Football League, 1990), pp. 105–28.

9 Schleppi, 'History of Professional Association Football', p. 412; Jack Rollin, *Soccer at War, 1939–45* (London: Collins Willow, 1985), p. 42; Anthony Bristowe, *Charlton Athletic Football Club, 1905–50* (London: Voice of the Valley, 1992 reprint [1st published 1951]), p. 49.

10 Football League Minutes, Report of Interview with the Ministry of War Transport, 3 December 1941; Sam Bartram, *My Autobiography* (London: Burke, 1951), pp. 101–2; Schleppi, 'History of Professional Association Football', pp. 405–8.

11 Peter Doherty, 'Footballers at War', reprinted in Stephen Kelly (ed.), *A Game of Two Halves* (London: Mandarin, 1992), p. 27.

12 Football Players' Union Minutes, 2 October 1939.

13 *Birmingham Post*, 12 September 1939; Eamon Dunphy, *A Strange Kind of Glory: Sir Matt Busby and Manchester United* (London: Heinemann, 1991), pp. 80–3; Schleppi, 'History of Professional Association Football', p. 329.

14 Willie Watson, *Double International* (London: Stanley Paul, 1956), p. 27; Tom Finney, *Football Round the World* (London: Sportsmans Book Club, 1955), p. 30.

15 James Walvin, *The People's Game: The History of Football Revisited* (Edinburgh: Mainstream, 1994), p. 151; Russell, *Football and the English*, p. 124; Pierre Lanfranchi and Matthew Taylor, 'Professional Football in World War Two Britain', in P. Kirkham and D. Thoms (eds), *War Culture: Social Change and Changing Experience in World War Two* (London: Lawrence & Wishart, 1995), p. 190.

16 Schleppi, 'History of Professional Association Football', pp. 439–42.

17 Baker, 'A More Even Playing Field', pp. 130–2; Juliet Gardiner, *Wartime: Britain 1939–45* (London: Headline, 2004), pp. 139–40.

18 Tom Harrisson and Charles Madge (eds), *War Begins at Home* (London: Chatto & Windus, 1940), p. 257.

19 Robert Mackay, *Half the Battle: Civilian Morale in Britain during the Second World War* (Manchester: Manchester University Press, 2002), pp. 117–19.

20 Quoted in Walvin, *Only Game*, p. 92.

21 Mackay, *Half the Battle*, pp. 117–19, 209–15; Thomas Taw, *Football's War and Peace: The Tumultuous Season of 1946–47* (Westcliff-on-Sea: Desert Island, 2003), p. 39. See also Simon Kuper, *Ajax, The Dutch, The War: Football in Europe During the Second World War* (London: Orion, 2003), p. 151.

22 Stanley Rous, *Football Worlds: A Lifetime in Sport* (London: Faber & Faber, 1978), pp. 104–14, 212; Baker, 'A More Even Playing Field', pp. 135–7.

23 Holt and Mason, *Sport in Britain*, pp. 23–5; Inglis, *League Football*, pp. 168–70; Crampsey, *First 100 Years*, pp. 129–33.

24 Sue Lopez, *Women on the Ball: A Guide to Women's Football* (London: Scarlet, 1997), p. 10; Baker, 'A More Even Playing Field', p. 146. On the issue of war and social change, see Arthur Marwick, *Britain in the Century of Total War* (London: Penguin, 1970); Harold Smith (ed.), *War and Social Change: British Society and the Second World War* (Manchester: Manchester University Press, 1986).

25 Phil Vasili, *Colouring Over the White Line: The History of Black Footballers in Britain* (Edinburgh: Mainstream, 2000), chapter 4; Alan Rowlands, *Trautmann: The Biography* (Derby: Breedon, 1990), pp. 43–71; Crampsey, *First 100 Years*, p. 128; Pierre Lanfranchi and Matthew Taylor, *Moving With the Ball: The Migration of Professional Footballers* (Oxford: Berg, 2001), p. 50.

26 Russell, *Football and the English*, p. 127.

27 Lanfranchi and Taylor, 'Professional Football', pp. 191, 193; Schleppi, 'History of Professional Association Football', pp. 420–2.

28 Joyce Woolridge, 'Mapping the Stars: Stardom in English Professional Football, 1890–1946', *Soccer and Society*, 3, 2 (Summer 2002), pp. 62–4.

29 Holt and Mason, *Sport in Britain*, p. 24; Schleppi, 'History of Professional Association Football', p. 427.

30 Baker, 'A More Even Playing Field', p. 127.

31 Walvin, *People's Game*, p. 154; Brian Tabner, *Through the Turnstiles . . .*

Again (Harefield: Yore, 2002); Peter Hutchins, 'Football and Regional Pride in the North-East, 1918–60', unpublished Ph.D. thesis, University of Sussex, 1991, pp. 249, 204–5; Crampsey, *First 100 Years*, p. 137; Roy Hay, 'Soccer and Social Control in Scotland, 1873–1978', in R. Cashman and M. McKernan (eds), *Sport: Money, Morality and the Media* (Brisbane: New South Wales University Press, 1981), p. 243 (Table 10.1); Dilwyn Porter, 'Amateur Football in England, 1948–63: The Pegasus Phenomenon', in A. Smith and D. Porter (eds), *Amateurs and Professionals in Post-War British Sport* (London: Frank Cass, 2000), p. 13; David McClone and Bill McLure, *The Juniors – 100 Years: A Centenary History of Scottish Junior Football* (Edinburgh: Mainstream, 1987), pp. 100–1.

32 Walvin, *People's Game*, p. 155.

33 Stephen Dobson and John Goddard, *The Economics of Football* (Cambridge: Cambridge University Press, 2001), p. 67.

34 Holt and Mason, *Sport in Britain*, p. 122; Neil Wigglesworth, *The Evolution of English Sport* (London: Frank Cass, 1996), p. 132.

35 Dobson and Goddard, *Economics of Football*, pp. 56–8; Russell, *Football and the English*, p. 133; Callum G. Brown, 'Sport and the Scottish Office in the Twentieth Century: The Promotion of a Social and Gender Policy' in J. A. Mangan (ed.), *Sport in Europe: Politics, Class, Gender* (London: Frank Cass, 1999), p. 192.

36 Ross McKibbin, *Classes and Cultures: England, 1918–1950* (Oxford: Oxford University Press, 1998), pp. 188–98; John H. Goldthorpe, David Lockwood, Frank Bechhofer and Jennifer Platt, *The Affluent Worker in the Class Structure* (Cambridge: Cambridge University Press, 1969); Ferdinand Zweig, *The Worker in an Affluent Society* (London: Heinemann, 1961); Russell, *Football and the English*, p. 135.

37 Quoted in Hutchins, 'Football and Regional Pride', p. 179; Walvin, *People's Game*, p. 166.

38 Russell, *Football and the English*, p. 134.

39 Nicholas Fishwick, *English Football and Society, 1910–1950* (Manchester: Manchester University Press, 1989); Russell, *Football and the English*; Walvin, *People's Game*.

40 Gavin Mellor, 'The Social and Geographical Make-Up of Football Crowds in the North-West of England, 1946–1962: "Super-Clubs", Local Loyalty and Regional Identities', *The Sports Historian*, 19, 2 (November 1999), pp. 25–32.

41 Mellor, 'Social and Geographical Make-Up' pp. 33–6.

42 Dave Russell, *Looking North: Northern England and the National Imagination* (Manchester: Manchester University Press, 2004), p. 245.

43 Hutchins, 'Football and Regional Pride', pp. 132–3, 249–50.

44 Mellor, 'Social and Geographical Make-Up, pp. 25–42; quotation p. 28.

45 Quoted in Jeffrey Richards, 'Football and the Crisis of British Identity' in S. Caunce, E. Mazierska, S. Sydney-Smith and J. Walton (eds), *Relocating Britishness* (Manchester: Manchester University Press, 2004), p. 97.

46 Eric Dunning, Patrick Murphy and John Williams, *The Roots of Football Hooliganism* (London: Routledge, 1988), pp. 133–41.

47 J. Kennedy, *Belfast Celtic* (Belfast: Pretani, 1989), p. 97, quoted in John Sugden and Alan Bairner, *Sport, Sectarianism and Society in a Divided Ireland* (Leicester: Leicester University Press, 1993), p. 83.

48 See Jonathan Magee, 'Northern Irish Society and Football in the Immediate Post-World War II Era: Jimmy Jones and Sectarianism' in J. Magee, A. Bairner and A. Tomlinson (eds), *The Bountiful Game?: Football Identities and Finance* (Oxford: Meyer & Meyer Sport, 2005), pp. 61–78; Sugden and Bairner, *Sport, Sectarianism and Society*, pp. 82–3; Malcolm Brodie, *100 Years of Irish Football* (Belfast: Blackstaff, 1980), pp. 63–4.

49 Bill Murray, *The Old Firm: Sectarianism, Sport and Society in Scotland* (Edinburgh: John Donald, 2000 [1st edition, 1984]), pp. 150–2; Crampsey, *First 100 Years*, p. 143; Callum G. Brown, 'Sport and the Scottish Office in the Twentieth Century: The Control of a Social Problem' in Mangan (ed.), *Sport in Europe*, p. 176; Dunning *et al.*, *Roots of Football Hooliganism*, p. 143.

50 Walvin, *People's Game*, p. 155.

51 Geoffrey Green, *The History of the Football Association* (London: Naldrett, 1953), pp. 373–4; 443–6; Porter, 'Amateur Football', pp. 1, 11–12; Edward Grayson, *Corinthians and Cricketers* (London: Sportsman Book Club, 1957), chapter 9.

52 Brown, 'Social and Gender Policy', p. 192; Porter, 'Amateur Football', pp. 8–11, 24.

53 Green, *History of the Football Association*, pp. 519–22; Tony Mason, 'Football', in T. Mason (ed.), *Sport in Britain: A Social History* (Cambridge: Cambridge University Press, 1989), p. 149; Stephen G. Jones, *Workers at Play: A Social and Economic History of Leisure, 1918–1939* (London: Routledge & Kegan Paul, 1986), pp. 190–3; Baker, 'A More Even Playing Field', pp. 150–2; Bill Murray, *The World's Game: A History of Soccer* (Urbana: University of Illinois Press, 1998), p. 117.

54 Murray, *World's Game*, p. 117; Archie Ledbrooke and Edgar Turner, *Soccer from the Press Box* (London: Sportsmans Book Club, 1955), pp. 28–30.

55 Holt and Mason, *Sport in Britain*, p. 24; Alan Tomlinson, 'FIFA and the Men Who Made It', *Soccer and Society*, 1, 1 (Spring 2000), p. 59.

56 Tony Mason, 'Defeat of the Soccer Exiles', *BBC History Magazine*, 1, 2 (June 2000), p. 34–5; FA Bulletin, December 1947; Rous, *Football Worlds*, p. 124; Geoffrey Green, *Soccer: The World Game* (London: Sportsmans Book Club, 1954), pp. 189–90; Ian Nannestad, 'Celebrating the Festival of Britain: The St Mungo Cup', *Soccer History*, 2 (Summer 2002), p. 30.

57 Ronald Kowalski and Dilwyn Porter, 'Political Football: Moscow Dynamo in Britain, 1945', *International Journal of the History of Sport*, 14, 2 (August 1997), pp. 100–21; Walvin, *People's Game*, pp. 157–8; Stanley Matthews, *Feet First Again* (London: Nicholas Kaye, 1952), p. 83; Tommy Lawton, *Football is my Business* (London: Sporting Handbooks, 1946), pp. 179–81; Green, *Soccer*, p. 189.

58 Quoted in Peter Beck, 'Political Football: The British Government and Anglo-Soviet Footballing Relations, 1945–54', paper presented to the British Society of Sports History Annual Conference, University of Liverpool, April 2000.

59 Kowalski and Porter, 'Political Football', pp. 101, 113–16; Murray, *World's Game*, pp. 87–8; Ivan Sharpe, *40 Years in Football* (London: Sportsmans Book Club, 1954), pp. 61–6; Orwell quoted in Beck, 'Political Football'.

60 Richard Weight, *Patriots: National Identity in Britain, 1940–2000* (London: Pan Macmillan, 2003), p. 262.

61 Simon Inglis, *The Football Grounds of Britain* (London: Collins Willow, 1993 [1st edition, 1983]), p. 43; Richard Haynes, 'A Pageant of Sound and Vision: Football's Relationship with Television, 1936–60', *International Journal of the History of Sport*, 15, 1 (April 1998), p. 219.

62 Roger MacDonald, *Britain versus Europe* (London: Pelham, 1968), pp. 17–18; Ronald Kowalski and Dilwyn Porter, 'England's World Turned Upside Down?: Magical Magyars and British Football', *Sport in History*, 23, 2 (Winter 2003/4), pp. 43–5; quotation p. 44.

63 Willy Meisl, *Soccer Revolution* (London: Panther, 1957 [1st edition, 1955]), pp. 175–8.

64 MacDonald, *Britain versus Europe*, pp. 12–16, 18–20; Anthony King, *The European Ritual: Football in the New Europe* (Aldershot: Ashgate, 2003), pp. 37–8; Murray, *World's Game*, pp. 104–5; Matthias Marschik, 'Mitropa: Representations of "Central Europe" in Football', *International Review for the Sociology of Sport*, 36, 1 (2001), pp. 9–12.

65 Alan Hardaker, *Hardaker of the League* (London: Pelham, 1977), pp. 114–17.

66   Hardaker, *Hardaker of the League*, pp. 117–18; Inglis, *League Football*, pp. 207, 209; King, *European Ritual*, p. 39; Rous, *Football Worlds*, pp. 145–9; MacDonald, *Britain versus Europe*, pp. 177–9.

67   Mason, 'Defeat of the Soccer Exiles', p. 36; Dunphy, *Strange Kind of Glory*, pp. 208–13.

68   Weight, *Patriots*, p. 263; Walvin, *Only Game*, p. 126; *People's Game*, p. 171.

69   Walvin, *Only Game*, pp. 113–16; Mason, 'Defeat of the Soccer Exiles', p. 36.

70   Eric Thornton, *Leeds United and Don Revie* (Newton Abbot: Sportsmans Book Club, 1971), p. 66; Ramon Melcon and Stratton Smith (eds), *The Real Madrid Book of Football* (London: Consul, 1962).

71   Holt and Mason, *Sport in Britain*, pp. 115, 129; Dilwyn Porter, '"Your Boys Took One Hell of a Beating!": English Football and British Decline, *c.*1950–80', in A. Smith and D. Porter (eds), *Sport and National Identity in the Post-War World* (London: Routledge, 2004), p. 38.

72   Bob Ferrier, *Soccer Partnership: Billy Wright and Walter Winterbottom* (London: Sportsmans Book Club, 1961), p. 105; Kenneth Wolstenholme, *Sports Special* (London: Sportsmans Book Club, 1958), pp. 51–2; Fabio Chisari, '"Definitely Not Cricket": *The Times* and the Football World Cup, 1930–1970', *The Sports Historian*, 20, 1 (May 2000), p. 49; Weight, *Patriots*, pp. 255–6; Martin Polley, *Moving the Goalposts: A History of Sport and Society Since 1945* (London: Routledge, 1998), p. 44.

73   Wolstenholme, *Sports Special*, pp. 53–4; Kowalski and Porter, 'England's World', p. 29; Jeffrey Hill, 'Narratives of the Nation: The Newspaper Press and England v Hungary, 1953', *Sport in History*, 23, 2 (Winter 2003/4), p. 50; Ferrier, *Soccer Partnership*, p. 109.

74   Meisl, *Soccer Revolution*, pp. 145–51; Hill, 'Narratives of the Nation', pp. 49–53. Nevertheless, Russell is probably right to point out that England's defeat 'was not ... the profound surprise to the English football establishment and the nation as a whole that has sometimes been claimed'. Dave Russell, 'Associating with Football: Social Identity in England, 1863–1998' in G. Armstrong and R. Giulianotti (eds), *Football Cultures and Identities* (Basingstoke: Macmillan, 1999), p. 25.

75   Green quoted in Mason, 'Defeat of the Soccer Exiles', p. 35; Arthur Hopcraft, *The Football Man: People and Passions in Soccer* (London: Simon & Schuster, 1988 [1st edition, 1968]), p. 216. See also John Moynihan, *The Soccer Syndrome: From the Primeval Forties* (London: Simon & Schuster, 1987 [1st edition, 1966]), p. 27. For press reactions on the games, see Kowalski and Porter, 'England's World', pp. 29–32, 37–9;

Hill, 'Narratives of the Nation', pp. 54–7. On the 1953 match itself, see Tony Mason, '"I Doubt If They Will Lose At All": Looking Back on England versus Hungary 1953', *Sport in History*, 23, 2 (Winter 2003/4), pp. 1–9.

76 Stephen Wagg, *The Football World: A Contemporary Social History* (Brighton: Harvester, 1984), p. 85; Meisl, *Soccer Revolution*. See also Hill, 'Narratives of the Nation', p. 56.

77 Bernard Joy, *Soccer Tactics* (London: Sportsmans Book Club, 1959), pp. 33–42; Ferrier, *Soccer Partnership*, pp. 110–17.

78 *The Times*, 1 January 1955, quoted in John Clarke and Chas Critcher, '1996 and All That: England's World Cup Victory', in A. Tomlinson and G. Whannel (eds), *Off the Ball: The Football World Cup* (London: Pluto, 1986), p. 120.

79 Holt and Mason, *Sport in Britain*, p. 129.

80 Weight, *Patriots*, pp. 259–60. For a more nuanced analysis of these developments, see Porter, 'English Football'.

81 George Raynor, *Football Ambassador at Large* (London: Soccer Book Club, 1960), p. 107; Wolstenholme, *Sports Special*, p. 56; John Rafferty, *One Hundred Years of Scottish Football* (London: Pan, 1973), p. 96.

82 Murray, *World's Game*, p. 98; Rafferty, *One Hundred Years*, p. 96; George Young, *George Young Talks Football* (London: Stanley Paul, 1958), pp. 15–16.

83 Porter, 'English Football', pp. 40–1; Murray, *World's Game*, p. 101; Jimmy McIlroy, *Right Inside Soccer* (London: Sportsmans Book Club, 1961), p. 27; Mario Risoli, *When Pele Broke our Hearts: Wales and the 1958 World Cup* (Cardiff: St David's, 1998); Martin Johnes, *A History of Sport in Wales* (Cardiff: University of Wales Press, 2005), pp. 72–3.

84 Raymond Boyle and Richard Haynes, *Power Play: Sport, the Media and Popular Culture* (Harlow: Longman, 2000), p. 43; Young, *Talks Football*, p. 45; Ferrier, *Soccer Partnership*, pp. 135–8; Tom Finney, *Finney on Football* (London: Sportsmans Book Club, 1960), pp. 12–13.

85 Raynor, *Football Ambassador*, pp. 106–16.

86 Wagg, *Football World*, chapters 7 and 10; Neil Carter, *The Football Manager: A History* (London: Routledge, 2006), pp. 81–2.

87 Tony Say, 'Herbert Chapman: Football Revolutionary?', *The Sports Historian*, 16 (May 1996), pp. 81–98; Stephen Studd, *Herbert Chapman, Football Emperor: A Study in the Origins of Modern Soccer* (London: Souvenir, 1998 [1st edition, 1981]).

88 Carter, *Football Manager*, chapter 3; Young, *History of British Football*,

pp. 253–4; Wagg, *Football World*, pp. 44–58; Russell, *Football and the English*, pp. 88–91, Murray, *Old Firm*, pp. 168–70; Fishwick, *English Football*, pp. 36–8; Martin Johnes, 'Football Managers in South Wales Between the Wars', *Soccer History*, 4 (Spring 2003), p. 12.

89 Young, *History of British Football*, chapter 14.

90 Carter, *Football Manager*, p. 83; Wagg, *Football World*, p. 80.

91 Stanley Cullis, *All for the Wolves* (London: Sportsmans Book Club, 1960), p. 102; Carter, *Football Manager*, p. 83.

92 Political and Economic Planning (PEP), 'English Professional Football', *Planning*, 32, 496 (1966), pp. 122–4.

93 Wagg, *Football World*, pp. 164–5; Carter, *Football Manager*, pp. 5–6, 85, 165–6.

94 Carter, *Football Manager*, pp. 91–2; Holt and Mason, *Sport in Britain*, p. 70.

95 Carter, *Football Manager*, pp. 90–1; Ron Flowers, *For Wolves and England* (London: Sportsmans Book Club, 1964), pp. 28, 56; McIlroy, *Right Inside Soccer*, p. 100; Wagg, *Football World*, p. 167.

96 Hopcraft, *Football Man*, pp. 126–7; Carter, *Football Manager*, p. 91; Russell, *Football and the English*, p. 127. Wagg, *Football World*, p. 52, disagrees, giving this accolade to Frank Buckley from his time managing Blackpool as early as 1923–7.

97 Johnny Rogan, *The Football Managers* (London: Queen Anne, 1989), p. 7; Dunphy, *Strange Kind of Glory*, pp. 105, 143–5, 161.

98 Carter, *Football Manager*, pp. 86–8; quotation p. 87; Raynor, *Football Ambassador*, pp. 81–8.

99 Wagg, *Football World*, pp. 157, 161–2, 159; Stephen Wagg, 'Whatever He Said to Them at Half-Time It Certainly Did the Trick: A Social History of the Football Manager', in A. Tomlinson (ed.), *Explorations in Football Culture* (Eastbourne: Leisure Studies Association, 1983), pp. 134–5.

100 Wagg, *Football World*, pp. 73.

101 Rous, *Football Worlds*, pp. 58–9; Green, *History of the Football Association*, pp. 445–8; *Sport and the Community: Report of the Wolfenden Committee on Sport* (London: Central Council for Physical Recreation, 1960), p. 42; Russell, *Football and the English*, pp. 128–30; Ferrier, *Soccer Partnership*, pp. 40, 43.

102 Wagg, *Football World*, pp. 31, 79; Carter, *Football Manager*, p. 84.

103 Matthews, *Feet First Again*, p. 124; Nick Varley, *Golden Boy: A Biography*

of *Wilf Mannion* (London: Aurum, 1997), p. 181; Finney, *Finney on Football*, pp. 93–7.

104 Taylor, *The Leaguers*, p. 159; Rogan Taylor and Andrew Ward, *Kicking and Screaming: An Oral History of Football in England* (London: Robson, 1995), pp. 90–2.

105 Wagg, *Football World*, pp. 79–80; Ferrier, *Soccer Partnership*, p. 44; Young, *Talks Football*, p. 112.

106 Charles Korr, *West Ham United: The Making of a Football Club* (London: Duckworth, 1986), pp. 104–9.

107 Say, 'Herbert Chapman', pp. 81–98; Tony Mason, 'Kick and Rush or Revolt into Style?: Football Playing Among English Professionals from Great Power to Image of Decline', paper presented to INSEP Conference, Paris, May 1998. Joy, *Soccer Tactics*, pp. 50–60.

108 Meisl, *Soccer Revolution*, p. 31; Chas Critcher, 'Football Since the war', in J. Clarke, C. Critcher and R. Johnson (eds), *Working Class Culture: Studies in History and Theory* (London: Hutchinson, 1979), p. 180.

109 Mason, 'Kick and Rush'; Joy, *Soccer Tactics*, pp. 65–71, 96, 100, 103.

110 Ledbrooke and Turner, *Soccer from the Pressbox*, p. 82.

111 Cullis, *All for the Wolves*, pp. 39–42; Mason, 'Kick and Rush'; Øyvind Larsen, 'Charles Reep: A Major Influence on British and Norwegian Football', *Soccer and Society*, 2, 3 (Autumn 2001), pp. 58–78.

112 Mason, Kick and Rush; Cullis, *All for the Wolves*, pp. 43–4, 29.

113 Matthew Taylor, 'Work and Play: The Professional Footballer in England, *c.*1900–*c.*1950', *The Sports Historian*, 22, 1 (May 2002), pp. 20–1; Holt and Mason, *Sport in Britain*, p. 67; John Harding with Gordon Taylor, *Living to Play: From Soccer Slaves to Soccerati – A Social History of the Professionals* (London: Robson, 2003), pp. 114–15.

114 Raich Carter, *Footballer's Progress* (London: Sporting Handbooks, 1950), pp. 220–1; Peter Doherty, *Soccer* (London: Foyles Handbooks, 1950), p. 71; Taylor, 'Work and Play', p. 22.

115 Cullis, *All for the Wolves*, pp. 79–81.

116 Harding, *Living to Play*, p. 116; Holt and Mason, *Sport in Britain*, pp. 67–8.

117 Taylor, 'Work and Play', p. 25; Braham Dabscheck, '"Defensive Manchester": A History of the Professional Footballers' Association', in R. Cashman and M. McKernan (eds), *Sport in History* (Brisbane: University of Queensland Press, 1979), pp. 236–7.

118 Harding, *Living to Play*, pp. 118–19, 122–4; Holt and Mason, *Sport in Britain*, p. 70; Derek Dougan, *The Sash He Never Wore* (St Albans: Mayflower, 1974), pp. 97–8.

119   Richard Giulianotti, *Football: A Sociology of the Global Game* (London: Polity, 1999), pp. 108–9; Gerhard Vinnai, *Football Mania* (London: Ocean, 1973), pp. 31–40; Bruno Rigauer, *Sport and Work* (New York: Colombia University Press, 1981); Jean-Marie Brohm, *Sport: A Prison of Measured Time* (London: Ink Links, 1978), p. 175.

120   Taylor, 'Work and Play', *passim*; Charles Korr, 'A Different Kind of Success: West Ham United and the creation of Tradition and Community' in R. Holt (ed.), *Sport and the Working Class in Modern Britain* (Manchester: Manchester University Press, 1990), p. 155.

121   Tony Mason, 'Stanley Matthews' in Holt (ed.), *Sport and the Working Class*, p. 175; Giulianotti, *Football*, p. 112.

122   Finney, *Finney on Football*, p. 137.

123   Martin Polley, *Moving the Goalposts: A History of Sport and Society since 1945* (London: Routledge, 1998), p. 115; Bartram, *His Autobiography*, p. 141.

124   Bob Crampsey, *The Scottish Footballer* (Edinburgh: William Blackwood, 1978), pp. 40–2.

125   Dabscheck, 'Defensive Manchester', pp. 251–2; Holt and Mason, *Sport in Britain*, p. 73; Cullis, *All For the Wolves*, pp. 175–7; PEP, 'English Professional Football', p. 131 (Table 6); Football League Minutes, 3 June 1950; A. J. Arnold, *A Game that Would Pay: A Business History of Professional Football in Bradford* (London: Duckworth, 1988), p. 112. For some idea of a comparison of wage figures over time, the £1,600 received by the Wolves championship squad represents something approaching £26,000 in 2006 money, while Billy Wright's £2,100 equates to approximately £33,700. The Bradford City players on £12 per week in 1954 were making an equivalent of around £227 while the £5 wage would represent about £94 in 2006.

126   Young, *Talks Football*, p. 102; Crampsey, *Scottish Footballer*, p. 41; Russell, *Football and the English*, p. 145; PEP, 'English Professional Football', p. 126; Tom Whittaker, *Tom Whittaker's Arsenal Story* (London: Sportsmans Book Club, 1958), p. 336.

127   Russell, *Football and the English*, p. 148.

128   John Harding, *For the Good of the Game: The Official History of the Professional Footballers' Association* (London: Robson, 1991), p. 249; Harding, *Living to Play*, pp. 36–7; Varley, *Golden Boy*, pp. 109–32.

129   Tony Mason, 'The Bogotá Affair', in J. Bale and J. Maguire (eds), *The Global Sports Arena: Athletic Talent Migration in an Interdependent World* (London: Frank Cass, 1994), p. 40; Lanfranchi and Taylor, *Moving With the Ball*, pp. 58–63; Rob Hughes, 'John Charles', in P. Stead and H.

Richards (eds), *For Club and Country: Welsh Football Greats* (Cardiff: University of Wales Press, 2000), p. 106; John Charles, *King of Soccer* (London: Stanley Paul, 1957), p. 146.

130 Fishwick, *English Football*, p. 86; Holt and Mason, *Sport in Britain*, p. 81.

131 Dabscheck, 'Defensive Manchester', pp. 247-8; Wagg, *Football World*, p. 112.

132 Jimmy Hill, *Striking for Soccer* (London: Peter Davies, 1961), pp. 29-32, 65-6.

133 Wagg, *Football World*, pp. 112-19; Hardaker, *Hardaker of the League*, p. 81.

134 Harding, *Good of the Game*, p. 277; Russell, *Football and the English*, p. 149.

135 Inglis, *League Football*, pp. 220, 222; Hill, *Striking for Soccer*, p. 21.

136 Hardaker, *Hardaker of the League*, pp. 79-85.

137 Harding, *Good of the Game*, pp. 283-8; Steve Greenfield and Guy Osborn, *Regulating Football: Commodification, Consumption and the Law* (London: Pluto, 2001), pp. 78-81; Crampsey, *First 100 Years*, p. 141.

138 George Eastham, *Determined to Win* (London: Sportsmans Book Club, 1966), p. 10.

139 Hardaker, *Hardaker of the League*, pp. 87-8; Harding, *Good of the Game*, p. 289; Steve Redhead, 'You've Really Got a Hold of Me: Footballers in the Market', in Tomlinson and Whannel (eds), *Off the Ball*, pp. 55-6; Polley, *Moving the Goalposts*, p. 117.

140 Inglis, *League Football*, p. 237; Greenfield and Osborn, *Regulating Football*, p. 82.

141 Martin Johnes and Gavin Mellor, 'The 1953 FA Cup Final: Modernity and Tradition in British Culture', *Contemporary British History*, 20, 2 (June 2006), pp. 270-2, quotation p. 271; Russell, *Football and the English*, p. 139; Holt and Mason, *Sport in Britain*, p. 97; Fabio Chisari, '"The Age of Innocence": A History of the Relationship between the Football Authorities and the BBC Television Service', unpublished Ph.D. thesis, De Montfort University, 2006, chapter 2.

142 Mason, 'Stanley Matthews', pp. 170-2; Alastair Revie, *All Roads Lead to Wembley* (London: Pelham, 1971), pp. 110-14; Tony Pawson, *100 Years of the FA Cup* (London: Heinemann, 1972), pp. 157-63.

143 Holt and Mason, *Sport in Britain*, p. 97; Johnes and Mellor, '1953 FA Cup', pp. 264-5, 276.

144 Russell, *Football and the English*, p. 139; Holt and Mason, *Sport in*

Britain, p. 97; Mason, 'Stanley Matthews', p. 172; Johnes and Mellor, '1953 FA Cup', p. 271.

145 Jeff Hill, 'Rite of Spring: Cup Finals and Community in the North of England' in J. Hill and J. Williams (eds), *Sport and Identity in the North of England* (Keele: Keele University Press, 1996), pp. 87–93; John Hargreaves, 'The State and Sport: Programmed and Non-Programmed Intervention in Britain' in L. Allison (ed.), *The Politics of Sport* (Manchester: Manchester University Press, 1986), pp. 243, 252; Johnes and Mellor, '1953 FA Cup', pp. 265, 268; Mason, 'Stanley Matthews', p. 172.

146 Hill, 'Rite of Spring', pp. 94–105; quotation p. 105; Johnes and Mellor, '1953 FA Cup', pp. 266–8.

147 Johnes and Mellor, '1953 FA Cup', p. 265.

148 Arthur Marwick, *British Society Since 1945* (London: Penguin, 1990 [1st edition, 1982]), pp. 105–6.

149 Johnes and Mellor, '1953 FA Cup', pp. 272, 274–5; Mason, 'Stanley Matthews', pp. 175–6.

CHAPTER 5

Glory and decline, 1961–85

During the 1960s British football was in many respects on top of the world. England became the first (and only) British national side to win the World Cup in 1966 and the following year Celtic became the first British club side to win the European Cup, overcoming Inter Milan in Lisbon. Manchester United followed in Celtic's footsteps in 1968, a 4–1 defeat of Benfica finally putting the ghost of the 1958 Munich disaster to rest. Over the next decade and a half, British (especially English) clubs came to dominate European competition. Between 1968 and 1985 they won 8 European Cups (appearing in 11 finals), 9 Inter-Cities Fairs/UEFA Cups (out of 11 finals) and 5 Cup Winners Cups (out of 8 finals). Its closest competitors could not match England's haul of 20 trophies: German clubs, by comparison, won 8, Dutch and Italian clubs 6 each, and Spanish clubs just 4.[1] But the triumphs of club football seemed to mask a more profound malaise. The national teams achieved considerably less success than the clubs. Scotland at least continued to qualify for World Cup competitions, even hoping in 1978 that it might win one, but the England team appeared to be in freefall, no longer able to hold its place among the elite of world or European football. What is more, the British style of play seemed to have become increasingly outdated and redundant, eclipsed by the more sophisticated approaches of the leading South American and European nations. It was in this context that 'decline' became the watchword of sports journalists as it had long been for economic and political commentators.

Off the pitch, there were still fewer reasons to be cheerful. Decreasing attendances, poor behaviour on the terraces and the pitch, the growth of racism and manipulation by commercial interests were all put forward as evidence of football's deteriorating health. Academics were to the fore in raising these issues. In his 1981 book *Condition of England*, the political scientist Lincoln Allison mused over 'the state of the game', concluding that it was 'less attractive and important than it used to be' and no longer held a central place in the nation's social and cultural life. In 1984 the sociologist Stephen Wagg could talk of the 'continuing crisis' in football, involving financial meltdown, television overexposure and the alienation of the public.[2] Two years later, in the aftermath of the Heysel Stadium disaster, James Walvin published *Football and the Decline of Britain*, a powerful analysis of the malaise into which the national game had sunk. Once considered a reflection of the qualities of British innovation and character, football had by the 1980s come to epitomise many of the ills of urban Britain. Resistance to modernisation had left clubs in a state of financial crisis and grounds in a dangerous condition of ill-repair. Players had been elevated to the status of stars but were more likely to cheat, moan and misbehave than ever before. Most seriously, hooliganism seemed to combine most of Britain's major social problems, such as organised violence, drunkenness and racism. The public affection accumulated by football over much of the twentieth century seemed to have been lost in a decade or two. What had been 'the people's game' was now, according to the *Sunday Times*, 'a slum sport, played in slum stadiums, watched by slum people'.[3] As Walvin argued, many such assessments of the game and its perceived decline were misleading and simplistic, devoid of any detailed understanding of recent social change.[4] Ultimately, however, even football's most ardent defenders could not avoid the fact that the game had changed for the worse and perhaps come to symbolise national decline more potently than anything else.

In charting this apparent path from glory to decline, we should remember that while football undoubtedly changed in this period so too did the meanings attached to the game by the society and culture of which it was a part. The story of British football in these decades was of a sport that, while still extremely popular, was increasingly falling out of favour with many people who had once supported it. The chapter focuses first on the problems encountered in the recreational game and then the changing business of elite professional football. It turns then to look at the way in which football was represented to the British public through the media, art and literature, before dealing with the supposed decline of English football in the wake of that nation's greatest sporting triumph in 1966 and the game's role in defining and refining national loyalty and identity in a crucial period in the histories of Scotland, Northern Ireland and Wales. The chapter closes with an extended analysis of the hooliganism issue and the heated debate that still dominates academic discussion of football.

Football for all?: playing the game

Patterns of participation

Playing football had always been popular among significant numbers of British people, but from the 1960s it reached new heights. At a time when spectatorship at professional matches was in decline, participation in recreational football was on the rise. The English FA recorded a gradual rise in affiliated adult male clubs from the 23,163 in 1949 to 25,217 by 1964 and a sharp increase to 30,862 by 1967. This figure then grew to 37,461 clubs in 1975 and a decade later had reached 41,069. To this latter figure one could add the 3,281 member clubs of the Scottish Amateur FA, along with 1,600 Welsh and 967 Northern Ireland clubs attached to their respective governing bodies in 1985. With an estimated average of 1.4 teams per club, this would mean that approximately 65,000 football teams turned out each week in Britain by the end of this period. What this represented in player numbers is less easy to calculate. The FA estimated around a million active footballers in England and Wales in 1968, with figures over the next decade or so ranging from 780,000 to 1,170,000. With the addition of the youngsters playing regularly at the 14,000 soccer-playing schools in Britain by 1968, the figures of 1.5 million players of all ages for the 1970s and 1.6 million by the 1980s might not be too wide of the mark.[5]

Considered in isolation, however, such figures mean very little. More people may have been playing football by the 1980s than ever before but this does not necessarily mean that the game was proportionately more popular. The *Planning for Leisure* survey of 1969 showed football to be the third most popular recreational activity (after swimming and dancing) for males aged over 15, with 10 per cent of the national sample participating at least once a month during the season. General household surveys (GHS) conducted during the 1970s and 1980s reveal a rather lower figure of between 3 and 3.3 per cent of the *overall* British adult population playing on a regular basis, with slightly higher percentages of 7.9 per cent and 4.9 per cent in Scotland and Wales respectively.[6] Not surprisingly, the game appealed to some sections of the population more than others. As had been the case a century earlier, the typical recreational footballer was a young male, generally single and often with the experience of having learnt the game at school. *Social Trends* estimated in 1979 that 20 per cent of males aged 16 to 24 played on a regular basis, while the 1983 GHS arrived at figures of 21 per cent at ages 16–19 and 19 per cent at 20–4, with 23 as the median age of the recreational footballer. Thereafter, as we might expect, participation declined with age and with greater domestic responsibility: table tennis, fishing, cricket and golf had all overtaken soccer as a participant sport for married men aged between 31 and 45 in the 1969 survey. More skilled manual workers played than either managers and professionals or the semi-skilled and unskilled, but there does appear to have been a broadening of the social base of the game at its grass roots. Certainly, there is little evidence that large numbers of potential footballers were excluded due to financial constraints – the average cost per match being just over 2s. in 1969 – or lack of leisure time, as they may well have been in relation to golf or even cricket.[7] Likewise, John Moynihan has related how, in London at least, the world of recreational soccer was opened up to professional groups from the late 1950s onwards. Moynihan's own team, Chelsea Casuals, co-founded with fellow journalist Brian Glanville and the painter Keith Critchlow, initially included in its ranks 'a master-baker from Swiss Cottage, an Olympian goalkeeper, a Chelsea butcher's boy, and a string of mysterious layabouts exuding beer and brandy breath'. From impromptu kick-a-bouts in Hyde Park, the Casuals organised themselves and went on to become a permanent feature in the capital's Sunday leagues for the next three decades.[8]

Despite general patterns of growth, recreational football was more widespread in certain parts of the country than others. Lancashire, Greater London, the West Riding of Yorkshire and Warwickshire remained the key centres in 1979, as they had been 30 years earlier, accounting for 35 per cent of all registered clubs in England and Wales. But looked at in *per capita* terms, higher levels of participation were evident in areas less traditionally associated with the professional game. Lincolnshire topped the table of *per capita* provision, with over twice the national norm at one club for every 573 people, followed by Powys (one per 655), Northamptonshire and Essex (both one per 702) and Surrey and Cornwall (both one per 790). Participation levels and rates of growth were also generally higher in the south of England than in the north. Only 6.1 per cent of males aged 11–40 played regularly in Tyne and Wear and 6.2 per cent in Lancashire by the 1980s, while the equivalent figure for London was 13.4 per cent and 11.1 per cent in the south-east. The greatest growth in the game tended to come in the midlands and south of

England, with counties such as Northamptonshire and Hampshire each registering three times as many clubs in the late 1970s compared with 30 years earlier. Growth was much more limited north of the Mersey and Humber rivers. Indeed one study of the north-west conducted in 1972 saw little latent demand for soccer in the region and envisaged limited future growth. What such studies show is that by the 1980s recreational football was not only widespread throughout the country but was increasingly coming to be defined as a southern, suburban, even rural game, in contrast with the northern, urban and industrial characteristics of the professional side of the sport.[9]

The belated acceptance of Sunday football was fundamental to the sport's post-1960 growth. Writing in 1989, Tony Mason identified it as 'the great participatory change of the last thirty years'.[10] The immediate effect of the FA's 1960 decision may simply have been to provide official recognition for a practice that was already well established, but in time it facilitated a growth in participation. Providing an opportunity for those who supported professional teams on a Saturday to participate themselves, Sunday play led to a burgeoning of local tournaments. Three of the major leagues in Leicestershire, for example, were Sunday competitions established after the mid-1960s. According to one estimate, by the early 1990s between 60 and 80 per cent of all adult football at local level took place on a Sunday. Over this time, the Sunday game developed its own particular characteristics. It tended to be of a lower standard and played on poorer pitches than its Saturday equivalent, with more committed and talented Saturday players often appearing for their 'second' clubs on a Sunday. From its beginnings, it was also often connected with drinking culture. Many of the teams were 'pub sides', organised around and taking on the names of public houses. Playing with hangovers after heavy drinking sessions the night before, as well as post-match and even pre-match drinking (for afternoon fixtures), have all been characteristically associated with Sunday football. So too have incidents of player indiscipline and verbal and physical abuse by players and spectators. Moynihan's recollection of one team who 'threatened the referee with violence ... if they lost' may not have been typical but was certainly frequent enough to make the recruitment and retention of referees a continual problem at local level.[11]

The provision of facilities remained a crucial determining factor in the progress of the recreational game. The influential Wolfenden Report of 1960 had noted the lack of sufficient playing field acreage throughout Britain, as well as the underuse of existing facilities, which were either poorly situated or closed to the general public. It concluded that 'potential demand far exceeds present supply' and thus that 'there is plenty of need for more facilities, in the right places, of the right kind'.[12] Yet football enjoyed better provision than most sports. In new towns such as Basildon, Crawley, Harlow and Hemel Hempstead, over 98 per cent of the population lived within a mile of a football pitch in 1969, with an equivalent figure of 93 per cent for inner London. In keeping with the participation rates noted above, there tended to be a greater provision of pitches in suburban than inner-city areas. By the late 1970s, for instance, there was only about one pitch per 3,935 people in South Tyneside compared with one for every 1,600 in Norwich. In London, Greenwich boasted one pitch per 1,497, while inner-city Southwark had one per 6,317. On a national level, a rough figure of one football pitch per 1,500 of the population was reported by 1990. The majority of these – 58 per cent in 1969 and at least 51 per cent by 1990 – were provided by local authorities rather than private clubs or companies. However, the degree to which football benefited from the general growth of leisure provision

PLATE 15 *An aerial view from 1962 of the 111 football pitches on Hackney Marshes in North London (© Popperfoto.com).*

during the 1970s and 1980s is far from clear. The gains made through the Sports Council and its 'Sport for All' campaign, working in tandem with local government, were undoubtedly substantial. Perhaps the major development was the arrival of the multi-facility sports centre, 'a characteristically late twentieth-century social institution' in Jeffrey Hill's words, which burgeoned from just 12 in 1971 to 770 by 1981. Neither these, nor the growing number of all-weather sports pitches constructed at a similar time, were intended primarily for football use, but soon developed into key venues for both training and the emerging five-a-side game.[13]

Despite these developments, there remained serious deficiencies in the provision and the quality of football facilities. Romantic descriptions of mass recreational grounds such as Hackney Marshes in London and Hough End in Manchester – where 'pitches are so close, side by side, that the balls whiz muddily from one game to another' and teams changed in 'little hut boxes without showers' – should not distract us from the poor conditions under which much Saturday and Sunday football was played.[14] Wolfenden had outlined the importance of improving changing and washing facilities 'if potential users are to be attracted to the playing fields themselves', while *Planning for Leisure* revealed soccer as the lowest rated of all recreational sports, with only 18 per cent of informants considering the facilities used 'very good' and 41 per cent describing them as 'fair', 'poor' or 'very poor'. Such was the paucity of facilities at some venues that 7 per cent of footballers had no changing accommodation at all, and 8 per cent were unable even to wash or shower after playing. Despite general improvements in drainage and turf management, local studies from the 1980s revealed between 10 and 50 per cent of the pitches in Derbyshire and Nottinghamshire, and at least 28 per cent in the west midlands, to be of inadequate quality for regular use. Few commentators doubted that there had been an increase in the overall provision of outdoor playing pitches from the 1960s, but new pressures on future growth were emerging. The Sports Council's John Coghlan cited the loss of recreational land to motorway and ring-road development as well as the selling off of school and factory playing fields as crucial factors in diminishing the provision in certain areas, particularly the inner-cities. Demand still often exceeded supply, as in Portsmouth where 24 Sunday teams were refused entry into local competition because there were not enough pitches to accommodate them.[15]

Excluded groups

Sociologists and scholars of sports development have written extensively of the problems involved in reaching those social groups who tended not to be active sports participants.[16] The availability of facilities has generally been considered of less significance here than issues of inequality and discrimination. Like all sports, football had its excluded groups, particularly working-class youths, ethnic minorities and women. It would be appropriate at this point to consider each of these in turn. The long-acknowledged gap in sports participation in the time between young people leaving school and joining adult clubs emerged as a key feature of official policy after its identification by Wolfenden. Many of the Sports Council and local authority initiatives of the 1970s and 1980s thus targeted young adults aged between about 15 and 20, particularly in areas of urban deprivation. Football was to the forefront in pilot schemes such as those aimed at the young unemployed in Derwentshire and Leicester, and 'Action Sport', which appointed 'leaders' and 'motivators' to work with school leavers and other young people in deprived neighbourhoods. Most

PLATE 16 *A group of children playing football in Juvenal Gardens, Liverpool, 1971 (© Hulton Archive/Getty).*

significant for our purposes, however, was the Football and the Community programme established in 1978 by the then Minister of Sport, Denis Howell, in conjunction with the Sports Council and the Football League. Aimed partly as a tool in the battle against hooliganism, the programme's main intention was to encourage the involvement of young supporters in sporting activity by using and improving the facilities of professional clubs. An initial £1 million grant was distributed among 39 schemes in the first two years, ranging from the construction of vast indoor sports halls, such as those at Aston Villa and Coventry City, to the conversion of existing facilities for community use. A number of schemes also employed full-time or part-time motivators, often ex-professional players, to increase participation by arranging coaching sessions, competitive leagues and other activities.[17]

In terms of facility provision, Football and the Community was an undoubted success. When seen alongside the Football Trust's investment in new and updated facilities – involving some £2 million to assist over 100 schemes in London alone in 1980 – the initiative managed significantly to boost recreational provision in inner-city areas. Coglan praised the schemes on this basis, arguing that they gave 'those seeking participation some choice where none had previously existed'.[18] However, others have queried whether the facilities were actually used by those for whom they were intended. Roger Ingham argues that there was considerable ambiguity and confusion over the programme's aims as it travelled down from government to the local authorities and participating clubs. In particular, the main target group – working-class youths from the locality who were not regular users of other facilities – were often overlooked in favour of middle-class youngsters travelling some distance to use the facility, those already in established teams and even talented players already identified by the club's scouting network. At Queens Park Rangers, according to Ingham's data, 72 per cent of the users were aged 21 or over, 47 per cent lived over 3 miles from the ground and 91 per cent played for a regular team. Moreover, the tendency of participating clubs to see the schemes in terms of revenue raising for themselves rather than developmental work with the community led to the prioritisation of those who could afford to hire the facilities and were organised into teams to make such bookings, at the expense of the original target group.[19] Another view is that the conventional focus on 'initiatives', 'schemes' and organised forms of football provision misses the point. As John Clarke and Chas Critcher have pointed out, not all young working-class men have fitted into formal patterns of recreation, preferring informal and spontaneous activities that placed them beyond the scrutiny and surveillance of the state. 'Street football', wrote Clarke and Critcher in the early 1980s, 'and the use of public pitches when the park keeper's not looking, remain the "popular" basis of football in Britain'.[20]

For African-Caribbean and Asian youths, the problems associated with active participation in football were greater still. There has been relatively little systematic study of the treatment of ethnic minority groups in the recreational game but the fragmentary evidence we do have points to the prevalence of racism and other cultural assumptions that have hampered widespread participation. Academic studies focused on the professional game outline the stereotypes and expectations that linked blacks with above-average sporting ability in the minds of teachers and educationalists and led to them being steered towards careers in sport rather than more intellectual endeavours.[21] Yet this identification of blacks as 'natural' athletes seemingly had little impact on local football, where opposition and exclusion, rather than assimilation and integration, was the norm. This was certainly the case in Leicester, where a group of young footballers from the largely African-Caribbean district of Highfields formed their own club – Highfield Rangers – in 1970. The club worked its way up the local leagues but faced continual racial abuse from opposing players and spectators, particularly when visiting teams in rural areas. One player remembered:

We were called niggers, coons, we had some nasty physical challenges. We had people jeering from the side ... We were seen as, 'Hey, black people can't play football, what are they doing on a football pitch?' We had some very, very physical, hard, competitive games because to be beaten by us, black guys – to them who weren't as good physically and socially – how could we go on the pitch and beat them? When we got abuse, we wanted to beat them more.[22]

Discrimination also manifested itself in the club's treatment by local football officialdom. Referees were perceived to be particularly hard on Rangers, from fraternising with the opposing white teams and awarding numerous controversial decisions against them to rationalising racial abuse as 'part of the game'. Similarly, despite continued success at junior level, the higher senior competitions in Leicestershire were effectively closed to Rangers for a number of years. Resentment at the 'outsider' status assigned to the club was marked: 'We don't really feel we are a part of county football ... it's like we are the county's Achilles heel. They know we are good, they know we are good enough, but I feel we have been denied the status and the avenues to cement our status'.[23]

Football clubs such as Highfield Rangers, run by and for black communities, offer a rather different perspective on the emergence of blacks in sport from the conventional gaze on the elite professional game. As well as being an important focal point for the expression of ethnic identity, John Williams has categorised this type of involvement in local football as a 'form of community politics' and 'a site of resistance' against the dominant structures of 'white' society. Others have argued that when blacks entered the world of amateur football they were automatically involved in 'the cultural politics of "race"', a dimension largely absent in the professional arena.[24] Similar observations could be made about the role of certain Asian football clubs. The origins and development of Paak FC, for example, a largely Pakistani club based in the town of Nelson in Lancashire, has remarkable parallels to the Highfield Rangers story. Founded in 1972 by a group of Pakistani schoolboys who felt themselves excluded from playground kick-abouts, the club progressed steadily through local competition to win the top division of the Burnley District League in 1981–2, by which time it had also expanded to incorporate a second eleven and a youth team. Racism and intimidation were rife but the team soon challenged preconceptions about the passivity of Asians by gaining a reputation as an aggressive side not afraid to look after itself: as one player confirmed, 'We're seen as good footballers and dirty so and sos. They know we won't be messed with.' Over time, Paak developed into a key representative of the town's Pakistani population, fulfilling some of the roles taken on for previous generations by traditional community leaders. Much more than a mere football club, it became, in the words of Jas Bains and Sanjiev Johal, 'a local institution serving and preserving the interests of the wider community'.[25]

These examples raise interesting questions about the degree to which grassroots football in this period was segregated by colour and ethnicity. While a few white and Asian players always turned out for Rangers and the occasional white for Paak, and there were undoubtedly many ethnically mixed clubs throughout Britain, much of the non-white experience of soccer nonetheless took place outside the conventional structures of the game. The rise of the Asian Games (or tournaments) provides a perfect illustration of this. Bains and Johal have highlighted how the linguistic and cultural exclusion of Sikh immigrants and their restricted access to sports clubs and facilities proved the specific context within which the tournaments developed from the mid-1960s. The tournaments were intended to bring together various Sikh communities from different towns in sporting competition, thereby helping to forge and consolidate community networks but also providing a vehicle for organised competition in a safe and friendly environment. Along with the tag sport of kabbadi, football emerged as a central feature of these events. The quality of play improved and competition grew fiercer over the years, with ambitious clubs 'importing' players from other cities or making use of the 'foreign' player rule, which allowed the inclusion of two non-Asians. Yet critics of the tournaments have complained that they reinforced the presumed insularity of Asians, showing that footballers from these communities were happier playing in their 'own' company and placing the best talent beyond the view of professional club scouts. Similar conclusions about isolation from 'mainstream' recreational football could be drawn from the apparent long-term preference for the five-a-side game among young Asians in Glasgow, Preston, Oldham and Blackburn.[26] Other studies have challenged the stereotypical views that young Indian, Pakistani and Bangladeshi males lacked interest in sport generally, and football particularly, while noting their preference for informal 'pick-up' games in streets, playgrounds or parks rather than organised teams and leagues. Scott Fleming's work on north London Asians indicated that though few of the schoolboys interviewed perceived football as anything other than a hobby, playing in informal kick-abouts was nonetheless an important and meaningful part of their lives.[27]

A number of writers have identified the mid to late-1960s as the dawn of a 'new age of women's football', brought on by the combined but contrasting influences of England's 1966 World Cup triumph and the rise of the women's movement.[28] Central to this so-called 'new age' was the institutionalisation of women's competition and its gradual recognition by the governing bodies of the male game. Sue Lopez has described the rapid spread of the female game around the Southampton area, from a handful of office-based teams partaking in charity matches to the creation of a district league and a representative Southampton side by early 1967. On a national level, a carpenter from Deal in Kent, Arthur Hobbs, launched his first tournament for women's soccer the same year, and by 1969 the Deal Tournament was capable of attracting 52 entries, including three teams from continental Europe. Out of this came the inauguration of the Women's Football Association (WFA) in 1969, representing 44 clubs and seven leagues throughout England, with a Scottish and a Northern Irish body following in 1971 and 1976 respectively. A WFA Cup competition began in 1971 and the first international fixture between England and

Scotland took place the following year. Based on numbers alone, the women's game seems to have progressed rapidly during the 1970s. By 1979 as many as 300 clubs were affiliated to the WFA, involving an estimated 6,000 registered players and 21 regional leagues. Although more popular in some areas than others (the south of England rather than the north, for instance) by the 1980s players and clubs throughout Britain had established themselves as part of a network of local, regional, national and international competition. Founded in 1978, Burton Wanderers were not untypical in playing numerous friendly matches and tournament games, in addition to their regular fixtures in the Midlands Women's League, the WFA Cup, the Midland Regional Cup, the Majestic Cup, the Lloyds Cup and the Geoff Gibbs Trophy.[29]

Despite these advances, however, female participation remained constrained by a host of administrative, ideological and legal barriers. Although the FA agreed in 1971 to rescind the 1921 ban on its clubs staging women's matches, as well as officially recognising the WFA and setting up a joint consultative committee, there was little in the way of financial or administrative assistance and it was not until 1984, much later than in most European countries, that the women's body was formally affiliated to the FA. Progress was even slower in Scotland, where recognition from the governing body was not received until 1974 and affiliation had to wait until the 1990s. Such reluctance to embrace the women's game was underpinned by a continued prejudice against females taking part in what many still considered to be a fundamentally male and masculine sport. FA secretary Ted Croker was certainly not alone in regarding it as 'unnatural' for women or girls to play football. Joanne Broadhurst, a midfielder with Doncaster Belles and England during the 1990s, remembered teachers trying to force her to give up football: 'They just said women had nowhere to go in football and I should play hockey'. Another future England international was accused of being 'unfeminine' by her parents after showing an early interest in the game and even had her football boots thrown away. Views of this kind gained legal legitimacy in 1978 when an FA ban on 12 year-old schoolgirl Theresa Bennett from playing for her local boys' team was confirmed by Appeal Court judge Lord Denning. The judge accepted that Bennett herself 'used to run rings round the boys' but rejected that her individual attributes could be considered separately from what he took to be the basic physiological differences between the 'average' male and female, even at such an early age.[30] John Williams and Jackie Woodhouse have interpreted the Bennett ruling as particularly significant in retarding the development of junior female football, although Lopez, conversely, argues that the accompanying media support ultimately boosted the opportunities existing for younger girls to play football and led eventually to the FA's 1991 decision to allow mixed football up to the age of 11.[31]

Rich and poor: the structure and economics of football

In the professional game, the prevailing atmosphere of crisis and decline was difficult to avoid. The idea that a crisis existed in the finances of British clubs, with falling attendances (along with increasing wages and transfer fees) the root cause, was commonplace for much of this period, and particularly from the late 1970s. Many clubs were unprofitable and in severe debt, and by the early 1980s a number – Derby County, Hull City, Tranmere Rovers and Wolverhampton Wanderers among others – were close to going out of business entirely. Discussions about how to deal with this crisis naturally focused on the finances of clubs and the organisational structure of leagues, but also touched upon broader debates over the relationship between clubs and their communities and the changing social and cultural role of the game.[32]

Attendances, sponsorship and television

Notwithstanding a slight revival in the seasons immediately after England's 1966 World Cup success, Football League attendances continued to drop gradually – to 28.2 million in 1971–2, 24.5 million by 1978–9 – and then declined more rapidly during the early 1980s, reaching a post-war low of 16.5 million by the 1985–6 season. Numbers at Scottish matches fell at a similar rate, from 4.2 million in 1964–5 to 3.8 million a decade later and 2.5 million by 1984–5. Even Celtic and Rangers failed at times to fill more than a third or a quarter of their grounds during the 1970s when playing lowly opposition. Writing in 1978, Bob Crampsey could declare with confidence that 'the great days of mass attendance at football matches in Scotland have gone'.[33] In both countries, the decline was steeper and more damaging in the lower divisions than at the top end of the game. The combined shortfall in Third and Fourth Division Football League attendances from 1960–1 to 1980–1 was 55.5 per cent, compared with 36.4 per cent in the First Division. Similarly, the highest division share of 43.3 per cent in 1962–3 had increased to 52.2 per cent by 1977–8, while the Third and Fourth

Division figures of 19.7 and 11.3 fell to 13.1 and 9.2 per cent respectively over the same period. Likewise, attendances in the Scottish First Division dropped by 58.7 per cent between 1976–7 and 1983–4, whereas there was a mere 5.3 per cent decline in the Premier Division over the same period.[34] Focusing on the fortunes of neighbouring clubs, Stefan Szymanski and Tim Kuypers have calculated that high-flying Manchester United drew eleven times as many supporters as lowly Bury in 1969–70 compared with only four times as many a decade earlier, while Leeds United's crowds increased from three to eight times those of nearby York City over the same period.[35]

The extent to which the football industry itself bore responsibility for spectator decline remains unclear. As was noted in the previous chapter, increasing post-war affluence, changing leisure patterns and the counter-attractions of television and other forms of entertainment all had their effect, as did the relocation of many of the game's traditional supporters away from the vicinity of grounds in city centres and towards the suburbs. Writing in the early 1980s, Lincoln Allison believed that football could 'no longer hold the centre of the communal stage in the lives of a huge class as it once did ... There is too much mobility, too many alterna-tives.'[36] In this respect, football underwent a similar fate as other established sports and leisure activities, such as cricket and the cinema, which both suffered significant audience decline over the same period. But other factors that emerged from the 1960s were more particular to foot-ball and its organisation. Hooliganism and crowd trouble, the most commonly cited explanations, seem to have had some impact on atten-dances. The second Chester Report in 1983 highlighted the fear of hooliganism as a key factor in driving supporters away from the terraces. Declining standards of play and conduct on the field also played their part. Some commentators accused teams of adopting increasingly negative tactics which stifled imagination and flair, thus reducing the goals scored and the consequent entertainment value of matches. There was no doubt that fewer goals were scored in England and Wales at the end of the period than had been at the beginning (2.4 per game in the First Division during 1979–80 compared with 3.6 30 years earlier) and that significantly more matches per season ended in a draw (11.8 per First and Second Division team in 1981 compared with 8.4 in 1956). Moreover, the foot-ball authorities, unlike those in cricket and rugby league, had arguably made little attempt to change the laws of the game so as to produce more goals and make the 'product' more attractive since altering the offside law back in 1925.[37]

Some studies, unconvinced of the correlation between factors such as hooliganism and goals on one hand and falling attendances on the other, have focused instead on the clubs' failure to respond to increasing commercial pressures. Both the Political and Economic Planning (PEP) report of 1966 and the Chester Report of 1968 highlighted the inadequacies of ground facilities, which in most cases had been untouched since the inter-war years. In 1964, for instance, only 12 per cent of the accommodation at English League clubs took the form of seating, in comparison to 20 per cent in Italy and 80 per cent in the Portuguese top division. PEP also observed that market research was 'hardly known' and advertising and public relations were 'of a rudimentary kind'. Szymanski and Kuypers likewise noted the absence of attempts to bring in new supporters through flexible pricing, marketing and the improvement of ground facilities, concluding that most clubs before the late 1970s 'were making no attempt to make the experience of going to a football match enjoyable other than through what was on offer on the pitch'.[38]

Although much of the shortfall in attendances was offset by increases in admission charges, clubs and leagues were nonetheless extremely reticent in exploiting new commercial opportunities. Beyond the traditional forms of advertising placed on hoardings around grounds and in programmes, the commercial activities of most clubs during the 1960s and 1970s can best be described as modest. Some appointed commercial managers, but their duties tended to be restricted to organising fund-raising ventures and lotteries and running the club shop. Shirt advertising was pioneered by non-league Kettering Town in 1976 and then by Queen's Park Rangers in the English and Hibernian in the Scottish leagues a year later, although all clubs carrying sponsor's logos were required to remove them when appearing on television. Such was the success of these initiatives that by 1981 Arsenal could announce a £500,000 three-year deal with JVC, with Liverpool and Manchester United hot on their heels with similarly sized deals and smaller clubs securing more modest arrangements. Shirt sponsorship was one thing, but the FA was still not ready to accept more overt forms of commercialisation, stepping in to scupper Coventry City's planned £250,000 deal in 1980 with the car manufacturer Talbot, which would have required the club to be renamed 'Coventry-Talbot'.[39]

The leagues themselves experimented with a series of new sponsored competitions at the beginning of the 1970s as a means of generating additional revenue. The Watney Mann Invitation Trophy (better known as the Watney Cup), a pre-season tournament introduced in 1970 for high-scoring teams from each English division, was closely followed by a Scottish equivalent, the Dryborough Cup, and the all-British Texaco Cup for 16 English, Scottish and northern and southern Irish clubs not involved in European competition. None of these were particularly successful. Celtic chairman Desmond White labelled the Dryborough Cup as a 'quite unimaginative' competition that offered 'nothing to the clubs that most need a financial lift', while the Texaco Cup was treated from the beginning with disdain by the leading Football League clubs and the English press. The winding-up of the Ford Sporting League – based on games in existing competitions but rewarding clubs for goals scored and penalising them for poor discipline – after a single season in 1970–1 prompted League secretary Alan Hardaker to bemoan the attitude of critics in the media and club management who objected to sponsored competitions. It was thus hardly surprising that the professional game took some time to follow the lead of amateur football in acquiring sponsors for existing tournaments. Bell's Whisky put its name to the Scottish League Cup in 1979, while the drink companies Morans, Hennessy's and Smirnoff had done likewise for Northern Ireland's leading cup and league competitions by 1982. In England it was a rather different drinks body, the National Dairy Council, which agreed a £2 million deal over four years for the League Cup to become the Milk Cup. A year later the championship itself acquired its first sponsor, when the Japanese camera and computer firm Canon signed a three-year £3.3 million deal to associate itself with the oldest football league in the world. The traditional anti-commercialism of the game's governing bodies was thus slowly being challenged and, as a number of writers have stressed, this gained greater impetus with the arrival of Thatcherism and the accompanying ideological and political shift towards a more competitive, free-market economy during the 1980s.[40]

Football's other major source of external revenue came from television and pools companies. Both had long been regarded with considerable distrust by the game's leaders, who tended to argue that football was being sold cheaply to, and thus being exploited by, these outside interests. Regular transmission by the BBC and independent television of league, cup and international matches had begun in the 1950s, but the financial rewards to the game were limited. BBC records reveal that the FA received just £13,500 from the corporation and £7,250 from the ITA in payment for cup and international highlights and the live FA Cup final during the 1955–6 season. The leagues were not making much more. PEP reported that the Football League received only £30,000 in television fees in 1966, largely due to its 'unduly restrictive and unimaginative' attitude to broad-casting. The Scottish League's television contracts yielded just £55,000 by the mid-1970s, a situation not helped by the fact that certain clubs, such as Hibernian, sometimes refused to allow cameras into their grounds. Modest increases in the total television income followed in England, from £120,000 (or £1,300 per League club) in 1968 to £534,000 (£5,800 per club) by 1978, but it took London Weekend Television's attempted breach of the informal BBC–ITV cartel that year to precipitate the first major escalation in payments. The resulting deal secured the League a total of £9.2 million over four years, equivalent to a much-increased annual sum of £25,000 per club, with an additional £2.6 million per season coming from the first contract for live matches in 1983. Yet even these higher figures represented 'peanuts', in the words of one study, to the wealthier clubs: Arsenal's £28,261 share of the television pool in 1983, for instance, accounted for only 1 per cent of its annual turnover.[41] The injection of pools money into football from the late 1950s was also regarded by many as an opportunity missed. At first sight, as the 1968 Chester Report suggested, it could be seen to have transformed the game. After all, in 1964 the pools companies provided some £500,000 to the Football League and Scottish League coffers, a figure which by 1981 had risen to £3 million and £1 million respectively. In particular, as Crampsey argues, this income was 'an absolute life-saver' for smaller Second Division clubs in Scotland, such as Stenhousemuir, whose £1,225 pools share in 1964 represented some five or six average league gates. Yet there is little doubt that more money could have been made from the pools. PEP noted that the English league received only 1 per cent of pools' takings, compared with 10 per cent in Germany and Portugal, and recommended that it negotiate 'a more favourable arrangement' with the Pools Promoters' Association. A decade later, Hardaker was still reporting the view of those clubs who felt that over the years the pools 'could have been milked to a much greater degree'.[42]

Competition and equality

Perhaps the most obvious explanation for the game's financial problems lay in its own economic and competitive structure. Drawing on a wealth of literature relating to North American sport, economists in Britain have argued that sporting leagues act in the same fundamental way as do indus-trial cartels but in this case to ensure the production and viability of the sporting 'product'. One of their key objectives is to maintain what is called uncertainty of outcome and competitive balance: the assumption, in other words, that teams should be as closely matched as possible on a match-by-match, seasonal and longer-term basis so as to increase consumer interest and stimulate spectator demand. To this end, leagues have traditionally acted to restrict competition in a variety of areas, from regulating entry prices, player movement and the size and composition of membership to redistributing income among member clubs.[43] What is more, these economic motives were underpinned for much of the twentieth century by the prevalence of an 'ideology of equality' amongst football administrators and the media, which stressed the importance of a fair competition where the strong helped out the weak, and the poorer clubs were able to vie with the richer ones for promotion and, ultimately, for championship honours. Yet given that British football clubs, following the work of Peter Sloane and others, tended to be recognised as utility rather than profit maximisers – aiming to maximise playing success while remaining solvent – a basic tension can be said to have existed between individual clubs, who wanted to win consistently, and league organisers (representing the collective interest of clubs), whose intention was to create a competitively balanced and attractive competition.[44]

Much of this tension between individual and collective interests was reflected in attitudes towards structural reform. Neither England nor Scotland had witnessed significant changes in the size and structure of their league competitions since the 1920s, but by the 1960s many observers believed them to be unwieldy, uncompetitive and in dire need of reform. The Football League had brought in four new clubs in 1950 to make up a total of 92 and soon after, in 1958, the regional Third Division sections were abandoned in favour of separate Third and Fourth Divisions. Championed mainly by those southern clubs eager to improve their chances of climbing to the top divisions, the restructuring also meant increased travel costs and fewer local derbies and became identified by some as one reason for the demise of Accrington Stanley in 1962. Indeed one economic historian has described the logic behind the 1958 change as 'a little obscure'.[45] Possibly more logical was the 'Pattern for Football' first introduced by secretary Alan Hardaker and president Joe Richards in 1963 as an attempt to streamline the league while at the same time increasing public interest. The plan was to reorganise the competition into five divisions of 20 clubs each, with four promoted and relegated each season, and to move the new Football League Cup competition to the beginning of the season, like its Scottish equivalent. That way there would be a greater number of meaningful matches throughout the course of the season. The clubs rejected the idea, however, deciding instead to add to an already congested fixture list by keeping the League Cup in its existing form and leading Hardaker to accuse them of 'selfishness and shallow thinking'. For Simon Inglis, the rejection of the 'Pattern for Football' was one of the most crucial mistakes in the Football League's history, increasing the likelihood of the financial collapse of its weaker members. In 1968 the equally progressive recommendations of the Chester Report were dismissed, as was Norman Chester's second report of 1983, which (in its majority form) called for a reduced First Division of 20 clubs, a Third Division split into four sections of 12 clubs, and play-offs for promotion and relegation.[46]

Change proved less easy to resist north of the border, where discrepancies in wealth and playing success had always been more pronounced. In 1961 the Scottish League consisted of 37 clubs divided into an 18-club First and 19-club Second Division, but declining attendances for rich and poor clubs alike forced a wholesale rethink. The League executive's 1964 proposal for three divisions of 14–12–12 was prefaced by the suggestion that 'as conditions now exist, big leagues stultify competition. Many clubs find themselves engaged in meaningless matches before the season has run half its course.' The clubs rejected the idea, and another along similar lines two years later, but the increasing financial problems of many, exacerbated by the long-term domination of Celtic, who won nine consecutive championships from the 1965–6 season, meant that talk of reconstruction never went away. In 1972 the journalist Hugh Taylor described the First Division as 'a farce': 'Celtic are so far out on their own that they can win the flag without looking round'. Others agreed, including Celtic's manager Jock Stein, who controversially called for the amalgamation of some of the League's smaller clubs. When restructuring was finally accepted in the mid-1970s it was in a more radical form than most previous proposals, involving a new Premier Division of ten members and restyled First and Second Divisions of 14 clubs each. The teams in the top division played each other four times and those in the lower divisions only twice, with a supplementary Spring Cup to boost the fixture list, although this was soon abandoned in favour of the somewhat awkward and inequitable arrangement of clubs meeting on three occasions. Reactions to the new League structure were mixed. Competition seemed to increase, with the so-called 'New Firm' of Aberdeen and Dundee United briefly emerging to challenge the dominance of Celtic and Rangers. One club representative observed that the new division was 'hard, tight, entertaining and uncompromising in every way' but that this intensity of competition and the fear of relegation could also bring about defensive and negative play. Others were so dissatisfied with the lack of media coverage given to the lower divisions under the new system that they advocated a return to a two-divisional structure.[47]

Economists disagree on the extent to which changes in the distribution of income affected the gap between rich and poor. There had always been a degree of income-sharing, or cross-subsidisation, in the British leagues but this was to increase from the 1960s, especially in England and Wales, as constraints on the labour market dwindled with the end of the maximum wage and modifications to the transfer system. Since the First World War, Football League gate receipts had been divided on an 80–20 per cent basis between home and away sides, meaning that clubs with large crowds within each division effectively subsidised those with smaller ones. A more equitable 50–50 split existed in the Scottish League and for the FA and League Cup competitions in the south. From 1949 clubs also paid 4 per cent of net gate receipts into a central Football League pool, while television and pools money tended also to be shared fairly equally, although cup and league sponsorship revenues were related more to performance.[48] A. J. Arnold has argued that the overall effect of these measures was 'a substantial transfer of receipts' from rich to poor which helped to keep the latter afloat. Indeed, during the 1974–5 season some 45 per cent of the gross revenue of Fourth Division clubs came from redistribution payments. The transfer market arguably acted as another important mechanism for redistributing income between clubs. Data collected by Stephen Dobson and John Goddard, for example, has shown that in almost every season during the 1970s and 1980s clubs in the top two divisions of the Football League were net spenders, and those in the bottom two net recipients, in the transfer market, and that the figures involved increased over time. Transfer money also flowed consistently from English to Scottish clubs – with £2.3 million being paid by the former to the latter between 1968–9 and 1972–3 alone – although a fair proportion of this was received by the wealthier sides north of the border and so worked as much to increase as to reduce financial disparities.[49]

Szymanski and Kuypers have questioned the degree to which these measures were actually successful in redistributing revenue and promoting league equality. The division of gate receipts, they argue, actually had little effect. Birmingham City, for example, a struggling club with one of the lowest home attendances in the First Division during the 1978–9 season, received a little over £43,000 as a result of the 20 per cent rule, a figure that accounted for just 5 per cent of its total revenue. Elsewhere they argue that the sums involved were simply too small to contribute significantly to a club's annual turnover. Szymanski and Kuypers have similarly found little evidence to support the redistributive function assigned to the transfer system by Dobson and Goddard among others. Indeed they argue that in the period from 1964 to 1966 it was the First Division members who showed a surplus, and the lower divisions a deficit, on transfer deals rather than vice-versa.[50] Surveying a range of reports conducted by the government and football bodies as well as his own research on Scottish clubs, H. F. Moorhouse has likewise criticised the 'common sense' view that transfers 'automatically' redistribute income from rich to poor as entirely unfounded, 'confirmed only by easy anecdote, obvious ... example, or statistics of dubious authenticity'. In reality, Moorhouse argued, the data either point to the flow of fees in precisely the opposite direction to that often assumed by the football authorities or suggest a more complicated picture, in which certain lower-division clubs used the transfer system to generate revenue but others suffered considerable losses and pursued alternative measures to ensure their financial viability.[51]

Moreover, it is important to recognise that the Scottish and Football Leagues did not become more competitive and open over this period as a result of restructuring or increased cross-subsidisation. Indeed quite the reverse seems to have been the case. Tables 5.1 and 5.2 indicate that in both countries a small elite of clubs increasingly dominated the championship of the top division. This was particularly evident in England, where the relative openness of the 1960s, with eight different clubs being crowned Football League champions, was to contrast sharply with the concentration of championships in the hands of four clubs during the 1980s. The virtual stranglehold that Liverpool was able to establish by winning eight of the eleven available titles between 1975–6 and 1985–6 may have been unprecedented in England, even taking into account the success of Huddersfield Town and Arsenal between the wars and Manchester United and Wolves in the 1950s, but this level of domination was nothing new in Scotland. In a top division that was smaller than its English equivalent throughout the period, Celtic and Rangers won a combined 77 per cent of the championships during these decades, with only five other clubs managing to break the duopoly (Table 5.1). This degree of championship concentration was not uncommon in other European leagues at the time. Indeed the Celtic–Rangers domination was paralleled closely by that of Real Madrid and Barcelona in Spain, and to a lesser extent by Juventus, Milan and Inter in Italy, Bayern Munich in Germany and St Etienne in France. Dobson and Goddard's analysis of six European leagues in the post-war period revealed the English to be the most democratic of all, with the highest number of different champions and top-three finishers, while the Scottish League came in fifth ahead only of Spain. But if we move away from domination in the long run to consider outcome uncertainty on a seasonal basis, Szymanski and Kuypers have shown that from the mid-1950s to the mid-1980s the championship races for the Football League were actually less close than in the Italian and Spanish leagues. Thus, although there existed a number of clubs who could win the league, the gap between this group and the rest was considerable and was clearly growing.[52]

By the mid-1980s British league football was thus more unequal and less competitive than it had ever been. Significantly, the leading clubs had finally been successful in gaining a greater share of the game's revenue by dismantling many of the cross-subsidisation arrangements that had aimed to provide some degree of competitive balance. Gate-sharing was abolished in 1981 in Scotland and two years later in England and Wales,

TABLE 5.1 *Football League and Scottish League champions, 1960–89*

Competition	1960–9	1970–9	1980–9
Football League	Liverpool 2 Manchester United 2 Burnley 1 Everton 1 Ipswich Town 1 Leeds United 1 Manchester City 1 Tottenham Hotspur 1	Liverpool 4 Derby County 2 Arsenal 1 Everton 1 Leeds United 1 Nottingham Forest 1	Liverpool 6 Everton 2 Arsenal 1 Aston Villa 1
Scottish League	Celtic 4 Rangers 3 Dundee 1 Hearts 1 Kilmarnock 1	Celtic 7 Rangers 3	Celtic 4 Aberdeen 3 Rangers 2 Dundee United 1

Source: Stephen Dobson and John Goddard, *The Economics of Football* (Cambridge: Cambridge University Press, 2001), pp. 44, 48 (Tables 2.4 and 2.5).

TABLE 5.2 *Comparison of Football League and Scottish League champions and top-three finishers, 1960–89*

Competition	No. of winning clubs	No. of top-three finishing clubs
Football League	12	20
Scottish League	7	14

Source: Dobson and Goddard, *Economics of Football*.

leaving clubs free to retain all the proceeds from their home fixtures. Modifications were also made to the division of television and sponsorship incomes and cup receipts in favour of the larger clubs. While such developments might be considered economically irrational at first glance, by increasing the inequalities between the rich and poor and thus reducing the uncertainty of outcome presumed essential to successful sporting leagues, they were in fact logical for the best clubs, who were increasingly coming to see themselves as competitors in a European as well as a domestic market. For the lower clubs, the financial future looked bleak. The Chester Report suggested that to continue a system where the rich helped out the poor was 'a failure to face the facts' and other analysts predicted that many clubs unable to fend for themselves would be forced either out of the professional game or out of business entirely.[53]

Representations of football: the media, art and literature

While in decline as a live spectacle and an industry during these decades, football was probably more pervasive than ever before in British social and cultural life. As we noted of earlier periods, the majority of those with an interest in the game did not actually play or attend themselves but gained their understanding and experience of football through various facets of the media. From the 1960s onwards the most important of these was television. In his comprehensive study of the phenomenon, Garry Whannel referred to 'television sport' (rather, significantly, than sport on television or television coverage of sport) as 'by any standards a component of popular culture'. Television, he went on:

must inevitably affect the ways in which we see and understand sports ... the coverage is not simply concerned with sport; it inevitably also continually makes implicit and explicit statements, in words and pictures, about our sense of nation, of class, of the place of men and women, our relation to other nations and so on.[54]

Such an observation points to the crucial way in which 'images' or 'representations' of sport helped to form and shape attitudes towards both it and society in a wider sense. Stephen Wagg went so far as to suggest that by the 1980s the main social significance of football was not as a live spectator event but as 'a television show', with players, for example, transformed from sportsmen into media 'personalities'.[55] This section takes up and examines the means by which football was communicated to various sections of British society in this period (through what we generally recognise to be the mass media but also the arts and popular literature) and the consequent meanings that became attached to it.

We saw in earlier chapters that the football–media relationship was already close but it became increasingly so over this period. Coverage of the game grew significantly. We know that twice as much space was devoted to sport in the *Daily Mirror*, for example, in 1968–75 than had been during the 1947–51 period. By the beginning of the 1980s the same newspaper was providing 17.36 per cent of its space to sport, a figure topped by other tabloids such as *The Sun* (20.4 per cent) and the *Daily Star* (22.16 per cent). Along with horse racing, soccer made up the bulk of this coverage and, while it is impossible to know how many bought these papers primarily to read about the game, there is evidence that a significant and increasing proportion of both men and women looked at the sports pages. Even the broadsheet press, traditionally less keen on popular professional sports, began to write about football at greater length and with more enthusiasm than ever before. *The Times*' treatment of football, for instance, was more extensive than that of rugby union by 1970. Fabio Chisari has argued that that year's World Cup 'made a massive impact on the pages of *The Times*'. Chief football correspondent Geoffrey Green was sent to Mexico along with four other journalists, and at least half a page was set aside for news and reports from the tournament each day.[56]

Television built upon and quickly surpassed the scope and significance of radio's coverage of football. Brief highlights of matches were already a feature of the BBC's Saturday evening *Sports Special* programme in the 1950s but the real breakthrough for televised soccer came with the launch of *Match of the Day* in 1964. From modest beginnings, with only 75,000 watching the first broadcast on the new and largely unavailable BBC 2 channel, the programme was to become a staple of the corporation's Saturday night schedule for the next three decades. With the advent of colour in the early 1970s, viewing figures for *Match of the Day* reached an average of some 12–13 million, with ITV's Sunday afternoon *Big Match* attracting a similarly impressive 9–10 million. Audiences declined somewhat in the late 1970s and early 1980s but seem to have improved with the introduction of live league matches. Tottenham's 2–1 defeat of Nottingham Forest at White Hart Lane in October 1983 was the first Football League fixture to be broadcast live. By the following season the live Sunday fixtures were attracting around 11 million viewers at a time when the established recorded highlights could only draw 4–6 million. Even with fewer people visiting grounds, football still 'possessed the power to colonise the weekend' of significant numbers through the papers they read and the television they watched.[57]

Assessments of the impact of television, in particular, have emphasised the way in which the supposedly 'real' game witnessed by the spectator was reconstructed and reinterpreted for the viewing public. Television could never of course 'show' a football match complete in time and space. Rather, the game was conveyed to the viewer through a series of mediations – camera, commentary and editing – with an emphasis on 'highlights', 'action' and 'incidents'. It was also given added context and drama by the build-up, half-time and after-game analysis of the anchorman and his team of expert 'pundits'. One study has seen in this the construction of the 'game-narrative', which offers the viewer 'a preferred reading of the event, the text, the match'.[58] Writing in 1979, Critcher was highly critical of the role of television in distancing the supporters from the game and manipulating their response to it. For Critcher, match commentary and expert opinion were unnecessary, offering analysis rather than basic description and thereby acting as a barrier between the audience and the event. Camerawork distorted the nature of the game by focusing on small areas of the pitch or, in the case of close-ups, individual players. Editing and action replays served to break up the game's natural flow and pattern into a series of unconnected moments of drama. All in all, Critcher suggested, the effect on football's traditional subculture was 'debilitative', with the game itself 'playing second fiddle to television's idea of a show'. John Hargreaves has likewise asserted that, despite their claims to be 'reproducing reality', television companies were unable, or rather disinclined, to present the football match 'as the spectator sees it'. The positioning of the main camera, for example, at one side of the ground on the halfway line represented a neutral or impartial perspective similar to that of the bourgeois spectator rather than the partisan working-class fan located at the end terraces. The continual use of close-ups and action replays (apparently for the benefit of 'mums and daughters') similarly indicated how British coverage was, in Hargreaves's view, focused on the individual personality rather than the team and, in short, heavily skewed towards the conventions of entertainment programming.[59]

Central to this discussion is the tension in televised soccer between realism and entertainment. Both Critcher and Hargreaves' assessments of soccer on television are premised on the rather simplistic notion that there is such a thing as a 'real' or 'authentic' experience of watching football against which the televised version can be compared. It is surely misleading to suggest that, even for the spectator on the terraces, there is a singularly 'genuine' view of what takes place on the pitch: the perspective obviously differs depending on where the spectators are positioned in relation to the action, who they support, whether they have watched previous games, and so on. As Jeff Hill has argued, one should not regard any type of experience, sporting or otherwise, 'as being subject to a fixed, authentic "essence" which has a prior validity'. In relation to the televising of sport, Whannel has suggested that rather than a single reality, there are a variety of realities and a number of modes of representing sporting 'actuality'. Indeed television sport should not, in this view, be seen in terms of the objective presentation of reality: rather, it should be understood as a combination of the three main practices in television production, relating respectively to journalism, entertainment and drama. From the beginnings of televised football, it is evident that the need to produce 'good television', in the form of an entertaining spectacle crammed full of action, personalities and stars, along with the dramatic practices of the theatre and storytelling, were equally as prominent as the journalistic conventions of impartiality, balance and objectivity usually associated with news and current affairs programmes. Thus when the raw material on offer failed to entertain, as was true of one *Match of the Day* episode in 1978 when the only available match was a dull 0–0 draw, the programme was nonetheless infused with action, drama and goals through its opening and closing montage sequences, a Goal of the Month competition and a review of the championship race.[60]

A useful illustration of the construction of football as television entertainment and drama comes from Iain Colley and Gill Davies' reading of the 1981 FA Cup final. The authors offer a detailed examination of the way in which the football match itself was contextualised and, in their words, 'recombined' by both BBC and ITV as a major television event. The emphasis was on the construction of a series of interconnected narratives which ran through the entire day's programming (not just the match), providing it with a meaning and structure that could be easily absorbed and understood by the audience at home. Thus Tottenham Hotspur was presented as a club traditionally associated with glamour and style, aided by its two new 'exotic' Argentinian stars Ossie Ardiles and Ricardo Villa, but also in terms of superstition and fate. Viewers were repeatedly reminded that the club had a habit of winning trophies when the year ended in a 'one' and that 1981 was the Chinese year of the cockerel (symbolised on the club badge). For Tottenham's opponents, Manchester City, the focus was on charismatic manager John Bond and his achievement in helping the club escape relegation and reach the final. The 'professional' analysis was provided by the teams of commentators at the stadium and pundits in the studio, mostly ex-players and all 'personalities' in their own right, whose chatty and informal discussion 'drew players, managers and officials into the same soap-opera narrative'. 'The match', Colley and Davies noted, with 'its skills, tactics and rhythms, functioned as storyline'. The final was also framed by images of sporting history and national unity. Along with the usual references to the 'tradition' and 'romance' of the oldest cup competition in the world, the 1981 match was significantly the hundredth FA Cup final. So the BBC ran a dial-a-Cup-final item for viewers to nominate past goals, while ITV took its audience 'down Memory Lane' in the half hour before kick-off. Through the attention paid to the military marching bands, the presence of the royalty and other dignitaries and the traditional pre-match hymn 'Abide With Me', both channels also framed the Cup final as a significant, shared 'national' ritual. While the authors resisted the suggestion that what was produced on television was a fictionalised version of the game, they argued nonetheless that football had been permanently changed by the relationship. The Cup final at least, they concluded, 'no longer exists independently of how it is experienced on television'.[61]

One of the key trends in both television and press coverage of football was the increasing focus placed on the deeds of the individual player. In Chapter 3 we argued that the 'star' footballer, known to a national public through the dissemination of his image in the media, emerged in embryonic form during the inter-war years, much earlier than most writers assumed. Having said this, there is little doubt that the 1960s heralded a new phase both in the professional status and economic fortunes of the player and the way in which he was represented to the public through the media. Richard Holt has argued that the modest, ordinary professional hero, exemplified in soccer by Stanley Matthews, was transformed in this period into the 'contemporary sporting hero who exists as performer and celebrity, an ostensibly classless product of market values and the media'.[62] For Critcher, the combination of increased wages and heightened media interest led to a select band of players being 'nominated' as 'superstars' and subsequently 'raised to new levels and kinds of public adulation and attention'. Despite initial dislocation from their familiar environment, these soccer 'superstars' soon adopted a new identity in the world of showbusiness and celebrity, positioned 'metaphorically and sometimes literally, alongside film and television stars'.[63] Whannel provides a rather more sophisticated account of how sporting stars have been represented through the media. In common with Colley and Davies, he focuses on the process whereby the media restructures and recomposes the actual sporting contest into narrative form, with the star performer naturally playing a leading role. In the same way as individual matches and seasons are narrated to the audience, so an entire sporting career or life can be constructed by the media into a long-running saga or soap-opera. The narrative of a star's life, Whannel suggests, is produced through four main cultural outlets: newspaper articles, magazine profiles, television previews of sporting events and biographies or autobiographies. In this way, the star is made familiar to his public but simultaneously mythologised, meaning that he can ultimately only be 'known' through his representation in the media. And his story is constantly being reinterpreted, in a process that Whannel refers to as 'reinscription', to fit with the changing preoccupations of the time. The narrative is thus never fixed but subject to continual revision.[64]

The career of George Best, regarded by many as football's first superstar, offers a perfect example of these processes in operation. From his earliest appearances, Best was portrayed as being 'different' from his predecessors and many of his contemporaries. This difference had little to do with his extra-curricula activities. He was, after all, hardly the first player to achieve notoriety through his romantic liaisons, his taste for alcohol and his failure to deal with the various pressures of the professional game. But the difference was that Best had, in the words of Whannel, a 'cool appeal'. He hung out in discotheques and opened boutiques. He dressed like a mod and had his hair cut like the Beatles (the Portuguese press dubbed him as 'El Beatle' after a particularly impressive display in Lisbon in 1965). Even his thin and wiry physique – one newspaper describing him as a 'wispy waif on the left wing' – made his stocky contemporaries in their baggy shorts seem out of date. More important, however, was the fact that Best operated as a fully fledged media personality, straddling the worlds of sport, showbiz, fashion and pop music. In what was to become a familiar pattern in later decades, for seven years Best's 'every move was plotted by journalists and photographers' and he responded by living out 'the newspapers' dream version of the superstar's life'. Thus, Best's career became arranged as a rise-and-fall narrative. He progressed from Belfast teenager to Manchester United regular by the mid-1960s and then European Cup winner and Footballer of the Year by 1968, only to fall into a pattern of indiscipline and unbridled hedonism during the early 1970s, initially retiring in 1972 before eventually leaving United in 1974 for a series of uninspired spells at other English, Scottish and American clubs. Significantly, it was another media personality, television presenter Michael Parkinson, who wrote an 'intimate biography' in 1975, which promised to tell 'the true, explosive story behind Best's dazzling success and tragic decline'. Whannel has seen such texts as crucial in the mythologising of Best. Yet he also argues convincingly that during the 1990s Best's story of alcohol and hedonism was reinscribed both in the context of the celebratory 'lad' culture of men's magazines such as *Loaded* and as 'a Victorian moral tract about the evils of drink' and the squandering of natural talent.[65]

Given soccer's perceived centrality to working-class or popular culture, it is hardly surprising that the game was rarely represented in forms of 'high' culture. Artistic depictions of football in the first half of the twentieth century were rare beyond the cartoons and caricatures appearing in newspapers and on cigarette cards. Perhaps the best-known artistic representations of the game between the wars came through the poster art commissioned by companies such as Shell and London Transport, who respectively utilised the work of artists like Paul Nash, and Cyril Power and Sybil Andrews. In 1953, the FA launched a competition for artists as part of its ninetieth anniversary celebrations, subsequently exhibited by the Arts Council as *Football and the Fine Arts*. A 'watershed in soccer's relationship with the visual arts' according to one writer, the exhibition tended to portray the game in its urban and industrial environment, as an escape from the mundane nature of working life. A typical example is Arthur Hackney's *Spectators Returning Home after Port Vale v. Accrington Stanley*, which depicts a bleak landscape in which a dour, faceless crowd head home against a dark and threatening sky. The best-known work from the exhibition, and possibly the most celebrated piece of British football 'art', was L. S. Lowry's *Going to the Match*. With Lowry's distinctive match-stick characters and typical industrial setting, the painting has been described as a 'vivid evocation of "football's golden age"'. John Bale has positioned it as one of a number of football-themed paintings that portray the game in an unambiguously 'northern' industrial landscape. The background detail of the terraced housing and factory chimneys, and the fact that it was based on Bolton's Burnden Park ground, certainly support Bale's view, but it is worth noting that the same exhibition featured alternative regional representations of the game such as Richard Slater's modernist *Entering the Stands, White Hart Lane*, Hubert Andrew Freeth's studies of the dressing room and crowd at Watford and Peter Peri's *The Village Game*, set in a very different England of rolling fields and rural solitude. Throughout the 1960s and 1970s a number of artists, some of them prominent figures such as William Roberts and Robert Blake, depicted the game in a variety of styles but there proved to be no focal point like the 1953 exhibition and little evident support or interest from the governing bodies or the clubs themselves.[66]

Dramatic representations were equally sparse during this period. Most compendiums of the game include reference to the short passages from Harold Pinter's plays *The Dumb Waiter* (1960) and *A Night Out* (1961), while Glenn Melvyn's 1953 three-act comedy *The Love Match* was made into a film the following year, with Arthur Askey starring as a train driver attempting to follow the fortunes of his football-playing son. Yet the game tended not to form the basis of the drama in these works. A possible exception came when young playwright Peter Terson dealt with the themes of hooliganism and youth culture in his *Zigger Zagger*, first performed by the National Youth Theatre in 1967. Thereafter community plays celebrating the achievements of a local club, such as Bill Grundy's Derby County-inspired *Up the Rams* (1970), or 'fringe' plays dealing with the game's problems, became increasingly popular.[67]

The difficulties of dramatising sport on stage have been considered in a fascinating paper by the playwright Ian Brown. He argues that sporting and theatrical events share a number of common elements, from the role of the hero and characterisation to plot and pacing and the importance of conventions or rules guiding the performance, which need to be recognised in any successful dramatic presentation of sport. Using the football example of Peter Flannery's 1978 production *The Boys Own Story*, Brown suggests that above all it is the pace and rhythm of a 'sporting' play, as well as its staging and use of dramatic conventions, that are crucial. Thus Flannery tells the story of a goalkeeper struggling with professional and personal crises through a monologue in which the audience represents the pitch and the sudden action and lulls of the script suggest the rhythm of a match in progress. But Flannery's play goes further than simply providing the audience with a sense of the sporting experience. According to Brown, it also presents football as inextricably a part of society in general through its depiction of an 'exploited, lonely and unbalanced' hero and a manipulative and corrupt business.[68]

Novelists were no keener than playwrights to embrace soccer as a central theme in their work. If, as Jeff Hill notes, sport has inhabited a ghetto in the British literary imagination when compared to the USA, this is especially true of football. Unlike cricket, it could be argued, few novelists have had sufficient interest in or knowledge of the game to write about it convincingly, while football fans have not been considered by some as typical readers of 'serious' fiction. D. J. Taylor has pointed out other obstacles for the aspirant soccer novelist, such as the stylistic difficulties involved in writing about physical activity in general and the problems of articulating the inner thoughts and desires of this notoriously inarticulate occupational group. For these reasons, and others besides, Peter Seddon has recently characterised football and literature as 'not comfortable bedfellows nor even casual friends – distant relatives would be nearer the mark'. From the pre-Second World War period only Arnold Bennett's fictional depiction of Potteries soccer rivalry in *The Card* (1911) and J. B. Priestley's short passage on football spectatorship in Bruddersford (quoted in Chapter 3) from his *The Good Companions* (1929) are normally counted as 'serious' literary representations of the game. Yet neither of these novels, nor many others which include football-related conversations or incidents, were actually *about* the game in the precise sense identified by Hill: that is, having a narrative 'whose meaning to the reader hinges decisively on the sporting milieu'. There are only a handful of novels from the 1950s to the 1980s that fit this 'realist' category. One of the best known is J. L. Carr's *How Steeple Sinderby Wanderers Won the FA Cup* (1975), a comic portrayal of a 1930s village football team whose progress to Wembley glory is told through parodies of newspaper reports and the club secretary's committee minutes. Less celebrated are Robin Jenkins' *The Thistle and the Grail* (1954), a novel that details the fortunes of the Scottish junior team Drumsagart Thistle, and Gordon Williams' *From Scenes Like These* (1968), 'only parenthetically a football novel' in Taylor's view, which tells the story of the adolescent Duncan Logan who plays for junior club Cartneuk in the West of Scotland League and whose dreams of being spotted by a professional club represent one way out of his otherwise bleak and violent lifestyle.[69]

Probably the chief exponent of what we might call 'realist' soccer literature has been the novelist and sports journalist Brian Glanville. Many of his short stories and novels were set in the world of amateur and professional soccer, an environment that he knew well and attempted to portray as authentically as possible. *Goalkeepers are Different* (first published in 1971), for example, follows the young Ronnie Blake from schoolboy to apprentice with First Division Borough United and then, having suffered injuries and loss of form, on to his appearance in the FA Cup final. Billed as a story of 'what it is really like to be a professional footballer', it is a self-conscious slice of realism, located firmly in the contemporary football scene. Indeed Blake and Borough face in the final not an imaginary team but an Everton side consisting of Alan Ball, Howard Kendall and Joe Royle.[70] Likewise, Hill has described Glanville's first football novel, *The Rise of Gerry Logan*, published in 1963, as 'a classic realist tale'. First, as the story of a Scottish inside-forward's career path from the north-east of England to London and then Italy and back, culminating in a European Cup final against Real Madrid, it not only echoes the real-life experiences of migrants such as John Charles, Denis Law, Gerry Hitchens and Jimmy Greaves (although Logan was evidently actually based on Danny Blanchflower) but also successfully mimics the rise-and-fall format of many real sporting biographies. Second, key themes such as the state of the British game and its relationship with the media were major obsessions of Glanville and other sports journalists at the time. Authenticity, as Hill has argued, was thus the 'keyword' in this as in most of Glanville's football novels.[71]

Representations of the game in popular and juvenile literature were almost certainly read by many more than these attempts at serious fiction. Russell has written extensively of the serialised football novels and magazines produced in the 1920s and 1930s for a largely teenage market. Combining established genres of popular fiction and featuring recognisable stock characters, these texts often shared a romantic storyline and the type of emphasis on the amateur footballer as hero which suggested the continued stylistic influence of the Victorian public school story as well as 'suppressed concerns about the professional game' which was still 'not quite to be trusted'. Although we can never know with any precision what readers took from these stories, Russell has suggested that, in common with most popular fiction, they doubtless provided 'both a rich source of inspiration for personal fantasy and a comforting imaginary landscape in which justice and goodness always prevailed'. They tended, moreover, to articulate a rather conservative take on sport and social relations in which fair play, honesty and 'proper' sporting behaviour were highly valued.[72] Hill has identified a similar ideological thread in Michael Hardcastle's children's novels from the late 1960s onwards, with their emphasis on dedication, hard work, masculinity and overcoming physical and social obstacles. Such themes were also prevalent in many post-war comics, in strips like 'Limp-along Leslie', 'Billy's Boots' and the most famous of all, 'Roy of the Rovers'. Roy Race, star of the latter, was portrayed in many respects as the model English soccer hero. Blonde, handsome and wholesome, daring in his dealings with international crooks and corrupt directors as well as with adversaries on the field, Race initially appeared as the young centre-forward of First Division Melchester Rovers in the first edition of *Tiger* in 1954, going on to captain and manage the team in his own eponymous weekly from 1976. He soon acquired such a central position in the game's culture that the phrase 'real "Roy of the Rovers" stuff' was (and continues to be) used to describe improbably dramatic events and exciting contests. Yet, by the 1980s, the world inhabited by Roy Race and others seemed increasingly anachronistic and out of step with a rapidly changing football industry. Thus the adult comic *Viz* could cleverly satirise the 'Roy of the Rovers' style in its depiction of Billy Thompson, goalkeeper for Fulchester Rovers, who just happened to be half man, half fish ('Billy the Fish'). The writers' own attempts at modernisation – through a sensational 'Who shot Roy Race?' storyline (reminiscent of the US soap opera *Dallas*), the incorporation of real-life pop stars Spandau Ballet as new owners of Melchester Rovers, and even marriage problems between Roy and wife Penny – were targeted at a more sophisticated, media-savvy readership, but ultimately failed, and Roy finally bowed out in a helicopter crash in 1993.[73]

1966 and the decline of English football?

At first glance, it seems rather odd that England's 1966 World Cup victory has not featured heavily in histories of the British, or even the English, game. Neither Walvin's nor Russell's book-length studies do more than mention the event in passing, linking it to broader trends in live crowds and television figures rather than considering it as an event in itself.[74] Such neglect might be explained by the failure of 1966 to fit neatly into the narratives of decline that characterise most studies of this period. It can certainly be argued that England's great moment of footballing glory on the international stage came at a time when the popularity of the sport as a live event was fading and the game itself was less attractive than it had ever been. Victory could thus be regarded as a glitch in the broader downward trend – 'a miracle', in the words of Percy Young – achieved when the British were beginning to come to terms with their inferior position (sporting and otherwise) in the global hierarchy.[75] Rather than seeing it as an anomaly, however, some writers have interpreted 1966 as central to the broader debate over national failure and decline. For Critcher, the event has gained mythical status, helping to sustain 'the notion of a golden age of English football' while disguising the fundamental weaknesses that continued to hamper performances in international competition for the next three decades.[76] In understanding the significance of 1966, therefore, we need to consider how it has been remembered and represented in subsequent decades. But we must first look at the meanings attached to the event itself, and the English victory, in the context of 1960s Britain.

1966, England and national identity

The staging of the World Cup in England was a major organisational and logistical operation. In straightforward statistical terms, it involved hosting 32 matches between 16 national teams at 8 venues over a mere 19 days. Nearly 1.6 million tickets were sold, a fair proportion of these to spectators coming from overseas, with more people attending overall than in any of the previous tournaments. Over 2,000 media representatives from 62 different countries were accommodated, providing some 445 live television commentaries and over 1,000 hours of radio broadcasts. With an estimated global television and radio audience of 600 million and record gate receipts of £204,805, the final tie between the hosts and West Germany became the most lucrative football match of all time, witnessed by more people than any previous game. The tournament allegedly made a £1 million profit, with the FA receiving about a fifth of this sum and those clubs hosting the matches making a combined £235,000. Yet these achievements were by no means guaranteed. It had after all required the government to donate £500,000 at the eleventh hour, after refusing numerous requests since 1963, to ensure that the facilities were adequate and completed in time.[77] Although there had been plenty of media build-up to whet the appetite of football fans, it arguably took the theft of the Jules Rimet trophy, and its subsequent discovery in a south London bush by a dog called Pickles, to underline the competition's significance to the general public.[78] Arthur Hopcraft's account pointed to the enthusiasm with which the English public embraced the tournament. He described the sense of carnival and 'communal exuberance' that accompanied the event:

It gave us a chance to spruce up a lot, to lighten the leaden character of the grounds where the matches were played, to throw off much of our inhibition of behaviour, particularly in the provinces, so that we became a gay, almost reckless people in our own streets, which is commonly only how we conduct ourselves when we put on our raffia hats in other countries' holiday resorts. Except in the celebrations that greeted the end of the Second World War, I have never seen England look so unashamedly delighted with life as it did during the World Cup.

Attendances may not have been great for all matches but Hopcraft was nonetheless impressed by the attachment of the English crowds to foreign teams and players. The best example was the support given to the little-known and un-fancied North Korean side in the course of their progress to the quarter-finals, where they were finally defeated 5–3 by Portugal in a dramatic match which they had led 3–0, after having previously knocked out Italy in the group stage. At the end of the Italy game, Hopcraft wrote, the Middlesbrough crowd 'fell upon them [the North Koreans] in hysterical acclaim'.[79]

The England team was, of course, the main focus of public attention. A great deal had changed since the nation's exit from the 1958 World Cup. Walter Winterbottom remained in charge for the next four years but continued to be criticised by the press, especially during the course of a disastrous 1959 tour of the Americas in which England lost to Brazil, Peru and Mexico. Results had improved by the 1960–1 season, with a relatively settled side recording five victories and scoring 38 goals, including a 9–3 demolition of Scotland, and qualifying for the 1962 World Cup. But the team was considered to be past its peak by 1962 and won just one match before being overwhelmed 3–1 in the quarter-final stage by eventual winners Brazil. Winterbottom resigned after 17 years in charge and was replaced as full-time manager by Ipswich Town's Alf Ramsey. Crucially, the FA's International Selection Committee was disbanded at the same time and Ramsey became the first England manager entrusted to pick his own team. Things did not start well for Ramsey's England. A 5–2 defeat by France in early 1963 meant elimination from the European Championships and subsequent losses to Brazil (5–1) and Argentina (1–0) in the 'Little World Cup' of 1964 shook the squad's confidence and revealed the gap in playing standards between England and the best South American nations. Yet despite these setbacks, results improved, with Ramsey moulding a strong defensive unit, based particularly around goalkeeper Gordon Banks and central defender Bobby Moore, which proved difficult to break down. He also employed a new, more defensive and 'wingless' 4–3–3 formation in away victories over Sweden, West Germany and European champions Spain in 1965. Public confidence in the team returned. The hosts were now installed as 5–1 second favourites (after holders Brazil) and for the first time seemed to be capable of fulfilling Ramsey's famous prediction shortly after taking the job that his England side would win the 1966 World Cup.[80]

The variable quality of England performances in the years preceding 1966 was reflected during the tournament itself. Despite the advantage of being able to play all its matches at Wembley, England started Group A inauspiciously with a dismal goalless draw against Uruguay. The Sunday newspapers reacted as if it were the end of the world, but Ramsey congratulated his players on not conceding a goal and took them off to Pinewood Studios to watch Sean Connery shooting scenes in a James Bond film. Goals from Bobby Charlton and Roger Hunt gave England a 2–0 victory in its second group game against Mexico, but neither this, nor the subsequent 2–0 win over France, were impressive performances. Roger Hutchinson, in his account of the tournament, described these as 'deeply unsatisfactory matches'. Geoff Hurst, who had witnessed these games from the bench, admitted that they were 'a torture to watch' but blamed the spoiling tactics of the opponents rather than the deficiencies of the hosts.[81] Hurst replaced the injured Jimmy Greaves for the quarter-final against Argentina, heading the only goal from a cross by West Ham teammate Martin Peters, but the game is now remembered more for the sending-off of Argentinian captain Antonio Rattin and Ramsey's after-match comment that the South Americans had acted like 'animals'. This hardly endeared England to South American commentators, who already sensed a conspiracy to ensure a European, specifically an English, victory. The sense of preferential treatment for the hosts grew when a FIFA committee decided that the semi-final against Portugal was to be played at Wembley, rather than Goodison Park as had been expected. But England played its best match of the tournament (and arguably of Ramsey's tenure) in a thrilling encounter, two Bobby Charlton strikes to one Eusebio penalty setting up a showdown with West Germany in the final.[82]

The twists and turns of that July afternoon are probably better known than any other sporting encounter in British history. An error by full-back Ray Wilson helped the Germans to an early lead, but an unmarked Hurst headed the equaliser and Peters put England 2–1 up with a mere 13 minutes left to play. A scrambled goal from Wolfgang Weber in the final minute took the game to extra-time, Ramsey famously exhorting his exhausted players: 'You've won the World Cup once. Now go out and win it again.' His words worked as England dominated extra-time, the crucial goal coming when Hurst's shot against the crossbar was controversially adjudged by the linesman to have bounced down over the goal line. With seconds remaining and while some supporters were celebrating prematurely by running on to the pitch, Hurst completed his hat-trick to make the score 4–2 and secure the World Cup for England.[83]

Reactions to the victory reveal a great deal about both English national identity and the place of football in 1960s Britain. Writers have remarked upon the 'intense patriotism' and euphoria generated by the outcome and the way in which this success was related to past glories. Particularly notable were the connections made between 1966 and previous occasions of national victory and celebration. A policeman watching the celebrating crowds in Piccadilly Circus was quoted as saying, 'This is Mafeking night and VE night rolled into one'. Others compared it to the coronation of 1953. Most common were the references to the Second World War, especially given the identity of the defeated opponents. 'If Germany beat us at Wembley this afternoon in our national game' ran the *Daily Mail* editorial on the morning of the final, 'we can always point out to them that we have recently beaten them twice at theirs.' Central defender Jack Charlton later recalled thinking minutes before the kick-off: 'For six years we had waged a war against Germany; now we were preparing to do battle on the football field'. Hutchinson has argued that this brand of militant, and militaristic, nationalism was commonplace among the English. It certainly shocked elements of the West German press. The television commentator Werner Schneider regarded it as 'strange and sad' that the English attached such symbolic significance to its national sport:

They want to fly flags and beat drums because they are winning at football … It is said that the Germans are the most militaristic people in the world but it is not so. The British are. Even winning at football is treated like a victory in battle.

For Richard Weight, England's win represented 'a peacetime version of the Finest Hour … stamping the Second World War on the national cortex' more dynamically than Winston Churchill's state funeral had the previous January. It also highlighted a link between football and war that was to reverberate for decades in British popular culture and find an outlet in films such as 1981's *Escape to Victory* as well as in the pages of the tabloid press.[84]

The year 1966 has also been regarded as crucial in sealing football's place as a barometer of national well-being. We saw in the previous chapter that this process was first identified with the Hungarian defeat of 1953 but it undoubtedly intensified in the aftermath of England's win. The popular base of the game's support was almost certainly broadened as a result, although this hardly pleased everyone, as Hopcraft's resentment at the presence at Wembley of supporters with 'rugby club blazers' and 'Home Counties accents' shows. Broadsheet as well as tabloid newspapers were increasingly likely to associate footballing success with the state of the nation. In this respect, football seems to have filled a gap left by the decline of English cricket. Mike Cronin and Richard Holt have outlined the faltering prestige and public interest associated with the England test team from the late 1950s as it suffered increasing defeats at the hands of its Commonwealth rivals during a time of mounting imperial uncertainty. In this context, the success of 1966 could be regarded as the type of 'vindication for the continued vitality of the nation on the world stage' no longer offered by the summer game. The progress of England's footballers also attracted the interest of establishment figures and politicians. Although his request to add his comment to the half-time analysis was rejected by the BBC, Prime Minister Harold Wilson nevertheless made sure he was a part of the team's celebrations that evening on the balcony of the Royal Garden Hotel and the victory banquet. In so doing, Wilson arguably became the first British premier to make political capital out of the exploits of the national football teams.[85]

That 1966 was actually an English rather than a British victory was apparently lost on the many supporters who waved the Union Jack (rather than the St George's Cross) in the stadium and on the streets. Yet whether this can be seen as proof of English ignorance of its own national identity and that of its neighbours, as Weight claims, is open to debate. Ramsey himself was certainly a confirmed English patriot, declaring his faith 'in England and Englishmen, as well as English football', and conscious of the antipathy felt towards the English by their Scottish rivals. The success was also widely credited to the application of traditionally English values such as pride, determination, courage and discipline.[86] The Scottish attitude to 1966 has been well documented: casual indifference as the tournament progressed, followed by resentment at the English victory. It was perhaps best summed up by Manchester United's Denis Law, who chose to play golf rather than watch the final and subsequently claimed that England had only won because it had played at home without having to qualify. Or by *The Scotsman*, which devoted the same two columns to the English victory the Monday after the final as it did to a university golf tournament. That the Scottish FA congratulated its English counterpart on a 'great *British* achievement' and Scots such as the journalist Hugh McIlvanney were prepared to heap praise on the England team did not, in Weight's view, contradict the general 'meanness of spirit' emanating from those associated with the Scottish game. We know less of the reaction to the tournament in Wales, although it does seem to have been followed with greater interest and enthusiasm. On the Monday after the final, an editorial in the *Western Mail* could even claim England's 'superb victory' as a triumph that 'the whole of Britain can feel proud of'.[87]

Modernisation and decline

In England at least, the victory was also connected to broader notions of modernisation and economic renewal. Reflecting a few months after the tournament had ended, a writer in *FA News* was sure that it had both bolstered the international prestige of England and helped provide a 'welcome boost' to 'many of our export industries'. Clarke and Critcher have linked it to the Wilson government's policy of technological change and innovation, specifically comparing Ramsey's approach to team affairs with an emerging spirit of rationalisation and scientific management. His role was to organise and co-ordinate his 'workers' to 'produce' as efficiently as possible for the team cause. In certain respects, Ramsey's team marked a transition towards a new style of playing the game. The traditional marking full-back was now expected to overlap; hardworking 'midfield' players such as Alan Ball and Nobby Stiles had replaced the dribbling wingers of previous decades; and the functional 'professionalism' of forwards such as Roger Hunt and Geoff Hurst was favoured ahead of the skill and flair of the established Jimmy Greaves. The important point that Clarke and Critcher make, however, is that any change that did occur, in football as in politics, turned out to be cosmetic and lacking in real substance. In the cases of both Wilson and Ramsey, they argue that short-term success served merely to cover up a lack of significant structural change.[88] English football may have found itself momentarily top of the world but it still suffered from an antiquated and unwieldy league system, dated coaching systems and a reliance on the established virtues of speed, strength and character, characterised by the domination of what Tony Pawson has called 'the hard and the fast'. It had won not by adapting to foreign developments and techniques but by obstinately sticking to its own game. Modernisation was floated but tradition ultimately preserved. 'The real victor of 1966', according to Clarke and Critcher, 'was the deeply conservative and nationally characteristic instincts of English football'.[89]

In contrast to notions of modernisation and renewal, such observations fit closely with the idea of 1966 as an essential chapter in the story of English decline. A number of writers have argued that in the long run the World Cup triumph had a negative effect on English football and the prospects of the national team. David Downing has dubbed 1966 'the fatal victory', in that it served to confirm the English in their misguided notion of leadership in international football while blinkering them from the progression in the game emanating from other parts of the world.

David Thomson has argued rather cryptically that 'there were ways in which England's victory in 1966 made later defeats a little more likely'.[90] The Liverpool and England defender Tommy Smith was more blunt, suggesting that the win was 'probably the worst thing that could have happened to us', encouraging as it did the hegemony of the coach at the expense of the professional player. Taking a broader perspective, Kevin Foster has suggested that 1966 'retarded the development' of English football, signifying a wider 'social inertia' and reluctance 'to adapt to or embrace the new order of a changing world'.[91]

For a short time, certainly, England did possess one of the strongest sides in world football. Entering the 1970 Mexico tournament as champions and with an arguably more talented squad than four years earlier, England matched but narrowly lost out to Pele's Brazil during the group stage, before letting a two-goal lead slip in a 3–2 extra-time defeat by the West Germans in the quarter-finals. But performances declined over the subsequent decade and it was not until 1982 that England qualified again for the World Cup finals. Ramsey stayed on as manager until 1974, when his team's inability to beat Poland home or away meant World Cup elimination and his subsequent dismissal. Critics now considered him tactically inflexible and over-cautious and his approach out of touch with modern football developments: Brian Glanville summed up the Ramsey years as 'one splendid success and eight years of anti-climax'.[92] His successors fared even worse. After caretaker Joe Mercer, former Leeds United manager Don Revie took over but failed to pick a consistent side and controversially left in 1977 for a well-paid job managing the United Arab Emirates national side. Results improved slightly under Revie's replacement, Ron Greenwood, an experienced and respected coach, but defeat to un-fancied Norway in a World Cup qualifier in September 1981 seemed to represent a new humiliating low comparable with the 1950 loss to the USA and the Hungarian reverses of 1953–4.[93]

In a particularly thought-provoking essay, Dilwyn Porter has outlined football's contribution to a post-war narrative of 'declinism' that became essential to the way the British, and especially the English, were beginning to see themselves. If 1953 was the effective starting point, 1966 did little to arrest perceptions of decline, serving only to raise expectations and make subsequent failure harder to bear. Over the following years and decades, the World Cup victory came to stand as an emblem of England's broader retreat from international pre-eminence, 'another item in the collection of cultural clutter symbolic of national greatness once possessed but now lost'. Porter also shows how the failures of the England team through the 1970s and early 1980s were articulated by the media as symptomatic of a wider economic, political and cultural stagnation. Parallels were easily drawn between the economic and sporting spheres: short-termism, resistance to change and institutional sclerosis were all offered as explanations of decline in both. Similarly, the economic journalist Peter Jay's depiction of the confusion and unhappiness of a nation suffering from what he termed 'Englanditis', a condition in which public expectations rose as political competence fell, could be equally applied to attitudes towards the national football team.[94] Yet it was not simply a case of football 'reflecting' these broader narratives: it could, and did, also feed into them. This was particularly true of the tabloid press, whose readers tended to consume newspapers back-to-front, and thus encounter and engage with notions of national decline via the sports section rather than the political or financial pages. Thus defeat to West Germany in a European Nations Championship tie in 1972 led columnists to comment on the English tendency to 'dwell in the past and rest complacently on past triumphs', comparing this stagnation with German vitality and progress. Previewing a World Cup qualifying fixture against Italy in November 1977, Frank McGhee of the *Daily Mirror* noted that: 'The days when you could beat the drum for England and make bold fighting forecasts with some certainty of success have long gone'. In *The Times*, Norman Fox spoke of 'England's football poverty', while the Norway defeat convinced *The Sun* that England was now 'the laughing-stock of the world', languishing among 'the banana republics of world football'.[95]

During the 1980s the England football team was increasingly used to evoke feelings of national pride by the popular press. Stephen Wagg has shown how *The Sun*, in particular, continually tapped into its readers' anxieties about imperial decline through ever more sensationalist reporting of the (mis)fortunes of the national side and the ineptitude of the England manager. As the battle for readers gained ground, so the style of *The Sun* and its competitors became increasingly blunt and unsubtle, moving 'further from the saloon bar and closer to the skinhead with the six-pack' and personalising criticism by attacking the manager himself. Bobby Robson, England manager for most of the decade, was a particular target. *The Sun* was never happy with his appointment, issuing 'Robson Out/Clough In' lapel badges after a 1–0 defeat by Wales in May 1984. A poor start to the 1986 World Cup in Mexico led to the manager being branded a 'fool' and his team dubbed 'the Mugs of Monterrey', while the England squad eliminated from the 1988 European Championships were labelled 'A GUTLESS, SPINELESS SHOWER!' with Robson pictured wearing a dunce's cap on his head. Wagg has outlined how *The Sun* based its assessment of the England team on a static and mythical notion of continued 'British' superiority. In its view, England would always be perceived as the nation that invented the game and gave it to the world; it would always be the master with rival football nations perpetually the pupils. Because England was still assumed to be best, any failure, especially against the weaker 'developing' nations, could only be explained by a lack of passion and guts, or by managerial blunders. To acknowledge the reality, that in the post-war world England had become 'a country like many others and the England football team … a football team like many others', was out of the question. With successive squads and managers unable to match these elevated expectations, it is hardly surprising that a discourse of decline continued to pervade the sports pages of the English tabloid press.[96]

By this time, the 1966 triumph had become not just an essential part of the nation's sporting heritage but also a cornerstone of English (if not British) popular culture and public memory. Those too young to have witnessed the tournament first hand are nonetheless probably able to recall the final match through a series of television images and the famous words of BBC commentator Kenneth Wolstenholme as Geoff Hurst scored the winning goal: 'There are some people on the pitch, they think it's all over, it is now!' As much a part of broadcasting history as sporting history, these images and words are continually replayed on British television, attaining almost mythical status and even inspiring a popular satirical sports quiz *They Think It's All Over*, which ran on the BBC from the mid-1990s.[97] This continual revisiting of 1966 is central to what Critcher means when he refers to it in terms of myth and folklore. The way the event has been interpreted is crucial here. With the death of Bobby Moore in February 1993, for example, the media once again set about contrasting the glory of the past with the ignominy of football's present. Moore was eulogised not only as a supremely talented footballer but also as a symbol of national triumph and of old-fashioned gentlemanly masculinity. An editorial in the *Daily Mirror* described his death as 'a loss not just to football but to Britain' as he 'represented a past which the nation desperately needs to recover'. Unlike the overpaid and pampered superstars of the early 1990s, it was felt that for Moore and his ilk 'there was true pride in pulling on an England shirt'. Such recollections of a perceived 'golden age', of course, were hardly the preserve of tabloid sports writers. The Conservative government's calls at around the same time for a return to the 'basic values' of the past in education, family life and religion were not dissimilar from the periodic evocations of the spirit of 1966, especially when England was eliminated from a major tournament. Indeed so potent was the myth of 1966, Critcher argues, that it prevented the game's leaders from modernising and learning from the success of others: obsessed by the need to look backwards and inwards rather than forwards and outwards, the England set-up remained stuck in the past and unable to move on for many decades.[98]

Football and the break-up of Britain?

Notions of decline and declinism, both inside and outside football, were always more closely associated with England and the English than with the other British nations. Loss of empire, a struggling economy and a diminishing status in world affairs undoubtedly affected the entire British population but were arguably felt more keenly by the politically and economically dominant English. Moreover, by the 1970s notions of decline had become bound up with what some regarded as a fundamental crisis of Britishness. The revival of nationalist politics in Scotland and Wales, coupled with the beginning of 'the Troubles' in Northern Ireland, convinced a number of political commentators that the British state itself was on the brink of collapse. Most famously, the Scottish intellectual Tom Nairn argued in his 1977 book *The Break-Up of Britain* that the growth of neo-nationalist sentiment in Scotland and Wales and calls for devolution meant that inevitably 'the old British state is going down'.[99]

Recent accounts have outlined the relatively weak and transient nature of British identity and the decline of Britishness in the late twentieth century. Building upon Linda Colley's portrayal of Britishness as an identity superimposed over, but coexistent with, Englishness, Scottishness, Welshness and Irishness, David McCrone has argued that Britishness always 'sat lightly on top of [these] constituent national identities' as a supranational rather than a genuinely 'national' identity. Forged by war against the continental 'Other' in the eighteenth century, and reinforced by the conflicts of the twentieth, British 'national' identity was nonetheless weakened and eventually 'unmade' as older alternative forms of national affiliation and consciousness reasserted themselves once again.[100] In a similar vein, Weight has suggested that since 1940 perceptions of Britishness have declined sharply to be replaced by a rejuvenated attachment to the 'core' national identities of the UK. He portrays Britishness as an identity that became associated with imperialism and Protestantism and fundamentally dominated by English interests; an identity, moreover, that was then imposed upon the peripheral nations of the union largely against their will. Its demise became almost inevitable as the Empire dissolved and wartime memories faded under the growing influence of US and European culture and an increasingly diverse multicultural population. As Britain, in Weight's words, 'turned in on itself' so 'the English, Scots and Welsh returned to their core nationalities, once more defining themselves against rather than with each other'.[101] While acknowledging the elusive and complex nature of English national identity and the persistence of notions of Britishness, Krishan Kumar has likewise accepted that by the mid to late twentieth century British national identity was 'on the defensive', and possibly even in terminal decline. Some have challenged this orthodox view. Paul Ward, for example, sees Britishness as a fluid and adaptable identity, which was continually 'made' and 'remade' over the course of the twentieth century. While it may not have been the only, or even the most important, identity of place, Britishness, according to Ward, was nonetheless an identity 'accepted, put together and lived by the majority of people within the United Kingdom'.[102]

Football in this period was more obviously associated with the decline than the resilience of Britishness. The historical organisation of competition along national rather than state lines meant that the game had rarely been a forum for the articulation of a merged British identity. Great Britain had not competed seriously at international level since a representative match against the Rest of Europe in 1947 and the London Olympics a year later. Unlike in some other sports, where British representative teams regularly competed instead of, or in addition to, national teams, football articulated a series of singular (though often far from coherent) national identities.[103] England, Scotland, Wales and Northern Ireland still played in the British International Championship during the 1960s and 1970s, but the competition had lost much of its earlier significance, appearing increasingly insular and marginal when set alongside the World Cup and European Championships. Rather than demonstrating the continued British orientation of the competing nations, these 'home internationals' were emerging as sites for the articulation of broader nationalist frustrations and tensions. By the mid-1980s, the competition had been shelved permanently. What is more, any expressions of British identity were difficult to locate in a sport that was increasingly nationalist in character. We have already shown that for Britain's peripheral nations, representative sport in general, and often football in particular, had a crucial symbolic meaning as a demonstration of nationhood. From the late 1960s, it could be argued that any sense of British football solidarity had disappeared: Scottishness and Welshness, in particular, were increasingly expressed through football in the form of anti-Englishness.

Scotland

Few would deny the important role the game played during these years in defining what it meant to be Scottish. Weight's claim that football in Scotland 'fostered national identity more than anywhere else in the UK' chimes with much of the academic literature on the subject. H. F. Moorhouse has talked of the 'over-determined significance' of football in Scottish society, while Richard Holt sees it as 'filling a cultural void'. Alan Bairner regards it simply as 'a symbol of Scottish nationality', every bit as distinctive as Scotland's own legal and educational systems, church and military regiments.[104] Many Scots had long believed that there was something special in the way they approached and played the game. Bolstered by the memory of the skilled Scottish 'professors' of the late nineteenth century and the legend of the 1928 'Wembley Wizards', this myth of Scottish football 'exceptionalism' continued to have a powerful hold on post-war followers of the game. Yet what was arguably emerging for the first time in the 1960s and 1970s was a link between football and a wider political nationalism. The rise of the Scottish National Party (SNP) was a key feature of the latter. Its campaign for independence, or at least devolutionary powers through the creation of a Scottish parliament, gained considerable support among Scots from the late 1960s. Bolstered by the discovery of oil off the north-east coast of Scotland, and subsequent resentment at the British government's decision to sell it off, in October 1974 the SNP put in its strongest electoral performance to date, securing 11 seats at Westminster and 30 per cent of the Scottish vote. Nationalist pressure eventually contributed to the Labour government's decision to offer a referendum on devolution, but on 1 March 1979 only 32.85 per cent voted in favour, some way short of the 40 per cent required.[105]

Whether football fuelled or merely rode upon this wave of nationalism is inevitably difficult to determine. Those who argue the former point to the increasing nationalist sentiment associated with the Scottish team. In 1967 Scotland beat England 3–2 at Wembley, less than a year after the latter had been crowned World Champions in the same stadium. The visitors ought to have won much more convincingly but, prompted by Rangers' supremely talented playmaker Jim Baxter, chose to humble the hosts by keeping hold of the ball rather than scoring more goals. *The Scotsman*'s John Rafferty described the performance as 'that peculiar

Scottish thing in which the scoreline is not as important as toying with beaten opponents, tormenting them, humiliating them'. Yet while undoubtedly an important exhibition of national pride there were few attempts to link the victory to broader political desires and no indication, as Ronald Kowalski notes, that either Scottish supporters or players desired to 'break up' the union. This seems to have changed by the 1970s. First, the jeering of the *British* national anthem, 'God Save the Queen', before matches with England became commonplace. It certainly occurred before Scotland's 2–0 defeat of England at Hampden Park in May 1974, a passionate affair at which a patriotic home crowd also chanted 'We hate the English'. This 'ugly manifestation of Scottish nationalism', as a Scottish Office junior minister later condemned it, was repeated two years later, but with resentment now further stoked by the Scottish FA's refusal to sanction the nationalist and anti-English 'Flower of Scotland' as a more appropriate accompaniment. The home crowd sang the song anyway, Scotland won 2–1 and 'Flower of Scotland' was officially adopted from that point on. Passions were running higher still in 1977, when Scotland's

PLATE 17 *Scotland fans before the group match against Brazil at the 1974 World Cup finals in West Germany (© Popperfoto.com).*

dramatic victory prompted visiting fans to invade the pitch, break the goalposts and dig up sections of the Wembley turf. The English press angrily condemned the drunken hooliganism of the Scottish 'hordes' but the political dimension of such acts during Silver Jubilee year was lost neither on the press nor on those jubilant Scots who chanted 'Give us an assembly, we'll give you back your Wembley'.[106]

Political and sporting self-confidence were often intertwined during the 1970s. As Scotland seemed to be moving closer to devolution, so the national football team became increasingly prominent on the international stage. After failing to reach the World Cup finals between 1962 and 1970, Scotland went on to qualify for the next five tournaments, and represented British interests alone in 1974 and 1978. In the first of these in West Germany, a talented Scottish squad narrowly failed to progress to the knock-out phase on goal difference after drawing with both Brazil and Yugoslavia but failing to beat an inexperienced Zaire by more than two goals. On the plus side, Scotland had finally arrived on the global football stage, winning its first World Cup match and considered unlucky not to beat the World Champions. More importantly, the 'performance' of both the players and the supporters had helped to create a near nationalist euphoria in Scotland. During the tournament, manager Willie Ormond called for Scotland to have its own national anthem, and the SNP claimed that if an election were held the following week they would have gained a landslide victory. Four years later, the squad that travelled to Argentina was expected to represent the nation even more proudly. Buoyed by the bravado of manager Ally McLeod, many thought the Scots might actually win the competition. But they played poorly in a defeat to Peru and were then unable to beat Iran. The squad was accused of being insufficiently prepared and lacking in discipline, an assumption borne out when one of its members, Willie Johnston, was sent home after testing positive for performance-enhancing drugs. The 3–2 win over accomplished eventual finalists Holland in the final group match only served to highlight what might have been. In the aftermath of its team's departure, the Scottish press pondered the role of football in projecting Scottishness. Many considered it wrong that a mere game should be assigned such significance, but others accepted that while Scotland remained ruled from London, international football would inevitably carry extra weight as an expression of Scottish pride and identity, with the players assuming the role of ambassadors. Journalists, political scientists and historians of nationalism have likewise regarded the 'disgrace' of Argentina '78 as a major factor in the failure of the 1979 devolution referendum. Tom

Gallagher, for one, argued that the team's exit from the tournament 'might have been the final blow to faith in Scottish capabilities' to govern itself; for Christopher Harvie, 'Matters political might have been a lot different had they [the Scottish side] won, and the "we were rubbish" hangover certainly contributed to the 1 March outcome'.[107]

This assumption of a direct link between sporting performance and nationalist feeling has, however, come under considerable scrutiny. Critics of Scottish football's nationalist pretensions have tended to regard the game as a form of 'subcultural nationalism' that operates as a substitute for genuine political nationalism. The best-known expression of this view came from the deputy leader of the SNP, Jim Sillars, who in 1992 chastised Scotland for having too many 'ninety minute patriots' whose nationalist passions failed to transfer from the terraces to the ballot box. Nairn had earlier been equally dismissive of football as one element of Scotland's distorted and mindless cultural output, which remained separate, and drew attention away, from the more important politics of nationalism.[108] Yet while it would be wrong to equate the nationalist emotions of the football crowd with mainstream political nationalism, it would equally be mistaken to ignore the linkages between the two. McCrone, for example, has highlighted the complex relationship between the cultural and political elements of neo-nationalism in 'stateless nations' like Scotland. Rather than regarding cultural nationalism as a simple alternative to its political variant – 'a safety valve which lets off the steam of nationalism lest it take a more challenging political form' – he argues that the two often grew together and fed off one another. The intensified nationalist passion of Scottish football fans in this period may not have been straightforwardly political – few, after all, transferred their allegiance to the SNP – but it undoubtedly helped forge a powerful sense of Scottish identity as well as reflecting sympathy with the quest for greater political autonomy. It was often through football and other aspects of popular culture that ideas about Scotland and Scottishness were kept alive.[109]

The nuances in the relationship between football and Scottish identity are nowhere more evident than in the treatment of the star players. We saw in an earlier chapter how those Scots employed by English clubs, the so-called 'Anglos', had always been looked upon somewhat suspiciously by the Scottish press. This attitude seems to have intensified in the light of a reinvigorated Scottish nationalism and explains why a player such as Denis Law, in spite of his extraordinary talent and achievements, could be treated with such ambivalence north of the border. In a career that saw him join Huddersfield Town as a 15-year old and play for Manchester City and Manchester United, interspersed with a spell in Italy, Law significantly never played club football in his native Scotland. This, as Holt has explained, was his 'fatal flaw' in the view of the nationalistic Scottish press, which, notwithstanding his fervent expressions of Scottish patriotism and anti-Englishness, often accused Law of lacking team spirit and passion and regularly campaigned to have him dropped from the national team. As a result, Law and other Anglos tended to be praised when Scotland performed well but singled out for criticism when the team lost. After being thrashed 9–3 by England in 1961, for example, the *Daily Record* argued that as 'the men who have let us down are the Anglos', an all-tartan team should be chosen in future. As for Law: 'I SUGGEST THE SELECTORS FORGET ALL ABOUT HIM'. Failure to qualify for the World Cup in 1962 and 1966 was blamed on the 'individualism' of the Anglos, who were too concerned with the praise and money they received in England and unwilling to give their all for the 'jersey'. Such sentiments persisted throughout the period, with the then Aberdeen (and later Scotland) manager Alex Ferguson commenting in 1983: 'I'm against Anglos being in the Scots team ... Players go south and return with their llama coats and their discipline on and off isn't as good as the lads at home.' This could equally have been said of Law's more wayward contemporaries like Jim Baxter and Jimmy Johnstone, but these were players who achieved their greatest feats in Scotland and thus became idolised in a way that Law never was. Living and working in England, Law's Scottishness always remained locked firmly into a British context.[110]

Changing styles of play and support also reveal the complex nature of the relationship between football and Scottishness. The existence of a distinct Scottish playing style 'identified with aggression, passion and ... skill', and personified in the figure of the small tricky winger, or 'tanner ba' player,[111] who 'never beat a man once when he could do it twice', was recognised and widely accepted well before the 1960s, when it was increasingly contrasted with the stereotypical view of English football as methodical and organised but lacking in inspiration and natural talent (epitomised by 'Ramsey's Robots'). Yet, in reality, the style of the national team oscillated between different versions of Scottishness: the Presbyterian work ethic of figures like George Young on one hand and the 'Celtic' individualism of men such as Baxter and Johnstone on the other. The more successful club sides attempted to combine effort and inspiration by including big, strong defenders alongside creative ball players, but at international level the debate between the two approaches was never adequately resolved.[112] The style of support adopted in respect of the national team also reflected changing notions of Scottishness. Gerry Finn and Richard Giulianotti have shown how the most passionate supporters of the so-called 'Tartan Army', so often associated with disorder and violence during the 1970s, made a conscious effort to revamp their public image from the early 1980s. Central to this was an attempt to embrace a 'carnival' identity, marked by gregariousness, sociability and good behaviour, and consciously set in opposition to the emerging 'hooligan' identity of English supporters. On overseas trips and during international tournaments, in particular, fans increasingly sported 'traditional' stereotypical markers of Scottishness such as tartan, kilts and bagpipes, with the aim of defining themselves, and being recognised by others, as distinctively 'Scottish-not-English'.[113] This reconstructed 'Tartan Army' may not have been fully formed by the mid-1980s but was certainly beginning to unsettle the established and largely negative media and public perceptions of Scottish fan identity.

While Moorhouse has emphasised the unified features of a shared Scottish football culture that was distinct from, and often antagonistic towards, its English counterpart, other writers continue to stress the divisions that worked against the development of a national football identity in Scotland. Foremost among these was sectarianism. Both 'Old Firm' clubs, in particular, projected identities that could be interpreted as being anti-Scottish and both were regularly accused of lacking loyalty to the national cause. Rangers, of course, had always been associated with Unionism as well as Protestantism, an association symbolised in its colours of red, white and blue and the supporters' waving of the Union flag.[114] Bill Murray, moreover, has argued that Rangers directors from the beginning of the twentieth century were overwhelmingly Conservative and unionist, and periodically expressed their allegiance to the monarchy and Northern Ireland and, later on, their opposition to devolution.[115] While acknowledging that Rangers supporters often sang the British national anthem and adorned banners with pictures of royalty, Graham Walker has countered that such expressions of British identity did not mean a downplaying of Scottishness. Rangers fans, he argues, had for some time regarded themselves among the core supporters of the Scottish national team, symbolising their Scottish allegiance by waving Lion Rampants alongside Union Jacks at club matches. Unionist sentiment here was essentially an element of a broader Protestant identity rather than the result of a close relationship with the English. Indeed contrary to what some writers have suggested, Walker argues that anti-English feeling was widespread among Rangers followers.[116]

In the case of Celtic, accusations of a lack of commitment to the Scottish cause are not so easy to deflect. The origins of the club in Glasgow's Irish immigrant community and its historical association with Ireland and Catholicism has led to some doubt over the extent and voracity of Celtic supporters' commitment to the Scottish national side. Although much of the evidence for this period is anecdotal, there is nonetheless broad agreement that at least some Celtic fans chose not to support Scotland and that some instead followed the fortunes of the Republic of Ireland. Joseph Bradley suggests that these allegiances emerged organically as a manifestation of the Irish ancestry and identity of most Celtic supporters, but others have argued that ambivalence towards the Scottish side was the result of 'prejudices symbolically directed against them [Celtic fans] – prejudices they have to face in order to support Scotland'.[117] The first of these alleged prejudices was the perceived bias against Celtic or ex-Celtic players, especially Catholics, by the national team selectors. From Jimmy McGrory between the wars, to Bobby Lennox and Jimmy Johnstone in the 1960s and 1970s, and Charlie Nicholas in the 1980s, there are a host of 'Celts' whom some supporters point to as having received fewer international caps than their talent merited. Second, and more significant, was the alleged antagonism by the Scottish crowd towards players with Celtic connections. Johnstone and Davie Hay were two Celtic players who were reportedly abused by Scottish supporters in the 1970s. In his autobiography, Johnstone, who for much of his career competed for selection with his Rangers counterpart Willie Henderson, recalled the barracking he received from the traditional Rangers end at Hampden Park: 'In those days these so-called fans seemed to hate the sight of a Celtic player in Scotland colours ... I had to endure chants of "Henderson, Henderson" throughout the game'. During another match against Northern Ireland in 1972, Johnstone was booed by a section of the Hampden crowd before the match even began, and whenever he touched the ball, and was finally replaced by Leeds United's Peter Lorimer 'to tumultuous acclaim'. Moorhouse is doubtless right to point out that the 'vast bulk of Celtic players and "catholics" ... who have played for Scotland have never been booed' but this did not prevent some Celtic followers *perceiving* that 'their' players were discriminated against in this way. This sense of being poorly treated, marginalised and frankly not 'wanted' by both the football authorities and other fans may go some way to explaining why a percentage of Celtic supporters remained indifferent to the Scotland team for much of this period.[118]

Northern Ireland and Wales

The connections between national identities, sectarianism and football are more complicated still in the case of Northern Ireland. Here the very legitimacy of the 'nation' has been contested. Northern Ireland was constitutionally a part of the UK but since the beginning of the modern Troubles in the late 1960s it had been 'a battle ground, both in a real and political/cultural sense, between those who want to remain within the United Kingdom and those who do not'. Cronin has described this as a division between a British and an Irish variant of national identity: the former espoused by the Protestant and unionist majority who sought to protect the existing links with mainland Britain and the latter by the Catholic and nationalist minority who aimed for independence as part of the Irish Republic. Operating as a crucial 'signifier of identity', sport in Northern Ireland, and in this case football, has tended to divide along the very same lines.[119]

In domestic football, Linfield continued to be the key Protestant club in Belfast, while the earlier identification of the city's Catholic and nationalist supporters with Belfast Celtic was transferred first to Distillery, then by the late 1970s to Cliftonville, due mainly to improved performances and the proximity of the club's Solitude ground to the Catholic population of north Belfast. In Northern Ireland's second city, Derry or Londonderry (even the name was contested), the premier club was Derry City. It had previously gained support, and recruited players, from both communities and had, by and large, avoided sectarian affiliation, but this was to change with the onset of the Troubles. The normal running of the football club became increasingly difficult in a city engulfed by rioting and communal violence, especially given the location of Derry's Brandywell ground at the heart of the Catholic 'Bogside' area. The reluctance of visiting clubs (especially Protestant ones) to play at Brandywell was hardly helped when the ground was used for nationalist and civil rights rallies, but the regular cancellation of matches was also a result of the unionist-dominated football establishment's tendency to regard nationalist violence in Derry as especially threatening to civil order. Tensions increased in September 1971 when a bus that had transported visitors Ballymena United was set on fire, and the football and security authorities forced the club to play the rest of its 1971–2 home fixtures 30 miles away at Coleraine. With increasing debts and no sign of a return to Brandywell, Derry City eventually withdrew from the Irish League in October 1973. It never went back and in the face of continued opposition in the north instead looked south, securing admission in 1985 to the League of Ireland.[120]

If Northern Irish football was rather unique in that nationalism was attached to domestic games, the Northern Ireland team provoked similar struggles over national identities. One way of looking at this is at the administrative level. As late as 1950, the IFA was still selecting players for its international squads born in the south of the island as well as the north and, even after this changed, resisted attempts made by the FAI (through FIFA) to force it to abandon the name 'Ireland'. Only in the 1970s did the more politically precise title 'Northern Ireland' become commonplace. Support for the 'national' team, meanwhile, tended to polarise the two main communities, but not necessarily in a straightforward fashion. Many Catholic/nationalists clearly rejected the Northern Ireland team as a symbol of the state and the union, and were unlikely to attend international games played at Windsor Park, Belfast, normally home of the fervently loyalist Linfield. Yet Catholics had always been selected for the Northern Ireland team and some, such as goalkeeper Pat Jennings, became admired and lauded as great international players and representatives of Northern Ireland. Equally, many Catholics in the north supported the team long before its World Cup appearances in Spain 1982 and Mexico 1986, even if by the early 1990s (and doubtless before) the overwhelming majority (91 per cent according to one survey) had transferred their allegiance to the increasingly successful Republic of Ireland.[121]

For Protestants in the province, the Northern Irish football team mattered a great deal, demonstrating to the wider world that Northern Ireland existed 'as a distinct entity'.[122] That it also reflected the changing identity of Ulster Protestants during the Troubles is something that is missed in Ward's simplistic connection of support for Northern Ireland with Britishness.[123] Writing in the mid-1980s, John Sugden and Alan Bairner outlined how the Union Jack and red, white and blue had been gradually replaced on the terraces of Windsor Park by scarves and rosettes in the team's playing colours of green and white, adorned, significantly, with the red hand of Ulster. This, they suggested, was indicative of the increasing Protestant distrust of the British government and a corresponding political and cultural shift away from an unalterable unionism and towards the possibilities of an autonomous Northern Ireland. This independent Northern Irish identity was articulated most forcefully in matches

PLATE 18 *The Northern Ireland team group before a 1–1 draw against Wales at Cardiff in 1984. Back row (l–r): John McClelland, Norman Whiteside, Gerry McElhinney, Billy Hamilton, Ian Stewart, Pat Stewart. Front row (l–r) Sammy McIlroy, Nigel Worthington, Martin O'Neill, Gerry Armstrong, Mal Donaghy (© Popperfoto.com).*

against England when Protestants and Catholics were allegedly united in their desire to 'beat the Brits'. By the end of the decade, however, Sugden and Bairner show how Windsor Park had become an increasingly unfriendly arena for Catholic supporters and players. At a time when Northern Ireland was falling and the Republic rising in the international football hierarchy, players with Catholic and nationalist connections were the target of considerable sectarian abuse. It was in this context that Protestant supporters targeted Anton Rogan, a Catholic and a Celtic employee, and Allan McKnight, a Protestant but also a Celtic player, regarding them as somehow disloyal to Northern Ireland, part of 'the enemy within'. Ultimately, support for the Northern Ireland side was bound up in the same sectarian rivalries that affected club football in the province, reflecting the divided 'national' allegiances of the two communities and complicating any assumed straightforward link between football and national identity.[124]

As far as the link between sport and Welsh national identity is concerned, football continued to be overshadowed by rugby union. The Welsh soccer team could hardly match the half dozen Five Nations Championships secured by their rugby counterparts between 1968–9 and 1979–80 or challenge the cross-class appeal of the oval ball game. A quarter-final place in the 1976 European Championships and a first-ever victory at Wembley against England in 1977 were the major achievements of these years. Cardiff City and Swansea City had brief stints at the top level of the Football League, but both they and the other Welsh professional clubs spent most of this period in the lower reaches of the competition. Cardiff reached the semi-final of the Cup-Winners Cup in 1967–8 and Newport County, a Third Division side at the time, made the last eight in 1980–1, but otherwise European triumphs were few and far between. Even if there was no great Welsh team, there was still a steady stream of exceptional Welsh players plying their trade, for the most part, at leading English clubs. Mike England at Spurs, John Toshack and Ian Rush at Liverpool and Mark Hughes at Manchester United, for example, all made their names as top-class sportsmen performing on an international stage, and were celebrated as such in their homeland.[125] Yet none of this was sufficient to transform football from a game the Welsh played into a Welsh sport. Martin Johnes has shown that ultimately it was rugby that continued to be the main sporting emblem of Welsh national pride and identity. Rugby rather than football internationals were the occasion for the expression of nationalist sentiments during the 1960s and 1970s, with some spectators openly endorsing the radical Free Wales Army and others simply booing the Queen. Unable to guarantee international success, football was often treated as 'another part of the nation's inferiority complex' but continued to reflect the dual national identity of Wales as both a distinct 'nation' and a part of the UK.[126]

Britain versus the world?

One context in which 'British football' did have some meaning was in European club competition. Here was where Britain excelled and where, in English club sides especially, the various talents of the 'home' nations were combined to the greatest effect. Celtic, of course, became the first British side to win the European Cup in 1967 with a side famously all born within a 30-mile radius of Glasgow. But this and later Scottish victories in the 1970s and 1980s were celebrated as Scottish rather than

British triumphs. By contrast, the phenomenal success of English clubs could hardly be credited to the English alone, although journalists often tried to do so by conflating 'England' and 'Britain' and contrasting English/British virtues with those of the 'continentals'. Manchester United's 1968 European Cup winning side was managed by a Scot, Matt Busby, and dependent upon the 'Celtic' flair of Glasgow's Pat Crerand, Belfast's George Best and Denis Law from Aberdeen.[127] The Tottenham Hotspur squad that won the first UEFA Cup in 1972 was predominantly English but also included a sprinkling of 'outer Britons' – Pat Jennings (Northern Ireland), Mike England (Wales) and Alan Gilzean (Scotland). More significantly, it was another Scot, Bill Shankly, who founded the Liverpool dynasty that went on to dominate European football between 1973 and 1984 – winning four European Cups and two UEFA Cups – with teams composed of players from all nations of the UK as well as the Irish Republic. It has indeed been argued that much of the success of English sides in Europe was based on the important role of managers and players who were 'British but not English' and the ability to harness the best of the various 'national' styles of play in Britain. Critcher has even talked of the development of a distinctively British style of play, emphasising tackling and harrying opponents and quick and direct delivery into the penalty area, in contrast to the 'overseas' concentration on good ball control, accurate passing and the slow build-up, with the ball patiently manoeuvred sideways and backwards (as well as forwards) until an opening presented itself. Critcher himself admits, however, that Liverpool's success was actually based on a unique ability to marry the best of the 'British' and 'continental' styles and 'blend' the various qualities of its playing staff 'to produce a whole which [was] often greater than the sum of its parts'.[128]

In other ways, connections with non-British football were becoming increasingly difficult to resist. The late 1970s witnessed the first significant influx of foreign footballers to the British game. The effective ban on the importation of non-British professionals that had been put in place way back in 1931 was reversed by the Football League in 1978 as a result of the European Commission's decision that footballers as workers should be guaranteed freedom of movement. There had been no such ban in the Scottish League, but only a handful of mainly Scandinavian amateurs had previously tried their luck. The arrival of world-class stars such as Ossie Ardiles and Ricky Villa at Tottenham and Arnold Muhren and Frans Thijssen at Ipswich Town was greeted positively by the press and the fans, but with caution by the football authorities. The Professional Footballers'

PLATE 19 *The Celtic team pictured with the European Cup at their celebration banquet in May 1967. Celtic beat Inter Milan 2–1 to become the first British club to win the competition (© Popperfoto.com).*

Association (PFA), in particular, was conscious of protecting the jobs and livelihood of its British membership. For PFA secretary Cliff Lloyd, 'Every foreign player of standing in our league represents a denial to a UK player of a place in the first team'. He was concerned about 'the bandwagon of buying foreign footballers' and feared that 'what starts as a trickle can finish as a deluge'.[129] While this 'foreign' deluge never fully materialised in this period, it is possible to detect the beginnings of what might be called the 'Europeanisation' or 'internationalisation' of British professional football. In his study of the post-war recruitment of 'foreign' labour into the Football League, for instance, Patrick McGovern has identified two overlapping phases: the 'Celtic phase', lasting from 1946 until the late 1970s, and the 'International phase', stretching from 1978 until the present. Scottish players were always the most prominent of the 'Celtic' contingent. H. F. Moorhouse found that some 1,653 Scots had played in the Football League between 1946 and 1981, the majority arriving in the 1950s and 1960s. Sixty-one players moved from the Scottish to the English League between 1968–9 and 1972–3 alone, but the trend was nonetheless downwards. A total of 258 Scots in the Football

League in 1965 had dropped to 198 by 1975. Indeed McGovern has shown that from the mid-1980s the volume of Scottish and Irish signings in English and Welsh football fell below those coming from 'international' destinations for the first time. In the recruitment of players as in the focus of competition, British football was increasingly looking outwards to Europe and beyond.[130]

The hooliganism debate

Historians looking back on football in the 1970s and 1980s could be forgiven for thinking that hooliganism was all that mattered. More than any other topic, it was the violent behaviour of some supporters that dominated discussions of the game in the media, in the political arena and in university seminar rooms. Writing in 1991, John Williams, one of the subject's leading researchers, noted that hooliganism had effectively become football's 'key defining characteristic over the past 25 years'. Given its significance both to the game itself and to broader transformations in, and perceptions of, social structure, criminal justice and deviance, it is hardly surprising that hooliganism effectively monopolised the agenda of those interested in the social role and politics of modern sport. It was, as Russell noted of England but with equal applicability to the rest of the UK, a central aspect of political culture during these decades.[131] Studies of hooliganism have differed significantly in the theories adopted and the methods used. The most influential interpretations have derived from the markedly different sociological perspectives of Ian Taylor and John Clarke on one hand and the Leicester researchers led by Eric Dunning on the other, and from the fieldwork of Peter Marsh and colleagues and, more recently, the anthropologist Gary Armstrong. Historians, not surprisingly, have been more reticent to engage with 'modern' manifestations of hooligan behaviour although some, like Richard Holt, have provided relatively detached analyses of what remains a particularly factious and bitter academic debate.[132]

Defining precisely what football hooliganism is and when and why it emerged are not easy tasks. Most writers agree on the complicated and multifaceted nature of the phenomenon and highlight the numerous variables that complicate the problem of definition: indeed some prefer to see hooliganism as 'several overlapping phenomena' rather than one specific type of occurrence. One useful way of perceiving hooliganism is as a continuum along which a range of different modes of behaviour can be placed. This might include relatively minor anti-social acts such as swearing and general rowdiness at one end to the more serious throwing of missiles and pitch invasions and then on to the often organised and orchestrated confrontations with police and fights with opposing groups of fans. Similarly, Gerry Finn has posited a continuum along which aggression and violence are positioned, with the naturally aggressive stance of the spectator sometimes providing the basis for the physical intimidation and violence of the hooligan.[133] Others, however, have been rather more exclusive in their definitions of hooliganism. Dunning *et al.*, whose work on the long history of hooliganism engages with all of its manifestations, nonetheless focus their analysis of 'present-day' hooliganism on the activities of the so-called 'hard core'. They differed from rank and file supporters in that they intended to engage in violent activity. Fighting, for them, was 'an integral part of "going to the match" '.[134] In a similar vein, Richard Giulianotti has talked of the 'subcultural identity' of hooligan groups, of their commitment to define themselves as 'hooligans' and engage competitively in violent activity against other similar groups. Hooliganism in this view is to be found and understood in the subculture of the 'firms' or 'mobs' associated with club sides and national teams. Excluded from this definition are many individualistic acts that take place within football grounds that are normally linked with hooliganism, such as incidents of vandalism and missile throwing and even the racial abuse of players.[135]

Hooliganism and working-class culture

The earliest sociological explanations of hooliganism had no doubt that it was a modern phenomenon. Writing at the beginning of the 1970s, Taylor acknowledged that, while violence had always been a part of the game, hooliganism in its modern form, involving, for example, the routine invasion by spectators of the playing area, was entirely new. Indeed he specifically dated its beginnings in England to a televised cup-tie in 1961 between Sunderland and Tottenham Hotspur. More broadly, Taylor sought to locate the emergence of hooliganism within football's changing power relations, especially those between the club and its largely working-class following. Before the Second World War, Taylor argued, football was not only marked by close connections between the clubs and their surrounding communities but also by the obligations of directors, managers and players towards the fans. Perceived by supporters as a 'participatory democracy', the football club was a genuine 'club' in the sense that the views of those who entered through the turnstiles were given some degree of recognition and credence. The players, for their part, were considered as representatives of the supporters, expected to play and behave according to the masculine values of the subculture from which they sprang. At the very least, it was important that the illusion of responsibility towards the supporters was maintained, often by virtue of the appearance of players at the latest pigeon race or the local public house. This changed, in Taylor's view, as directors attempted to attract and promote the game to a new type of wealthy, middle-class leisure 'consumer'. The illusion of participatory control was undermined as football became increasingly commodified, professionalised and embourgeoisified, leaving the game's core working-class supporters marginalised and alienated. It was in this context that disorder and violence could be explained by Taylor as a form of 'resistance' to football's changing structure and values; a 'democratic response' to the supporters' loss of control of what had previously been 'their' game.[136]

Other explanations of hooliganism focused more explicitly on the structural changes at work in post-war British society, particularly those involving young working-class males. While sharing Taylor's emphasis on the increasing 'professionalisation' and 'spectacularisation' of football, Clarke also looked at the way in which this coincided with industrial decline and the breakdown of the traditional bonds of community, neighbourhood and family. Working-class youngsters brought with them to football the traditional masculine and aggressive qualities associated with the workplace but, with less guidance and supervision from older relatives than had previously been the case, the 'old' ways of supporting manifested themselves in 'new' forms of antisocial, and increasingly violent, behaviour. For these young men, particularly those from the lowest socio-economic groups, football offered the only real opportunity for the 'magical recovery' of a community identity that had been lost to them. The idea of territory was important in this context, with hooligan groups increasingly committed to the defence of their own 'ends' of the ground and the 'taking' of those of their rivals. Holt neatly summed up the game's developing significance in this respect as 'a kind of surrogate community for the young; the club defines their identity and the "end" is their territory'.[137]

These attempts to account for hooliganism by highlighting changes in the culture of football and the fragmentation of working-class communities have been challenged on a number of levels. First, there is little evidence that football clubs were ever regarded as 'participatory democracies' in the way Taylor suggested; most fans had long recognised, even if they did not always accept, that it was the directors who in reality controlled the clubs. If fans did influence club policy, it was more often middle-class rather than working-class groups that did so, often through the vehicle of supporters' clubs and other organised protest campaigns. Second, most commentators now accept that the assumed 'bourgeoisification' and 'professionalisation' of football was insufficiently developed by the 1960s and early 1970s to prompt the emergence of Taylor's hooligan 'resistance'. Third, and turning to Clarke's work, critics have argued that there was nothing novel in young males attending matches with peers and without adult supervision. Underpinning these criticisms of the theories of Taylor and Clarke is the suggestion that their work lacks both empirical and historical grounding. Dunning *et al.*, for instance, dismissed these approaches as entirely 'present-centred', based on a romanticised view of working-class history and a misguided emphasis on the solidarity and cohesion of 'traditional' working-class communities.[138] Taylor evidently recognised the weaknesses in his own thesis, modifying his rather romantic and naïve view of hooligans as 'resistance fighters' during the 1980s and belatedly accepting them instead as a serious social threat.[139]

The 'Leicester school' and its critics

It was the team based around Eric Dunning at Leicester University that was most critical of these previous approaches and which, in the course of the 1980s, developed an influential theory of hooliganism combining rigorous historical research with sociological analysis. We already noted in Chapter 3 one of the key arguments of Dunning *et al.*, that hooliganism in some form had always existed in British football and that, as such, there was a fundamental continuity between the behaviour of spectators in the late nineteenth century and the 'modern' examples dating from the 1960s onwards. Dunning *et al.* chart this long history (as far as England is concerned) not in terms of a steady increase in reported incidents, or of consistent levels from decade to decade, but as a U-shaped curve, with considerable violence before the First World War, which then fell between the wars and in the immediate post-war years before a steady rise from the mid-1950s and a more rapid increase after the mid-1960s. All types of hooligan activity were evident throughout these years, although before the First World War attacks on players and officials predominated, whereas from the 1960s fights between rival fans were most common. The 1966 World Cup is identified here as a major catalyst in the move towards modern hooliganism. Existing media concern over the fighting between mods and rockers became connected to the increased coverage of football to create a disproportionate fear of violent disorder at grounds, which simultaneously served to 'advertise' the football ground as a venue for 'masculine' confrontations between young males. Dunning *et al.* quote a *Sun* editorial written in the aftermath of disturbances at a Liverpool and Celtic match in April 1966 which speculated that continued incidents would destroy the game and lead the world to conclude 'that all the British are hooligans'. There were, they argue, 'elements of self-fulfilling prophecy' in such media reporting which, though it may not have caused hooliganism as such, did play a crucial role in its subsequent development.[140]

Utilising the notion of the 'civilizing process' developed by the sociologist Norbert Elias, the Leicester researchers argue it was those groups that resisted 'incorporation' into mainstream society, and the 'civilising' pressures this entailed, that tended to engage in hooligan activity. For these members of the so-called 'rough' (as opposed to the 'respectable') working class, located towards the lower end of the social scale, football hooliganism was an outlet for a particular form of aggressive masculine behaviour. Socialised by peers and parents to be able to 'handle oneself' in physical confrontations, and denied the possibility of achieving status and identity through education or work, these young men tended instead to gain prestige through, among other things, their ability to fight. This assertion of 'aggressive masculinity' was combined with a keen territorial identification with, and sense of ownership over, the street, neighbourhood and, by extension, the local football ground, and a corresponding hostility towards any outsiders who might attempt to 'invade' this territory. Support for the theory was found in statistical data unearthed on the social background of hooligans. Evidence drawn from the late 1960s through to the 1980s confirmed for Dunning *et al.* that the overwhelmingly majority (ranging from 70 to 90 per cent) of hooligans came from the lower working-class, had limited formal education and worked in semi-skilled or unskilled manual jobs, or were unemployed. But while there was little change over time in their social composition, what did alter significantly was the organisation of hooligan groups. As police and clubs sought to control behaviour within football grounds, the loose allegiances that had characterised 'skinhead' hooligan groups in the late 1960s began to tighten and 'crews' or 'firms' were formed to co-ordinate and plan confrontations with opponents, many of which increasingly took place away from grounds.[141]

Critics of the work of Dunning *et al.* have attacked it from a number of angles.[142] First, they have challenged the theoretical approach of the Leicester group, particularly its reliance on Elias's 'civilising process' to explain the emergence of hooliganism. Some object to what they see as the 'evolutionist' nature of the theory, although Dunning has countered that it was never intended to suggest 'unilinear, progressive and irreversible evolution'. Others, notably Williams, a former member of the Leicester team, have expressed disquiet at the 'high level of generality at which the theory operates' and its assumed applicability to other (non-English) national and cultural settings.[143] Second, critics have attacked the team's social location of hooliganism within the 'rough' working class. In fact, Dunning *et al.* never suggested that hooligans were drawn exclusively from poorer social groups and always acknowledged the presence in hooligan firms of those from skilled and middle-class occupations. Nonetheless, many remained unconvinced of the dominance of the lower working class in hooligan activity, pointing out weaknesses in the empirical data and suggesting that the examples chosen, such as West Ham United's notorious 'Inner City Firm', were far from typical of the phenomenon as a whole. Giulianotti has argued, for example, that in Scotland during the 1960s and 1970s it tended to be the more skilled and 'incorporated' Protestant Rangers fans that engaged in violent activity rather than the poorer and 'rougher' Catholic supporters of Celtic. Moreover, Giulianotti and others have found little evidence of 'rougher' hooligan elements in their own studies of the more prosperous and style-conscious 'casual' hooligans emerging from the early 1980s. Rather, they argue that hooligans actually came (and continue to come) from a variety of socio-economic backgrounds and that class structure and relationships thus provide little explanation for their activity.[144]

There have also been quite legitimate misgivings concerning Dunning *et al.*'s 'continuity' thesis. From an historian's point of view, certainly, some sections of their work are based on rather generalised understandings of social change and developing class relationships and structures. That said, some critics seem to have misread the Leicester team's recognition of 'the balance between continuity and discontinuity' as a more simplistic thesis that post-1960s hooliganism had always existed. In fact, as we have seen, Dunning *et al.* outline in some detail the discontinuities separating 'older' from 'modern' forms of hooliganism and the specific conjunctures that help to explain the rise of the latter. In this respect, their conclusions were not markedly dissimilar from those of Holt, who argued lucidly that football hooliganism 'can neither be explained in terms of simple continuities nor as an abrupt discontinuity'. In its *specific* forms' it was undeniably new, even if, as the Leicester team argued, it had existed in some form for as long as the game itself.[145]

Weaknesses in the Leicester methodology are more difficult to deny. Armstrong and Giulianotti have both highlighted the shortcomings of the relatively 'detached' approach of the group, particularly its failure to engage in extended fieldwork and study hooligans at first hand. As the Argentinian scholars Eduardo Archetti and Amilcar Romero note in their critique of the Leicester work: 'We never hear the voices of the hooligans themselves; in most cases they are transformed into statistical facts'.[146] Back in the 1970s, Peter Marsh and his colleagues had conducted research of this type with Oxford United supporters. Their conclusions, based on three years of observing the actions and assessing the verbal accounts of young fans, were that much of what was considered hooligan behaviour by the authorities and the press was in reality a less severe form of 'ritualised aggression'. When studied closely, the mayhem and disorder that was assumed to occur at and around football matches was revealed as a highly ordered form of social action, guided and determined by specific internal rules. Violent confrontations did take place, but these were far less frequent and significant than chants, threats and ritual insults. There was, indeed, 'far more talk about violence than actual fighting'.[147] Armstrong's more recent study of the Sheffield United 'Blades' made similar points regarding the relative infrequency of football-related violence, its exaggeration by the police and media, and the ritualistic nature of confrontations between rival fans. But he differed in his conception of hooligan groups such as the 'Blades' as 'neo-tribes', which, far from being highly organised, were in fact 'fluid, unstable and transient' entities based around loose networks of friends and acquaintances who gathered and acted together as a means of 'promoting self-identity and self-definition'.[148]

Other explanations of hooliganism have focused directly on its psychological appeal. First-hand accounts from former hooligans themselves (dismissed by some as 'hooligan porn') often emphasise the intense 'buzz', adrenalin rush and excitement arising from violent encounters; sensations that can hardly be matched in the routine of day-to-day existence.[149] '[Y]ou cannot take away the thrill that is associated with a confrontation at football', wrote Colin Ward in his account of life on the terraces during the 1970s and 1980s. 'People who in everyday life have to perform monotonous tasks, who haven't got paper qualifications and never will have, come to life, making crucial and instantaneous decisions.'[150] Finn has used the concepts of 'peak' and 'flow' experiences to describe this aspect of the appeal of hooliganism. Such experiences allow the individual to become immersed in the 'flow' of the activity and feel an intense emotional closeness and identification with others. Most supporters achieve 'peak' and 'flow' merely by watching the game, but others seek these experiences more directly by crossing the boundary between fan and hooligan.[151] Pursuing these ideas a little further, Giulianotti has suggested that hooliganism might be understood in a similar context as extreme, dangerous or high-risk sports such as scuba-diving, sky-diving or hang-gliding, in which 'the pleasure of facing danger is socially acquired'. Such activities involve the participant maintaining some degree of control over what appears to be a chaotic situation from the outside. Likewise, argues Giulianotti, the hooligan's intention 'is to walk in and out of an apparent maelstrom with mind and body intact'.[152]

Yet explanations that place the actions and experiences of the hooligans themselves centre-stage have their own weaknesses. Foremost of these is an absence of sociological and historical grounding. The tendency to regard hooliganism as a modern version of the type of ritualistic aggression found in all human societies fails, as critics have pointed out, to explain why some become involved in this supposedly universal phenomenon while others do not. It leaves us unable to account for the uneven development of hooliganism and its attraction to certain social groups during specific periods in particular societies. There is also the danger that it can blind us to the complex cultural and historical dimension of 'traditional' rivalries between specific hooligan groups, although Armstrong, at least, was conscious of the particular antagonisms at work when the 'Blades' met their adversaries from Sheffield Wednesday and Leeds United.[153] More profoundly, perhaps, both Marsh and colleagues and Armstrong have been accused of underplaying the serious nature of the encounters they witnessed. Much 'aggro' at football may indeed have been primarily ritualistic or symbolic but it could easily escalate into genuinely violent encounters, especially before and after matches when police control over the crowd was inevitably loosened. Moreover, just as the Leicester team was criticised for being distanced from the groups it purported to study, Armstrong and others have been accused of getting too close.[154] Indeed one particularly strident reviewer castigated Armstrong for even trying to understand the hooligans he studied, dismissing his account of their 'sorry behaviour' as 'a vain attempt to sanitize senseless violence and wasted lives'.[155]

The significance of hooliganism

Notwithstanding the entrenched and strangely defensive positions of many of the academics involved in the debate, there is more compatibility between these theories than is normally acknowledged. The emphasis on aggressive masculinity, the sense of identity and status offered by membership of hooligan firms and the media's role in exaggerating the extent of the 'problem' are common to almost every approach. Most authorities on the subject, however, have tended to eschew a multi-disciplinary perspective that would pay due attention to the range of sociological, historical, anthropological and psychological approaches outlined above. Moreover, whichever perspective we choose to take, the danger of overstating the contemporary significance of hooliganism remains equally pertinent in this as in earlier periods (see Chapter 3). Garry Crawford is surely right to note that 'for far too long academic attention has focused on extreme cases of supporter violence, largely at the expense of "ordinary" forms of support'.[156] It is true that many clubs, particularly at the lower levels of the professional game, experienced few major outbreaks of hooliganism during these decades and that 'good humour and moderately impolite badinage' were more characteristic of the average football crowd than aggression and violence. Russell has pointed out the continuation over these decades of older styles of support characterised by chanting, singing and wisecracking (exemplified by the infamous Kop 'end' at Liverpool's Anfield ground), which he takes to have 'tempered the more aggressive elements of terrace culture'.[157] Tom Watt has similarly concluded that for the majority of Arsenal fans 'fighting remained ... a marginal (albeit regular) part of what life on the North Bank was all about'. The increasingly passionate and vocal devotion of supporters to the team, mixed with a liberal dose of scepticism and sarcasm, meant that the 1970s 'traditionally seen as the worst of times on the terraces ... were to prove the best of times on the North Bank'.[158]

Arrest figures also tended to be low. The McElhone Report of 1977 revealed that of the nearly 4 million spectators who passed through the turnstiles at Scottish grounds in 1976 only 1,079 were arrested, an arrest rate of just 0.028 per cent. David Canter and his team mention a less precise figure of under 5 per 10,000 spectators (0.05 per cent) pertaining to English football in the 1980s. Not only were such figures lower than might have been expected, they were also comparable to the number of arrests arising from other leisure pursuits, such as those indulged in on the average Saturday night. Steve Frosdick and Peter Marsh have recently highlighted the limitations of McElhone's data, but few have objected to his conclusion that the media's concern over hooliganism was 'out of proportion to the level which actually occurs at matches'.[159]

For all this, hooliganism remains important to any study of this period because it dominated the internal politics of football and brought the game more closely into contact than ever before with the government and the law. Giulianotti has argued that the political discourse on spectator disorder passed through four distinct stages from the late 1960s to the mid-1980s. The first period, from 1968 to 1970, marked the initial recognition by government of hooliganism as a social policy issue. The reports conducted by Harrington in 1968 and Lang in 1969, though flawed in many respects, were important in raising the link between hooliganism and crowd safety and outlining the importance of co-operation between football clubs and the police authorities. By 1971 football hooliganism was, according to Giulianotti, 'embedded in the national and governmental consciousness'. Increasing concern over the behaviour of British supporters at home and abroad between 1971 and 1978 led to the first signs of reflection upon existing measures of crowd control and efforts to adopt a national approach. As it turned out, it was only in Scotland that significant legislation was enacted, following on from the recommendations of the aforementioned McElhone Report. The resultant Criminal Justice (Scotland) Act of 1980, made more urgent in the wake of fighting between Celtic and Rangers fans at that year's Scottish Cup final, attempted to sever the perceived link between alcohol and disorder by prohibiting the possession of alcohol at grounds. Heightened government involvement in combating hooliganism marked Giulianotti's third stage, dating from 1979 to 1984. The behaviour of English supporters abroad became a particular concern, leading to the first significant House of Commons debate on the issue in February 1984 and a report by a Department of the Environment Working Group following trouble at England fixtures in Luxemburg and France.[160]

Attitudes to hooliganism, however, and football in general, were altered radically by the events of 1985. This was to be the game's 'crisis year', or its 'annus horribilis'.[161] Alongside a continued decline in attendances, English football suffered an unprecedented series of stadium disasters and high-profile incidents of crowd disorder. In March, Millwall fans tore up seats and clashed with police and opposition supporters during a televised FA Cup tie at Luton. The ramifications of this incident were still being felt when, on the final day of the English season, a supporter was killed during disturbances between Birmingham City and

Leeds United fans and, more significantly, a fire at Bradford's Valley Parade ground took the lives of 56 people and injured over 200 more. Caused by a discarded cigarette dropped on to rubbish underneath a decrepit wooden grandstand, the Bradford fire was the worst disaster at a British football ground since the death of 66 spectators at Ibrox in 1971. An inquiry conducted by Justice Popplewell controversially linked the problems of spectator disorder and stadium safety, recommending, among other things, consideration of a national membership scheme for football supporters. By this time, the standing of the game had further plummeted with the death of 38 fans prior to the European Cup final between Liverpool and Juventus at the Heysel Stadium in Brussels. The outcry and recriminations that followed were, as Walvin noted, extraordinary, with politicians, critics and the quality and popular press eager to provide explanation and solutions to football's (often barely defined) problems. Few veered from the view that British football was in a deep crisis; some journalists pronounced it effectively dead. English clubs were soon banned indefinitely from European competition and, initially at least, from playing outside their own country. Ostracised and isolated from Europe and the world, English football, in particular, had reached its nadir. In the despair of Bradford and Heysel, however, the seeds of football's eventual revolution were being sown.[162]

References

1 See Steve Greenfield and Guy Osborn, *Regulating Football: Commodification, Consumption and the Law* (London: Pluto, 2001), p. 3.

2 Lincoln Allison, *Condition of England: Essays and Impressions* (London: Junction, 1981), p. 134; Stephen Wagg, *The Football World: A Contemporary Social History* (Brighton: Harvester, 1984), pp. 220–3.

3 James Walvin, *Football and the Decline of Britain* (Basingstoke: Macmillan, 1986); Dave Russell, 'Associating with Football: Social Identity in England, 1863–1998', in G. Armstrong and R. Giulianotti (eds), *Football Cultures and Identities* (Basingstoke: Macmillan, 1999), p. 22.

4 Walvin, *Football and the Decline of Britain*, pp. 6–14.

5 Tony Mason, 'Football', in T. Mason (ed.), *Sport in Britain: A Social History* (Cambridge: Cambridge University Press, 1989), pp. 149–50; Sports Council, *Digest of Sports Statistics for the UK* (London: Sports Council, 1991), pp. 21–2; Arthur Hopcraft, *The Football Man* (London: Simon & Schuster, 1988 [1st edition, 1968]), p. 198; John Bale, *Sport and*

Place: A Geography of Sport in England, Scotland and Wales (London: C. Hurst, 1982), p. 45; Dave Russell, *Football and the English: A Social History of Association Football in England, 1863–1995* (Preston: Carnegie, 1997), p. 171.

6 K. K. Sillitoe, *Planning for Leisure* (London: HMSO, 1969), p. 120 (Table 62); Sports Council, *Digest of Sports Statistics*, p. 20.

7 Bale, *Sport and Place*, p. 45; Chris Gratton and Peter Taylor, *Leisure in Britain* (Letchworth: Leisure Productions, 1987), p. 21 (Table 3.1); Sillitoe, *Planning for Leisure*, pp. 121–9.

8 John Moynihan, *The Soccer Syndrome: From the Primeval Forties* (London: Simon & Schuster, 1987 [1st edition, 1966]), pp. 192–203; Brian Glanville, *Football Memories* (London: Virgin, 1999), pp. 135–8, 142–8.

9 Bale, *Sport and Place*, pp. 45–9; North West Sports Council, *Leisure in the North West* (Salford: North West Sports Council, 1972), pp. 113–14.

10 Mason, 'Football', p. 149.

11 John Williams, '"Rangers is a Black Club": "Race", Identity and Local Football in England' in R. Giulianotti and J. Williams (eds), *Game Without Frontiers: Football, Identity and Modernity* (Aldershot: Arena, 1994), p. 154–9; Mason, 'Football', p. 149; Moynihan, *Soccer Syndrome*, p. 201.

12 *Sport and the Community: The Report of the Wolfenden Committee on Sport* (London: Central Council of Physical Recreation, 1960), p. 34.

13 Sillitoe, *Planning for Leisure*, pp. 243–4 (Tables A45, A46i), 146 (Table 77); Bale, *Sport and Place*, p. 51; Sports Council, *Digest of Sports Statistics*, pp. 22–3; Jeffrey Hill, *Sport, Leisure and Culture in Twentieth-Century Britain* (Basingstoke: Palgrave, 2002), p. 173; John F. Coglan with Ida M. Webb, *Sport and British Politics Since 1960* (London: Falmer, 1990), p. 84; Richard Holt and Tony Mason, *Sport in Britain, 1945–2000* (London: Blackwell, 2000), p. 150.

14 Hopcraft, *Football Man*, pp. 198–200; Moynihan, *Soccer Syndrome*, p. 200.

15 *Sport and the Community*, p. 34; Sillitoe, *Planning for Leisure*, pp. 147–52 (Tables 79 and 83); Sports Council, *Digest of Sports Statistics*, p. 23; Coglan with Webb, *Sport and British Politics*, pp. 202, 226 (n. 16).

16 See, for example, Michael F. Collins with Tess Kay, *Sport and Social Exclusion* (London: Routledge, 2003).

17 Coglan with Webb, *Sport and British Politics*, pp. 88, 206, 218–19; John Hargreaves, 'The State and Sport: Programmed and Non-Programmed Intervention in Britain' in L. Allison (ed.), *The Politics of Sport* (Manchester: Manchester University Press, 1986), p. 256; Roger Ingham,

'The Fate of a Good Intention: The "Football and the Community" Schemes' in A. Tomlinson (ed.), *Explorations in Football Culture* (Eastbourne: Leisure Studies Publications, 1983), pp. 57–61.

18 Coglan, *Sport and British Politics*, pp. 206, 215.

19 Ingham, 'Fate of a Good Intention', pp. 61–70.

20 John Clarke and Chas Critcher, *The Devil Makes Work: Leisure in Capitalist Britain* (Basingstoke: Macmillan, 1985), p. 134. See also John Hargreaves, *Sport, Power and Culture: A Social and Historical Analysis of Popular Sports in Britain* (Cambridge: Polity, 1986), p. 174.

21 See Ellis Cashmore, *Making Sense of Sports* (London: Routledge, 1996 [1st edition, 1990]), chapter 6.

22 Highfield Rangers Oral History Group (HROHG) and the Sir Norman Chester Centre for Football Research (SNCCFR), *Highfield Rangers: An Oral History* (Leicester: Leicester City Council, 1993), p. 53.

23 HROHG and SNCCFR, *Highfield Rangers*, pp. 51–7, 91; Williams, 'Rangers is a Black Club', pp. 174–6.

24 Williams, 'Rangers is a Black Club', pp. 161–2.

25 Jas Bains and Sanjiev Johal, *Corner Flags and Corner Shops: The Asian Football Experience* (London: Victor Gollancz, 1998), pp. 180–8.

26 Bains and Johal, *Corner Flags and Corner Shops*, pp. 51–7, 138; Sanjiev Johal, 'Playing Their Own Game: A South Asian Football Experience' in B. Carrington and I. McDonald (eds), *'Race', Sport and British Society* (London: Routledge, 2001), pp. 161–5.

27 Scott Fleming, 'Sport, Schooling and Asian Male Youth Culture' in G. Jarvie (ed.), *Sport, Racism and Ethnicity* (London: Falmer, 1991), pp. 30–57.

28 John Williams and Jackie Woodhouse, 'Can Play, Will Play?: Women and Football in Britain' in J. Williams and S. Wagg (eds), *British Football and Social Change: Getting into Europe* (Leicester: Leicester University Press, 1991), p. 96; Sue Lopez, *Women on the Ball: A Guide to Women's Football* (London: Scarlet, 1997), p. 31; Jessica Macbeth, 'The Development of Women's Football in Scotland', *The Sports Historian*, 22, 2 (November 2002), p. 158. The significance of 1966 as a pivotal moment in the women's game is challenged by Jean Williams, who suggests a more gradual development involving many clubs that had been playing from the 1950s and early 1960s. Jean Williams, *A Game for Rough Girls?: A History of Women's Football in Britain* (London: Routledge, 2003), p. 38.

29 Lopez, *Women on the Ball*, pp. 31–42, 55–60, 145, 155–9; Williams, *Game for Rough Girls*, pp. 41–2, 52–4; Bale, *Sport and Place*, pp. 51–4.

30 Williams and Woodhouse, 'Can Play, Will Play', pp. 97–8; Macbeth, 'Development of Women's Football', pp. 159–60; David McArdle, *From Boot Money to Bosman: Football, Society and the Law* (London: Cavendish, 2000), pp. 136–7; Williams, *Game for Rough Girls*, pp. 125–7; Celia Brackenridge and Diana Woodward, 'Gender Inequalities in Leisure and Sport in Post-War Britain' in J. Obelkevich and P. Catterall (eds), *Understanding Post-War British Society* (London; Routledge, 1994), p. 200.

31 Williams and Woodhouse, 'Can Play, Will Play', p. 99; Lopez, *Women on the Ball*, p. 226–7.

32 See Wagg, *Football World*, p. 220; Hargreaves, *Sport, Power and Culture*, p. 115; John Harding, *For the Good of the Game: The Official History of the Professional Footballers' Association* (London: Robson, 1991), pp. 331–7; A. J. Arnold, *A Game That Would Pay: An Economic History of Professional Football in Bradford* (London: Duckworth, 1988).

33 Stephen Dobson and John Goddard, *The Economics of Football* (Cambridge: Cambridge University Press, 2001), pp. 57–8, 65; *Scottish Abstract of Statistics* (Edinburgh: HMSO, 1980), p. 81 (Table 8.2); *Scottish Abstract of Statistics* (Edinburgh: HMSO, 1986), p. 88 (Table 8.8a); Bob Crampsey, *The Scottish Footballer* (Edinburgh: William Blackwood, 1978), p. 73.

34 W. E. Skinner, *The Football Industry: A Discussion Paper* (Sheffield: Sheffield City Polytechnic, 1982), p. 24; Dobson and Goddard, *Economics of Football*, pp. 57–8; calculated from *Scottish Abstract of Statistics* (Edinburgh: HMSO, 1985), p. 89 (Table 8.5a).

35 Stefan Szymanski and Tim Kuypers, *Winners and Losers: The Business Strategy of Football* (London: Penguin, 2000), pp. 48–9.

36 Allison, *Condition of England*, pp. 134–5

37 Szymanski and Kuypers, *Winners and Losers*, pp. 45–50; Skinner, *Football Industry*, pp. 36–8.

38 N. Jennett and P. J. Sloane, *Football in Decline: An Economic Analysis of the Report of the Chester Committee of Enquiry* (Paisley: Paisley College Social Science Working Papers, 1983); Political and Economic Planning (PEP), 'English Professional Football', *Planning*, 32, No. 496, 1966, pp. 111, 154; Department of Education and Science, *Report of the Committee on Football* (London: HMSO, 1968); Szymanski and Kuypers, *Winners and Losers*, pp. 46–7.

39 Russell, *Football and the English*, pp. 200–1; Szymanski and Kuypers, *Winners and Losers*, pp. 68–9, 323–4 (n. 29); Simon Inglis, *League Football and the Men Who Made It* (London: Collins Willow, 1988),

p. 313; Anthony King, *The End of the Terraces: The Transformation of English Football in the 1990s* (Leicester: Leicester University Press, 1998), pp. 49–52; Bob Crampsey, *The First 100 Years: The Scottish Football League* (Glasgow: Scottish Football League, 1990), p. 218.

40 Inglis, *League Football*, pp. 428–9, 313–15; Crampsey, *First 100 Years*, pp. 183–6, 202; Alan Hardaker, *Hardaker of the League* (London: Pelham, 1977), pp. 73–4; Russell, *Football and the English*, pp. 201–2; Mason, 'Football', p. 166; Hill, *Sport, Leisure and Culture*, p. 32.

41 BBC Written Archives Centre, Football Association, Broadcasting and Television of Matches (season 1956–7); PEP, 'English Professional Football', pp. 101, 152; Crampsey, *First 100 Years*, p. 198; Dobson and Goddard, *Economics of Football*, p. 81; Peter J. Sloane, *Sport in the Market?*, (London: Institute of Economic Affairs, Hobart Paper No. 85, 1980), p. 44; Szymanski and Kuypers, *Winners and Losers*, p. 56. Stephen Dobson and John Goddard, 'Performance, Revenue and Cross Subsidisation in the Football League, 1927–1994', *Economic History Review*, 51, 4 (1998), pp. 777, 779.

42 Inglis, *League Football*, p. 254; Hardaker, *Hardaker of the League*, p. 72; Szymanski and Kuypers, *Winners and Losers*, p. 76; Crampsey, *First 100 Years*, p. 165; PEP, 'English Professional Football', pp. 100, 83.

43 P. J. Sloane, 'Restriction of Competition in Professional Team Sports', *Bulletin of Economic Research*, 28, 1 (May 1976), pp. 3–22 and *Sport in the Market?*; Chris Gratton and Bernard Lisewski, 'The Economics of Sport in Britain: A Case of Market Failure?', *British Review of Economic Issues*, 3, 8 (Spring 1981), pp. 64–8. Useful summaries of this literature are provided in Andrew Cooke, *The Economics of Leisure and Sport* (London: Routledge, 1994), pp. 205–10; Chris Gratton, 'The Peculiar Economics of English Professional Football', *Soccer and Society*, 1, 1 (Spring 2000), pp. 11–15; Dobson and Goddard, *Economics of Football*, pp. 3–11; Szymanski and Kuypers, *Winners and Losers*, pp. 277–80; Stephen Morrow, *The New Business of Football: Accountability and Finance in Football* (Basingstoke: Palgrave, 1999), pp. 8–25.

44 Matthew Taylor, *The Leaguers: The Making of Professional Football in England, 1900–1939* (Liverpool: Liverpool University Press, 2005), chapter 5; Alan Tomlinson, 'North and South: The Rivalry of the Football League and the Football Association' in Williams and Wagg (eds), *British Football and Social Change*, pp. 25–47; Peter J. Sloane, 'The Economics of Professional Football: The Football Club as a Utility Maximiser', *Scottish Journal of Political Economy*, 17 (June 1971), pp. 121–45.

45 PEP, 'English Professional Football', p. 98; Inglis, *League Football*, pp. 229–32; Arnold, *A Game That Would Pay*, p. 125.

46 Inglis, *League Football*, pp. 229–32; Hardaker, *Hardaker of the League*, pp. 97–106; Jennett and Sloane, *Football in Decline*, pp. 15–16.

47 Crampsey, *First 100 Years*, pp. 167–70, 188, 192–4, 197–98, 206–9, 211; Bill Murray, *The Old Firm: Secretarianism, Sport and Society in Scotland* (Edinburgh: John Donald, 2000 [1st edition, 1984]), p. 210.

48 A. J. Arnold and Ivor Benveniste, 'Wealth and Poverty in the English Football League', *Accounting and Business Research*, 17, 67 (1987), pp. 195–203 and 'Cross Subsidisation and Competition Policy in English Professional Football', *Journal of Industrial Affairs*, 15 (1988), pp. 2–14; Sloane, 'Economics of Professional Football', pp. 126–7 and 'Restriction of Competition', pp. 10–14.

49 Tony Arnold, 'Rich Man, Poor Man: Economic Arrangements in the Football League' in Williams and Wagg (eds), *British Football and Social Change*, p. 56; N. C. Wiseman, 'The Economics of Football', *Lloyds Bank Review* (January 1977), p. 35; Dobson and Goddard, 'Performance, Revenue and Cross Subsidisation', pp. 777–8; H. F. Moorhouse, 'Blue Bonnets over the Border: Scotland and the Migration of Footballers' in J. Bale and J. Maguire (eds), *The Global Sports Arena: Athletic Talent Migration in an Interdependent World* (London: Frank Cass, 1994), p. 81.

50 Szymanski and Kuypers, *Winners and Losers*, pp. 265–6, 111–15.

51 H. F. Moorhouse, 'The Economic Effects of the Traditional Transfer System in European Professional Football', *Football Studies*, 2, 1 (1999), pp. 92–7.

52 Dobson and Goddard, *Economics of Football*, pp. 43–51; Szymanski and Kuypers, *Winners and Losers*, pp. 257–63.

53 Morrow, *New Business of Football*, pp. 16–17; Arnold and Benvensite, 'Wealth and Poverty', pp. 202–3; Jennett and Sloane, *Football in Decline*, p. 23.

54 Garry Whannel, *Fields in Vision: Television Sport and Cultural Transformation* (London: Routledge, 1992), p. 2.

55 Wagg, *Football World*, p. 121.

56 Russell, *Football and the English*, p. 197; Hargreaves, *Sport, Power and Culture*, pp. 138–9; Hill, *Sport, Leisure and Culture*, pp. 46–7; Fabio Chisari, '"Definitely Not Cricket": The Times and the Football World Cup, 1930–1970', *The Sports Historian*, 20, 1 (May 2000), pp. 60–4. See also Fred Inglis, *The Name of the Game: Sport and Society* (London: Heinemann, 1977), p. 102.

57 Raymond Boyle and Richard Haynes, *Power Play: Sport, the Media and Popular Culture* (London: Longman, 2000), p. 42; Russell, *Football and the English*, p. 195; Inglis, *League Football*, p. 320.

58 Iain Colley and Gill Davies, 'Kissed by History: Football as TV Drama' in M. Green and C. Jenkins (eds), *Sporting Fictions* (Birmingham: Centre for Contemporary Cultural Studies, 1981), pp. 195–6.

59 Chas Critcher, 'Football Since the War' in J. Clarke, C. Critcher and R. Johnson (eds), *Working Class Culture: Studies in History and Theory* (London: Hutchinson, 1979), pp. 174–5; Hargreaves, *Sport, Power and Culture*, pp. 141–4.

60 Whannel, *Fields in Vision*, pp. 60–2, 92–5, 106–7; Rod Brookes, *Representing Sport* (London: Arnold, 2002), pp. 24–5; Hill, *Sport, Leisure and Culture*, p. 52.

61 Colley and Davies, 'Kissed by History', pp. 189–208.

62 Richard Holt, 'Champions, Heroes and Celebrities: Sporting Greatness and the British Public' in *The Book of British Sporting Heroes* (London: National Portrait Gallery, 1998), p. 13.

63 Critcher, 'Football since the War', p. 164.

64 Garry Whannel, *Media Sport Stars: Masculinities and Moralities* (London: Routledge, 2002), pp. 52–63.

65 Matthew Taylor, 'Football, History and Memory: The Heroes of Manchester United', *Football Studies*, 3, 2 (October 2000), pp. 32–4; Whannel, *Media Sport Stars*, pp. 112–14, 123–7; Critcher, 'Football since the War', p. 166; Wagg, *Football World*, pp. 142–3; Michael Parkinson, *Best: An Intimate Biography* (London: Arrow, 1975), back cover.

66 Tom Preston, 'Art', in R. Cox, D. Russell and W. Vamplew (eds), *Encyclopedia of British Football* (London: Frank Cass, 2002), pp. 35–7; Pierre Lanfranchi, Christiane Eisenberg, Tony Mason and Alfred Wahl, *100 Years of Football: The FIFA Centennial Book* (London: Weidenfeld & Nicolson, 2004), p. 208; *Muddied Oafs: An Exhibition of Football* (London: Gallery 27, 1998), nos. 23, 28, 32–5, 74–5; Hunter Davies, *Boots, Balls and Haircuts: An Illustrated History of Football from Then to Now* (London: Cassell Illustrated, 2003), pp. 223–7; John Bale, 'Identity, Identification and Image: Football and Place in the New Europe', in S. Gehrmann (ed.), *Football and Regional Identity in Europe* (Münster: Lit Verlag, 1997), p. 281.

67 See the Pinter extracts 'Playing Away' and 'His Normal Game' in Brian Glanville (ed.) *The Footballer's Companion* (London: Eyre & Spottiswoode, 1962) and *The Joy of Football* (London: Hodder & Stoughton, 1986). Dave Russell and Jean Williams, 'Drama', in Cox, Russell and Vamplew (eds), *Encyclopedia of British Football*, pp. 91–2; Peter Seddon, *A Football Compendium* (Wetherby: The British Library, 1995), pp. 311–12.

68 Ian Brown, 'Play Sport: Problems of Sport as a Theme for the Playwright', in Green and Jenkins (eds), *Sporting Fictions*, pp. 82–104.

69 Jeff Hill, 'Bascombe, Machin and Logan: Explorations in Sport and Literature', paper presented to the British Society of Sports History Annual Conference, Leicester, April 2002; D. J. Taylor, '"Rally Round You Havens!": Soccer and the Literary Imagination', in S. Kuper (ed.), *Perfect Pitch 1: Home Ground* (London: Headline, 1997), pp. 81–3, 93–7; Seddon, *Football Compendium*, pp. 291–4. See also Robin Jenkins, *A Would-Be Saint* (Edinburgh: Black & White, 1994 [1st edition, 1978]), a novel set in an inter-war Scottish mining community that uses football as a setting to reflect upon attitudes to violence and morality.

70 Brian Glanville, *Goalkeepers are Different* (Harmondsworth: Puffin edition, 1974).

71 Hill, 'Bascombe, Machin and Logan'; Glanville, *Football Memories*, p. 170.

72 Russell, *Football and the English*, pp. 108–13.

73 Hill, *Sport, Leisure and Culture*, p. 56; Davies, *Boots, Balls and Haircuts*, p. 231; Tony Remnick, 'Comic Characters', in Cox, Russell and Vamplew (eds), *Encyclopedia of British Football*, pp. 69–71.

74 James Walvin, *The People's Game: The History of Football Revisited* (Edinburgh: Mainstream, 1994), pp. 181–2; Russell, *Football and the English*, pp. 159, 184, 185.

75 Percy Young, *A History of British Football* (London: Arrow, 1973 [1st edition, 1968]), p. 278.

76 Chas Critcher, 'England and the World Cup: World Cup Willies, English Football and the Myth of 1966', in J. Sugden and A. Tomlinson (eds), *Hosts and Champions: Soccer Cultures, National Identities and the USA World Cup* (Aldershot: Arena, 1994), p. 79. See also Kevin Foster, 'Dreaming of Pelé: Football and Society in England and Brazil in the 1950s and 1960s', *Football Studies*, 6, 1 (2003), pp. 70–86.

77 Harold Mayes, *The Football Association World Cup Report* (London: Heinemann, 1967), pp. 13–14, 51, 63, 86–7; Young, *History of British Football*, pp. 280, 288; Tony Mason, 'England 1966: Traditional and Modern?' in A. Tomlinson and C. Young (eds), *National Identity and Global Sports Events: Culture, Politics, and Spectacle in the Olympics and the Football World Cup* (Albany, NY: SUNY Press, 2006), pp. 85–6.

78 Holt and Mason, *Sport in Britain*, pp. 129–30.

79 Hopcraft, *Football Man*, pp. 219–21. See also Dave Russell, *Looking North: Northern England and the National Imagination* (Manchester: Manchester University Press, 2004), p. 254; Mason, 'England 1966', p. 87.

80 Jimmy Greaves with Norman Giller, *Don't Shoot the Manager: The Revealing Story of England's Soccer Bosses* (London: Boxtree, 1993), pp. 22, 24, 39–40; Roger Hutchinson, *'66!: The Inside Story of England's World Cup Triumph* (Edinburgh: Mainstream, 2002 [1st edition, 1995]), pp. 55–7, 64, 78–80, 92–7.

81 Hutchinson, *'66!*, pp. 138, 149; Geoff Hurst, *The World Game* (London: Stanley Paul, 1967), pp. 31–2.

82 Hutchinson, *'66!*, pp. 161–4; Critcher, 'England and the World Cup', pp. 80–2; Pablo Alabarces, Alan Tomlinson and Christopher Young, 'Argentina versus England at the France '98 World Cup: Narratives of Nation and the Mythologizing of the Popular', *Media, Culture & Society*, 23, 5 (2001), p. 550.

83 See David Thomson, *4–2* (London: Bloomsbury, 1996); Hutchinson, *'66!*, p. 196; David Miller, *England's Last Glory: The Boys of '66* (London: Pavilion, 2006 [1st edition, 1986]), chapter 10.

84 Richard Weight, *Patriots: National Identity in Britain, 1940–2000* (London: Pan Macmillan, 2002), pp. 458–62; Hutchinson, *'66!*, pp. 179–80; Paul Ward, *Britishness Since 1870* (London: Routledge, 2004), p. 76. Weight's interpretation is contradicted to some extent by Tony Mason, who has emphasised the relatively modest celebrations that greeted the victory and the 'restrained patriotism' of English supporters throughout the competition. Mason, 'England 1966', pp. 91, 95.

85 Weight, *Patriots*, pp. 462–3; Hopcraft, *Football Man*, p. 222; Mike Cronin and Richard Holt, 'The Imperial Game in Crisis: English Cricket and Decolonisation' in S. Ward (ed.), *British Culture and the End of Empire* (Manchester: Manchester University Press, 2001), p. 119; Richard Holt, *Sport and the British: A Modern History* (Oxford: Clarendon, 1989), pp. 269–70; Holt and Mason, *Sport in Britain*, p. 165.

86 Weight, *Patriots*, pp. 464, 459; Dave Bowler, *Winning Isn't Everything . . .: A Biography of Alf Ramsey* (London: Orion, 1999), pp. 155, 222–3; John Clarke and Chas Critcher, '1966 and All That: England's World Cup Victory', in A. Tomlinson and G. Whannel (eds), *Off the Ball: The Football World Cup* (London: Pluto, 1986), p. 120; Dilwyn Porter, '"Your Boys Took One Hell of a Beating!": English Football and British Decline, *c*.1950–80', in A. Smith and D. Porter (eds), *Sport and National Identity in the Post-War World* (London: Routledge, 2004), p. 43.

87 Rogan Taylor and Andrew Ward, *Kicking and Screaming: An Oral History of Football in England* (London: Robson, 1995), p. 173; Denis Law with Bernard Bale, *The Lawman: An Autobiography* (London: André Deutsch, 1999), pp. 126–8; Mason, 'England 1966', p. 92. Weight, *Patriots*, p. 464; Martin Johnes, '"Every day when I Wake Up I Thank the Lord I'm Welsh":

Sport and National Identity in Post-War Wales', in Smith and Porter (eds), *Sport and National Identity*, p. 60.

88 Clarke and Critcher, '1966 and all that', pp. 122–5; Weight, *Patriots*, p. 462.

89 Tony Pawson, *The Football Managers* (London: Eyre Methuen, 1973), p. 51; Clarke and Critcher, '1966 and All That', p. 118.

90 Downing quoted in Porter, 'English Football and British Decline', p. 43; Thomson, 4–2, p. 221.

91 Taylor and Ward, *Kicking and Screaming*, p. 174, Foster, 'Dreaming of Pelé', pp. 70, 72.

92 Jeff Dawson, *Back Home: England and the 1970 World Cup* (London: Orion, 2001); Glanville quoted in Bowler, *Winning Isn't Everything*, p. 286.

93 Stephen Wagg, 'Naming the Guilty Men: Managers and Media', in Tomlinson and Whannel (eds), *Off the Ball*, 46–7.

94 Porter, 'English Football and British Decline', pp. 43, 35–7, 46. See also Richard English and Michael Kenny (eds), *Rethinking British Decline* (Basingstoke: Macmillan, 2000).

95 Quoted in Porter, 'English Football and British Decline', pp. 44–7.

96 Stephen Wagg, 'Playing the Past: The Media and the England Football Team', in J. Williams and S. Wagg (eds), *British Football and Social Change: Getting into Europe* (Leicester: Leicester University Press, 1991), pp. 222, 225–30, 237.

97 Boyle and Haynes, *Power Play*, pp. 78–9; Mason, 'England 1966', p. 94.

98 Critcher, 'England and the World Cup', pp. 83–7, 90–1. See also Joseph Maguire, *Global Sport: Identities, Societies, Civilizations* (Cambridge: Polity, 1999), pp. 193–8; Barrie Houlihan, 'Sport, National Identity and Public Policy', *Nations and Nationalism*, 3, 1 (1997), p. 119.

99 Tom Nairn, *The Break-Up of Britain: Crisis and Neo-Nationalism* (London: Verso, 1977), p. 13.

100 Linda Colley, *Britons: Forging the Nation, 1707–1837* (London: Pimlico, 2003 [1st edition, 1992]), p. 6; David McCrone, 'Unmasking Britannia: The Rise and Fall of British National Identity', *Nations and Nationalism*, 3, 4 (1997), p. 587.

101 Weight, *Patriots*, pp. 1–16, 727.

102 Krishan Kumar, *The Making of British National Identity* (Cambridge: Cambridge University Press, 2003), p. 239; Ward, *Britishness Since 1870*, pp. 6–8.

103 Brian Glanville, 'Britain Against the Rest: The Decline of British Sporting Prestige' in M. Sissons and P. French (eds), *The Age of Austerity, 1945–1951* (Harmondsworth: Penguin, 1964), pp. 155–72; Martin Polley, *Moving the Goalposts: A History of Sport and Society Since 1945* (London: Routledge, 1998), pp. 35–8; Houlihan, 'Sport, National Identity and Public Policy', p. 121.

104 Weight, *Patriots*, pp. 255–6; H. F. Moorhouse, 'On the Periphery: Scotland, Scottish Football and the New Europe', in Williams and Wagg (eds), *British Football*, p. 201; Holt, *Sport and the British*, p. 260; Alan Bairner, 'Football and the Idea of Scotland', in G. Jarvie and G. Walker (eds), *Scottish Sport in the Making of the Nation: Ninety-Minute Patriots?* (Leicester: Leicester University Press, 1994), pp. 9–10.

105 Ronald Kowalski, '"Cry For Us, Argentina": Sport and National Identity in Late Twentieth-Century Scotland', in Smith and Porter (eds), *Sport and National Identity*, pp. 70–1, 74; Christopher Harvie, *Scotland and Nationalism: Scottish Society and Politics, 1707–1994* (London: Routledge, 1994 [1st edition, 1977]), pp. 173–97; Vernon Bogdanor, *Devolution in the United Kingdom* (Oxford: Oxford University Press, 1999), chapter 4; Anthony H. Birch, *Political Integration and Disintegration in the British Isles* (London: George Allen & Unwin, 1977), pp. 98–115.

106 Kowalski, 'Cry for us', pp. 74–5; Grant Jarvie and Irene Reid, 'Sport, Nationalism and Culture in Scotland', *The Sports Historian*, 19, 1 (May 1999), p. 117; Weight, *Patriots*, pp. 556–8. See also John Rafferty, *One Hundred Years of Scottish Football* (London: Pan, 1973), pp. 40–2.

107 Stuart Cosgrove, 'And the Bonny Scotland Will Be There: Football in Scottish Culture', in Tomlinson and Whannel (eds), *Off the Ball*, pp. 105–6; Kowalski, 'Cry for us', pp. 75–6; Ian Archer, 'World Cup '74', in I. Archer and T. Royle (eds), *We'll Support You Evermore: The Impertinent Saga of Scottish Fitba'* (Edinburgh: Mainstream, 2000 [1st edition, 1976]), pp. 102–21; Gallagher quoted in Bairner, 'Football and the Idea of Scotland', p. 10; Harvie, *Scotland and Nationalism*, p. 197; Holt and Mason, *Sport in Britain*, p. 134.

108 Nairn, *Break-Up of Britain*, pp. 173–4; Sillars quoted in Grant Jarvie and Graham Walker, 'Ninety Minute Patriots?: Scottish Sport in the Making of the Nation', in Jarvie and Walker (eds), *Scottish Sport*, p. 1.

109 David McCrone, *The Sociology of Nationalism* (London: Routledge, 1998), pp. 135–7; Richard Holt, 'King over the Border: Denis Law and Scottish Football', in Jarvie and Walker (eds), *Scottish Sport*, p. 60; Jarvie and Reid, 'Sport, Nationalism and Culture', p. 117.

110 Holt, 'King over the Border', pp. 58–74; H. F. Moorhouse, 'Scotland

against England: Football and Popular Culture', *International Journal of the History of Sport*, 4, 2 (September 1987), pp. 193–5 and 'Blue Bonnets over the Border: Scotland and the Migration of Footballers', in J. Bale and J. Maguire (eds), *The Global Sports Arena: Athletic Talent Migration in an Interdependent World* (London: Frank Cass, 1994), pp. 81–6; Bob Crampsey, *The Scottish Footballer* (Edinburgh: William Blackwood, 1978), pp. 56–64.

111 Named after the small, cheap ball he honed his skills with.

112 Bairner, 'Football and the Idea of Scotland', p. 12; Holt, 'King over the Border', pp. 66–7; Holt and Mason, *Sport in Britain*, p. 134; Hargreaves, *Sport, Power and Culture*, p. 156.

113 Gerry P. T. Finn and Richard Giulianotti, 'Scottish Fans, Not English Hooligans!: Scots, Scottishness and Scottish Football', in A. Brown (ed.), *Fanatics!: Power, Identity and Fandom in Football* (London: Routledge, 1998), pp. 190–2; Kowalski, 'Cry for us', pp. 77–8; Stuart Cosgrove, *Hampden Babylon: Sex and Scandal in Scottish Football* (Edinburgh: Canongate, 2001 [1st edition, 1991]), pp. 70–7.

114 Moorhouse, 'Scotland against England', p. 200, and his 'Scotland, Football and Identities: The National Team and Club Sides', in S. Gehrmann (ed.), *Football and Regional Identity in Europe* (Munster: Lit Verlag, 1997), pp. 183–4; Alan Bairner, 'Football', in G. Jarvie and J. Burnett (eds), *Sport, Scotland and the Scots* (East Linton: Tuckwell, 2000), p. 90; Bairner, 'Football and the Idea of Scotland', pp. 18–19; Richard Giulianotti and Michael Gerrard, 'Cruel Britannia? Glasgow Rangers, Scotland and "Hot" Football Rivalries', in G. Armstrong and R. Giulianotti (eds), *Fear and Loathing in World Football* (Oxford: Berg, 2001), pp. 34–5.

115 Bill Murray, *The Old Firm: Sectarianism, Sport and Society in Scotland* (Edinburgh: John Donald, 2000 [1st published, 1984]), pp. 265–6.

116 Graham Walker, '"There's Not a Team Like the Glasgow Rangers": Football and Religious Identity in Scotland', in G. Walker and T. Gallagher (eds), *Sermons and Battle Hymns: Protestant Popular Culture in Modern Scotland* (Edinburgh: Edinburgh University Press, 1990), p. 146.

117 Bairner, 'Football and the Idea of Scotland', pp. 20–1; Joseph M. Bradley, 'Football in Scotland: A History of Political and Ethnic Identity', *International Journal of the History of Sport*, 12, 1 (April 1995), p. 91 and 'Integration or Assimilation? Scottish Society, Football and Irish Immigrants', *International Journal of the History of Sport*, 13, 1 (August 1996), pp. 71–3; G. P. T. Finn, 'Racism, Religion and Social Prejudice: Irish Catholic Clubs, Soccer and Scottish Society – 2 Social Identities and Conspiracy Theories', *International Journal of the History of Sport*, 8, 3 (December 1991), p. 391. See also Raymond Boyle, '"We are Celtic

Supporters ...": Questions of Football and Identity in Modern Scotland' in Giulianotti and Williams (eds), *Game Without Frontiers*, pp. 86, 87–9.

118 Finn, 'Racism, Religion and Social Prejudice', pp. 391–3; Bairner, 'Football and the Idea of Scotland', pp. 19–20; Murray, *Old Firm*, p. 187; Moorhouse, 'Scotland, Football and Identities', pp. 195–6; Boyle, 'We are Celtic', pp. 88–9.

119 Mike Cronin, *Sport and Nationalism in Ireland: Gaelic Games, Soccer and Irish Identity Since 1884* (Dublin: Four Courts, 1999), pp. 146, 144.

120 John Sugden and Alan Bairner, *Sport, Sectarianism and Society in a Divided Ireland* (Leicester: Leicester University Press, 1993), pp. 84–6; Cronin, *Sport and Nationalism*, pp. 170–84, and his 'Playing Away from Home: Identity in Northern Ireland and the Experience of Derry City Football Club', *National Identities*, 2, 1 (2000), pp. 65–79; Vic Duke and Liz Crolley, *Football, Nationality and the State* (Harlow: Longman, 1996), pp. 70–5.

121 Cronin, 'Playing Away from Home', p. 78; H. F. Moorhouse, 'One State, Several Countries: Soccer and Identities in the "United" Kingdom', European University Institute Colloquium Papers, 1989, p. 6; Sugden and Bairner, *Sport, Sectarianism and Society*, pp. 74, 75–9 and their 'Observe the Sons of Ulster: Football and Politics in Northern Ireland', in Tomlinson and Whannel (eds), *Off the Ball*, p. 155; David Hassan, 'A People Apart: Soccer, Identity and Irish Nationalists in Northern Ireland', *Soccer and Society*, 3, 3 (Autumn 2002), pp. 71–2, 74–5.

122 Alan Bairner, 'Where Did It All Go Right? George Best, Manchester United and Northern Ireland', in D. L. Andrews (ed.), *Manchester United: A Thematic Study* (London: Routledge, 2004), p. 137.

123 Ward, *Britishness Since 1870*, pp. 79–80.

124 John Sugden and Alan Bairner, 'Northern Ireland: Sport in a Divided Society', in Allison (ed.), *Politics of Sport*, pp. 113–14; 'Observe the Sons', pp. 155–6; *Sport, Sectarianism and Society*, pp. 76–8; 'Ireland and the World Cup: "Two Teams in Ireland, There's Only Two Teams in Ireland ..."', in Sugden and Tomlinson (eds), *Hosts and Champions*, pp. 127–30.

125 Martin Johnes, 'Eighty Minute Patriots? National Identity and Sport in Modern Wales', *International Journal of the History of Sport*, 17, 4 (December 2000), pp. 105–6; Holt and Mason, *Sport in Britain*, p. 136; Peter Stead and Huw Richards (eds), *For Club and Country: Welsh Football Greats* (Cardiff: University of Wales Press, 2000).

126 Johnes, 'Eighty Minute Patriots?', pp. 105–6, 108; Polley, *Moving the Goalposts*, p. 61.

127 Murray, *Old Firm*, p. 178; Rafferty, *One Hundred Years*, pp. 145–9; Holt and Mason, *Sport in Britain*, pp. 140–1; Anthony King, *The European Ritual: Football in the New Europe* (Aldershot: Ashgate, 2003), pp. 4–8.

128 Hunter Davies, *The Glory Game* (Edinburgh: Mainstream, 1992 [1st edition, 1972]); Chas Critcher, 'Putting on the Style: Aspects of Recent English Football', in Williams and Wagg (eds), *British Football and Social Change*, pp. 69–72.

129 Matthew Taylor, 'The Migration of Footballers: An Historical Approach', *Moving Bodies*, 1, 1 (2003) pp. 32–7 and 'The Foreigner in English Football before the 1980s', paper presented to the British Society of Sports History Annual Conference, University of Lancaster, April 2001; Nick Harris, *England, Their England: The Definitive Story of Foreign Footballers in the English Game since 1888* (Hove: Pitch, 2003), pp. 157–85.

130 Patrick McGovern, 'Globalization or Internationalization?: Foreign Footballers in the English League, 1946–95', *Sociology*, 36, 1, pp. 28–30; Moorhouse, 'Blue Bonnets', p. 81.

131 John Williams, 'Having an Away Day: English Football and the Hooligan Debate', in Williams and Wagg (eds), *British Football and Social Change*, p. 160; Russell, *Football and the English*, p. 189.

132 Ian Taylor, '"Football Mad": A Speculative Sociology of Football Hooliganism', in E. Dunning (ed.), *The Sociology of Sport* (London: Frank Cass, 1971), pp. 352–77; John Clarke, 'Football and Working Class Fans: Tradition and Change', in R. Ingham (ed.), *Football Hooliganism: The Wider Context* (London: Inter-Action, 1978), pp. 37–60; Eric Dunning, Patrick Murphy and John Williams, *The Roots of Football Hooliganism: An Historical and Sociological Study* (London: Routledge & Kegan Paul, 1988); Patrick Murphy, John Williams and Eric Dunning, *Football on Trial: Spectator Violence and Development in the Football World* (London: Routledge, 1990); Peter Marsh, Elizabeth Rosser and Rom Harre, *The Rules of Disorder* (London: Routledge & Kegan Paul, 1978); Gary Armstrong, *Football Hooligans: Knowing the Score* (Oxford: Berg, 1998); Holt, *Sport and the British*, pp. 326–43.

133 Richard Giulianotti, 'Social Identity and Public Order: Political and Academic Discourses on Football Violence', in R. Giulianotti, N. Bonney and M. Hepworth (eds), *Football, Violence and Social Identity* (London: Routledge, 1994), pp. 10–11; Steve Redhead, 'Always Look on the Bright Side of Life', in S. Redhead (ed.), *The Passion and the Fashion: Football Fandom in the New Europe* (Aldershot: Avebury, 1993), p. 3; Murphy, Williams and Dunning, *Football on Trial*, p. 10; Steve Frosdick and Peter Marsh, *Football Hooliganism* (Cullompton: Willan, 2005), pp. 27–9; Holt, *Sport and the British*, p. 343; Gerry P. T. Finn, 'Football Violence: A

Societal Psychological Perspective', in Giulianotti, Bonney and Hepworth (eds), *Football, Violence and Social Identity*, pp. 90–1.

134 Dunning, Murphy and Williams, *Roots of Football Hooliganism*, pp. 5–7.

135 Richard Giulianotti, 'A Different Kind of Carnival', in M. Perryman (ed.), *Hooligan Wars: Causes and Effects of Football Violence* (Edinburgh: Mainstream, 2001), p. 141.

136 Taylor, 'Football Mad'.

137 Clarke, 'Football and Working Class Fans', pp. 44–57; John Hughson, 'The Bad Blue Boys and the "Magical Recovery" of John Clarke', in G. Armstrong and R. Giulianotti (eds), *Entering the Field: New Perspectives on World Football* (Oxford: Berg, 1997), pp. 239–41; David Waddington, *Contemporary Issues in Public Disorder* (London: Routledge, 1992), pp. 134–6; Holt, *Sport and the British*, p. 337.

138 Dunning, Murphy and Williams, *Roots of Football Hooliganism*, pp. 28–31; Giulianotti, *Football*, pp. 41–2; Wagg, *Football World*, pp. 198–201; Russell, *Football and the English*, p. 191; Armstrong, *Football Hooligans*, pp. 15–16; Waddington, *Contemporary Issues*, p. 137.

139 Ian Taylor, 'On the Sports Violence Question: Soccer Hooliganism Revisited', in J. Hargreaves (ed.), *Sport, Culture and Ideology* (London: Routledge & Kegan Paul, 1982), pp. 152–96.

140 See Dunning, Murphy and Williams, *Roots of Football Hooliganism*, chapter 7; Murphy, Williams and Dunning, *Football on Trial*, pp. 82–4; Eric Dunning, *Sport Matters: Sociological Studies of Sport, Violence and Civilization* (London: Routledge, 1999), pp. 142–5.

141 Dunning, Murphy and Williams, *Roots of Football Hooliganism*, chapter 9; Murphy, Williams and Dunning, *Football on Trial*, pp. 86–92; Eric Dunning, 'The Social Roots of Football Hooliganism: A Reply to the Critics of the "Leicester School" ' in Giulianotti, Bonney and Hepworth (eds), *Football, Violence and Social Identity*, pp. 152–3; Dunning, *Sport Matters*, pp. 148–53.

142 For an extended analysis of the Leicester School and its critics, see Alan Bairner, 'The Leicester School and the Study of Football Hooliganism', *Sport in Society*, 9, 4 (October 2006), pp. 583–98.

143 See Giulianotti, *Football*, pp. 44–6; Eric Dunning, 'Social Roots', pp. 137–49, 152; Williams, 'Having an Away Day', pp. 177–8; Bairner, 'Leicester School', pp. 591–2, 594.

144 Dunning, Murphy and Williams, *Roots of Football Hooliganism*, pp. 186–91, 213–14; Waddington, *Contemporary Issues*, pp. 133–4; Giulianotti, *Football*, pp. 46–7, 51–2; Armstrong, *Football Hooligans*, pp. 323–2.

145   D. Hobbs and D. Robins, 'The Boy Done Good: Football Violence, Changes and Continuities', *Sociological Review*, 39, 3 (1991), pp. 551–79; Dunning, 'Social Roots', pp. 136–7; Holt, *Sport and the British*, pp. 341, 343.

146   Armstrong, *Football Hooligans*, pp. 14–18; Giulianotti, *Football*, pp. 46–7; Eduardo P. Archetti and Amilcar G. Romero, 'Death and Violence in Argentinian Football' in Giulianotti, Bonney and Hepworth (eds), *Football, Violence and Social Identity*, pp. 42–3. See also Bairner, 'Leicester School', pp. 590–1.

147   Marsh, Rosser and Harre, *Rules of Disorder*; Peter Marsh, 'Life and Careers on the Soccer Terraces', in Ingham (ed.), *Football Hooliganism*, pp. 61–81; Frosdick and Marsh, *Football Hooliganism*, p. 93.

148   Armstrong, *Football Hooligans*, p. 306. See also Guilianotti, *Football*, p. 51; Garry Crawford, *Consuming Sport: Fans, Sport and Culture* (London: Routledge, 2004), p. 93.

149   Frosdick and Marsh, *Football Hooliganism*, pp. 80–1.

150   Colin Ward, *Steaming In: Journal of a Football Fan* (London: Pocket Books, 1994 [1st edition, 1989]), p. 52

151   Finn, 'Football Violence', pp. 105–18.

152   Giulianotti, *Football*, pp. 52–3.

153   Dunning, Murphy and Williams, *Roots of Football Hooliganism*, pp. 29–30; Dunning, *Sport Matters*, pp. 141–2; John Williams, 'Who You Calling a Hooligan?', in Perryman (ed.), *Hooligan Wars*, p. 49; Giulianotti, *Football*, pp. 43–4; Gary Armstrong, 'False Leeds: The Construction of Hooligan Confrontations', in Giulianotti and Williams (eds), *Game Without Frontiers*, pp. 299–325; Armstrong, *Football Hooligans*, pp. 203–20.

154   Dunning, Murphy and Williams, *Roots of Football Hooliganism*, pp. 21–3; Wagg, *Football World*, pp. 214–15; Waddington, *Contemporary Issues*, pp. 130–1; Frosdick and Marsh, *Football Hooliganism*, p. 94; Eric Dunning, Patrick Murphy and Ivan Waddington, 'Anthropological versus Sociological Approaches to the Study of Soccer Hooliganism: Some Critical Notes', *Sociological Review*, 39, 3 (1991), pp. 467–8.

155   Shirl J. Hoffman, Review of *Football Hooligans*, *Contemporary Sociology*, 28, 2 (1999), pp. 191–2.

156   Frosdick and Marsh, *Football Hooliganism*, pp. 86, 101; David Canter, Miriam Comber and David L. Uzzell, *Football in its Place: An Environmental Psychology of Football Grounds* (London: Routledge, 1989), pp. 124–5; Waddington, *Contemporary Issues*, pp. 138–9; Crawford, *Consuming Sport*, p. 89.

157 Russell, *Football and the English*, pp. 193–4; Canter, Comber and Uzzell, *Football in its Place*, p. 17.

158 Tom Watt, *The End: 80 Years of Life on the Terraces* (Edinburgh: Mainstream, 1995 [1st edition, 1993]), pp. 136, 135. See also Hopcraft, *Football Man*, pp. 191–4; John Williams, 'Kopites, "Scallies" and Liverpool Fan Cultures: Tales of Triumph and Disasters', in J. Williams, S. Hopkins and C. Long (eds), *Passing Rhythms: Liverpool FC and the Transformation of Football* (Oxford: Berg, 2001), pp. 100–10.

159 Frosdick and Marsh, *Football Hooliganism*, p. 39; Canter, Comber and Uzzell, *Football in its Place*, p. 17; John Bale, *Sport, Space and the City* (London: Routledge, 1993), p. 29.

160 Giulianotti, 'Social Identity', pp. 12–18; Greenfield and Osborn, *Regulating Football*, pp. 9–11.

161 Giulianotti, 'Social Identity', p. 18; Russell, *Football and the English*, p. 206.

162 Walvin, *Football and the Decline of Britain*, pp. 6–8; Russell, *Football and the English*, p. 208.

CHAPTER 6

Football's revolution, 1985–2000

Revolutions have always played a key role in the trajectory of history. As significant turning points in the history of societies and markers of change, they help historians to divide eras, centuries and decades into discrete frames of time. They are one of those 'events', along with war and the death of monarchs, for example, that form part of the periodisation so central to the historians' task. We are most familiar with the term 'revolution' as applied to major periods of political upheaval and transformation, such as the French Revolution and the Russian Revolution. Neither of these, nor the Industrial Revolution of the late eighteenth and nineteenth centuries, could really be described as 'events' as such, although in the case of France and Russia, the dates 1789 and 1917 have acted as useful emblems both to signify the beginning of change and, in Ludmilla Jordanova's words, 'conjure up a whole historical era'.[1] What is more, the term 'revolution' has been applied to a range of political, economic, social and cultural transformations, where change has appeared to be radical and dramatic, and resulted in significant shifts in the structures, forms and power relations of societies.[2]

It is in this respect that the notion of 'revolution' might be applicable to what happened to British football during the late 1980s and 1990s. John Williams, for example, has written of an '*English* football revolution' in which the game 'began to hum to the new rhythms of global capitalism', appealing to new types of supporters, sponsors and investors and, with the help of satellite television, repositioning itself as a central feature of British culture. Others have talked of these years as witnessing the 'transformation' or 'reinvention' of football, characterised most dramatically by the creation of the Premier League and the reconstruction or relocation of the grounds of professional clubs. Not since the late nineteenth century, it has been argued, when football was effectively 'made' as a popular recreation and a cultural form, had the game been subject to such fundamental change.[3] Moreover, it could be suggested that much of what occurred was a quite conscious attempt at reform, if not revolution, from above and below. The Football Supporters' Association (FSA), the Taylor Report and the FA's *Blueprint for the Future of Football*, to take just three examples, were all part of a conscious attempt at restructuring, refashioning and effectively remaking a game that it was widely agreed had lost much of its commercial and popular appeal. That those driving forward these changes, and those reacting to them, acknowledged their 'revolutionary' character is not without significance. The belief among contemporaries that a dark era in the history of football was ending and a 'new football' coming into being underscores the 'revolutionary' interpretation of these years.[4]

Yet we ought not to get carried away with all the talk of change and revolution. There are in fact already signs of a revisionist approach to the period, with some accounts challenging the completeness of football's structural, economic and cultural transformation and emphasising important elements of continuity between the pre- and post-'revolution' decades.[5] Weaknesses in the orthodox interpretation are being highlighted. One example is the tendency to concentrate on developments in England and Wales and ignore what was going on in Scotland. Whether football north of the border changed along the same lines, and to the same extent, as in the south has not been adequately considered. Similarly neglected is the extent to which changes at the elite level affected grassroots football. From the 1990 World Cup onwards, the professional side of the sport undoubtedly loomed larger than ever in the public mind, but we should be careful not to read the transformation of the highest leagues as a transformation of football as a whole. Furthermore, even among those who have not challenged the notion of a football 'revolution' there is disagreement over whether it has in fact rejuvenated or irreparably damaged the sport.[6] This chapter will focus on issues of gender, race, class and place, among others, in the light of these debates over the degree and nature of change within British football since the mid-1980s.

Hillsborough, the Taylor Report and the Premier League

On 15 April 1989, 96 football supporters were killed at Hillsborough stadium in Sheffield at the beginning of an FA Cup semi-final between Liverpool and Nottingham Forest. As hundreds of Liverpool fans arrived at the Leppings Lane end of the ground, a serious bottleneck developed at the terraces and the police opened an exit gate to relieve the crushing. This decision, and the subsequent failure to direct supporters into the sparsely populated side-pens of the terrace, was to have fatal consequences. With even the narrow gates at the front locked, fans had no means of escape and were crushed to death against the perimeter fence that kept them from the pitch. The police were not only slow to respond to the tragedy unfolding but also initially informed watching FA officials, and by extension the media, that the disturbing scenes they were witnessing were the result of crowd trouble.[7]

What happened at Hillsborough was undoubtedly an important catalyst for change in British football. There are a number of reasons why it had such a profound impact, especially when compared with earlier football disasters. The number dead and injured was not the main one. More people were killed at Hillsborough than at previous disasters at Burnden Park in 1946 and Ibrox Stadium in 1971, but its perceived significance was more to do with the context in which it occurred. First, the public reaction was unprecedented. BBC's popular *Grandstand* programme reported the events from Sheffield live, providing an immediacy that was reinforced by the vivid nature of newspaper accounts over the following days. That many of these reports continued the theme of hooligan responsibility first alleged by senior police officers, but subsequently refuted by Lord Justice Taylor, only served to make the genuine public safety issues when they were uncovered seem more urgent.[8] The event was also followed by an outpouring of public grief that had rarely been associated with football before, demonstrated by the building of shrines of flowers, wreaths and club memorabilia both at Hillsborough and Liverpool's Anfield ground.[9] The second crucial context of Hillsborough was that it not only came soon after the tragedies at Bradford and Heysel but also followed a series of high-profile disasters in the transport and public services. It now joined a list that included the sinking of the *Herald of Free Enterprise* ferry and the King's Cross Underground fire in 1987, the Piper Alpha oil rig explosion and the Clapham rail crash in 1988, as well as the fire at Manchester Airport in 1985 and the Lockerbie plane crash of 1988. Not since the Aberfan landslide of 1966 had catastrophes of this type had such an impact on the public consciousness. Although some denied that there was any common pattern to these disasters, others drew attention to the recurring disregard for public safety, poor emergency procedures and dilapidated facilities outlined in the public inquiries that followed each. For Ian Taylor, this 'disaster theme' was key to understanding Hillsborough as part of a broader failing in English culture exemplified by the authorities' disregard 'for the provision of well-being and security of others'.[10]

Third, the government reacted to Hillsborough in a different way than it had to previous football disasters. In the wake of the events of 1985, and in line with the subsequent Popplewell Report, political discussion had focused on the question of hooliganism rather than safety. The government's chief post-Heysel measure, a proposed national membership scheme requiring all supporters attending English league fixtures to affiliate to a central Football Membership Authority, reflected this assumption that containing the behaviour of fans, rather than ensuring their safety, would resolve the game's problems. It also showed the government's increasing determination to force change on the football authorities instead of relying on the industry to regulate itself. According to Graham Kelly, chief executive of the Football League and then the FA during the 1980s, the Thatcher administration showed little understanding or sympathy for football. He notes how Margaret Thatcher herself 'despised football' and 'drove those around her who were interested in the national game underground'.[11] Football, in this view, was narrowly perceived as a public order 'problem' that could be solved through a regulatory framework designed to control its spectators. The government's determination to press ahead with the membership card scheme in the face of opposition from the football authorities and football supporters was a clear indication that it intended to deal with hooliganism through central regulation and legislation. Anthony King has argued that the resulting Football Spectators' Bill of 1989 was the apotheosis of the Thatcherite preference for strong state control and authoritarianism. Hillsborough only served to increase the regulatory impulse, although the focus changed as the national membership scheme fell out of favour and the physical environment of football grounds was opened up to scrutiny.[12]

Most significantly of all, the impact of Hillsborough was sharpened and reinforced by the subsequent findings and recommendations of the Taylor Report.[13] There was some feeling at the time that the appointment of a judge, Lord Justice Taylor, to lead the official inquiry into

Hillsborough would result in the type of narrowly focused and conservative recommendations that had characterised previous judicial inquiries. Yet what was most remarkable about the Taylor Report when it was published in January 1990 was how broad-minded and radical it was. It dealt with the problems of security and safety at sports grounds but also embraced more fundamental questions about club–fan relations and the governance of the game. What was needed, according to Taylor, was nothing short of 'a new ethos in football': 'Attitudes should be more welcoming. The aim should be to provide more modern and comfortable accommodation, better and more varied facilities, more consultation with the supporters and more positive leadership.' The report made 76 recommendations in total, the vast majority of which were eventually implemented. Most importantly, Taylor required all grounds in the top two divisions of the Football League and the Scottish Premier Division to become all-seated within four seasons (by the beginning of 1994–5). Linked to this, he advised that perimeter fencing should be torn down, a safety officer appointed at each club and a central Football Licensing Authority established to inspect and regulate grounds. Detailed theoretical and practical criticisms of the government's membership scheme also led Taylor to reject it as a solution to hooliganism, which effectively meant that it was never implemented.[14]

While some critics lauded the report as an enlightened response written '*for* football ... and in the name of the football crowd as a whole', it nonetheless elicited considerable opposition from within the football world. The objections of supporters and supporters' organisations were particularly powerful, although they have tended to be downplayed or misunderstood in subsequent accounts. Some of the resistance to the removal of terraces could accurately be dismissed as the nostalgic glorification of a traditional 'terrace culture', which was in reality often typified by racist, sexist and aggressive behaviour.[15] Yet we should not disregard what Vic Duke has called the 'communal tradition' of watching football from the terraces and the sense of sociability and belonging that many gained from it, an experience that, it was argued, could not be replicated by sitting on seats. Moreover, it was perfectly legitimate for supporters to challenge many of the assumptions that underpinned Taylor's recommendations, from the notion that the built environment determined social behaviour (that, in other words, people would act more reasonably in more reasonable surroundings) to the idea that seating was necessarily safer than terracing.[16] Likewise, while some clubs simply resisted change of any kind, others highlighted the financial obstacles that stood in the way of Taylor's plans. Taylor estimated that £130 million would be needed to fund the necessary renovations in England and Wales alone, but it soon became clear that this was a massive underestimation. Money released by the government from betting duty and a levy from 'spot the ball' competitions met some of the costs, which were administered through grants from the Football Trust. But this still represented a small percentage of the money needed by most clubs to implement Taylor's recommendations. The FA had recognised by 1992 that as much as £600 million might be required for clubs in the First Division of the Football League alone. There was criticism of some clubs, particularly the poorer ones, for dragging their feet on the reconstruction and modernisation of grounds, but this often ignored the quite legitimate concerns over where the money was coming from and the real weaknesses in Taylor's scheme for financing change through public funding.[17]

The financial implications of the Taylor Report also fed into existing debates over the structure of the professional game in England and Wales. We need to take a step back at this point and consider the internal politics of football during the 1980s. Particularly important here was the growing assertiveness and power of a handful of elite clubs and their cohering alignment with a network of media and commercial interests. We noted in the last chapter how many of the economic arrangements of British football had been based on a philosophy of equality and mutual support that stressed the importance of the rich clubs looking after, and subsidising, the poor. This was particularly true in the Football League, where from the late nineteenth century until the 1980s administrators had consistently fostered policies of income redistribution and power sharing. Yet this core philosophy was under increasing attack from the so-called 'Big Five' – Arsenal, Everton, Liverpool, Manchester United and Tottenham Hotspur – who argued that the smaller clubs were holding them back and restricting their potential for commercial growth.[18] The objections of these clubs to the representation and voting rights of the Management Committee (the League's executive body) became increasingly vocal during the 1980s. As Maurice Watkins, a director of Manchester United, commented in 1986: 'We are committed ... to retaining the Football League, but the feeling is that there has got to be a restructuring and there has to be a change in the financial side'. With television coverage and sponsorship interest directed almost exclusively at such 'glamour' clubs, it was hardly surprising that, for these clubs, 'the metaphor of the family network ... was giving way to that of the League as Robin Hood'.[19]

Behind the increasingly powerful commercial ethic of the elite clubs was the emergence of a new breed of director. King has dated this precisely to the FA's decision in 1982 to rescind the infamous regulation limiting shareholders' dividends to 7.5 per cent. It was after this, he argues, that entrepreneurial businessmen such as Irving Scholar, Martin Edwards and David Dein established themselves as directors of Tottenham Hotspur, Manchester United and Arsenal respectively. These 'new directors' rejected the 'traditional' view of football as a 'peculiar' business in which the club was run as a public utility rather than a profit-making venture. Football, for these men, was *primarily* a business: their main goal became the 'pursuit of profit through the commodification' of the game. Scholar, a property developer, went furthest in attempting to transform his club into an entrepreneurial enterprise. He employed a strategist from a leading advertising company, Saatchi & Saatchi, to promote the club, diversified into leisurewear through a four-year deal with Hummel and, most significant of all, made Tottenham the first British club to be floated on the Stock Exchange in 1983. Not all Scholar's schemes or those of other entrepreneurial directors proved successful during the 1980s, but such serious attempts to apply a free-market rationale to football marked an important turning point in the game. There is no denying that some directors continued to become involved in football clubs for a range of 'traditional' reasons, including local pride, social standing and a fundamental affection for the game. Yet, as King has convincingly shown, the move towards a new philosophy in the administration of football clubs – marked by the need to turn them into businesses – was increasingly difficult to resist, even for those who remained tied to older styles of management.[20]

The importance of what one historian has called this 'commercial turn' in English football was demonstrated in the growing power base of the elite clubs during the 1980s. On two occasions, in particular, considerable pressure, and the threat of a breakaway 'super league', enabled the elite clubs substantially to increase both their share of the income generated by the Football League and their control over its administrative machinery.[21] The Ten-Point Plan agreed in April 1986 increased the First Division's representation on the Management Committee to four of the nine members, improved their voting power and reduced the majority needed for rule changes from three-quarters to two-thirds. The top division also secured a 50 per cent slice of all television and sponsorship income and a reduction of the League gate levy from 4 per cent to 3 per cent. Two years later, the 'super league' idea re-emerged in the context of ITV's decision to break its cartel with the BBC and negotiate independently with the 'Big Five' clubs and five others for exclusive rights to televise matches of a proposed ten-club breakaway league. A compromise was reached whereby the top clubs accepted an improved 75 per cent share of the £44 million deal eventually agreed with ITV. However, the divisions between rich and poor could no longer be glossed over: as Adrian Goldberg and Stephen Wagg suggested, a '*de facto* financial super league' had been created. The developing schism in the value systems and priorities of Football League clubs had become effectively institutionalised in the recognised notion of the 'Big Five' and the assumption that a breakaway 'super league' would be established at some point in the future. By the end of the 1980s, the League had become 'less a community of interests and more a vehicle for individual advancement by clubs'.[22]

The role of television was crucial in reinforcing the independence of the leading clubs. Much of this was due to its financial input. There is no doubt that the elite clubs were the principal beneficiaries of the television deals of 1986 and 1988. It is estimated that the 'Big Five' received just under a third (£3.5 million of a total £11 million) of the ITV money invested in the Football League in 1988–9. Some writers have identified the formation of an 'informal trading bloc' between ITV and the 'Big Five' after 1988, whereby each club was guaranteed two home and away games (or £390,000 in facility fees) per season. Jeff Foulston, producer of ITV's *The Match*, admitted that there was indeed 'a gentleman's agreement to put the big clubs on television'.[23] The developing relationship between television and the elite clubs had important implications for the organisation and structure, as well as the finances, of English football. It was not insignificant that as early as 1985 the television companies were bypassing the formal decision-making structures and negotiating independently with the elite clubs. David Lacey of *The Guardian* could comment that, in the wake of the proposed ITV-sponsored breakaway of 1988, the most powerful man in English football was now Greg Dyke, ITV's head of programming, who had become 'both paymaster and ringmaster'. By 1991, with the ITV deal soon to run out and revenue desperately needed to meet the requirements of the Taylor Report, there was considerable talk of a new breakaway threat. Yet while the potential of increased income for the larger clubs through a new television deal was undoubtedly an important factor, it would be wrong to assume that it was television alone that brought about the final split that led to the creation of the Premier League.[24]

More significant was the role of the Football Association (FA) and its power struggle with the Football League. In theory, the two bodies had always occupied distinct roles. The FA was the governing body, responsible for all facets of the game, from the grassroots level of junior, local and county associations to professional football. The Football League, meanwhile, administered its own 92-club competition in accordance with, and under the licence of, the FA. Yet in practice the relationship between the two had become muddled and responsibilities blurred. Unlike bodies such as the Italian and French football federations, the FA had only ever been able to exercise partial control over the professional game, which constrained its leadership role within the sport as a whole.[25] In this context, and with Taylor's criticisms of how football was governed loudly echoed by politicians, journalists and academics, the early 1990s witnessed a leadership crisis in the game. Patrick Murphy and his colleagues at Leicester University, for example, argued at the time that the ruling bodies were ill-equipped to deal with the problems confronting them. The professional arm of the sport, in particular, was 'loosely organized', with power tending to move away from the executive at the centre and towards individual clubs. The Football League responded first by publishing its plans for how the game should be restructured under the title *One Game, One Team, One Voice* in October 1990. It proposed the creation of a Joint Board, comprising equal representation from the League and FA, to develop 'a coherent and consistent set of policies ... across all the issues which are of joint concern', such as finance, crowd control, commercial affairs and even the organisation of the England team.[26] But the League's plans for power-sharing were soon set to one side when the FA produced its own *Blueprint for the Future of Football* the following June. The document was premised on the plan for the creation of an FA-controlled Premier League, which, as well as securing increased commercial opportunities for the elite clubs involved, would reaffirm the FA's status as 'the highest parliament in English football' and guarantee the marginalisation of the Football League.[27] The First Division clubs quickly fell into line with the plan and by August 1991 had formally resigned en bloc from the Football League. A year later, they were playing in a new competition, the FA Premier League.

Whether this administrative revolution would have occurred without the intervention of the FA is difficult to tell. The fact that the proposals emanated from the governing body and not the leading clubs certainly gave them a legitimacy that would otherwise have been missing. What is more, because the changes were initially premised on improving the performances of the England team by creating a leaner 18-club elite division, they could be seen as promoting the national game as a whole rather than a small clique of clubs. However, most writers have recognised that after the Taylor Report an elite league based on increased commercial revenue and television exposure was likely to occur in one form or another. Indeed King has convincingly argued that a breakaway was essential after 1990. The way in which Taylor's recommendations were interpreted, in particular, reflected the hegemony of free-market ideas in any discussions over the reform of football. King has identified three strands in this free-market argument: the necessary attrition of any football clubs that were badly managed or economically unviable; the adoption by clubs of proper management and business practices; and a reappraisal of the relationship between clubs and supporters, with fans being treated the same way as customers in any other sector of the leisure industry.[28] Such ideas were fundamental to the FA *Blueprint* and the subsequent formation of the Premier League. The former, in the words of one journalist, envisaged 'top-class football played in luxurious stadiums and watched by upmarket crowds'.[29] According to this new commercial terminology, the 'consumer' had replaced the fan, and the dictates of the modern leisure industry had been substituted for the needs of the local culture. The birth of the Premier League was an important step in this new free-market approach to football, but it was not to be its culmination. In the course of the 1990s the new league was to become the vehicle for a more profound and far-reaching transformation in the consumption of football and its broader cultural profile.[30]

A Scottish revolution?

If most of the discussion on the regeneration of football has centred on England and Wales, this does not mean that Scotland was insulated from these developments. Alan Bairner has argued that here the traditional dominance of city-based clubs had created 'a climate of suspicion and dislike' in which the leading clubs resented the disproportionate influence of the small provincial teams, while the latter, in turn, complained of the arrogance of the former.[31] It is thus hardly surprising that disputes similar to those in the south over management and league structure, voting rights and the allocation of sponsorship and television monies plagued the Scottish Football League during the 1980s. These led to breakaway threats by the leading Premier Division clubs in 1983 and 1986 that were only quelled by a series of significant concessions by the minnows, including a reallocation of pools money, a new voting structure that gave absolute power to the elite clubs, and a decision to move by the 1988–9 season to a one-up one-down system of promotion and relegation between the Premier and the First Divisions. Unlike its English counterpart, the Scottish Football League managed to keep hold of its most ambitious members even if, by mopping up the bulk of the game's extra-curricular revenue and almost sealing themselves off from their weaker brethren, they were increasingly operating like an independent 'super league'.[32]

Significantly, however, despite the success of Aberdeen and Dundee United in the early 1980s, the 'Old Firm' continued to represent an elite within an elite. Indeed, with English clubs banned from European competition after Heysel and a European-wide 'super league' on the agenda more than ever before, there were signs that the two leading Glasgow clubs were beginning to position themselves not in terms of Scottish or even British football but as part of an emerging European elite. Always with an eye on international developments, Rangers, in particular, was at the forefront of the commercial and structural regeneration of the British game from the 1980s. The redesign and rebuilding of Ibrox between 1978 and 1983, funded largely by the club's own pools scheme, already meant that Rangers had the most modern and one of the most impressive stadiums in Britain, with 36,000 of its 45,000 capacity designated for seated spectators and 20,000 feet of office space created to generate additional income. At boardroom level, a more commercial outlook was heralded by the arrival of Lawrence Marlborough, a grandson of former chairman John Lawrence, and his appointment in 1985 of David Holmes as chief executive. Holmes, in turn, appointed the former Scottish and Liverpool midfielder Graeme Souness as player-manager in April 1986. A couple of years later, David Murray, a young Edinburgh-based businessman and friend of Souness, bought out Marlborough's interest in Rangers and replaced Holmes, who had since become chairman. Very much one of the new breed of entrepreneurial directors, Murray continued to modernise the club's commercial operations, diversifying into broadcasting and continuing the redevelopment of Ibrox into a multipurpose leisure facility catering to an increasingly corporate market.[33]

Murray and Souness also attempted to modernise Rangers in its 'ways of thinking'.[34] By signing a number of English players, including high-profile international stars like Chris Woods and Terry Butcher, they temporarily reversed the subordinate status of Scottish football vis-à-vis England, and in so doing, Fynn and Guest argue, 'overturned a century of tradition'.[35] More significantly still, Souness broke the 80-year old club policy prohibiting the buying of Catholic players in 1989 by signing Maurice 'Mo' Johnston, a former Celtic employee who had been widely expected to return to Parkhead. The move upset some supporters of both clubs, but many more seem to have accepted that sectarian 'traditions' of this type were incompatible with Rangers' emerging commercial and European ambitions. Both the club and the press justified the signing by emphasising the importance of attracting big business and multinational sponsors, who would not, it was argued, want to be associated with the club's outdated sectarian image. The Glasgow *Evening News* ran the story under the headline 'WHY IT HAD TO HAPPEN: SECTARIANISM HAS NO PLACE IN THE EUROPEAN SUPER LEAGUE' and censured those supporters against the signing for 'looking backwards, at a time when Rangers must look forwards'.[36] H. F. Moorhouse has argued that the relatively muted reaction to the Johnston signing reflected an increasingly cosmopolitan and 'modern' Glasgow that had little in common with the mythical view of 'warring communities' in a 'divided city' so beloved of the media and a number of academics. While stopping short of arguing that Rangers was in the process of losing its Protestant identity or that sectarianism had become an irrelevant factor either in Scottish football or society more generally, Moorhouse was nonetheless convinced that Rangers was emerging as the exemplar of the 'new soccer world' of the early 1990s, defined by entrepreneurial chairmen, stadium reconstruction, commercial interests, big business and European markets.[37]

The Rangers 'revolution' took some time to impact upon the rest of Scottish football. Celtic, notably, was left behind by its rival in the boardroom and on the field of play. Controlled by members of the same three families that had effectively owned the club for decades, the club resisted pleas both to match Rangers' high spending on non-Scottish players and to open up the directorate to new blood and new money. It won the League and Cup double in its centenary season of 1987–8, but thereafter was overshadowed by its resurgent 'Old Firm' rival, which began to accumulate the first of nine consecutive titles to match the achievement of Celtic 20 years earlier. It was only after a lengthy boardroom battle, and the orchestrated protest of supporter groups, that the families were removed and a new millionaire owner, Fergus McCann, a Canadian citizen but lifelong Celtic supporter, gained control in 1994. Bill Murray has, rather awkwardly, likened the events at Celtic to the French and Russian Revolutions, with the 'families' representing the ruling class, determined to protect their right to rule and defend the 'soul' of Celtic against the forces of progression and liberalism represented by McCann and 'the people'. In this reading, the old regime was swept away after a bitter 'civil war' and replaced by a new leadership intent upon complete transformation of the club's administrative and ideological structure. Moorhouse has similarly portrayed the Celtic of the early 1990s as reflective of an older, 'pre-modern' Glasgow bound by traditional notions of loyalty and community, at a time when Rangers was successfully projecting a more modern image of itself as the progressive representative of Scotland in Europe.[38] Yet Raymond Boyle has challenged these interpretations, arguing that they set up a 'false dichotomy' between tradition, on one hand, and modernisation on the other. In certain respects, he argues, the two were closely linked. Supporters of Celtic, in particular, were not as backward as those who ran the club and were conscious of the commercial potential in harnessing, rather than downplaying, the club's distinctive Irish-Catholic identity and marketing Celtic on 'its sense of difference' rather than as 'another bland football club'.[39]

Outside the 'Old Firm', resistance to 'modernisation' was strong. Wallace Mercer's attempt in 1990 to create an amalgamated 'Edinburgh United' through his own club, Hearts, taking over its city rival Hibernian showed the obstacles that free-trade arguments faced when set against claims of club identity and tradition. Mercer's idea of combining the resources and support base of the two clubs by creating a 'superclub' capable of representing the capital city and the surrounding region in a future European league was based entirely on an appeal to financial logic and reason. Amalgamation would give Edinburgh a club capable of reaching European-standard criteria on 'quality of stadia, size of supporting population catchment, financial strength and management'.[40] Yet opponents of the scheme stressed that it would devastate the established loyalties and identities on which football in Edinburgh was based. A document published by the owners of Hibernian defended the status quo through an emphasis on passion and emotion and the inclusion of pictures of the successful teams of the 1920s and 1950s, while supporters of both clubs argued that the scheme ignored the ethnic and sectarian divide between the two. In response to Mercer's claim that 'the eradication of the tribalistic element in Edinburgh football' would attract 'new corporate customers', a solicitor and Hearts shareholder answered that 'whether he [Mercer] likes it or not, football is a form of tribalism. The two clubs quite literally live off each other.' Mercer claimed that he had won 'the business argument' but lost 'the social argument' and in the end Hibernian was saved by the financial intervention of a group of Catholic entrepreneurs intent on ensuring that Edinburgh retained two clubs 'in the interests of the city's community'.[41] Scottish football was also lauded (mistakenly, according to certain accounts) in the Taylor Report for the modernisation of some of its grounds, particularly Ibrox, but also the more modest all-seater venues of Aberdeen's Pittodrie, Clydebank's New Kilbowie Park and St Johnstone's recently built McDiarmid Park. But this alone hardly represented a revolution in the Scottish game. Indeed the vast majority of Scottish clubs faced the same financial dilemmas as their English and Welsh counterparts in a post-Taylor era in which the modernisation agenda continued to clash with a football culture still rooted in notions of history, tradition and local identity.[42]

Place and space

Most football clubs come from, and represent, a specific place. We saw in previous chapters how some of the earliest organised clubs were linked to social institutions, but many more became attached to, and took their name from, streets, communities or districts in the expanding towns and cities of late nineteenth-century Britain. Moving into regional and then national competition, the most successful teams carried the name of their place of foundation with them and represented their locality on a broader geographical stage. As the decades passed, there was a remarkable continuity in the connection between football and place in Britain. Not only did the vast majority of professional clubs retain their original names and stay in the same area, most spent the bulk of the twentieth century in exactly the same location. Indeed, as many as 70 of the 92 Premier League and Football League clubs during the 1992–3 season had been situated at their present ground since before the First World War. No more than a handful had relocated since the Second World War and only three English and one Scottish club – Scunthorpe United (1988), St Johnstone (1989), Walsall (1990) and Chester City (1992) – had moved home in the previous decade.[43] This could be contrasted with US professional sports such as baseball and football, whose teams frequently moved at the intra-urban level, from the inner cities to the suburbs, and at the inter-urban level, from one city to another. In baseball, for example, owners relocated their teams (or franchises) from one part of the country to another on no less than 11 occasions between 1953 and 1972. Between 1970 and 1990, 15 sports franchises moved to new sites and many more secured better stadiums from local municipal authorities by threatening to leave. Such dramatic shifts in location reflect the fundamental distinction between sports teams in the USA, which as *franchises* are the property of the owner and the respective league, and football *clubs* in Britain (and Europe more generally), which have tended to retain their autonomy and their close links with the communities from which they originally emerged.[44]

Football has thus always been considered important in providing a sense of pride in place. John Bale has highlighted the role of the game as a vehicle for place-bonding, whereby 'insiders' identify with their local club, and place-boosting, a similar identification or recognition among 'outsiders'.[45] Through the former, people are bonded or brought together in support of their place, sentiments that are heightened when the club representing that place is particularly successful. Football thus helps to tighten the bonds of loyalty and attachment to place and enhance its self-image. Through the latter, football allows the profile of a place to be projected outwards and promoted beyond the locality and the region. It is difficult to imagine anything comparable that exists 'to project a place-name to a national audience each week', which is why civic leaders and politicians put so much time and effort into gaining membership of, or avoiding demotion from, the top leagues.[46] The few studies conducted on the subject tend to support these assumptions. Research on the reaction to Sunderland's unexpected 1973 FA Cup final victory over Leeds United showed that productivity in the city increased and feelings of place-pride were enhanced: according to one resident, 'a not particularly glamorous town feels more proud of itself after a win of this sort'.[47] A study by Euan Hague and John Mercer focused on the 'geographical memories' associated with Raith Rovers and the small town of Kirkcaldy in Fife. They found not only that the local club acted as an important reference point for deeper memories of family and life in the town but also that for some respondents Raith Rovers was 'the prime *geographical* text of Kirkcaldy'.[48] Interviewees continually referred to Raith Rovers putting Kirkcaldy 'on the map', particularly in the wake of the club's Coca-Cola Cup victory over Celtic in 1995 and its short run in the UEFA Cup the following season. Hague and Mercer also showed how stories about the club were shared by supporters and passed down the generations, reflecting how, in the words of another writer, the idea of the club 'as a metaphor for pride in the working-class community' could become 'deeply embedded in the identities of football fans'.[49]

It has tended to be the ground itself on which the most significant place-related meanings and emotions have focused. Writing in the late 1960s, the journalist Arthur Hopcraft recognised the appeal of these 'cavernous and stark' grounds to those who visited them regularly: 'Football grounds are not often attractive places in the ornamental sense. Their beauty is the special, environmental kind, appreciable only to people who relate the setting to their emotional attachment.'[50] A number of academic studies have developed this link between football, place and the emotions. David Canter, Miriam Comber and David Uzzell, for example, applied the skills of the environmental psychologist to football, recognising the powerful meanings that people attach to their surroundings and the symbolic significance of grounds for spectators. They found that the ground was 'one of the most important physical symbols of a club ... The social history of the club is embedded in and complemented by the grounds.'[51] Richard Giulianotti has outlined the way in which the football ground 'evokes memories and excites anticipation' and how the individual and idiosyncratic features of the pitch, stands and surrounding landscape signify each ground's 'special status relative to other stadia'. As such, he argues that grounds 'possess their own socio-geographical character, emblematic of the fans' community', even if that 'community' is dispersed spatially and some members retain an emotional attachment from a distance.[52] Ian Taylor, meanwhile, saw the football ground as 'an emblem of identity', particularly in towns and cities with no other outstanding architectural features. For the working people of Sheffield, for instance, Hillsborough, ironically one of the most modern and impressive sporting stadiums in Britain before the 1989 disaster, had been 'the symbol of the city's local pride'.[53]

Topophilia and topophobia

Most influential of all has been the work of Bale, who in a series of articles and books has outlined how football grounds can become a source of 'topophilia', or love of place. To illustrate the various ways in which the British football ground could foster topophilia, Bale used five key metaphors.[54] First, the stadium is a 'sacred place', analogous to a temple or a cathedral. On a match day at least, it is awash with ritual and ceremony and the quasi-religious worship of the team by its 'congregation'. Those who see football as a surrogate religion have made much of this spiritual dimension, emphasising particularly the way in which stadiums have at times (such as post-Hillsborough or after the death of Chelsea director Matthew Harding in 1996) become shrines where supporters gather to pay their respects to the deceased.[55] Second, the stadium is a 'scenic place' that can provide players and supporters alike with visual pleasure and gratification, a feeling that is heightened by the distinctiveness of the ground and 'the visual connection between the stadium and the town'.[56] More recently, Bale has extended this metaphor to incorporate the affection people feel for the sound and smell of stadiums and other 'sportscapes'.[57] Third, many football spectators maintain similar bonds of affection with the stadium of the team they support as with their own home. Not only does the notion of the ground as 'home' provide acknowledged psychological advantages over 'visiting' teams and supporters but, as we shall see later, it can elicit powerful emotional reactions from supporters when the decision is made to move to another 'home'. Fourth, the stadium is a 'tourist place', a heritage site or a museum, literally in an increasing number of cases, where visitors can connect with the club's history and traditions through touring the ground or looking at material artefacts of the past. Finally, the stadium is important in engendering the type of local pride and patriotism that we discussed earlier. The football club, in Bale's words, became over the years 'a focus for community bonding and the source of "reconstruction" of some former *Gemeinschaft*'.[58] And at the heart of the club's relationship with the local community, as Taylor argued, was and is the stadium.

The most significant form of topophilia floated by Bale is the notion of the stadium as home. There is no shortage of supporting examples from academic and popular writing. Hague and Mercer have shown how Raith Rovers' Stark's Park ground became a 'home' to spectators who attended matches for decades – one of their respondents in 1995 had been visiting the ground since 1918, and another since 1950 – and bred comforting feelings of 'rootedness' and security among supporters.[59] Søren Nagbøl, a Danish academic, articulated similar sentiments when he visited his first English football ground, Crewe Alexandra's Gresty Road, in 1992:

Those who are from Crewe, and support the home team, can take their usual places, the places where they have come year after year, generation after generation. A world that is as it has always been, where people have been able to leave their own mark on memories. In this stadium, memories from decades of local games surface every time those who have influenced the place are gathered there. The sense of familiarity and the set of memories have been jointly created. They belong to the place as their legacy to each other. Innumerable visits and meetings with friends have left their traces, marks of security and stability ... Here you know your place, you have, so to speak, grown up here.[60]

Some fans have been so attached emotionally to the ground that they considered it more significant than the team itself. As one Manchester City supporter told Bale:

I have been a supporter since birth, well, since my parents first took me when I was around two years old. Since that time my interest has revolved more around the stadium than the team. Of course, I support the team through and through, but to me the club is Maine Road as that is the only part of the club that rarely changes. Managers, players, directors, and even supporters come and go but the stadium never disappears.[61]

Martin Lacey, a lifelong supporter of Southern League Wealdstone, has recalled his reaction when the club was forced in the early 1990s to play its matches at the ground of nearby Watford: 'I continued to watch Wealdstone at Watford … but the soul had been ripped out of the club … To me, Wealdstone was Lower Mead and Lower Mead was Wealdstone. The club I loved is dead.'[62]

Such feelings were invariably intensified when a club moved or threatened to move. The classic example of this was the saga involving Charlton Athletic's move away from its ground, The Valley, and the activism of supporters in securing its return.[63] When Charlton's directors announced that from the 1985–6 season the club would share Crystal Palace's Selhurst Park ground 7 miles away, the affection felt by some supporters was articulated in the *Voice of the Valley* fanzine. It may just have been a case of a football club leaving its ground, but 'to many, many people it was so much more. For the older fans it was the destruction of something that had run like a thread through their lives.'[64] The local paper started a campaign called 'Our home is The Valley' and collected some 15,000 signatures in support of a return 'home'. When it was first announced in 1989 that the club planned to play again at The Valley, the fanzine's editor explained the strength of feeling:

We know that there are people who argue that they support the team and not the ground but they miss the point. The two cannot be separated without compromising the club's identity. Do that and you lose the deep emotional hold that even today football clubs exert over their supporters. Now, in the nick of time, the soul of Charlton Athletic will be recovered.[65]

When the club finally returned to The Valley in 1992, after seven years away at Selhurst Park and then West Ham United's Upton Park, and a long campaign that even involved the fans fielding candidates in local council elections, the *Voice of the Valley* celebrated with the front-page headline 'LET'S GO HOME!'[66] Raith Rovers supporters expressed similar feelings when a move away from Stark's Park to a nearby town was mooted in the early 1990s: 'Even if they moved to Glenrothes [and were] still called Raith Rovers, it would be a disaster. You can't take a team away from its roots.'[67] And when the Luton Town board suggested a move from Kenilworth Road to a new stadium 20 miles north in Milton Keynes, there was an outcry from those who accused the directors of 'tearing the club from its most loyal supporters'. In both cases, the planned relocations were shelved. Such reactions confirm, for Bale, the strength of the identification and attachment to place felt among at least the most committed football supporters, and the way in which passive forms of topophilia could be converted into more active expressions of love of place manifest in the resistance to ground relocation.[68]

Despite the emphasis on topophilia, however, Bale's work also concentrated on the way in which football grounds could be regarded as 'landscapes of fear' or sources of 'topophobia'. The same experiences, images and memories that might have positive meanings for some, he argued, could easily have negative connotations and 'create hostility' in others.[69] As far as spectators themselves were concerned, two studies conducted in the late 1980s revealed that a significant percentage had identified football grounds at one time or another with feelings of fear or danger. A project conducted by Leicester University's Sir Norman Chester Centre for Football Research (SNCCFR) found that more than half of the members of supporters' clubs sampled felt threatened at matches, especially at grounds associated with crowd trouble, such as Chelsea's Stamford Bridge and Liverpool's Anfield. Canter et al., meanwhile, discovered that over a third of the fans surveyed at nine English and one Scottish club were worried for their safety while going to and from, or during, a match. At all but one club, at least one in four respondents recorded being worried; at Coventry City as many as two-thirds did. Most reported incidents of violence by fans, but others recounted being crushed by crowds or mounted police.[70] Perhaps more significant, however, were the concerns of those local residents who, far from considering themselves 'represented' by the club and emotionally attached to the ground, regarded football more as a nuisance to their everyday lives. Responses from interviews with people living within 1¼ miles of 37 Football League grounds in 1989 revealed that 41 per cent thought football created a nuisance, with most of the complaints concerning issues relating to parking and traffic rather than more serious matters such as hooliganism. Some resident groups, meanwhile, mounted successful campaigns to prevent the potential nuisance that would result from stadium relocation close to where they lived. In Oxford, Bristol and Portsmouth, residents who opposed plans to build new grounds in suburban sites appealed to specific notions of 'community'. Rejecting the club's claim that a new stadium for Bristol Rovers would benefit the city as a whole, residents close to the site complained that it signified for them increased disorder, traffic problems, noise, litter and a negative impact on the value of property.[71]

The relocation and redevelopment of grounds

Notions of topophilia and topophobia were to prove especially important in the post-Taylor Report era of ground rebuilding and relocation. At the beginning of the 1990s clubs faced three main options if they were to fulfil the all-seater demand of the Report: they could redevelop the existing ground, relocate to a new one, or ground share with another club. At first, relocation seemed the most cost-effective option for many. A town planning survey from 1990 reported that 42 Football League clubs were considering relocation, while 37 intended to redevelop in situ. Plans for relocation were driven forward by what Duke has termed 'the supermarket imperative'. Many grounds were located in inner-city sites, crammed in by surrounding streets, and had poor parking and transport access. They may therefore have been in the wrong place for modern football, as some critics claimed, but they were in exactly the right place for supermarket chains eager to acquire prime plots of urban land.[72] The idea of selling the ground to a supermarket or property developer to fund the move to a new stadium on the outskirts

TABLE 6.1 *English stadium relocations as part of the post-Taylor Report initiative, 1992–8*

Club	Stadium	Year
Chester City	Deva Stadium	1992
Millwall	New Den	1993
Northampton Town	Sixfields Stadium	1994
Huddersfield Town	McAlpine Stadium	1995
Middlesbrough	Riverside Stadium	1995
Derby County	Pride Park Stadium	1997
Sunderland	Stadium of Light	1997
Bolton Wanderers	Reebok Stadium	1997
Stoke City	Britannia Stadium	1997
Reading	Madejski Stadium	1998

Source: Adapted from Sir Norman Chester Centre for Football Research, 'Fact Sheet Number 2: Football Stadia After Taylor' (Leicester: Sir Norman Chester Centre for Football Research, 2002), p. 14.

of the town or city thus seemed a popular solution initially, but the objections of local residents and the planning authorities meant that only a small number of clubs took this option (see Table 6.1). The most common solution was to modernise the stadium where it stood. Between 1991 and 1997, over £500 million was spent by British clubs on ground improvements or new stadiums. In Williams's words, this represented 'an extraordinary national rebuilding programme', completely transforming the physical environment in which professional football was played and watched.[73] It meant significantly reduced capacities at most grounds and the destruction of the most famous (and notorious) parts of many, such as the Kop at Liverpool, the 'Jungle' at Celtic and the North Bank at Arsenal.

Supporters and commentators were initially less than impressed by these developments. Duke analysed the reactions of supporters, mediated through club fanzines, to the first 'new wave' English grounds: Scunthorpe United's Glanford Park and Walsall's Bescot Stadium. The comments tended to be negative, with criticisms of the poor view, uninspired architecture and overall lack of character. Duke also compared photographs of the old and new grounds, concluding that while the mixture of styles and structures had made the former 'a unique home for the supporters', the latter were 'functional but soulless . . . they both look the same and further clones may well ensue'.[74] Nagbøl described the new Walsall ground as 'a neutral place . . . a football stadium in no-man's land. A package solution stadium where everything except football has been considered.'[75] Similar criticisms were made of many of the rebuilt all-seated grounds. One Newcastle United supporter wrote in the leading national fanzine, *When Saturday Comes*, of his disappointment at the lack of 'atmosphere' at the reconstructed St James's Park. With the terraces had gone the noise, wit and commitment of fans. Seated fans, he argued, were 'alienated from the action' and less able to contribute to the spectacle of the game: 'Yes, goals are celebrated, but not in the same ape-shit way. You stand, then applaud a bit, as if in appreciation of a good performance at the ballet.'[76] A national survey of members of the Football Supporters' Association (FSA) in 1989 revealed 69.3 per cent opposed to seating at their own ground, while 93 per cent of the readers of Millwall's *The Lion Roars* fanzine believed they should retain 'the right to stand'. Bale is thus surely right to note a 'preference for the traditional English ground' and an opposition to all-seater stadiums among fanzine writers and activist supporters, even if we accept that these groups were hardly representative of football supporters in general.[77]

PLATE 20 *The new North Stand at Arsenal's Highbury stadium during redevelopment in the 1990s (© Popperfoto.com).*

But opposition to change was far from universal. Boyd Hilton, an Arsenal fan, put much of the resistance to the destruction of the old terraces down to sentimentality, and applauded the new all-seated Highbury as 'an opportunity to make [the fans'] home as pleasant, comfortable and appealing as possible'.[78] Such views seem to have become increasingly widespread. While *When Saturday Comes*' own survey of readers in 1991 revealed that 80 per cent were 'against all-seater stadiums', a similar survey in 1994 showed that a majority (albeit a small one of 55 per cent) approved of the structural changes made to grounds in general and 80 per cent endorsed the modernisation of facilities at their own clubs. Indeed, similar endorsements of the modernised grounds of Aberdeen and Rangers in the 1980s seemed to show that 'people come to accept seating'.[79] Moreover, relocation and the building of new stadiums at clubs such as Middlesbrough, Bolton Wanderers and Sunderland (Table 6.1) tended to be interpreted positively by supporters as a sign of the club's ambitions and aspirations. While far from conclusive, by the late 1990s research showed that most supporters were 'reasonably happy' with the development of stadiums over the previous decade, even if there were still concerns about high ticket prices and the loss of atmosphere in all-seated grounds.[80]

Academics tended not to be so optimistic about what two of them have called the 'traditional "topophilic" triangle' connecting the club, the ground and the surrounding community.[81] Underpinning much of Bale's work is the suggestion that space is likely to become more important than place in football's future. His concern that modern stadiums would evolve into 'dehumanised landscapes' which, though safe and comfortable, could be 'inauthentic', 'placeless' and 'Disney-fied', was echoed elsewhere.[82] In an assessment of the staging of the 1994 World Cup in the USA, Williams and Giulianotti posited that the 'concrete bowl' architecture of venues like the Foxboro Stadium in Boston, located 30 miles out of town and 'detached' from any supporting network or community, offered 'little of the historical purchase of "place" of the kind more regularly associated with sport in Europe'. Yet in the post-Taylor environment, there was a genuine fear that the US model of sport might become increasingly influential in Britain, leading to football played in 'soulless, "American style", "production line" concrete bowls in front of passive and affluent "consumers" or customers (not supporters)'.[83] The sports economist and historian Wray Vamplew expressed similar concerns in an economic impact report he wrote for Newcastle United in 1997 on its options in either redeveloping the facilities close to St James's Park or moving to a new out-of-town site. Supporting the former, he argued that it was important that the club stayed physically close to the scene of its past glories at the heart of the city rather than moving to 'some soulless suburban bowl'. 'Traditions do matter', Vamplew argued, 'and they should not be set aside as of little consequence. A move to another site would not be the same. Something irreplaceable would be lost.'[84] In this view, relocation meant the severing of the emotional connection of the supporter with place and the devaluing of topophilia.

The redevelopment of grounds also raised broader concerns about the social control of football supporters. A number of writers have argued that with the introduction of all-seater stadiums, supporters became subject to increasing levels of containment, control and discipline.[85] Organised in numbered rows and designated seats, there is an order to the seated stadium that, it is argued, inevitably has an effect on the way crowds behave. Seats serve not only as physical impediments to the spontaneous swaying and rushing of bodies common on the terraces, but also act as a moral inducement to sit still, contain one's behaviour and not disrupt the experience of others. The theoretical approach of French social theorist Michel Foucault has proved particularly useful in this respect.[86] His concept of the 'gaze' has been applied to explain how sports spectators have found themselves distanced from the game in modern stadiums. While most grounds have been rebuilt to provide the spectator with a better view of the action, this has coincided with a more withdrawn and reactive form of spectatorship. The passive viewer has replaced the participating fan, previously as essential a part of the spectacle of the match as the players themselves. In this view, football 'becomes less a process to interact with, and more an event at which to gaze'.[87] As one Millwall supporter commented, the club's new stadium had 'sanitized the experience of supporting Millwall. Rather than moaning and cussing in the comfortably grubby surroundings, people tend to sit in their plastic seats and drift off if the game isn't up to much.' Similar views were expressed by the Manchester United fans interviewed by King: 'When it was all paddocks, it was all crushed in and everyone was swaying about and jumping about, and waving their fist at the opposition over the fence and all that. Now, it's not the same at all, it's almost like going to the cinema'.[88] Moreover, the modern football stadium allows the authorities to control and regulate the crowd as never before through the introduction of family enclosures or ends but, more significantly, via surveillance techniques such as CCTV. Like prisons and other buildings that adopted a 'panopticon' form of surveillance, stadiums have become arenas in which individuals are perpetually monitored and, as a result of their awareness of being watched, regulate their own behaviour (and that of those around them) accordingly.

Such views have not been left unchallenged, however. Garry Crawford, for example, has accused Bale and other writers of romanticising the experience of the 'traditional' football supporter, leading to a nostalgic preference for football grounds of the pre-Taylor Report period. What is more, he argues that while certain forms of behaviour have undoubtedly been regulated and stifled within modern stadiums, methods of surveillance and social control have also created 'a safe environment where people feel free to celebrate and be entertained'.[89] Crawford is surely right to draw attention to this tendency to embrace the notion of topophilia wholeheartedly and downplay the numerous topophobic experiences associated with visiting football grounds before the 1990s. He is also correct to note that not all football spectators have become docile and pacified in this environment and that not all modern stadiums offer the type of 'sanitised' versions of the football 'experience' identified by Bale.[90] It is to the various, and often complex, ways in which the changes to the game during the 1990s affected supporters, and how supporters dealt with these changes, that we now turn.

Fans and fandom

In no respect did football seem to change more than in the character and composition of its audience. The orthodox view is that the emergence of the new business-oriented, commercial model of football, buoyed by the popularity of the 1990 World Cup and the injection of money from satellite television, effectively transformed spectatorship during the 1990s. Changes in the way football was consumed heralded the arrival of a new socially diverse football audience alongside, and sometimes in place of, the predominantly working-class men who had supposedly constituted the game's core support. Adorned in club merchandise and unversed in traditional styles of support, these were 'promiscuous consumers' willing to take their place in the new all-seater stadiums and acquiesce to the free-market strategy of the new directors.[91] Writers often expressed this in terms of a dichotomy between 'authentic' and 'inauthentic' forms of support, the former generally identified as loyal, local and anti-commercial, the latter as fickle, non-local and consumerist. Indeed for many, the main story of British football in the 1990s involved the attempts of 'authentic' supporters to resist the forces of business and commodification and thus protect the 'soul' of the 'people's game'.[92] Yet while such debates over the 'ownership' of football and attempts to democratise the game were undeniably important, they hardly represented the totality of fan experiences. As we noted in Chapter 3, football has always been 'followed' or 'consumed' in a variety of ways, not all of which involve live attendance or even commitment to a particular team. We therefore need to look beyond the most active supporters involved in fanzines or fan organisations, and the relatively limited number who regularly attended live matches, to focus also on those who connected with football in a seemingly more mundane but equally meaningful way through purchasing merchandise, watching television, browsing websites and so on.[93]

There have been a number of attempts to categorise different types of football supporter and their relationship to the game. The most straightforward of these have drawn on the aforementioned distinctions between 'older' and 'newer' fans and their respective 'authentic' and 'inauthentic' modes of support. Giulianotti, for example, has talked about the emergence of what he calls the 'post-fan' in this post-modern era. Post-fans are characterised here by a critical and ironic attitude towards those who control football and, as such, are often at the forefront of supporter move-ments and fanzines directed against the club and its directors. They tend to be better educated than other supporters, middle class in background and employed in sales, marketing, the media and other 'knowledge' indus-tries. There is no suggestion here that the 'traditional' fan was displaced but rather that the post-fan emerged alongside them as 'a new and critical kind of football spectator', helping to define the game's changing class identity in the 1990s.[94] Steve Redhead, meanwhile, uses the term 'post-fandom' in a slightly different way, relating it to the privatisation, marketisation and increasing regulation of football culture since 1990. The post-fan experiences the game by watching on television at home or in public bars as much as at the stadium. Redhead had no doubt that, though the two always coexisted to some extent, the predominantly terrace culture of 'fandom' had now been replaced by the more self-con-scious, reflexive culture of post-fandom.[95]

Less elusive are the three main fan groups sketched out by King: 'the lads', the 'new football writing' and the 'new consumer fans'. The lads were young working-class males characterised by a distinctive masculine type of support based on drinking, singing and casual styles of dress. They in turn were distinguished by King, and distinguished themselves, from the somewhat inelegantly named new football writing group, members of the educated, professional middle classes who produced and consumed the fanzines and emerging football literature of the period. The final group, the new consumer fans, included long-standing supporters, family groups and teenage girls, bound together, in King's view, by their general approval of the commercial transformation of football. This attitude was displayed most clearly by the tendency to wear the club shirt and other official merchandise. Although based on interviews with supporters of just one club (Manchester United) during a specific period (the early to mid-1990s), the categories have a wider applicability, demonstrating the perspectives and strategies adopted by different groups in response to the perceived commodification of the game.[96]

More recently, Giulianotti has built upon his notion of the post-fan by outlining a more detailed taxonomy of spectator identities (see Figure 6.1). In this view, spectators can be classified into four ideal-type cat-egories – supporter, fan, follower and flâneur – based on the fundamental oppositions represented by the traditional–consumer and the hot–cool axes. The traditional–consumer axis is based on a spectator's personal investment in a club, ranging from the long-term, localised commitment of the traditional spectator to the market-centred relationship of the

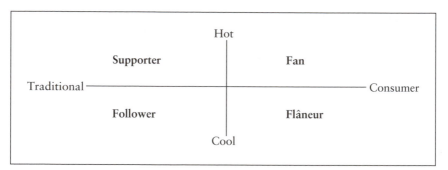

FIGURE 6.1 *Spectator categories (simplified)*
Source: Stephen Morrow, The People's Game: Football, Finance and Society *(Basingstoke: Palgrave, 2003), p. 85 (figure 3.1); an adaptation of Richard Giulianotti's spectator categories in 'Supporters, Followers, Fans and* Flâneurs: A Taxonomy of Spectator Identities in Football', *Journal of Sport and Social Issues, 26, 1 (February 2002), p. 31 (figure 1).*

consumer. The hot–cool axis, meanwhile, represents the role of the club in the self-identity and self-formation of the spectator. Hot loyalties involve intense emotional solidarity and identification, while cool loyalties denote detachment and transience. Giulianotti suggests that the general trend among football spectators is away from the supporter, with their close emotional attachment to, and investment in, the club and its ground, and towards the flâneur, who has little or no connection with specific clubs or the game's broader culture but instead engages with football through 'a depersonalized set of market-dominated virtual relationships', interacting particularly with the 'cool media' of television and the Internet.[97]

What both King and Giulianotti's models show is that the complexity and diversity of football fandom in the 1990s can never be satisfactorily grasped by a simplistic division between the old and new or the supporter and the consumer. In this as in other periods, the football crowd was not a monolithic group. Supporters reacted to changes in the game in a variety of ways, often expressed by writers in terms of resistance or compliance. Yet it is significant that change was also negotiated and adapted by supporters, who were often successful in remaking and reinventing the culture of fandom, and what it meant to be a fan, on their own terms. The remainder of this section will focus in more detail on the ways in which the commodification of football impacted upon fans, leading to the various forms of resistance, compliance and negotiation identified by King and others.[98]

New football, new fans?

Most analyses of British football during the 1990s proceed from the assumption that the social constituency of the game was radically altered. Within a few years of the Hillsborough disaster, Holt and Mason suggest, football managed to acquire 'a new "classless" (i.e. more middle class) following'.[99] What had once been 'the working man's theatre' quickly became, in many people's eyes, a form of middle-class entertainment.[100] We know that the roots of this 'embourgeoisification' of football stretched a long way back. Some historians have traced it to the 1930s (see Chapter 3), while sociologists have identified similar developments in the post-war years. Taylor, for instance, noted how even before the 1970s football clubs had been forced to adapt to their role in a competitive entertainment industry by marginalising the working-class supporter and appealing to a middle-class clientele. The game was thus opened up to the bourgeoisie, with even academics and serious journalists becoming interested in it: what had previously been a characteristically working-class occasion 'was legitimised for the middle class'.[101] Building on Taylor's ideas, Chas Critcher wrote of the emergence of the customer and consumer at the expense of the established supporter, who had always regarded themself, 'however illusorily', as a genuine 'member' of the club.[102] Another writer went further, arguing in 1973 that the image of the traditional fan – 'the dedicated team supporter, done up in striped scarf and woolly hat, and waving a rattle' – was already 'about ten years out of date'. They had been replaced, it was argued, by a new more affluent and discriminating supporter who 'can take his choice of the games he will go and see out of a variety of entertainment on offer any Saturday afternoon [sic]'.[103]

Notwithstanding these earlier signs of change, the beginning of the 1990s still stands as the key moment in the broadening of football's social complexion. The first World Cup of the decade, Italia '90, was crucial in this respect, although its significance in remaking football's public image is usually asserted rather than demonstrated.[104] Some of its impact was certainly due to the fact that the England team performed well, reaching the semi-finals before losing to West Germany in a penalty shoot-out. It was also important that the England midfielder Paul Gascoigne (or 'Gazza' as he was affectionately known) emerged as one of the star players of the tournament. But most significant was the way in which Italia '90 was represented by the media and experienced as a television event. The BBC's decision to link football with 'high' culture through the use of Pavarotti's rendition of Puccini's 'Nessun dorma' aria as the theme tune of its coverage was a conscious attempt, some have argued, to appeal to those social groups who had previously shown little interest in the game. The BBC's success in attracting a new audience to football was underlined by the broadsheet press, which reported on the interest shown in the World Cup at charity balls and metropolitan dinner parties, and in so doing further underlined football's appeal to a wider market. A television audience of 25.2 million (the largest ever in the UK at the time) watched the semi-final and witnessed the defining moment of the competition when Gascoigne, having been booked for a rash challenge on a German opponent, realised that he would miss the final if England qualified and struggled to hold back his tears. The image of Gazza's tears was to have resonance beyond the world of sport: it became a 'human interest' story, prompting discussion about the emotional shortcomings of males, the nature of English patriotism and the like. A television documentary was even commissioned by Channel 4 on men who cry in public.[105] For this reason, Gascoigne became a central figure in what has been called the 'repackaging myth in English football', in which the game acquired a new range of associations with skill, technicality, sophistication and cosmopolitanism to replace its existing link in the public mind with unimaginative styles of play, crowd violence and dilapidated grounds. Italia '90 was thus crucial to the cultural rebranding of football, connecting the high-brow with the popular and opening the game up to a much wider market than had previously been imagined.[106]

Football's new respectability was consolidated by the publication in 1992 of Nick Hornby's *Fever Pitch*.[107] An autobiographical account of Hornby's obsessive support for Arsenal since the age of 11, *Fever Pitch* soon became a best-seller, was made into a stage play and a film and influenced a range of similar, and often derivative, writing. There is no doubt that the book has become emblematic of football's cultural rehabilitation. Hornby and *Fever Pitch* are often linked to what one writer has called the 'literaturisation of soccer' and the development of the so-called *soccerati*, a group of writers who aimed to provide serious literary expression for their fascination with football and its meanings.[108] In 1993, Hornby published an edited anthology of 'new football writing' called *My Favourite Year*, with contributors reflecting on the ups and downs of supporting their favoured clubs and national teams. *The Observer* proclaimed it as heralding 'the emergence of a new class of soccer fan – cultured and discerning'.[109] A few years later the *Financial Times* journalist Simon Kuper (author of an influential and widely read soccer travel book, *Football Against the Enemy*) launched *Perfect Pitch*, a shortlived football-themed literary periodical. Its first number included essays by the poet Dannie Abse and the novelist D. J. Taylor alongside a contribution from the former Argentinian international Jorge Valdano. Hornby, a Cambridge graduate from a comfortable suburban middle-class background, was in many respects typical of the *soccerati*'s social roots. The contributors to *My Favourite Year*, for instance, included a number of journalists and novelists as well as a university lecturer, a translator, a pharmacist and another Cambridge graduate who was managing director of a market research company.[110] Giulianotti has linked the emergence of this *soccerati* with another group he has dubbed the 'football *arrivistes*', white-collar professionals from London who '"do football" to flesh out the popular culture dimension of their social curriculum vitae'. Neither group, in his view, had any deep knowledge of the game or 'a long personal immersion' in it, which distinguished them from those middle-class fans in northern England and Scotland who tended to maintain strong affiliations with their hometown clubs and were thus closer to the traditional, 'authentic' culture of football.[111]

Other forms of literature flourished in this post-1990, 'post-fan' culture. Most significant was the growth of independent fanzines, an idea borrowed from music (particularly the do-it-yourself approach of punk) and benefiting from the development of cheap printing and desktop publishing. From a mere handful of titles in the mid-1980s, fanzines boomed in popularity in the late 1980s and early 1990s. There were around 35 produced in 1988–9, at least 350 by 1991 and over 1,000 by 1997.[112] The most influential of these was *When Saturday Comes*, a national fanzine founded in March 1986 by Chelsea fan Mike Ticher. From a print-run of 200 copies for its first issue, by 1993 the 'half-decent football magazine', as it styled itself, had a readership of nearly 40,000 and eight full and part-time employees. From its own marketing data, we can see that the readership of *When Saturday Comes* fitted closely with the middle-class complexion of the *soccerati*. Overwhelmingly males aged between 18 and 34, the majority (63 per cent) of its readers in 1992 were drawn from the ABC1 classes, ranging from the professional to the skilled manual worker. A further 15 per cent were students and, significantly, a majority admitted also to buying the *The Guardian* or *Independent* newspapers, indicating a left-leaning and liberal perspective.[113] The impact of this newer form of football literature carried over into the publication of a number of more mainstream glossy magazines, such as *Four-Four-Two*, *90 Minutes* and *Total Football*, which attempted to package and market football along the lines of existing fashion, style and music publications. The fanzine influence was also evident in the format and style of radio and television programmes such as Radio 5's *Six-O-Six* (a phone-in presented initially by former music journalist and Millwall fan Danny Baker), and BBC 2's *Standing Room Only* and *Fantasy Football League*.[114]

Football's broadening appeal was also due to its ability to tap into other aspects of popular culture, becoming more respectable but increasingly fashionable too. An important element of this was the game's crossover with popular music. Some groups and pop stars had always shown an interest in football but it was not until the mid to late-1980s that the culture of the two became closely intertwined. Cult independent artists such as Half Man Half Biscuit, Billy Bragg and I, Ludicrous had written songs on football themes, while terrace songs and chants had been appropriated by dance music producers, but before the late 1980s the most common link between soccer and pop music in the public mind remained the deeply unfashionable 'football record' released to coincide with a team's upcoming FA Cup or World Cup appearance. In this context, 'World in Motion', the official England single for Italia '90, written and recorded by the popular Manchester band New Order, represented a genuine breakthrough. Magazines such as *The Face* and the *New Musical Express* reported on this football–music crossover, while a number of British bands – Eusebio, Saint Etienne, Mexico '70, Pele – began to take their names from the world of football. By the mid-1990s, leading 'Britpop' bands were self-consciously linking themselves with football and football culture. Oasis, in particular, were avid Manchester City fans, regularly appearing in replica shirts for photo-shoots and playing two sell-out concerts at Maine Road in 1996. The supporters, in return, adapted the Oasis hit 'Wonderwall' as a tribute to the manager at the time, Alan Ball.[115] The ironic humour and nostalgia of the fanzine permeated the football-themed music of alternative bands such as Flyscreen and Halftime Oranges, as well as the enduringly popular England theme song for Euro '96, 'Three Lions', written and performed by the comedians (and *Fantasy Football* hosts) Frank Skinner and David Baddiel and the Liverpool pop group the Lightning Seeds.[116]

Central to football's cultural and social realignment was the perceived exclusion of its traditional fan base. Rising ticket prices and changing ticketing policies were often blamed for squeezing out those on low or irregular incomes.[117] Despite the fact that Taylor's recommendations and the Premier League had both been delivered with the promise of keeping admission fees down, clubs were quick to increase prices in order to fund ground refurbishment and generate the revenue to buy and pay the best players. At Everton, for instance, an average admission price of £4.79 in 1988–9 had leapt to £9.71 by 1994–5, a 102.7 per cent increase over seven seasons. These figures were by no means untypical. The equivalent increase was 99.3 per cent at Swindon Town, 178.8 per cent at Blackburn Rovers and a massive 240.9 per cent at Manchester United. The government's Football Task Force found that Premier League prices had risen 312 per cent between 1989 and 1999, well above the 54.8 per cent rise in the retail price index over the same decade. Minimum ticket prices had by now reached £25 at some venues, while season tickets at certain London clubs topped £1,000. In addition, the relatively small capacities of post-Taylor stadiums (in comparison with their pre-Taylor and continental equivalents), and the moves towards advance sales through season tickets and credit cards, were seen as factors limiting the attendance of the lower paid.[118] Yet, the evidence to support these claims of social exclusion is surprisingly patchy. A SNCCFR report from 1998 found that 70 per cent of those who no longer went to football matches highlighted ticket prices as the main reason, while 'the lads' at Manchester United reported friends who had stopped going to Old Trafford due to spiralling ticket prices. But beyond these fragments of evidence, there is nothing particularly concrete and little to substantiate the claim that ticketing policies represented 'a form of social exclusion for the low-paid and unwaged, young and old'.[119]

Dominic Malcolm and colleagues have taken this issue further by challenging the common assumption that the demographics of football crowds changed significantly in the 1990s.[120] Comparing data from ten club and league surveys conducted between 1983 and 1997, Malcolm et al. found little to support the suggestions that football had attracted either a new family audience or an increasingly middle-class one. Results naturally varied from club to club, but overall the age, sex and occupational composition of the spectators remained remarkably constant. Indeed, contrary to the interpretation drawn from the findings of the widely publicised 1994–5 Carling Survey, that increasing numbers of female supporters were being attracted to Premiership grounds, Malcolm et al. found female spectatorship consistent at between 10 and 13 per cent across all the surveys.[121] Likewise, they saw no significant decline in the percentage of working-class, retired or unemployed spectators emerging from the data, with regional differences (the larger proportion of middle-class fans attached to Home Counties clubs Watford and Luton Town than Coventry City and Aston Villa of the west midlands, for example) more striking than change over time. Indeed, if anything, the proportion of

TABLE 6.2 *Football fans and social class, 1993–4 to 1996–7*

	Middle class (Non-manual) (%)	*Working class (Manual) (%)*
1993–4	67.3	32.7
1994–5	71.4	28.6
1995–6	67.4	32.6
1996–7	66.4	33.6

Source: Dominic Malcolm, 'The People's Game?': Football Crowds and the New Marketing of the Game', *Singer & Friedlander's Review*, 1999–2000 season, p. 32 (Table 5).

middle-class (defined crudely as non-manual) spectators had decreased slightly between 1993–4 and 1996–7, while working class (manual) attendance had marginally increased (see Table 6.2).

What was being suggested here was not that football crowds were static and unchanging in their composition but rather that the notion of an increasingly affluent, middle-class and female clientele may well have been more perceived than real. In fact, the traditional fan base was much more resilient, Malcolm *et al.* argued, than had often been assumed. Ian Jones's study of fandom at Luton Town provides useful evidence here, confirming that the level of commitment of existing fans was sufficiently strong to resist changes in the physical environment of the stadium and the image of the game. Jones found that the vast majority of supporters he questioned during the 1996–7 season exhibited a strong level of identification with the club: 73 per cent identified themselves 'very strongly' as fans and a third considered being a fan the most important aspect of their identity. The relationships these supporters forged with the club, and with fellow supporters, were long-standing (the average length of support at Luton was 21.9 years) and they remained loyal and positive irrespective of success or failure on the pitch.[122] This 'love of the team', which King found so prominent among 'the lads' at Manchester United, did not preclude resistance to the ways in which football was changing, as we shall see below, but it suggests that many supporters accommodated change and modified their experience of fandom rather than cutting their ties with the game altogether. Football was thus not a casual interest but a serious leisure pursuit for a considerable proportion of supporters and, as such, Malcolm *et al.* argued that the composition of British spectatorship over time was likely to remain stable.[123]

Fan democracy and protest

Those supporters who stayed loyal to their clubs, however, did not necessarily comply with the agenda of the directors and owners. Indeed it was a sense of a loss of control over the game and its future trajectory – the feeling that football was being 'taken away' from fans in the wake of the Hillsborough disaster and the Taylor Report – that underpinned the emergence from the late 1980s of the independent fan movement and what one writer has called 'fan democracy'.[124] Key to this was the establishment of the Football Supporters' Association (FSA) on a national basis and Independent Supporters' Associations (ISAs) at club level, as well as the associated growth of football fanzines, all of which provided fans with a forum to challenge modernisation and organise resistance. Established in Liverpool in 1985 in the aftermath of the Heysel disaster, the FSA managed to establish itself as an independent and autonomous voice of the grassroots supporter in a way that had eluded the existing club-based National Federation of Football Supporters' Clubs. A high media profile and articulate representatives helped in a number of successful campaigns, such as the opposition to compulsory identity cards, the poor image and treatment of England fans abroad and racism at grounds. The FSA was also instrumental in persuading the media, the government and the football authorities to seek out and consult the views of fans on issues relating to the future of the game and, more broadly, in helping to change the public perception of supporters as thugs and hooligans.[125] After Hillsborough, in particular, it has been argued that the FSA, led by its charismatic chairman Rogan Taylor, was successful in making 'the views of the "ordinary" supporter seem ever more the stuff of common sense'.[126]

It was at individual clubs and through ISAs, however, that most campaigns were waged. Adam Brown has distinguished between two types of campaign: those which challenged plans to restrict participation in the context of the move to all-seater stadiums; and those directed more specifically against chairmen, boards of directors, managers and the people who ran the club.[127] As far as the first of these is concerned, we can point to the work of ISAs in the defeat of proposed 'bond schemes' (requiring fans to buy expensive bonds to fund the rebuilding of stands) at Arsenal and West Ham United in the early 1990s. At West Ham, for example, the Hammers Independent Supporters' Association (HISA) demonstrated by waving red cards urging 'Don't buy the bond' during matches, selling independent merchandise and organising petitions. When ticket prices increased for the 1992–3 season following the club's relegation from the top division, members of HISA began to boycott home matches and organise independent travel for away trips in competition with the club's own arrangements. Declining attendances forced the board to reduce ticket prices and, with only 576 of the 19,500 bonds sold by

March 1993, the scheme was shelved. *Time Out* felt that the board had been defeated 'because of a well-run vigorous campaign by the people who care most about their club, the fans'.[128] At Manchester United, it was increased admission prices that prompted the formation of HOSTAGE – Holders of Season Tickets Against Gross Exploitation – with over 1,000 fans attending a meeting in February 1992. Its attempts to force price reductions by seeking meetings with club officials failed, and a new body, the Independent Manchester United Supporters' Association (IMUSA) formed in 1995, also found the club unwilling to engage in regular dialogue about the continued redevelopment of Old Trafford and the possible establishment of designated singing and standing areas to improve the atmosphere at the stadium.[129]

Other ISAs emerged as what Rex Nash has called 'emergency services', provoked by crises involving the team, manager or directors. Sheffield United fans, for example, formed Blades Independent Supporters' Association in 1994 primarily to remove unpopular chairman Reg Brearley, although the initial aims also included securing a fan representative on the board and creating a supporters' shareholding co-operative. A similar association at Southampton coalesced in 1993 around opposition to manager Ian Branfoot and the general decline of the club. Both achieved their objectives but then found membership difficult to sustain with no immediate crisis and an absence of long-term objectives.[130] Yet we should not underestimate the significance of these achievements, demonstrating the 'politicisation of football's fandom' and the ability of supporters to influence the way in which clubs were run.[131] The best illustration of organised fan power was the success of Manchester United supporter groups in halting BSkyB's attempted takeover of the club in 1998–9. Working together with Shareholders United Against Murdoch, an organisation set up by the journalist, writer and United supporter Michael Crick, IMUSA launched a sophisticated public relations and legal battle which culminated in the Monopolies and Mergers Commission and Trade and Industry secretary Stephen Byers blocking the deal.[132] More recently, the growth of supporter trusts (beginning at Northampton Town in 1992) designed to provide fans with a genuine say in the policies of their clubs, as well as the increasing role of supporter representatives on boards of directors, provide evidence of what might be considered the first steps toward the democratisation of football. By 2000 there were almost 20 trusts established or in the process of formation and fan representatives on the board at AFC Bournemouth, Chester City, Enfield, Lincoln City and Luton Town in addition to Northampton.[133] According to the leading experts in football governance at Birkbeck College, these trusts constituted 'an effective bottom-up mechanism for making clubs more accountable to widespread public interests'.[134]

Fanzines underpinned these campaigns, acting as a focus and a mouthpiece for fan protest. The link between fanzines and activism was established early on. We have seen that *Voice of the Valley* played a fundamental role in returning Charlton Athletic to its former ground, as did Fulham (*There's Only One F in Fulham*), Queen's Park Rangers (*A Kick Up the R's*) and Hibernian (*The Proclaimer*) fanzines in opposing planned mergers involving their clubs in the late 1980s and early 1990s. Fanzines and their editors were likewise instrumental in the Arsenal, West Ham and Manchester United campaigns, working closely with ISAs in each case to publicise and sustain enthusiasm for the cause. Many also played a part in the wider *political* campaigns fought against identity cards, racism and criminal justice legislation. Aberdeen fanzines, for example, consistently granted space to national movements organised by the Commission for Racial Equality and Football Fans Against the Criminal Justice Act.[135] Some academics have placed considerable emphasis on this political dimension of fanzine culture. In an influential article, David Jary and colleagues argued that football fanzines provide an important example of 'cultural and political contestation' with the dominant commercial agenda of the professional game. On a similar line, Haynes located them as part of a 'culture of defence' that evolved in opposition to the various modernising tendencies of late twentieth-century football.[136] H. F. Moorhouse has taken a different tack, admonishing 'English analysts' for being uncritical of the content of fanzines and exaggerating their significance. Drawing on a case study of the principal Rangers and Celtic fanzines (*Follow Follow* and *Not the View* respectively), Moorhouse argued that far from being progressive, radical and inclusive, they could be myopic in vision and conservative in outlook, reflecting a strand of working-class values that were essentially 'accommodative, defensive and parochial'.[137] Yet ultimately, in his view, this narrow-mindedness and negativity hardly mattered as the influence of these fanzines over the affairs of the clubs tended to be minimal, with small percentages of the readership responding to initiatives, and plans for protest through demonstrations, sit-ins and non-attendance garnering little support.

Similar debates have informed discussion of the overall impact of the independent fan movement. The contention that the alliance of the FSA, ISAs and fanzines built up an effective 'culture of opposition' has been persuasively countered by those who emphasise the limits to fan democracy and solidarity.[138] Despite its early successes, it is difficult to deny that the FSA has been a marginal body reflecting the interests of a minority of active and politicised supporters; ISAs and fanzines have likewise tended to be dominated by a coterie of committed organisers and campaigners. As such, they could hardly claim to represent the majority, or even a significant minority, of supporters.[139] The influence of these organisations has also been constrained by the fractured nature of football fandom. National bodies such as the FSA will always find it hard to overcome geographical differences as well as the inherent divisions between fans of competing and rival clubs. The attitude of activists in the Newcastle United ISA, who made it clear that they were 'not interested in ... fucking Mackems [Sunderland fans] or Mancs [Manchester United]' but only in their own supporters, was probably not untypical.[140] Most importantly, we need to bear in mind the obvious but crucial point that few fans have wanted to oppose or damage the clubs they support: they were (and are) 'too addicted to the game to threaten the structures that provide it'.[141] For Brown, the centrality of football in British social life and the levels of emotional attachment and loyalty to clubs 'make it very difficult for fans to challenge the running of the game'.[142] Often, supporters could be simultaneously resistant *and* compliant, opposing the directors and their ideology while still wanting the club to achieve financial and sporting ascendancy over its rivals.[143] Under such circumstances, it was hardly surprising that the power structures of the 'new football' of the 1990s were left largely undisturbed by fan protest.

The media and 'virtual' fandom

Nothing shaped the relationship between football and its supporters more than television. From the first historic £304 million deal in 1992 between BSkyB (with the BBC) and the Premier League, satellite broadcasting was crucial in altering the way in which the game was consumed. There were a number of aspects to this. First, there was widespread concern that satellite control would limit the access of supporters to top-flight football. The initially small audiences for BSkyB's soccer coverage – an average of just 525,000 per game in the 1992–3 season compared with over 7 million for terrestrial live matches in the previous three seasons – and the prospect of increasing restrictions through the introduction of pay-per-view hinted at a two-tier system in which football would still be shown on terrestrial television but the best of the British game would increasingly be removed to a satellite ghetto. Linked to this was the fear that satellite coverage would distort the experience and fragment the established rituals of fandom.

Although recognised national and international events such as the FA Cup final and the World Cup continued to be open to a large audience on terrestrial channels, the trend in satellite broadcasting was towards exclusive audiences and fractured viewing patterns. The BBC was no longer central, as it had been before the 1980s, in making 'shared national rituals' out of football and other sporting events.[144] Significantly, television companies also began to dictate when football was played and watched. The traditional 'FA Cup Saturday' became scattered over a week, and half-time breaks were lengthened to accommodate more advertisements. BSkyB's Premier League coverage introduced Monday night matches (the old Saturday league programme extended to resemble a long weekend) and 4.00 p.m. kick-offs.[145]

More fans consumed football through the mass media in this period than ever before. Watching football on television, in particular, was considerably more common in the 1990s than attending 'live' matches. Yet it is noteworthy that academics and journalists have tended to downplay the experience of the media fan, defining it as vicarious, individualistic and passive and significantly less fulfilling than actually 'being there'. Thus Raymond Boyle and Richard Haynes, in their study of sport and the media, discuss the stereotypes of the 'armchair supporter' and the 'couch potato' and the 'passive experience of watching televised sport'.[146] For Cornel Sandvoss, meanwhile, 'television football' was a simulated version, or a copy, of the 'real' thing in which fans did not in fact consume the game 'but an image of the game'.[147] In this view, the atmosphere and experience of attending in person were downgraded when viewing on a screen and the fans lost their crucial role in participating in the spectacle of the event itself.

However, the media consumption of football has never been as straightforward as these perspectives suggest. For one thing, there was a communal context to watching satellite matches from the beginning. Too much emphasis on the 'armchair supporter' neglects the extent to which fans were able to recreate the atmosphere of live matches in clubs, pubs and even at home. As a Chelsea fan put it: 'you can stand, shout and other people shout and that is something of getting the atmosphere back to the extent that I go down to the pub to watch Chelsea play, even when they are on terrestrial TV'.[148] Indeed a number of researchers have noted the *preference* among some supporters for the communality, participation and social interaction of television fandom, which was difficult to recreate within many stadiums.[149] A similar point can be made about the increasing engagement with football through the Internet or digital gaming, often dismissed as passive and isolated activities. Crawford has convincingly argued that neither should be seen primarily as 'static texts' that are passively consumed. Rather, those who create fan websites, contribute to newsgroups or discussion sites, or play interactive games such as Championship Manager, are engaging in active forms of participation that often develop their interest and knowledge in football more generally.[150]

The media consumption of football has also enabled the growth of distant forms of fan identification. It has become a cliché that Manchester United supporters, in particular, live everywhere apart from Manchester. Gavin Mellor has shown that the club drew support from across Britain, Ireland and beyond from at least the 1960s due to a combination of sporting success, an association with glamour and broader socio-cultural and economic changes, such as a decline in local identity and the influence of televised football.[151] Bale agrees that television's role 'in reducing fan attachment to place' has been crucial. The concentration of television coverage on certain 'super clubs', along with increased geographical mobility, meant that by the late 1980s significant proportions of fans supported clubs outside their area of residence. Thus two-thirds of English schoolchildren in their early teens surveyed in 1987 supported just four clubs, 34 per cent opting for Liverpool and 17 per cent for Manchester United. Moreover, while only 20 per cent of respondents came from the northwest of England, 60 per cent supported clubs from that region.[152] If the core of regular supporters and season-ticket holders at most clubs (including Manchester United) still came from the locality or the region, the spatial fan base of British football was nonetheless expanding in the 1990s. By 1997, 36 per cent of West Ham United supporters lived more than 50 miles from Upton Park, while two-thirds of Chelsea season-ticket holders in 1998–9 came from outside London (Table 6.3).[153]

TABLE 6.3 *Geographical distribution of Chelsea season-ticket holders, 1998–9*

Postcode area	No.	%
Fulham and Chelsea	674	4.35
South-west London, other	1,611	10.40
London, other	2,821	18.21
UK, outside London	10,335	66.73
Overseas	34	0.21
Total*	15,488	99.9

*No postcode information available for 13 season-ticket holders.
Source: Cornel Sandvoss, *A Game of Two Halves: Football, Television and Globalization* (London: Routledge, 2003), p. 88 (Table 5.1).

Perhaps the best example of what Bale calls this 'community without propinquity', or what Sandvoss refers to as deterritorialised fan communities, are the Scandinavian supporters of British clubs.[154] The live transmission from 1969 of Football League games in Denmark, Norway and Sweden was the start of a 'satellite transmitted passion' for British football in Scandinavia.[155] The first supporters' club, organised around Manchester City, was formed in 1974, and by 1985 the Supporterunionen for Britisk Fotball had been created to unite Scandinavian fans of all British clubs. In 1997 it covered fans of 45 clubs with a total membership of 53,000. For many, visiting the chosen club, often in search of the 'genuine' or 'authentic' experience of local fans, augmented the virtual connections of satellite television and the Internet. As with Finnish and Israeli long-distance supporters, studies have shown the Scandinavian fans of British clubs to be committed enthusiasts with deep and long-standing loyalties rather than 'pseudo' fans or 'glory hunters'. Notwithstanding the geographical distance, many were closer to Giulianotti's hot/traditional supporters than his cold/consumer flâneurs.[156]

'Race' and racism

One of the most significant developments in British football in the 1990s was the foregrounding of racism as a problem to be addressed and combated. Yet recent research has highlighted the complexity and multifaceted nature of the phenomenon and the failure of commentators and policy makers to grasp its many and often insidious manifestations. An influential study by Les Back and colleagues, for example, has criticised the 'commonsense' approach that links racism in football exclusively with hooliganism (what they call the 'racist-hooligan couplet') and thus neglects more mundane examples prevalent throughout the culture of the game. This, they argue, has also led to the denial of racism within football's institutions, exemplified by the view that 'you can speak about racism in the ... stands but you can't talk about it in the board rooms'.[157] Jon Garland and Michael Rowe have taken a similar position, arguing against a simplistic and narrow conception of racism and in favour of thinking about the diversity of *racisms* within football. They also emphasise the importance, long acknowledged in academic discourse, of recognising 'race' as a concept that is socially constructed rather than biologically determined.[158] In Scotland the issue is further complicated by the significance of sectarianism in football and a lack of agreement over whether it should be seen as a facet of racism or something qualitatively different.[159] While few historians or social scientists would deny that prejudice towards white ethnic minorities constitutes a form of racism, most discussions of the phenomenon within football have centred on black–white relations. As such, it is football's treatment of the black (defined for our purposes as Afro-Caribbean) and Asian population of Britain that will be the main focus here.

Black and Asian players and racial abuse

The presence of black players in the professional game dates back to before the First World War. Thanks mainly to the work of Phil Vasili, a great deal is now known about the extraordinary lives of England's first two black professionals, Arthur Wharton and Walter Tull.[160] Wharton, a goalkeeper with Darlington, Preston North End and Sheffield United among other clubs during the 1880s and 1890s, was an all-round sportsman born in the Gold Coast (modern-day Ghana) who also became the first British athlete to run 100 yards in under 10 seconds. The son of a Barbadian father and a white English mother, Tull played professionally for Tottenham Hotspur and Northampton Town between 1908 and 1914. He became Britain's first black army combat officer during the First World War but was killed in March 1918 at the second Battle of the Somme. Between 1914 and the 1970s a number of prominent black footballers played at the highest level of British football, including Plymouth Argyle's prolific goalscorer Jack Leslie and Welsh international John 'Eddie' Parris in the interwar years; two Jamaican-born strikers, Celtic's Giles Heron (father of jazz musician Gil-Scott) and Portsmouth and Middlesbrough's Lindy Delapenha in the 1950s; and Leeds United's South African-born Albert Johanneson and Clyde Best of West Ham United during the 1960s. It was not until the mid to late 1970s, however, as the sons of post-war immigrants from the West Indies began to come of age, that the so-called 'black explosion' took place.[161] A key moment was the selection of Nottingham Forest's Viv Anderson as the first black player to be capped by England in November 1978. The position of black players in England was consolidated by Bobby Robson's tenure as national team manager between 1982 and 1990 and his public commitment to pick the best players regardless of colour. He introduced a number of promising black players, such as Cyrille Regis, Luther Blissett, Mark Chamberlain, Ricky Hill and John Barnes, into his early England squads. Of these, Barnes made the greatest impact, scoring a memorable goal in England's 2–0 victory against Brazil in the Maracana Stadium in the summer of

PLATE 21 *John Barnes, one of the best young black footballers of the 1980s, playing for England (© Popperfoto.com).*

1984, although many felt that his early promise at international level was never fulfilled. Another landmark was reached in 1993, when Manchester United's Paul Ince became the first black player to captain England.[162]

Statistical studies have confirmed the remarkable growth in the quantity and quality of black talent in the Football League from the mid-1970s. Not only did overall numbers rise from only three black players in the 1972–3 season to 244 by 1993–4; the proportion of clubs with black players in their squads increased in the same period from 2 per cent to 88 per cent. Black Britons were also grossly over-represented in elite football, accounting for 11.5 per cent of the professional workforce in 1989–90 as against just 1.4 per cent of the population. Equally noteworthy was their concentration in the League's highest divisions. During the 1982–3 season, 64 per cent of black footballers played in the top two divisions, a proportion that was almost unchanged (63 per cent) in 1993–4. By 1997 a BBC survey could reveal that the number of black footballers in the Football League and Premier League had doubled since 1985 to some 15 per cent of the total, although other estimates put the figure at 20–25 per cent. Scottish football, by contrast, remained decidedly white. Despite the presence of high-profile black stars such as Mark Walters at Rangers and Paul Elliot at Celtic during the late 1980s, by the 1994–5 season there were only seven black players out of 1,084 (just over 1 per cent of the total) competing in the Scottish Football League.[163] British Asians, meanwhile, made relatively little impact at the professional level. Most of those that did make the grade, from the Cowther brothers, Jack and Eddie, who played for Southern League Watford at the end of the nineteenth century to Brian 'Bud' Houghton, Kevin Keelan, Ricky Heppolete and Paul Wilson in the 1960s and 1970s, were Anglo-Asians, which arguably made it easier for them to downplay their ethnic difference and become 'one of the lads'. In the 1990s the presence of British Hindus, Muslims and Sikhs as professionals was negligible: only 16 out of 62 clubs in a 1996 national survey admitted to having an Asian on its books.[164]

Racism in football has taken a variety of forms. The most overt of these has involved individual or collective abuse from spectators. Although Tull was apparently racially taunted by 'a section of spectators [who] made a cowardly attack upon him in language lower than Billingsgate' during a league fixture at Bristol in 1909, collective racist chanting does not seem to have emerged until the 1960s and 1970s.[165] It increased significantly from the late 1970s due to the involvement of far-right political groups, such as the National Front, at certain clubs but also because of fans' increasing exposure to black footballers. John Barnes, for example, was subjected to various forms of racial abuse after moving from Watford to Liverpool. Dave Hill has written about the notorious cup-tie against Everton in November 1987 when visiting fans chanted 'Niggerpool' and 'Everton are White', while Hornby noted how Liverpool supporters hurled bananas on to the pitch before Barnes's first away match at Arsenal. Similar treatment was dished out to Mark Walters, particularly by those Hearts fans who subjected him to a torrent of racial and physical abuse in what has been described as one of the worst examples of overt racism in British sport.[166]

A number of studies attempted to determine how widespread this type of racial abuse was. Canter et al. found in 1989 that the percentage of supporters who believed there was a lot of racist chanting at matches ranged from 15 at Fulham to 66 at Celtic, with most clubs registering a figure of around 20 to 30 per cent. Concerns about such 'openly expressed racism' tended to be high among the fans of all clubs, although this probably declined after the Football Offences Act of 1991 made racist chanting unlawful.[167] Brian Holland's fieldwork at Leeds United and Newcastle

United between the 1989–90 and 1992–3 seasons was subtler in focusing both on the content of the abuse and the intended target. Holland found that black players were not only subjected to overtly racist chants and songs but also received a proportionate amount of non-racist abuse. What he terms the 'burden of abuse' fell most heavily on black players, whether playing for the home team or the opposition. Thus of the 28 abusive incidents recorded when Portsmouth visited Newcastle in September 1992, 16 were directed at the two 'opposition' black players, representing a 'burden' 80 times that of a home player and eight times that of their white teammates.[168] Back *et al.* have similarly analysed the more banal forms of racism that developed at football grounds in the 1990s. They argue that a song such as 'I'd rather be a Paki than a Scouse', as sung by Millwall fans against Merseyside clubs during the 1995–6 season (but used, with variations, by many clubs against a range of targets), represented a less explicit but equally important form of racism. Designed to insult the predominantly white fans of the opposing club, it was based both on an assumption that whiteness represents the norm and that 'Pakis' were outsiders, located at the bottom of a racialised hierarchy. Songs of this type, which relied on the fact that both performers and audience were largely white, indicated the prevalence of coded expressions of racism within fan culture alongside the cruder examples mentioned above.[169]

Stereotyping and institutional racism

The normalisation of whiteness within British football was also demonstrated through the racial stereotyping of blacks and Asians. Although neither necessarily negative nor historically fixed, stereotypes relating to the physical characteristics of black footballers have been accepted and reinforced by coaches, administrators and the media throughout the twentieth century. Much of this stereotyping was derived from nineteenth-century scientific racism and imperialist thought concerning the natural physical prowess but weak mental capacities of blacks. The notion of the black footballer as highly gifted, quick, instinctive and graceful but unreliable, immature and lacking in courage and intelligence was widely expressed.[170] It had arguably been epitomised by Albert Johanneson, described in one retrospective portrait as 'a mercurial performer, full of craft and daring one moment, but likely to be cowed by a ferocious opponent'. Brendan Batson, one of West Bromwich Albion's trio of black stars in the late 1970s, recalled the prevalence of white assumptions about black players: 'no bottle, unreliable, don't like training, don't like the cold . . . All those ignorant views that have got no foundation whatsoever.'[171] One of the most notorious expressions of racial stereotyping came from then Crystal Palace chairman Ron Noades, who in 1991 told a television interviewer that few black players could 'read' the game and that when the going got tough in the English winter 'you need the hard white man to carry the artistic black players through'. Graham Taylor, meanwhile, a relatively progressive manager in many respects, reportedly bemoaned the 'laid-back attitude' of Barnes and talked of the 'free spirit' of other black players.[172] Asian players, meanwhile, have tended to be stereotyped as physically frail, lacking in stamina and culturally unsuited to playing at the highest level. As one Luton Town coach allegedly claimed: 'they don't like the physical element [and] . . . their eating habits are a problem'.[173]

More significant still was the way in which racial stereotyping and discrimination became institutionalised in many football clubs and associations. One example of this was the apparent concentration of black players in peripheral positions on the field of play and their exclusion from central, decision-making roles. Despite some doubts over the applicability of the North American work on 'stacking' and 'centrality' to a more free-flowing sport such as football, Joseph Maguire's analysis of the Football League in the 1980s confirmed that black players were under-represented in central positions and over-represented in non-central positions. Indeed, of the 152 black players in the League in 1989–90, only five played in central midfield and there was not a single goalkeeper, while there were 24 black full backs and 57 'wide' forwards. Such data, taken together with qualitative evidence from interviews with players and managers, convinced Maguire that black players were indeed 'stacked' into particular non-central positions and that this position allocation was connected to prevailing stereotypes about their physical and mental capabilities. More studies are needed, however, to determine the extent to which these patterns changed during the 1990s, as 'hard', muscular and 'typically English' black midfielders and defenders such as Paul Ince and Sol Campbell became increasingly prominent at the 'core' of many professional teams.[174]

Perhaps the most important vehicle for reinforcing racial stereotypes was the media. Specialists on sport and television have emphasised the contradictory nature of representations of race. While sports such as football offered positive images of talented and successful black athletes, they also helped to reproduce stereotypes about the natural ability and technical or tactical shortcomings of these athletes.[175] A study by David

McCarthy and Robyn L. Jones found that television commentators tended to be overwhelmingly positive in their evaluation of the physical characteristics of black players but less positive in their psychological assessment. When looking at the opening sequences of the *Match of the Day* programme, they also identified images of black players that highlighted speed and physicality, in contrast with those of white players that suggested skill and organisational abilities. As such, the authors concluded that 'an image of the physically powerful, athletic, but unintelligent Black athlete was being covertly suggested'.[176] Patrick Ismond has similarly drawn attention to the division between 'instinct' and 'intelligence' in the media portrayal of black and white footballers. He argues, for example, that while white centre-forwards such as Teddy Sheringham, Alan Shearer and Eidur Gudjohnsen were often noted for their intelligent play, sports commentators rarely described black forwards like Jimmy Floyd Hasselbaink and Thierry Henry as 'intelligent', emphasising instead their pace, strength and shooting power.[177] The general absence of blacks in media roles as presenters, commentators or pundits – roles requiring thought, reflection and analysis – was arguably another facet of this stereotyping. That said, during the 1990s a number of black former professionals such as Garth Crooks, Ian Wright and Mark Bright did become more prominent on television. Wright is a particularly interesting example, as he developed an increasing public profile as his football career came to an end. His exuberant personality and association with flair and style in dress as well as play made him attractive to advertisers and television producers, but it is noteworthy that, in keeping with historical racial stereotypes, Wright was portrayed primarily as an entertainer rather than an expert or analyst.[178]

It is on the subject of institutional racism, however, that the most innovative recent research has focused. The Macpherson Report of 1999 into the murder of black teenager Stephen Lawrence had clearly shown that institutional racism was less about the holding of overtly racist views than the existence of discriminatory procedures and policies within organisations and a culture that tended to reinforce 'unwitting prejudice'.[179] Thus while many of the crude stereotypes concerning black footballers may not have been as widely held in the 1990s as in previous decades, those players seeking to enter management, coaching or other administrative positions still faced a whole series of institutional restrictions and barriers. Back *et al.*'s explanation of the relative absence of black managers focused on three main factors: misconceptions over their basic ability to lead, organise and effectively manage multiracial teams; their exclusion from the networks that provide access to such posts; and the reluctance of white directors to hand over power and responsibility to a black manager. Stella Orakwue covered many of the same points, forcefully arguing that clubs and associations 'are still pristinely white institutions where even black footballers with excellent pasts dare not tread'.[180] The recruitment procedures of many clubs, based on personal contacts and 'word of mouth', ensured that 'outsiders' found it difficult to penetrate the 'white ... administrative core' of the professional game.[181] Similarly, it has been argued that systems of player recruitment '"naturally" discriminate against Asian players'. The assumption within clubs that 'talent will always come through' ignored the fact that Asian teams and leagues were not a part of established scouting networks, meaning that many talented players were probably never seen and thus denied the opportunity of playing at the highest level. As one writer commented in 1995: 'It's not that Asians have accidentally slipped the net, more that the net's got huge holes in strategic places'.[182]

It would of course be wrong to overlook the considerable effort made in challenging racism in its various guises. Anti-racist campaigns among supporters pre-dated the 1990s but it took until 1993 for the first major national campaign to be launched. In that year the Commission for Racial Equality (CRE) joined forces with the PFA to establish 'Let's Kick Racism Out of Football' (relaunched in 1997 independently as 'Kick It Out'), a campaign that, on the surface at least, seemed to enjoy widespread support from the football establishment. Although this and other campaigns were successful in raising awareness of racism as an issue to be tackled, a number of studies have pointed out that many clubs adopted a superficial commitment to anti-racism that might involve displaying anti-racist messages and removing racist graffiti but rarely extended to wholesale programmes of reform or equal opportunities policies. Doubts were also raised about the applicability of English-based anti-racism campaigns in Scotland.[183] Even taking into account the success of a handful of club-based initiatives such as Charlton Athletic's 'Red, White and Black' scheme and Sheffield United's 'Football Unites, Racism Divides', David McArdle could suggest that the response of 'some of the country's biggest clubs' had been 'lamentable'.[184] Similar criticisms have been made of the anti-racist initiatives of the Labour government's Football Task Force. In 1998 it published a report, *Eliminating Racism from Football*, which, building upon the work of 'Kick It Out', featured a shaft of recommendations designed to tackle racism at all levels of the sport and so encourage wider involvement of ethnic minority groups as players, fans and administrators. But what it failed to address, according to its many critics, was the question of institutionalised racism. For Back *et al.*, the fundamental problem with the report was its narrow understanding of 'racism' and its inability to get to grips with the way in which the culture of football normalised whiteness and marginalised 'otherness'. It was only in this context that it was possible to sustain the erroneous assumption that racism was a problem imported from outside football rather than one embedded in the game's own culture and structures.[185]

Gender

The concept of gender has tended to be neglected, or else marginalised, in orthodox accounts of British football. As we saw in earlier chapters, the game's connection with the construction of masculinity and manliness has long been recognised, but few historians chose to pursue it beyond the Victorian and Edwardian era. To paraphrase Richard Holt, the history of football in Britain has largely been written as 'a history of men', with women's involvement as players and supporters explained in terms of exclusion from this male preserve.[186] Reflecting broader trends in history and the social sciences, however, a number of recent studies have focused more seriously on football as a gendered activity. Often drawing explicitly or implicitly on feminist theory, they have sought to understand football as an institution and an associated culture dominated by men and defined in relation to masculinity. The very terms used to describe the game reflect this: while the men's game is simply referred to as 'football', the game played by females is usually termed 'women's football', a deviation from the male norm. Building on the work of pioneering sociologists and historians, there has been an emphasis on the power relations of sport and issues of patriarchy and inequality but, most of all, on the particular experiences of women involved in football and the meanings they attach to the game.[187] Likewise, much recent work on football has recognised what Martin Polley called 'the centrality of common-sense masculinity' in perceptions of the game and begun to make good 'the silences and blind spots that common sense has allowed to develop'.[188] Although much remains to be done, we now have a more sophisticated understanding of the complex and changing nature of masculine identities within football and the various ways in which dominant discourses of masculinity have shaped male and female responses to the game.

Football and femininity

The 1990s was in many respects a decade of progress for women in football. Participation rates increased significantly. The available figures reveal that in 1991 there were 334 women's clubs and 9,000 registered players in England but some 1,500 clubs and 35,000 players by 2000. Growth was particularly dramatic at school, youth and university level: a 1996 poll estimated that 2 million girls were involved in some form of football activity.[189] The gradual assumption of control by national associations over the women's game, beginning with the FA and the FAW in 1993, has been widely regarded as crucial to these developments. Donna Woodhouse and John Williams have emphasised the administrative and commercial benefits that flowed from the takeover of power. A more professional and forward-thinking structure, they argue, had replaced the ad hoc voluntarism of the WFA. A clear 'pyramid' structure of regional and national leagues was established to improve competition, and some 20 FA-licensed Centres of Excellence created to develop future talent. With an annual budget of £1 million, a kit deal for the England squad and a sponsorship deal for the domestic game, it could be suggested that, by the end of the 1990s, women's football had 'a sound financial basis for real progress'.[190] Some also pointed to an increasing media profile, with weekly columns in broadsheet newspapers and Channel 4's broadcasting of Women's FA Cup matches and internationals in the late 1980s, along with a series of general programmes on the women's game. Yet despite promising viewing figures, Channel 4, and subsequently Sky, failed to establish women's football as a television sport and the game ironically tended to feature more as the backdrop for dramas such as *Playing the Field* and the later film *Bend it like Beckham!*.[191]

Indeed, optimistic views of the imminent 'breakthrough' of women's football have been rigorously challenged in some quarters. Jean Williams has written persuasively of the ignorance and insensitivity displayed by the male governing bodies to the traditions of the women's game. The low priority accorded to long-established independent clubs provides a good example of this. Doncaster Belles, for instance, the dominant side of the late 1980s and early 1990s, nonetheless found itself deprived of the financial backing, sponsorship and facilities enjoyed by rivals such as Arsenal and Croydon who had been integrated into men's clubs. Although logical in administrative and financial terms, the 'arrogant' refusal of the governing bodies to support independent women's clubs has arguably led to a loss of identity for many and an unwelcome future as appendages of

Premiership, Football League and Scottish League clubs. Linked to this is the concern that women have lost control over the sport. At both club and association level, it was increasingly men who ran the game: even the FA's new Women's Committee was predominantly male. Although generally positive in their assessment, Woodhouse and Williams were thus alarmed that power rested in the hands of 'a small number of senior individuals within the FA, some of whom have little experience of the women's game pre-1993'.[192] Jennifer Hargreaves, meanwhile, has pointed to the way in which the women's game came to be dominated by 'male-defined practices and ideas'. The predominance of male coaches and a desire by female players to emulate masculine styles of play are important here. Hargreaves offers a fascinating alternative example of the Newham club in London, controlled entirely by women and advocating a 'women's philosophy of football' defined by positive, imaginative and attacking play, which suggests the possibilities of a female variant of football distinct from the men's game. Yet in the main, as Williams found, female players 'did not want to play a different form of football, either as an alternative game or as a critique of the values of sport'.[193]

Recent studies of the subculture of women's football have perhaps provided the most revealing insights in this area. The starting point for much of this work was the tension involved for females playing a sport traditionally considered inappropriate for their sex. Many played football because they enjoyed the game and the social life surrounding it; others were more serious about developing their own football career and improving the status of the women's game more generally. But all had to negotiate the stereotypes associated with women's football.[194] Jayne Caudwell's work, in particular, has probed the image of the game and its connection with sexuality and gender. The stereotype of the 'butch lesbian' player, in particular, was regarded by some of her interviewees as problematic, giving the sport a negative image and compromising the feminine identity of its participants. Jessica Macbeth's analysis of Scottish players has similarly drawn out the tension between what she calls the 'conformers' to the gay stereotype and the non-conformers, showing, in line with Caudwell, how this led to attempts to marginalise and even deny the indisputable lesbian presence in the game. The link between sexuality and gender was evident in the way in which players displaying masculine traits – through how they played or how they looked – tended to be labelled as lesbians and, by extension, excluded from the largely heterosexual feminine identity of women's football.[195] John Harris, meanwhile, has linked the experiences of players themselves to the media representation of women and football. His conclusion, that the game's dominant masculine ideal continued to exclude and marginalise women, fits with the relatively pessimistic consensus of many of these studies. For Harris, like Williams and many others, the constant claim by the governing bodies that the future of football was 'feminine' seemed 'a little quixotic'.[196]

Doubts over the so-called 'feminisation' of football in the 1990s extended to the role of women in the men's game.[197] Despite disagreements over the changing sexual composition of the crowd (mentioned earlier in this chapter), many commentators have regarded increased female interest as a key element in football's reinvention. Anne Coddington, for example, wrote in 1997 about what she termed football's 'sexual revolution' post-Italia '90, measured by an increasing female involvement in supporting, playing and reporting on the game. She argues that girls and women overcame barriers relating to male patterns of socialisation, language and sociability to establish a significant minority presence on the terraces and stands. Yet it remained difficult to overcome the assumption that they were somehow less committed and 'authentic' in their support than male fans.[198] 'All men', one female supporter told Coddington, 'grow up with this idea that football is intrinsic to their masculinity. Women are excluded from that'. For another, the difference was less about commitment than the way in which males and females engaged with the game:

Men collect – they collect football experiences. I think they are more obsessed with detail but not necessarily with the game, the passion or supporting the team. Women are just as capable of that, we have an emotional commitment.[199]

Liz Crolley has outlined how female football supporters were marginalised through both overt and covert forms of sexism. The tendency to 'insult' opponents by 'feminising' them was common but largely condoned: few supporters were ejected from grounds for calling male players 'women', 'tarts' or wolf-whistling them, although this certainly caused considerable offence to female fans. Equally significant was the trivialisation of female support by ignoring or dismissing their opinions and regarding them as interested only in the physical attributes of players.[200] Yet objections to sexism did not always equate to a desire to 'femininise' the masculine environment of football. Indeed not only did many female fans oppose attempts to make the game more 'female friendly' by, for example, forbidding swearing, they also showed little interest in attracting more women if it meant a dilution of the game's fundamental appeal. It is crucial to note that, for many women, football's masculine aura was a key part of its attraction. As Crolley and Cathy Long argued, there was an element of female fandom that wanted football 'to remain a mainly male domain, but one in which those "privileged" few women can peek – and even become part of – thereby awarding us with a special status denied other females'.[201]

Football and masculinity

Studies of the occupational culture of football have emphasised the game's role in 'celebrating, displaying, and reproducing' what Polley has termed 'orthodox masculine qualities'.[202] In a fascinating study of the inner world of North American professional ice hockey, Michael A. Robidoux looked in detail at the way in which a privileged model of masculinity was 'articulated repeatedly through occupational demands and the informal behaviours of the workplace'.[203] 'Insider' accounts of British soccer have outlined how a similar model of masculinity pervaded dressing rooms and training grounds. Studies by Hunter Davies and Eamon Dunphy in the 1970s and Garry Nelson in the 1990s revealed the importance of physical toughness and inter-group competition but also the male camaraderie and group solidarity of football culture. While some writers have seen the 'groupishness' and masculinity of the football club as an extension of male adolescence, others have drawn parallels with the culture of the male workplace or the shop floor. Being 'one of the lads' involved behaving in a particular way: being able to 'have a laugh' and endure 'piss takes' and 'wind ups'.[204] Andrew Parker's research on football trainees is particularly illuminating here. He shows how these apprentice footballers, aged between 16 and 19 years old, were influenced by a series of 'official' norms that emphasised the importance of discipline and professionalism as well as the 'unofficial' values of a lifestyle of fast cars, designer clothes and heterosexual relations. Being a football trainee was, in short, 'about becoming a man', although Parker is keen to stress that trainees negotiated these norms and values in different ways and so developed a range of individual masculine identities.[205]

Throughout much of the 1990s English football, at least, seemed to exhibit an unreconstructed masculine identity. A series of high-profile incidents involving players in the abuse of drink, violence and assault and the sexual humiliation of women were dismissed by some as 'new-laddism' but could also be perceived as 'an aggressive, almost virulent conception of masculinity'.[206] Those who did not fit the masculine norm were subject to ridicule. This explains the treatment of Graham Le Saux, an ex-England international and full-back with Chelsea, whose preference for broadsheet newspapers, art and antiques over the normal trappings of football fame marked him as an outsider in the eyes of some of his fellow professionals. In February 1999 Le Saux (a married man with children) was subjected to homophobic baiting by Liverpool's Robbie Fowler.[207] 'Fowler's point was simple', according to *When Saturday Comes*:

Football is for men who conform to a certain ideal of what a man is: aggressive, inarticulate, misogynic and definitely one of the lads. Players who don't conform ... are favoured with the worst insult the lads can think of.[208]

The vilification of Justin Fashanu when he 'came out' in 1990 seemed to provide further proof of the game's preservation of narrow masculine and hetereosexual norms.[209] If being a successful footballer involved being mentally as well as physically tough, there was also little room for those who suffered from depression or mental distress. In a thought-provoking study, Wagg has shown how the sports press effectively denied the possibility that young athletes, earning thousands of pounds a week, could be depressed at all. When Stan Collymore, a talented but 'difficult' forward with a controversial reputation, was diagnosed with clinical depression in early 1999, the press and the football world remained sceptical. Collymore, they thought, was being self-indulgent and mentally weak: what he really needed, according to one journalist, was 'a hefty kick up the backside'. Mental distress was thus not a legitimate 'illness' in the macho and competitive football industry, where men had to dig deep and get on with things when the going got tough.[210]

All this is not to suggest, however, that football offered only one version of masculinity. Crolley and Long highlighted aspects of supporting culture, expressive of adoration, emotions and sensitivity, which indicated a more complicated notion of masculinity than is normally recognised. Discussing the diverse nature of supporting and playing styles, Giulianotti similarly argued that football cultures 'have always enabled the expression and appreciation of different forms of masculinity'.[211] Nobody demonstrated this more clearly than the best-known English footballer of the late 1990s: David Beckham. Much of Beckham's popularity, it has been argued, lay in the fluid nature of his 'identity' and his broad appeal. For some, he reflected a new type of masculinity: he was a loyal husband and a devoted father, who famously missed training at Manchester United in February 2000 to look after his baby son and was subsequently dropped from the first team by manager Alex Ferguson. He was comfortable with his status as a gay icon and his rapid absorption (with the help of his ex-Spice Girl wife as well as agents and marketing men) into the worlds of fashion, style and celebrity. Garry Whannel described Beckham as 'a post-"new lad" man', noting that his rise to celebrity status coincided with a broader cultural shift in masculinity and sexual politics.[212] Others regarded him as combining aspects of traditional working-class masculinity with a classless 'new mannishness'. According to one account, Beckham stood 'at the precise juncture at which "new man" meets the masculine remnants of a bygone age, where caring husband and father meets physical labourer and breadwinner'.[213] Yet the notion that Beckham represented a subversion of soccer's key masculine conventions is ultimately unconvincing. At the heart of Beckham's identity were his qualities as a footballer and in this respect he was not so far removed from the likes of Stanley Matthews, Kevin Keegan and Paul Gascoigne. In his sheer enthusiasm, driving commitment, determination and loyalty to colleagues on the field of play, it has been argued, Beckham exemplified 'the very qualities of masculinity that are most central to football'.[214]

British football, national identities and globalisation

The 1990s was a troubling decade for defenders of the British state and proponents of a unitary British identity. Writing in 1995, the historian Raphael Samuel could suggest that, in the context of the increasing restlessness and self-confidence of its peripheral nations, Britain faced 'a very uncertain future'. 'As a source of symbolic capital', he went on, 'Britain's credit seems to be exhausted.'[215] Within two years, aided by Tony Blair's reformist New Labour government, the process of political devolution was well under way. In September 1997 the Scottish voted overwhelmingly for their own parliament, while the Welsh narrowly opted for a national assembly. Where did this leave the so-called 90-minute patriotism of the football crowd? Some commentators felt it had been rendered irrelevant and trivial in the context of devolution. According to Iain Macwhirter of *The Scotsman*, the emerging sense of national self-confidence and autonomy felt by the young members of the 'Tartan Army' at the French World Cup of 1998 had 'nothing whatever to do with football'.[216] Other Scottish observers felt that the regaining of some degree of national sovereignty would at least result in a more rational

attitude to international football and less need to regard the performances of the Scottish team (or its fans) as a barometer of national
pride.[217] Yet the links between football, nation and identity did not
simply fade away during the 1990s: quite the opposite in some cases. In
England, it could be argued that the national team came to represent the
cornerstone of a newly acquired sense of Englishness as distinct from
Britishness. Reinforced by the aggressive nationalism and xenophobia of
the popular press, football patriotism in England acquired 'a sharper political edge' which was fed by, and fed into, broader anxieties concerning
national decline, devolution and European integration.[218] At the same
time, the British game was affected by economic and cultural trends at
the European and global level, which served to complicate any simplistic
notion of a fixed and straightforward relationship between football and
national identity.

Scottishness, Welshness and football

The Scottish football team continued to qualify for international competitions throughout the 1980s and 1990s but offered little more to enliven
the population's sense of nationhood. Defeats to Costa Rica and Morocco
at the 1990 and 1998 World Cups respectively extended Scotland's international 'role of dishonour'.[219] The termination in 1989 of the annual
fixture against England, meanwhile, denied the Scots their traditional
opportunity to get one over the despised 'auld enemy'. By this point, it
was arguably the Scottish fans rather than the team who had come to represent the nation best on the international stage. We saw in the last
chapter how Scotland's 'Tartan Army' consciously adopted a carnivalesque style of support in direct contrast to the hooligan image of the
English fan abroad. The identification of Scottish fans with friendly exuberance and non-violence was reinforced in the course of Italia '90, and at
the 1992 European Championships in Sweden, where the 'Tartan Army'
was recognised by UEFA as having the best behaved supporters at the
tournament. A number of studies have outlined the role of the Scottish
press in building up a positive image of the 'Tartan Army' as 'ambassadors for Scotland'. By the 1996 European Championships in England
(Euro '96), Scottish fans seemed to have overtaken the players 'as central
representatives of Scottish identity' and even of 'the new Scotland to
come'.[220] Scotland on Sunday, for one, was more concerned that the supporters' reputation was kept intact than that the Scottish team beat
England at Wembley. Significantly, in 1997 the Daily Record illustrated

the announcement of the publication of the Home Rule Bill and an accompanying article titled 'Scottish and proud of it!' with what it saw as an unequivocal image of Scottish pride: the 'Tartan Army' partying at London's Trafalgar Square.[221]

For others, however, the Scottish team and its supporters seemed to be an inappropriate symbol for a new politically mature Scotland. The anti-Englishness that had helped to define the 'Tartan Army' and unite its membership was increasingly criticised by social and academic commentators as embarrassing and anachronistic. Many saw it as suggestive of a negative, insular and backward-looking version of Scottishness that fitted poorly with more modern 'internationalist' perspectives. With Scotland eliminated from France '98, the *Daily Record* exhorted its readers not to cheer too loudly if England lost, but most Scots still celebrated when their neighbours were knocked out at the quarter-final stage by Argentina. One poll indicated that 75 per cent of Scots chose not to support England and that 40 per cent would have liked any team other than England to win the 1998 tournament. Some journalists also felt that the tartan and kilt imagery of the supporters needed urgent updating and that the Scots ought to stop making fools of themselves 'on and off the park'.[222] Other evidence pointed to the decline of football in general, and the national team in particular, as a symbol of Scottish identity. Moorhouse's 1994 survey of Rangers supporters revealed a widespread lack of interest in the Scotland side, which was perceived as being poorly managed and administered by the Scottish FA. Joseph Bradley's small survey of fans of the leading Scottish clubs indicated higher levels of support for the national team but also suggested that considerable numbers of Scottish fans (and not only Celtic supporters of the Republic of Ireland) spread their allegiances to other British and international teams.[223] Things may have been different if Scotland had won more often. Yet by the time the team lost to England in November 1999 in a play-off for Euro 2000, it seemed that more Scots were prepared to accept defeat in sporting rather than nationalistic terms. The match still mattered a great deal but, as Ronald Kowalski has argued, probably less so than it had done in previous decades. Whether football was now 'less central to most Scots' sense of identity' is difficult to say.[224] Devolution and a new parliament had certainly helped forge a positive sense of Scottishness but this did not mean that Scots would start rooting for England rather than England's opponents.

Football continued to illustrate the complicated nature of Welsh identity into the 1990s. Despite attempts to forge autonomous structures,

PLATE 22 *John Charles, star of Leeds United, Juventus and Wales in the late 1950s and 1960s, pictured in 1994 with miniature statues of his all time Great Britain team (© Popperfoto.com).*

Welsh football still 'operated firmly within an English context'.[225] The independence of Welsh football was probably questioned more towards the end of the twentieth century than it ever had been before. The FAW's decision to set up the League of Wales in 1992 derived from a need to assert its separate identity in the context of international pressure from those countries who demanded the amalgamation of the four UK associations, as well as UEFA and FIFA, who insisted that new national associations should control their own league. But without the three leading Welsh professional clubs – Cardiff City, Swansea City and Wrexham – and a number of semi-professional sides who also chose to stay within the English 'pyramid', the new competition failed to garner popular support and was only a limited success.[226] What is more, Martin Johnes has argued that a familiarity with televised Premiership football and the persistent failure of the national side meant that a proportion of Welsh fans felt able to follow England 'without feeling they were compromising their Welsh identity', although many more probably lined up with the Scots in cheering for whoever England was playing.[227] Club sides rather than the national eleven have been the main conveyors of national feeling and anti-English sentiment. It may be that the flying of Welsh flags and the aggressive anti-English chanting at Welsh grounds was evidence of a radicalisation of nationalist sentiment. But most writers are more circumspect, arguing that choruses of 'You cheating English bastard' and 'England's full of shit' ought not be taken literally but understood instead in the context of the ritualised nature of football rivalries. Such an interpretation is also in keeping with the pluralistic and divided identities evidenced by the marginal vote for devolution, and surveys in which the vast majority of Welsh people continued to define themselves as at least partly 'British'. Even with its own assembly and a new Millenium Stadium, built in 1999, the Welsh remained committed to Britain, and in football as in politics the British (or English) stage still afforded the best opportunity for Wales to make its mark and express its complex sense of nationhood.[228]

Englishness and football

Historians of national identity have made much of the role of football in sparking a renewal of English patriotism. Richard Weight has suggested that in the wake of the resurgence of Scottish and Welsh nationalism, the English 'found a sense of direction in football'. He argues strongly that the national team emerged as 'the focal point of a new, self-conscious and separatist Englishness'; according to Jeffrey Richards, it became 'a vehicle for the affirmation of the new national identity'.[229] Euro '96 seemed to be a key turning point in this respect. Senses of history and nostalgia were crucial to the presentation of the event – the first major football tournament in Britain since 1966 – and a number of important slogans and symbols illustrated the complicated relationship between past and present. One example was the FA's official tournament slogan, 'Football's coming home', popularised in the 'Three Lions' song that reached Number One in the charts and resounded around Wembley during England matches. Garland and Rowe have argued that the phrase reflected a persistent but outdated belief in England's superiority as the nation that invented the game and kindly bestowed it on the world. Others saw it as an overtly nationalistic attempt to 'reconstruct an imperial Britain'. Polley, by contrast, has seen the song (if not the slogan) not as backward-looking nostalgia but as an example of a type of post-modern humour that 'revisits and recycles past sport in a celebratory manner as an inspiration for the present'.[230] Debate also centred on the apparent reclamation of the Cross of St George as a symbol of Englishness. Weight thought that the proliferation of red and white flags and painted faces in 1996 in comparison with the Union Jacks of 1966 showed that the English had 'shed their Britishness', but others disagreed. The fact that the Union flag did not disappear altogether and that St George's flags were often combined with choruses of 'God Save the Queen' and 'Rule Britannia' suggested a continued English confusion over national identity.[231] There were also those, as we shall see below, who doubted whether the St George's Cross could really be considered a legitimate symbol of a modern, multicultural and inclusive England.

Studies of the media coverage of major tournaments in the 1990s suggest that this 'new Englishness' was no more benign than the aggressive xenophobia of English hooligans in previous decades. In an analysis of the newspaper reporting of Euro '96, Garland and Rowe showed how an overt form of patriotism developed as the tournament progressed, culminating in the extreme xenophobia and militaristic vocabulary and imagery published before the semi-final clash with Germany. *The Sun* proclaimed 'LET'S BLITZ FRITZ' while the *Daily Mirror* infamously declared 'soccer war' on the Germans and superimposed tin helmets on two England players under the headline 'ACHTUNG! SURRENDER! FOR YOU FRITZ, ZE EURO 96 CHAMPIONSHIP IS OVER!'[232] A more systematic analysis by Joseph Maguire and colleagues at Loughborough University, comparing the English press with its German equivalent, similarly identified the interweaving of nostalgic references to former glories with a more assertive and defensive nationalism. The constant harking back to 1945 and 1966 was in marked contrast to the German newspapers, which, secure in the nation's contemporary role in European politics, were happy 'to let their football team do the talking'. Coverage of the 1998 World Cup was generally more restrained but continued many of the themes of two years earlier, with Argentina replacing Germany as the main foreign foe and the memories of the Falklands War of 1982 and Diego Maradona's 'hand of God' in 1986 revived alongside those of 1945 and 1966.[233] It would be mistaken to dismiss all this as the characteristic excess and hyperbole of the English tabloid press. Each of these studies recognise, to varying degrees, that the media coverage of the England team reflected a strand of jingoism and aggressive nationalism rooted in the wider political culture. As Peter Beck has perceptively argued in respect of Anglo-German relations, the negative stereotyping, irrational prejudices and anti-European mentality of the English press was often mirrored in politics, where wartime images became 'fossilised' and attitudes could appear 'stuck in a time warp'.[234]

For all this, Weight has maintained that football played a key role in articulating a new, far-reaching English identity. This, he argues, was much more than a 90-minute form of patriotism: it flowed into, and took strength from, popular campaigns to revive St George's Day and define 'Englishness', as well as a growing feeling of political separateness prompted by the ongoing process of devolution. It also involved, in his view, an acceptance of non-white players and supporters as representatives of the nation. The media's conversion of Paul Ince and Ian Wright into national heroes after gaining a draw for England in Rome to secure qualification for France '98 supports this idea. So does the adulation of the same two players, along with Sol Campbell and their white teammate Paul Gascoigne, for leading the singing of the national anthem before a friendly against Morocco in 1998. For Weight, incidents of this kind 'did more for race relations than a dozen earnest reports by the Commission for Racial Equality'.[235] Yet such an argument simplifies the relationship between notions of Britishness, Englishness and black identity and ignores the fact that the acceptance of black sportspeople as icons of the nation has been 'contingent and limited'. Ben Carrington, for example, has argued that implicit in the discourse of Euro '96, with its 'Football's coming home' and 'return to '66' messages, was a coded form of cultural racism that marginalised images of blacks and Asians and identified Englishness as exclusively white.[236] The degree to which non-whites could legitimately embrace the St George's Cross and other symbols of English identity was also open to question. Ian Wright may have been happy to wrap himself in the flag at France '98 but many black supporters were not. As Krishan Kumar has argued: 'For a black or Asian fan to drape himself in it [the St George's Cross] had become almost as unthinkable as wrapping himself in the Union Jack', the flag previously associated with the far-right National Front and British National Party. There is anecdotal evidence that non-whites began to support England in greater numbers but many undoubtedly remained alienated from the team and what it represented. Unlike Britishness, Englishness continued to be widely perceived in terms of cultural and racial exclusion.[237]

Football, Europeanisation and globalisation

This emphasis on national identities should not lead us to ignore the effect on British football of wider processes often termed Europeanisation and globalisation. These took a variety of forms. First, the expansion of European competition over the course of the 1990s, and the increasing financial rewards that flowed from European success, meant that the leading British clubs were increasingly competing within a continental as well as a national context. Influenced by a proposal submitted by Rangers chairman David Murray, UEFA reformed the European Cup in 1991–2 to include a league format. The competition was subsequently renamed the 'Champions League' and expanded in 1997 to include runners-up from national leagues. Further restructuring in 1999 led to the creation of a bloated two-round, 32-club, group stage open to the third and fourth-placed teams in the Premier League and other lucrative national leagues (France, Germany, Italy and Spain) and the absorption of the Cup Winners' Cup into an expanded UEFA Cup competition.[238] Significantly, in 1998 Liverpool and Manchester United were also involved in forming the independent G14 group consisting of the continent's most successful and powerful clubs, the rise of which threatened the sovereignty of national federations and contributed to 'the emergence of a transnational regime' in European football.[239]

Second, the 1990s witnessed a considerable influx of foreign players and coaches at British clubs. From 11 foreign registrations in the first Premier League season in 1992–3, the non-British contingent grew to 66 in 1995–6 and 166 by 1998–9. By 1997 there were 218 foreign players in all English leagues, a figure that had reached over 400 by the opening day of the 2000–1 season. These players were also recruited from a range of different countries: by 1995 41 nationalities were represented in the English leagues and 22 in the top division alone.[240] Foreign coaches were also engaged at a number of leading clubs, most notably Frenchmen Arsene Wenger and Gerard Houllier (at Arsenal and Liverpool respectively), Italy's Gianluca Vialli (at Chelsea), and the Dutchmen Ruud Gullit (at Chelsea and Newcastle United) and Dick Advocaat (at Rangers). A number of explanations have been forwarded for this relatively recent burst of cosmopolitanism. The Bosman ruling of 1995 was undoubtedly significant in facilitating greater player mobility, ensuring as it did the free movement of players whose contracts had expired between European Union states and effectively 'open[ing] up the European "player pool" to British clubs'.[241] Yet equally important, if not more so, were the high transfer fees and wages that could now be paid (by English clubs particularly) as the result of wealthy owners and the lucrative deals with satellite broadcasters throughout the 1990s. Such developments led to Britain's transformation from an oasis of foreign talent into a prime destination for the modern football migrant. By the end of the decade, Premier League clubs had moved alongside their Italian and Spanish rivals as 'major "brokers" in the global market'.[242]

Finally, global developments in the televising, marketing and sponsorship of football have significantly impacted upon the British game at a number of levels. Vast audiences watched those clubs involved in the Champions League, the highest tier of European competition: an aggregate European audience of some 3.5 billion was registered in 1995–6. The progress of satellite and digital television also meant that Europe's leading national competitions were effectively globalised. By the 2000–1 season, the Premier League had become 'the world's most popular national football league', broadcast to 450 million homes and a cumulative audience of 1.3 billion in 141 different countries. It was particularly popular in Australasia, Africa and in south-east Asian countries such as Indonesia, Malaysia and Japan, as well as China, the largest market of all, where interest was thought to be rapidly increasing.[243] At club level, sponsorship and international capital has helped to lift some clubs out of national markets and into European and even global ones. The best example is Manchester United, which emerged during the 1990s as football's leading global brand. The club's eagerness to exploit its existing international reputation was demonstrated through a number of initiatives, such as the opening of club megastores in Kuala Lumpa and Singapore and the 'Theatre of Dreams' project, providing its estimated 30 million fans in the Far East with Internet access to club merchandise and other resources. Sponsorship agreements in 2000 with global companies such as Vodafone (worth over £30 million over four years) and Nike (£300 million over 13 years) were crucial in developing the club's position as a genuinely transnational brand. Manchester United's decision to reposition itself as a global concern was also demonstrated by the undertaking of summer tours to the Far East and the USA and its decision in early 2000 to withdraw from the FA Cup in order to compete in FIFA's inaugural World Club Championships in Brazil.[244]

It would be mistaken to assume, however, that the British game simply jettisoned local and national concerns for European and global ones. Few theorists of globalisation equate it with homogeneity: most recognise the continued ability of local and national communities to resist, adapt and remake global culture. Richard Giulianotti and Roland Robertson, for example, have applied Robertson's notion of 'glocalisation' to football, acknowledging that while the world has increasingly become a single place, individual societies have managed to retain particular identities. Thus although they see the wealthiest clubs as transnational corporations with the ability to trade across national borders, they recognise that these clubs remain tied to 'home' locations through name, stadium, colours and local support, and connected financially and historically to national structures and competitions.[245] It is indeed important not to overstate British football's newly acquired cosmopolitanism. Despite the alleged arrival of a more sophisticated approach to tactics and preparation, there is little evidence that styles of play changed markedly or that the game's masculine occupational culture was transformed. More often it was foreign players and coaches who had to adapt to the British game, rather than vice-versa. At Liverpool, as Wagg has shown, new ideas from abroad were reconciled with the local tradition of the Anfield 'boot room' by initially appointing Houllier as joint-manager with Roy Evans, a survivor of the old regime. Few clubs assembled genuinely 'global' teams. Most still relied on a core of home-grown talent and kept 'home' players at the 'heart' of the team, often as captain. And despite the importation of leading players from France, Italy and South America, player recruitment continued to be based largely on well-established international networks linking Britain to culturally and linguistically compatible regions and nations, such as Scandinavia, the Netherlands and the British Commonwealth.[246]

Nor did the development of a new European consciousness among some British supporters necessarily threaten other layers of identification. As we have seen, from its beginnings European club football undoubtedly broadened the worldview of British supporters. We might also legitimately see it as part of a complex and contested political discourse concerning the meaning of 'Europe' and its proper relationship with Britain. The game may not have offered a solution to the uncertainty of whether Britain was really a part of Europe or not, but football's development in the late twentieth century increasingly suggested a position at the heart of the continent rather than detached and isolated from it. While football continued to be an obvious vehicle for national rivalry and division, Donald McNeill is surely right that, in Britain and elsewhere, it did 'as much as anything to engender the idea of a "Europe" in the popular imagination'.[247] This certainly seems to have been true of many of the Manchester United fans interviewed by King in his study of European football. Increasing involvement in European competition and familiarity with continental destinations led this group of male supporters to develop a type of post-national identity that seemed to reject Englishness and domestic competition. Yet, crucially, these supporters were not becoming European in any straightforward sense: they embraced Europe only as far as it offered a platform for elevating the status of Manchester and

Manchester United 'into a new transnational context'. European success certainly helped forged new rivalries with continental clubs such as Feyenoord and Juventus, but it was at the local level that such European adventures had the greatest impact, in terms of asserting pride in one's club and city and reinforcing superiority over long-established rivals such as Liverpool, Leeds United and Manchester City.[248] Like all identities, those relating to football were thus fluid and difficult to pin down: they shifted and overlapped according to context and circumstance. What is clear is that the influence of Europeanisation and globalisation did not mean that people ceased to care about local, regional and national affiliations. Indeed a global world offered more opportunities than ever before for followers of all teams – large or small, national or club – to express their allegiances and share or compare their passion with others.[249]

References

1 Ludmilla Jordanova, *History in Practice* (London: Arnold, 2000), p. 119; Pat Hudson, *The Industrial Revolution* (London: Edward Arnold, 1992).

2 For an earlier sporting example, see the discussion of the nineteenth-century British 'sporting revolution' in Neil Tranter, *Sport, Economy and Society in Britain, 1750–1914* (Cambridge: Cambridge University Press, 1998), chapter 2.

3 John Williams, 'The Fall of Liverpool FC and the English Football "Revolution"', in J. Williams, S. Hopkins and C. Long (eds), *Passing Rhythms: Liverpool FC and the Transformation of Football* (Oxford: Berg, 2001), p. 147; 'The "New Football" in England and Sir John Hall's New "Geordie Nation"' in S. Gehrmann (ed.), *Football and Regional Identity in Europe* (Münster: Lit Verlag, 1997), pp. 243–77; Anthony King, *The End of the Terraces: The Transformation of English Football in the 1990s* (Leicester: Leicester University Press, 1998); Dave Russell, *Football and the English: A Social History of Association Football in England, 1863–1995* (Preston: Carnegie, 1997), p. 209; James Walvin, *The People's Game: The History of Football Revisited* (Edinburgh: Mainstream, 1994), p. 199.

4 Russell, *Football and the English*, chapter 9; Williams, 'New Football'; Paul Dempsey and Kevan Reilly, *Big Money, Beautiful Game* (London: Nicholas Brealey, 1998), chapter 2.

5 See John Williams, *Is It All Over?: Can Football Survive the Premier League?* (Reading: South Street, 1999), p. 21; Dominic Malcolm, Ian Jones and Ivan Waddington, 'The People's Game?: Football Spectatorship and Demographic Change', *Soccer and Society*, 1, 1 (Spring 2000), pp. 129–43;

Garry Crawford, *Consuming Sport: Fans, Sport and Culture* (London: Routledge, 2004), pp. 10–11; Tim Crabbe and Adam Brown, '"You're Not Welcome Anymore": The Football Crowd, Class and Social Exclusion', in S. Wagg (ed.), *British Football and Social Exclusion* (London: Routledge, 2004), p. 31.

6   Williams, *Is It All Over?*, pp. 17–21.

7   The most detailed account of the disaster and its aftermath is Phil Scraton, *Hillsborough: The Truth* (Edinburgh: Mainstream, 1999). See also Phil Scraton, 'Death on the Terraces: The Contexts and Injustices of the 1989 Hillsborough Disaster' in P. Darby, M. Johnes and G. Mellor (eds), *Soccer and Disaster: International Perspectives* (London: Routledge, 2005), pp. 59–76. For other perspectives, see Ian Taylor, 'English Football in the 1990s: Taking Hillsborough Seriously?' in J. Williams and S. Wagg (eds), *British Football and Social Change: Getting into Europe* (Leicester: Leicester University Press, 1991), pp. 3–24; John Williams, 'Kopites, "Scallies" and Liverpool Fan Cultures: Tales of Triumph and Disasters' in Williams, Hopkins and Long (eds), *Passing Rhythms*, pp. 114–17.

8   Martin Johnes, '"Heads in the Sand": Football, Politics and Crowd Disasters in Twentieth-Century Britain' in Darby, Johnes and Mellor (eds), *Football and Disaster*, pp. 19–21; Scraton, *Hillsborough*, pp. 81, 112–16.

9   Taylor, 'English Football', p. 5; Tony Walter, 'The Mourning After Hillsborough', *Sociological Review*, 39, 3 (1991), pp. 599–625; Dave Russell, '"We All Agree, Name the Stand after Shankly": Cultures of Commemoration in Late Twentieth-Century English Football Culture', *Sport in History*, 26, 1 (April 2006), pp. 6–7.

10 Taylor, 'English Football', pp. 10–12; Patrick Murphy, John Williams and Eric Dunning, *Football on Trial: Spectator Violence and Development in the Football World* (London: Routledge, 1990), pp. 20–1; Johnes, 'Heads in the Sand', p. 20; King, *End of the Terraces*, pp. 74–5.

11 Richard Giulianotti, 'Social Identity and Public Order: Political and Academic Discourses on Football Violence' in R. Giulianotti, N. Bonney and M. Hepworth (eds), *Football, Violence and Social Identity* (London: Routledge, 1994), pp. 21–4; Johnes, 'Heads in the Sand', pp. 20–3; Graham Kelly, *Sweet FA* (London: Collins Willow, 1999), p. 170.

12 Steve Greenfield and Guy Osborn, *Regulating Football: Commodification, Consumption and the Law* (London: Pluto, 2001), pp. 1, 12–14; King, *End of the Terraces*, pp. 77–86; Alex Fynn and Lynton Guest, *The Secret Life of Football* (London: Macdonald Queen Anne, 1989), pp. 243–53; Murphy, Williams and Dunning, *Football on Trial*, pp. 217–22; Kelly, *Sweet FA*, pp. 178–9.

13 Lord Justice P. Taylor, *The Hillsborough Stadium Disaster 15th April 1989: Final Report* (London: HMSO, 1990). For summaries of and commentaries on the findings, see Scraton, *Hillsborough*; King, *End of the Terraces*, pp. 97–106; Taylor, 'English Football', pp. 12–16; Williams, *Is It All Over?*, p. 13; David McArdle, *From Boot Money to Bosman: Football, Society and the Law* (London: Cavendish, 2000), pp. 90–4; Greenfield and Osborn, *Regulating Football*, pp. 14–16; Richard Holt and Tony Mason, *Sport in Britain, 1945–2000* (Oxford: Blackwell, 2000), pp. 159–60.

14 Taylor, 'English Football', pp. 12–13; Williams, 'New Football', pp. 245–6; Taylor, *Hillsborough Stadium Disaster*, pp. 12, 76–82; King, *End of the Terraces*, pp. 97–8.

15 Taylor, 'English Football', pp. 13–15; quotation p. 13; Walvin, *People's Game*, pp. 197–8.

16 Vic Duke, 'The Drive to Modernization and the Supermarket Imperative: Who Needs a New Football Stadium?', in R. Giulianotti and J. Williams (eds), *Game Without Frontiers: Football, Identity and Modernity* (Aldershot: Arena, 1994), pp. 132–3; Williams, 'New Football', p. 248; David Canter, Miriam Comber and David L. Uzzell, *Football in its Place: An Environmental Psychology of Football Grounds* (London: Routledge, 1989), pp. 41–2, 48; John Bale, *Landscapes of Modern Sport* (Leicester: Leicester University Press, 1994), p. 83.

17 King, *End of the Terraces*, pp. 100–2; Richard Giulianotti, *Football: A Sociology of the Global Game* (Cambridge: Polity, 1999), p. 76; H. F. Moorhouse, 'On the Periphery: Scotland, Scottish Football and the New Europe' in Williams and Wagg (eds), *British Football*, pp. 215–16; Football Association, *A Manifesto for Football*, June 1992 (London: Football Association, 1992), p. 1; Walvin, *People's Game*, p. 198; Taylor, 'English Football', p. 16.

18 See King, *End of the Terraces*, pp. 55–69; Alan Tomlinson, 'North and South: The Rivalry of the Football League and the Football Association', pp. 25–47 and Adrian Goldberg and Stephen Wagg, 'It's Not a Knockout: English Football and Globalisation', both in Williams and Wagg (eds), *British Football*, pp. 242–5.

19 Goldberg and Wagg, 'It's Not a Knockout', p. 242; Tomlinson, 'North and South', p. 40.

20 King, *End of the Terraces*, pp. 120–31; Fynn and Guest, *Secret Life*, pp. 10–27; Russell, *Football and the English*, pp. 217–18.

21 Russell, *Football and the English*, p. 217. For details of the breakaway threats of the 1980s, see Fynn and Guest, *Secret Life*, pp. 148–67; King, *End of the Terraces*, pp. 59–64.

22 Goldberg and Wagg, 'It's Not a Knockout', p. 244.

23 Goldberg and Wagg, 'It's Not a Knockout', pp. 244–5; Fynn and Guest, *Secret Life*, p. 145.

24 Fynn and Guest, *Secret Life*, pp. 119–47; King, *End of the Terraces*, p. 64. Holt and Mason, *Sport in Britain*, p. 105, are rather confused in their chronology and surely wrong to claim that television was responsible for 'the biggest change in the game since the FA agreed to the setting up of the Football League in 1888.'

25 On the power struggle between the FA and the Football League, see Tomlinson, 'North and South'; Matthew Taylor, *The Leaguers: The Making of Professional Football in England, 1900–1939* (Liverpool: Liverpool University Press, 2005), pp. 35–44; Barrie Houlihan, *The Government and Politics of Sport* (London: Routledge, 1991), pp. 132–4.

26 Murphy, Williams and Dunning, *Football on Trial*, pp. 214–15; Football League, *One Game, One Team, One Voice: Managing Football's Future* (London: Football League, 1990), p. 1.

27 Football Association, *Blueprint for the Future of Football* (London: Football Association, 1991); Alex Fynn and Lynton Guest, *Out of Time: Why Football Isn't Working* (London: Pocket Books, 1994), pp. 20–43; Geoffrey Green, 'The Football Association', in A. H. Fabian and G. Green (eds), *Association Football*, Vol. 1 (London: Caxton, 1960), p. 47.

28 Russell, *Football and the English*, pp. 211–12; Fynn and Guest, *Out of Time*, pp. 44–55; King, *End of the Terraces*, pp. 102–3, 106, 88–96.

29 David Lacey, 'FA Promises Bolt from the Blue', *The Guardian*, 20 June 1991.

30 Tomlinson, 'North and South', pp. 41–3; King, *End of the Terraces*, pp. 67–8.

31 Alan Bairner, 'Football and the Idea of Scotland', in G. Jarvie and G. Walker (eds), *Scottish Sport and the Making of the Nation: Ninety-Minute Patriots?* (Leicester: Leicester University Press, 1994), pp. 13–14.

32 Bob Crampsey, *The First 100 Years: The Scottish Football League* (Glasgow: Scottish Football League, 1990), pp. 219–21, 225–8; Fynn and Guest, *Secret Life*, pp. 156–7.

33 Fynn and Guest, *Secret Life*, pp. 45–66; Moorhouse, 'On the Periphery', pp. 203–11, 217; Simon Inglis, *The Football Grounds of Britain* (London: Collins Willow, 1993 [1st edition, 1983]), p. 294; Bill Murray, *The Old Firm: Sectarianism, Sport and Society in Scotland* (Edinburgh: John Donald, 2000 [1st edition, 1984]), pp. 220–8.

34 Murray, *Old Firm*, p. 226.

35 Fynn and Guest, *Secret Life*, pp. 56–7. See also Murray, *Old Firm*, p. 227.

36 Quoted in Moorhouse, 'On the Periphery', p. 206.

37 Moorhouse, 'On the Periphery', pp. 204–7. See also Bairner, 'Football and the Idea of Scotland', p. 14; Walvin, *People's Game*, pp. 206–8.

38 Murray, *Old Firm*, pp. 230–2, 235–42, 221; Moorhouse, 'On the Periphery', pp 208–9.

39 Raymond Boyle, '"We Are Celtic Supporters …": Questions of Football and Identity in Modern Scotland', in Giulianotti and Williams (eds), *Game Without Frontiers*, pp. 81–4. See also Neil Blain and Raymond Boyle, 'Battling Along the Boundaries: The Marking of Scottish Identity in Sports Journalism', in Jarvie and Walker (eds), *Scottish Sport*, pp. 133–4.

40 Quoted in Moorhouse, 'On the Periphery', p. 211. See also Bairner, 'Football and the Idea of Scotland', p. 15.

41 Quoted in Moorhouse, 'On the Periphery', pp. 212–13.

42 Inglis, *Football Grounds*, p. 7; Moorhouse, 'On the Periphery', pp. 214–15.

43 John Bale, *Sport, Space and the City* (London: Routledge, 1993), p. 136; 'The Changing Face of Football: Stadiums and Communities', *Soccer and Society*, 1, 1 (Spring 2000), p. 91; Duke, 'Drive to Modernization', pp. 129–30.

44 John Bale, *Sports Geography* (London: Routledge, 2003 [1st edition, 1989]), pp. 96–7; Charles C. Euchner, *Playing the Field: Why Sports Teams Move and Cities Fight to Keep Them* (Baltimore: Johns Hopkins University Press, 1993), p. 5; John Williams and Richard Giulianotti, 'Introduction: Stillborn in the USA?', in Giulianotti and Williams (eds), *Game Without Frontiers*, p. 13.

45 John Bale, 'Identity, Identification and Image: Football and Place in the New Europe', in Gehrmann (ed.), *Football and Regional Identity*, pp. 280–1.

46 John Bale, 'Football and Topophilia: The Public and the Stadium', European University Institute Colloquium Papers, 1989, p. 7; 'Playing at Home: British Football and a Sense of Place', in Williams and Wagg (eds), *British Football*, pp. 135–6.

47 Quoted in Bale, *Sports Geography*, p. 19.

48 Euan Hague and John Mercer, 'Geographical Memory and Urban Identity in Scotland: Raith Rovers FC and Kirkcaldy', *Geography*, 83, 2 (1998), p. 113.

49 Hague and Mercer, 'Geographical Memory', pp. 112–14; Jack Fawbert, 'Football Fandom and the "Traditional" Football Club: From "Cockney

Parochialism" to a European Diaspora?', in J. Magee, A. Bairner and A. Tomlinson (eds), *The Bountiful Game?: Football Identities and Finances* (Oxford: Meyer & Meyer Sport, 2005), p. 99.

50 Arthur Hopcraft, *The Football Man* (London: Simon & Schuster, 1988 [1st edition, 1968]), p. 141.

51 Canter, Comber and Uzzell, *Football in its Place*, pp. 2, 7–8; 82.

52 Giulianotti, *Football*, p. 70.

53 Taylor, 'English Football', pp. 5–6.

54 See Bale, 'Playing at Home', pp. 131–6; *Sport, Space and the City*, pp. 65–77. For discussions of the metaphors employed by Bale, see Crawford, *Consuming Sport*, pp. 67–9; Richard Giulianotti, *Sport: A Critical Sociology* (Cambridge: Polity, 2005), pp. 122–3; Simon Inglis, *Sightlines: A Stadium Odyssey* (London: Yellow Jersey Press, 2000), pp. 31–2.

55 Taylor, 'English Football', p. 5; Desmond Morris, *The Soccer Tribe* (London: Jonathan Cape, 1981), pp. 22–4; Raymond Boyle, 'Football and Religion: Merseyside and Glasgow', in Williams, Hopkins and Long (eds), *Passing Rhythms*, pp. 39–52; Wray Vamplew, John Coyle, Julie Heath and Brian Naysmith, 'Sweet FA: Fans' Rights and Club Relocations', *Football Studies*, 1, 2 (August 1998), p. 57. On football and religion, see Alan Edge, *Faith of Our Fathers: Football as a Religion* (London: Mainstream, 1999); Martin Percy and Rogan Taylor, 'Something for the Weekend Sir?: Leisure, Ecstacy and Identity in Football and Contemporary Religion', *Leisure Studies*, 16 (1997), pp. 37–49.

56 Bale, 'Playing at Home', p. 132; *Sport, Space and the City*, pp. 73–74.

57 Bale, *Landscapes of Modern Sport*, pp. 139–42; Chris Gaffney and John Bale, 'Sensing the Stadium', in P. Vertinsky and J. Bale (eds), *Sites of Sport: Space, Place and Experience* (London: Routledge, 2004), pp. 25–38.

58 Bale, 'Playing at Home', p. 135.

59 Hague and Mercer, 'Geographical Memory', pp. 108–10.

60 Søren Nagbøl and John Bale, *A View of English Football: Sport and Sense of Place* (Jyväskylä: Department of Social Policy, University of Jyväskylä Working Papers, 1994), p. 6.

61 Bale, *Landscapes of Modern Sport*, p. 133.

62 Martin Lacey, 'The End of Something Small and the Start of Something Big', in D. Bull (ed.), *We'll Support You Evermore: Keeping Faith in Football* (London: Duckworth, 1992), pp. 91–2.

63 For details, see Rick Everitt, *Battle for the Valley* (London: Voice of the Valley, 1991); Joseph Maguire and Catherine Possamai, '"Back to the Valley": Local Responses to the Changing Culture of Football' in Joseph

Maguire, *Power and Global Sport: Zones of Prestige, Emulation and Resistance* (London: Routledge, 2005), pp. 41–60; Inglis, *Football Grounds*, pp. 267–9.

64 Quoted in Bale, 'Playing at Home', p. 133.

65 Vamplew, Coyle, Heath and Naysmith, 'Sweet FA', p. 62; Bale, 'Playing at Home', pp. 133–4.

66 Bale, *Landscapes of Modern Sport*, p. 132.

67 Hague and Mercer, 'Geographical Memory', p. 108.

68 Bale, 'Playing at Home', p. 134; Maguire and Possamai, 'Back to the Valley', p. 58.

69 Bale, *Sport, Space and the City*, pp. 94–133; *Landscapes of Modern Sport*, p. 145; 'Playing at Home', pp. 136–7.

70 Bale, 'Playing at Home', p. 136; Canter, Comber and Uzzell, *Football in its Place*, pp. 37–41.

71 John Bale, 'In the Shadow of the Stadium: Football Grounds as Urban Nuisances', *Geography*, 75 (1990), pp. 325–34; 'Football and Topophilia', pp. 7–15; 'Changing Face of Football', pp. 93–9. See also Colin Mason and Andrew Moncrieff, 'The Effect of Relocation on the Externality Fields of Football Stadia: The Case of St Johnstone FC', *Scottish Geographical Magazine*, 109, 2 (1993), pp. 96–105.

72 Duke, 'Drive to Modernization', pp. 136–7.

73 Sir Norman Chester Centre for Football Research (SNCCFR), 'Fact Sheet Number 2: Football Stadia After Taylor' (Leicester: SNCCFR, 2002), p. 10; Williams, 'New Football', p. 257.

74 Duke, 'Drive to Modernization', pp. 140–7.

75 Nagbøl and Bale, *View of English Football*, pp. 11–13. See also a Blackpool fan's description of Walsall and Scunthorpe as 'DIY-kit grounds': Eugene Ring, 'Blackpool: Illuminations of a Distant Fan', in Bull (ed.), *We'll Support You*, p. 114.

76 Ken Sproat, 'The Best Seats in the House?', *When Saturday Comes*, May 1994, pp. 16–17.

77 Bale, *Sport, Space and the City*, pp. 49, 43; Crawford, *Consuming Sport*, p. 99. See also Russell, *Football and the English*, p. 232.

78 Boyd Hilton, 'Out With the Old ... In With the New?', *When Saturday Comes*, November 1994, pp. 19–20.

79 Bale, *Sport, Space and the City*, pp. 191, 49; *When Saturday Comes*, August 1994, pp. 20–2.

80 SNCCFR, 'Football Stadia After Taylor', p. 17; Giulianotti, *Football*, p. 77.

81 Williams and Giulianotti, 'Stillborn in the USA', p. 12. See also Williams, 'New Football', p. 247.

82 Bale, *Sport, Space and the City*, p. 40.

83 Williams and Giulianotti, 'Stillborn in the USA', p. 12; Williams, 'New Football', p. 248.

84 Wray Vamplew, *Newcastle United Football Club: An Economic Impact Assessment. A Report by the De Montfort International Centre for Sports History and Culture* (Leicester: De Montfort University, 1997), pp. 33–4. See also Vamplew, Coyle, Heath and Naysmith, 'Sweet FA', pp. 58–9.

85 See Gary Armstrong, *Football Hooligans: Knowing the Score* (Oxford: Berg, 1998), pp. 127–37; Giulianotti, *Football*, pp. 80–2; *Sport*, pp. 128–33; Bale, *Sport, Space and the City*, pp. 50–3; *Landscapes of Modern Sport*, pp. 82–4; King, *End of the Terraces*, pp. 160–2; Carlton Brick, 'Taking Offence: Modern Moralities and the Perception of the Football Fan', *Soccer and Society*, 1, 1 (2000), pp. 159–63.

86 See Michel Foucault, *The Birth of the Clinic* (New York: Vintage, 1975); *Discipline and Punish* (London: Allen Lane, 1977).

87 Giulianotti, *Football*, p. 80.

88 Lance Bellers, 'Haven't You Got Homes to Go To?', *When Saturday Comes*, July 1995; King, *End of the Terraces*, p. 161.

89 Crawford, *Consuming Sport*, pp. 99–100.

90 Crawford, *Consuming Sport*, pp. 100–1.

91 Williams, *Is It All Over?*, pp. 20–1; 'New Football', p. 244.

92 Crabbe and Brown, 'You're Not Welcome', pp. 35–6; John Williams, 'The Changing Face of Football: A Case for National Regulation', in S. Hamil, J. Michie, C. Oughton and S. Warby (eds), *Football in the Digital Age: Whose Game Is It Anyway?* (Edinburgh: Mainstream, 2000), p. 102; David Conn, *The Beautiful Game?: Searching for the Soul of Football* (London: Yellow Jersey, 2004).

93 Crawford, *Consuming Sport*, pp. 105–7.

94 Giulianotti, *Football*, pp. 148–9, 169.

95 Steve Redhead, *Post-Fandom and the Millennial Blues: The Transformation of Soccer Culture* (London: Routledge, 1997), pp. 29–31.

96 Anthony King, 'The Lads: Masculinity and the New Consumption of Football', *Sociology*, 31, 2 (May 1997), pp. 329–46; *End of the Terraces*, pp. 148–203.

97 Richard Giulianotti, 'Supporters, Followers, Fans, and *Flaneurs*: A Taxonomy of Spectator Identities in Football', *Journal of Sport and Social*

Issues, 26, 1 (February 2002), pp. 25–46; p. 38. See also Richard Giulianotti and Michael Gerrard, 'Cruel Britannia?: Glasgow Rangers, Scotland and "Hot" Football Rivalries', in G. Armstrong and R. Giulianotti (eds), *Fear and Loathing in World Football* (Oxford: Berg, 2001), pp. 39–40.

98 King, *End of the Terraces*, pp. 148–50, 201–2.

99 Holt and Mason, *Sport in Britain*, p. 4.

100 Conn, *Beautiful Game?*, p. 10. See also Dempsey and Reilly, *Big Money*, pp. 236–40; Craig McGill, *Football Inc.: How Soccer Fans Are Losing the Game* (London: Vision, 2001), pp. 7–23.

101 Ian Taylor, '"Football Mad": A Speculative Sociology of Football Hooliganism', in E. Dunning (ed.), *The Sociology of Sport* (London: Frank Cass, 1971), pp. 364–5.

102 Chas Critcher, 'Football Since the War', in J. Clarke, C. Critcher and R. Johnson (eds), *Working Class Culture: Studies in History and Theory* (London: Hutchinson, 1979), pp. 169–70.

103 Peter Douglas, *The Football Industry* (London: George Allen & Unwin, 1973), p. 161.

104 See, for example, Russell, *Football and the English*, p. 210.

105 King, *End of the Terraces*, pp. 103–5; Garry Whannel, *Fields in Vision: Television Sport and Cultural Transformation* (London: Routledge, 1992), pp. 147–8; Richard Giulianotti and Michael Gerrard, 'Evil Genie or Pure Genius?: The (Im)moral Football and Public Career of Paul "Gazza" Gascoigne', in D. L. Andrews and S. J. Jackson (eds), *Sport Stars: The Cultural Politics of Sporting Celebrity* (London: Routledge, 2001), pp. 126–7, 132–3; Simon Kuper, *Football Against the Enemy* (London: Orion, 1994), p. 73.

106 Giulianotti and Gerrard, 'Evil Genie', p. 133; Greenfield and Osborn, *Regulating Football*, p. vii.

107 Nick Hornby, *Fever Pitch: A Fan's Life* (London: Victor Gollancz, 1992).

108 Redhead, *Post-Fandom*, p. 88. See also Raymond Boyle and Richard Haynes, *Power Play: Sport, the Media and Popular Culture* (London: Longman, 2000), pp. 180–5; Russell, *Football and the English*, pp. 219, 229–30; James Walvin, *The Only Game: Football in Our Times* (Harlow: Longman, 2001), pp. 241–3.

109 Nick Hornby (ed.), *My Favourite Year: A Collection of New Football Writing* (London: H. F. & G. Witherby, 1993); Redhead, *Post-Fandom*, p. 88.

110 Simon Kuper (ed.), *Perfect Pitch 1: Home Ground* (London: Headline,

1997); King, *End of the Terraces*, pp. 177–8; Hornby (ed.), *My Favourite Year*, pp. 219–20.

111   Giulianotti, *Football*, pp. 150–1.

112   Richard Haynes, *The Football Imagination: The Rise of Football Fanzine Culture* (Aldershot: Arena, 1995), pp. 39–45; Russell, *Football and the English*, pp. 231–2; Adam Brown, 'Let's All Have a Disco?: Football, Popular Music and Democratization', in S. Redhead, with D. Wynne and J. O'Connor (eds), *The Clubcultures Reader* (Oxford: Blackwell, 1997), p. 91; list of general and Club magazines in *When Saturday Comes*, July 1991, pp. 30–1. Redhead included as an appendix to one of his books a list of 1,287 soccer fanzines (still existing and defunct) published up to the mid-1990s. Redhead, *Post-Fandom*, pp. 104–29.

113   Richard Haynes, 'Vanguard or Vagabond?: A History of *When Saturday Comes*', in S. Redhead (ed.), *The Passion and the Fashion: Football Fandom in the New Europe* (Aldershot: Avebury, 1993), pp. 45–6; Haynes, *Football Imagination*, pp. 69–79; King, *End of the Terraces*, pp. 178–9.

114   Russell, *Football and the English*, pp. 218, 233; Walvin, *Only Game*, p. 244.

115   Redhead, *Post-Fandom*, pp. 80–8; Richard Newson, 'Music To Your Ears?', *When Saturday Comes*, April 1996, pp. 24–6; Adam Brown, '"Ratfink Reds": Montpellier and Rotterdam 1991', in Redhead, *Passion and the Fashion*, pp. 33–4; Haynes, *Football Imagination*, pp. 50–1.

116   Newport band Flyscreen's *Size Five Leather E.P.* (Endangered, 1996) featured 'Stamford Bridge' and 'Charlie George on Super8'. Norwich-based Halftime Oranges' *Clive Baker Set Fire To Me* (Rutland, 1996) and *Rotterdamnation* (Rutland, 1997) albums included tracks such as 'The Only Halifax Supporter', 'What's the Fuss About Ryan Giggs?', 'Blues for John Gidman' and 'Six Point Christmas'.

117   See David Conn, *The Football Business: Fair Game in the 1990s* (Edinburgh: Mainstream, 1997); Rex Nash, 'The Sociology of English Football in the 1990s: Fandom, Business and Future Research', *Football Studies*, 3, 1 (2000), pp. 50–2; Crabbe and Brown, 'You're Not Welcome', p. 30; Giulianotti, 'Supporters, Followers', p. 25; McGill, *Football Inc.*.

118   King, 'The Lads', pp. 334–6; *King, End of the Terraces*, pp. 134–5; Adam Brown, 'The Football Task Force and the "Regulator Debate"', in Hamil, Michie, Oughton and Warby (eds), *Football in the Digital Age*, p. 252; Williams, *Is It All Over?*, pp. 35–7.

119   John Williams and Sean Perkins, 'Ticket Pricing, Football Business and "Excluded" Football Fans', in *A Report to the Football Task Force*

(Leicester: University of Leicester, 1998), quoted in Brown, 'Football Task Force', p. 252; King, *End of the Terraces*, pp. 158–9; Williams, 'Changing Face of Football', p. 104.

120 Malcolm, Jones and Waddington, 'People's Game?', pp. 129–43; Dominic Malcolm, 'The People's Game?: Football Crowds and the New Marketing of the Game', *Singer & Friedlander's Review*, 1999–2000 season, pp. 29–33.

121 For discussion of the methodology of the Carling Survey, see Ivan Waddington, Eric Dunning and Patrick Murphy, 'Research Note: Surveying the Social Composition of Football Crowds', *Leisure Studies*, 15 (1996), pp. 209–14; John Williams, 'Surveying the Composition of Football Crowds: A Reply to Waddington, Dunning and Murphy', *Leisure Studies*, 15 (1996), pp. 215–19; Rex Nash, 'Research Note: Concept and Method in Researching the Football Crowd', *Leisure Studies*, 16 (1997), pp. 127–31.

122 See Malcolm, Jones and Waddington, 'People's Game?', pp. 138–40; Ian Jones, 'Football Fandom: Football Fan Identity and Identification at Luton Town Football Club', unpublished Ph.D. thesis, University of Luton, 1998.

123 King, 'The Lads', pp. 332–33, 340–41; Ian Jones, 'A Model of Serious Leisure Identification: The Case of Football Fandom', *Leisure Studies*, 19 (2000), pp. 283–98; Malcolm, Jones and Waddington, 'People's Game?', p. 140.

124 Adam Brown, 'United We Stand: Some Problems with Fan Democracy', in A. Brown (ed.), *Fanatics!: Power, Identity and Fandom in Football* (London: Routledge, 1998), pp. 50–67.

125 Rogan Taylor, *Football and its Fans: Supporters and their Relations with the Game, 1885–1985* (Leicester: Leicester University Press, 1992), pp. 72–3; Brown, 'Let's All Have a Disco', pp. 87–93; David Jary, John Horne and Tony Bucke, 'Football "Fanzines" and Football Culture: A Case of Successful "Cultural Contestation" ', *Sociological Review*, 39, 3 (1991), pp. 581–97.

126 Russell, *Football and the English*, p. 230.

127 Brown, 'United We Stand', pp. 52–3.

128 Brown, 'United We Stand', pp. 54–7; Denis Campbell and Andrew Shields, *Soccer City: The Future of Football in London* (London: Mandarin, 1993), pp. 214–37; Fynn and Guest, *Out of Time*, pp. 105–11.

129 Simon Lee, 'Grey Shirts to Grey Suits: The Political Economy of English Football in the 1990s', in Brown (ed.), *Fanatics*, pp. 42–6; Brown, 'United We Stand', pp. 58–61; King, *End of the Terraces*, pp. 188–90.

130 Rex Nash, 'English Football Fan Groups in the 1990s: Class, Representation and Fan Power', *Soccer and Society*, 2, 1 (Spring 2001), pp. 39–58. The quotation is from p. 44.

131 Brown, 'United We Stand', p. 53.

132 Adam Brown and Andy Walsh, *Not for Sale: Manchester United, Murdoch and the Defeat of BskyB* (Edinburgh: Mainstream, 1999); Michael Crick, 'Shareholders United Against Murdoch', *Soccer and Society*, 1, 3 (Autumn 2000), pp. 64–9; Greenfield and Osborn, *Regulating Football*, pp. 54–61. On the details of the judgment and broader implications of the case, see Peter Crowther, 'The Attempted Takeover of Manchester United by BskyB', pp. 64–70; Nicholas Finney, 'The MMC's Inquiry into BskyB's Merger with Manchester United PLC', pp. 71–80; Adam Brown, 'Sneaking in through the Back Door?: Media Company Interests and Dual Ownership of Clubs', pp. 81–92, all in Hamil, Michie, Oughton and Warby (eds), *Football in the Digital Age*.

133 Brian Lomax, 'Democracy and Fandom: Developing a Supporters' Trust at Northampton Town FC', *Soccer and Society*, 1, 1 (Spring 2000), pp. 79–87; Phil Frampton, Jonathan Michie and Andy Walsh, *Fresh Players, New Tactics: Lessons from the Northampton Town Supporters' Trust* (London: Football Governance Research Centre, 2001); Stephen Morrow, *The People's Game?: Football, Finance and Society* (Basingstoke: Palgrave, 2003), pp. 52–5; Dominic Malcolm, 'Football Business and Football Communities in the Twenty-First Century', *Soccer and Society*, 1, 3 (Autumn 2000), p. 103.

134 Sean Hamil, Jonathan Michie, Christine Oughton and Steven Warby, 'Recent Developments in Football Ownership', *Soccer and Society*, 1, 3 (Autumn 2000), p. 4.

135 Haynes, *Football Imagination*, pp. 89–98; Vic Duke, 'Local Tradition Versus Globalisation: Resistance to the McDonaldisation and Disneyisation of Professional Football in England', *Football Studies*, 5, 1 (2002), p. 18; Richard Giulianotti, 'Enlightening the North: Aberdeen Fanzines and Local Football Identity', in G. Armstrong and R. Giulianotti (eds), *Entering the Field: New Perspectives on World Football* (Oxford: Berg, 1997), pp. 227–8, 236.

136 Jary, Horne and Bucke, 'Football "Fanzines"', p. 592; Haynes, *Football Imagination*, p. 146. See also Giulianotti, 'Enlightening the North', pp. 211–37.

137 H. F. Moorhouse, 'From Zines Like These?: Fanzines, Tradition and Identity in Scottish Football', in Jarvie and Walker (eds), *Scottish Sport*, pp. 173–93; quotation p. 190. For criticism of Moorhouse's research on Scottish fanzines see John Horne, 'Kicking Racism Out of Soccer in

England and Scotland', *Journal of Sport and Social Issues*, 20, 1 (February 1996), p. 60.

138 Brown, 'Let's All Have a Disco', p. 91.

139 Brown, 'Let's All Have a Disco', pp. 91–2; Brown, 'United We Stand', p. 64; Nash, 'English Football Fan Groups', pp. 48–53; Crawford, *Consuming Sport*, p. 99; King, *End of the Terraces*, chapter 13.

140 Nash, 'English Football Fan Groups', p. 52. See also Eric Dunning, *Sport Matters: Sociological Studies of Sport, Violence and Civilization* (London: Routledge, 1999), p. 127.

141 Dave Russell, 'Associating with Football: Social Identity in England, 1863–1998', in G. Armstrong and R. Giulianotti (eds), *Football Cultures and Identities* (Basingstoke: Macmillan, 1999), p. 16.

142 Brown, 'United We Stand', p. 54.

143 King, 'The Lads', pp. 340–3.

144 John Williams, 'The Local and the Global in English Soccer and the Rise of Satellite Television', *Sociology of Sport Journal*, 11 (1994), pp. 376–97; Whannel, *Fields in Vision*, p. 15.

145 Goldberg and Wagg, 'It's Not a Knockout', p. 249; Vic Duke, 'The Politics of Football in the New Europe', in Williams and Wagg (eds), *British Football*, p. 199.

146 Boyle and Haynes, *Power Play*, pp. 188–9.

147 Cornel Sandvoss, *A Game of Two Halves: Football, Television and Globalization* (London: Routledge, 2003), p. 144. See also John Bale, 'Virtual Fandoms: Futurescapes of Football', in Brown (ed.), *Fanatics*, pp. 265–77.

148 Quoted in Sandvoss, *Game of Two Halves*, p. 157.

149 Gary Armstrong, *Football Hooligans: Knowing the Score* (Oxford: Berg, 1998), p. 322; Nash, 'Sociology of English Football', p. 58; King, 'The Lads', p. 336.

150 Crawford, *Consuming Sport*, pp. 141–51; Garry Crawford, 'Sensible Soccer: Sport Fandom and the Rise of Digital Gaming', in Magee, Bairner and Tomlinson (eds), *Bountiful Game?*, pp. 249–66.

151 Gavin Mellor, 'The Genesis of Manchester United as a National and International "Super-Club", 1958–68', *Soccer and Society*, 1, 2 (Summer 2000), pp. 151–66; 'The Rise of the Reds: An Historical Analysis of Manchester United as a "Super-Club"', *Singer & Friedlander's Review*, 1999–2000 season, pp. 18–21. See also Carlton Brick, 'Can't Live With Them. Can't Live Without Them: Reflections on Manchester United', in Armstrong and Giulianotti (eds), *Fear and Loathing*, pp. 10–13; Matthew

Taylor, 'Football, History and Memory: The Heroes of Manchester United', *Football Studies*, 3, 2 (October 2000), pp. 27–8; Claude Boli, *Manchester United, L'invention d'un Club: Deux siècles de metamorphoses* (Paris: Éditions de La Martinière, 2004), pp. 320–49.

152   Bale, *Sport, Space and the City*, pp. 62–3.

153   Adam Brown, '"Manchester Is Red"?: Manchester United, Fan Identity and the "Sport City"', pp. 184–5 and David Hand, 'Love Thy Neighbour or a Red Rag to a Blue?: Reflections on the City-United Dynamic in and around Manchester', p. 193, both in D. L. Andrews (ed.), *Manchester United: A Thematic Study* (London: Routledge, 2004); Fawbert, 'Football Fandom', pp. 102–3; Sandvoss, *Game of Two Halves*, pp. 87–8.

154   Bale, *Sport, Space and the City*, p. 61; 'Changing Face of Football', p. 91; Sandvoss, *Game of Two Halves*, pp. 89–100.

155   Matti Goksøyr and Hans Hognestad, 'No Longer Worlds Apart?: British Influences and Norwegian Football', in Armstrong and Giulianotti (eds), *Football Cultures*, p. 206.

156   Goksøyr and Hognestad, 'No Longer Worlds Apart', pp. 205–7; Bo Reimer, 'For the Love of England: Scandinavian Football Supporters, Manchester United and British Popular Culture', in Andrews (ed.), *Manchester United*, pp. 265–77; Rex Nash, 'Globalised Football Fandom: Scandinavian Liverpool FC Supporters', *Football Studies*, 3, 2 (October 2000), pp. 5–23; Fawbert, 'Football Fandom', pp. 104–5; Harri Heinonen, 'Finnish Football Supporters: Couch Potatoes or Partisan Fans?', *Moving Bodies*, 1, 1 (2003), pp. 101–9; Amir Ben-Porat, 'Overseas Sweetheart: Israeli Fans of English Football', *Journal of Sport and Social Issues*, 24, 4 (November 2000), pp. 344–50; Bale, *Sport, Space and the City*, p. 63; Giulianotti, 'Supporters, Followers'.

157   Les Back, Tim Crabbe and John Solomos, *The Changing Face of Football: Racism, Identity and Multiculture in the English Game* (Oxford: Berg, 2001), pp. 23–9; 'Racism in Football: Patterns of Continuity and Change' in Brown (ed.), *Fanatics!*, p. 85.

158   Jon Garland and Michael Rowe, 'Selling the Game Short: An Examination of the Role of Antiracism in British Football', *Sociology of Sport Journal*, 16 (1999), pp. 36–7; *Racism and Anti-Racism in Football* (Basingstoke: Palgrave, 2001), pp. 8–11, 50–3.

159   See G. P. T. Finn, 'Racism, Religion and Social Prejudice: Irish Catholic Clubs, Soccer and Scottish Society – 1 The Historical Roots of Prejudice', *International Journal of the History of Sport*, 8, 1 (May 1991), p. 74; Paul Dimeo and Gerry P. T. Finn, 'Scottish Racism, Scottish Identities: The Case of Partick Thistle' in Brown (ed.), *Fanatics!*, pp. 124–38; 'Racism, National Identity and Scottish Football' in B. Carrington and I. McDonald (eds),

'Race', Sport and British Society (London: Routledge, 2001), pp. 32–6; Horne, 'Kicking Racism Out of Soccer', pp. 49–51.

160 See Phil Vasili, *Colouring Over the White Line: The History of Black Footballers in Britain* (Edinburgh: Mainstream, 2000), pp. 17–56. On Wharton, see Ray Jenkins, 'Salvation for the Fittest? A West African Sportsman in Britain in the Age of New Imperialism', *International Journal of the History of Sport*, 7, 1, (May 1990), pp. 23–60; Phil Vasili, *The First Black Footballer: Arthur Wharton, 1865–1930* (London: Frank Cass, 1998). On Tull, see Phil Vasili, 'Walter Daniel Tull, 1888–1918: Soldier, Footballer, Black', *Race and Class*, 38, 2 (1996).

161 See Vasili, *Colouring Over the White Line*, chapters 2, 5 and 7; Martin Johnes, *A History of Sport in Wales* (Cardiff: University of Wales Press, 2005), pp. 62–3; Garland and Rowe, *Racism and Anti-Racism*, pp. 28–42.

162 Martin Polley, *Moving the Goalposts: A History of Sport and Society Since 1945* (London: Routledge, 1998), pp. 148–9; Brian Woolnough, *Black Magic: England's Black Footballers* (London: Pelham, 1983), pp. 8–14; Dave Hill, *Out of His Skin: The John Barnes Phenomenon* (London: Faber & Faber, 1989), pp. 44–8.

163 Brian Holland, 'Surviving Leisure Time Racism: The Burden of Racial Harassment on Britain's Black Footballers', *Leisure Studies*, 16 (1997), pp. 270–1; Joe Maguire, 'Sport, Racism and British Society: A Sociological Study of England's Elite Male Afro/Caribbean Soccer and Rugby Union Players' in G. Jarvie (ed.), *Sport, Racism and Ethnicity* (London: Falmer, 1991), pp. 94–123; Vasili, *Colouring Over the White Line*, p. 190; Russell, *Football and the English*, p. 174; Brendon McGuire, Kelly Monks and Rob Halsall, 'Young Asian Males: Social Exclusion and Social Injustice in British Professional Football?', *Culture, Sport, Society*, 4, 3 (Autumn 2001), p. 66; Horne, 'Kicking Racism Out', pp. 52–3; Stuart Cosgrove, *Hampden Babylon: Sex and Scandal in Scottish Football* (Edinburgh: Canongate, 2001 [1st edition, 1991]), pp. 118–23.

164 Daniel Burdsey, '"One of the Lads": Dual Ethnicity and Assimilated Ethnicities in the Careers of British Asian Professional Footballers', *Ethnic and Racial Studies*, 27, 5 (September 2004), pp. 757–79; Sanjiev Johal, 'Playing their own Game: A South Asian Football Experience' in Carrington and McDonald (eds), *'Race', Sport* pp. 159; Vasili, *Colouring Over the White Line*, pp. 155–76. This was despite considerable involvement at grassroots level. Surveys conducted through the 1990s found the participation rates of Bangladeshi, Indian and Pakistani males on a par with, if not higher than, those of whites, black Caribbeans and black Africans. See Michael F. Collins with Tess Kay, *Sport and Social Exclusion* (London: Routledge, 2003), pp. 127–32; Matthew Brown, 'Asian Games', *When Saturday Comes*, February 1995, pp. 14–16.

165   Vasili, 'Walter Daniel Tull', p. 61.

166   Hill, *Out of his Skin*, pp. 135–8; 'From Barnes to Camara: Football, Identity and Racism in Liverpool' in Williams, Hopkins and Long (eds), *Passing Rhythms*, pp. 129–45; Back, Crabbe and Solomos, *Changing Face of Football*, pp. 47–55; Hornby, *Fever Pitch*, pp. 188–90; Dimeo and Finn, 'Racism', pp. 40–2.

167   Canter, Comber and Uzzell, *Football in its Place*, pp. 72–4. On the legal dimensions of racism at football grounds and the impact of the Football Offences Act, see Greenfield and Osborn, *Regulating Football*, pp. 154–62; Brian Holland, '"Kicking Racism Out of Football": An Assessment of Racial Harassment in and around Football Grounds', *New Community*, 21, 4 (October 1995), pp. 578–81; Simon Gardiner and Roger Welch, 'Sport, Racism and the Limits of "Colour Blind" Law' in Carrington and McDonald (eds), *'Race', Sport*, pp. 133–49; Garland and Rowe, *Racism and Anti-Racism*, pp. 103–5; Back, Crabbe and Solomos, *Changing Face of Football*, pp. 202–6.

168   Holland, 'Surviving Leisure Time Racism', pp. 266–70.

169   Back, Crabbe and Solomos, 'Racism in Football', pp. 80–4; *Changing Face of Football*, pp. 55–9, 72–4.

170   See Michael Pickering, *Stereotyping: The Politics of Representation* (Basingstoke: Palgrave, 2001), pp. 115–36; Colin Holmes, *John Bull's Island: Immigration and British Society, 1871–1971* (Basingstoke: Macmillan, 1988), p. 82; Ellis Cashmore, *Making Sense of Sports* (London: Routledge, 1996 [1st edition, 1990]), pp. 99–106; Patrick Ismond, *Black and Asian Athletes in British Sport and Society: A Sporting Chance?* (Basingstoke: Palgrave, 2003), pp. 92–6; Polley, *Moving the Goalposts*, pp. 153–3; John Hoberman, *Darwin's Athletes: How Sport has Damaged Black America and Preserved the Myth of Race* (New York: Mariner, 1997), pp. 99–114. On the similar stereotyping of black African footballers in France, see Pierre Lanfranchi, 'The Migration of Footballers: The Case of France, 1932–1982' in J. Bale and J. Maguire (eds), *The Global Sports Arena: Athletic Talent Migration in an Interdependent World* (London: Frank Cass, 1994), pp. 73–5; Pierre Lanfranchi and Matthew Taylor, *Moving With the Ball: The Migration of Professional Footballers* (Oxford: Berg, 2001), p. 176.

171   Hoberman, *Darwin's Athletes*, p. 125; Hill, *Out of his Skin*, p. 54.

172   Hoberman, *Darwin's Athletes*, p. 126; Back, Crabbe and Solomos, *Changing Face of Football*, pp. 174–5; Hill, *Out of his Skin*, pp. 53–4.

173   Polley, *Moving the Goalposts*, p. 136; Scott Fleming, 'Racial Science and South Asian and Black Physicality', pp. 105–20 and Johal, 'Playing Their Own Game', pp. 160–1, both in Carrington and McDonald (eds),

'*Race*', *Sport*; McGuire, Monks and Halsall, ''Young Asian Males',
p. 68.

174 Maguire, 'Sport, Racism and British Society', pp. 101–13; Ismond, *Black and Asian*, pp. 93, 99–100. See also Merrill Melnick, 'Racial Segregation by Playing Position in the English Football League: Some Preliminary Observations', *Journal of Sport and Social Issues*, 12, 2 (1988), pp. 122–30; Joseph Maguire, 'Race and Position Assignment in English Soccer: A Preliminary Analysis of Ethnicity and Sport in Britain', *Sociology of Sport Journal*, 5, 3 (1988), pp. 257–69; Tony Mason, *Sport in Britain* (London: Faber & Faber, 1988). Discrimination was also evident in the labour market. By analysing the wage bills and sporting performance of clubs, Stefan Szymanski found evidence that black players, who tended to have longer careers, make more appearances and score more goals than their white counterparts, were nonetheless under-rewarded, though later work confirmed that this was not the result of the racial discrimination of supporters. Stefan Szymanski, 'A Market Test for Discrimination in the English Professional Leagues', *Journal of Political Economy*, 108, 3 (2000), pp. 590–603; Ian Preston and Stefan Szymanski, 'Racial Discrimination in English Football', *Scottish Journal of Political Economy*, 47, 4 (September 2000), pp. 342–63.

175 Whannel, *Fields in Vision*, pp. 129–31; Rod Brookes, *Representing Sport* (London: Arnold, 2002), p. 107; Boyle and Haynes, *Power Play*, pp. 112–13; Hoberman, *Darwin's Athletes*, pp. xxiii–xxvi.

176 David McCarthy and Robyn L. Jones, 'Speed, Aggression, Strength, and Tactical Naïveté: The Portrayal of the Black Soccer Player on Television', *Journal of Sport and Social Issues*, 21, 4 (November 1997), pp. 348–62; quotation from p. 357.

177 Ismond, *Black and Asian*, p. 117.

178 Boyle and Haynes, *Power Play*, p. 113; Polley, *Moving the Goalposts*, pp. 150–1; Garry Whannel, *Media Sport Stars: Masculinities and Moralities* (London: Routledge, 2002), pp. 185–8; Ben Carrington, 'Postmodern Blackness and the Celebrity Sports Star: Ian Wright, "Race" and English Identity' in Andrews and Jackson (eds), *Sport Stars*, pp. 105–6.

179 Quoted in Garland and Rowe, *Racism and Anti-Racism*, p. 65.

180 Back, Crabbe and Solomos, *Changing Face of Football*, pp. 180–2; Stella Orakwue, *Pitch Invaders: The Modern Black Football Revolution* (London: Vista, 1999), p. 220.

181 Steven Bradbury, *The New Football Communities: A Survey of Professional Football Clubs on Issues of Community, Ethnicity and Social Inclusion* (Leicester: Sir Norman Chester Centre for Football Research, 2001).

182 McGuire, Monks and Halsall, 'Young Asian Males', pp. 74–5; Johal, 'Playing their own Game', pp. 156–9; Brown, 'Asian Games', p. 16.

183 Garland and Rowe, *Racism and Anti-Racism*, pp. 53–81; 'Selling the Game Short', pp. 40–1; Back, Crabbe and Solomos, *Changing Face of Football*, pp. 192–4; Horne, 'Kicking Racism Out', pp. 55–60.

184 McArdle, *From Boot Money*, p. 128.

185 Back, Crabbe and Solomos, *Changing Face of Football*, p. 201; Steven Bradbury and John Williams, 'New Labour, Racism and "New" Football in England', *Patterns of Prejudice*, 40, 1 (2006), 69–79.

186 Richard Holt, *Sport and the British: A Modern History* (Oxford: Clarendon, 1989), p. 8.

187 Jean Williams, *A Game for Rough Girls?: A History of Women's Football in Britain* (London: Routledge, 2003); 'An Equality Too Far?: Historical and Contemporary Perspectives of Gender Inequality in British and International Football', *Historical Social Research*, 31, 1 (2006), pp. 159–64; Jayne Caudwell, 'Women's Football in the United Kingdom: Theorizing Gender and Unpacking the Butch Lesbian Image', *Journal of Sport and Social Issues*, 23, 4 (November 1999), pp. 390–402; 'Women's Experiences of Sexuality Within Football Contexts: A Particular and Located Footballing Epistemology', *Football Studies*, 5, 1 (2002), pp. 24–45; John Harris, 'Still a Man's Game?: Women Footballers, Personal Experience and Tabloid Myth' in Wagg (ed.), *British Football*, pp. 110–26. See also Michael A. Messner and Donald F. Sabo (eds), *Sport, Men and the Gender Order: Critical Feminist Perspectives* (Champaign, Illinois: Human Kinetics, 1990); Jennifer Hargreaves, *Sporting Females: Critical Issues in the History and Sociology of Women's Sports* (London: Routledge, 1994); Grant Jarvie and Joseph Maguire, *Sport and Leisure in Social Thought* (London: Routledge, 1994), pp. 161–82; Giulianotti, *Sport*, pp. 80–101; Dunning, *Sport Matters*, pp. 219–39.

188 Polley, *Moving the Goalposts*, pp. 89, 90.

189 Jean Williams, 'The Fastest Growing Sport?: Women's Football in England' in F. Hong and J. A. Mangan (eds), *Soccer, Women, Sexual Liberation: Kicking Off a New Era* (London: Frank Cass, 2004), pp. 122–3; *Game for Rough Girls*, pp. 41–3, 58–65; Sue Lopez, *Women on the Ball: A Guide to Women's Football* (London: Scarlet, 1997), pp. 226–36; John Williams and Jackie Woodhouse, 'Can Play, Will Play?: Women and Football in Britain' in Williams and Wagg (eds), *British Football*, p. 102; Donna Woodhouse and John Williams, *Offside?: The Position of Women in Football* (Reading: South Street, 1999), p. 26.

190 Woodhouse and Williams, *Offside?*, pp. 19–32; quotation from p. 20.

191 Lopez, *Women on the Ball*, pp. 218–21; Williams and Woodhouse, 'Can Play, Will Play?', p. 101; Woodhouse and Williams, *Offside?*, pp. 23, 42–52; Williams, *Game for Rough Girls*, pp. 80–3.

192 Williams, *Game for Rough Girls*, pp. 54–7; 'Fastest Growing Sport?', pp. 119–20; Hargreaves, *Sporting Females*, p. 252; Woodhouse and Williams, *Offside?*, pp. 21–2. There were a number of criticisms of the FA's control of the women's game from those on the inside in Pete Davies' account of his season with the Doncaster Belles in 1994–5. Pete Davies, *I Lost My Heart to the Belles* (London: Mandarin, 1997), pp. 68–9, 205–6.

193 Hargreaves, *Sporting Females*, pp. 280, 252–3; Williams, *Game for Rough Girls*, p. 21. See also Anita White, 'Women and Sport in the UK' in I. Hartmann-Tews and G. Pfister (eds), *Sport and Women: Social Issues in International Perspective* (London: Routledge, 2003), pp. 35–52.

194 Jessica Macbeth, 'The "Pals", the "Professionals" and the "Conformers": The Meaning of Football in the Lives of Women Footballers in Scotland' in Magee, Bairner and Tomlinson (eds), *Bountiful Game*, pp. 79–97.

195 Caudwell, 'Women's Football'; 'Women's Experiences'; 'Out on the Field: Women's Experiences of Gender and Sexuality in Football' in Wagg (ed.), *British Football*, pp. 127–46; Macbeth, 'Meaning of Football', pp. 84–6, 93–7; Harris, 'Still a Man's Game?', pp. 113–20; Williams, *Game for Rough Girls*, pp. 96–7.

196 Harris, 'Still a Man's Game?', p. 126; Williams, 'An Equality Too Far?', pp. 167–9.

197 Giulianotti, *Football*, p. xi; Liz Crolley and Cathy Long, 'Sitting Pretty?: Women and Football in Liverpool' in Williams, Hopkins and Long (eds) *Passing Rhythms*, pp. 195–214.

198 Anne Coddington, *One of the Lads: Women Who Follow Football* (London: Harper Collins, 1997), pp. 1, 45–75; Woodhouse and Williams, *Offside?*, pp. 59–60. See also Nick Hornby's comment: 'I have met women who have loved football, and go to a number of games a season, but I have not yet met one who would make that Wednesday night trip to Plymouth … I am not saying that the anally retentive woman does not exist, but she is vastly outnumbered by her masculine equivalent.' Hornby, *Fever Pitch*, p. 103.

199 Coddington, *One of the Lads*, pp. 71, 70.

200 Crolley and Long, 'Sitting Pretty?', pp. 206–8, 211; Vic Duke and Liz Crolley, *Football, Nationality and the State* (Harlow: Longman, 1996), p. 141; Giulianotti, *Football*, p. 155; Williams, *Game for Rough Girls*, p. 71.

201 Crolley and Long, 'Sitting Pretty?', pp. 210–12; Duke and Crolley, *Football*, pp. 139–40; Liz Crolley, 'The Green, Green Grass of Anfield' in

S. Kuper and M. Mora Y Araujo (eds), *Perfect Pitch 3: Men and Women* (London: Headline, 1998), pp. 46–7, 53; Coddington, *One of the Lads*, pp. 86–8, 99–101; Williams and Woodhouse, 'Can Play, Will Play?', pp. 104–5; Gill Lines, 'The Sports Star in the Media: The Gendered Construction and Youthful Consumption of Sports Personalities' in J. Sugden and A. Tomlinson (eds), *Power Games: A Critical Sociology of Sport* (London: Routledge, 2004), p. 212.

202 Polley, *Moving the Goalposts*, p. 106.

203 Michael A. Robidoux, *Men at Play: A Working Understanding of Professional Hockey* (Montreal: McGill-Queen's University Press, 2001), pp. 188, 127–50.

204 Hunter Davies, *The Glory Game* (Edinburgh: Mainstream, 1992, [1st edition, 1972]); Eamon Dunphy, *Only a Game?: The Diary of a Professional Footballer* (London: Penguin, 1987 [1st edition, 1976]); Garry Nelson, *Left Foot Forward: A Year in the Life of a Journeyman Footballer* (London: Headline, 1995); Alan Tomlinson, 'Tuck Up Tight Lads: Structures of Control within Football Culture' in A. Tomlinson (ed.), *Explorations in Football Culture* (Eastbourne: Leisure Studies Association, 1983), pp. 149–77; Andrew Parker, 'Soccer, Servitude and Sub-Cultural Identity: Football Traineeship and Masculine Construction', *Soccer and Society*, 2, 1 (Spring 2001), pp. 72–6; John Harding with Gordon Taylor, *Living to Play: From Soccer Slaves to Soccerati – A Social History of the Professionals* (London: Robson, 2003), pp. 153–7. See also Lee Chapman, *More Than a Match: A Player's Story* (London: Arrow, 1993); Rick Gekoski, *Staying Up: A Fan Behind the Scenes in the Premiership* (London: Warner, 1999).

205 Parker, 'Soccer, Servitude', pp. 59–80; quotation from p. 57. See also Andrew Parker, 'Great Expectations – Grimness or Glamour?: The Football Apprentice in the 1990s', *The Sports Historian*, 15 (1995), pp. 107–28.

206 Ellis Cashmore and Andrew Parker, 'One David Beckham?: Celebrity, Masculinity and the Soccerati', *Sociology of Sport Journal*, 20 (2003), pp. 224, 223; Harding with Taylor, *Living to Play*, pp. 162–6; Jeffrey Richards, 'Football and the Crisis of British Identity' in S. Caunce, E. Mazierska, S. Sydney-Smith and J. Walton (eds), *Relocating Britishness* (Manchester: Manchester University Press, 2004), pp. 101–2.

207 Ellis Cashmore, *Beckham* (Cambridge: Polity, 2002), p. 122; Cashmore and Parker, 'One David Beckham?', p. 222; Whannel, *Media Sport Stars*, p. 212.

208 Quoted in Sandvoss, *Game of Two Halves*, p. 62.

209 Harding with Taylor, *Living to Play*, pp. 169–72; Cashmore, *Beckham*, pp. 123–4; Polley, *Moving the Goalposts*, pp. 108–9; Holt and Mason, *Sport in Britain*, pp. 12–13.

210 Stephen Wagg, 'With His Money, *I* Could Afford to be Depressed: Markets, Masculinity and Mental Distress in the English Football Press', *Football Studies*, 3, 2, (2000), pp. 67–87; quotation from p. 75. An updated version of this article is contained in Wagg (ed.), *British Football*, pp. 90–109.

211 Crolley and Long, 'Sitting Pretty?', pp. 204–6; Giulianotti, *Football*, p. 156.

212 Cashmore and Parker, 'One David Beckham?', pp. 214–15, 220–2; Cashmore, *Beckham*, pp. 124–32; Garry Whannel, 'Punishment, Redemption and Celebration in the Popular Press: The Case of David Beckham' in Andrews and Jackson (eds), *Sport Stars*, p. 148; Whannel, *Media Sport Stars*, p. 212. The notion of Beckham as a 'loyal husband' became less sustainable after 2004, however, when details of his alleged infidelities were revealed by the tabloid press.

213 Julie Burchill, *Burchill on Beckham* (London: Yellow Jersey, 2002), pp. 110–11; Zoe Williams, 'End of an Era', *The Guardian* (G2 supplement), 4 July 2006, p. 8; Cashmore and Parker, 'One David Beckham?', p. 223.

214 Barry Smart, *The Sport Star: Modern Sport and the Cultural Economy of Sporting Celebrity* (London: Sage, 2005), p. 165. See also Garry Whannel, 'From Pig's Bladders to Ferraris: Media Discourses of Masculinity and Morality in Obituaries of Stanley Matthews', *Culture, Sport, Society*, 5, 3 (Autumn 2002), pp. 73–94.

215 Raphael Samuel, *Island Stories: Unravelling Britain* (London: Verso, 1998), p. 41.

216 Quoted in Tom Nairn, *After Britain: New Labour and the Return of Scotland* (London: Granta, 2000), pp. 301–2.

217 Alan Bairner, 'Football' in G. Jarvie and J. Burnett (eds), *Sport, Scotland and the Scots* (East Linton: Tuckwell, 2000), p. 87.

218 Richard Weight, *Patriots: National Identity in Britain, 1940–2000* (London: Pan Macmillan, 2003), p. 708; Joseph Maguire, Emma Poulton and Catherine Possamai, 'The War of the Words?: Identity Politics in Anglo-German Press Coverage of Euro 96', *European Journal of Communication*, 14, 1 (1999), pp. 61–89.

219 Bairner, 'Football', p. 99.

220 Richard Giulianotti, 'Hooligans and Carnival Fans: Scottish Football Supporter Cultures' in Armstrong and Giulianotti (eds), *Football Cultures*, pp. 35–40; 'Scotland's Tartan Army in Italy: The Case for the Carnivalesque', *Sociological Review*, 39, 3 (1991), pp. 503–27; Gerry P. T. Finn and Richard Giulianotti, 'Scottish Fans, Not English Hooligans!: Scots, Scottishness and Scottish Football' in Brown (ed.), *Fanatics!*,

pp. 195–9. See also Boyle and Haynes, *Power Play*, pp. 154–9; Garland and Rowe, *Racism and Anti-Racism*, pp. 131–4; Bairner, 'Football and the Idea of Scotland', pp. 21–4.

221 Boyle and Haynes, *Power Play*, p. 156; Finn and Giulianotti, 'Scottish Fans', p. 199.

222 Giulianotti, 'Hooligans', pp. 37–8; Bairner, 'Football and the Idea of Scotland', pp. 22–4; Garland and Rowe, *Racism and Anti-Racism*, pp. 132–3; Weight, *Patriots*, p. 711.

223 H. F. Moorhouse, 'Scotland, Football and Identities: The National Team and Club Sides' in S. Gehrmann (ed.), *Football and Regional Identity*, pp. 193–6; Joseph M. Bradley, '"We Shall Not Be Moved"! Mere Sport, Mere Songs?: A Tale of Scottish Football' in Brown (ed.), *Fanatics!*, pp. 210–12. See also Boyle, 'We Are Celtic', pp. 87–9.

224 Ronald Kowalski, '"Cry For Us, Argentina": Sport and National Identity in Late Twentieth-Century Scotland' in A. Smith and D. Porter (eds), *Sport and National Identity in the Post-War World* (London: Routledge, 2004), pp. 78–9, 84; Holt and Mason, *Sport in Britain*, p. 135.

225 Johnes, *History of Sport*, p. 113.

226 Duke and Crolley, *Football*, pp. 19–23; Johnes, *History of Sport*, p. 92; Garland and Rowe, *Racism and Anti-Racism*, p. 137.

227 Martin Johnes, '"Every Day When I Wake Up I Thank the Lord I'm Welsh": Sport and National Identity in Post-War Wales' in Smith and Porter (eds), *Sport and National Identity*, pp. 60–1; *History of Sport*, pp. 91–2, 113–14. See also Stuart Smith and Matt Johnson, 'Unusual Support?: Welsh Fans of the English Game', *Soccer Review* (2003), pp. 38–41.

228 Johnes, 'Every day', pp. 61–3; *History of Sport*, pp. 92, 113–14, 119–20; Garland and Rowe, *Racism and Anti-Racism*, pp. 137–8.

229 Weight, *Patriots*, p. 708; Jeffrey Richards, 'Football', p. 105.

230 Jon Garland and Mike Rowe, 'War Minus the Shooting?: Jingoism, the English Press, and Euro 96', *Journal of Sport and Social Issues*, 23, 1 (February 1999), pp. 80–95; *Racism and Anti-Racism*, p. 149; Ben Carrington, '"Football's Coming Home" But Whose Home? And Do We Want It?: Nation, Football and the Politics of Exclusion' in Brown (ed.), *Fanatics!*, p. 113; Polley, *Moving the Goalposts*, p. 2.

231 Weight, *Patriots*, p. 709; Paul Ward, *Britishness Since 1870* (London: Routledge, 2004), p. 76; Holt and Mason, *Sport in Britain*, p. 143; Richards, 'Football', p. 105.

232 Garland and Rowe, 'War Minus the Shooting?', pp. 84–6. See also Peter J.

Beck, 'The Relevance of the "Irrelevant": Football as a Missing Dimension in the Study of British Relations with Germany', *International Affairs*, 79, 2 (2003), pp. 401–2; Polley, *Moving the Goalposts*, p. 3; Weight, *Patriots*, pp. 709–10.

233 Maguire, Poulton and Possamai, 'War of the Words?', p. 70; 'Weltkrieg III?: Media Coverage of England versus Germany in Euro 96', *Journal of Sport and Social Issues*, 23, 4 (November 1999), pp. 439–54; Joseph Maguire, *Global Sport: Identities, Societies, Civilizations* (Cambridge: Polity, 1999), pp. 182–3, 199–202; Garland and Rowe, *Racism and Anti-Racism*, pp. 159–72; Pablo Alabarces, Alan Tomlinson and Christopher Young, 'Argentina versus England at the France '98 World Cup: Narratives of Nation and the Mythologising of the Popular', *Media, Culture & Society*, 23, 5 (2001), pp. 547–66. For similar studies of the England team and the media post-2000, see Jon Garland, 'The Same Old Story?: Englishness, the Tabloid Press and the 2002 Football World Cup, *Leisure Studies*, 23, 1 (January 2004), pp. 79–92; Emma Poulton, 'New Fans, New Flags, New England?: Changing News Values in the English Press Coverage of World Cup 2002', *Football Studies*, 6, 1 (April 2003), pp. 19–36; Joseph Maguire and Michael Burrows, '"Not the Germans Again": Soccer, Identity Politics and the Media' in Joseph Maguire, *Power and Global Sport: Zones of Prestige, Emulation and Resistance* (London: Routledge, 2005), pp. 130–42.

234 Maguire, Poulton and Possamai, 'War of the Words?', pp. 84–5; Maguire, *Global Sport*, p. 201; Garland and Rowe, *Racism and Anti-Racism*, pp. 172–5; Beck, 'Relevance of the "Irrelevant"', pp. 396–9, 406–10.

235 Weight, *Patriots*, pp. 711–15. See also Carrington, 'Postmodern Blackness', p. 107; Martin Polley, 'Sport and National Identity in England' in Smith and Porter (eds), *Sport and National Identity*, pp. 17–22.

236 Ward, *Britishness*, pp. 82–3, 85; Carrington, 'Football's Coming Home', pp. 101–23.

237 Polley, 'Sport and National Identity', pp. 10–11, 27–8; Krishan Kumar, *The Making of English National Identity* (Cambridge: Cambridge University Press, 2003), pp. 262–3; Les Back, Tim Crabbe and John Solomos, '"Lions and Black Skins": Race, Nation and Local Patriotism in Football' in Carrington and McDonald (eds), *'Race', Sport*, pp. 94–100; *Changing Face of Football*, pp. 221–51; Richards, 'Football', pp. 105–6.

238 Anthony King, *The European Ritual: Football in the New Europe* (Aldershot: Ashgate, 2003), pp. 141–4; Stephen Dobson and John Goddard, *The Economics of Football* (Cambridge: Cambridge University Press, 2001), pp. 425–6.

239 King, *European Ritual*, p. 154.

240 Williams, *Is It All Over?*, pp. 40–1; Jon Magee, 'Shifting Balances of Power in the New Football Economy' in Sugden and Tomlinson (eds), *Power Games*, p. 221; Patrick McGovern, 'Globalization or Internationalization?: Foreign Footballers in the English League, 1946–95', *Sociology*, 36, 1 (2002), p. 30.

241 Garland and Rowe, *Racism and Anti-Racism*, p. 115. The literature on the Bosman ruling and its consequences is vast. See, for example, Roger Blanpain and R. Inston, *The Bosman Case: The End of the Transfer System?* (Brussels: Bruylants, 1996); Fiona Miller, 'Beyond *Bosman*', *Sport and the Law Journal*, 3, 1 (1996), pp. 45–9; David McArdle, 'They're Playing R. Song: Football and the European Union after *Bosman*', *Football Studies*, 3, 2 (2000), pp. 42–66; *From Boot Money*, pp. 31–59; King, *European Ritual*, pp. 69–96; Lanfranchi and Taylor, *Moving With the Ball*, pp. 213–29; Greenfield and Osborn, *Regulating Football*, pp. 83–93.

242 Joseph Maguire and David Stead, 'Border Crossings: Soccer Labour Migration and the European Union', *International Review for the Sociology of Sport*, 33, 1 (1998), p. 66.

243 Smart, *Sport Star*, p. 91; Denis Campbell, 'United (versus Liverpool) Nations', *Observer Sport Monthly*, 21 (January 2002), pp. 44–6. See also Maguire, *Global Sport*, chapter 7.

244 Kirsten Rosaaen and John Amis, 'From the Busby Babes to the Theatre of Dreams: Image, Reputation and the Rise of Manchester United' in Andrews (ed.), *Manchester United*, pp. 43–61; Brick, 'Can't Live With Them', p. 11; King, *European Ritual*, pp. 128–9. On the 'Europeanisation' of West Ham United, a less prestigious football 'brand', see Fawbert, 'Football Fandom', pp. 99–119.

245 Richard Giulianotti and Roland Robertson, 'The Globalization of Football: A Study in the Glocalization of the "Serious Life"', *British Journal of Sociology*, 55, 4 (2004), pp. 545–68.

246 Stephen Wagg, '"No Scouse, Please. We're Europeans": Liverpool FC and the Decline of the Boot Room Mystique' in Magee, Bairner and Tomlinson (eds), *Bountiful Game?*, pp. 121–41; Stephen Hopkins and John Williams, 'Gérard Houllier and the New Liverpool "Imaginary"' in Williams, Hopkins and Long (eds), *Passing Rhythms*, pp. 173–94; Giulianotti and Robertson, 'Globalization of Football', pp. 552–3; McGovern, 'Globalization or Internationalization?', pp. 28–30; Bill Gerrard, 'Why does Manchester United Keep Winning On and Off The Field?: A Case Study of Sustainable Advantage in Professional Team Sports' in Andrews (ed.), *Manchester United*, pp. 76–8; Matthew Taylor, 'Global Players?: Football, Migration and Globalization, *c*.1930–2000', *Historical Social Research*, 31, 1 (2006), pp. 22–8; David Stead and Joseph Maguire, '"Rite De Passage"

or Passage to Riches?: The Motivation and Objectives of Nordic/Scandinavian Players in English League Soccer', *Journal of Sport and Social Issues*, 24, 1 (February 2000), pp. 36–60. See also Jonathan Magee and John Sugden, '"The World at Their Feet": Professional Football and International Labor Migration', *Journal of Sport and Social Issues*, 26, 4 (November 2002), pp. 421–37; Patrick McGovern, 'The Irish Brawn Drain: English League Clubs and Irish Footballers, 1946–95', *British Journal of Sociology*, 51, 3 (2000), pp. 401–15; Ann Bourke, 'The Road to Fame and Fortune: Insights on the Career Paths of Young Irish Professional Footballers in England', *Journal of Youth Studies*, 5, 4 (2002), pp. 375–89.

247 Piers Ludlow, 'Us or Them?: The Meaning of Europe in British Political Discourse' in M. af Malmborg and B. Stråth (eds), *The Meaning of Europe* (Oxford: Berg, 2002), pp. 101–24; Donald McNeill, *New Europe: Imagined Spaces* (London: Arnold, 2004), p. 42.

248 Anthony King, 'Football Fandom and Post-National Identity in the New Europe', *British Journal of Sociology*, 51, 3 (September 2000), pp. 419–42; quotation from p. 427. Moorhouse's survey of Rangers fans found a clear attachment to European competition, with the vast majority supporting the club's involvement in a future European league and many seemingly unconcerned about whether it remained in the Scottish League. Moorhouse, 'Scotland, Football and Identities', pp. 188–90.

249 See Alan Bairner, 'Sport and the Nation in the Global Era' in L. Allison (ed.), *The Global Politics of Sport: The Role of Global Institutions in Sport* (Abingdon: Routledge, 2005), pp. 99–100; Polley, 'Sport and National Identity', pp. 24–7.

Into the twenty-first century

British football may have been reinvented during the 1990s but the 'new' game was far from universally popular. Indeed assessments of the state of football in the early twenty-first century have varied dramatically. Optimists could point to the game's cultural and commercial advances. With increasing media interest, it could be argued, football's relatively narrow social base widened to embrace sections of the population who had been driven out in previous decades: the affluent middle class, female supporters and families, in particular. In this sense, it was arguably more a 'people's game' than it had been at almost any point in its history. Outside the stadiums themselves, football became difficult to escape. Stephen Wagg has talked of the 'ubiquitous' nature of the twenty-first century game: 'it has become a sea of public discourse in which we all care to swim' and 'part of the popular cultural air that the people of many societies breathe'.[1] Politicians and public figures could no longer decry or ignore it as most had done for much of the previous century. Football clearly mattered to the media and significant sections of the population, and, as such, the state of the game and the fortunes of its representative sides emerged as key topics of public interest. Writers focusing specifically on England have also outlined the changing public perception of the England football team during the 1990s and the way in which the older image of the aggressive hooligan fan was replaced by a newly inclusive 'sense of national community' and 'a new national sporting identity for English football'.[2]

The establishment of the Premier League was central to the commercial transformation of football in England and beyond. In many respects,

PLATE 23 *An England fan watching the 4–2 win over Croatia at the 2004 European Championships in Portugal (© Popperfoto.com).*

its achievements have been unprecedented. Most significantly, its arrival led to a reversal in the downward trend in attendances. From an aggregate of 9.8 million in 1992–3, the first Premier League season, attendances had climbed to 11.6 million by 1998–9 and 13.5 million in 2002–3. Below the elite level, Football League attendances also increased, from 10.9 million in 1992–3 to 14.9 million by 2002–3. Such figures represented a virtual resurrection of popular support for football in England and a return to the spectatorship levels of the 1970s. On a European level, the Premier League became not only the most widely watched but also the biggest league in financial terms. The total income of its clubs rose from 534 million euros in 1995–6 to 1.748 billion euros by 2001–2. England now accounted for 25 per cent of the overall European market, compared with 16 per cent in Italy, 15 per cent in Germany and 3 per cent in Scotland. Much of this revenue came from its substantial broadcasting deals, but by 2001 the Premier League also topped the European list in commercial and matchday income. Supporters of the Premier League could celebrate its financial transformation of English football and the 'stellar decade of growth and commercial success' that it heralded.[3] If we add to this the modernisation of stadiums, the decline in hooliganism and an increasingly cosmopolitan workforce and fan base, the assessment of the Premier League as 'a global, as well as a local, success story' is particularly persuasive. So too is the notion that it effectively saved the English game from the malaise into which it sank in the 1980s.[4]

Increasingly, however, more pessimistic views have come to dominate discussion of the state of British football in the media and the academy. The apparent cultural and financial success of the 'new' football, according to these views, could not hide the more fundamental crises threatening the status and future of the game. Critics focus on a range of problems, but three interconnected themes are particularly prominent, relating to money, morality and social exclusion. First, the inequalities between the elite clubs and leagues and the rest have now become impossible to ignore. Competitive imbalance in the Scottish and English leagues, though hardly new (see Chapter 5), was increasingly pronounced throughout the 1990s and early 2000s. In the former, Celtic and Rangers continued to dominate the top two positions but were also losing fewer games and stretching the annual points gap between themselves and their competitors. South of the border, Manchester United and Arsenal established a similar stranglehold over the Premier League title, while the sporting and financial divide between the Premier League and the Football League grew. Promoted clubs found it increasingly difficult to survive in the top division: 75 per cent were relegated within two seasons between 1996–7 and 2001–2. The financial gap widened to the point where, by 2001, the average Premier League club brought in four times more income than its counterpart in Division One of the Football League and was making an average of £4 million profit as against a £4.2 million loss in the lower division. An over-reliance on television revenue, exacerbated in England by the 2002 collapse of ITV Digital, along with spiralling wage costs, meant that an increasing number of clubs faced mounting debt and periods in administration.[5] The soccer accountants Deloitte & Touche referred to this as 'a financial crisis bigger than ever before' in the Football League, while Stephen Morrow talked about 'a systematic crisis in Scottish football' with 'negative financial implications for all'.[6]

In this context, football as 'sport' seemed to have given way to money and business considerations. The popular assumption that rich clubs could buy success appeared to be borne out by the strong correlation between player salaries and league position. It was also evident in the arrival of new foreign owners such as the Russian billionaire Roman Abramovic at Chelsea, and, to a lesser extent, the Lithuanian businessman

Vladimir Romanov at Hearts, both eager to challenge the domination of the high payers in their respective competitions. The hegemony of the wealthy was perhaps most evident in dramatic salary rises. The annual wage bill of the 20 Premier League clubs was £475 million in 2001–2, representing an enormous 780 per cent increase in the nine-year history of the competition. By 2000, over 100 Premier League players were making a basic wage of over £1 million per year (equivalent to £25,000 a week), with average annual earnings topping £600,000 in 2001–2. A few years later, in 2004, top salaries had reached something like £50,000 to £100,000 per week. Wage increases were less significant further down the English and Welsh divisions, and in Scotland, but had still escalated to the point where many clubs were struggling to survive and forced to cut wages and release players.[7] During the close season of 2002, at the time when England captain David Beckham was about to sign a new deal worth £92,000 a week with Manchester United, *The Guardian* could report that an estimated 619 of the 2,650 professionals in the Football League and Scottish leagues were being made redundant.[8]

Excessive earnings were increasingly regarded as not just inequitable but morally indefensible. Professional footballers at the turn of the century were paradoxically among the most celebrated and the most derided of public figures. Continually compared to the working-class heroes of the maximum wage era and the more glamourous but moderately paid stars of the 1960s and 1970s, the 'pampered' celebrities of the noughties, with their £1 million-plus annual salaries, had few supporters. Such high earnings could be justified economically not just on the basis that footballers possessed a unique talent that was in scarce supply but also because, unlike providers of more valuable services such as nurses and teachers, they were able to service large paying audiences at stadiums and also, crucially, via terrestrial and satellite television.[9] Morally, however, these salaries were increasingly regarded as 'obscene' and 'indecent' by those who continued to doubt the social utility of the footballers' occupation. There was little sympathy for individuals who, it was felt, should count themselves lucky to be able to 'play' for the public *and* get paid for it. 'Distrust of the motives and moral character of men who play for pay' was, as Charles Korr noted some years earlier, hardly new in Britain, but the players' deteriorating public image at the turn of the century undoubtedly sharpened it.[10] Newspaper accounts of violence, heavy drinking and sexual abuse and humiliation reinforced the notion of a profession out of control, dominated by arrogant young men with too much money and no sense of social responsibility. On the field, too, there

was a widespread assumption that the behaviour of players was deteriorating and that, in a game increasingly dominated by money, the will to
win invariably overshadowed any lingering sense of sportsmanship or 'fair
play'. As such, it is hardly surprising that journalists and academics often
saw the crisis in British soccer in terms of moral degeneration and
decline.[11]

A further aspect of the game's contemporary crisis has been the perceived exclusion of certain social and ethnic groups. We noted in Chapter
6 that claims that football crowds had become gentrified during the 1990s
and the 'traditional' supporter (often defined as young, poor and working-
class) excluded were often overstated and that, in fact, there was
considerable continuity over time in the social make-up of football spectators. Nevertheless, by the turn of the century it was becoming difficult
to deny that many clubs were disregarding, if not disenfranchising, their
less wealthy 'customers' and failing to connect with the communities of
which they were a part. For all the schemes and educational projects for
'disadvantaged' groups, and the 'community' agenda promoted by the
Labour government's policy of 'social inclusion', it seemed that professional football was increasingly losing touch with 'the people'
(assuming such a 'connection' had ever really existed).[12] A report drawing
on data from Leeds United, Manchester City and Sheffield United revealed
that only small percentages of these clubs' season ticket holders and
members came from areas with large ethnic minority populations or high
levels of social deprivation, many of which were located close to the
respective stadium. Given the general failure to attract local populations
and the large number of supporters drawn from affluent areas, there was,
the authors argued, considerable doubt 'over the game's capacity to continue engaging supporters from across the social spectrum'.[13] David
Hassan's work on Northern Ireland has highlighted similar long-standing
concerns over the exclusion of particular groups, especially Catholics,
many of whom tended to stay away from domestic and international
matches administered by an organisation – the IFA – they associated with
unionist hegemony.[14]

Problems of social exclusion have extended to participation in football
at the grassroots. At first glance, participatory figures seemed to hold up
well through the 1990s and the early twenty-first century. National statistics showed that the proportion of the adult British population playing
football regularly stayed fairly consistent at between 4.5 and 5 per cent
from the late 1980s to 2002–3. In 1995 there were approximately 47,500
clubs affiliated to the governing bodies and an estimated 1.65 million reg-

istered members, although with unaffiliated players included, the figure was well over 2 million and probably not much short of the 2.2 million adult footballers recorded in 1987.[15] The game was especially popular among the young, with 42.7 per cent of 6–16 year-olds (66.9 per cent of boys and 18.1 per cent of girls) in England playing on a regular basis in 1999. The other success story was the rise of the female game, from 9,000 registered players in 1991 in England alone to some 85,000 by 2002–3, and 80 girls' teams in 1993 to 6,209 in 2005.[16] Beneath such bald figures, however, there was evidence of a decline in football as it had traditionally been played and understood. A special report by *The Observer* newspaper in April 2005 talked of a 'steep decline at grassroots level' in popular team sports such as cricket and football. It argued that the two sports together had lost some 1.5 million participants in the previous ten years, a decline reflected by the case of the Sussex Sunday League in Brighton and Hove, which had shed 150 of its 260 teams since the late 1970s. Deteriorating facilities, lack of support from outside agencies, changing lifestyles and wider social and economic trends were all identified as important factors, along with the competition from individual forms of exercise and 'lifestyle' sports. Significantly, however, the popularity of less formalised small-sided varieties of soccer, such as the five-a-side game, had increased rapidly over the same period, suggesting a shift in the form and setting of football at the grassroots rather than any straightforward decline.[17]

Such assessments of the state of British football often highlight the crucial tension between the grassroots game as simple recreation, on one hand, and as a form of development for the elite level on the other. This is particularly true in relation to children's football, a facet of the sport that has often been overlooked by academics but has become increasingly central to the policies of public bodies and the football authorities. H. F. Moorhouse, for example, has written of the sparse and 'often physically unpleasant, costly and quite dangerous' facilities for youth soccer in Scotland and the game's failure to 'reach out to modern youth'. With shortages of good coaching and high quality facilities, he argues, Scotland lacks a formal and organised system for ensuring both mass participation in football and the production of 'an elite of great players'.[18] A number of recent English studies, meanwhile, have suggested that FA initiatives such as the 1997 'Charter for Quality' may actually have been counter-productive by encouraging the clashing objectives of social inclusion and the development of excellence.[19] While the shift of responsibility for the 'football education' of youngsters away from schools and 'well-meaning parents and unqualified coaches' to the youth academies of professional clubs might be seen to benefit the elite game in the long term, it could be argued that it has also led to the increasing control, exploitation and alienation of the children themselves. Interviews and fieldwork with children have revealed that the friendships and social connections that came from playing football and belonging to a team far outweigh the pursuit of cups and championships or a desire to become a professional in the future. One study of a local youth league concluded that above all else the boys in the survey 'wanted to play football for its own sake and were focused very much on the present'.[20] Winning may have mattered, and competition certainly did, but for the majority of children taking part really was what football was all about.

Without doubt, football faces considerable problems. Just like British society, it seems to be in a perpetual state of crisis and imminent collapse. In certain respects, its difficulties reflect and reinforce broader debates in British political culture. Issues concerning the control and ownership of football are, as we have seen, as old as the game itself and recent debates over football's democratisation have clearly tapped into wider anxieties about the failures and inadequacies of the British political system and the effective disenfranchisement of large sections of the electorate. Likewise, football has undoubtedly been important in helping the British to work through their attitudes to 'Europe'. In football, the debate over whether Britain should be a part of Europe or not has long been resolved, but the tensions inherent in that relationship certainly have not. Concerns over levels of immigration, the 'influx' of asylum seekers and the possible impact of these on 'British' identity have often been conflated with similar fears over the 'domination' of foreign players and coaches in the domestic leagues. Most obviously, perhaps, football's 'health' has long been used as a convenient barometer of the state of the British (or the English, Scottish, Welsh and Northern Irish) 'nation'. Since the game's transformation in the 1990s, decline and degeneration, shot through with a dose of nostalgia, have been recurring themes in the sporting and political pages of the British press.

Yet the foundations of British football seem rather more secure than is often assumed. Despite a crisis in the economics of the game and the absence of a 'coherent "vision" or national plan for Scottish football as the whole', football still matters to many Scots and seems as central to Scottish identity as ever.[21] Support for the domestic game in Wales and Northern Ireland remains relatively weak, but English and Scottish football is still popular there and the smaller nations continue to provide a consistent supply of players to the more powerful British leagues. In

England, meanwhile, though many seem to have lost faith in football, the media show no signs of losing interest in the game. Football continues to feature heavily in the schedules of satellite and terrestrial broadcasters and in the sporting pages, and increasingly the news and business sections, of the popular and quality press. If anything, poor publicity seems to have strengthened rather than weakened soccer's 'symbiotic relationship with the media'.[22] Most significantly, football does seem to have planted new roots among parts of the population who had been, or felt themselves to be, excluded. Increasing numbers of females and ethnic minorities play, read about and watch the game, although institutional prejudice means that they still have little say in the way the sport is run. Most important for the future, football also plays a central role in the lives of increasing numbers of young people. Indeed, while it may not seem as deeply rooted in local communities as it once did, the game has probably never meant as much to as many British people as it does in the early twenty-first century. It is part of the social and cultural fabric of these islands. In many respects, football's past, present and future are bound up in what it means to be British.

References

1 Stephen Wagg, 'Fat City?: British Football and the Politics of Social Exclusion at the Turn of the Twenty-First Century' in S. Wagg (ed.), *British Football and Social Exclusion* (London: Routledge, 2004), pp. 2–3.

2 Steve Greenfield and Guy Osborn, *Regulating Football: Commodification, Consumption and the Law* (London: Pluto, 2001), pp. vii–ix; John Williams, '"Protect Me From What I Want": Football Fandom, Celebrity Cultures and "New" Football in England', *Soccer and Society*, 7, 1 (January 2006), pp. 98–100.

3 Deloitte & Touche, *Deloitte & Touche Annual Review of Football Finance* (Manchester: Deloitte & Touche, 2003), pp. 54, 9–12, 1.

4 Williams, 'Protect Me', p. 102.

5 Stephen Morrow, *The People's Game?: Football, Finance and Society* (Basingstoke: Palgrave, 2003), pp. 5–8, 17–18; 'Uncertainty of Outcome: Where Next for Scottish Football?', *Soccer Review* (2002), pp. 37–9; Deloitte & Touche, *Deloitte & Touche Annual Review of Football Finance* (Manchester: Deloitte & Touche, 1999), pp. 56–60; Deloitte & Touche, *Annual Review* (2003), pp. 28–9, 32, 69; Wagg, 'Fat City?', p. 10.

6 Deloitte & Touche, *Annual Review* (2003), p. 34; Stephen Morrow, 'A

Critical Analysis of the State of Scottish Football: Reasons, Excuses, Solutions' in J. Magee, A. Bairner and A. Tomlinson (eds), *The Bountiful Game?: Football Identities and Finances* (Oxford: Meyer & Meyer Sport, 2005), p. 183.

7 Deloitte & Touche, *Annual Review* (2003), pp. 41–3; Stephen Dobson and John Goddard, *The Economics of Football* (Cambridge: Cambridge University Press, 2001), p. 209; Wagg, 'Fat City?', p. 8.

8 Dominic Fifield, 'As Beckham Gets Set for £92,000 a Week, 600 Fellow Footballers Prepare for the Dole', *The Guardian*, 7 May 2002.

9 Dobson and Goddard, *Economics of Football*, pp. 209–15.

10 Charles P. Korr, 'Two Cheers for the Professional: Some Anglo-American Comparisons', *British Journal of Sports History*, 2, 3 (December 1985), p. 301.

11 Williams, 'Protect Me', p. 105; Wagg, 'Fat City?', pp. 8–9; Germaine Greer, 'Nothing New about Ugly Sex', *The Guardian*, 16 December 2003; J. A. Mangan, 'Series Editor's Foreword' to Wagg (ed.), *British Football*, p. ix.

12 Williams, 'Protect Me', pp. 108–9; Wagg, 'Fat City?', pp. 14–24; Neil Watson, 'Football and the Community: "What's the Score?" ', *Soccer and Society*, 1, 1 (Spring 2000), pp. 114–25; Neil Taylor, '"Giving Something Back": Can Football Clubs and their Communities Co-Exist?' in Wagg (ed.), *British Football*, pp. 47–66.

13 Adam Brown, Tim Crabbe, Gavin Mellor, Tony Blackshaw and Chris Stone, *Football and Its Communities: Final Report* (Manchester: Football Foundation and Manchester Metropolitan University, 2006), pp. 52, 59.

14 David Hassan, 'An Opportunity for a New Beginning: Soccer, Irish Nationalists and the Construction of a New Multi-Sports Stadium for Northern Ireland', *Soccer and Society*, 7, 2–3 (April–July 2006), pp. 339–52.

15 *Annual Abstract of Statistics* (London: The Stationery Office, 2002), 'Lifestyles', Table 12.6; *Social Trends* (London: The Stationery Office, 2002), p. 216; *Social Trends* (Basingstoke: Palgrave, 2006), p. 197; Sports Council, *Sport in the Nineties: New Horizons – Part Two: The Context* (London: Sports Council, n.d.); *Lifestyle Pocket Book 1996* (Henley-on-Thames: NTC Publications, 1996), pp. 96–9; Sports Council, *A Digest of Sports Statistics for the UK* (London: Sports Council, 1991), p. 20.

16 Sport England, *Participation in Sport: Past Trends and Future Prospects – The General Household Survey* (Wetherby: UK Sport/Sport England, 2001), pp. 2–5; *Social Trends* (2006), p. 197; Jean Williams, *A Game for Rough Girls?: A History of Women's Football in Britain* (London: Routledge, 2003), p. 42 (Table 1.1); Louise France, 'Not So Jolly', *The Observer* (Sports Section), 24 April 2005.

17 Denis Campbell, Kevin Mitchell and Jamie Jackson, 'Hang Up Your Boots and Dance', *The Observer* (Sports Section), 17 April 2005.

18 H. F. Moorhouse, 'The Organisation of Scottish Football', invited submission to the Scottish Parliament's Reporters' Investigation into Scottish Football 2005, www.scottish.parliament.uk-business-committees-enterprise-inquiries-sfi-fie_pt01_Moorhouse_pdf [accessed 22 March 2006].

19 See Andy Pitchford, Celia Brackenridge, Joy D. Bringer, Claudi Cockburn, Gareth Nutt, Zofia Pawlaczek and Kate Russell, 'Children in Football: Seen But Not Heard', *Soccer and Society*, 5, 1 (Spring 2004), pp. 43–60; Paul Daniel, 'Football for Children or Children for Football?: A Contemporary Boys' League and the Politics of Childhood', pp. 205–23 and Simon Thorpe, 'Pick the Best, Forget the Rest?: Training Field Dilemmas and Children's Football at the Turn of the Century', pp. 224–41, both in Wagg (ed.), *British Football*; Colm Kerrigan, *A History of the English Schools' Football Association, 1904–2004* (Trowbridge: English Schools' Football Association, 2004), pp. 124–5.

20 Daniel, 'Football for Children', pp. 208, 222.

21 Moorhouse, 'Organisation of Scottish Football'.

22 Dave Russell, *Football and the English: A Social History of Association Football in England, 1863–1995* (Preston: Carnegie, 1997), p. 240.

Bibliography

Af Malmborg, M. and Stråth, B. (eds), *The Meaning of Europe* (Oxford: Berg, 2002).

Alabarces, P., Tomlinson, A. and Young, C. (eds), 'Argentina versus England at the France '98 World Cup: Narratives of Nation and the Mythologising of the Popular', *Media, Culture & Society*, 23, 5 (2001).

Allison, L., *Condition of England: Essays and Impressions* (London: Junction, 1981).

Allison, L. (ed.), *The Politics of Sport* (Manchester: Manchester University Press, 1986).

Allison, L. (ed.), *The Global Politics of Sport: The Role of Global Institutions in Sport* (Abingdon: Routledge, 2005).

Andrew, C., '1883 Cup Final: "Patricians" v "Plebeians" ', *History Today* (May 1983).

Andrews, D. L. (ed.), *Manchester United: A Thematic Study* (London: Routledge, 2004).

Andrews, D. L. and Jackson, S. J. (eds), *Sport Stars: The Cultural Politics of Sporting Celebrity* (London: Routledge, 2001).

Annual Abstract of Statistics (London: The Stationery Office, 2002).

Archer, I., 'World Cup '74' in I. Archer and T. Royle (eds), *We'll Support You Evermore: The Impertinent Saga of Scottish Fitba'* (Edinburgh: Mainstream, 2000 [1st edition, 1976]).

Archer, I. and Royle, T. (eds), *We'll Support You Evermore: The Impertinent Saga of Scottish Fitba'* (Edinburgh: Mainstream, 2000 [1st edition, 1976]).

Archetti, E. P., 'The Spectacle of a Heroic Life: The Case of Diego Maradona' in D. L. Andrews and S. J. Jackson (eds), *Sport Stars: The Cultural Politics of Sporting Celebrity* (London: Routledge, 2001).

Archetti, E. P. and Romero, A. G., 'Death and Violence in Argentinian Football' in R. Giulianotti, N. Bonney and M. Hepworth (eds), *Football, Violence and Social Identity* (London: Routledge, 1994).

Armstrong, G. 'False Leeds: The Construction of Hooligan Confrontations' in R. Giulianotti and J. Williams (eds), *Game Without Frontiers: Football, Identity and Modernity* (Aldershot: Arena, 1994).

Armstrong, G., *Football Hooligans: Knowing the Score* (Oxford: Berg, 1998).

Armstrong, G. and Giulianotti, R. (eds), *Entering the Field: New Perspectives on World Football* (Oxford: Berg, 1997).

Armstrong, G. and Giulianotti, R. (eds), *Football Cultures and Identities* (Basingstoke: Macmillan, 1999).

Armstrong, G. and Giulianotti, R. (eds), *Fear and Loathing in World Football* (Oxford: Berg, 2001).

Arnaud, P. and Riordan, J. (eds), *Sport and International Politics: The Impact of Fascism and Communism on Sport* (London: E & FN Spon, 1998).

Arnold, A. J., *A Game That Would Pay: A Business History of Professional Football in Bradford* (London: Duckworth, 1988).

Arnold, A. J., 'The Belated Entry of Professional Soccer into the West Riding Textile District of Northern England: Commercial Imperatives and Problems, *International Journal of the History of Sport*, 6, 3 (December 1989).

Arnold, A. J., '"Not Playing the Game"?: Leeds City in the Great War', *International Journal of the History of Sport*, 7 (May 1990).

Arnold, A. J., 'Rich Man, Poor Man: Economic Arrangements in the Football League' in J. Williams and S. Wagg (eds), *British Football and Social Change: Getting into Europe* (Leicester: Leicester University Press, 1991).

Arnold, A. J. and Benveniste, I., 'Wealth and Poverty in the English Football League', *Accounting and Business Research*, 17, 67 (1987).

Arnold, A. J. and Benveniste, I., 'Cross Subsidisation and Competition Policy in English Professional Football', *Journal of Industrial Affairs*, 15 (1988).

Ayers, P., 'The Making of Men: Masculinities in Interwar Liverpool' in M. Walsh (ed.), *Working Out Gender: Perspectives from Labour History* (Aldershot: Ashgate, 1999).

Back, L., Crabbe, T. and Solomos, J., 'Racism in Football: Patterns of Continuity and Change' in A. Brown (ed.), *Fanatics!: Power, Identity and Fandom in Football* (London: Routledge, 1998).

Back, L., Crabbe, T. and Solomos, J., *The Changing Face of Football: Racism, Identity and Multiculture in the English Game* (Oxford: Berg, 2001).

Back, L., Crabbe, T. and Solomos, J., '"Lions and Black Skins": Race, Nation and Local Patriotism in Football' in B. Carrington and I. McDonald (eds), *'Race', Sport and British Society* (London: Routledge, 2001).

Bailey, P., *Leisure and Class in Victorian England: Rational Recreation and the Contest for Control, 1830–1885* (London: Methuen, 1987 [1st edition, 1978]).

Bains, J. and Johal, S., *Corner Flags and Corner Shops: The Asian Football Experience* (London: Victor Gollancz, 1998).

Bairner, A., 'Football and the Idea of Scotland' in G. Jarvie and G. Walker (eds), *Scottish Sport and the Making of the Nation: Ninety-Minute Patriots?* (Leicester: Leicester University Press, 1994).

Bairner, A., 'Football' in G. Jarvie and J. Burnett (eds), *Sport, Scotland and the Scots* (East Linton: Tuckwell, 2000).

Bairner, A., 'Where Did It All Go Right? George Best, Manchester United and Northern Ireland' in D. L. Andrews (ed.), *Manchester United: A Thematic Study* (London: Routledge, 2004).

Bairner, A., 'Sport and Nation in the Global Era' in L. Allison (ed.), *The Global Politics of Sport: The Role of Global Institutions in Sport* (Abingdon: Routledge, 2005).

Bairner, A., 'The Leicester School and the Study of Football Hooliganism', *Sport in Society*, 9, 4 (October 2006).

Baker, N., 'A More Even Playing Field?: Sport During and After the War' in N. Hayes and J. Hill (eds), *'Millions Like Us'?: British Culture in the Second World War* (Liverpool: Liverpool University Press, 1999).

Baker, W. J., 'The Making of a Working-Class Football Culture in Victorian England', *Journal of Social History*, 13 (Winter 1979).

Bale, J., 'Geographical Diffusion and the Adoption of Professionalism in Football in England and Wales', *Geography*, 63 (1978).

Bale, J., *Sport and Place: A Geography of Sport in England, Scotland and Wales* (London: C. Hurst, 1982).

Bale, J., 'Football and Topophilia: The Public and the Stadium', European University Institute Colloquium Papers, 1989.

Bale, J., 'In the Shadow of the Stadium: Football Grounds as Urban Nuisances', *Geography*, 75 (1990).

Bale, J., 'Playing at Home: British Football and a Sense of Place' in J. Williams and S. Wagg (eds), *British Football and Social Change: Getting into Europe* (Leicester: Leicester University Press, 1991).

Bale, J., *Sport, Space and the City* (London: Routledge, 1993).

Bale, J., *Landscapes of Modern Sport* (Leicester: Leicester University Press, 1994).

Bale, J., 'Identity, Identification and Image: Football and Place in the New Europe' in S. Gehrmann (ed.), *Football and Regional Identity in Europe* (Münster: Lit Verlag, 1997).

Bale, J., 'Virtual Fandoms: Futurescapes of Football' in A. Brown (ed.), *Fanatics!: Power, Identity and Fandom in Football* (London: Routledge, 1998).

Bale, J., 'The Changing Face of Football: Stadiums and Communities', *Soccer and Society*, 1, 1 (Spring 2000).

Bale, J., *Sports Geography* (London: Routledge, 2003 [1st edition, 1989]).

Bale, J., Christiansen, M. K. and Pfister, G. (eds), *Writing Lives in Sport: Biographies, Life-Histories and Methods* (Langelandsgade: Aarhus University Press, 2004).

Bale, J. and Maguire, J. (eds), *The Global Sports Arena: Athletic Talent Migration in an Interdependent World* (London: Frank Cass, 1994).

Bartram, S., *My Autobiography* (London: Burke, 1951).

Bassett, W. I., 'Big Transfers and the Transfer System' in C. Leatherdale (ed.), *The Book of Football* (Westcliff-on-Sea: Desert Island, 1997 [1st edition, 1906]).

Bassett, W. I., 'The Making of a Player: Part 1 – The Forward Game' in C. Leatherdale (ed.), *The Book of Football* (Westcliff-on-Sea: Desert Island, 1997 [1st edition, 1906]).

Beaven, B., *Leisure, Citizenship and Working-Class Men in Britain, 1850–1945* (Manchester: Manchester University Press, 2005).

Beck, P., *Scoring for Britain: International Football and International Politics, 1900–1939* (London: Frank Cass, 1999).

Beck, P., 'Political Football: The British Government and Anglo-Soviet Footballing Relations, 1945–54', paper presented to the British Society of Sports History Annual Conference, University of Liverpool, April 2000.

Beck, P., 'Leisure and Sport in Britain, 1900–1939' in C. Wrigley (ed.), *A Companion to Early Twentieth-Century Britain* (London: Blackwell, 2003).

Beck, P., 'The Relevance of the "Irrelevant": Football as a Missing Dimension in the Study of British Relations with Germany', *International Affairs*, 79, 2 (2003).

Bellers, L., 'Haven't You Got Homes to Go To?', *When Saturday Comes*, July 1995.

Ben-Porat, A., 'Overseas Sweetheart: Israeli Fans of English Football', *Journal of Sport and Social Issues*, 24, 4 (November 2000).

Benson, J. (ed.), *Working Class in England, 1875–1914* (London: Croom Helm, 1984).

Benson, J., *The Working Class in Britain, 1850–1939* (London: Longman, 1989).

Bilsborough, P., 'The Development of Sport in Glasgow, 1850–1914', unpublished M. Litt. thesis, University of Stirling, 1983.

Bingham, A. C., 'Debating Gender: Approaches to Femininity and Masculinity in the Popular National Daily Press in Interwar Britain', unpublished D.Phil. thesis, University of Oxford, 2002.

Birch, A. H., *Political Integration and Disintegration in the British Isles* (London: George Allen & Unwin, 1977).

Birley, D., *Land of Sport and Glory: Sport and British Society, 1887–1910* (Manchester: Manchester University Press, 1995).

Birley, D., *Playing the Game: Sport and British Society, 1910–45* (Manchester: Manchester University Press, 1995).

Blanpain, R. and Inston, R., *The Bosman Case: The End of the Transfer System?* (Brussels: Bruylants, 1996).

Blythe Smart, J., *The Wow Factor: A Concise History of Early Soccer and the Men Who Made It* (Hailsham: Blythe Smart, 2003).

Bogdanor, V., *Devolution in the United Kingdom* (Oxford: Oxford University Press, 1999).

Boli, C., *Manchester United, L'invention d'un Club: Deux siècles de metamorphoses* (Paris: Éditions de La Martinière, 2004).

Booth, K., *The Father of Modern Sport: The Life and Times of Charles W. Alcock* (Manchester: Parrs Wood, 2002).

Bourke, A., 'The Road to Fame and Fortune: Insights into the Career Paths of Young Irish Professional Footballers in England', *Journal of Youth Studies*, 5, 4 (2002).

Bourke, J., *Working-Class Cultures in Britain, 1890–1960: Gender, Class and Ethnicity* (London: Routledge, 1994).

Bourne, J., Liddle, P. and Whitehead, I. (eds), *The Great World War, 1914–45*, Vol. 2: *The People's Experience* (London: HarperCollins, 2001).

Bowker, D., 'Parks and Baths: Sport, Recreation and Municipal Government in Ashton-under-Lyme Between the Wars' in R. Holt (ed.), *Sport and the Working Class in Modern Britain* (Manchester: Manchester University Press, 1990).

Bowler, D., *Winning Isn't Everything …: A Biography of Alf Ramsey* (London: Orion, 1999).

Boyle, R., '"We Are Celtic Supporters …".: Questions of Football and Identity in Modern Scotland' in R. Giulianotti and J. Williams (eds), *Game Without Frontiers: Football, Identity and Modernity* (Aldershot: Arena, 1994).

Boyle, R., 'Battling Along the Boundaries: The Making of Scottish Identity in Sports Journalism' in G. Jarvie and G. Walker (eds), *Scottish Sport and the Making of the Nation: Ninety-Minute Patriots?* (Leicester: Leicester University Press, 1994).

Boyle, R., 'Football and Religion: Merseyside and Glasgow' in J. Williams, S. Hopkins and C. Long (eds), *Passing Rhythms: Liverpool FC and the Transformation of Football* (Oxford: Berg, 2001).

Boyle, R. and Haynes, R., *Power Play: Sport, the Media and Popular Culture* (London: Longman, 2000).

Brackenridge, C. and Woodward, D., 'Gender Inequalities in Leisure and Sport in Post-War Britain' in J. Obelkevich and P. Catterall (eds), *Understanding Post-War British Society* (London: Routledge, 1994).

Bradbury, S., *The New Football Communities: A Survey of Professional Football Clubs on Issues of Community, Ethnicity and Social Inclusion* (Leicester: Sir Norman Chester Centre for Football Research, 2001).

Bradbury, S. and Williams, J., 'New Labour, Racism and "New" Football in England', *Patterns of Prejudice*, 40, 1 (2006).

Bradley, J. M., *Ethnic and Religious Identity in Scotland: Politics, Culture and Football* (Aldershot: Avebury, 1995).

Bradley, J. M., 'Football in Scotland: A History of Political and Ethnic Identity', *International Journal of the History of Sport*, 12, 1 (April 1995).

Bradley, J. M., 'Integration or Assimilation?: Scottish Society, Football and Irish Immigrants', *International Journal of the History of Sport*, 13, 1 (August 1996).

Bradley, J. M., '"We Shall Not Be Moved"! Mere Sport, Mere Songs?: A Tale of Scottish Football' in A. Brown (ed.), *Fanatics!: Power, Identity and Fandom in Football* (London: Routledge, 1998).

Brick, C., 'Taking Offence: Modern Moralities and the Perception of the Football Fan', *Soccer and Society*, 1, 1 (2000).

Brick, C., 'Can't Live With Them. Can't Live Without Them: Reflections on Manchester United' in G. Armstrong and R. Giulianotti (eds), *Fear and Loathing in World Football* (Oxford: Berg, 2001).

Bristowe, A., *Charlton Athletic Football Club, 1905–50* (London: Voice of the Valley, 1992 reprint [1st published 1951]).

Brocklehurst, H. and Phillips, R. (eds), *History, Nationhood and the Question of Britain* (Basingstoke: Palgrave, 2004).

Brodie, M., *100 Years of Irish Football* (Belfast: Blackstaff, 1980).

Brohm, J-M., *Sport: A Prison of Measured Time* (London: Ink Links, 1978).

Bromberger, C. with Hayot, A. and Mariottini, J-M., '"Allez l'O.M., Forza Juve": The Passion for Football in Marseille and Turin' in S. Redhead (ed.), *The Passion and the Fashion: Football Fandom in the New Europe* (Aldershot: Avebury, 1993).

Brookes, R., *Representing Sport* (London: Arnold, 2002).

Brown, A., '"Ratfink Reds": Montpellier and Rotterdam 1991' in S. Redhead (ed.), *The Passion and the Fashion: Football Fandom in the New Europe* (Aldershot: Avebury, 1993).

Brown, A., 'Let's All Have a Disco?: Football, Popular Music and Democratization' in S. Redhead, with D. Wynne and J. O'Connor (eds), *The Clubcultures Reader* (Oxford: Blackwell, 1997).

Brown, A. (ed.), *Fanatics!: Power, Identity and Fandom in Football* (London: Routledge, 1998).

Brown, A., 'United We Stand: Some Problems with Fan Democracy' in A. Brown (ed.), *Fanatics!: Power, Identity and Fandom in Football* (London: Routledge, 1998).

Brown, A., 'Sneaking in through the Back Door?: Media Company Interests and the Dual Ownership of Clubs' in S. Hamil, J. Michie, C. Oughton and S. Warby (eds), *Football in the Digital Age: Whose Game Is It Anyway?* (Edinburgh: Mainstream, 2000).

Brown, A., 'The Football Task Force and the "Regulator Debate"' in S. Hamil, J. Michie, C. Oughton and S. Warby (eds), *Football in the Digital Age: Whose Game Is It Anyway?* (Edinburgh: Mainstream, 2000).

Brown, A., '"Manchester Is Red"?: Manchester United, Fan Identity and the "Sport City"' in D. L. Andrews (ed.), *Manchester United: A Thematic Study* (London: Routledge, 2004).

Brown, A., Crabbe, T., Mellor, G., Blackshaw, T. and Stone, C., *Football and Its Communities: Final Report* (Manchester: Football Foundation and Manchester Metropolitan University, 2006).

Brown, A. and Walsh, A., *Not for Sale: Manchester United, Murdoch and the Defeat of BSkyB* (Edinburgh: Mainstream, 1999).

Brown, C. G., 'Sport and the Scottish Office in the Twentieth Century:

The Control of a Social Problem' in J. A. Mangan (ed.), *Sport in Europe: Politics, Class, Gender* (London: Frank Cass, 1999).

Brown, C. G., 'Sport and the Scottish Office in the Twentieth Century: The Promotion of a Social and Gender Policy' in J. A. Mangan (ed.), *Sport in Europe: Politics, Class, Gender* (London: Frank Cass, 1999).

Brown, I., 'Play Sport: Problems of Sport as a Theme for the Playwright' in M. Green and C. Jenkins (eds), *Sporting Fictions* (Birmingham: Centre for Contemporary Cultural Studies, 1981).

Brown, M., 'Asian Games', *When Saturday Comes*, February 1995.

Bull, D. (ed.), *We'll Support You Evermore: Keeping Faith in Football* (London: Duckworth, 1992).

Burchill, J., *Burchill on Beckham* (London: Yellow Jersey, 2002).

Burdsey, D., '"One of the Lads": Dual Ethnicity and Assimilated Ethnicities in the Careers of British Asian Professional Footballers', *Ethnic and Racial Studies*, 27, 5 (September 2004).

Burke, P., *What is Cultural History?* (Cambridge: Polity, 2004).

Calder, A., *The People's War: Britain 1939–45* (London: Jonathan Cape, 1969).

Campbell, D., 'United (versus Liverpool) Nations', *Observer Sport Monthly*, 21 (January 2002).

Campbell, D., Mitchell, K. and Jackson, J., 'Hang Up Your Boots and Dance', *The Observer* (Sports Section), 17 April 2005.

Campbell, D. and Shields, A., *Soccer City: The Future of Football in London* (London: Mandarin, 1993).

Campbell, J. D., '"Training for Sport is Training for War": Sport and the Transformation of the British Army, 1860–1914', *International Journal of the History of Sport*, 17, 4 (December 2000).

Canter, D., Comber, M. and Uzzell, D. L., *Football in its Place: An Environmental Psychology of Football Grounds* (London: Routledge, 1989).

Capel-Kirby, W. and Carter, F. W., *The Mighty Kick: Romance, History and Humour of Football* (London: Jarrolds, 1933).

Carrington, B., '"Football's Coming Home" But Whose Home? And Do We Want It?: Nation, Football and the Politics of Exclusion' in A. Brown (ed.), *Fanatics!: Power, Identity and Fandom in Football* (London: Routledge, 1998).

Carrington, B., 'Postmodern Blackness and the Celebrity Sports Star: Ian Wright, "Race" and English Identity' in D. L. Andrews and S. J. Jackson (eds), *Sport Stars: The Cultural Politics of Sporting Celebrity* (London: Routledge, 2001).

Carrington, B. and McDonald, I., 'Introduction: "Race", Sport and British Society' in B. Carrington and I. McDonald (eds), *'Race', Sport and British Society* (London: Routledge, 2001).

Carrington, B. and McDonald, I. (eds), *'Race', Sport and British Society* (London: Routledge, 2001).

Carter, N., *The Football Manager: A History* (London: Routledge, 2006).

Carter, R., *Footballer's Progress* (London: Sporting Handbooks, 1950).

Cashman, R. and McKernan, M. (eds), *Sport in History* (Brisbane: University of Queensland Press, 1979).

Cashman, R. and McKernan, M. (eds), *Sport: Money, Morality and the Media* (Brisbane: New South Wales University Press, 1981).

Cashmore, E., *Making Sense of Sports* (London: Routledge, 1996 [1st edition, 1990]).

Cashmore, E., *Beckham* (Cambridge: Polity, 2002).

Cashmore, E. and Parker, A., 'One David Beckham?: Celebrity, Masculinity and the Soccerati', *Sociology of Sport Journal*, 20 (2003).

Caudwell, J., 'Women's Football in the United Kingdom: Theorizing Gender and Unpacking the Butch Lesbian Image', *Journal of Sport and Social Issues*, 23, 4 (November 1999).

Caudwell, J., 'Women's Experiences of Sexuality Within Football Cultures: A Particular and Located Footballing Epistemology', *Football Studies*, 5, 1 (2002).

Caunce, S., Mazierska, E., Sydney-Smith, S. and Walton, J. (eds), *Relocating Britishness* (Manchester: Manchester University Press, 2004).

Chandler, T. J. L., 'The Structuring of Manliness and the Development of Rugby Football at the Public Schools and Oxbridge, 1830–1880' in J. Nauright and T. J. L. Chandler (eds), *Making Men: Rugby and Masculine Identity* (London: Frank Cass, 1996).

Chapman, L., *More Than a Match: A Player's Story* (London: Arrow, 1993).

Charles, J., *King of Soccer* (London: Stanley Paul, 1957).

Chisari, F., '"Definitely Not Cricket": *The Times* and the Football World Cup, 1930–1970', *The Sports Historian*, 20, 1 (May 2000).

Chisari, F., '"The Age of Innocence": A History of the Relationship between the Football Authorities and the BBC Television Service', unpublished Ph.D. thesis, De Montfort University, 2006.

Clapson, M., *A Bit of a Flutter: Popular Gambling and English Society, c.1823–1961* (Manchester: Manchester University Press, 1992).

Clarke, J., 'Football and Working Class Fans: Tradition and Change' in

R. Ingham (ed.), *Football Hooliganism: The Wider Context* (London: Inter-Action, 1978).

Clarke, J. and Critcher, C., *The Devil Makes Work: Leisure in Capitalist Britain* (Basingstoke: Macmillan, 1985).

Clarke, J. and Critcher, C., '1966 and All That: England's World Cup Victory' in A. Tomlinson and G. Whannel (eds), *Off the Ball: The Football World Cup* (London: Pluto, 1986).

Clarke, J., Critcher, C. and Johnson, R. (eds), *Working Class Culture: Studies in History and Theory* (London: Hutchinson, 1979).

Coddington, A., *One of the Lads: Women Who Follow Football* (London: HarperCollins, 1997).

Coglan, J. F. with Webb, I. M., *Sport and British Politics Since 1960* (London: Falmer, 1990).

Colley, I. and Davies, G., 'Kissed by History: Football as TV Drama' in M. Green and C. Jenkins (eds), *Sporting Fictions* (Birmingham: Centre for Contemporary Cultural Studies, 1981).

Colley, L., *Britons: Forging the Nation, 1707–1837* (London: Pimlico, 2003 [1st edition, 1992]).

Collins, M. with Kay, T., *Sport and Social Exclusion* (London: Routledge, 2003).

Collins, T., *Rugby's Great Split: Class, Culture and the Origins of Rugby League Football* (London: Frank Cass, 1998).

Collins, T., 'English Rugby Union and the First World War', *The Historical Journal*, 45, 4 (2002).

Collins, T., 'The End of the "Creeping Barrage": The Introduction of Rugby League's Limited Tackle Rule', paper presented to the British Society of Sports History Annual Conference, University of Southampton, April 2003.

Collins, T., 'History, Theory and the "Civilizing Process"', *Sport in History*, 25, 2 (August 2005).

Conn, D., *The Football Business: Fair Game in the 1990s* (Edinburgh: Mainstream, 1997).

Conn, D., *The Beautiful Game?: Searching for the Soul of Football* (London: Yellow Jersey, 2004).

Connell, R. M., 'The Association Game in Scotland' in C. Leatherdale (ed.), *The Book of Football* (Westcliff-on-Sea: Desert Island, 1997 [1st edition, 1906]).

Connell, R. M., 'The Scottish Football League and its History' in C. Leatherdale (ed.), *The Book of Football* (Westcliff-on-Sea: Desert Island, 1997 [1st edition, 1906]).

Cooke, A., *The Economics of Leisure and Sport* (London: Routledge, 1994).

Cosgrove, S., 'And the Bonny Scotland Will Be There: Football in Scottish Culture' in A. Tomlinson and G. Whannel (eds), *Off the Ball: The Football World Cup* (London: Pluto, 1986).

Cosgrove, S., *Hampden Babylon: Sex and Scandal in Scottish Football* (Edinburgh: Canongate, 2001 [1st edition, 1991]).

Cox, R., Russell, D. and Vamplew, W. (eds), *Encyclopedia of British Football* (London: Frank Cass, 2002).

Coyle, J., 'English Sports Leagues, Franchising and the Management of Expansion: The Football League and the Northern Union up to 1923', unpublished MA dissertation, De Montfort University, 1997.

Crabbe, T. and Brown, A., '"You're Not Welcome Anymore": The Football Crowd, Class and Social Exclusion' in S. Wagg (ed.), *British Football and Social Exclusion* (London: Routledge, 2004).

Crampsey, B., *The Scottish Footballer* (Edinburgh: William Blackwood, 1978).

Crampsey, B., *The First 100 Years: The Scottish Football League* (Glasgow: Scottish Football League, 1990).

Crawford, G., *Consuming Sport: Fans, Sport and Culture* (London: Routledge, 2004).

Crawford, G., 'Sensible Soccer: Sport Fandom and the Rise of Digital Gaming' in J. Magee, A. Bairner and A. Tomlinson (eds), *The Bountiful Game?: Football Identities and Finances* (Oxford: Meyer & Meyer Sport, 2005).

Crick, M., 'Shareholders United Against Murdoch', *Soccer and Society*, 1, 3 (Autumn 2000).

Critcher, C., 'Football Since the War' in J. Clarke, C. Critcher and R. Johnson (eds), *Working Class Culture: Studies in History and Theory* (London: Hutchinson, 1979).

Critcher, C., 'Putting on the Style: Aspects of Recent English Football' in J. Williams and S. Wagg (eds), *British Football and Social Change: Getting into Europe* (Leicester: Leicester University Press, 1991).

Critcher, C., 'England and the World Cup: World Cup Willies, English Football and the Myth of 1966' in J. Sugden and A. Tomlinson (eds), *Hosts and Champions: Soccer Cultures, National Identities and the USA World Cup* (Aldershot: Arena, 1994).

Croll, A., *Civilizing the Urban: Popular Culture and Public Space in Merthyr, c.1870–1914* (Cardiff: University of Wales Press, 2000).

Crolley, L., 'The Green, Green Grass of Anfield' in S. Kuper and M. Mora

Y Araujo (eds), *Perfect Pitch 3: Men and Women* (London: Headline, 1998).

Crolley, L. and Long, C., 'Sitting Pretty?: Women and Football in Liverpool' in J. Williams, S. Hopkins and C. Long (eds), *Passing Rhythms: Liverpool FC and the Transformation of Football* (Oxford: Berg, 2001).

Cronin, M., *Sport and Nationalism in Ireland: Gaelic Games, Soccer and Irish Identity Since 1884* (Dublin: Four Courts, 1999).

Cronin, M., 'Playing Away from Home: Identity in Northern Ireland and the Experience of Derry City Football Club', *National Identities*, 2, 1 (2000).

Cronin, M. and Holt, R., 'The Imperial Game in Crisis: English Cricket and Decolonisation' in S. Ward (ed.), *British Culture and the End of Empire* (Manchester: Manchester University Press, 2001).

Crowhurst, A., 'The "Portly Grabbers of 75 per cent": Capital Investment in the British Entertainment Industry, 1885–1914', *Leisure Studies*, 20 (2001).

Crowther, P., 'The Attempted Takeover of Manchester United by BSkyB' in S. Hamil, J. Michie, C. Oughton and S. Warby (eds), *Football in the Digital Age: Whose Game Is It Anyway?* (Edinburgh: Mainstream, 2000).

Cubitt, G. and Warren, A. (eds), *Heroic Reputations and Exemplary Lives* (Manchester: Manchester University Press, 2000).

Cullis, S., *All for the Wolves* (London: Sportsmans Book Club, 1960).

Cunningham, H., *Leisure in the Industrial Revolution* (London: Croom Helm, 1980).

Cunningham, H., 'Leisure' in J. Benson (ed.), *Working Class in England, 1875–1914* (London: Croom Helm, 1984).

Curry, G., 'The Trinity Connection: An Analysis of the Role of Members of Cambridge University in the Development of Football in the Mid-Nineteenth Century', *The Sports Historian*, 22, 2 (November 2002).

Curry, G., 'Playing for Money: James J. Lang and Emergent Soccer Professionalism in Sheffield', *Soccer and Society*, 5, 3 (Autumn 2004).

Curry, G., Dunning, E. and Sheard, K., 'Sociological Versus Empiricist History: Some Comments on Tony Collins's "History, Theory and the Civilizing Process"', *Sport in History*, 26, 1 (April 2006).

Dabscheck, B., '"Defensive Manchester": A History of the Professional Footballers' Association' in R. Cashman and M. McKernan (eds), *Sport in History* (Brisbane: University of Queensland Press, 1979).

Dahlgren, P. and Sparks, C. (eds), *Journalism and Popular Culture* (London: Sage, 1992).

Daniel, P., 'Football for Children or Children for Football?: A Contemporary Boys' League and the Politics of Childhood' in S. Wagg (ed.), *British Football and Social Exclusion* (London: Routledge, 2004).

Darby, P., Johnes, M. and Mellor, G. (eds), *Soccer and Disaster: International Perspectives* (London: Routledge, 2005).

Davies, A., *Leisure, Gender and Poverty: Working Class Culture in Salford and Manchester, 1900–1939* (Buckingham: Open University Press, 1992).

Davies, A., 'Leisure in the "Classic Slum", 1900–1939' in A. Davies and S. Fleming (eds), *Workers' Worlds: Cultures and Communities in Manchester and Salford, 1880–1939* (Manchester: Manchester University Press, 1992).

Davies, A. and Fielding, S. (eds), *Workers' Worlds: Cultures and Communities in Manchester and Salford, 1880–1939* (Manchester: Manchester University Press, 1992).

Davies, H., *The Glory Game* (Edinburgh: Mainstream, 1992 [1st edition, 1972]).

Davies, H., *Boots, Balls and Haircuts: An Illustrated History of Football from Then to Now* (London: Cassell Illustrated, 2003).

Davies, N., *The Isles* (Basingstoke: Permac, 1999).

Davies, P., *I Lost My Heart to the Belles* (London: Mandarin, 1997).

Davis, A., 'The Southern League: Its Rise and Progress' in C. Leatherdale (ed.), *The Book of Football* (Westcliff-on-Sea: Desert Island, 1997 [1st edition, 1906]).

Dawson, J., *Back Home: England and the 1970 World Cup* (London: Orion, 2001).

Deloitte & Touche, *Deloitte & Touche Annual Review of Football Finance* (Manchester: Deloitte & Touche, 1999).

Deloitte & Touche, *Deloitte & Touche Annual Review of Football Finance* (Manchester: Deloitte & Touche, 2003).

Delves, A., 'Popular Recreation and Social Conflict in Derby, 1800–1850' in E. Yeo and S. Yeo (eds), *Popular Culture and Class Conflict, 1590–1914* (Brighton: Harvester, 1981).

Dempsey, P. and Reilly, K., *Big Money, Beautiful Game* (London: Nicholas Brealey, 1998).

Department of Education and Science, *Report of the Committee on Football* (London: HMSO, 1968).

Dimeo, P. and Finn, G. P. T., 'Scottish Racism, Scottish Identities: The Case of Partick Thistle' in A. Brown (ed.), *Fanatics!: Power, Identity and Fandom in Football* (London: Routledge, 1998).

Dimeo, P. and Finn, G. P. T., 'Racism, National Identity and Scottish Football' in B. Carrington and I. McDonald (eds), *'Race', Sport and British Society* (London: Routledge, 2001).

Dixon, P., Garnham, N. and Jackson, A., 'Shareholders and Shareholding: The Case of the Football Company in Late Victorian England', *Business History*, 46, 4 (October 2004).

Dobson, S. and Goddard, J., 'Performance, Revenue and Cross Subsidisation in the Football League, 1927–1994, *Economic History Review*, 51, 4 (1998).

Dobson, S. and Goddard, J., *The Economics of Football* (Cambridge: Cambridge University Press, 2001).

Doherty, P., *Soccer* (London: Foyles Handbooks, 1950).

Dougan, D., *The Sash He Never Wore* (St Albans: Mayflower, 1974).

Douglas, P., *The Football Industry* (London: George Allen & Unwin, 1973).

Duke, V., 'The Politics of Football in the New Europe' in J. Williams and S. Wagg (eds), *British Football and Social Change: Getting into Europe* (Leicester: Leicester University Press, 1991).

Duke, V., 'The Drive to Modernization and the Supermarket Imperative: Who Needs a New Football Stadium?' in R. Giulianotti and J. Williams (eds), *Game Without Frontiers: Football, Identity and Modernity* (Aldershot: Arena, 1994).

Duke, V., 'Local Tradition Versus Globalisation: Resistance to the McDonaldisation and Disneyisation of Professional Football in England', *Football Studies*, 5, 1 (2002).

Duke, V. and Crolley, L., *Football, Nationality and the State* (Harlow: Longman, 1996).

Dunning, E. (ed.), *The Sociology of Sport* (London: Frank Cass, 1971).

Dunning, E., 'The Development of Football' in E. Dunning (ed.), *The Sociology of Sport* (London: Frank Cass, 1971).

Dunning, E., 'The Social Roots of Football Hooliganism: A Reply to the Critics of the "Leicester School" ' in R. Giulianotti, N. Bonney and M. Hepworth (eds), *Football, Violence and Social Identity* (London: Routledge, 1994).

Dunning, E., *Sport Matters: Sociological Studies of Sport, Violence and Civilization* (London: Routledge, 1999).

Dunning, E., 'Something of a Curate's Egg', *International Journal of the History of Sport*, 18, 4 (December 2001).

Dunning, E. and Curry, G., 'The Curate's Egg Scrambled Again: Comments on "The Curate's Egg Put Back Together"!', *International Journal of the History of Sport*, 19, 4 (December 2002).

Dunning, E. and Curry, G., 'Public Schools, Status Rivalry and the Development of Football' in E. Dunning, D. Malcolm and I. Waddington (eds), *Sport Histories: Figurational Studies of the Development of Modern Sports* (London: Routledge, 2004).

Dunning, E., Malcolm, D. and Waddington, I. (eds), *Sport Histories: Figurational Studies of the Development of Modern Sports* (London: Routledge, 2004).

Dunning, E., Murphy, P. and Waddington, I., 'Anthropological versus Sociological Approaches to the Study of Soccer Hooliganism: Some Critical Notes', *Sociological Review*, 39, 3 (1991).

Dunning, E., Murphy, P. and Williams, J., *The Roots of Football Hooliganism: A Historical and Sociological Study* (London: Routledge & Kegan Paul, 1988).

Dunning, E. and Sheard, K., *Barbarians, Gentlemen and Players: A Sociological Study of the Development of Rugby Football* (London: Routledge, 2005 [1st edition, 1979]).

Dunphy, E., *Only a Game?: The Diary of a Professional Footballer* (London: Penguin, 1987 [1st edition, 1976]).

Dunphy, E., *A Strange Kind of Glory: Sir Matt Busby and Manchester United* (London: Heinemann, 1991).

Eastham, G., *Determined to Win* (London: Sportsmans Book Club, 1966).

Edge, A., *Faith of Our Fathers: Football as a Religion* (London: Mainstream, 1999).

Eisenberg, C., 'From England to the World: The Spread of Modern Football, 1863–2000', *Moving Bodies*, 1, 1 (2003).

English, R. and Kenny, M., *Rethinking British Decline* (Basingstoke: Macmillan, 2000).

Euchner, C. C., *Playing the Field: Why Sports Teams Move and Cities Fight to Keep Them* (Baltimore: Johns Hopkins University Press, 1993).

Everitt, R., *Battle for the Valley* (London: Voice of the Valley, 1991).

Fabian, A. H. and Green, G. (eds), *Association Football*, Vol. 1 (London: Caxton, 1960).

Fawbert, J., 'Football Fandom and the "Traditional" Football Club: From

"Cockney Parochialism" to a European Diaspora?' in J. Magee, A. Bairner and A. Tomlinson (eds), *The Bountiful Game?: Football Identities and Finances* (Oxford: Meyer & Meyer Sport, 2005).

Ferrier, B., *Soccer Partnership: Billy Wright and Walter Winterbottom* (London: Sportsmans Book Club, 1961).

Fielding, S., *Class and Ethnicity: Irish Catholics in England, 1880–1939* (Buckingham: Open University Press, 1993).

Fifield, D., 'As Beckham Gets Set for $92,000 a Week, 600 Fellow Footballers Prepare for the Dole', *The Guardian*, 7 May 2002.

Finn, G. P. T., 'Racism, Religion and Social Prejudice: Irish Catholic Clubs, Soccer and Scottish Society – 1 The Historical Roots of Prejudice', *International Journal of the History of Sport*, 8, 1 (May 1991).

Finn, G. P. T., 'Racism, Religion and Social Prejudice: Irish Catholic Clubs, Soccer and Scottish Society – 2 Social Identities and Conspiracy Theories', *International Journal of the History of Sport*, 8, 3 (December 1991).

Finn, G. P. T., 'Football Violence: A Societal Psychological Perspective' in R. Giulianotti, N. Bonney and M. Hepworth (eds), *Football, Violence and Social Identity* (London: Routledge, 1994).

Finn, G. P. T. and Giulianotti, R., 'Scottish Fans, Not English Hooligans!: Scots, Scottishness and Scottish Football' in A. Brown (ed.), *Fanatics!: Power, Identity and Fandom in Football* (London: Routledge, 1998).

Finney, N., 'The MMC's Inquiry into BSkyB's Merger with Manchester United PLC' in S. Hamil, J. Michie, C. Oughton and S. Warby (eds), *Football in the Digital Age: Whose Game Is It Anyway?* (Edinburgh: Mainstream, 2000).

Finney, T., *Football Round the World* (London: Sportsmans Book Club, 1955).

Finney, T., *Finney on Football* (London: Sportsmans Book Club, 1960).

Fishwick, N., *English Football and Society, 1910–1950* (Manchester: Manchester University Press, 1989).

Fleming, S., 'Sport, Schooling and Asian Male Youth Culture' in G. Jarvie (ed.), *Sport, Racism and Ethnicity* (London: Falmer, 1991).

Fleming, S., 'Racial Science and South Asian and Black Physicality' in B. Carrington and I. McDonald (eds), *'Race', Sport and British Society* (London: Routledge, 2001).

Flowers, R., *For Wolves and England* (London: Sportsmans Book Club, 1964).

Football Association, *Blueprint for the Future of Football* (London: Football Association, 1991).

Football Association, *A Manifesto for Football* (London: Football Association, 1992).

Football League, *One Game, One Team, One Voice: Managing Football's Future* (London: Football League, 1990).

Foster, K., 'Dreaming of Pelé: Football and Society in England and Brazil in the 1950s and 1960s', *Football Studies*, 6, 1 (2003).

Foucault, M., *The Birth of the Clinic* (New York: Vintage, 1975).

Foucault, M., *Discipline and Punish: The Birth of the Prison* (London: Allen Lane, 1977).

Frampton, P., Michie, J. and Walsh, A., *Fresh Players, New Tactics: Lessons from Northampton Town Supporters' Trust* (London: Football Governance Research Centre, 2001).

France, L., 'Not So Jolly', *The Observer* (Sports Section), 24 April 2005.

Frosdick, S. and Marsh, P., *Football Hooliganism* (Cullompton: Willan, 2005).

Frykholm, P. A., 'Soccer and Social Identity in Pre-Revolutionary Moscow', *Journal of Sport History*, 24, 2 (Summer 1997).

Fuller, J. G., *Troop Morale and Popular Culture in the British and Dominion Armies 1914–1918* (Oxford: Clarendon, 1991).

Fynn, A. and Guest, L., *The Secret Life of Football* (London: Macdonald Queen Anne, 1989).

Fynn, A. and Guest, L., *Out of Time: Why Football Isn't Working* (London: Pocket Books, 1994).

Gaffney, C. and Bale, J., 'Sensing the Stadium' in P. Vertinsky and J. Bale (eds), *Sites of Sport: Space, Place and Experience* (London: Routledge, 2004).

Gardiner, S. and Welch, R., 'Sport, Racism and the Limits of "Colour Blind" Law' in B. Carrington and I. McDonald (eds), *'Race', Sport and British Society* (London: Routledge, 2001).

Garland, J., 'The Same Old Story?: Englishness, the Tabloid Press and the 2002 Football World Cup', *Leisure Studies*, 23, 1 (January 2004).

Garland, J., and Rowe, M., 'War Minus the Shooting?: Jingoism, the English Press, and Euro 96', *Journal of Sport and Social Issues*, 23, 1 (February 1999).

Garland, J. and Rowe, M., 'Selling the Game Short: An Examination of the Role of Antiracism in British Football', *Sociology of Sport Journal*, 16 (1999).

Garland, J. and Rowe, M., *Racism and Anti-Racism in Football* (Basingstoke: Palgrave, 2001).

Garnham, N. (ed.), *The Origins and Development of Football in Ireland* (Belfast: Ulster Historical Foundation, 1999).

Garnham, N., 'The Origins and Development of Irish Football' in N. Garnham (ed.), *The Origins and Development of Football in Ireland* (Belfast: Ulster Historical Foundation, 1999).

Garnham, N., 'Football and National Identity in Pre-Great War Ireland', *Irish Economic and Social History*, 28 (2001).

Garnham, N., 'Patronage, Politics and the Modernization of Leisure in Northern England: The Case of Alnwick's Shrove Tuesday Football Match', *English Historical Review*, 117, 474 (2002).

Garnham, N., 'Professionals and Professionalism in Pre-Great War Irish Soccer', *Journal of Sport History*, 29, 1 (Spring 2002).

Garnham, N., *Association Football and Society in Pre-Partition Ireland* (Belfast: Ulster Historical Foundation, 2004).

Garnham, N. and Jackson, A., 'Who Invested in Victorian Football Clubs?: The Case of Newcastle-upon-Tyne', *Soccer and Society*, 4, 1 (Spring 2003).

Gastaut, Y. and Mourlane, S. (eds), *Le Football dans nos sociétés: Une culture populaire, 1914–1998* (Paris: Autrement, 2006).

Gehrmann, S. (ed.), *Football and Regional Identity in Europe* (Münster: Lit Verlag, 1997).

Gekoski, R., *Staying Up: A Fan Behind the Scenes in the Premiership* (London: Warner, 1999).

Gerrard, B., 'Why does Manchester United Keep Wining On and Off the Field?: A Case Study of Sustainable Advantage in Professional Team Sports' in D. L. Andrews (ed.), *Manchester United: A Thematic Study* (London: Routledge, 2004).

Gibbons, P., *Association Football in Victorian England: A History of the Game from 1863–1900* (Leicestershire: Upfront, 2002).

Gibson, A. and Pickford, W., *Association Football and the Men Who Made It*, Vol. 2 (London: Caxton, 1906).

Giulianotti, R., 'Scotland's Tartan Army in Italy: The Case for the Carnivalesque', *Sociological Review*, 39, 3 (1991).

Giulianotti, R., 'Social Identity and Public Order: Political and Academic Discourses on Football Violence' in R. Giulianotti, N. Bonney and M. Hepworth (eds), *Football, Violence and Social Identity* (London: Routledge, 1994).

Giulianotti, R., 'Enlightening the North: Aberdeen Fanzines and Local

Football Identity' in G. Armstrong and R. Giulianotti (eds), *Entering the Field: New Perspectives on World Football* (Oxford: Berg, 1997).

Giulianotti, R., *Football: A Sociology of the Global Game* (Cambridge: Polity, 1999).

Giulianotti, R., 'Hooligans and Carnival Fans: Scottish Football Supporter Cultures' in G. Armstrong and R. Giulianotti (eds), *Football Cultures and Identities* (Basingstoke: Macmillan, 1999).

Giulianotti, R., 'A Different Kind of Carnival' in M. Perryman (ed.), *Hooligan Wars: Causes and Effects of Football Violence* (Edinburgh: Mainstream, 2001).

Giulianotti, R., 'Supporters, Followers, Fans and *Flâneurs*: A Taxonomy of Spectator Identities in Football', *Journal of Sport and Social Issues*, 26, 1 (February 2002).

Giulianotti, R., *Sport: A Critical Sociology* (Cambridge: Polity, 2005).

Giulianotti, R., Bonney, N. and Hepworth, M. (eds), *Football, Violence and Social Identity* (London: Routledge, 1994).

Giulianotti, R. and Gerrard, M., 'Cruel Britannia?: Glasgow Rangers, Scotland and "Hot" Football Rivalries' in G. Armstrong and R. Giulianotti (eds), *Fear and Loathing in World Football* (Oxford: Berg, 2001).

Giulianotti, R. and Gerrard, M., 'Evil Genie or Pure Genius?: The (Im)moral Football and Public Career of Paul "Gazza" Gascoigne' in D. L. Andrews and S. J. Jackson (eds), *Sport Stars: The Cultural Politics of Sporting Celebrity* (London: Routledge, 2001).

Giulianotti, R. and Robertson, R., 'The Globalization of Football: A Study in the Glocalization of "Serious Life" ', *British Journal of Sociology*, 55, 4 (2004).

Giulianotti, R. and Williams, J. (eds), *Game Without Frontiers: Football, Identity and Modernity* (Aldershot: Arena, 1994).

Glanville, B. (ed.), *The Footballer's Companion* (London: Eyre & Spottiswoode, 1962).

Glanville, B., 'Britain Against the Rest: The Decline of British Sporting Prestige' in M. Sissons and P. French (eds), *Age of Austerity, 1945–51* (Harmondsworth: Penguin, 1964).

Glanville, B., *Goalkeepers are Different* (Harmondsworth: Puffin edition, 1974).

Glanville, B. (ed.), *The Joy of Football* (London: Hodder & Stoughton, 1986).

Glanville, B., *Football Memories* (London: Virgin, 1999).

Goksøyr, M. and Hognestad, H., 'No Longer Worlds Apart?: British

Influences and Norwegian Football' in G. Armstrong and R. Giulianotti (eds), *Football Cultures and Identities* (Basingstoke: Macmillan, 1999).

Goldberg, A. and Wagg, S., 'It's Not a Knockout: English Football and Globalisation' in J. Williams and S. Wagg (eds), *British Football and Social Change: Getting into Europe* (Leicester: Leicester University Press, 1991).

Goldthorpe, J. H., Lockwood, D., Bechhofer, F. and Platt, J., *The Affluent Worker in the Class Structure* (Cambridge: Cambridge University Press, 1969).

Goulstone, J., 'The Working Class Origins of Modern Football', *International Journal of the History of Sport*, 17, 1 (March 2000).

Goulstone, J., *Football's Secret History* (Upminster: 3–2 Books, 2001).

Grant, A. and Stringer, K., 'Introduction: The Enigma of British History' in A. Grant and K. Stringer (eds), *Uniting the Kingdom?: The Making of British History* (London: Routledge, 1995).

Grant, A. and Stringer, K. (eds), *Uniting the Kingdom?: The Making of British History* (London: Routledge, 1995).

Gratton, C., 'The Peculiar Economics of English Professional Football', *Soccer and Society*, 1, 1 (Spring 2000).

Gratton, C. and Lisewski, B., 'The Economics of Sport in Britain: A Case of Market Failure?', *British Review of Economic Issues*, 3, 8 (Spring 1981).

Gratton, C. and Taylor, P., *Leisure in Britain* (Letchworth: Leisure Publications, 1987).

Gray, R., *The Labour Aristocracy in Victorian Edinburgh* (Oxford: Clarendon, 1976).

Grayson, E., *Corinthians and Cricketers* (London: Sportsmans Book Club, 1957).

Greaves, J. with Giller, N., *Don't Shoot the Manager: The Revealing Story of England's Soccer Bosses* (London: Boxtree, 1993).

Green, G., *The History of the Football Association* (London: Naldrett, 1953).

Green, G., *Soccer: The World Game* (London: Sportsmans Book Club, 1954).

Green, G., 'The Football Association' in A. H. Fabian and G. Green (eds), *Association Football*, Vol. 1 (London: Caxton, 1960).

Green, M. and Jenkins, C. (eds), *Sporting Fictions* (Birmingham: Centre for Contemporary Cultural Studies, 1981).

Greenfield, S. and Osborn, G., *Regulating Football: Commodification, Consumption and the Law* (London: Pluto, 2001).

Greer, G., 'Nothing New about Ugly Sex', *The Guardian*, 16 December 2003.

Griffiths, T., *The Lancashire Working Classes, c.1880–1930* (Oxford: Clarendon, 2001).

Gunn, S., *History and Cultural Theory* (Harlow: Longman, 2006).

Hague, E. and Mercer, J., 'Geographical Memory and Urban Identity in Scotland: Raith Rovers FC and Kirkcaldy', *Geography*, 83, 2 (1998).

Hamil, S., Michie, J., Oughton, C. and Warby, S. (eds), *Football in the Digital Age: Whose Game Is It Anyway?* (Edinburgh: Mainstream, 2000).

Hamil, S., Michie, J., Oughton, C. and Warby, S., 'Recent Developments in Football Ownership', *Soccer and Society*, 1, 3 (Autumn 2000).

Hamilton, A., *An Entirely Different Game: The British Influence on Brazilian Football* (Edinburgh: Mainstream, 1998).

Hamilton, I. (ed.), *The Faber Book of Soccer* (London: Faber & Faber, 1992).

Hamish Fraser, W., 'Developments in Leisure' in W. Hamish Fraser and R. J. Morris (eds), *People and Society in Scotland*, Vol. 2, *1830–1914* (Edinburgh: John Donald, 1990).

Hamish Fraser, W. and Morris, R. J. (eds), *People and Society in Scotland*, Vol. 2, *1830–1914* (Edinburgh: John Donald, 1990).

Hand, D., 'Love Thy Neighbour or a Red Rag to a Blue?: Reflections on the City-United Dynamic in and around Manchester' in D. L. Andrews (ed.), *Manchester United: A Thematic Study* (London: Routledge, 2004).

Hardaker, A., *Hardaker of the League* (London: Pelham, 1977).

Harding, J., *Football Wizard: The Story of Billy Meredith* (Derby: Breedon, 1985).

Harding, J., *Alex James: Life of a Football Legend* (London: Robson, 1988).

Harding, J., *For the Good of the Game: The Official History of the Professional Footballers' Association* (London: Robson, 1991).

Harding, J., 'Billy Meredith' in P. Stead and H. Richards (eds), *For Club and Country: Welsh Football Greats* (Cardiff: University of Wales Press, 2000).

Harding, J. with Taylor, G., *Living to Play: From Soccer Slaves to Soccerati – A Social History of the Professionals* (London: Robson, 2003).

Hargreaves, J. (ed.), *Sport, Culture and Ideology* (London: Routledge & Kegan Paul, 1982).

Hargreaves, J., *Sport, Power and Culture: A Social and Historical Analysis of Popular Sports in Britain* (Cambridge: Polity, 1986).

Hargreaves, J., 'The State and Sport: Programmed and Non-Programmed Intervention in Britain' in L. Allison (ed.), *The Politics of Sport* (Manchester: Manchester University Press, 1986).

Hargreaves, J., *Sporting Females: Critical Issues in the History and Sociology of Women's Sports* (London: Routledge, 1994).

Harris, J., 'The Early History and Development of Association Football in Breconshire' in C. Harte (ed.), *One Day in Leicester* (Association of Sport Historians, 1996).

Harris, J., "Still a Man's Game?: Women Footballers, Personal Experience and Tabloid Myth' in S. Wagg (ed.), *British Football and Social Exclusion* (London: Routledge, 2004).

Harris, N., *England, Their England: The Definitive Story of Foreign Footballers in the English Game since 1888* (Hove: Pitch, 2003).

Harrison, P., *Southern League Football: The First Fifty Years* (Gravesend: P. Harrison, 1989).

Harrisson, T. and Madge, C. (eds), *War Begins at Home* (London: Chatto & Windus, 1940).

Harte, C. (ed.), *One Day in Leicester* (Association of Sport Historians, 1996).

Hartmann-Tews, I. and Pfister, G. (eds), *Sport and Women: Social Issues in International Perspective* (London: Routledge, 2003).

Harvey, A., 'Football's Missing Link: The Real Story of the Evolution of Modern Football' in J. A. Mangan (ed.), *Sport in Europe: Politics, Class, Gender* (London: Frank Cass, 1999).

Harvey, A., '"An Epoch in the Annals of National Sport": Football in Sheffield and the Creation of Modern Soccer and Rugby', *International Journal of the History of Sport*, 18, 4 (December 2001).

Harvey, A., 'The Curate's Egg Put Back Together: Comments on Eric Dunning's Response to "An Epoch in the Annals of National Sport"', *International Journal of the History of Sport*, 19, 4 (December 2002).

Harvey, A., 'Curate's Egg Pursued by Red Herrings: A Reply to Eric Dunning and Graham Curry', *International Journal of the History of Sport*, 21, 1 (January 2004).

Harvey, A., *The Beginnings of a Commercial Sporting Culture in Britain, 1793–1850* (Aldershot: Ashgate, 2004).

Harvey, A., *Football: The First Hundred Years* (London: Routledge, 2005).

Harvie, C., *Scotland and Nationalism: Scottish Society and Politics, 1707–1994* (London: Routledge, 1994 [1st edition, 1977]).

Harvie, C., 'Sport and the Scottish State' in G. Jarvie and G. Walker (eds), *Scottish Sport and the Making of the Nation: Ninety-Minute Patriots?* (Leicester: Leicester University Press, 1994).

Harvie, C., *No Gods and Precious Few Heroes: Twentieth-Century Scotland* (Edinburgh: Edinburgh University Press, 2000 [1st edition, 1981]).

Hassan, D., 'A People Apart: Soccer Identity and Irish Nationalists in Northern Ireland', *Soccer and Society*, 3, 3 (Autumn 2002).

Hassan, D., 'An Opportunity for a New Beginning: Soccer, Irish Nationalists and the Construction of a New Multi-Sports Stadium for Northern Ireland', *Soccer and Society*, 7, 2–3 (April–July 2006).

Hay, R., 'Soccer and Social Control in Scotland, 1873–1978' in R. Cashman and M. McKernan (eds), *Sport: Money, Morality and the Media* (Brisbane: New South Wales University Press, 1981).

Hayes, N. and Hill, J. (eds), *'Millions Like Us'?: British Culture in the Second World War* (Liverpool: Liverpool University Press, 1999).

Haynes, R., 'Vanguard or Vagabond?: A History of *When Saturday Comes*' in S. Redhead (ed.), *The Passion and the Fashion: Football Fandom in the New Europe* (Aldershot: Avebury, 1993).

Haynes, R., *The Football Imagination: The Rise of Football Fanzine Culture* (Aldershot: Arena, 1995).

Haynes, R., 'A Pageant of Sound and Vision: Football's Relationship with Television, 1936–60', *International Journal of the History of Sport*, 15, 1 (April 1998).

Haynes, R., '"There's Many a Slip 'Twixt the Eye and the Lip": An Exploratory History of Football Broadcasts and Running Commentaries on BBC Radio, 1927–1939', *International Review for the Sociology of Sport*, 34, 2 (1999).

Heinonen, H., 'Finnish Football Supporters: Couch Potatoes or Partisan Fans?', *Moving Bodies*, 1, 1 (2003).

Hélal, H. and Mignon, P. (eds), *Football: Jeu et société* (Paris: INSEP, 1999).

Highfield Rangers Oral History Group and the Sir Norman Chester Centre for Football Research, *Highfield Rangers: An Oral History* (Leicester: Leicester City Council, 1993).

Hill, D., *Out of His Skin: The John Barnes Phenomenon* (London: Faber & Faber, 1989).

Hill, D., 'From Barnes to Camara: Football, Identity and Racism in Liverpool' in J. Williams, S. Hopkins and C. Long (eds), *Passing Rhythms: Liverpool FC and the Transformation of Football* (Oxford: Berg, 2001).

Hill, J., *Striking for Soccer* (London: Peter Davies, 1961).

Hill, J., 'Reading the Stars: Towards a Post-Modernist Approach to Sports History', *The Sports Historian*, 14 (May 1994).

Hill, J., 'British Sports History: A Post-Modern Future?', *Journal of Sport History*, 23, 1 (Spring 1996).

Hill, J., 'Rite of Spring: Cup Finals and Community in the North of England' in J. Hill and J. Williams (eds), *Sport and Identity in the North of England* (Keele: Keele University Press, 1996).

Hill, J., 'Cocks, Cats, Caps and Cups: A Semiotic Approach to Sport and National Identity', *Culture, Sport, Society*, 2, 2 (1999).

Hill, J., *Sport, Leisure and Culture in Twentieth-Century Britain* (Basingstoke: Palgrave, 2002).

Hill, J., 'Bascombe, Machin and Logan: Explorations in Sport and Literature', paper presented to the British Society of Sports History Annual Conference, Leicester, April 2002.

Hill, J., 'Narratives of the Nation: The Newspaper Press and England v Hungary, 1953', *Sport in History*, 23, 2 (Winter 2003/4).

Hill, J., '"Brylcreem Boy": Inter-Textual Signification in the Life of Denis Compton' in J. Bale, M. K. Christiansen, and G. Pfister (eds), *Writing Lives in Sport: Biographies, Life-Histories and Methods* (Langelandsgade: Aarhus University Press, 2004).

Hill, J., '"The Day was an Ugly One": Wembley, 28th April 1923' in P. Darby, M. Johnes and G. Mellor (eds), *Soccer and Disaster: International Perspectives* (London: Routledge, 2005).

Hill, J., 'Anecdotal Evidence: Sport, the Newspaper Press and History' in M. G. Phillips (ed.), *Deconstructing Sport History: A Postmodern Analysis* (New York: SUNY Press, 2006).

Hill, J. and Williams, J. (eds), *Sport and Identity in the North of England* (Keele: Keele University Press, 1996).

Hill, K., '"Thoroughly Imbued with the Spirit of Ancient Greece": Symbolism and Space in Victorian Civic Culture' in A. Kidd and D. Nicholls (eds), *Gender, Civic Culture and Consumerism: Middle Class Identity in Britain, 1800–1940* (Manchester: Manchester University Press, 1999).

Hilton, B., 'Out With the Old ... In With the New?', *When Saturday Comes*, November 1994.

Hobbs, D. and Robins, D., 'The Boy Done Good: Football Violence, Changes and Continuities', *Sociological Review*, 39, 3 (1991).

Hoberman, J., *Darwin's Athletes: How Sport has Damaged Black America and Preserved the Myth of Race* (New York: Mariner, 1997).

Hobsbawm, E., 'Mass-Producing Traditions: Europe, 1870–1914' in E. Hobsbawm and T. Ranger (eds), *The Invention of Tradition* (Cambridge: Cambridge University Press, 1983).

Hobsbawm, E., *Worlds of Labour: Further Studies in the History of Labour* (London: Weidenfeld & Nicolson, 1984).

Hobsbawm, E., *Nations and Nationalism Since 1870: Programme, Myth, Reality* (Cambridge: Cambridge University Press, 1990).

Hobsbawm, E. and Ranger, T. (eds), *The Invention of Tradition* (Cambridge: Cambridge University Press, 1983).

Hoffman, S., review of *Football Hooligans*, *Contemporary Sociology*, 28, 2 (1999).

Holland, B., '"Kicking Racism Out of Football": An Assessment of Racial Harassment in and around Football Grounds', *New Community*, 21, 4 (October 1995).

Holland, B., 'Surviving Leisure Time Racism: The Burden of Racial Harassment on Britain's Black Footballers', *Leisure Studies*, 16 (1997).

Holmes, C., *John Bull's Island: Immigration and British Society, 1871–1971* (Basingstoke: Macmillan, 1988).

Holt, R., 'Football and the Urban Way of Life in Nineteenth-Century Britain' in J. A. Mangan (ed.), *Pleasure, Profit and Proselytism: British Culture and Sport at Home and Abroad, 1700–1914* (London: Frank Cass, 1988).

Holt, R., *Sport and the British: A Modern History* (Oxford: Clarendon, 1989).

Holt, R. (ed.), *Sport and the Working Class in Modern Britain* (Manchester: Manchester University Press, 1990).

Holt, R., 'King over the Border: Denis Law and Scottish Football' in G. Jarvie and G. Walker (eds), *Scottish Sport and the Making of the Nation: Ninety-Minute Patriots?* (Leicester: Leicester University Press, 1994).

Holt, R., 'Cricket and Englishness: The Batsman as Hero' in R. Holt, J. A. Mangan and P. Lanfranchi (eds), *European Heroes: Myth, Identity, Sport* (London: Frank Cass, 1996).

Holt, R., 'Heroes of the North: Sport and the Shaping of Regional Identity' in J. Hill and J. Williams (eds), *Sport and Identity in the North of England* (Keele: Keele University Press, 1996).

Holt, R., 'Champions, Heroes and Celebrities: Sporting Greatness and the British Public' in *The Book of British Sporting Heroes* (London: National Portrait Gallery, 1998).

Holt, R., 'The Foreign Office and the Football Association: British Sport and Appeasement, 1935–1938' in P. Arnaud and J. Riordan (eds), *Sport and International Politics: The Impact of Fascism and Communism on Sport* (London: E & FN Spon, 1998).

Holt, R., 'The Batsman as Gentleman: Inter-War Cricket and the English Hero' in G. Cubitt and A. Warren (eds), *Heroic Reputations and Exemplary Lives* (Manchester: Manchester University Press, 2000).

Holt, R., 'Sport and History: The State of the Subject in Britain', *Twentieth Century British History*, 7, 2 (1966).

Holt, R. and Mangan, J. A., 'Prologue: Heroes of a European Past' in R. Holt, J. A. Mangan and P. Lanfranchi (eds), *European Heroes: Myth, Identity, Sport* (London: Frank Cass, 1996).

Holt, R., Mangan, J. A. and Lanfranchi, P. (eds), *European Heroes: Myth, Identity, Sport* (London: Frank Cass, 1996).

Holt, R. and Mason, T., *Sport in Britain, 1945–2000* (Oxford: Blackwell, 2000).

Hong, F. and Mangan, J. A. (ed.), *Soccer, Women and Sexual Liberation: Kicking Off a New Era* (London: Frank Cass, 2004).

Hopcraft, A., *The Football Man: People and Passions in Soccer* (London: Simon & Schuster, 1988 [1st edition, 1968]).

Hopkins, S. and Williams, J., 'Gérard Houllier and the New Liverpool "Imaginary"' in J. Williams, S. Hopkins and C. Long (eds), *Passing Rhythms: Liverpool FC and the Transformation of Football* (Oxford: Berg, 2001).

Hornby, N., *Fever Pitch: A Fan's Life* (London: Victor Gollancz, 1992).

Hornby, N. (ed.), *My Favourite Year: A Collection of New Football Writing* (London: H. F. & G. Witherby, 1993).

Horne, J., 'Kicking Racism Out of Soccer in England and Scotland', *Journal of Sport and Social Issues*, 20, 1 (February 1996).

Horrall, A., *Popular Culture in London, c.1890–1918: The Transformation of Entertainment* (Manchester: Manchester University Press, 2001).

Houlihan, B., *The Government and Politics of Sport* (London: Routledge, 1991).

Houlihan, B., 'Sport, National Identity and Public Policy', *Nations and Nationalism*, 3, 1 (1997).

Houlihan, B. (ed.), *Sport and Society: A Student Introduction* (London: Sage, 2003).

Hudson, P., *The Industrial Revolution* (London: Edward Arnold, 1992).

Huggins, M., 'The Spread of Association Football in North-East England, 1876–90: The Pattern of Diffusion', *International Journal of the History of Sport*, 6, 3 (December 1989).

Hughes, R., 'John Charles' in P. Stead and H. Richards (eds), *For Club and Country: Welsh Football Greats* (Cardiff: University of Wales Press, 2000).

Hughson, J., 'The Bad Blue Boys and the "Magical Recovery" of John Clarke' in G. Armstrong and R. Giulianotti (eds), *Entering the Field: New Perspectives on World Football* (Oxford: Berg, 1997).

Humphries, S., *Hooligans or Rebels?: An Oral History of Working-Class Childhood and Youth, 1889–1939* (Oxford: Basil Blackwell, 1981).

Hunt, B., *Northern Goalfields Revisited: The Millennium History of the Northern Football League, 1889–2000* (Northern Football League, 2000).

Hunter, A., *Triumphs of the Football Field* (Smethwick: Sports Projects, 1997 [first published in *Birmingham Weekly Mercury*, 1890]).

Hurst, G., *The World Game* (London: Stanley Paul, 1967).

Hutchins, P., 'Football and Regional Pride in the North-East, 1918–60', unpublished Ph.D. thesis, University of Sussex, 1991.

Hutchinson, J., 'Some Aspects of Football Crowds before 1914', paper presented to the Society for the Study of Labour History, University of Sussex, 1975.

Hutchinson, J., *The Football Industry* (Edinburgh: Richard Drew, 1982).

Hutchinson, R., *'66!: The Inside Story of England's World Cup Triumph* (Edinburgh: Mainstream, 2002 [1st edition, 1995]).

Ingham, R. (ed.), *Football Hooliganism: The Wider Context* (London: Inter-Action, 1978).

Ingham, R., 'The Fate of Good Intention: The "Football and the Community" Schemes' in A. Tomlinson (ed.), *Explorations in Football Culture* (Eastbourne: Leisure Studies Association, 1983).

Inglis, F., *The Name of the Game: Sport and Society* (London: Heinemann, 1977).

Inglis, S., *Soccer in the Dock* (London: Willow, 1985).

Inglis, S., *League Football and the Men Who Made It: The Official*

Centenary History of the Football League, 1888–1988 (London: Collins Willow, 1988).

Inglis, S., *The Football Grounds of Britain* (London: Collins Willow, 1987 [1st edition, 1983]).

Inglis, S., *Sightlines: A Stadium Odyssey* (London: Yellow Jersey Press, 2000).

Ismond, P., *Black and Asian Athletes in British Sport and Society: A Sporting Chance?* (Basingstoke: Palgrave, 2003).

Jaquiss, K., 'Football, Fans and Fat Cats: Whose Football Club is it Anyway?' in S. Hamil, J. Michie, C. Oughton and S. Warby (eds), *Football in the Digital Age: Whose Game Is It Anyway?* (Edinburgh: Mainstream, 2000).

Jarvie, G. (ed.), *Sport, Racism and Ethnicity* (London: Falmer, 1991).

Jarvie, G. and Burnett, J. (eds), *Sport, Scotland and the Scots* (East Linton: Tuckwell, 2000).

Jarvie, G. and Maguire, J., *Sport and Leisure in Social Thought* (London: Routledge, 1994).

Jarvie, G. and Reid, I., 'Sport, Nationalism and Culture in Scotland', *The Sports Historian*, 19, 1 (May 1999).

Jarvie, G. and Walker, G., 'Ninety Minute Patriots?: Scottish Sport in the Making of the Nation' in G. Jarvie and G. Walker (eds), *Scottish Sport and the Making of the Nation: Ninety-Minute Patriots?* (Leicester: Leicester University Press, 1994).

Jarvie, G. and Walker, G. (eds), *Scottish Sport and the Making of the Nation: Ninety-Minute Patriots?* (Leicester: Leicester University Press, 1994).

Jary, D, Horne, J. and Bucke, T., 'Football "Fanzines" and Football Culture: A Case of Successful "Cultural Contestation" ', *Sociological Review*, 39, 3 (1991).

Jenkins, R., 'Salvation for the Fittest?: A West African Sportsman in Britain in the Age of New Imperialism', *International Journal of the History of Sport*, 7, 1, (May 1990).

Jenkins, R., *A Would-Be Saint* (Edinburgh: Black & White, 1994 [1st edition, 1978]).

Jenkins, R., *Social Identity* (London; Routledge, 2004 [1st edition, 1996]).

Jennett, N. and Sloane, P. J., *Football in Decline: An Economic Analysis of the Report of the Chester Committee of Enquiry* (Paisley: Paisley College Social Science Working Papers, 1983).

Johal, S., 'Playing Their Own Game: A South Asian Football Experience' in B. Carrington and I. McDonald (eds), 'Race', Sport and British Society (London: Routledge, 2001).

Johnes, M., 'Fred Keenor: A Welsh Soccer Hero', The Sports Historian, 18, 1 (May 1998).

Johnes, M., 'Hooligans and Barrackers: Crowd Disorder and Soccer in South Wales, c.1906–36', Soccer and Society, 1, 2 (Summer 2000).

Johnes, M., 'Eighty Minute Patriots?: National Identity and Sport in Modern Wales', International Journal of the History of Sport, 17, 4 (December 2000).

Johnes, M., Soccer and Society: South Wales, 1900–1939 (Cardiff: University of Wales Press, 2002).

Johnes, M., 'Football Managers in South Wales Between the Wars', Soccer History, 4 (Spring 2003).

Johnes, M., '"Every Day When I Wake Up I Thank the Lord I'm Welsh": Sport and National Identity in Post-War Wales' in A. Smith and D. Porter (eds), Sport and National Identity in the Post-War World (London: Routledge, 2004).

Johnes, M., A History of Sport in Wales (Cardiff: University of Wales Press, 2005).

Johnes, M., '"Heads in the Sand": Football, Politics and Crowd Disasters in Twentieth-Century Britain' in P. Darby, M. Johnes and G. Mellor (eds), Soccer and Disaster: International Perspectives (London: Routledge, 2005).

Johnes, M. and Garland, I., '"The New Craze": Football and Society in North-East Wales, c.1870–90', Welsh History Review, 22, 2 (December 2004).

Johnes, M. and Mason, R., 'Soccer, Public History and the National Football Museum', Sport in History, 23, 1 (Summer 2003).

Johnes, M. and Mellor, G., 'The 1953 FA Cup Final: Modernity and Tradition in British Culture', Contemporary British History, 20, 2 (June 2006).

Johnson, P. (ed.), Twentieth-Century Britain: Economic, Social and Cultural Change (London: Longman, 1994).

Jones, I., 'Football Fandom: Football Fan Identity and Identification at Luton Town Football Club', unpublished Ph.D. thesis, University of Luton, 1998.

Jones, I., 'A Model of Serious Leisure Identification: The Case of Football Fandom', Leisure Studies, 19 (2000).

Jones, S. G., 'The Economic Aspects of Association Football in England, 1918–39', British Journal of Sports History, 1, 3 (December 1984).

Jones, S. G., *Workers at Play: A Social and Economic History of Leisure, 1918–1939* (London: Routledge & Kegan Paul, 1986).

Jones, S. G., 'State Intervention in Sport and Leisure in Britain between the Wars', *Journal of Contemporary History*, 22 (1987).

Jones, S. G., 'Cotton Employers and Industrial Welfare Between the Wars' in J. A. Jowitt and A. J. McIvor (eds), *Employers and Labour in the English Textile Industries, 1850–1939* (London: Routledge, 1988).

Jones, S. G., *Sport, Politics and the Working Class: Organised Labour and Sport in Interwar Britain* (Manchester: Manchester University Press, 1988).

Jones, S. G., 'Working-Class Sport in Manchester Between the Wars' in R. Holt (ed.), *Sport and the Working Class in Modern Britain* (Manchester: Manchester University Press, 1990).

Jordanova, L., *History in Practice* (London: Arnold, 2000).

Jowitt, J. A. and McIvor, A. J. (eds), *Employers and Labour in the English Textile Industries, 1850–1939* (London: Routledge, 1988).

Joy, B., *Soccer Tactics* (London: Sportsmans Book Club, 1959).

Joyce, P., *Visions of the People: Industrial England and the Question of Class, 1848–1914* (Cambridge: Cambridge University Press, 1991).

Kearney, H., *The British Isles: A History of Four Nations* (Cambridge: Cambridge University Press, 1989).

Kelly, G., *Sweet FA* (London: Collins Willow, 1999).

Kelly, G., *Terrace Heroes: The Life and Times of the 1930s Professional Footballer* (London: Routledge, 2005).

Kelly. S. (ed.), *A Game of Two Halves* (London: Mandarin, 1992).

Kennedy, A. E., 'The History of Woolwich Arsenal' in C. Leatherdale (ed.), *The Book of Football* (Westcliff-on-Sea: Desert Island, 1997 [1st edition, 1906]).

Keogh, D., *Twentieth-Century Ireland: Nation and State* (Dublin: Gill & Macmillan, 1994).

Kerrigan, C., 'London Schoolboys and Professional Football', *International Journal of the History of Sport*, 11, 2 (August 1994).

Kerrigan, C., '"Thoroughly Good Football": Teachers and the Origins of Elementary School Football', *History of Education*, 29, 1 (2000).

Kerrigan, C., *A History of the English Schools' Football Association, 1904–2004* (Trowbridge: English Schools' Football Association, 2004).

Kidd, A. and Nicholls, D. (eds), *Gender, Civic Culture and Consumerism: Middle Class Identity in Britain, 1800–1940* (Manchester: Manchester University Press, 1999).

King, A., 'The Lads: Masculinity and the New Consumption of Football', *Sociology*, 31, 2 (May 1997).

King, A., *The End of the Terraces: The Transformation of English Football in the 1990s* (Leicester: Leicester University Press, 1998).

King, A., 'Football Fandom and Post-National Identity in the New Europe', *British Journal of Sociology*, 51, 3 (September 2000).

King, A., *The European Ritual: Football in the New Europe* (Aldershot: Ashgate, 2003).

Kirk, N., '"Traditional" Working-Class Culture and "the Rise of Labour": Some Preliminary Questions and Observations', *Social History*, 16, 2 (May 1991).

Kirk, N., *Change, Continuity and Class: Labour in British Society, 1850–1920* (Manchester: Manchester University Press, 1998).

Kirkham, P. and Thoms, D. (eds), *War Culture: Social Change and Changing Experience in World War Two* (London: Lawrence & Wishart, 1995).

Knox, W. W., *Industrial Nation: Work, Culture and Society in Scotland, 1800–Present* (Edinburgh: Edinburgh University Press, 1999).

Korr, C., 'West Ham United Football Club and the Beginnings of Professional Football in East London, 1895–1914', *Journal of Contemporary History*, 13 (1978).

Korr, C., 'Two Cheers for the Professional: Some Anglo-American Comparisons', *British Journal of Sports History*, 2, 3 (December 1985).

Korr, C., *West Ham United: The Making of a Football Club* (London: Duckworth, 1986).

Korr, C., 'A Different Kind of Success: West Ham United and the Creation of Tradition and Community' in R. Holt (ed.), *Sport and the Working Class in Modern Britain* (Manchester: Manchester University Press, 1990).

Kowalski, R., '"Cry For Us, Argentina": Sport and National Identity in Late Twentieth-Century Scotland' in A. Smith and D. Porter (eds), *Sport and National Identity in the Post-War World* (London: Routledge, 2004).

Kowalski, R. and Porter, D., 'Political Football: Moscow Dynamo in Britain, 1945', *International Journal of the History of Sport*, 14, 2 (August 1997).

Kowalski, R. and Porter, D., 'England's World Turned Upside Down?: Magical Magyars and British Football', *Sport in History*, 23, 2 (Winter 2003/4).

Kumar, K., *The Making of English National Identity* (Cambridge: Cambridge University Press, 2003).

Kuper, S., *Football Against the Enemy* (London: Orion, 1994).

Kuper, S. (ed.), *Perfect Pitch 1: Home Ground* (London: Headline, 1997).

Kuper, S., *Ajax, The Dutch, The War: Football in Europe During the Second World War* (London: Orion, 2003).

Kuper, S. and Mora Y Araujo, M. (eds), *Perfect Pitch 3: Men and Women* (London: Headline, 1998).

Lacey, D., 'FA Promises Bolt from the Blue', *The Guardian*, 20 June 1991.

Lacey, M., 'The End of Something Small and the Start of Something Big' in D. Bull (ed.), *We'll Support You Evermore: Keeping Faith in Football* (London: Duckworth, 1992).

Lamont, W. (ed.), *Historical Controversies and Historians* (London: UCL Press, 1998).

Lanfranchi, P., 'Unaccomplished Heroes: Three Sporting Biographies between Algeria and France', unpublished paper, n.d.

Lanfranchi, P., 'Exporting Football: Notes on the Development of Football in Europe' in R. Giulianotti and J. Williams (eds), *Game Without Frontiers: Football, Identity and Modernity* (Aldershot: Arena, 1994).

Lanfranchi, P., 'The Migration of Footballers: The Case of France, 1932–1982' in J. Bale and J. Maguire (eds), *The Global Sports Arena: Athletic Talent Migration in an Interdependent World* (London: Frank Cass, 1994).

Lanfranchi, P., '"Mister" Garbutt: The First European Manager', *The Sports Historian*, 22, 1 (May 2002).

Lanfranchi, P., Eisenberg, C., Mason, T. and Wahl, A., *100 Years of Football: The FIFA Centennial Book* (London: Weidenfeld & Nicolson, 2004).

Lanfranchi, P. and Taylor, M., 'Professional Football in World War Two Britain' in P. Kirkham and D. Thoms (eds), *War Culture: Social Change and Changing Experience in World War Two* (London: Lawrence & Wishart, 1995).

Lanfranchi, P. and Taylor, M., *Moving With the Ball: The Migration of Professional Footballers* (Oxford: Berg, 2001).

Lanfranchi P., with Wagg, S., 'Cathedrals in Concrete: Football in Southern European Society' in S. Wagg (ed.), *Giving the Game Away: Football, Politics and Culture on Five Continents* (Leicester: Leicester University Press, 1995).

Langhamer, C., *Women's Leisure in England, 1920–60* (Manchester: Manchester University Press, 2000).

Larson, Ø., 'Charles Reep: A Major Influence on British and Norwegian Football', *Soccer and Society*, 2, 3 (Autumn 2001).

Law, D. with Bale, B., *The Lawman: An Autobiography* (London: André Deutsch, 1999).

Lawton, T., *Football is my Business* (London: Sporting Handbooks, 1946).

Laybourn, K. (ed.), *Social Conditions, Status and Community, 1860–c.1920* (Stroud: Sutton, 1997).

Leatherdale, C. (ed.), *The Book of Football* (Westcliff-on-Sea: Desert Island, 1997 [1st edition, 1906]).

Ledbrooke, A. and Turner, E., *Soccer From the Press Box* (London: Sportsmans Book Club, 1955).

Lee, S., 'Grey Shirts to Grey Suits: The Political Economy of English Football in the 1990s' in A. Brown (ed.), *Fanatics!: Power, Identity and Fandom in Football* (London: Routledge, 1998).

Lewis, R. W., 'The Development of Professional Football in Lancashire, 1870–1914', unpublished Ph.D. thesis, University of Lancaster, 1993.

Lewis, R. W., 'Football Hooliganism in England before 1914: A Critique of the Dunning Thesis', *International Journal of the History of Sport*, 13, 3 (1996).

Lewis, R. W., 'The Genesis of Professional Football: Bolton-Blackburn-Darwen, the Centre of Innovation, 1878–85', *International Journal of the History of Sport*, 14, 1 (April 1997).

Lewis, R. W., '"Touched Pitch and Been Shockingly Defiled": Football, Class, Social Darwinism and Decadence in England, 1880–1914' in J. A. Mangan (ed.), *Sport in Europe: Politics, Class, Gender* (London: Frank Cass, 1999).

Lifestyle Pocket Book 1996 (Henley-on-Thames: NTC Publications, 1996).

Lile, B. and Farmer, D., 'The Early Development of Association Football in South Wales, 1890–1906', *Transactions of the Honourable Society of Cymmrodorion* (1984).

Lines, G., 'The Sports Star in the Media: The Gendered Construction and Youthful Consumption of Sports Personalities' in J. Sugden and A. Tomlinson (eds), *Power Games: A Critical Sociology of Sport* (London: Routledge, 2004).

Lomax, B., 'Democracy and Fandom: Developing a Supporters' Trust at Northampton Town FC', *Soccer and Society*, 1, 1 (Spring 2000).

Lopez, S., *Women on the Ball: A Guide to Women's Football* (London: Scarlet, 1997).

Lowenthal, D., *The Heritage Crusade and the Spoils of History* (Cambridge: Cambridge University Press, 1998).

Lowerson, J., *Sport and the English Middle Classes, 1870–1914* (Manchester: Manchester University Press, 1993).

Lowerson, J., 'Opiate of the People or Stimulant for the Historian? – Some Issues in Sports History' in W. Lamont (ed.), *Historical Controversies and Historians* (London: UCL Press, 1998).

Ludlow, P., 'Us or Them?: The Meaning of Europe in British Political Discourse' in M. af Malmborg and B. Stråth (eds), *The Meaning of Europe* (Oxford: Berg, 2002).

Lynch, M., *Scotland: A New History* (London: Pimlico, 1992).

McArdle, D., *From Boot Money to Bosman: Football, Society and the Law* (London: Cavendish, 2000).

McArdle, D., "They're Playing R. Song: Football and the European Union after *Bosman*', *Football Studies*, 3, 2 (2000).

McCarthy, D. and Jones, R. L., 'Speed, Aggression, Strength and Tactical Naïveté: The Portrayal of the Black Soccer Player on Television', *Journal of Sport and Social Issues*, 21, 4 (November 1997).

McCrone, D., 'Unmasking Britannia: The Rise and Fall of British National Identity', *Nations and Nationalism*, 3, 4 (1997).

McCrone, D., *The Sociology of Nationalism* (London: Routledge, 1998).

McGill, C., *Football Inc.: How Soccer Fans Are Losing the Game* (London: Vision, 2001).

McGlone, D. and McLure, B., *The Juniors – 100 Years: A Centenary History of Scottish Junior Football* (Edinburgh: Mainstream, 1987).

McGovern, P., 'The Irish Brawn Drain: English League Clubs and Irish Footballers, 1946–95', *British Journal of Sociology*, 51, 3 (2000).

McGovern, P., 'Globalization or Internationalization?: Foreign Footballers in the English League, 1946–95', *Sociology*, 36, 1 (2002).

McGregor, W., 'The £ s. d. of Football' in C. Leatherdale (ed.), *The Book of Football* (Westcliff-on-Sea: Desert Island, 1997 [1st edition, 1906]).

McGregor, W., 'Birmingham (late Small Heath) Football Club in C. Leatherdale (ed.), *The Book of Football* (Westcliff-on-Sea: Desert Island, 1997 [1st edition, 1906]).

McGuire, B., Monks, K. and Halsall, R., 'Young Asian Males: Social Exclusion and Social Injustice in British Professional Football?', *Culture, Sport, Society*, 4, 3 (Autumn 2001).

McIlroy, J., *Right Inside Soccer* (London: Sportsmans Book Club, 1961).

McKernan, L., 'Sport and the First Films' in C. Williams (ed.), *Cinema: The Beginnings and the Future* (London: University of Westminster Press, 1996).

McKibbin, R., *Classes and Cultures: England, 1918–1951* (Oxford: Oxford University Press, 1998).

McKibbin, R., 'Class, Politics, Money: British Sport Since the First World War', *Twentieth Century British History*, 13, 2 (2002).

McNeill, D., *New Europe, Imagined Spaces* (London: Arnold, 2004).

Macbeth, J., 'The Development of Women's Football in Scotland', *The Sports Historian*, 22, 2 (November 2002).

Macbeth, J., 'The "Pals", the "Professionals" and the "Conformers": The Meaning of Football in the Lives of Women Footballers in Scotland' in J. Magee, A. Bairner and A. Tomlinson (eds), *The Bountiful Game?: Football Identities and Finances* (Oxford: Meyer & Meyer Sport, 2005).

MacDonald, R., *Britain versus Europe* (London: Pelham, 1968).

Mackay, R., *Half the Battle: Civilian Morale in Britain during the Second World War* (Manchester: Manchester University Press, 2002).

MacRaild, D. M and Martin, D. E., *Labour in British Society* (London: Macmillan, 2000).

Magee, J., 'Shifting Balances of Power in the New Football Economy' in J. Sugden and A. Tomlinson (eds), *Power Games: A Critical Sociology of Sport* (London: Routledge, 2004).

Magee, J., 'Northern Irish Society and Football in the Immediate Post-World War II Era: Jimmy Jones and Sectarianism' in J. Magee, A. Bairner and A. Tomlinson (eds), *The Bountiful Game?: Football Identities and Finances* (Oxford: Meyer & Meyer Sport, 2005).

Magee, J., Bairner, A. and Tomlinson, A. (eds), *The Bountiful Game?: Football Identities and Finances* (Oxford: Meyer & Meyer Sport, 2005).

Magee, J. and Sugden, J., '"The World at Their Feet": Professional Football and International Labour Migration', *Journal of Sport and Social Issues*, 26, 4 (November 2002).

Maguire, J., 'Race and Position Assignment in English Soccer: A Preliminary Analysis of Ethnicity and Sport in Britain, *Sociology of Sport Journal*, 5, 3 (1988).

Maguire, J., 'Sport, Racism and British Society: A Sociological Study of England's Elite Male Afro/Caribbean Soccer and Rugby Union Players' in G. Jarvie (ed.), *Sport, Racism and Ethnicity* (London: Falmer, 1991).

Maguire, J., *Global Sport: Identities, Societies and Civilizations* (Cambridge: Polity, 1999).

Maguire, J., *Power and Global Sport: Zones of Prestige, Emulation and Resistance* (London: Routledge, 2005).

Maguire, J. and Burrows, M., '"Not the Germans Again": Soccer, Identity Politics and the Media' in J. Maguire, *Power and Global Sport: Zones of Prestige, Emulation and Resistance* (London: Routledge, 2005).

Maguire, J. and Possamai, C., '"Back to the Valley": Local Responses to the Changing Culture of Football' in J. Maguire, *Power and Global Sport: Zones of Prestige, Emulation and Resistance* (London: Routledge, 2005).

Maguire, J., Poulton, E. and Possamai, C., 'The War of the Words?: Identity Politics and the Anglo-German Press Coverage of Euro 96', *European Journal of Communication*, 14, 1 (1999).

Maguire, J., Poulton, E. and Possamai, C., 'Weltkrieg III?: Media Coverage of England versus Germany in Euro 96', *Journal of Sport and Social Issues*, 23, 4 (November 1999).

Maguire, J. and Stead, D., 'Border Crossings: Soccer Labour Migration and the European Union', *International Review for the Sociology of Sport*, 33, 1 (1998).

Malcolm, D., 'The People's Game?: Football Crowds and the New Marketing of the Game', *Singer & Friedlander's Review*, 1999–2000 season.

Malcolm, D., 'Football Business and Football Communities in the Twenty-First Century', *Soccer and Society*, 1, 3 (Autumn 2000).

Malcolm, D., Jones, I. and Waddington, I., 'The People's Game?: Football Spectatorship and Demographic Change', *Soccer and Society*, 1, 1 (Spring 2000).

Malcolmson, R. W., *Popular Recreations in English Society, 1700–1850* (Cambridge: Cambridge University Press, 1973).

Mangan, J. A., *Athleticism in the Victorian and Edwardian Public School* (London: Frank Cass, 2002 [1st edition, 1981]).

Mangan, J. A. (ed.), *Pleasure, Profit and Proselytism: British Culture and Sport at Home and Abroad, 1700–1914* (London: Frank Cass, 1988).

Mangan, J. A. (ed.), *Sport in Europe: Politics, Class, Gender* (London: Frank Cass, 1999).

Mangan, J. A., 'Series Editor's Foreword' to S. Wagg (ed.), *British Football and Social Exclusion* (London: Routledge, 2004).

Mangan, J. A. and Hickey, C., 'English Elementary Education Revisited and Revised: Drill and Athleticism in Tandem' in J. A. Mangan (ed.), *Sport in Europe: Politics, Class, Gender* (London: Frank Cass, 1999).

Marschik, M., "Mitropa: Representations of "Central Europe" in Football', *International Review for the Sociology of Sport*, 36, 1 (2001).

Marsh, P., 'Life and Careers on the Soccer Terraces' in R. Ingham (ed.), *Football Hooliganism: The Wider Context* (London: Inter-Action, 1978).

Marsh, P., Rosser, E. and Harre, R., *The Rules of Disorder* (London: Routledge & Kegan Paul, 1978).

Marwick, A., *Britain in the Century of Total War* (London: Penguin, 1970).

Marwick, A., *British Society Since 1945* (London: Penguin [1st edition, 1982]).

Mason, C. and Moncrieff, A., 'The Effect of Relocation on the Externality Fields of Football Stadia: The Case of St Johnstone FC', *Scottish Geographical Magazine*, 109, 2 (1993).

Mason, T., 'Rise and Strange Decline of Women's Football', unpublished paper, n.d.

Mason, T., *Association Football and English Society, 1863–1915* (Brighton: Harvester, 1980).

Mason, T., 'Football and the Workers in England, 1880–1914' in R. Cashman and M. McKernan (eds), *Sport: Money, Morality and the Media* (Brisbane: New South Wales University Press, 1981).

Mason, T., 'Some Englishmen and Scotsmen Abroad: The Spread of World Football' in A. Tomlinson and G. Whannel (eds), *Off the Ball: The Football World Cup* (London: Pluto, 1986).

Mason, T., *Sport in Britain* (London: Faber & Faber, 1988).

Mason, T., 'Football and the Historians', *International Journal of the History of Sport*, 5 (1988).

Mason, T., 'Football' in T. Mason (ed.), *Sport in Britain: A Social History* (Cambridge: Cambridge University Press, 1989).

Mason, T., (ed.), *Sport in Britain: A Social History* (Cambridge: Cambridge University Press, 1989).

Mason, T., 'Stanley Matthews' in R. Holt (ed.), *Sport and the Working Class in Modern Britain* (Manchester: Manchester University Press, 1990).

Mason, T., 'All the Winners and the Half Times ...', *The Sports Historian*, 13 (May 1993).

Mason, T., 'The Bogotá Affair' in J. Bale and J. Maguire (eds), *The Global*

Sports Arena: Athletic Talent Migration in an Interdependent World (London: Frank Cass, 1994).

Mason, T., 'Sport and Recreation' in P. Johnson (ed.), *Twentieth-Century Britain: Economic, Social and Cultural Change* (London: Longman, 1994).

Mason, T., *Passion of the People?: Football in South America* (London: Verso, 1995).

Mason, T., 'Football, Sport of the North?' in J. Hill and J. Williams (eds), *Sport and Identity in the North of England* (Keele: Keele University Press, 1996).

Mason, T., '"Our Stephen and Our Harold": Edwardian Footballers as Local Heroes' in R. Holt, J. A. Mangan and P. Lanfranchi (eds), *European Heroes: Myth, Identity, Sport* (London: Frank Cass, 1996).

Mason, T., 'Kick and Rush or Revolt into Style?; Football Playing Among the English Professionals from Great Power to Image of Decline', paper presented to the Jeu et société conference, INSEP Paris, May 1998.

Mason, T., 'Grandeur et déclin du Kick and Rush Anglais ou la revolt d'un style' in H. Hélal and P. Mignon (eds), *Football: Jeu et société* (Paris: INSEP, 1999).

Mason, T., "Defeat of the Soccer Exiles', *BBC History Magazine*, 1, 2 (June 2000).

Mason, T., '"I Doubt If They Will Lose At All": Looking Back on England versus Hungary 1953', *Sport in History*, 23, 2 (Winter 2003/4).

Mason, T., 'England 1966: Traditional and Modern?' in A. Tomlinson and C. Young (eds), *National Identity and Global Sports Events: Culture, Politics, and Spectacle in the Olympics and the Football World Cup* (Albany, NY: SUNY Press, 2006).

Matthews, S., *Feet First Again* (London: Nicholas Kaye, 1952).

Mayes, H., *The Football Association World Cup Report* (London: Heinemann, 1967).

Meisl, W., *Soccer Revolution* (London: Panther Edition, 1957 [1st edition, 1955]).

Melcon, R. and Smith, S. (eds), *The Real Madrid Book of Football* (London: Consul, 1962).

Meller, H. E., *Leisure and the Changing City, 1870–1914* (London: Routledge & Kegan Paul, 1976).

Meller, H., *European Cities 1890s–1930s: History, Culture and the Built Environment* (Chichester: John Wiley, 2001).

Melling, A., '"Ray of the Rovers": The Working-Class Heroine in Popular Football Fiction, 1915–25', *International Journal of the History of Sport*, 15, 1 (April 1998).

Melling, A., '"Plucky Lasses", "Pea Soup" and Politics: The Roles of Ladies' Football during the 1921 Miners' Lock-Out in Wigan and Leigh', *International Journal of the History of Sport*, 16, 1 (March 1999).

Melling, A., 'Cultural Differentiation, Shared Aspiration: The Entente Cordiale of International Ladies' Football, 1920–45' in J. A. Mangan (ed.), *Sport in Europe: Politics, Class, Gender* (London: Frank Cass, 1999).

Mellor, G., 'The Social and Geographical Make-Up of Football Crowds in the North-West of England, 1946–1962: "Super-Clubs", Local Loyalty and Regional Identities', *The Sports Historian*, 19, 2 (November 1999).

Mellor, G., 'The Rise of the Reds: An Historical Analysis of Manchester United as a "Super-Club"', *Singer and Friedlander's Review*, 1999–2000 season.

Mellor, G., 'The Genesis of Manchester United as a National and International "Super-Club", 1958–68', *Soccer and Society*, 1, 2 (Summer 2000).

Mellor, G., 'Football and its Supporters in the North West of England, 1945–85', unpublished Ph.D. thesis, University of Central Lancashire, 2003.

Melnick, M., 'Racial Segregation by Playing Position in the English Football League: Some Preliminary Observations', *Journal of Sport and Social Issues*, 12, 2 (1988).

Messner, M. A. and Sabo, D. F. (eds), *Sport, Men and the Gender Order: Critical Feminist Perspectives* (Champaign, Illinois: Human Kinetics, 1990).

Metcalfe, A., 'Football and the Mining Communities of East Northumberland, 1882–1914', *International Journal of the History of Sport*, 5, 3 (December 1988).

Miller, D., *England's Last Glory: The Boys of '66* (London: Pavilion, 2006 [1st edition, 1986]).

Miller, F., 'Beyond *Bosman*', *Sport and the Law Journal*, 3, 1 (1996).

Molyneux, D. D., 'The Development of Physical Recreation in the Birmingham District from 1871 to 1892', unpublished MA thesis, University of Birmingham, 1957.

Moorhouse, H. F., 'Scotland against England: Football and Popular

Culture', *International Journal of the History of Sport*, 4, 2 (September 1987).

Moorhouse, H. F., 'One State, Several Countries: Soccer and Identities in the "United" Kingdom', European University Institute Colloquium Papers, 1989.

Moorhouse, H. F., 'Football Hooliganism: Old Bottle, New Whines?', *Sociological Review*, 39 (1991).

Moorhouse, H. F., 'On the Periphery: Scotland, Scottish Football and the New Europe' in J. Williams and S. Wagg (eds), *British Football and Social Change: Getting into Europe* (Leicester: Leicester University Press, 1991).

Moorhouse, H. F., 'Shooting Stars: Footballers and Working-Class Culture in Twentieth-Century Scotland' in R. Holt (ed.), *Sport and the Working Class in Modern Britain* (Manchester: Manchester University Press, 1990).

Moorhouse, H. F., 'Blue Bonnets over the Border: Scotland and the Migration of Footballers' in J. Bale and J. Maguire (eds), *The Global Sports Arena: Athletic Talent Migration in an Interdependent World* (London: Frank Cass, 1994).

Moorhouse, H. F., 'From Zines Like These?: Fanzines, Tradition and Identity in Scottish Football' in G. Jarvie and G. Walker (eds), *Scottish Sport and the Making of the Nation: Ninety-Minute Patriots?* (Leicester: Leicester University Press, 1994).

Moorhouse, H. F., 'Scotland, Football and Identities: The National Team and Club Sides' in S. Gehrmann (ed.), *Football and Regional Identity in Europe* (Münster: Lit Verlag, 1997).

Moorhouse, H. F., 'The Economic Effects of the Traditional Transfer System in European Professional Football', *Football Studies*, 2, 1 (1999).

Moorhouse, H. F., 'The Organisation of Scottish Football', invited submission to the Scottish Parliament's Reporters' Investigation into Scottish Football 2005, www.scottish.parliament.uk/business/commit tees/enterprise/inquiries/sfi/fie_pt01_Moorhouse_pdf [accessed 22 March 2006].

Morgan, K. O., *Rebirth of a Nation: Wales 1880–1980* (Oxford: Clarendon, 1980).

Morris, D., *The Soccer Tribe* (London: Jonathan Cape, 1981).

Morrow, S., *The New Business of Football: Accountability and Finance in Football* (Basingstoke: Palgrave, 1999).

Morrow, S., 'Uncertainty of Outcome: Where Next for Scottish Football?', *Soccer Review* (2002).

Morrow, S., *The People's Game?: Football, Finance and Society* (Basingstoke: Palgrave, 2003).

Morrow, S., 'A Critical Analysis of the State of Scottish Football: Reasons, Excuses, Solutions' in J. Magee, A. Bairner and A. Tomlinson (eds), *The Bountiful Game?: Football Identities and Finances* (Oxford: Meyer & Meyer Sport, 2005).

Moynihan, J., *The Soccer Syndrome: From the Primeval Forties* (London: Simon & Schuster, 1987 [1st edition, 1966]).

Muddied Oafs: An Exhibition of Football (London: Gallery 27, 1998).

Munting, R., 'The Games Ethic and Industrial Capitalism before 1914: The Provision of Company Sports', *Sport in History*, 23, 1 (Summer 2003).

Murphy, P., Williams, J. and Dunning, E., *Football on Trial: Spectator Violence and Development in the Football World* (London: Routledge, 1990).

Murray, B., *The Old Firm in the New Age* (Edinburgh: Mainstream, 1998).

Murray, B., *The World's Game: A History of Soccer* (Urbana: University of Illinois Press, 1998).

Murray, B., *The Old Firm: Sectarianism, Sport and Society in Scotland* (Edinburgh: John Donald, 2000 [1st edition, 1984]).

Nagbøl, S. and Bale, J., *A View of English Football: Sport and Sense of Place* (Jyväskylä: Department of Social Policy, University of Jyväskylä Working Papers, 1994).

Nairn, T., *The Break-Up of Britain: Crisis and Neo-Nationalism* (London: Verso, 1977).

Nairn, T., *After Britain: New Labour and the Return of Scotland* (London: Granta, 2000).

Nannestad, I., '"The Charge at Football is Good, That With the Bayonet Finer": The Formation of the Footballers' Battalion, 1914', *Soccer History*, 1 (Spring 2002).

Nannestad, I., 'Celebrating the Festival of Britain: The St Mungo Cup', *Soccer History*, 2 (Summer 2002).

Nash, R., 'Research Note: Concept and Method in Researching the Football Crowd', *Leisure Studies*, 16 (1997).

Nash, R., 'The Sociology of Football in the 1990s: Fandom, Business and Future Research', *Football Studies*, 3, 1 (2000).

Nash, R., 'Globalised Football Fandom: Scandinavian Liverpool FC Supporters', *Football Studies*, 3, 2 (October 2000).

Nash, R., 'English Football Fan Groups in the 1990s: Class, Representation and Fan Power', *Soccer and Society*, 2, 1 (Spring 2001).

Nauright, J. and Chandler, T. J. L. (eds), *Making Men: Rugby and Masculine Identity* (London: Frank Cass, 1996).

Nelson, G., *Left Foot Forward: A Year in the Life of a Journeyman Footballer* (London: Headline, 1995).

Newsham, G., *In a League of Their Own!: The Dick, Kerr Ladies Football Team* (London: Scarlet, 1997 [1st edition, 1994]).

Newson, R., 'Music To Your Ears?', *When Saturday Comes*, April 1996.

North West Sports Council, *Leisure in the North West* (Salford: North West Sports Council, 1972).

Nottingham, C. J., 'More Important Than Life or Death: Football, the Working Class and the Social Order' in L. H. van Voss and F. van Holthoon (eds), *Working Class and Popular Culture* (Amsterdam: Stichting Beheer IISG, 1988).

Obelkevich, J. and Catterall, P. (eds), *Understanding Post-War British Society* (London: Routledge, 1994).

Offord, H. J. W., 'Schoolboy Football' in C. Leatherdale (ed.), *The Book of Football* (Westcliff-on-Sea: Desert Island, 1997 [1st edition, 1906]).

Orakwue, S., *Pitch Invaders: The Modern Black Football Revolution* (London: Vista, 1999).

Oriard, M., *Reading Football: How the Popular Press Created an American Spectacle* (Chapel Hill: University of North Carolina Press, 1993).

Osborne, J. M., '"To Keep the Life of the Nation on the Old Lines": *The Athletic News* and the First World War', *Journal of Sport History*, 14, 2 (Summer 1987).

Oxford Dictionary of National Biography (Oxford: Oxford University Press, 2004).

Parker, A., 'Great Expectations – Grimness or Glamour?: The Football Apprentice in the 1990s', *The Sports Historian*, 15 (1995).

Parker, A., 'Soccer, Servitude and Sub-Cultural Identity: Football Traineeship and Masculine Construction', *Soccer and Society*, 2, 1 (Spring 2001).

Parkinson, M., *Best: An Intimate Biography* (London: Arrow, 1975).

Pawson, T., *100 Years of the FA Cup* (London: Heinemann, 1972).

Pawson, T., *The Football Managers* (London: Eyre Methuen, 1973).

Percy, M. and Taylor, R., 'Something for the Weekend Sir?: Leisure, Ecstacy and Identity in Football and Contemporary Religion', *Leisure Studies*, 16 (1997).

Perryman, M. (ed.), *Hooligan Wars: Causes and Effects of Football Violence* (Edinburgh: Mainstream, 2001).

Pfister, G., Fasting, K., Scraton, S. and Vzquez, B., 'Women and Football – A Contradiction?: The Beginnings of Women's Football in Four European Countries' in J. A. Mangan (ed.), *Sport in Europe: Politics, Class, Gender* (London: Frank Cass, 1999).

Phelps, N. A., 'The Southern Football Hero and the Shaping of Local and Regional Identity in the South of England', *Soccer and Society*, 2, 3 (Autumn 2001).

Phelps, N. A., 'Professional Football and Local Identity in the "Golden Age": Portsmouth in the Mid-Twentieth Century', *Urban History*, 32, 3 (2005)

Phillips, M. G. (ed.), *Deconstructing Sport History: A Postmodern Analysis* (New York: SUNY Press, 2006).

Phillips, S., '"Fellowship in Recreation, Fellowship in Ideals": Sport, Leisure and Culture at Boots Pure Drug Company, Nottingham *c*.1883–1945', *Midland History*, 29 (2004).

Pickering. M., *Stereotyping: The Politics of Representation* (Basingstoke: Palgrave, 2001).

Pitchford, A. Brackenridge, C., Bringer, J. D., Cockburn, C., Nutt, G., Pawlaczek, Z. and Russell, K., 'Children in Football: Seen But Not Heard', *Soccer and Society*, 5, 1 (Spring 2004).

Pocock, J. G. A., 'The Limits and Divisions of British History: In Search of the Unknown Subject', *American Historical Review*, 87 (1982).

Political and Economic Planning, 'English Professional Football', *Planning*, 32, 496, (1966).

Polley, M., 'The Foreign Office and International Sport, 1918–1948', unpublished Ph.D. thesis, St David's University College, University of Wales, 1991.

Polley, M., *Moving the Goalposts: A History of Sport and Society Since 1945* (London: Routledge, 1998).

Polley, M., 'History and Sport' in B. Houlihan (ed.), *Sport and Society: A Student Introduction* (London: Sage, 2003).

Polley, M., 'Sport and National Identity in England' in A. Smith and D. Porter (eds), *Sport and National Identity in the Post-War World* (London: Routledge, 2004).

Poole, R., *Popular Leisure and the Music Hall in Nineteenth-Century*

Bolton (University of Lancaster: Centre for North-West Regional Studies, Occasional Paper No. 12, 1982).

Pope, S. W., 'Decentring "Race" and (Re)presenting "Black" Performance in Sport History: Basketball and Jazz in American Culture, 1920–1950' in M. G. Phillips (ed.), *Deconstructing Sport History: A Postmodern Analysis* (New York: SUNY Press, 2006).

Porter, D., 'Amateur Football in England, 1948–63: The Pegasus Phenomenon' in A. Smith and D. Porter (eds), *Amateurs and Professionals in Post-War British Sport* (London: Frank Cass, 2000).

Porter, D., '"Your Boys Took One Hell of a Beating!": English Football and British Decline, *c.*1950–80' in A. Smith and D. Porter (eds), *Sport and National Identity in the Post-War World* (London: Routledge, 2004).

Poulton, E., 'New Fans, New Flags, New England?: Changing News Values in the English Press Coverage of World Cup 2002', *Football Studies*, 6, 1 (April 2003).

Preston, I. and Szymanski, S., 'Racial Discrimination in English Football', *Scottish Journal of Political Economy*, 47, 4 (September 2000).

Preston, T., 'Art' in R. Cox, D. Russell and W. Vamplew (eds), *Encyclopedia of British Football* (London: Frank Cass, 2002).

Priestley, J. B., *The Good Companions* (London: Heinemann, 1976 [1st edition, 1929]).

Rafferty, J., *One Hundred Years of Scottish Football* (London: Pan, 1973).

Raynor, G., *Football Ambassador at Large* (London: Soccer Book Club, 1960).

Redhead, S., 'You've Really Got a Hold of Me: Footballers in the Market' in A. Tomlinson and G. Whannel (eds), *Off the Ball: The Football World Cup* (London: Pluto, 1986).

Redhead, S. (ed.), *The Passion and the Fashion: Football Fandom in the New Europe* (Aldershot: Avebury, 1993).

Redhead, S., 'Always Look on the Bright Side of Life' in S. Redhead (ed.), *The Passion and the Fashion: Football Fandom in the New Europe* (Aldershot: Avebury, 1993).

Redhead, S., *Post-Fandom and the Millennial Blues: The Transformation of Soccer Culture* (London: Routledge, 1997).

Redhead, S., with Wynne D. and O'Connor, J. (eds), *The Clubcultures Reader* (Oxford: Blackwell, 1997).

Reid, D., 'Folk Football, the Aristocracy and Cultural Change: A Critique of Dunning and Sheard', *International Journal of the History of Sport*, 5, 2 (1988).

Reimer, B., 'For the Love of England: Scandinavian Football Supporters, Manchester United and British Popular Culture' in D. L. Andrews (ed.), *Manchester United: A Thematic Study* (London: Routledge, 2004).

Reiss, S., 'From Pitch to Putt: Sport and Class in Anglo-American Sport', *Journal of Sport History*, 21, 2 (Summer 1994).

Reiss, S., *Sport in Industrial America, 1850–1920* (Wheeling, Illinois: Harlan Davidson, 1995).

Remnick, T., 'Comic Characters' in R. Cox, D. Russell and W. Vamplew (eds), *Encyclopedia of British Football* (London: Frank Cass, 2002).

Revie, A., *All Roads Lead to Wembley* (London: Pelham, 1971).

Richards, J., 'Football and the Crisis of British Identity' in S. Caunce, E. Mazierska, S. Sydney-Smith and J. Walton (eds), *Relocating Britishness* (Manchester: Manchester University Press, 2004).

Rigauer, B., *Sport and Work* (New York: Colombia University Press, 1981).

Ring, E., 'Blackpool: Illuminations of a Distant Fan' in D. Bull (ed.), *We'll Support You Evermore: Keeping Faith in Football* (London: Duckworth, 1992).

Risoli, M., *When Pele Broke Our Hearts: Wales and the 1958 World Cup* (Cardiff: St David's, 1998).

Robbins, K., *Nineteenth-Century Britain: Integration and Diversity* (Oxford: Clarendon, 1988).

Robbins, K., 'British History and the Generation of Change' in H. Brocklehurst and R. Phillips (eds), *History, Nationhood and the Question of Britain* (Basingstoke: Palgrave, 2004).

Roberts, J., '"The Best Football Team, The Best Platoon": The Role of Football in the Proletarianization of the British Expeditionary Force, 1914–1918', *Sport in History*, 26, 1 (April 2006).

Robidoux, M. A., *Men at Play: A Working Understanding of Professional Hockey* (Montreal: McGill-Queen's University Press, 2001).

Rogan, J., *The Football Managers* (London: Queen Anne, 1989).

Rollin, J., *Soccer at War, 1939–45* (London: Collins Willow, 1985).

Rosaaen, K. and Amis, J., 'From the Busby Babes to the Theatre of Dreams: Image, Reputation and the Rise of Manchester United' in D. L. Andrews (ed.), *Manchester United: A Thematic Study* (London: Routledge, 2004).

Rous, S., 'Football as an International Sport', *The Listener*, 4 May 1938.

Rous, S., *Football Worlds: A Lifetime in Sport* (London: Faber & Faber, 1978).

Rowe, D., 'Modes of Sports Writing' in P. Dahlgren and C. Sparks (eds), *Journalism and Popular Culture* (London: Sage, 1992).

Rowe, D., *Sport, Culture and the Media: The Unruly Trinity* (Maidenhead: Open University Press, 1999).

Rowlands, A., *Trautmann: The Biography* (Derby: Breedon, 1990).

Russell, D., '"Sporadic and Curious": The Emergence of Rugby and Soccer Zones in Yorkshire and Lancashire, *c.*1860–1914', *International Journal of the History of Sport*, 5, 2 (September 1988).

Russell, D., 'Sport and Identity: The Case of Yorkshire County Cricket Club, 1890–1939', *Twentieth Century British History*, 7, 2 (1996).

Russell, D., *Football and the English: A Social History of Association Football in England, 1863–1995* (Preston: Carnegie, 1997).

Russell, D., 'Associating with Football: Social Identity in England, 1863–1998' in G. Armstrong and R. Giulianotti (eds), *Football Cultures and Identities* (Basingstoke: Macmillan, 1999).

Russell, D., 'Football and Society in the North-East, 1919–1939', *North West Labour History*, 24 (1999/2000).

Russell, D., *Looking North: Northern England and the National Imagination* (Manchester: Manchester University Press, 2004).

Russell, D., '"We All Agree, Name the Stand after Shankly": Cultures of Commemoration in Late Twentieth-century English Football Culture', *Sport in History*, 26, 1 (April 2006).

Russell, D. and Williams, J., 'Drama' in R. Cox, D. Russell and W. Vamplew (eds), *Encyclopedia of British Football* (London: Frank Cass, 2002).

Samuel, R., 'British Dimensions: "Four Nations History"', *History Workshop Journal*, 40 (Autumn 1995).

Samuel, R., *Island Stories: Unravelling Britain* (London: Verso, 1998).

Sandvoss, C., *A Game of Two Halves: Football, Television and Globalization* (London: Routledge, 2003).

Savage, M. and Miles, A., *The Remaking of the British Working Class, 1840–1940* (London: Routledge, 1994).

Say, T., 'Herbert Chapman: Football Revolutionary?', *The Sports Historian*, 16 (May 1996).

Schleppi, J. R., 'A History of Professional Association Football in England during the Second World War', unpublished Ph.D. thesis, Ohio State University, 1972.

Scottish Abstract of Statistics (Edinburgh: HMSO, 1980).

Scottish Abstract of Statistics (Edinburgh: HMSO, 1985).

Scottish Abstract of Statistics (Edinburgh: HMSO, 1986).

Scraton, P., *Hillsborough: The Truth* (Edinburgh: Mainstream, 1999).

Scraton, P., 'Death on the Terraces: The Contexts and Injustices of the 1989 Hillsborough Disaster' in P. Darby, M. Johnes and G. Mellor (eds), *Soccer and Disaster: International Perspectives* (London: Routledge, 2005).

Seddon. P., *A Football Compendium* (Wetherby: The British Library, 1995).

Seddon, P., *Steve Bloomer: The Story of Football's First Superstar* (Derby: Breedon, 1999).

Sharpe, I., *40 Years in Football* (London: Sportsmans Book Club, 1954).

Sharpe, G., *Gambling on Goals: A Century of Football Betting* (Edinburgh: Mainstream, 1997).

Shearman, M. (ed.), *Football* (London: Badminton Library Series, 1899).

Sillitoe, K. K., *Planning for Leisure* (London: HMSO, 1969).

Sir Norman Chester Centre for Football Research, 'Fact Sheet Number 2: Football Stadia After Taylor' (Leicester: Sir Norman Chester Centre for Football Research, 2002).

Sissons, M. and French, P. (eds), *Age of Austerity, 1945–51* (Harmondsworth: Penguin, 1964).

Skinner, W. E., *The Football Industry: A Discussion Paper* (Sheffield: Sheffield City Polytechnic, 1982).

Sloane, P. J., 'The Economics of Professional Football: The Football Club as a Utility Maximiser', *Scottish Journal of Political Economy*, 17 (June 1971).

Sloane, P. J., 'Restriction of Competition in Professional Team Sports', *Bulletin of Economic Research*, 28, 1 (May 1976).

Sloane, P. J., *Sport in the Market?* (London: Institute of Economic Affairs, Hobart Paper No. 85, 1980).

Smart, B., *The Sport Star: Modern Sport and the Cultural Economy of Sporting Celebrity* (London: Sage, 2005).

Smith, A. and Porter, D. (eds), *Amateurs and Professionals in Post-War British Sport* (London: Frank Cass, 2000).

Smith, A. and Porter, D. (eds), *Sport and National Identity in the Post-War World* (London: Routledge, 2004).

Smith, G. O., 'Origin and Benefits of the League and the Effects of Professionalism on the Game' in M. Shearman (ed.), *Football* (London: Badminton Library Series, 1899).

Smith, H. (ed.), *War and Social Change: British Society and the Second World War* (Manchester: Manchester University Press, 1986).

Smith, S. and Johnson, M., 'Unusual Support?: Welsh Fans of the English Game', *Soccer Review* (2003).

Social Trends (London: The Stationery Office, 2002).

Social Trends (Basingstoke: Palgrave, 2006).

Sport and the Community: Report of the Wolfenden Committee on Sport (London: Central Council for Physical Recreation, 1960).

Sport England, *Participation in Sport: Past Trends and Future Prospects – The General Household Survey* (Wetherby: UK Sport/Sport England, 2001).

Sports Council, *Digest of Sports Statistics for the UK* (London: Sports Council, 1991).

Sports Council, *Sport in the Nineties: New Horizons – Part Two: The Context* (London: Sports Council, n.d.)

Sproat, K., 'The Best Seats in the House?', *When Saturday Comes*, May 1994.

Stead, D. and Maguire, J., '"Rite De Passage" or Passage to Riches?: The Motivation and Objectives of Nordic/Scandinavian Players in English League Soccer', *Journal of Sport and Social Issues*, 26, 4 (February 2000).

Stead, P. and Richards, H. (eds), *For Club and Country: Welsh Football Greats* (Cardiff: University of Wales Press, 2000).

Stedman Jones, G., 'Working-Class Culture and Working-Class Politics in London, 1870–1900, *Journal of Social History*, 7 (1975).

Stedman Jones, G., *Languages of Class: Studies of English Working-Class History, 1832–1982* (Cambridge: Cambridge University Press, 1983).

Stobart, J., 'Building an Urban Identity: Cultural Space and Civic Boosterism in a "New" Industrial Town. Burslem, 1761–1911', *Social History*, 29, 4 (November 2004).

Studd, S., *Herbert Chapman, Football Emperor: A Study in the Origins of Modern Soccer* (London: Souvenir, 1998 [1st edition, 1981]).

Sugden, J. and Bairner, A., 'Northern Ireland: Sport in a Divided Society' in L. Allison (ed.), *The Politics of Sport* (Manchester: Manchester University Press, 1986).

Sugden, J. and Bairner, A., 'Observe the Sons of Ulster: Football and Politics in Northern Ireland' in A. Tomlinson and G. Whannel (eds), *Off the Ball: The Football World Cup* (London: Pluto, 1986).

Sugden, J. and Bairner, A., *Sport, Sectarianism and Society in a Divided Ireland* (Leicester: Leicester University Press, 1993).

Sugden, J. and Bairner, A., 'Ireland and the World Cup: "Two Teams in Ireland, There's Only Two Teams in Ireland . . ."' in J. Sugden and A. Tomlinson (eds), *Hosts and Champions: Soccer Cultures, National Identities and the USA World Cup* (Aldershot: Arena, 1994).

Sugden, J. and Tomlinson, A. (eds), *Hosts and Champions: Soccer Cultures, National Identities and the USA World Cup* (Aldershot: Arena, 1994).

Sugden, J. and Tomlinson, A. (eds), *Power Games: A Critical Sociology of Sport* (London: Routledge, 2004).

Sutcliffe, C. E. and Hargreaves, F., *History of the Lancashire Football Association, 1878–1928* (Harefield: Yore, 1992 [1st edition, 1928]).

Szymanski, S., 'A Market Test for Discrimination in the English Professional Leagues', *Journal of Political Economy*, 108, 3 (2000).

Szymanski, S. and Kuypers, T., *Winners and Losers: The Business Strategy of Football* (London: Penguin, 2000).

Tabner, B., *Through the Turnstiles . . . Again* (Harefield: Yore, 2002).

Taw, T., *Football's War and Peace: The Tumultuous Season of 1946–47* (Westcliff-on-Sea: Desert Island, 2003).

Taylor, D. J., '"Rally Round You Havens!": Soccer and the Literary Imagination' in S. Kuper (ed.), *Perfect Pitch 1: Home Ground* (London: Headline, 1997).

Taylor, Lord Justice P., *The Hillsborough Stadium Disaster 15th April 1989: Final Report* (London: HMSO, 1990).

Taylor, I., '"Football Mad": A Speculative Sociology of Football Hooliganism' in E. Dunning (ed.), *The Sociology of Sport* (London: Frank Cass, 1971).

Taylor, I., 'On the Sports Violence Question: Soccer Hooliganism Revisited' in J. Hargreaves (ed.), *Sport, Culture and Ideology* (London: Routledge & Kegan Paul, 1982).

Taylor, I., 'English Football in the 1990s: Taking Hillsborough Seriously?' in J. Williams and S. Wagg (eds), *British Football and Social Change: Getting into Europe* (Leicester: Leicester University Press, 1991).

Taylor, M., 'Little Englanders: Tradition, Identity and Professional Football in Lancashire, 1880–1930' in S. Gehrmann (ed.), *Football and Regional Identity in Europe* (Münster: Lit Verlag, 1997).

Taylor, M., 'Football, History and Memory: The Heroes of Manchester United', *Football Studies*, 3, 2 (October 2000).

Taylor, M, 'Labour Relations and Managerial Control in English Professional Football, 1890–1939', *Sport History Review*, 31, 2 (November 2000).

Taylor, M., 'Beyond the Maximum Wage: The Earnings of Football Professionals in England, 1900–1939', *Soccer and Society*, 2, 3 (Autumn 2001).

Taylor, M., 'Leisure and Entertainment' in J. Bourne, P. Liddle and I. Whitehead (eds), *The Great World War, 1914–45*, Vol. 2: *The People's Experience* (London: Harper Collins, 2001).

Taylor, M., 'The Foreigner in English Football before the 1980s', paper presented to the British Society of Sports History Annual Conference, University of Lancaster, April 2002.

Taylor, M., 'Work and Play: The Professional Footballer in England, c.1900–1950', *The Sports Historian*, 22, 1 (May 2002).

Taylor, M., 'The Migration of Footballers: An Historical Approach', *Moving Bodies*, 1, 1 (2003).

Taylor, M., 'Building a National League?: The Football League and the North of England, 1888–1939', *International Journal of Regional and Local Studies*, 1, 1 (2005).

Taylor, M., *The Leaguers: The Making of Professional Football in England, 1900–1939* (Liverpool: Liverpool University Press, 2005).

Taylor, M., 'Football et culture politique en Grande-Bretagne' in Y. Gastaut and S. Mourlane (eds), *Le Football dans nos sociétés: Une culture populaire, 1914–1998* (Paris: Autrement, 2006).

Taylor, M., 'Global Players?: Football, Migration and Globalization, c.1930–2000', *Historical Social Research*, 31, 1 (2006).

Taylor, N., '"Giving Something Back": Can Football Clubs and their Communities Co-Exist?' in S. Wagg (ed.), *British Football and Social Exclusion* (London: Routledge, 2004).

Taylor, R., *Football and its Fans: Supporters and their Relations with the Game, 1885–1985* (Leicester: Leicester University Press, 1992).

Taylor, R. and Ward, A., *Kicking and Screaming: An Oral History of Football in England* (London: Robson, 1995).

Tennant, J., *Football: The Golden Age* (London: Cassell, 2001).

Thompson, F. M. L., 'Social Control in Victorian Britain', *Economic History Review*, 34 (1981).

Thomson, D., *4–2* (London: Bloomsbury, 1996).

Thornton, E., *Leeds United and Don Revie* (Newton Abbot: Sportsmans Book Club, 1971).

Thorpe, S., 'Pick the Best, Forget the Rest?: Training Field Dilemmas and Children's Football at the Turn of the Century' in S. Wagg (ed.), *British Football and Social Exclusion* (London: Routledge, 2004).

Tischler, S., *Footballers and Businessmen: The Origins of Professional Soccer in England* (New York: Holmes & Meier, 1981).

'Tityrus', *The Rise of the Leaguers, 1863–1897* (London: Sporting Chronicle, 1897).

Tomlinson, A. (ed.), *Explorations in Football Culture* (Eastbourne: Leisure Studies Association, 1983).

Tomlinson, A., 'Tuck Up Tight Lads: Structures of Control within Football Culture' in A. Tomlinson (ed.), *Explorations in Football Culture* (Eastbourne: Leisure Studies Association, 1983).

Tomlinson, A., 'Going Global: The FIFA Story' in A. Tomlinson and G. Whannel (eds), *Off the Ball: The Football World Cup* (London: Pluto, 1986).

Tomlinson, A., 'North and South: The Rivalry of the Football League and the Football Association' in J. Williams and S. Wagg (eds), *British Football and Social Change: Getting into Europe* (Leicester: Leicester University Press, 1991).

Tomlinson, A., 'FIFA and the Men Who Made It', *Soccer and Society*, 1, 1 (Spring 2000).

Tomlinson, A. and Whannel, G. (eds), *Off the Ball: The Football World Cup* (London: Pluto, 1986).

Tomlinson, A. and Young, C. (eds), *National Identity and Global Sports Events: Culture, Politics, and Spectacle in the Olympics and the Football World Cup* (Albany, NY: SUNY Press, 2006).

Toulmin, V., '"Vivid and Realistic": Edwardian Sport in Film', *Sport in History*, 26, 1 (April 2006).

Tranter, N., 'The Chronology of Organized Sport in Nineteenth-century Scotland: A Regional Study, 1 – Patterns', *International Journal of the History of Sport*, 7, 2 (September 1990).

Tranter, N., 'The Cappielow Riot and the Composition and Behaviour of Soccer Crowds in Late Victorian Scotland', *International Journal of the History of Sport*, 12, 3 (December 1995).

Tranter, N., *Sport, Economy and Society in Britain, 1750–1914* (Cambridge: Cambridge University Press, 1998).

Vamplew, W. 'Playing for Pay: The Earnings of Professional Sportsmen in England, 1870–1914' in R. Cashman and M. McKernan (eds), *Sport: Money, Morality and the Media* (Brisbane: New South Wales University Press, 1981).

Vamplew, W., 'The Economics of a Sports Industry: Scottish Gate-Money Football, 1890–1914', *Economic History Review*, 35 (1982).

Vamplew, W., *Pay Up and Play the Game: Professional Sport in*

Britain, 1875–1914 (Cambridge: Cambridge University Press, 1988).

Vamplew, W., 'Sport and Industrialization: An Economic Interpretation of the Changes in Popular Sport in Nineteenth-Century England' in J. A. Mangan (ed.), *Pleasure, Profit and Proselytism: British Culture and Sport at Home and Abroad, 1700–1914* (London: Frank Cass, 1988).

Vamplew, W., *Newcastle United Football Club: An Economic Impact Assessment. A Report by the De Montfort International Centre for Sports History and Culture* (Leicester: De Montfort University, 1997).

Vamplew, W., Coyle, J., Heath, J. and Naysmith, B., 'Sweet FA: Fans' Rights and Club Relocations', *Football Studies*, 1, 2 (August 1998).

Vande Berg, L. R., 'The Sports Hero Meets Mediated Celebrityhood' in L. A. Wenner (ed.), *MediaSport* (London: Routledge, 1998).

Van Voss, L. H. and van Holthoon, F. (eds), *Working Class and Popular Culture* (Amsterdam: Stichting Beheer IISG, 1988).

Varley, N., *Golden Boy: A Biography of Wilf Mannion* (London: Aurum, 1997).

Vasili, P., 'Walter Daniel Tull, 1888–1918: Soldier, Footballer, Black', *Race and Class*, 38, 2 (1996).

Vasili, P. *The First Black Footballer: Arthur Wharton, 1865–1930* (London: Frank Cass, 1998).

Vasili, P., *Colouring Over the White Line: The History of Black Footballers* (Edinburgh: Mainstream, 2000).

Veitch, C., '"Play Up! Play Up! And Win the War!": Football, the Nation and the First World War, 1914–15', *Journal of Contemporary History*, 20, 3 (July 1985).

Vertinsky, P., 'Time Gentlemen Please: The Space and Place of Gender in Sport History' in M. G. Phillips (ed.), *Deconstructing Sport History: A Postmodern Analysis* (New York: SUNY Press, 2006).

Vertinsky, P. and Bale, J. (eds), *Sites of Sport: Space, Place and Experience* (London: Routledge, 2004).

Vincent, J. E., 'The Antiquities of Football' in C. Leatherdale (ed.), *The Book of Football* (Westcliff-on-Sea: Desert Island, 1997 [1st edition, 1906]).

Vinnai, G., *Football Mania* (London: Ocean, 1973).

Waddington, D., *Contemporary Issues in Public Disorder* (London: Routledge, 1992).

Waddington, I., Dunning, E. and Murphy, P., 'Research Note: Surveying the Social Composition of Football Crowds', *Leisure Studies*, 15 (1996).

Wagg, S., 'Whatever He Said to Them at Half-Time It Certainly Did the Trick: A Social History of the Football Manager' in A. Tomlinson (ed.), *Explorations in Football Culture* (Eastbourne: Leisure Studies Association, 1983).

Wagg, S., *The Football World: A Contemporary Social History* (Brighton: Harvester, 1984).

Wagg, S., 'Naming the Guilty Men: Managers and the Media' in A. Tomlinson and G. Whannel (eds), *Off the Ball: The Football World Cup* (London: Pluto, 1986).

Wagg, S., 'Playing the Past: The Media and the England Football Team' in J. Williams and S. Wagg (eds), *British Football and Social Change: Getting into Europe* (Leicester: Leicester University Press, 1991).

Wagg, S. (ed.), *Giving the Game Away: Football, Politics and Culture on Five Continents* (Leicester: Leicester University Press, 1995).

Wagg, S., 'With His Money, *I* Could Afford to be Depressed: Markets, Masculinity and Mental Distress in the English Football Press', *Football Studies*, 3, 2 (2000).

Wagg, S. (ed.), *British Football and Social Exclusion* (London: Routledge, 2004).

Wagg, S., 'Fat City?: British Football and the Politics of Social Exclusion at the Turn of the Twenty-First Century' in S. Wagg (ed.), *British Football and Social Exclusion* (London: Routledge, 2004).

Wagg, S., '"No Scouse, Please. We're Europeans": Liverpool FC and the Decline of the Boot Room Mystique' in J. Magee, A. Bairner and A. Tomlinson (eds), *The Bountiful Game?: Football Identities and Finances* (Oxford: Meyer & Meyer Sport, 2005).

Walker, G., '"There's Not a Team Like the Glasgow Rangers": Football and Religious Identity in Scotland' in G. Walker and T. Gallagher (eds), *Sermons and Battle Hymns: Protestant Popular Culture in Modern Scotland* (Edinburgh: Edinburgh University Press, 1990).

Walker, G., 'Identity Questions in Contemporary Scotland: Faith, Football and Future Prospects', *Contemporary British History*, 15, 1 (Spring 2001).

Walker, G. and Gallagher, T. (eds), *Sermons and Battle Hymns: Protestant Popular Culture in Modern Scotland* (Edinburgh: Edinburgh University Press, 1990).

Waller, P. J., *Town, City and Nation: England, 1850–1914* (Oxford: Clarendon, 1983).

Walsh, M. (ed.), *Working Out Gender: Perspectives from Labour History* (Aldershot: Ashgate, 1999).

Walter, T., 'The Mourning after Hillsborough', *Sociological Review*, 39, 3 (1991).

Walton, J. K., 'Leisure Towns in Wartime: The Impact of the First World War in Blackpool and San Sebastián', *Journal of Contemporary History*, 31, 4 (1996).

Walvin, J., *The People's Game: A Social History of British Football* (London: Allen Lane, 1975).

Walvin, J., *Leisure and Society, 1830–1915* (Harlow: Longman, 1978).

Walvin, J., *Football and the Decline of Britain* (Basingstoke: Macmillan, 1986).

Walvin, J., *The People's Game: The History of Football Revisited* (Edinburgh: Mainstream, 1994).

Walvin, J., *The Only Game: Football in Our Times* (Harlow: Longman, 2001).

Wann, D. L., Melnick, M. J., Russell, G. W. and Pease, D. G., *Sport Fans: The Psychology and Social Impact of Spectators* (London: Routledge, 2001).

Ward, C., *Steaming In: Journal of a Football Fan* (London: Pocket Books, 1994 [1st edition, 1989]).

Ward, P., *Britishness Since 1870* (London: Routledge, 2004).

Ward, S. (ed.), *British Culture and the End of Empire* (Manchester: Manchester University Press, 2001).

Watson, N., 'Football and the Community: "What's the Score?"', *Soccer and Society*, 1, 1 (Spring 2000).

Watson, W., *Double International* (London: Stanley Paul, 1956).

Watt, T., *The End: 80 Years of Life on the Terraces* (Edinburgh: Mainstream, 1993).

Weight, R., *Patriots: National Identity in Britain, 1940–2000* (London: Pan Macmillan, 2003).

Wenner, L. A. (ed.), *MediaSport* (London: Routledge, 1998).

Whannel, G., *Fields in Vision: Television Sport and Cultural Transformation* (London: Routledge, 1992).

Whannel, G., 'Punishment, Redemption and Celebration in the Popular Press: The Case of David Beckham' in D. L. Andrews and S. J. Jackson (eds), *Sport Stars: The Cultural Politics of Sporting Celebrity* (London: Routledge, 2001).

Whannel, G., *Media Sport Stars: Masculinities and Moralities* (London: Routledge, 2002).

Whannel, G., 'From Pig's Bladders to Ferraris: Media Discourses of

Masculinity and Morality in Obituaries of Stanley Matthews', *Culture, Sport, Society*, 5, 3 (Autumn 2002).

Whitcher, A. E., *The Voice of Soccer* (Brighton: Southern Publishing, 1946).

White, A., 'Women and Sport in the UK' in I. Hartmann-Tews and G. Pfister (eds), *Sport and Women: Social Issues in International Perspective* (London: Routledge, 2003).

Whittaker, T., *Tom Whittaker's Arsenal Story* (London: Sportsmans Book Club, 1958).

Wigglesworth, N., *The Evolution of English Sport* (London: Frank Cass, 1996).

Williams, C. (ed.), *Cinema: The Beginnings and the Future* (London: University of Westminster Press, 1996).

Williams, G., *The Code War: English Football Under the Historical Spotlight* (Harefield: Yore, 1994).

Williams, J., 'Churches, Sport and Identities in the North, 1900–1939' in J. Hill and J. Williams (eds), *Sport and Identity in the North of England* (Keele: Keele University Press, 1996).

Williams, J., '"One Could Literally Have Walked on the Heads of the People Congregated There": Sport, the Town and Identity' in K. Laybourn (ed.), *Social Conditions, Status and Community, 1860–c.1920* (Stroud: Sutton, 1997).

Williams, J., *A Game for Rough Girls?: A History of Women's Football in Britain* (London: Routledge, 2003).

Williams, J., 'The Fastest Growing Sport?: Women's Football in England' in F. Hong and J. A. Mangan (ed.), *Soccer, Women and Sexual Liberation: Kicking Off a New Era* (London: Frank Cass, 2004).

Williams, J., 'An Equality Too Far?: Historical and Contemporary Perspectives of Gender Inequality in British and International Football', *Historical Social Research*, 31, 1 (2006).

Williams, J., 'Having an Away Day: English Football Spectators and the Hooligan Debate' in J. Williams and S. Wagg (eds), *British Football and Social Change: Getting into Europe* (Leicester: Leicester University Press, 1991).

Williams, J., 'The Local and the Global in English Soccer and the Rise of Satellite Television', *Sociology of Sport Journal*, 11 (1994).

Williams, J., '"Rangers is a Black Club": "Race", Identity and Local Football in England' in R. Giulianotti and J. Williams (eds), *Game Without Frontiers: Football, Identity and Modernity* (Aldershot: Arena, 1994).

Williams, J., "Surveying the Social Composition of Football Crowds: A Reply to Waddington, Dunning and Murphy', *Leisure Studies*, 15 (1996).

Williams, J., 'The "New Football" in England and Sir John Hall's New "Geordie Nation"' in S. Gehrmann (ed.), *Football and Regional Identity in Europe* (Münster: Lit Verlag, 1997).

Williams, J., *Is It All Over?: Can Football Survive the Premier League?* (Reading: South Street, 1999).

Williams, J., 'The Changing Face of Football: A Case for National Regulation' in S. Hamil, J. Michie, C. Oughton and S. Warby (eds), *Football in the Digital Age: Whose Game Is It Anyway?* (Edinburgh: Mainstream, 2000).

Williams, J., 'Kopites, "Scallies" and Liverpool Fan Cultures: Tales of Triumph and Disasters' in J. Williams, S. Hopkins and C. Long (eds), *Passing Rhythms: Liverpool FC and the Transformation of Football* (Oxford: Berg, 2001).

Williams, J., 'The Fall of Liverpool FC and the English Football "Revolution" in J. Williams, S. Hopkins and C. Long (eds), *Passing Rhythms: Liverpool FC and the Transformation of Football* (Oxford: Berg, 2001).

Williams, J., 'Who You Calling a Hooligan?' in M. Perryman (ed.), *Hooligan Wars: Causes and Effects of Football Violence* (Edinburgh: Mainstream, 2001).

Williams, J., '"Protect Me From What I Want": Football Fandom, Celebrity Cultures and "New" Football in England', *Soccer and Society*, 7, 1 (January 2006).

Williams, J. and Giulianotti, R., 'Introduction: Stillborn in the USA?' in R. Giulianotti and J. Williams (eds), *Game Without Frontiers: Football, Identity and Modernity* (Aldershot: Arena, 1994).

Williams, J., Hopkins, S. and Long, C. (eds), *Passing Rhythms: Liverpool FC and the Transformation of Football* (Oxford: Berg, 2001).

Williams, J. and Wagg, S. (eds), *British Football and Social Change: Getting into Europe* (Leicester: Leicester University Press, 1991).

Williams, J. and Woodhouse, J., 'Can Play, Will Play?: Women and Football in Britain' in J. Williams and S. Wagg (eds), *British Football and Social Change: Getting into Europe* (Leicester: Leicester University Press, 1991).

Williams, Z., "End of an Era', *The Guardian* (GS supplement), 4 July 2006.

Williamson, D., *Belles of the Ball* (Devon: R & D Associates, 1991).

Wiseman, N. C., 'The Economics of Football', *Lloyds Bank Review* (January 1977).

Wolstenholme, K., *Sports Special* (London: Sportsmans Book Club, 1958).

Woodhouse, D. and Williams, J., *Offside?: The Position of Women in Football* (Reading: South Street, 1999).

Woolnough, B., *Black Magic: England's Black Footballers* (London: Pelham, 1983).

Woolridge, J., 'Mapping the Stars: Stardom in English Professional Football, 1890–1946', *Soccer and Society*, 3, 2 (Summer 2002).

Wrigley, C. (ed.), *A Companion to Early Twentieth-Century Britain* (London: Blackwell, 2003).

Yeo, E. and Yeo, S. (eds), *Popular Culture and Class Conflict, 1590–1914* (Brighton: Harvester, 1981).

Yeo, S., *Religion and Voluntary Organisations in Crisis* (London: Croom Helm, 1976).

Young, G., *George Young Talks Football* (London: Stanley Paul, 1958).

Young. P., *Football in Sheffield* (London: Sportsmans Book Club, 1964).

Young, P., *A History of British Football* (London: Arrow, 1973 [1st edition, 1968]).

Zweig, F., *The Worker in an Affluent Society* (London: Heinemann, 1961).

Index